76 THE DIFFERENCE BETWEEN MORALITY + RELIGION.
252 THE WAY OF ALL THE EARTH

D0029216

Anna Akhmatova

Poet and Prophet

ROBERTA REEDER

PICADOR USA 🐾 *New York*

Except where otherwise noted, quotations of poems are translated by Judith Hemschemeyer and reprinted, with permission, from *The Complete Poems of Anna Akhmatova* (Zephyr Press, 1990). Copyright © 1990 by Judith Hemschemeyer, edited by Roberta Reeder.

Production Editor: DAVID STANFORD BURR

Design: JUDITH A. STAGNITTO

ANNA AHKMATOVA. Copyright © 1994 by Roberta Reeder. All rights reserved. Printed in the United States of America. No part of this book may be used or reproduced in any manner whatsoever without written permission except in the case of brief quotations embodied in critical articles or reviews. For information, address Picador USA, 175 Fifth Avenue, New York, NY 10010.

Picador® is a U.S. registered trademark and is used by St. Martin's Press under license from Pan Books Limited.

Library of Congress Cataloging-in-Publication Data

Reeder, Roberta.
    Anna Akhmatova : poet and prophet / Roberta Reeder.
      p. cm.
    ISBN 0-312-13429-0
    1. Akhmatova, Anna Andreevna, 1889–1966—Biography. 2. Poets,
Russian—20th century—Biography. I. Title.
PG3476.A324Z85   1995
891.71'42—dc20
    [B]   95-21676
                                                CIP

First published by St. Martin's Press

First Picador USA Edition: November 1995
10 9 8 7 6 5 4 3 2 1

Akhmatova brought me back
To Kiev, and Yakov, and the cupolas
—AUGUST 1993

Contents

. . . But in the world there is no power more threatening and terrible
Than the prophetic word of the poet.

—Akhmatova, 1958

Acknowledgments

Throughout the preparation and writing of this book, I have received valuable advice and encouragement from my colleagues and friends. I would like to thank the many people in Russia and Ukraine who knew Akhmatova, and the scholars who provided me with insights into her life, which include Lev Ozerov, V. G. Admoni, Irina Punina, Anna Kaminskaya, Lev Zykov, Alexey and Tamara Shileiko, Andrey and Olga Sreznevskaya, Galina Shapovalova, Mikhail Meilakh, Zoya Tomashevskaya, Lev Kopelev, Mikhail Kralin, Anatoly Naiman, Nina Korolyova, Evdokiya Olshanskaya, Valery Kukharenko, Alexander Moskalets, and Konstantin Azadovsky. I wish specially to thank Svetlana Kovalenko, who helped me find materials on Akhmatova and solutions to many problems. I would like to thank Alla Demidova for the many hours she spent discussing and reciting "Poem Without a Hero," and the German government, which provided me with a DAAD grant to work with students at the Gießen Theater Institute on performing and analyzing a dance-drama version of this poem. I would like to thank the many others who helped me with my research, including Wendy Rosslyn, Elaine Rusinko, Rosemarie Düring, Arkady Nebolsin, Michael Hagemeister, Sergei Dorzweiler, Astrid Scheunemann, Alma Law, Fritz Mierau, Irina Graham, Amanda Haight, Detlef Gojowy, Sidney Monas, Lev Loseff, and Peter Brown. I am grateful to Sir Isaiah Berlin for the discussion of his relationship with Akhmatova, and to Joseph Brodsky for discussing Akhmatova while we planned the Poet's Theater "Homage to Akhmatova" at Harvard University. I enjoyed the many talks I had with Yevgeny and Yelena Pasternak about Akhmatova and Russian culture during their stay in Marburg. I would like to thank Zephyr Press for permission to use the translations in their edition of Akhmatova's poems. I would like to show my appreciation to the publisher "Ada" and Vladimir Stolyarov for the collection of photographs which they allowed me to use. I am grateful to the RFE/RL Research Institute archive in Munich, its director A. Ross Johnson, Gabriel Superfin, and to Inna Burger, whose personal archive on Akhmatova was invaluable. Special thanks to Nina Popova, director of the Akhmatova Museum in St. Petersburg, and to the many colleagues there who helped me, especially Sophia Starkina, director of the photograph archive. I would like to thank the Harvard Ukrainian Research Institute and the Widener Library for their valuable resources, and the library at Phillips University in Marburg, Germany, which enabled me to continue my research while abroad. I am also grateful to the International Research & Exchanges Board, which provided me with a travel grant to visit the key cities relevant to my research, St. Petersburg, Moscow, Kiev, and Odessa. My very special thanks to Yakov Gubanov, for reading the manuscript carefully and correcting it, and for giving me the emotional encouragement during the final and most difficult stages of writing the book. I would like to thank those who helped me with my manuscript at St. Martin's Press—Leslie Sharpe, Ann Adelman, David Stanford Burr, and Rebecca Koh, and also Madeline Morel who first contacted me and continued to give me help and encouragement during the writing of it. I am extremely grateful to Robert Weil, my editor, who was the first to suggest writing a book on Anna Akhmatova, who gave me encouragement and support in every possible way, when I most needed it.

Blessed is he
who has visited life
in its fatal moments.
　　—TYUTCHEV

Anna Akhmatova has taken her place as one of the greatest poets and prophets of the twentieth century. At first compared with Sappho because of her exquisitely lyrical love poems, Akhmatova later assumed the role of Cassandra, becoming a prophetess of doom; and like Antigone, she was left behind to bury the dead and to teach us that it is an ethical imperative to remember them.

Akhmatova was writing poetry at the beginning of the twentieth century, when "for a woman to be a poet—is absurd."[1] Many Russian women had been allowed to take an active part in the political and social life of their country, but few had been accepted as equals to their male peers in the artistic world. This situation changed radically at the turn of the century, when instead of joining feminist movements, young women like Anna Akhmatova and Marina Tsvetayeva wrote great poetry, or like Natalya Goncharova and Alexandra Exter, they painted magnificent abstract works and revolutionized stage design.

The evolution of Akhmatova's poetry represents the evolution of her personal response to the dramatic events occurring in her country. Recognition of her poetic gifts began in 1912, with her first collection of poetry, *Evening,* when Russia was already in the throes of chaos and revolution. These poems do not reflect political chaos, but are, rather, introverted: with great sensitivity and restraint Akhmatova portrays the subtle twists and turns of the female psyche through various stages of a love affair. But World War I marked a significant change in Akhmatova's work, and soon she began to take on the role of the traditional village "Wailer": overcome by grief, those in the village who lost someone turned to the Wailer to articulate what they felt. Then, as the dreams of the Revolution turned into a Stalinist nightmare, Akhmatova became the voice of an entire people—of the women who lost men in the apocalyptic events of this century, and her own son, who was among them.

This book is a biography of a great poet; it is also a biography of the Russian intelligentsia struggling for survival in this century, and the tragedy of those, like Akhmatova, Mandelstam, and Pasternak, who loved Russia so much that they stayed, in spite of an atmosphere marked by fear and terror. Early in the history of the Soviet State, Akhmatova wrote, "I am not with those who abandoned this land," and warned that foreign bread smells like wormwood. What these poets loved was the beauty of a landscape of birches and pines, high mountains and endless steppes; the beauty of the Russian tongue, with its complexity and richness that enables the language to convey an incredible range of subtle nuances of emotion and thought. They shared a love for art and poetry that could not be equaled in any other country, for it was a country where hungry people gathered in cold rooms to read poetry to each other and performed experimental music based on traditions of the Russian past. And they shared a love for a people who had suffered so much and had yet endured, a love for a people who asked questions about the meaning of life and death that others had often been afraid to ask. In the process, these poets came up with answers that have influenced most major Western thinkers throughout the twentieth century. Akhmatova never regretted her decision to remain in Russia, and watched as those who left often lost their creative urge, were misunderstood or merely ignored. As she saw those who had remained with her suffer, she began to express more philosophical themes.

Although her poetry reflects a particular reality—a young Russian aristocrat in love at the turn of the century, a woman reacting to the Revolution and Terror, to the horrors of war and the loneliness of exile, and finally to the confrontation with death in her old age—she raises these themes to a universal level that we can all understand. And she has conveyed these thoughts and feelings in a new poetic language. Her poetry marks a radical break with the erudite, ornate style and mystical themes of the poetry of the period in which she was writing. Her lyrics are composed of short fragments of simple speech, which do not form a logical, coherent pattern. Instead, they reflect the way we actually think—the links between the images are emotional, and simple, everyday objects are important for the psychological associations we attach to them. Her style is concise, yet organized in such a way that every detail, every gesture carries meaning. Like the great nineteenth-century Russian poet Alexander Pushkin, whom she admired so much, Akhmatova was the master of conveying so much by so little.

A complex individual, Akhmatova combined Tatar and Eastern European ancestry and traditions with an education that acquainted her with the cultural legacy of Western Europe. The wisdom of her Tatar ancestors, and the solace and mysticism of the Russian Orthodox Church, were elements that endured in her. However, she always appreciated and admired what the West had given to Russia, and her poetry is filled with images from world culture. Her poetry teaches people everywhere that love of one's own country does not mean hatred of other countries. If we are to be ruled by compassion rather than logic, then it must be a compassion for all our fellow human beings; that compassion is an integral part of Akhmatova's great masterpieces.

Below is a list of editions of Akhmatova's poetry published during her lifetime in Russia and the Soviet Union, based on Amanda Haight, *A Poetic Pilgrimage* (New York: Oxford University Press, 1990), p. 199.

Vecher (Evening). St. Petersburg, 1912.
Chyotki (Rosary). St. Petersburg, 1914; 9th enlarged edition, Petersburg-Berlin, 1923.
Belaya staya (White Flock). Petrograd, 1917; 2nd edition, 1918; 3rd edition, 1922; 4th edition, Petersburg-Berlin, 1923.
Podorozhnik (Plantain). Petrograd, 1921.
Anno Domini MCXMXXI. Petersburg, 1922; 2nd enlarged edition, Petersburg-Berlin, 1923.
Iz shesti knig (From Six Books). Leningrad, 1940.
Izbrannoye (Selected Poems). Tashkent, 1943.
Izbrannye stikhi (Selected Poems). Moscow, 1946.
Stikhotvoreniya 1909–1945 (Poems 1909–1945). Moscow-Leningrad, 1946.
Stikhotvoreniya (Poems). Moscow, 1958.
Stikhotvoreniya (1909–1960). Moscow, 1961.
Requiem. Munich, 1963.
Beg vremeni (The Flight of Time). Moscow-Leningrad, 1965.

All translations of Akhmatova's poems, unless indicated otherwise, are from *The Complete Poems of Anna Akhmatova*, trans. Judith Hemschemeyer, ed. Roberta Reeder (Somerville, MA: Zephyr Press, 1990).

Anna Akhmatova

The Wild Child Becomes a Poet: 1889–1909

Believe me, not the serpent's sharp sting,
But longing has drunk my blood.
In the white fields I became a quiet girl,
With the voice of a bird I cry out for love.
    —AKHMATOVA (I, p. 245), 1912

Anna Akhmatova was born in a period of relative calm, before the approach of impending chaos when the wings of the Angel of Death would hover over the land. It was the twilight of Imperial Russia, as Nicholas II, a weak and indecisive ruler, ascended the throne in 1894 and made frantic efforts to preserve the foundations of the crumbling Romanov dynasty.[1] She was born in 1889—the same year as Charlie Chaplin. Tolstoy's *Kreutzer Sonata* was written that year; the Eiffel Tower was completed, and the French celebrated the one hundredth anniversary of the fall of the Bastille.[2]

    Anna Andreyevna Akhmatova was born Anna Gorenko in the Ukraine, in a small cottage on the seashore in Bolshoy Fontan near Odessa. When she was fifteen years old, the family visited the area. Again, Akhmatova and her mother happened to pass by the cottage where Anna was born, and her mother suggested she have a look at it. At the entrance Akhmatova declared, "Here one day there will be a memorial plaque." She says in her autobiographical notes that she only meant it as a joke, that she was not being vain; but the remark indicates that even as a child she had a sense of her own destiny. Not understanding the full implications of her daughter's remarks, Akhmatova's mother replied, "My God, how badly I've brought you up!" Today the plaque stands there, set up by the city of Odessa to show their pride in a great national poet.[3]

Not only was the year of Akhmatova's birth special, but even the actual date, for it was June 23 (June 11, Old Style), St. John's Eve. In Russia it was believed that all of nature's forces, good and evil, were most effective on this one night. Purification rituals took the form of bathing in rivers and streams and jumping over bonfires, while Satan summoned his followers to a celebration on Bald Mountain in the Ukraine.[4] Akhmatova received the name "Anna," which means "grace," from her maternal grandmother. Like all Russians, she would always celebrate her saint's day, in this case February 3, the day of St. Anna, the prophetess who met Christ in the Temple in Jerusalem.[5]

Akhmatova's parents belonged to the generation of the 1870s, when, young people from the upper classes were politically active. Akhmatova's godfather, Stepan Romanenko, the son of a wealthy landowner from Bessarabia, was imprisoned several times for his political activities at the university. Her godmother, Maria Valtzer, taught French and was one of the liberated women of her generation; she had studied at the Bestuzhev courses set up for women in Petersburg to allow them some semblance of a university education. It was still considered quite radical for women to study at this level.[6] Both of Akhmatova's parents had close contacts with the "People's Will," a terrorist organization which believed that the assassination of key members of the government would bring it down. An irony of history was that the tsar who liberated the serfs, Alexander II, was also assassinated. The result was one of the most tyrannical regimes in Russian history, when the new tsar, Alexander III, took revenge for his father's death by brutally oppressing the masses. Other members of Akhmatova's family, including her father's sisters, were involved in political activity and joined the "People's Will" movement.[7]

Akhmatova's childhood was not a very happy one. She had a philandering father and an intelligent but hopelessly impractical mother. The insecurity of her childhood and the disharmony between her parents may have accounted for her own difficulties in her relations with the men she later lived with, and with her own son. By 1905, her parents had separated and Akhmatova saw her father only on rare occasions. Andrey Gorenko was a naval engineer. Through her father, Akhmatova added more romantic details to her ancestry: Ukrainian Cossacks and Greek pirates. The Gorenko family's high rank came about when Andrey's father acquired hereditary nobility after winning awards for his service in the navy.[8]

Gorenko was born in Sebastopol in the Crimea on January 13, 1848, and began his career as an instructor in the naval corps in Nikolayev. According to one version, it was here in 1880 that letters "of a suspicious nature" were found that had been written by him several years earlier.[9] However, according to Akhmatova's brother Viktor, it was when their father was appointed to the Naval Academy in Petersburg that he got into trouble. His friend, Lieutenant Nikitenko, a specialist in explosives, made a bomb used by the revolutionaries to kill someone in the tsar's family. Nikitenko was hanged and Gorenko was called in for questioning. Although not accused of anything specific, he was ordered to retire from the navy.[10]

Both of Akhmatova's parents had been married before. Gorenko had two sons by a previous marriage to the daughter of a sea captain. In 1885 he married Akhmatova's mother, the young and very beautiful Inna Stogova, a descendant of the Stogovs, rich and powerful landowners who moved to Moscow after they had fled Novgorod in the fifteenth century when it came under siege by Ivan III. Akhmatova's grandfather, Erazm Stogov, was another romantic ancestor. After graduating from the Naval Academy, he sailed around the world for seven years. He then volunteered to go to Kamchatka in Siberia, where he became involved in the fur trade. Twenty years later he came to Petersburg, retired from the navy, and moved to Kiev, where he made a fortune raising sugar beets for refineries. There he married Akhmatova's grandmother, Anna Motovilova. When he died, he was considered one of the richest men in the Ukraine.[11]

Akhmatova left a beautiful portrait of her mother in her first "Northern Elegy." In it she defined the trait that meant most to her—her mother's kindness—what she called a "useless gift," but which she inherited and which would mean so much to the many people who were touched in some way by Akhmatova.

> And a woman with translucent eyes
> (Of such deep blue, that to gaze into them
> And not think of the sea was impossible)
> With the rarest of names and white hands,
> And a kindness that as an inheritance
> I have from her, it seems—
> Useless gift for my harsh life . . .[12]

Inna's life had been difficult, which may account for why she later had trouble running a household and leading an ordinary life. When she was three years old her mother died, and she and her five sisters and brother were raised by their capricious father and various governesses. Her brother had been thrown out of the house for insubordination and deprived of his inheritance. Like many liberal young women of her generation, Inna attended the Bestuzhev courses, but hid this from her father. She was also politically active; much later, in 1927, when she was visiting Akhmatova, she was full of memories of the "People's Will," recalling with great pleasure the Petersburg of her youth in the 1870s when terrorism flourished.[13] She was forced to marry an older man whom she did not love, named Zmunchilla, but soon after the marriage he shot himself.[14] Inna then fell in love with a dashing naval officer, Andrey Gorenko, who was tall and attractive, with a wonderful sense of humor. Andrey was also a great success with women, a trait that eventually led to the breakup of their marriage.[15] His romantic affairs were well known, and everyone in Tsarskoye Selo was aware that a certain young man, Leonid Galakhov, was his father's illegitimate son. His main affair was with Yelena Strannolyubskaya, the widow of a rear admiral, for whom he eventually abandoned his family.[16]

The inability of Akhmatova's mother to maintain any semblance of domestic order may explain the helplessness Akhmatova would later exhibit throughout her life in her own household affairs. A witness of this domestic disaster, Ariadna Williams, living in Tsarskoye Selo at the time, said that Inna had many servants but no order, and the governesses did whatever they pleased.[17]

The Gorenkos made an interesting pair. Akhmatova's childhood friend Valeriya Sreznevskaya described them both: "Imagine a small woman, rosy, with exceptional hands, spoke French, her pince-nez was always falling off, and she could not do a thing, not a blessed thing." Anna's father was handsome, elegant, and dressed beautifully in a tall hat worn slightly to the side as they used to do under Napoleon III. He had met Inna in Constantinople [Istanbul] and thought she was the most beautiful woman in the world.[18]

Akhmatova would claim that her maternal ancestor was Khan Akhmat, the last Tatar to accept tribute from the Russian rulers. He was killed in his tent in 1481 by a paid assassin, and this essentially ended the Tatar rule. Akhmat was a descendant of Genghis Khan, which means the royal blood of the Tatars flowed in Akhmatova's veins. The Akhmatovas were first baptized as Christians under Empress Anna in the eighteenth century. Around this time Akhmatova's great-grandmother Praskovya married a rich and powerful Simbirsk landowner, Yegor Motovilov. Their daughter Anna was the grandmother after whom Anna was named.[19] When Akhmatova's father said she would bring shame to the family by publishing poetry as Anna Gorenko, she chose the name "Akhmatova" and made it famous.

The Gorenko family was large. There were six children in all: Andrey and Inna were older than Akhmatova; Iya, Irina (Rika), and Viktor were younger. In 1887, Akhmatova's father retired with the rank of captain, and he and his family settled in Odessa, where he worked in the government control office and on a newspaper, keeping in contact with such politically radical figures as Stepan Romanenko, Akhmatova's godfather.[20]

In 1890, Akhmatova's father received a modest post in the civil service in Petersburg, and in August 1890 the family moved to Pavlovsk, a lovely little town outside of Petersburg, where many members of the upper classes had their summer dachas. The Gorenkos soon moved to Tsarskoye Selo, near Petersburg, site of the palace where the Russian tsars often spent their summers. Akhmatova lived from the age of two to sixteen in the more ordinary suburban part of Tsarskoye Selo, except for one winter in Kiev when her sister Iya was born, and another in Sebastopol in the Crimea.[21]

In Akhmatova's childhood there were premonitions that eventually came true. She had a presentiment that she was destined to do something special, that she was moving toward some mysterious goal in her future. Several incidents in her childhood seemed to point to the fact that the finger of God was upon her. When she was staying in Kiev, she once found a pin in the form of a lyre in the park called the "Tsar's Garden." Her governess told her, "This means you will be a poet." In 1894, in Gungerburg where the family was spending the summer, she found a rare type of mushroom—a "tsar-mushroom"—which was supposed to bring good luck. This incident caused Akhmatova's superstitious nanny to pour out a whole stream of sayings, "This is like white soot," "There will be pepper," in the belief that a special fate awaited Akhmatova.[22]

Tsarskoye Selo ("Tsar's Village") was an extraordinarily beautiful place in which to grow up. Set amidst elegant pavilions, *allées* of tall trees, and a superb park with replicas of ancient statues stood the Baroque Catherine Palace. At the beginning of the nineteenth century, part of the palace had been transformed into a lyceum that Pushkin attended. Akhmatova felt his poetic presence keenly while growing up. In a passage in her autobiographical notes, she describes the beauty of Tsarskoye: "My childhood is as unique and grand as the childhood of all children in the world. . . . My first memories are those of Tsarskoye Selo— the green grandeur of the parks, the groves where my nanny took me, the hip- podrome where small, mottled ponies jumped, and the old train station."[23] The powerful effect of Tsarskoye on those who lived there was summed up by Valentin Krivich, son of the headmaster and famous poet Innokenty Annensky: "Tsarskoye always possessed an attraction for anyone who happened to settle here. 'You will be poisoned by Tsarskoye,' Father said frequently. The charm of this enchanting garden-city, whose *alleés* are filled with history become legend and legend become history, literally enters your blood and poisons you, and for many years I met people who could not sever their ties with this town."[24]

It was an atmosphere of restrained elegance. In discussing a Moscow Art Theater production of *Anna Karenina,* in which they depicted the aristocratic residents of Tsarskoye in lavish attire, Akhmatova once commented on the dis- torted vision many had of Tsarskoye: "The people of the upper classes dressed modestly, never according to the latest fashion. Only the wives of famous lawyers, actresses, and coquettes went around in gold slippers and outrageously extravagant gowns." It is a telling comment that partly explains Akhmatova's own subtle taste in clothes and restrained behavior, which some found cold but which was typical of the time and place in which she grew up.[25]

Tsarskoye was not only a place of parks and palaces, however. It was really two quite distinct worlds: one was the solemn world of elegant courtiers, palaces, and enormous parks, with lawns, classical colonnades, Turkish minarets, even Chinese pagodas. The second world was around the corner—the world dusty in summer and snowy in winter, a semi-provincial garrison town with one-story wooden houses behind picket fences, a white church on an empty square, and ordinary stores.[26]

Of all the houses she lived in, Akhmatova remembered best the one in which she spent most of her childhood—the home of the merchant's wife, Yelizaveta Shukhardina, in Tsarskoye Selo. The dark green wooden house was said to have been a tavern until 1838. In the cellar was a milk store with a loud bell by the door and the unforgettable smell associated with this type of shop. On the other side of Bezymyanny Street was a bootmaker's shop, with a colorful sign: "Bootmaker B. Nevolin." During the summer through the window he could be seen working in his green apron; he had the deadly pallor of a drunkard, and the odor of boot polish drifted out his window. In front of the house along Shirokaya Street were magnificent oak trees.

Akhmatova recalled that almost every half hour a procession of vehicles passed by on the way to the station—carriages from the court, rich people's trotters, the police chief standing in a sleigh, three-horse troikas. In the winter Bezymyanny Street was covered with deep snow, pure and white, and in the summer it was overgrown with weeds—nettles and burdock, from which Akhmatova would make little baskets. On one side of the street there were no houses, but a very old, unpainted wooden fence. Like so many places in which she lived, this would all disappear afterwards, replaced by a park. The loss of homes in which she lived was to become a major theme in Akhmatova's later poetry—the inability to return physically to her past because of houses shifted or destroyed symbolized the inability ever to capture the elusive, fragile world of her youth. Akhmatova's own room was Spartan—an iron bed, a desk to prepare her lessons, a stand for her books, a candle in a brass candlestick, and an icon in the corner.[27]

No one in the family wrote poetry, although Akhmatova traced her lineage to the first woman Russian poet, Anna Bunina, the aunt of her grandfather Erazm Stogov. In a family where there was more interest in social reform than aesthetics, Akhmatova heard the verses of Nikolay Nekrasov, whose poetry was full of sympathy for the plight of the lower classes. A large volume of Nekrasov was virtually the only book the family owned.[28] This was typical of the intelligentsia of the time, who grew up with the ideas of Nikolay Chernyshevsky, Dmitry Pisarev, and Nikolay Dobrolyubov, who had written in the 1860s but whose thought continued to influence subsequent generations. They espoused a utilitarian aesthetics, defending art only if it was functional, if it taught people how to achieve social and political reform. Nekrasov's works admirably fulfilled this requirement. Many of the intelligentsia of the next generation rebelled against their socially committed elders. They turned away from politically engaged works, instead writing verses devoted to philosophical meditations, creating worlds of great beauty produced by the imagination, or like Akhmatova, poems centered on one's own personal longings rather than the problems of the suffering masses. However, in spite of her lack of interest in Nekrasov's social themes, Akhmatova was attracted to his sensitive perception of the beauty of the Russian countryside and his love of the Russian land. His poems also provide examples of strong female characters— Russian women of all classes, from the young peasant who had just buried her husband and faced starvation, to the brave wives of the Decembrists, the aristocrats who rebelled against the tsar in 1825 and were either hanged or sent to Siberia. These women followed their husbands and displayed a fortitude that Akhmatova herself would later emulate.

In the Shukhardina house lived another family, the Tulpanovs, and their young daughter Valeriya (whose name was Sreznevskaya after her marriage) became Akhmatova's lifetime friend. They had first met at the Gungerburg spa, a very fashionable resort, when Akhmatova's family was living in a dacha nearby. Both had governesses, both chattered in French and German, and both went with their "madames" to the square near the spa where children and their governesses sat on benches. Sreznevskaya describes Akhmatova at that time: thin, her hair cropped, not really very remarkable in any way. Akhmatova was rather quiet and introverted, in contrast to her lively friend, who was full of mischief and very sociable. Their real friendship began when they lived in the same house in Tsarskoye Selo. Sreznevskaya described the transformation she witnessed in Akhmatova over these years and the loneliness she must have felt as it became increasingly clear how strange and different she was from the more ordinary residents of Tsarskoye Selo:

> Anya wrote poems and read a lot of books which were allowed and not allowed, and she changed greatly both inwardly and outwardly. She grew up, and became an elegant young woman, with a charming frail figure, long, thick, straight black hair like seaweed, with beautiful white hands, and with an almost deathlike pallor on her carefully carved face, with large, deep, brightly sparkling eyes standing out strangely against the background of her black hair and dark brows and lashes. She was a sparkling water sprite, an avid wanderer on foot, climbed like a cat, and swam like a fish. For some reason, she was considered a "lunatic," and she did not impress the self-righteous and ill-bred inhabitants of the stagnant Tsarskoye Selo, which had all the drawbacks of a spot near the capital without any of the virtues. . . . Our families were close. Our fathers were mainly concerned with their affairs in Petersburg and our mothers, with their many children, or constantly worrying about the household. . . . The governesses mainly Swiss and German . . . It was not easy growing up in a large family. It's understandable why we wandered off, away from vigilant eyes, roaming in the gardens and groves of the lovely abandoned melancholy Tsarskoye Selo.[29]

Another feature that marked Akhmatova off from others was her somnambulism, her moon-walking. On moonlit nights a thin little girl could be seen in a white nightdress walking along the roof of their house in her sleep.[30]

Her strangeness, however, did not prevent Akhmatova from assimilating the proper behavior of a turn-of-the-century aristocratic young woman. Akhmatova did everything a well-brought-up young Russian lady was supposed to do. She knew how to fold her hands, curtsy, respond politely but briefly to an old lady's questions in French, and prepare for Holy Week in the school chapel. Once in a while her father brought her to Petersburg. Dressed in her gymnasium uniform, she went with her father to the opera at the Mariinsky Theater. She visited the Hermitage, the museum of Alexander III and art exhibits.

Pushkin captured the beauty of Petersburg in the prologue to *The Bronze Horseman:*

> I love you, Peter's creation, I love your severe, graceful appearance, the Neva's majestic current, the granite of her banks, the tracery of your cast-iron railings and transparent twilight, the moonless gleam of your still nights. . . . I love the warlike animation of the playing field of Mars, the uniform beauty of the troops. . . . City of Peter, stand in all your splendour, stand unshakeable as Russia![31]

Pushkin wrote these lines at the beginning of the nineteenth century, when the glory of Petersburg was at its height. It was still lovely when Akhmatova visited it as a child, but in many people's eyes neither Petersburg nor Russia was "unshakeable" any longer. Tragically, Akhmatova was born at the time of the inevitable collapse of her beloved city. Akhmatova lovingly described Petersburg as she remembered it in her childhood:

> This is the Petersburg of Dostoyevsky, before trams, full of horses. . . . Petersburg covered from head to foot with signs which mercilessly covered the houses. [This Petersburg] was most perceptible after the quiet and fragrant Tsarskoye. Inside the Gostinny Dvor [department store] were clusters of pigeons, in corner niches of galleries were large icons covered with gold embossing, and icon lamps burning. The Neva was full of vessels, and you could hear many foreign tongues on the streets. The houses were painted in lovely colors—red, purple, rose. Magnificent wooden houses, mansions of the nobility, lined Kamenni Ostrov Avenue and the streets near the Tsarskoye Selo train station. . . . It lacked parks and greenery at that time—it was mainly a city of granite and water.[32]

She remembered that there were two staircases in Petersburg houses: the front one, which smelled of the perfume of visiting ladies and the cigars of visiting gentlemen; and the back stairs, which reeked of the smells of the kitchen—of pancakes during Carnival week, of mushrooms and butter during Lent, of smelts from the Neva in May. But most of all, the back staircases of Petersburg houses smelled of cats.[33]

In her autobiographical notes, Akhmatova created a Petersburg symphony of sights and sounds. She fondly recalled the sounds of Petersburg courtyards—the thud of wood being thrown into cellars, the organ grinders playing "Sing, sweet lark, sing, calm the heart," the knife grinders calling out, "I grind knives, scissors," the secondhand clothes men, who were always Tatars, yelling, "Robes, robes," the tinsmiths and pretzel sellers. She also recalled visual images: the smoke over the rooftops, Petersburg Dutch tile ovens, fireplaces, and bonfires during the bitter frosts. But she returned to the sounds: the peal of bells deafening the entire city, the roar of a cannon, the drum roll signaling someone's execution, the clash of sleighs colliding on humpbacked bridges.[34]

As a young girl, Akhmatova attended the famous concerts at the hall in the Pavlovsk train station. She wrote that she would never forget the smells there, the smoke of the antediluvian train that brought her, nor the park, the music salon, the polished parquet floors, the strawberries one could buy, and flowers and fresh wet bouquets at the kiosk, cigars, food from the restaurant, and the specter of the famous character from Dostoyevsky's *The Idiot,* Nastasya Fillipovna, who was associated with Pavlovsk. Akhmatova said that for her Pavlovsk was always very special, like a holiday, because it was far from home.[35]

One of the most enigmatic figures of Tsarskoye Selo was the poet and head-master of the boys' gymnasium from 1896 to 1905, Innokenty Annensky. He was soon to have a decisive influence on Akhmatova's work. Although sharing many features of Symbolism, the prevailing literary movement of the period, Annensky made dramatic attempts to write in a simpler language, to convey the subtle psychological states of ordinary individuals through simple objects of everyday life. Akhmatova firmly believed he had a powerful impact on the work of such diverse poets of her generation as Vladimir Mayakovsky and Boris Pasternak: "While Balmont and Bryusov were culminating what had been begun by them. . . . Annensky put life into the next generation. . . . I don't wish to say everyone was influenced by him, but he went along so many paths at the same time. He carried within him so many new things, so all innovators seemed like him in a certain way."[36]

While still schoolgirls, Akhmatova and Sreznevskaya read Annensky's works, and once they went looking for the subject of one of his poems, the statue of *Pace (Peace)* in the park. They finally found it in a remote spot:

> For a long time we looked at its face, wounded by rain, white with dark spots . . . and in a horrible and strange way we repeated (how insightful into the future, isn't it?) the last exclamation of this amazing poem, "Give me eternity and I will give back eternity for indifference to insults and

the years." And how strange, almost children, adolescents, young girls, how we loved to observe from afar the tall figure of the poet walking along, and behind him always his old valet carrying a small folding chair—he was suffering at that time from chest pains.[37]

Akhmatova was touched after she learned that when Annensky heard that his sister-in-law's brother had married Akhmatova's sister Inna, he replied he would have married the younger Gorenko (Akhmatova). The remark remained one of Akhmatova's treasured compliments.[38]

Akhmatova attended the Mariinsky Gymnasium from 1900 to 1905. She remembered the intellectual paucity of those years:

I hate it when fifty-year-old ladies today claim that in their youth things were better than they are now. It's not true. When we were young, we did not love poetry and did not understand it. Poetry had been forgotten, because our fathers and mothers, because of Pisarev, considered it pure nonsense . . . I remember very well how I once brought [Alexander Blok's] poems of the "Beautiful Lady" to school, and the first thing one of the pupils said was, "Gorenko, you're certainly reading a lot of nonsense!" Plump, fair, with a white collar and ribbon in her hair—everything ahead of her clear for the rest of her life. There was no way of getting through to her. And that's the way they all were.

She mentioned her fellow classmates in the gymnasium—rich young girls who were brought their lunch by valets at noon on silver trays, and poor ones, daughters of tailors or orphans. Neither breed liked poetry. And that was why the Symbolists were so important for her generation, who had mainly grown up on prose, not verse. "They taught people to love poetry again."[39]

The famous poet Marina Tsvetayeva once described her peer Akhmatova as "Anna Chrysostom [the golden-mouthed] of *all* the Rus." Indeed, Akhmatova did not spend all her time in the north. Every summer the family traveled to different points in the south, including little towns near Odessa, and to Sebastopol in the Crimea. Here Akhmatova became "friends with the sea."[40]

That trace of the wild child of the south behind the austere woman of the north would later be noted by Korney Chukovsky, an important critic who wrote about Akhmatova at various key points in her career:

Critics who stress that Akhmatova had many features of someone brought up in Northern Russian culture have forgotten she was born by the Black Sea, and in her youth was a wild southern child. . . . For days at a time she would find herself . . . on the shores of Khersones, barefoot, merry, tanned by the sun. No matter in what attire she appeared in her books and in her life, I always sensed within her that unkempt impetuous little girl who, regardless of what the weather was like, was always ready to hurl herself from any cliff into the sea.[41]

The typical beach attire for young ladies at the time was a corset, bodice, two skirts (one starched) and a silk dress, rubber slippers, and a special cap. They "swam" daintily tiptoeing into the water, splashing a bit, and running back to shore. "And then there appeared the monster—me, in a thin dress over my naked body, barefoot. I jumped into the sea, and swam for two hours."[42]

Often her mother sent her to Khersones by rowboat to buy melons at the bazaar. Once on the way back the other children insisted she should row, but she refused. They began to quarrel and make fun of her. Standing on the edge of the boat, Anna leapt into the sea. The others did not even bother to look back, but continued rowing. When her mother asked them, "Where is Anya?" they replied, "She threw herself overboard." Anna swam all the way back, even though it was far from shore.[43]

Christmas 1903 introduced a figure into Akhmatova's life whose fate would be forever linked with her own—her future husband Nikolay Gumilyov. She was on her way to buy Christmas ornaments with her friend Valeriya when they met the Gumilyov brothers near Gostinny Dvor, the large department store in Petersburg. After this Gumilyov often came over to see Akhmatova, gaining access through her brother Andrey. Andrey and Gumilyov became close friends, sharing many interests. Andrey was extremely cultured in the classics, knew ancient poetry, but was enthusiastic too about modern poets. He proved a perfect audience for Gumilyov's poems and for his literary theories.

Sreznevskaya says Akhmatova did not find Gumilyov particularly attractive, possibly because at this age girls dream about disillusioned older men who have tasted forbidden fruit and are bored. However, many others said that Gumilyov was not handsome, which perhaps accounted for his arrogant facade—one way to hide his insecurity over his physical appearance. He was born April 15, 1886 (April 3, Old Style), in Kronstadt, the son of a naval doctor and the grandson of an admiral, L. I. Lvov, on his mother's side.[44] Those who knew him well said that by nature he was kind and generous, but shy. He did not like to express his feelings, and many mistook his coldness for disdain or indifference. His father had been married before, and his daughter by this marriage, Alexandra Sverchkova, lived with the family. She would subsequently help raise Lev, the son of Akhmatova and Gumilyov.

Soon after Nikolay Gumilyov was born, his father retired and the family moved to Tsarskoye. Nikolay was a sickly child, a precocious poet who began writing verses and fables at the age of six. The family spent summers in the south on his father's estate in Ryazan. Then in 1893 for a brief period they moved to Petersburg. Because of his brother Dmitry's tuberculosis, in 1900 the family moved again, to Tbilisi, Georgia. Gumilyov found the city a hotbed of revolutionary activity and as a boy of fourteen, he was drawn into politics for the first and last time. He read Marx and agitated among the local population.[45]

When his family moved back to Tsarskoye Selo in 1903, Gumilyov's reading habits changed, and he turned from politics to philosophy and French Symbolism. His love for the French Symbolists was shared by Akhmatova, but his interest in Nietzsche marks an important difference between them. By this time Nietzsche had become a powerful influence among Russian intellectuals, proving an attractive figure to those aesthetes who rebelled against the social activism of their parents' generation. They attacked charity and altruism as signs of weakness, preferring instead individualism, ego, and will.[46] One of the reasons why Nietzsche's ideas were so readily adopted by this generation was that they were concepts derived from ideas already generated by Dostoyevsky's protagonists— men like Raskolnikov—that God is dead, and therefore all is permitted; that the man-god is beyond good and evil; and that beauty will save the world. Dostoyevsky himself attacked such concepts vigorously, but they were found to be attractive to a generation that replaced moral virtue with an aesthetic sensualism.

When Gumilyov returned to Tsarskoye Selo in 1903, he attended the gymnasium where the poet Annensky was headmaster. The impression Gumilyov made on his fellow students is described by Nikolay Punin, the art critic with whom Akhmatova would live during the mid-1920s and 1930s, and who attended the same gymnasium as Gumilyov. Gumilyov always went around in a uniform with a white lining and was considered very chic among the students. He was a loner, taking no active interest in school life, but generating numerous rumors. They talked about his arrogance, his wicked behavior and strange poems. Though no one dared to tease him to his face, he evoked mockery and respect rather than love. Like Akhmatova, he was considered odd and eccentric by the ordinary residents of Tsarskoye Selo. Her father also found it difficult to get along with him.[47]

For someone so attached to beauty, it disturbed Gumilyov greatly that he was not attractive. "I began to pay a lot of attention to my external appearance," he wrote later, "and thought I was ugly. I tormented myself over this. I really was ugly then—too thin and awkward." In the evening he would lock himself in his room and stand in front of a mirror, hypnotizing himself: he firmly believed that strength of will could change his external appearance, and thought each day he would become a little more handsome.[48]

Like the Symbolists and aesthetes at the turn of the century, Gumilyov began to look at his own life as a continuation of his creative work. Life was perceived as material for art rather than art as an illumination of life. In a letter dated July 12, 1908, he says, "What is life if not the realization of ideas created by art? Wouldn't it be wonderful to create your life like an artist creates his pictures, like a poet creates a poem? True, the material is stubborn, but can't you carve the most wonderful statue out of hard stone?"[49] Sergey Makovsky, editor of the journal *Apollon,* describes the Nietzschean aspect of Gumilyov and its relationship to aesthetic hedonism, the concept of "life as a work of art," which was central to interpreting Gumilyov's behavior and understanding his poetry: "His whole life he did not accept life as it is, but escaped into the past, into distant centuries, into the deserts of Africa. He wanted to be like the gods, 'beyond good and evil.' "[50] Gumilyov was imitating the sentiments expressed in Valery Bryusov's famous poem, "To the Poet":

Be a dispassionate witness of all things
And turn your gaze to everything
Let your virtue be ready
To mount the pyre

It may be that everything in life
Is but a means for the creation
Of vivid and melodious verses
So from your carefree childhood
Search for combinations of words.[51]

Akhmatova and Gumilyov began spending more time together. They went to events at the town hall, to student evenings, took part in performances in a club, went skating, took long walks, went to see Isadora Duncan dance, and had rendezvous by the artificial ruins on the palace grounds of Tsarskoye Selo. Akhmatova began writing poems dedicated to Gumilyov, speaking about him as if he were dead, and always referring to him as "brother." These poems were written when she was between thirteen and fourteen years old, and she never showed them to anyone.

They attended the weekly receptions at Inna and Sergey von Shtein's, Akhmatova's sister and brother-in-law. It was more like a modest student party than a real literary salon: they drank tea, read poetry, and engaged in polite conversation. However, there was another interesting salon they visited: one of Gumilyov's classmates had married Shtein's sister Natasha and their receptions were much more elegant. Akhmatova's father would not allow her to go to either one, but her mother secretly let her go when her father was not at home.[52]

The year 1905 marked a turning point for Akhmatova—and for Russia. Akhmatova's parents separated. Her father went to live with his mistress, and her mother left with her children in August for Evpatoriya on the Black Sea. It was difficult for a sensitive young girl in her teens to leave the calm, womblike atmosphere of Tsarskoye Selo and have to begin her life again. Her anxiety was exacerbated by vague rumors of the 1905 Revolution, which made their way to isolated Evpatoriya. She wrote later that "January 9 and Tsushima [the defeat of the Russian fleet] were a shock to me for my entire life, and since they were the first, it was particularly terrible."[53] In 1905, Russia was an enormous empire still ruled by one man, Tsar Nicholas II. Although reforms had been introduced, conditions were oppressive. People were subject to arbitrary search and arrest;

the press was under heavy censorship; universities were closely supervised by the state; and the situation of the peasants and the working conditions in mills, factories, and mines were often intolerable. For decades the progressive movements urging reform had become increasingly radical, and the unrest among the lower classes increased. Soon all the seething forces exploded in the events known as "the 1905 Revolution." Valery Bryusov captured the feeling of doom hovering in the air:

Like a giant in the nocturnal fog
The new year arose, stern and blind
It held in its merciless palm
The scales of mysterious fates.
    . . .
And in intoxication and in fear
We, contemporaries, watch
How the bones wander, in blood and dust
And fall as a fatal sign.[54]

The events began on January 9, a day that would go down in history as "Bloody Sunday." A mass demonstration of unarmed workers led by a priest, Father Gapon, came in a procession to the Winter Palace in Petersburg, looking not for revolution but reform. They had come to see their beloved *batyushka,* their dear father the tsar, to beg him for help in making improvements in their living and working conditions. Around 200,000 people marched, some carrying icons and portraits of Nicholas, and many singing the national anthem. In spite of the fact that the police had assured the authorities it was going to be a peaceful demonstration, the state ministers decided to disband it by force and summoned troops to scatter the crowds. Over 40,000 infantrymen, cavalry, and police were ready for action. As the procession approached Palace Square, their way was barred and shooting began. Over a thousand people were killed and five thousand wounded. Although the tsar was not present, the people interpreted the events as the result of his orders. Never again would he have the respect and love of the masses which they had shown him before this event.

Then, in May, the Russo-Japanese War culminated in the humiliating defeat of the Russian Navy at Tsushima. The news reverberated throughout the land. It was also the year of the mutiny on the battleship *Potyomkin* in the port of Odessa, immortalized in Sergey Eisenstein's film. Alexander Blok's poem "Retribution" (1911) associates the downfall of the poet's ancestral home with chaos and revolution. That retribution, he believed, had been imposed on Russia for the sins of many generations:

Already the bloody dawn
Has spread across the boundless horizon,

Warning of Port Arthur and Tsushima,
Warning of January 9th.
The son pays for the sins of the fathers,
Born to be destroyed
The son of a homeless wanderer.[55]

For Akhmatova and others of her generation, Blok was more than just a great poet; he was the very symbol of the age. Growing up as the darling of his grandparents and a doting mother on the estate of Shakhmatovo near Moscow, Blok was a handsome young man with chiseled features, thick curly hair, exquisite manners, and elegant clothes.[56] He was a member of the second generation of Symbolists, who looked to the philosopher Vladimir Solovyov for their inspiration, introducing mysticism into the Russian literary movement. They believed humanity would be cleansed in spirit as a result of a universal cataclysm that would destroy the old and introduce a new and better life. The political events and chaos enveloping Russia were interpreted through the prism of this vision—the old world, they believed, was at the end of a cycle, and a new one predicted by the Apocalypse was fast approaching, when there would be peace, justice, and Christian love. The World Soul, which Solovyov called the "Eternal Feminine," or Sophia (universal wisdom), would save mankind.

Blok's early works expressed Solovyov's ideal in poetic form, but he gradually became disillusioned, and by 1905 he had begun writing about imps and demons that corrupted the soul of modern man, and about whores and prostitutes who replaced Sophia. One critic says that Blok was "a man split between the irreconcilable concept of an ideal mystical world and the real world. The harmony created between a fusion of his 'I' with the ideal Beautiful Lady he found to be illusory, but he could not find a place for himself either in real society."[57] Blok began to spend time in bars drinking, which stimulated his imagination, enabling him to transform tedious reality into a magic vision. He was convinced the old world was doomed. Georgy Chulkov describes the 1905 Revolution as a torch illuminating the twilight of the culture—a culture that was fated soon to end—and how the events produced such a strong feeling of anxiety and alienation that people tried to meet with each other, even loners like Blok. Chulkov recalls the sleepless "white nights" of summer when he would wander through the city with Blok, the nocturnal conversations behind a glass of wine at some dubious pub.[58]

In 1906 Blok wrote a play, *The Fairground Booth,* in which he ridiculed his former mystical views: Columbine, the beautiful woman who earlier in Blok's work would have symbolized the Eternal Feminine, turns out to be the harbinger of death. (This whole world of Columbine, masks, and mysticism would later become the subject of one of Akhmatova's most famous works, *Poem Without a Hero,* and Blok the prototype for one of the main characters.)

In 1905 the great ballet impressario Sergey Diaghilev mounted an exhibition

of historical portraits at the Tauride Palace, and his prophetic speech at a banquet
in honor of the exhibition added to the feeling of doom:

> We are witnesses of the greatest moment of summing up in history, in
> the name of a new and unknown culture, which will be created by us,
> and which will also sweep us away. . . . The only wish that I, an incor-
> rigible sensualist, can express is that the forthcoming struggle should not
> damage the amenities of life, and that the death should be as beautiful
> and as illuminating as the resurrection.[59]

Akhmatova was writing poetry at this turbulent time, but she considered her
early verses to be very poor: "These poems were terrible! Somehow I reread
them and almost burned them from shame. Not a single one of my thoughts, not
a single one of my intonations [was valid], everything alien and somehow wretched.
It is totally incomprehensible how I overcame this shame and somehow became
a poet."[60]

When Akhmatova came south, she spent several months preparing for her
entrance exam, which she had to take to be accepted at the gymnasium in Kiev.
Her personal life and her relationship with Gumilyov were becoming increasingly
difficult. Gumilyov had proposed to her, but she refused, and they stopped corresponding. However, he still knew what was happening in her life through her
brother Andrey.[61]

Akhmatova returned to Evpatoriya after passing her exams. Gumilyov graduated the gymnasium in June 1906 and left for Paris in July to study literature at
the Sorbonne. He came to see Akhmatova on the way, and they became friends
again.[62]

Unlike the poetry of Akhmatova, the young Gumilyov's verses were heavily
influenced by the ornate style and erudite and exotic themes of Symbolist poetry.
Valery Bryusov, who was living in Moscow—the representative of the earlier
generation of Symbolists, the aesthetes rather than the mystics—became Gumilyov's idol, and soon through their correspondence a master-disciple relationship
was established. Bryusov was described by a contemporary:

> For someone in Petersburg, literary Moscow seemed to be the king-
> dom of Bryusov, an unpleasant monarchy. He was the arbiter of artistic
> taste—no one really loved him. He had no real social or family life. He
> kept any passion or strong feeling under a stern mask. What did this
> mannequin in his black frock coat have in common with what was ex-
> pressed in his poems—"passion," "despair," "madness," "trembling" or
> "death"?[63]

Akhmatova said later that she thought Bryusov's influence on Gumilyov was
pernicious, but that his power over the fate of young poets was enormous at this

time, especially through critical articles, which appeared in his journal *Vesy (Scales)*. In 1905 Bryusov reviewed Gumilyov's first collection of poems, *The Path of the Conquistador*, noting that although there were several pleasant images, the book did indeed represent the path of a new conquistador whose real conquests still lay ahead.

One of Gumilyov's talents was in initiating new groups and maintaining journals around them. An early attempt was in Paris in 1906, when he founded a journal called *Sirius*. The purpose, he wrote in the first issue, was to acquaint his readers with the aesthetic beauty of all ages, from antiquity to the present. Only three issues appeared, and most of the prose and poems were written by Gumilyov himself under various pseudonyms. *Sirius* also marked Akhmatova's debut as a poet. Her poem "On his hand are lots of shining rings" appeared under the name "Anna Gorenko." She did not take the publication very seriously, writing to her brother-in-law von Shtein: "Why has Gumilyov gotten involved with *Sirius*? I'm absolutely amazed and find it very funny. How many tragedies our Mikolay [Nikolay] has lived through, and all in vain! You've noticed that everyone taking part is about as well known as I am. I think his star must be in eclipse. These things happen."[64]

In the spring of 1907, Anna was in her last year at the Fundukleyevskaya Gymnasium in Kiev. A fellow classmate, Vera Beer, tells of one memorable evening. Akhmatova's unusual physical appearance had already marked her off as striking and different from other young women of the time. It was twilight and Beer entered the beautiful church of St. Sophia in Kiev. There in the semi-darkness among the few people standing in the church she saw the unique profile:

> Standing motionless, slender, elegant, staring ahead, seeing no one and hearing no one, barely breathing, I said to myself, "How strange Gorenko is, how different!" I left the church, but Akhmatova remained and merged with the building. I wanted to tell Akhmatova about this, but something always prevented me. It was as if I had been let in on a stranger's secret which no one should divulge.[65]

Akhmatova was clearly much more well read and way above her peers in her sensitivity and her awareness of world culture. Beer describes another incident which took place during a psychology lesson devoted to associative thinking. The instructor was Gustav Shpet, later to become a famous philosophy professor in Moscow, and among his students was Boris Pasternak. The passage also proves that Akhmatova was already conscious of the process of associative thinking, and possibly of Henri Bergson's theories. It was a process that had a marked influence on her early style, typified by fragments of images strung together through associative links of thought and emotion. Beer describes how Shpet was giving examples of associative thinking from life and literature, when suddenly a voice rang out:

One-hundred-year-old street lamps!
Oh, so many of you in the mist
On the firm thread of time
Stretched out in the mind!

The solemn meter, the strange manner of recitation, the images which appeared so unusual forced us to pay attention. We all looked at Anya Gorenko, who did not stand up but spoke as if in a dream. A slight smile played on Shpet's face, and then it disappeared as he asked: "Whose verses are those?" A slightly disdainful answer rang out: "Valery Bryusov's." Very few of us had ever heard of Bryusov at that time, and certainly no one knew him as well as Anya. "Miss Gorenko's example is very interesting," Shpet said. And he continued reading and commenting on the poem she had begun. On her compressed lips played a self-satisfied smile.[66]

Akhmatova graduated from the gymnasium at the end of May 1907, receiving good grades.[67] She then entered the Kiev College for Women, where she studied law. She continued to correspond with Gumilyov, who was spending the year in Paris visiting museums and various exhibitions, reading books by Russian and French authors, medieval French chronicles, and knightly romances. The arrogant young poet had a humiliating experience in Paris when he went to visit two equally arrogant but by then quite famous Russian Symbolists, Dmitry Merezhkovsky and his wife Zinaida Gippius, who were seeking a synthesis of the sensuality of paganism and the spirituality of the Christian religion. They had been forced to flee abroad because of Merezhkovsky's opposition in the 1905 Revolution to the autocracy, which he called the Anti-Christ. Gippius was known for her coldness, her lack of human warmth; one contemporary describes her as a "decadent Madonna." "Slender, fragile, a mass of copper hair, green eyes and thickly powdered face, she wore an ebony cross and rings on her fingers, smoking fragrant cigarettes and played with a glittering lorgnette."[68]

In a letter to Bryusov, Gippius described her version of the visit:

Oh, Valery Yakovlevich! Have you actually seen him? [Bryusov had not yet met Gumilyov] We absolutely died. Boris [Boris Bogayev, pseudonym Andrey Bely] had enough strength to make fun of him, but I was absolutely paralyzed. Twenty years old, sickly and pale, full of old clichés, inhaling ether and saying that he alone could change the world. "There have been attempts before me—Buddha, Christ . . . but they were unsuccessful." He then put on his top hat and left. I found some issues of *Vesy* with his poems, wishing at least to justify your interest in the brilliance of his verse, but could not. Absolute nonsense. . . . Why do you find him so fascinating?"[69]

Andrey Bely, the Symbolist poet mentioned in Gippius's letter, noted that listening to the lisping voice of Gumilyov, one could hardly have envisaged the great pedagogue soon to emerge. Bely says that Gumilyov probably never forgot this evening for the rest of his life.[70] He is correct. Gumilyov and Akhmatova avoided Gippius and Merezhkovsky when they returned in 1912 to Russia, and in 1917, when Gippius later invited Akhmatova to see her, Akhmatova declined the offer.[71]

Gumilyov soon set off on his first adventure. Using the money he had saved from his monthly allowance from his parents, he set out in 1907 for Istanbul, Izmir, Port Said, and Cairo. Like Hemingway, he sought unusual and often dangerous situations to prove his manhood, but his quest was colored by his reading of Nietzsche, and the attempt to prove—to oneself and others—that by overcoming extreme tests and trials one could indeed become one of the elect, a Superman. Before he left Paris, Gumilyov had written letters to his parents, and his friends posted them off every ten days. He slept in the prison aboard ship with a group of pilgrims and was arrested in Normandy for attempting to stow away.[72]

In April Gumilyov stopped in Kiev to see Akhmatova on his way back home from Paris and then stayed briefly in Moscow to make the acquaintance of Bryusov, who made the following cryptic diary entry (dated May 15, 1907) about the meeting: "I was in a nasty hotel near the train station. We spoke about poetry and the occult . . . apparently he is in his decadent period. He reminded me of myself in 1895."[73]

In a letter of July 21, Gumilyov described to Bryusov his trip to Petersburg, his two weeks in the Crimea, how he then set out for Constantinople (Istanbul), an affair he had with a Greek woman in Smyrna, and a fight with gangsters in Marseilles on his way back to Paris.[74] Presumably the two weeks in the Crimea were when Gumilyov went to see Akhmatova in Sebastopol. Her face was muffled up to her eyes because she had the mumps and did not want anyone to see the swelling. He learned from her that she was no longer a virgin, and this along with her refusal to come away with him led him to attempt suicide.[75] He describes this incident in his poem "Rejection," written that same year:

A tsarina or, perhaps, only a sad child
She leaned over the sleepily sighing sea,
And her figure, graceful and lithe, seemed so slender,
It secretly strained to meet the silver dawns.

Twilight descended quickly. Some bird cried out,
And before her dolphins gleamed on the moist expanse,
So that she could swim to the turquoise realms of the beloved prince
They offered her their glistening backs.

But the crystal voice rang out,
When it stubbornly uttered the fatal: "There's no need" . . .

A tsarina or, perhaps, only a capricious child,
A tired child with a look of helpless torment.

When Gumilyov arrived in Paris in the fall, friends could not relieve his depression or his humiliation at being rejected by Akhmatova. Although her brother Andrey, who was in Paris at the time, attempted to cheer him up, Gumilyov went to Trouville in Normandy and attempted to drown himself. Luckily the guards on the empty beach restrained him. When he returned to Paris, he wrote Bryusov that there are times in life when one loses any sense of aim or purpose, when it is difficult to imagine any "tomorrow" and everything seems like a wearisome, fantastic dream.

In Paris, one of Gumilyov's best friends was the Russian writer Alexey Tolstoy, a member of the nobility who was later to play the role of a leading writer under the Soviet regime. But at this time he was young and unknown. They frequently met at a café, where they discussed poetry, their future fame, and travels to tropical countries. Gumilyov returned to Kiev in October, but Akhmatova again refused him, and this time upon his return he attempted to poison himself in the Bois de Boulogne. Tolstoy describes Gumilyov narrating this incident in the café:

> As usual, Gumilyov sat up very straight, tall, wooden, with his derby pulled down over his eyes, his long fingers lying on the knob of his cane. There was something of the pompous peacock about him, but his mouth was like that of a child, with a kind, tender smile. His story—white figures passing before him with covered heads moving on a turquoise field, and he thought to himself sadly, "This is death." He felt he was dying, as the figures floated upward. He realized he was lying on his back looking at the sky, and when he attempted to raise himself up, he saw he was sitting on the grass at the edge of a moat in the Bois de Boulogne. On the ground he found a small flask which was open and empty . . . He had been carrying a large piece of cyanide potassium in it for over a year. . . . "Why did I want to die—there was a young girl."

Tolstoy said death was always close to Gumilyov, and he thought this proximity excited him. Gumilyov was courageous and stubborn, always reflecting a certain sadness and self-importance. "He was pensive and brave—a captain of a transparent ship with sails out of clouds."[77]

Many of the Russians with whom Gumilyov was close in Paris, including Akhmatova's brother Andrey, left at the end of 1907, and it became very lonely. He wrote Akhmatova that he was bored and missed Russia.

Akhmatova was writing a series of letters to her brother-in-law, von Shtein, at this time. He was now living in Petersburg and was a widower, since Akhmatova's sister Inna had died on July 15, 1906. Shtein was a philologist and a scholar of Pushkin's works, and he served as a good confidante for Akhmatova's problems with her family and her infatuation with Vladimir Golenishchev-Kutuzov, a young student of Oriental studies. Little is known from the available sources about Kutuzov; he does not appear in Amanda Haight's biography, which was written with the advice of Akhmatova. However, although Kutuzov did not seem important to the poet by the end of her life, he plays a significant role in the letters she wrote to Shtein.

While attending the Fundukleyevskaya Gymnasium in Kiev, Anna had lived in the family of her cousin Mariya Zmunchilla, but she found it increasingly difficult to be with her relatives. Another cousin, Alexander Demyanovsky, said she exhibited an "unearthly indifference," which was her way of coping with the situation. She wrote von Shtein that she was most happy when everyone left for a tavern or the theater, when she could sit quietly alone and listen to the silence in the dark parlor. On holidays she visited her mother's sister, Anna Vakar (*née* Stogova) and her husband Viktor Vakar, where the situation was even more impossible. She did not get along with her aunt, and her uncle shouted all the time and used foul language. By 1906 she missed Tsarskoye terribly, but there seemed no possibility of her going there for Christmas as she had hoped. Her dream of visiting Tsarskoye Selo was only fulfilled in August 1908, when she briefly saw both Sreznevskaya and Gumilyov.

Akhmatova's letters to von Shtein reflect a pattern of coping that appears in her poems as well as in her personal life. When someone tried to hurt her—a lover, a critic, the state—Akhmatova built a psychological wall around her inner self, which it was difficult for others to penetrate. She withdrew into her own spiritual and creative resources, overcoming the situation imposed from without, and achieving not so much a state of numbness or indifference as one of inner peace that allowed her to endure. However, this pattern also made her appear remote and cold in contrast to her counterpart from Moscow, the poet Marina Tsvetayeva, whose solution to pain inflicted from without was an explosion of fury and wrath.

Akhmatova's inner peace was shattered now by despair not only over her family situation but over her infatuation for Kutuzov, which was not reciprocated. She constantly asked her brother-in-law for a photograph of him, and in one letter (suggested date 1906) admitted that she had attempted suicide: "Sergey Vladimirovich, if only you could realize how spiritual and unwanted I feel. No one will ever really need me. It's easy to die. Did Andrey tell you that I attempted to hang myself in Evpatoriya and the nail pulled out of the wall? Mama cried and I was ashamed—it was awful."[78]

From her letters we learn that she finally accepted Gumilyov's proposal. Why she gave in at last remains a mystery. In one letter she said she believed it was her "fate" to become his wife; but she did not feel that before, when for three years she constantly rejected his proposals. Perhaps she was tired of fighting his persistence. However, Gumilyov also offered her a chance to leave the provinces and enter the exciting life of Petersburg—the capital not only politically but culturally as well. While Kiev and Odessa were intellectually and artistically active, they could not compete with Petersburg. Another important point is that until the twentieth century most people married for other reasons than passion and love. Nikolay Gumilyov had been her close companion and intimate friend for many years. They had many interests in common and felt comfortable with each other. Her letters at this period reflect Akhmatova's ambiguous attitude toward her impending marriage, and her continued longing for Kutuzov. In a letter to von Shtein (suggested date 1907), she says:

> I have decided to tell you about an event which must basically change my life, but it turned out to be so difficult that until this evening I couldn't make up my mind to send this letter. I'm marrying the friend of my youth, Nikolay Gumilyov. He has loved me for three years, and I believe it's my fate to be his wife. Whether or not I love him I really do not know, but I think I do.[79]

Yet in another letter (suggested date February 1907), she seems excited about her impending marriage, even considering marrying Gumilyov against her father's will:

> I think my Kolya [Nikolay] is coming to see me—I am so insanely happy. He writes me incomprehensible words, and I go with his letter to friends and ask them to explain them to me. Every time a letter comes from Paris, they hide it from me and are very careful about delivering it to me. Then I have a nervous attack, and there are cold compresses and confusion. This is from my passionate nature, nothing else. He loves me so much it is positively terrifying. . . . What do you think Papa will say when he finds out? If he is against my marriage, I'll run away and marry Nikolay secretly. I cannot respect my father; I never loved him, so why should I obey him?[80]

The image of Akhmatova as prophet first appears in this letter, when she compares herself to Cassandra—an image that the poet Osip Mandelstam would later use in a famous poem about her. Complaining about her unrequited love for Kutuzov, she says: "I have murdered my soul, and my eyes are created for tears, as Iolanthe says. Or do you remember Schiller's prophetic Cassandra? One facet of my soul adjoins the dark image of this prophetess, so great in her suffering. But I am far from greatness."[81] A letter dated February 11, 1907, to von Shtein thanks him for finally sending her a photo of Kutuzov:

> I waited five months for this picture; he looks exactly the way I knew him, loved him, and madly feared him: elegant and so coldly indifferent; he looks at me with the tired, serene gaze of his myopic, light eyes. *Il*

est intimidant. . . . I can't tear my soul away from him. I'm crippled for life; bitter is the poison of my unrequited love! Can I begin to live again? Of course not! But Gumilyov is my fate, and I will obediently submit to him. Don't judge me if you can. I swear to you by all that's sacred to me that this unhappy man will be happy with me.[82]

Akhmatova's enthusiasm for Blok is expressed in this same letter: Talking of his poem "The Stranger," she comments on the poet's new muse; the prostitute has replaced the Eternal Feminine. Blok sees an enchanted shore behind her dark veil, and a treasure, his creative instinct, is released by the wine he has drunk:

You are right, you drunken monster;
I know, truth lies in wine.

"It's splendid, this interlacing of the vulgar commonplace with the bright, divine vision," Akhmatova exclaims. She also says she has asked her cousin to subscribe to *Vesy,* Bryusov's Symbolist journal. Akhmatova was interested in keeping up with this literary movement. But in strong contrast to Gumilyov, who imitated his Symbolist masters, Akhmatova's verse from the very beginning was simple, clear, and conveyed emotions and ideas that occur in ordinary rather than extraordinary reality.

Although Akhmatova told her brother-in-law that she was sick and hoped to leave Russia for a long period of time, she stayed on in the Crimea, living in Sebastopol and making trips to visit her relatives in Kiev. In January 1908 Gumilyov's second book, *Romantic Flowers,* appeared. It was dedicated to Akhmatova. In the spring, weary of Paris, Gumilyov returned home, and on the way back, he stopped in April in Sebastopol to see her. Akhmatova had indicated in her earlier letters to Shtein that she intended to marry Gumilyov, yet at this point she was still ambivalent. Now she turned him down, and they returned their gifts to each other. Gumilyov spent the summer in the province of Tver, where his mother had inherited the estate of Slepnyovo. He was accepted by the law faculty of Petersburg University, but soon after he began his studies, he transferred to the faculty of history and philology. Back in Petersburg, he renewed his acquaintance with Annensky and met two old friends from Paris, Maximilian Voloshin and Alexey Tolstoy.[83]

Even while pursuing Akhmatova, Gumilyov continued to have affairs with other women, one of whom was Lydia Arens. It was a pattern he would pursue after his marriage. Akhmatova would always remain the most important woman in his life, but there were also always to be other women with whom he was romantically involved.

Gumilyov set off for another trip to Africa in the fall of 1908, hoping to find inspiration for his poetry, or, as he wrote Bryusov in July, to "find new words in a new environment." Without much money, he sailed from Odessa on September

10 to Constantinople, then on to Athens, Alexandria, and Cairo. He bathed in the Nile, visited the Sphinx, and lay on the stones of Memphis, but still had not reached the depths of Africa. That would come on his next trip.[84]

In 1908, while still in Petersburg, Gumilyov had become a regular visitor to the "Tower," the famous salon of the mystical Symbolist poet Vyacheslav Ivanov, where a few years later Akhmatova was to become a featured guest. This was the so-called Silver Age which, like the Golden Age of Russian culture during the time of Pushkin, marked a special confluence of some of the greatest minds in creative thought in Russian history. It was a constellation that included the philosopher Nikolay Berdyaev, the poets Blok and Bely, Akhmatova and Gumilyov, the composer Scriabin, and the artists Vroubel and Bakst. Many of them at one time or another appeared in the Tower. The name originated from the apartment on the top floor of a building overlooking the Tauride Gardens. The round corner room was shaped like a tower, and here meetings and lectures were held. Often people spent weeks there, lying on soft couches, writing, playing musical instruments, conversing, or sitting quietly by themselves, withdrawn from the crowd.[85] Ivanov and his wife Lydia Zinovyeva-Annibal entertained the most brilliant artistic and intellectual figures of the day. Nikolay Berdyaev was an early devotee of Ivanov's tower and comments:

> He [Ivanov] was one of the most remarkable people of that epoch. . . . Russia of the nineteenth century did not know such people. He was totally Russian by blood . . . but while at times close to nationalism, he was a man of Western culture, living abroad for a long time and coming to Petersburg armed with Greek and European culture. He was a universal man—a poet, scholar, philosopher, and thinker. He would talk to each person about his specialty; he was a real charmer. But he gave the impression he was always changing his views depending on whom he was speaking with. Yet in the end I think he remained himself—a combination of conservative and anarchist, nationalist and communist, Orthodox and Catholic, mystic and positivist. His talent was enormous, but as a poet he was scholarly and difficult.[86]

Akhmatova found Ivanov a "remarkable poet who wrote bad poetry." He understood everything, she said, and foresaw what would happen, had poetic vision, but without being able to encompass his vision in rhythmic images. His poems were too scholarly, too complex.[87]

In the 1940s, when the Silver Age became a major theme in Akhmatova's poetry and she looked back "as if from a tower" to reevaluate this epoch, which was so important in her own life and the life of her country, she turned to Berdyaev's autobiography for his insights. Berdyaev condemned both the aesthetic and the mystical aspects of Symbolism. He did not admire Bryusov's elevation of the aesthetic creativity over life itself, nor did he believe in Ivanov's pagan metaphysical exaltation, derived from the ancient Dionysian religions. Although once an ardent Marxist, Berdyaev soon realized that the logical end of Marxism was the loss of freedom, as the individual was forced to merge with the collective. For Berdyaev, what was sacred was not art, society, or the state, but the individual and his/her inner freedom—a belief shared by Akhmatova and practiced in her life and poetry.

Yet Berdyaev admired the beauty of this age, the great blossoming of Russian culture which greeted Akhmatova when she finally came to Petersburg to begin her career as a young poet. It was the era of the Ballets Russes, of Alexander Blok, Alexander Scriabin, and Igor Stravinsky; there was an atmosphere of decline, but also of hope for a transformation of life. However, as Berdyaev points out:

> All this took place within a very small, elite circle totally cut off from the masses. There was a feeling of breathing the putrefied air of a hothouse rather than fresh air. There was *Angst,* tension, but no joy. Serious creativity was combined with cheap imitation and a following of fashion. There were too many aesthetes, mystics, disciples of the occult, with a dominance of the erotic and aesthetic over the ethical. The ethical element, so strong in the nineteenth century, had grown weak. There was something poisonous in the air of Petersburg at this time.[88]

Berdyaev found the occult and anthroposophy, the mysticism and aestheticism, just as repellent as the revolutionary element. He believed that aesthetic amoralism was indifferent to the dignity of man.

Akhmatova had mixed feelings about Ivanov. She once said, "I was born to unmask Ivanov. He was a great hoaxer, a Count Germain. He latched on to people and then would not let them go—a 'fisher of men.' "[89] But despite her reservations about Ivanov's influence, she respected him, especially in comparison to Bryusov. It was also clear from her remarks that Ivanov was replacing Bryusov as Gumilyov's "master," which is apparent in a frank letter from Gumilyov to Bryusov that Akhmatova discusses:

> I never knew him personally [Bryusov], but I did not like his poetry or prose . . . no images, nothing. Neither the image of a poet nor a hero. His poems are all about different subjects, but they are really all the same. . . . He recommended that Gumilyov should not meet Ivanov. He obviously wanted to keep the hopes of young poets for himself. Ivanov was intelligent, a magnificently educated man, refined, wise. After a while Gumilyov wrote Bryusov, "I have met Ivanov and only now understand what poetry is really about."[90]

Berdyaev touched on another problem that would become the major theme of Akhmatova's *Poem Without a Hero:* the indifference of the literary salon to the suffering beyond. He was struck by the contrast between the refined conversation carried on by the cultural elite and the revolutionary activity raging outside. Two disparate worlds, but sometimes they impinged upon one another. For example, one evening Anatoly Lunacharsky, the future Soviet Minister of Culture, visited the Tower: there was a search, which produced a sensation. A tsarist soldier with a rifle stood at every door, and everybody's name was noted down.[91]

However, the Silver Age made an important contribution to Russia and the world, for it was the period when after almost two hundred years of looking to the West, Russians turned inward, to their own traditions, which is why this period is often referred to as the Russian Renaissance. It was also a time of resurrection of the past:

> [The Silver Age] resurrected Petersburg, the ancient Russian icon, returned the sensitivity to the word and melody of verse, revivified again everything that Russia had once lived by and again discovered anew for her the entire spiritual and artistic life of the West. This could not have occurred without a creativity of its own, and no matter how severely this period may be condemned, what was created during these twenty years was an awareness of Russian consciousness, a revitalization in philosophy, the sciences, literature, music, painting, theater. What these years lived by and what they gave to the spiritual world will not die. This could have been the threshold of a renaissance but it became instead the presentiment of the end.[92]

One of the favorites at the Tower was Alexander Blok, who was tormented at the time by the problem of the relationship of the intelligentsia to the masses. In a talk given in 1908, he maintained that there was an insurmountable barrier between the Russian people and the intelligentsia. The only solution was for the intelligentsia to join the people, who possessed a "will to live," whereas the intelligentsia were obsessed by a "will to die." He admitted there were exceptions, intellectuals who were devoting their lives to helping the masses. He then turned to one of the great passages in Russian literature, *Dead Souls,* where Gogol portrays Russia as a troika, a sleigh drawn by three horses, flying into the unknown. "What if this troika is flying straight at us?" Blok asks. "What if it tramples us and razes our culture to the ground? What if in rushing to the people we are rushing straight under the hoofs of that mad troika to our certain death?" And he frames the question he was to formulate again in his great poem, "The Twelve," written after the Revolution: An elemental force was being unleashed, but would it be destructive or creative?

In another talk given in 1909, Blok turned to the terrible earthquake that had just destroyed Messina, and asked just what their supposed triumphant civilization had really achieved. Was this Fate, he asked, showing us that some elemental force at any moment can wreak vengeance for our pride, our assumption that man can control nature and rule the universe through his technology? Man had created machines, artistic works of genius, but then "the pendulum of the seismograph in the observatory swings" and a catastrophe occurs in the face of which people are helpless. "We are going through a terrible crisis. We do not know yet exactly what is going to happen, but in our hearts the pendulum of the seismograph is already swinging."[93]

Gumilyov apparently thought a good deal about Akhmatova at this time, for she often figured in his poems. He was having his portrait painted by O. L. Dellavos-Kardovskaya, and during the sessions he read her his poems celebrating demonic imagery. Once the artist asked him who the heroine of these poems was. Not wishing to mention it was Akhmatova, he replied: "A gymnasium student with whom I am still friends. She also writes poetry."[94]

He began another journal in 1909, *Ostrov (Island),* with Alexey Tolstoy, but only one issue was published because of lack of funds. A more successful venture was the launching of one of the most important journals before the Revolution, *Apollon,* where Akhmatova's poems also appeared. In early January 1909 at an art exhibition, Gumilyov made the acquaintance of Sergey Makovsky. Makovsky liked Gumilyov's reserve, his calm arrogance, his remarkable intuition and ability to grasp a new idea and comprehend it immediately.[95] They soon became friends, and along with other acquaintances of Gumilyov, they founded *Apollon.* Gumilyov was also responsible for founding a new literary society, the "Academy of Verse," at this time, at which poets and literary figures met to read and discuss their works. Akhmatova was later to attend sessions of this important literary group.

In 1909, Gumilyov began to frequent the Tower regularly. Although not giving up on marrying Akhmatova, he began an affair with the poet Yelizaveta Dmitriyeva, whom he had met in Paris some years before, but who had then found him rather pale and uninteresting. In the spring she helped him with some medieval French songs, and in the summer they went to visit Voloshin at his home in Koktebel in the Crimea. After taking walks in the mountains, drinking Turkish coffee, going boating, and spending their evenings at the literary gatherings in Voloshin's studio, the affair began to cool. Voloshin says that when Dmitriyeva grew tired of Gumilyov, he spent the rest of the time catching tarantulas.[96]

Spurned by Dmitriyeva, at the beginning of July Gumilyov went to see Akhmatova, who was living at Lustdorf near Odessa. He spent several days there trying to convince her to come with him to Africa, but she refused. On the tram from Lustdorf to Odessa, Gumilyov asked Akhmatova if she loved him. She replied, "I don't love you, but I consider you an important person." Gumilyov then smiled and asked, "Like Buddha or like Mahomet?"[97]

In August, a strange event occurred, one of the more memorable incidents in the literary history of the time. A letter arrived at *Apollon* with a black border around it (normally indicating a death announcement). It was signed with the large letter "CH" from an unknown poet, who hoped her poems would be considered for publication. The poems portrayed a beautiful woman with a sad fate, and the paper smelled of an elegant perfume. Soon the poet herself began to call on the telephone in a magnificent, sensual voice. Her name was finally revealed— Cherubina de Gabriak. She was allegedly a Spanish aristocrat, alone in the world, and her priest confessor was a Jesuit. Makovsky as well as the rest of the board fell in love with her and agreed to print her poems. Gumilyov vowed to seduce her, but she refused to meet with anyone. After a while she said she had to leave for two months on doctor's orders. Dmitriyeva in particular made fun of her and wrote parodies of her verse. Johannes von Günther, a colleague on the journal, said that Dmitriyeva finally revealed to him that it was all a joke. She and Voloshin had thought it all up that summer while still in the Crimea, and Dmitriyeva herself wrote the poems and was the voice on the phone. The name "Gabriak" was derived from a book on demonology, and Cherubina was the heroine in a Bret Harte story which Dmitriyeva had read.[98]

Later Akhmatova blamed the death of Annensky on the de Gabriak incident. Bryusov had rejected Annensky's poems for *Vesy,* but Makovsky praised the poems and said he would print them in the first issue of *Apollon,* which made Annensky very happy. However, he decided to publish de Gabriak's poems instead. Stunned and very disappointed, Annensky wrote a strong letter to Makovsky telling him how upset he was. A few days later he collapsed and died at the Tsarskoye Selo train station on December 13, 1909.

The relationship between Gumilyov and Voloshin had become strained after Voloshin heard that Gumilyov had been discussing his romance with Dmitriyeva in crude language. Frequently all the colleagues of *Apollon* would gather in the studio of the set designer Alexander Golovin, who was painting their portraits. One evening Voloshin was posing. They could hear the performance of *Faust* below. Voloshin decided to wait until Chaliapin finished singing his aria. Then Voloshin went up to Gumilyov, who was talking to Alexey Tolstoy, and slapped him. Gumilyov stepped back and said, "You will answer for this."[99] Annensky, Golovin, and Ivanov ran up to Gumilyov, who was standing tall and straight and, as usual, very tense. Gumilyov put his hands behind his back and kept his self-control.

The duel took place on November 22, 1909. Prince Shevashidze served as Voloshin's second, and the poets Znosko-Borovsky and Mikhail Kuzmin as Gumilyov's. They had chosen as the site Chyornaya Rechka, because that was where the fatal duel between Pushkin and Baron Georges d'Anthès took place. It was a wet and windy day. Gumilyov and his comrades drove out of the city and soon caught up with their opponents' car, which was stuck in the snow. They had to call some yardmen to come with shovels, and soon everyone was dragging the car out of the snowdrift. Calm and serious, Gumilyov watched them working, his hands in his pockets. They finally abandoned the car and walked to Chyornaya Rechka on foot. Voloshin lost one of his galoshes in the snow and would not go on until he found it.

In Russia, duels were fought with one person shooting at a time. They chose lots to see who went first, and if the first person missed, then it was the second person's turn to shoot. Tolstoy handed out the pistols and counted the steps. Gumilyov stood there, a black silhouette in the misty dawn, in his characteristic tall hat and frock coat. He had tossed his fur coat onto the snow. Tolstoy says:

> Running up to him, I fell down in a pit up to my waist in water. Gumilyov calmly bided his time until I got out. He took the pistol and looked at Voloshin with cold hatred. . . . I began to count . . one, two . . . not having the strength to stand up, Kuzmin sat shivering in the snow and hid behind a metal box full of medical supplies so he would not have to witness the horror. "Three!" I shouted. A shot rang out—Gumilyov— several seconds passed. A second shot did not follow. Gumilyov shouted, "I demand that this gentleman shoot." Voloshin said, "I misfired." He raised his pistol and I heard the cock of the trigger, but no shot. I ran up to him, tore the pistol out of his hand, and aiming at the snow, shot. Gumilyov refused to shoot.

The newspapers reported this episode with great delight. *Rech (Speech)* expostulated: "The duel? Absolutely fabulous. Especially in winter. How can there be a duel in winter without cognac and champagne? And certainly the very best. Duels support the wine industry . . . and just imagine . . . there were seven seconds. And not a hint of danger."[100]

Gumilyov was continuing to publish his poetry: "Descendants of Cain" appeared in 1909 in the third issue of *Apollon*. It is another work celebrating the Nietzschean ideal of "beyond good and evil." The poet admits one may have certain moments of doubt when confronted by Christianity, a twinge of conscience when suddenly a cross appears. But one should overcome these and live like a god.

> He did not lie to us, spirit sad-stern
> Who took the name of the morning star,
> When he said: "Don't be afraid of revenge from above
> Taste the fruit and you will be like the gods."
>
> For young men all roads are open,
> For old men—all forbidden labors,
> For young girls—amber fruit
> And white as snow unicorns.
>
> But why do we bow down helplessly,
> Why do we think someone has forgotten us
> Why is the horror of the ancient temptation so clear

When by chance someone's hand
Combines two poles, two blades of grass, two sticks
For a moment in the form of a cross?[101]

On November 26, Gumilyov came to Kiev to participate in a literary evening entitled the "Island of Arts." He was joined by Mikhail Kuzmin, Peter Potyomkin, and Alexey Tolstoy. Akhmatova attended, and when it was over, Gumilyov invited her to the Hotel Europe for a coffee and once again proposed. This time, to his surprise, she accepted. He spent the next three days with her in Kiev. They stayed with Kuzmin at the home of the artist Alexandra Exter. On November 30 he left for Odessa, where he took a boat for Africa. This trip included Port Said, Djedda, Cairo, and Djibouti. At last his dreams were coming to fruition: Akhmatova had promised to become his wife and he was now entering into the relatively uncharted heart of Africa. As for Akhmatova, her decision to marry Gumilyov and to go to Petersburg would change her life dramatically.[102]

Petersburg, Poetry, and the Cabaret: 1910–1914

Once more St. Isaac's wears robes
Of cast silver.
And frozen in fierce impatience
Stands the horse of Peter the Great.
    —AKHMATOVA (I, p. 355)

The couple was married on April 25, 1910, in the small Nikolayevsky Church in Nikolska Slobodka where Anna's mother was living, a little town close to the Dnieper River on the opposite shore from Kiev.[1] The marriage had an important impact on Akhmatova's life, helping define her as a woman and an artist. Through Gumilyov she would meet the literary elite of the day, and her relationship with Gumilyov would provide the subtext of her first book of poetry.

Petersburg remained a city full of activity. In January 1910, *Apollon* had put on a small exhibition of contemporary Russian women's portraits.[2] Among them was the painting of Olga Glebova-Sudeikina by her husband, Sergey Sudeikin. She was portrayed as "Confusion," one of her favorite roles in Yury Belyaev's play by that name. Olga and the portrait would become the centerpiece of Akhmatova's *Poem Without a Hero* (1940–60).

Before her marriage, Akhmatova had come to Petersburg in February to visit

Gumilyov, who had returned from Africa. His father had just died. It was Carnival week when Akhmatova arrived, and together they went to museums and concerts. It was at this time that Gumilyov showed her proofs from Annensky's poetry collection, *The Cypress Box,* which had such a powerful impact on her work.[3]

After the marriage they stayed in Kiev until the end of the month, and then at the beginning of May set out for their honeymoon to Paris. They went to museums, visited the medieval monastery at Cluny and the zoo, drank coffee at Gumilyov's favorite cafés in the Latin Quarter, and went to cabarets.[4] They appeared to be a happy couple, but Sreznevskaya wrote that she knew sooner or later the relationship would become strained, viewing it as a power struggle between two very independent, creative people. "Their relationship was like a secret dueling—from her side, for her own affirmation of her status as a free woman; from his, because of a desire not to submit to any bewitchment and to remain independent and powerful . . . alas, without power over this eternally elusive, many-sided woman, who refused to submit to anyone!"[5]

The trip to Paris marked the first time Akhmatova had gone abroad. For generations of Russians Paris was the symbol of culture and fashion, of good manners and good taste. It was a magical time for Akhmatova. Other Russians were in Paris. In her memoirs she mentions that Marc Chagall had brought "his magic Vitebsk to Paris." She went to the Taverne du Panthéon, where at one table sat the Bolsheviks, the more radical wing of the Social Democrats, and at another table the Mensheviks, the wing that believed in social reform. Ida Rubenstein was performing *Salome* and the Ballets Russes was becoming famous. Stravinsky's *Firebird* opened in 1910 and *Petrouchka* in 1911. Charlie Chaplin (Akhmatova called him "the great Mute") was still eloquently silent, and in Paris, strolling along the boulevards.[6] Many Parisians had exotic ideas about Russia. They asked her, "Can you get to Russia by dry land?" and, "Is it true you wear sarafans and kokoshniks [traditional Russian costume and headdress] in Russia?"[7]

Akhmatova and Gumilyov returned from Paris at the end of June and met Makovsky on the train back. They shared opinions on the Diaghilev productions. Makovsky was impressed by Akhmatova, not just as Gumilyov's wife but for her striking appearance—tall, slender, quiet, very pale, with a sad mouth and bangs, which were the latest fashion in Paris and soon, along with her shawl, became her trademark. He said when Gumilyov spoke to her, one felt he loved her very deeply and was proud of her. Gumilyov had not told Makovsky anything about his marriage, and only later revealed that this was his childhood sweetheart. Makovsky also believed theirs would be a troubled marriage, for it would not be easy for Gumilyov to reconcile his poetic will and thirst for new impressions with a settled family life, yet he needed emotional support as much as the very air he breathed, and Akhmatova might not be prepared to give it to him.[8]

In Tsarskoye Selo the newlyweds lived with the Gumilyov family. Akhmatova found Tsarskoye very different now. "After Paris, Tsarskoye seemed quite dead. There was nothing surprising there. Where had my Tsarskoye Selo life gone after five years? I did not find a single one of my classmates, I did not cross a single threshold of a Tsarskoye Selo house. A new Petersburg life began."⁹ Her old friend Sreznevskaya described what it was like when Akhmatova returned: "For some reason we were tired of the Tsarskoye Versailles and Trianon. We walked in a field which was half pasture, half swamp . . . into a huge, burning sunset . . . apparently Akhmatova was no longer attracted by the poetic 'spirit of the living past,' by the beauty of the palace landscape, but by the ordinary aspects of Tsarskoye Selo."¹⁰

Sreznevskaya was just as surprised at Akhmatova's marriage as Makovsky. Her friend had written only of the proposals and the rejections, but had told her nothing of the marriage itself. Sreznevskaya offers significant—and surprising—insight into Akhmatova as a bride: "She spoke little about her marriage, and I thought she had not changed at all—I did not find that desire to talk about their fate that one often encounters in newlyweds. It was as if this event had absolutely no significance for her or me. She read poetry, and I found no images whatsoever in them of Gumilyov . . . in contrast to his poems, which were full of her until the end of his life. First as a water sprite, then as a witch, then simply as a woman hiding 'evil solemnity.' "¹¹

When Akhmatova entered Petersburg literary circles, the first impression she made was of a sweet, shy young woman who wrote poetry, and she was recognized only as the wife of Gumilyov.¹² The Tower especially became an important part of her new life. She made her first public appearance there on a Sunday, June 1, 1910, and wrote of it:

> He [Ivanov] needed his flatterers. He also knew how to seduce and work his charms on me. I came to see him and was taken to his studio. "Read!" Well, what could I read then! Twenty-one years old . . . something I had made up about unhappy love. I read something like "Over the water." Vyacheslav was ecstatic, "from the time of Catullus," etc. Then he led me out into the parlor—"Read!" I read the same thing. And Vyacheslav criticized me.¹³

Ivanov's insight and understanding of Akhmatova so early in her career is clear from his immediate realization that she was the heir of Annensky. She would be the one, he said, to develop and bring to perfection the brilliant innovations incipient in his poetry. Ivanov invited Akhmatova to sit on his right, the very seat that used to be reserved for Annensky. He announced: "Here is a new poet, to reveal to us what still lay deep within the the soul of Innokenty Annensky."¹⁴

The year 1910 marked a crisis in the Symbolist movement as well as a premonition of worse days to come in Russia. Blok prophesied:

> Oh, if you only knew, children,
> The cold and gloom of the days to come . . .

The Marxist critic Georgy Plekhanov called Symbolism "the pallid disease of an anemic social class in decline,"[15] and both Ivanov and Blok gave speeches before the Academy of Verse admitting the movement was in trouble. Ivanov continued to defend the role of the poet as a priest who comprehended the mysteries of the universe, and through symbol and myth could arouse intimations of these secrets in the reader. Blok's solution was to reject the idea of the poet as priest, isolated and rising above the people. Instead, the artist must return to life and share the fate of his nation, even to the point of supporting revolution.[16] Bryusov later wrote an article polemicizing both these views, defending his belief that art must be autonomous, without any message—mystical, political, or otherwise.[17] Thus Akhmatova entered the literary scene just at the moment when Symbolism was in its death throes, and the literary world was looking for new and fresh ideas to revitalize it.

One response to this crisis was Mikhail Kuzmin's article "About Beautiful Clarity," which appeared in *Apollon* in 1910. It was specifically about prose, and most of the ideas expressed had little to do with the ornate style of his own poetic works, but others saw it as the harbinger of a new way of writing, based on clarity and simplicity.[18] Some critics would later perceive the influence of this piece on Akhmatova's own works, although the poems she had already written in Kiev were typical of the concise, simple style for which she became famous.

Before the end of the summer Akhmatova went to see her mother in Kiev and then returned to the literary life in Petersburg, appearing at meetings of the Academy of Verse. One of the members, Vladimir Pyast, describes Akhmatova's appearance there:

> During the summer there had been a rumor that Gumilyov had married and—in contrast to all expectations—"A most ordinary *baryshnya* [young noblewoman]. . . . Obviously, since Gumilyov had already made a trip to Abyssinia, we expected him to bring back a Zulu wife or, at least, a mulatto; we certainly thought only an exotic wife would suit him. Of course, it would not now occur to anyone to say that Akhmatova was "a very ordinary woman." This "very ordinary woman," as we soon found out, wrote poetry "for herself." As a compliment Ivanov allowed her once to recite in the non-official part of the program of the Academy meetings. All the poems from the evening were soon printed. And yet she had just begun to write poetry. The fact is that this "very ordinary woman" grew up all at once and became a poetess who from the very beginning entered the ranks of the most distinguished Russian poets. In about two years the "Akhmatova" direction began to appear in almost every woman's lyrics in Russia.[19]

Gumilyov made another trip to Africa that year. After a farewell party with his colleagues from *Apollon,* he left on September 25, traveling to Beirut, Port

Said, Djedda, and Djibouti.[20] He did not return until the end of March, 1911, leaving his young bride alone. This constant desire to leave the domestic hearth to seek adventure would dominate their marriage and eventually helped to destroy it.

While he was away, Akhmatova studied at Professor Rayev's Historical Literary Courses.[21] She was already beginning to impress notable members of artistic circles. The writer Georgy Chulkov describes meeting Akhmatova in 1910 at an opening of one of the World of Art exhibitions:

I noticed a tall, gray-eyed woman surrounded by colleagues of *Apollon,* standing in front of a picture by Sudeikin. A few days later I met her at Fyodor Sologub's . . . I accompanied her to the station. In the evening Petersburg fog she resembled a large bird which was used to flying high in the air, but was now dragging her wounded wing along the ground. "You know, I write poetry," she said as we waited for the train. Assuming she was one of those many poetesses of the time, I nonchalantly asked her to recite something. She began to recite some of the poems which became *Evening* [*Vecher*]. It was a new, unique melody. "You are an authentic poet," I said in a voice no longer indifferent. I'm proud I had the chance to predict for her a great place in Russian poetry at a time when she had not yet printed a single verse.[22]

Akhmatova characterized the year 1911 in her memoirs as being marked by the Chinese Revolution, which changed the face of Asia, and as the year of Blok's notebooks, full of forebodings.[23] Makovsky, the editor of *Apollon,* says that when Gumilyov went off to Africa, Akhmatova came over to visit and read her poems, and he offered to publish them.[24] He says Gumilyov would not allow Akhmatova to publish them, which was not true, since by then she had already published in three different journals. Moreover, she did not publish the poems in Makovsky's journal until April 1911, after Gumilyov was already home. But while Gumilyov was in Africa, she began writing the poems for her first book, *Evening.* Some critics maintained that after they married, Gumilyov began to teach her how to write poetry, and soon the pupil surpassed the teacher. "This is all nonsense!" says Akhmatova. "I'd been writing poetry since I was eleven years old, totally independently of Gumilyov. While they were not very good, Gumilyov, being honest, told me so."[25] When Gumilyov returned from Africa after six months on March 25, 1911, he asked her whether she had written any verse. She read him what she had done, and he responded with praise. Whenever they were apart, he would ask about the progress of her poems, provide useful commentary, and tell her which were his favorites.

In the middle of May, the couple went to Paris, but Gumilyov soon left to return to the family estate in Slepnyovo. Left alone, Akhmatova became involved with the Italian Jewish painter Amedeo Modigliani, who was still unknown at the time, poor and very lonely. He found this enigmatic young Russian woman very attractive. They had already met on her trip to Paris the year before, but had seen each other only rarely. He wrote to her all winter, and they spent much time together when she returned in 1911. They visited the Louvre, walked through the Luxembourg Gardens and the Latin Quarter, and explored the old streets behind the Panthéon in the moonlight. Inspired at this time by the art of ancient Egypt, Modigliani drew Akhmatova's head with the coiffure of the queens and dancers of the Nile. (One of these drawings always remained with Akhmatova later, no matter where she was residing.) Often on rainy days she and Modigliani would sit on a bench under an enormous umbrella in the Luxembourg Gardens reciting verses by Verlaine. "It was Modigliani who acquainted me with the true Paris," she wrote later. She also noted what a major turning point the affair was in the artistic lives of both of them:

> Everything that had happened to us up until that point was the prehistory of our lives. The spirit of art had not yet transformed these two beings; it was the hour just before the dawn. But the future, as we know, throws its shadow long before it arrives, knocks at the window, hides behind the street lamps, breaks into dreams and frightens you with the grotesque Paris of Baudelaire, which is hiding somewhere nearby.[26]

One time she came to see Modigliani and he was not at home. She was carrying red roses in her arms. The window over the studio was open, so she tossed the roses into the studio, then left. He was bewildered as to how she had managed to get into the locked room, and when she explained what she had done, he exclaimed, "Impossible! They were lying there so beautifully." Modigliani liked to wander the streets at night. When Akhmatova heard his footsteps in the quiet street, she would go to the window and watch his shadow, which lingered down below. Modigliani was struck by her ability to divine people's thoughts, to see others' dreams. He greatly regretted he did not speak Russian and could not understand her poems, but suspected there were marvels hidden within them, even though they were her first timid efforts.

In Paris, Akhmatova also met Georgy Chulkov's wife, who describes the time they spent together:

> We took walks and visited small cafés in the evening and then usually went to shows featuring comedy acts, popular singers, and dancers. Akhmatova was very young then—not more than twenty. She was very beautiful and everyone on the street would turn around to look at her. . . . She was tall, elegant, and wore a white dress and a wide-brimmed straw hat with a large ostrich feather which her husband, the poet Gumilyov, had brought her. He had recently returned from Abyssinia. . . . Once we visited a restaurant in Montmartre, a gilded palace, and left at dawn,

admiring Paris awakening from its sleep and preparing for the approaching day. . . . We stopped at a milk shop and drank hot, steaming milk. It was so nice to refresh ourselves from the night's drunken trance in the noisy gatherings in Montmartre.[27]

Upon her return home, Akhmatova joined Gumilyov at Slepnyovo. It was not a typical nobleman's estate, but more like a dacha, a summer cottage with land around it that had been cut off from the original Lvov estate, Boriskovo, on which relatives lived, the Kuzmin-Karavayevs.

Akhmatova described Slepnyovo in her memoirs, saying flatly, "This is not a picturesque spot: fields ploughed in even squares on a hilly spot, mills, bogs, dried-out swamps, wheat." She added that "Verses came with a light, free step."[28] A poem from 1913 sums up her ambivalence:

You know, I languish in captivity,
Praying to the Lord for death.
But I remember, to the point of pain,
Tver's barren, meager earth.

The crane on the decrepit well,
Over it, boiling, the clouds,
In the field a creaking little gate,
And the smell of wheat, and weariness.

And those pale expanses,
Where even the voice of the wind is weak,
And the condemning way
Those quiet, sunburnt peasant women look at me.

(I, p. 333)

Akhmatova wrote many of her most lyrical poems during the time she spent in Tver on her mother-in-law's estate.[29] She described her strange reception when she first arrived there from Paris in 1911:

A hunchbacked servant in the waiting room at the Bezhetsk station, who had known everyone in Slepnyovo for ages, refused to recognize me as a Russian lady [*barynya*] and told someone: "A French lady has come to visit the Slepnyovo gentleman." The steward, Ivan Derin . . . a bearded country bumpkin, happened to be sitting next to me at lunch, and dying of embarrassment because he could not think of anything to ask, said: "You probably find it very cold here after Egypt?" It turned out that he had heard of my legendary slenderness so typical of young women of that time, and so I was mysteriously called the "London mummy" that brought misfortune. I didn't ride horseback and didn't play tennis. I just collected mushrooms, and over my shoulder Paris seemed to still blaze in a last sunset.[30]

Akhmatova wore a malachite necklace and a cap of fine lace. In her room hung a large icon, *Christ in Prison,* and over the divan was a small portrait of Tsar Nikolay I. In the cupboard were the remains of an old library. She thought, "at that time the old peasant women and young girls seemed more elegant than ancient statues."[31]

The artist Dmitry Bushen, who lived with his aunt Yekaterina Kuzmina-Karavayeva on the neighboring estate, noted his impressions of Gumilyov at the time—tall, not at all handsome, but when he spoke, it was so fascinating that you forgot what he looked like. Bushen believed Akhmatova was very much in love with Gumilyov then, although the tension between them was already apparent.[32]

Gumilyov's Aunt Varvara Lvova was living at Slepnyovo that summer, and her daughter Konstantsiya Kuzmina-Karavayeva came to visit with her two daughters, Masha and Olga. Gumilyov fell in love with Masha, who was kind, intelligent, but very ill with tuberculosis.

On another of the neighboring estates lived Vera Nevedomskaya, who returned in July 1911 from her honeymoon, and to her delight found new neighbors at Slepnyovo. Nevedomskaya wrote that "Akhmatova had the face of an Old Believer from a convent, features too sharp to be called beautiful, gray eyes without a smile. . . . At the table she was silent, and one immediately sensed she was a stranger in her husband's family, this patriarchal family—Nikolay and his wife were white crows."[33]

Nevedomskaya added that Gumilyov's mother was upset that her son did not want to serve in either the military or diplomatic corps, but had become a poet and gone off to Africa; he had picked out a very strange wife who also wrote poetry, was very quiet and went around in strange get-ups—either a dark cotton dress that resembled a peasant's sarafan or an extravagant Parisian-style narrow skirt with a slit.

The Slepnyovo estate was quite modest, but Nevedomskaya lived in a large house with empire columns, a huge park, and horses. Here Gumilyov could let his fantasies flow. Akhmatova felt stifled and bored in the surroundings of her husband's family, but when she came to visit Nevedomskaya's estate, Podobino, she could feel free to express herself. However, Nevedomskaya says Akhmatova became really lively only when poetry was discussed. In contrast to Gumilyov, Akhmatova always appeared introverted and strange.

Nevedomskaya described the various games the young people played when they came to Podobino. Gumilyov would make them up. Once he improvised a circus: He became a trick rider, standing on his saddle and jumping the barriers. Akhmatova, the "snake woman," had the amazing ability to put her leg behind her neck. Gumilyov was the master-of-ceremonies and wore a frock coat and top hat. Another time some of the group went off to a nearby village and were asked by the peasants crowding around them who they were. Gumilyov replied that they were a traveling circus. The peasants begged them to perform, and were so excited by what they saw that they started taking up a collection, but the performers became embarrassed and quickly escaped.

That summer Akhmatova and Gumilyov visited Moscow, then she traveled to Petersburg and Kiev, returned to Slepnyovo, and then on to Tsarskoye Selo, where she and Gumilyov spent the rest of the year. Gumilyov's mother had bought a house on 63, Malaya Street, where the Gumilyovs lived until 1916.[34] It was a two-story house, painted green, with a small fence and garden. Gumilyov had a yellow room and table on which he wrote poems; often he slept on the couch in the library. He had a small bedroom designated the "Abyssinian room," hung with pictures of Abyssinia and animal skins on the walls. Akhmatova's room was bright blue, with silk upholstery. When their rooms were given to a relative in the spring of 1916, Akhmatova moved into the study and Gumilyov lived upstairs in a small room. Makovsky says Akhmatova's room had a canvas by the avant-garde artist Alexandra Exter, and old-fashioned and Art Nouveau furniture. When people came to visit, Gumilyov would act like a child, showing off his trophies— elephant tusks and jaguar skins. Akhmatova was not very interested in these exotic props; "she looked at life more simply and deeply." As Makovsky came to know them better, he said it was clear Gumilyov expected submission and obedience from Akhmatova: "He loved her but did not understand her. She was proud and more intelligent than he was. Behind her extreme fragility was a strong will and a healthy mind."[35]

Anna Gumilyova, who had married Gumilyov's brother Dmitry, lived in the same house with them. In her memoirs she says that Akhmatova generally lived her own life. She got up very late, and after eating, would disappear into her room. In the evening she would either write in her room or leave for Petersburg, whereas Gumilyov was always a lively companion.[36]

Although Akhmatova may have appeared taciturn and withdrawn to her sister-in-law and their acquaintances, she described herself as being quite different when entertaining her own friends. "When I was young I was very sociable, loved guests, loved to go visiting. Kolya explained my sociability: when left alone, I constantly wrote poems. I needed people to rest from poetry, otherwise I would keep writing, never tearing myself away, never resting."[37]

Akhmatova's life was not just limited to literature at this time. She went to concerts given in the large room next to the *Apollon* office. Makovsky had a wonderful Bechstein piano: Igor Grastinuk played excerpts from Stravinsky's *Petrouchka* and the *Firebird*, Prokofiev performed his first piano sonatas, and Serge Koussevitsky amazed them with his virtuosity on the bass. Pianists often gave concerts here of the works of Rimsky-Korsakov, Mussorgsky, Debussy, and Ravel.[38]

* * *

Akhmatova soon became so identified with the artistic society of Petersburg that in a contemporary's memoir, she appears as one of the details typical of the capital in 1910–15: "Fog, streets, bronze horses, triumphal arches over the gates, Akhmatova, sailors and academics, the Neva, railings, murmuring lines at the bread shops, stray bullets of light from broken street lamps have settled in my memory . . . of the past, like love, like a disease, like the years."[39]

Within a few years she had developed from a shy young girl to a self-assured, regal woman. Korney Chukovsky says that she reminded him then of a passage from a poem by Nekrasov:

> There are women in Russian villages
> With a calm importance on their faces
> With beautiful power in their movements
> With the walk, the gaze of a tsarina.

Chukovsky, who was to write so many articles on Akhmatova's work, met her for the first time in 1915.

> The young poet Nikolay Gumilyov led her over to me. Slender, elegant, she resembled a shy, fifteen-year-old girl. She did not make a move without her husband; she was publishing her first poems at that time and experiencing unusual, unexpectedly enormous triumphs. Two or three years passed, and in her eyes, her bearing, in her treatment of people, one of the main features of her personality became apparent: her dignity. Not conceit, not arrogance, not insolence, but dignity based on the invincible feeling of the great importance of her mission as a writer.

He credited her upbringing in Tsarskoye Selo as the source of her unique refinement:

> At times, especially among guests, among strangers, she behaved with an intentional regal air, like an elegant woman of the world. That's when you sensed within her that polish by which we native Petersburgians unmistakably recognize people raised in Tsarskoye Selo. I always felt that imprint in her voice, manner and gestures. . . . The signs of this rare type of person are a strong sensitivity to music, poetry, and art, refined taste, an irreproachable correctness of carefully polished speech, extreme (slightly cold) politeness regarding strangers, and a total absence of passionate, strong, unrestrained gestures typical of a vulgar lack of control. Akhmatova had absorbed all these Tsarskoye Selo qualities.[40]

Akhmatova continued to appear at the Tower. Fyodor Fidler, a member of the literary circles and one of Gumilyov's instructors at the gymnasium, noted that he saw Akhmatova in March 1911, "the young wife of my lazy former pupil, who was wandering around Africa," there. He describes the chaotic atmosphere of the Tower: "Yesterday I was invited to Vycheslav Ivanov's. I ended up in a decadent nest, but everything turned out all right. At first they spoke about the probability of war, then about Scriabin's symphony *Prometheus,* and finally read some rather decent poetry."[41] Alexander Scriabin's name was on everyone's lips at the time. He combined innovations in musical style with Nietzschean content in his tone poems. Pasternak, who was much influenced by Scriabin as a young man, said that the composer preached Nietszche's ideas of the Superman.[42] Scriabin created philosophical tone poems in which leitmotifs or a particular melodic sequence were associated with abstract concepts such as "will," "chaos," and "lethargy." Works like *Toward the Flame, Poem of Ecstasy,* and *Prometheus* portray a world weak and lethargic. Suddenly energy, a glimmer of divine will, is introduced, which becomes increasingly stronger until man and the cosmos are revitalized; the music culminates in a merging of man and the universe in a state of Dionysian ecstasy.[43]

It was at the Tower in the spring of 1911 that Akhmatova met Osip Mandelstam, who would become one of her dearest friends, and one of the few of her generation of poets to remain in Russia after the Revolution. In her beautiful memoir of him, she wrote, "At that time he was a thin boy, with a lily-of-the-valley in his buttonhole and long eyelashes."[44]

Mandelstam was born in Warsaw in 1891, two years after Akhmatova. His father was a leather merchant who moved his family to Petersburg soon after Osip's birth. When Akhmatova met him, Mandelstam had just returned from a year in Heidelberg, and was now studying in Petersburg at the university. He often appeared dressed in an elegant English suit, sported sideburns, and projected the very image of a Romantic poet. He had fallen in love with Salomea Andronikova, a Georgian aristocrat and good friend of Akhmatova's. A contemporary described Andronikova as "not a writer, not a poetess, not an actress, not a ballerina and not a singer—but she was recognized as the most interesting woman of our circle."[45] What everyone loved about her was her ability to listen— and her ability to speak.

Mandelstam too was loved, not only for his great poetic sensibility but for his very special personal qualities. The art critic Nikolay Punin captured the attraction of this very vulnerable and gifted human being, and described his special relationship with Akhmatova. The two poets created their own magical world:

> Here was a creature more perfect than most people. He listened to his interlocutor with his lowered long lashes, as if listening not to words but what was hidden behind the words. . . . A conversation between him and other people very often turned into a poetic improvisation in a special spiritual space, witty without being nasty; with a certain delicacy he would throw a challenge to his partner and then catch it himself, but from the other end, as if he had run from one point to the other in the conversation.

He was not handsome, but attractive—and charming, especially when he squinted and threw his head back like a bird. Later I was often present at conversations between Akhmatova and Mandelstam. It was a brilliant dialogue which made me both excited and envious—they would speak together for hours, perhaps without saying anything remarkable, but it was a genuine poetic game totally inaccessible to me. . . . This small exultant Jew was magnificent—grand—like a fugue.[46]

Mandelstam perceived intuitively that Akhmatova had been marked by destiny with the gift of creation, for which she would pay by great suffering. He spoke of this in a poem entitled "Like a Black Angel on the Snow," written at the time:

Today you were like
A Black Angel in the snow,
And it's difficult to keep this secret

God's seal is upon you,
So strange a seal—
Granted by heaven—
That you seemed to stand
In a church, in a niche.
May it be that love not of this earth
And love of this earth will intermix,
May it be that storm-blood
Will not appear on your cheeks,
And magnificent marble will set off
All the deceptions of this wrath,
All the nakedness of your softest flesh,
But not your blushing cheeks.[47]

Another poet who appeared at the Tower was Velemir Khlebnikov. Born in 1885 in Astrakhan on the coast of the Caspian Sea, he changed his name from Victor to Velemir, which was more Slavic. He was the son of an ornithologist, and studied bird behavior when he was young. Khlebnikov had been a student of mathematics at the University of Kazan, then came to Petersburg, where he studied Sanskrit, Slavic studies, and biology, but was writing poetry at the same time. He soon became part of Ivanov's circle, attending meetings at the Academy of Verse and turning up at the Tower. Khlebnikov also practiced numerology, attempting to find mathematical patterns of prediction in the past in order to predict the future. At that time, though he dressed like a dandy, "Velimir the Great" was characterized by the composer Arthur Lourie as a "holy fool,"

close to those eccentric and strange beings created by E. T. A. Hoffmann. Like these strange creatures, one could not expect any sober, rational action. He was in the realm of the irrational, the fantastic. He was very poor, no furniture. He would arrange his notebooks and pieces of paper on his bed and work while standing on his knees in front of it. He was like a holy fool, one of those mad men gifted by God with great insight, but generally considered mad. He was impeccably polite and delicate in his treatment of people. He possessed an oral purity, never used a vulgar word, never lied, and was very kind. His mathematical calculations were a mystery for most—they were of an eschatological nature, predicting the end of the world.[48]

The relations between Gumilyov and Ivanov were becoming increasingly strained at this point. At a meeting of the Academy of Verse, Ivanov criticized one of Gumilyov's poems harshly. In turn, in 1912 Gumilyov gave a sarcastically negative review of Ivanov's collection *Cors ardens* in *Apollon*.

Mandelstam discussed the increasing disillusionment with Symbolism felt by his generation. By then the movement had outlived itself, its creative ideas reduced to empty forms and formulas:

> In place of the Symbolists' forms of correspondences we are left with a workshop producing scarecrows. . . . Nothing is real, genuine. Nothing is left but a terrifying quadrille of "correspondences" all nodding to one another. Never a clear thing, but hints and whispers. The rose nods to the girl, the girl to the rose. No one wants to be himself. No longer wonder at the phenomena of this world as phenomena in and of themselves.[49]

In response to this crisis, Gumilyov and the poet Sergey Gorodetsky decided to form a new literary organization, the Poets' Guild. The group founded the journal *Hyperborean* (1912–14), edited by Mikhail Lozinsky. The first meeting of the Guild took place in autumn 1911. Little held the group together except their rejection of Symbolism. Kuzmin and Blok attended one meeting, but soon found they had no interest in it, and left. Georgy Adamovich described what the sessions were like: "Gumilyov had an amazing ear for poetry, an exceptional feeling for the verbal texture of poems. But he was better at judging other people's verses than his own. Akhmatova spoke little and became animated only when Mandelstam read his works."[50]

Six of the members—Gumilyov, Akhmatova, Mandelstam, Gorodetsky, Narbut, and Mikhail Zenkevich—soon formed a new movement called "Acmeism," or "Adamism." "Acmeism in Greek," wrote Gumilyov, "means the point of highest achievement, the time of blossoming; Adamism means a virile, firm and clear outlook on life."[51] In his discussion of Acmeism, the poet Gorodetsky emphasized the need for poetry to turn to the beauty of this world, and like Mandelstam, he urged poets to cease looking at objects from everyday reality as merely symbols of another, mystical world: "For the Acmeist, the rose has once more become beautiful in and of itself. Its petals are beautiful, its fragrance and color, and not the thoughts, correspondences, mystical love and other things of that sort which are evoked by it."[52]

Akhmatova later became quite cynical about Gorodetsky's interest in Acmeism, saying that for him Acmeism was just another passion—first he was a mystical anarchist, then he became interested in the theories of Vyacheslav Ivanov, then the Acmeists and folklore, patriotic verse; finally he ended up as a Communist. The only thing that bound Gumilyov and Gorodetsky together was a desire to follow new principles of art and create their own tradition. They had never been particularly close before.[53]

The critic Vasily Gippius wrote of the Guild and Acmeism:

A new school did not grow out of Acmeism because schools are not created only by world views. Rejecting symbolism and mysticism, the Acmeists did not know where to go and ended up in the open sea. They had no disciples, no followers. It lasted about two years as a simple group of poets. The role of the Guild was important—here Akhmatova was recognized, her first steps grew firm. In the eyes of the Guild, Gumilyov grew from an imitator of Bryusov into an independent poet. . . . Mandelstam became popular. His transformation from a refined Symbolist into an Acmeist was sudden and unexpected.[54]

However, in an article published in 1913, Bryusov attacked Acmeism, "such a great topic of discussion recently," calling it "a hothouse plant cultivated under the glass hood of a literary circle by several young poets who certainly wish to say something new. . . . Acmeism is an invention, a whim. It is possible to take it seriously only because under its transparent banner there are several poets who are definitely talented." His reaction was predictable. As Akhmatova pointed out, how could the person who considered himself the founder of Russian Symbolism and one of its creators reject what was his own?[55]

There were many analogies between Acmeism and Imagism in the West. Imagists like Ezra Pound also believed in modernizing diction and, like T. E. Hulme, objected to the Romantic confusion of poetry and religion. Pound emphasized the importance of craftsmanship and technique, warning against inspired poetry. Yet Pound and Gumilyov alike agreed that no amount of craft or knowledge would replace talent, which is vital to a genuine poet. Both Acmeism and Imagism contributed to a renewal of aesthetic taste in Russia and elsewhere—a taste for simplicity, clarity, economy, and craftsmanship.[56]

For Akhmatova, the highlight of the meetings of the Guild were the poems by Mandelstam. Akhmatova told Georgy Adamovich how boring the meetings could be. "You sat for several hours and read poetry, some good, some ordinary.

Then suddenly your attention would be distracted. You listened because you had to—and suddenly, as if some swan flew in above you . . . Osip reads."

"In my memory, the image of Mandelstam is indissolubly connected with the memory of Akhmatova," Adamovich wrote later.

> Their names should go together in the history of Russian poetry. He valued her no less than she did him. . . . I remember one meeting of the Guild at which Akhmatova read the poem "Noiselessly they wandered," which she had just written, evoking an excited, feverish monologue by Mandelstam in reply—to Akhmatova's surprise thinking that these lines were not particularly successful.[57]

At the end of 1911 Gumilyov went to Finland to visit Masha Kuzmina-Karavayeva, who was very ill; he accompanied her to Italy, hoping she would be cured, but she died there in January 1912.[58] It was a great loss to him, for he loved her deeply.

In February, Gumilyov became more aggressive in his attacks on Symbolism. At a meeting of the Academy of Verse, when Ivanov and Bely delivered speeches, he attacked them. Then he wrote an article—"The Legacy of Symbolism and Acmeism"— describing and defending Acmeism, which appeared in *Apollon,* no. 1 (1913). His poems in his new collection *Strange Sky* (1912) exhibited a new direction, simpler in theme and style. Akhmatova analyzed Gumilyov's development perceptively: "One must understand Gumilyov's character and what is most important in his character: as a boy he believed in Symbolism, as people believe in God. This was sacred, untouchable, but the closer he came to Symbolism, the more his belief wavered. He began to be upset by it."[59]

Viktor Zhirmunsky summed up the literary struggles of the past few years in another important article, entitled "Overcoming Symbolism," written in 1915. He pointed out that by 1912, when Akhmatova published her own first collection, *Evening (Vecher)*, she and the Acmeists had left behind much of the Symbolist aesthetic:

> Poets became tired of going to the Golgotha of mysticism; they wanted to be simpler, more direct, more human in their experiences. They were tired of so much lyricism, spiritual excitement. . . . They did not feel a sacred obligation to proclaim divine truths, but wanted to speak about objects from external life simply and clearly, stories about intimate ordinary life. They continued the Symbolists' focus on artistic technique, but produced not so much melodious lines, a musical effect, as the pictorial, graphic clarity of visual images.[60]

One of the inspirations for the new turn to simplicity and clarity was Innokenty Annensky. He linked objects from the everyday world to a psychic state rather than imbuing them, as the Symbolists did, with transcendental meaning.[61] A deflated child's balloon, a worn-out barrel organ, or a broken watch corresponded to internal psychological states such as fear, disillusionment, or creative joy. While the Symbolists turned mainly to the city, Annensky also wrote about the countryside and landed estates. His innovations, including the use of images with emotional rather than logical connotations, and sudden transitions from one subject to the next, influenced Akhmatova considerably.[62] In his use of conversational language, the preciseness of his poetic world, and subjects more typical of psychological prose than contemporary poetry, Annensky also had an important impact on Akhmatova's style.

Akhmatova published forty-six poems in her first collection, *Evening*. The three hundred copies sold out quickly. In his preface to the book, Mikhail Kuzmin grasped the dramatic turn Russian poetry had taken with the appearance of these poems. He compared Akhmatova to members of an ancient Alexandrian society, who each day pretended they were condemned to death in order to make their everyday impressions more poignant.[63] Imagery appeared in their memory as vivid fragments, yet these fragments did not come in sequence, but in a stream of images. Kuzmin believed Akhmatova's work reflected this same heightened sensitivity, as well as the thought processes of the Alexandrian society.

Though the response to *Evening* was generally positive, Akhmatova herself was later critical of it, saying rather coyly:

> These are the poor poems of a very vapid little girl which for some reason were reprinted thirteen times. . . . The little girl herself did not foresee such a fate for them and hid a number of journals under the sofa pillow. Because of the anxiety caused by their appearance, she went to Italy [the spring of 1912] and sitting in a tram, thought, looking at her neighbors: "How happy they are—they haven't had a little book published."[64]

Nevertheless, as Chukovsky points out, the youth of two or three generations fell in love to the accompaniment of Akhmatova's poems, finding in them the embodiment of their own feelings.[65]

Evening concentrates on the many facets of love—from awakening hope to joyful fulfillment, from disillusionment to the last embers of a dying relationship. The themes and language are, as Mandelstam said, not "ladylike" (as was typical of Akhmatova's imitators) but more comparable to Russian women's folk songs, where emotion is generally human rather than specifically feminine, just as in the so-called male poems of Pushkin or Goethe. As with the appearance of Pushkin's clear, concise verse, her contemporaries were struck not only by what was present, but by what she had left out in her poetic diction. The sparseness is characteristic, as is the absence of any overwhelming melodiousness or the complex mystical, mythological, and erudite images so typical of Symbolist verse. The sparseness itself was a form of experimentation. Chulkov commented, "Schopenhauer, annoyed by feminine chattiness, suggested they [female poets] be shut up. What would he have said if he had read Akhmatova's poems? She is one of the most silent of poets; her words are sparse, restrained, severe; strained and concentrated emotions are couched in simple, precise and harmonic form." He noted the lack of metaphors, strict selection of words, daring use of rhyme, unique rhythm, juxtaposition of images, and the touching irony of her verse.[66]

Certain themes continually recur in Akhmatova's verse, especially the theme of Fate, which often is cruel to the heroine. In *Evening,* it is mainly personal fate in a love relationship that is the focus of attention. There is a sense that if the heroine experiences a precious moment of happiness, she will have to pay dearly for it. There are various ways she can deal with her suffering: passivity, a feeling of helplessness, numbness, or finally the idea that unhappiness is a normal state and one must learn to endure it and find compensation by looking at the positive aspects of the situation. Already in these poems the key themes of retribution, punishment for self-indulgent behavior, indifference to the pain of others, and a guilty conscience are apparent. Another motif in the early verse is that of memory, which can preserve the valuable moments in life but also those moments that may be a source of torment. Memory becomes linked with guilt and atonement, retribution and expiation; for by recalling the moments that make us feel guilty and atoning for them, we can expiate our sins. This would prove a major theme in *Poem Without a Hero.*[67]

One of Akhmatova's most innovative techniques is her use of abrupt shifts in perspective. In describing concrete setting and landscapes, a character's actions, she chooses what at first may seem a chance detail, and then rearranges reality through the use of a highly selective eye. Objects and events appear not in causal or chronological sequence, but through the personal associations which she attaches to them.[68] In this sense her works reflect the ideas of Henri Bergson, as well as Freud's analysis of dreams, where normally unrelated people and events occur together because of the private associations of the dreamer. In her poems there is that same technique of flashback, multi-exposure of events, the manipulation of time that we see in the works of Marcel Proust, James Joyce, Andrey Bely, and T. S. Eliot.[69]

The Russian psychological novel also played an important role in Akhmatova's development. As Mandelstam noted: "Akhmatova brought to the Russian lyric the enormous complexity and richness of the Russian novel of the nineteenth century. There never would have been an Akhmatova without Tolstoy and *Anna Karenina,* Turgenev with *Nest of Gentry,* and all of Dostoyevsky. The genesis of Akhmatova lies in Russian prose and not in poetry. Her poetic form, strong and unique, was developed with a glance at psychological prose."[70]

Symbols still are relevant in Akhmatova's poems, but they are of a different nature from those used by the Symbolists. They are metonymic symbols, where, for example, an ordinary object associated with somebody may stand for him— a tall hat and ivory-tipped cane for a dandy; the crown for a king. However, often these objects also have particular associations. Black, shiny boots became associated with the police, and therefore oppressive authority in Sergey Eisenstein's films, while champagne and jazz became associated with Western decadence in early Soviet posters. Similarly, in Akhmatova, the woven belt in "My husband whipped me . . . " (1911) indicates the class of the protagonist—she is a peasant woman who is being beaten by her husband, but the belt also represents the hateful authority he has over her. A riding crop and a glove left behind on a table in "The door is half open" (1911) immediately calls to mind someone from the middle or upper class; but the fact they have been left behind indicates something has occurred to distract the owner of these objects and make him forget them. They become symbols of a psychological event, of a turning point in a relationship. In "He loved three things in life" (1910), the beauty of evensong, white peacocks, and old maps of America not only represent things the speaker's husband is fond of but are associated with someone who is an aesthete and an intellectual. Those objects and events associated with her—children crying, tea with jam, and women's hysteria—reveal that she spends her days in an entirely different realm of psychological existence, and the two worlds are incompatible.

Critics frequently mention the influence of Alexander Pushkin's concise style on Akhmatova. Like her, Pushkin wrote verses in clear language in an age when poetic style was typically rhetorical and ornate. Like her, he often turned to metonymic symbolism, choosing one telling facial expression, detail of clothing, or element of nature. But beneath these simple details was a subtext—they reveal the state of mind or character of the protagonist, a historical situation, even a philosophical concept. In Pushkin's poem "Doride," the shyness, careless dress and speech, and endearing names of his sweetheart are enough to reveal to the speaker that he is loved:

> I believe: I am loved; my heart must believe this,
> No, my sweetheart is not hypocritical.
> Nothing is feigned: the languorous head of desire,
> Shy embarrassment, the invaluable gift,
> The lovely carelessness of dress and speech,
> And the young tenderness of endearing names.[71]

Inner feelings are not described directly, but indirectly through simple outward signs. A poem by Akhmatova that is similar in style to Pushkin is "The Fisherman," which was written in April 1911:

> Her cheeks are pale, her hands are weak,
> Her wary glance is deep,
> Crabs crawl out along the sand,
> Tickling her feet.

But she no longer
Reaches out to catch them.
The blood beats ever stronger
In a body wounded by desire.

(I, p. 261)

Although some are lyrical monologues, frequently her poems are in the form of a dialogue with narration. Laconic remarks, interrupted conversation, monologue and dialogue alternate, crossing on several psychological levels.

Akhmatova also creates unusual combinations of adjectives and nouns to produce a metaphorical effect—"broad sound," "trembling February." The same adjective may be positive or negative, depending on the context: white may be the color of a bridal veil or a shroud, yellow roses may signify joy, but a yellow sky evokes anxiety. She devises oxymorons, combinations of opposites, such as "bitter fame" and "joyful grief."[72] Wendy Rosslyn points out that the use of everyday words gives the impression that Akhmatova's verses are deceptively simple. "Though Akhmatova uses simple, ordinary, and therefore very familiar words, she clothes them with new and personal associations so that the emotional load which they carry differentiates them from the same words used in ordinary speech."[73]

Akhmatova's meters are interesting but not totally innovative. She is often cited for her extensive use of a meter that was unusual in nineteenth-century Russian poetry, the *dolnik*—a poem with a fixed number of accents but not a fixed number of syllables. However, this meter was used extensively among the Symbolists, especially by Bryusov and Blok. Akhmatova cannot be viewed as a metrical innovator, but she continued the experiments of her immediate predecessors.[74] Her poetry also exhibits the influence of Russian folk lyrics (usually sung by women) both in their concise manner of conveying emotion and through specific techniques such as parallelism—the juxtaposition of events from nature and the outside world with events relating to the human condition. A typical song compares a bush with no leaves on it to a young girl pining:

There is a bush in the middle of the field
All alone it stands
It does not dry up, does not wither,
But there are no leaves on it.
And I, bitter, unhappy,
Will always cry for my sweetheart.
During the day I pine, at night I grieve,
Quietly I shed tears.
The tears burn, the snow melts,
Grass will grow on it.[75]

Akhmatova sometimes alluded directly to Russian folklore in *Evening*. In "High in the Sky . . . " (1911), for example, the speaker's lover refers to the famous Russian tale of the Snow Maiden who falls in love with a mortal. Because the Snow Maiden is caught up in the divine plan of revenge of the sun god Yarilo, she must suffer: The sun's rays melt her on her wedding day. Akhmatova implies that her heroine will experience the same grief in love as this poetic figure. At the end of the poem, Akhmatova refers to another Russian custom: on Epiphany Eve, young girls tell their fortunes and guess who their bridegroom will be. The heroine also takes part in this hopeful ritual, even though she seems to feel that her love, like that of the Snow Maiden, will bring her grief by the spring. (The same ritual later played an important role in *Poem Without a Hero*.)

In "My husband whipped me . . . ," Akhmatova takes on the persona of the peasant woman. Here she picks up a theme that is typical of Russian women's folk lyrics—an unhappy young wife, beaten and held psychological prisoner by her unloved husband, sits by the window thinking of her lover:

> My husband whipped me with his woven belt
> Folded in two.
> All night I've been at the little window
> With a taper, waiting for you.
>
> Day breaks. And over the forge
> Puffs a puff of smoke.
> Ah, once more you couldn't be here
> With this sad prisoner.
>
> It's a gloomy fate, a torturous fate
> I've accepted for you.
> Are you in love with someone fair?
> Or is your sweetheart auburn-haired?
>
> How can I suppress you, my long, low moans!
> In my heart there is dark, stifling drunkenness,
> And a few slender sunbeams lie down
> On the unrumpled bed.
>
> (I, p. 239)

Akhmatova's main interest in Russian folk poetry was not to imitate devices of oral literature, but to present the peasant's point of view.[76] Even the device of parallelism, though perhaps originally derived from folk lyrics, is used throughout and becomes an integral part of her own technique.

In an early poem not included in *Evening*, "On his hand are lots of shining rings . . . " (1907), published by Gumilyov in *Sirius*, Akhmatova began using metonymic symbols. Each of the rings worn by the speaker's lover was given to him by a different woman, and thus metonymically represents her. But the poet has another gift—the gift of poetry—which she will never bestow upon him, even if it means the loss of love.

Several of Akhmatova's early poems show traces of the Symbolist aesthetic, with its love of fantasy, costume, and the eighteenth century. "Masquerade in the Park," which bears the same trappings as Bely's poem "Declaration of Love"— a cornice, a marquise—is one example. Sometimes Akhmatova turns to Shakespeare. In her two-poem cycle *Reading Hamlet* (Kiev, 1909), like Ophelia, the speaker defends herself against her beloved's cruel words. The heroine wishes to marry a prince, but life presents her only with the choice of marrying a fool or going into a nunnery.[77]

One of Akhmatova's most popular poems, "The Gray-Eyed King" (1910) is related to this theme. According to some critics, the apparent fairy tale reflects Akhmatova's own dilemma: she married Gumilyov thinking he was a fairy prince, and he turned out to be a very ordinary human being. According to another interpretation, she had waited for her prince, her ideal love, to come along before she married, and never viewed Gumilyov as someone with whom she could ever be passionately involved. The death of the gray-eyed king indicates that she has given up any hope of meeting this ideal:

Hail to thee, everlasting pain!
The gray-eyed king died yesterday.

Scarlet and close was the autumn eve,
My husband returning, said calmly to me:

"They brought him back from the hunt, you know,
They found his body near the old oak.

Pity the queen. So young! . . .
Overnight her hair has turned gray."

Then he found his pipe on the hearth
And left, as he did every night, for work.

I will wake my little daughter now,
And look into her eyes of gray.

And outside the window the poplars whisper:
"Your king is no more on this earth. . . . "

(I, p. 259)

The reader does not realize the relationship between the female speaker and the gray-eyed king until the color of the child's eyes is mentioned. This is the poet's way of telling us it is the king's child, and that the speaker as well as the queen will be grieving. The calm way the husband picks up his pipe and leaves for work implies he knows nothing of the relationship between the speaker and the king. Typically in this early work Akhmatova conveys abstract ideas and reveals psychological relationships through a few carefully selected details. (Prokofiev later set this poem to music.)

Throughout her career Akhmatova would write poems about her Muse, who for centuries has appeared as a female figure inspiring male poets. For Akhmatova, she often appears as the poet's sister. In "To the Muse" (1911), Akhmatova introduces a crucial theme: that the woman poet must give up normal life in order to create. The Muse takes away from the poet the golden ring, the marriage ring, symbolizing normal family happiness:

> Muse! You see how happy they all are,
> Girls, wives, widows . . .
> Better to perish on the wheel,
> But not these chains.
>
> (II, p. 249)

What she does have in common with other ordinary women is the chance to play the game of love, picking off daisy petals to see whether "he loves me or he loves me not." But she is destined to lose. She shares with other women not the emotional security of family life but only the torments of love.

The cycle of poems in *Evening* devoted to Tsarskoye Selo initiates a theme that would develop over the course of her life, as Akhmatova faced increasingly tragic experiences. Her life there eventually becomes symbolic of the calm before the storm of revolution and war. In 1911, although the speaker has complaints, life is still relatively peaceful. The cycle *In Tsarsykoye Selo* portrays the refined cultivation of nature that was so typical of the time—extending even to the combed-out manes of horses and the *allée* with its planted trees. In this toy town it is difficult to take relationships seriously, and she, too, has been reduced to a toy, like her "rosy-friend the cockatoo."

The last poem in this cycle refers to Pushkin.[78] In two marvelous images Akhmatova captures Pushkin as a young boy: his three-cornered hat, which places him in the early nineteenth century; and the book of Parny, the poet of light, amorous verse which the early Pushkin imitated before he developed his own classical style.[79] While attending the Lyceum in Tsarskoye Selo, Pushkin wandered along these same *allées* and wrote lyrically of the landscape so dear to him:

> In mute silence slumber the vale and the groves,
> In the gray mist, a distant forest.
> Barely heard is the brook, rushing into a canopy of oaks.
> Barely breathes the zephyr, falling asleep in the leaves.
> And the quiet moon, like a magnificent swan,
> Floats in the silver clouds.
> . . .

There, in the quiet lake, water sprites splash.
. . .
Didn't earthly gods spend peaceful days here?[80]

"First Return" (1919) was not included in the first edition of *Evening*. This poem reflects the time when Akhmatova returned to Tsarskoye Selo after her marriage. It has been five years since she last lived here. Instead of being overjoyed by the beauty of the palace and parks, the poet now looks at the "other" Tsarskoye Selo, where ordinary people live, and finds it tedious, "dead and dumb."

One of the most famous poems from this collection, "Under her dark veil" (1911), is a masterpiece of gesture and indirect discourse. Two brief gestures—she wrings her hands, she rushes down the stairs so fast she does not touch the bannister—reveal the heroine's overwrought state of mind. The hero is just as upset, which again is revealed through gesture and facial expression—he staggers, his mouth twists in agony. At the end Akhmatova achieves a masterful Chekhovian touch in which there is a clear contrast between the spoken words and the real subject. After an intensely emotional scene, the lover's calm smile, his remark, "Don't stand in the wind," indicate he wishes to end the affair, that he wishes to discuss it no longer—not that he is worried whether the heroine will catch cold.

Another very famous poem, "The Song of the Last Meeting" (1911), begins with a slight but revealing gesture—putting a glove on the wrong hand—to convey the heroine's troubled state of mind:

So helplessly my breast grew cold,
But my steps were light.
I put on my right hand
The glove for my left.
(II, p. 225)

In "At the new moon . . . " (1911), the poet takes on the persona of a tightrope walker abandoned by her lover. While at first feigning indifference when her lover tells her he is leaving, she soon admits how painful is her loss. Her feelings are expressed through the prism of her world—the circus—comparing the terror she feels when performing to the strong emotion that overwhelms her because her lover has abandoned her. Typically, her lover's absence is noted indirectly, by the fact that the box in which he used to sit to watch the tightrope walker's performance is now empty.

But the poem "He loved three things in life" referred to earlier illustrates the danger of using Akhmatova's poetry as evidence of her own personal autobiography. This work is often interpreted as describing Akhmatova's role as the wife of Gumilyov. The hero is depicted through elegant, aesthetic images such as white peacocks and evensong, while the woman is portrayed in a world filled with ordinary details—strawberry jam and screaming children. Akhmatova saves the most important detail for last: the speaker is the hero's wife. Clearly these two people cohabit the same space but live in two mutually incomprehensible worlds. However, Akhmatova was no more capable of being an ordinary housewife than her mother. She wrote this poem before she had a child, but soon after her son was born he was sent to her mother-in-law's at Slepnyovo because Akhmatova felt she could not take on the responsibilities of motherhood. Numerous friends recounted how helpless Akhmatova was in running a household. In a few simple lines Akhmatova's poem brilliantly conveys the plight of the ordinary woman married to an aesthete or intellectual, but not the real-life situation and character of the poet herself.

In discussing the poems in *Evening,* Vasily Gippius praised Akhmatova's "feminine soul": "Here everything is feminine: the penetrating eye, the beloved memory of things precious, grace—refined and just a bit capricious. . . . Akhmatova is a genuine lyric poet." He then examined Akhmatova's poetic genealogy, predecessors who could have influenced her verse, but showed how she differs from them: "There is none of the strong grief and bitterness of Annensky, the melancholy of Kuzmin, the mystical languor of Sologub, the outbursts of ecstasy and despair of Blok. . . . Here it is rather restrained pain, compressed lips, and eyes just about to cry. . . . In these colorful and ironic stories, elegantly stylized and almost precious verses, the voice of Akhmatova grows strong." Gippius singled out Akhmatova from the enormous number of other "young poets" who were publishing at the time, saying that she was distinguished by the nobility of her poetic images and her "daring technique exemplifying poetic mastery."[81]

Roman Timenchik, the Akhmatova scholar, said that *Evening* appeared just at the time when Russian literature was looking for a great woman poet. However, the contemporary reader was not simply hoping for poems written by a nice lady (he already had several such little volumes on his shelf) but a new literary personality who would be able to speak in the name of sincere but inarticulate women.[82] In 1909, a few days before he died, Innokenty Annensky had written: "Lyrics have become so individualistic . . . that they now *need* a feminine musicality. Perhaps she will reveal new lyric horizons, this woman who is no longer condemned to silence, but is our comrade."[83] Akhmatova herself spoke of the vacuum in Russian poetry which existed around 1910, saying, "Fate wanted it to be occupied by me."[84]

In spite of Bryusov's general animosity toward Acmeism and the fact that Akhmatova's poetry was so very different from his own, he wrote a positive review of *Evening,* saying the basic feature of Akhmatova's work was her ability to portray psychological experience "as if a whole novel were condensed into a series of poems."[85]

In *Apollon* (1912) Valerian Chudovsky also distinguished Akhmatova's verse from the many other poems written by women. He emphasized how innovative and experimental these apparently simple poems were; just when people began to think it was impossible to go further in explaining the real world in all its endless complexity of detail and beauty, "the secret of *synthetic perception* [italics mine] was discovered—a few successfully selected partial aspects provide the same complete synthesis of a picture as a lengthy enumeration of details." He then went on to compare Akhmatova's poetry to Japanese painting, where a whole landscape is represented by a few lines, a technique that was introduced by Annensky into Russian literature.

> In Akhmatova's poems there is much of Japanese art. The same refracted perspective, a disregard for space distinguishing the foreground from the background, one detail serving for the whole atmosphere. What is important is not the event as such, but the state of the soul revealed through it—Love fills the book. "He" is the one who leaves, abandons, forgets. "She" best describes the state of the soul after it has gone through a strong shock, grief, loss.[86]

Akhmatova's greatness, Chudovsky concluded, was her ability to reveal, "à la Japanese," an entire landscape or state of mind through two or three features.

While the Acmeists were attracting attention in Petersburg, in Moscow another group, the Futurists, was beginning to have an impact. They rejected all art of the past, embracing instead the age of modernism and technology, speed and energy. They rebelled against the heavily ornate style of the Symbolists and enlarged the vocabulary considered permissible in poetry not only by using ordinary words, as the Acmeists did, but vulgar ones as well, often breaking all grammatical rules. The works of the poets varied radically from each other, yet they shared a common disdain for tradition and "good taste." Some, like Khlebnikov, worked with a new transrational language, *zaum*, composed of pure sounds or neologisms, new words formed from Slavic roots. It was a language "beyond reason" that was supposed to communicate directly, without being logical or directly reflecting objects in the real world.

Khlebnikov's themes were often related to Slavic paganism and a numerological, mathematical interpretation of history, while Mayakovsky's were derived from urban images, modern technology, politics and revolution. What the Futurists shared was a focus on the future and a rebellion against the past. Their 1912 manifesto, *A Slap in the Face of Public Taste,* declared bravely: "Throw Pushkin . . . Tolstoy and all others overboard from the ship of modernity." Their dress and behavior were meant to shock. They walked down the main streets of Moscow with painted faces, wooden spoons in their lapels, and often disrupted pompous banquets or meetings with their outrageous behavior. Mayakovsky appeared at readings wearing a tunic of wide yellow and black stripes, a silk top hat, and no necktie. He was big and burly, resembling a boxer rather than an aesthete. He was the diametrical opposite of Blok, the idealized image of the poet. Yet beneath the tough facade was a very sensitive, vulnerable man, and the poet Benedikt

Livshits remarked that all the shouting and carrying on by Mayakovsky was "theater for its own sake."[87]

In one of his greatest poems before the Revolution, "Cloud in Trousers," Mayakovsky combines the personal theme of rejected love with the public theme of revolution. He receives no reply when he challenges God to help humanity, just as he receives no answer from his mistress, who will not let him in. The "new" kind of poetry that should be written for the new age of Futurism is also a theme: earlier, "a poet came, lightly opened his lips, and the inspired fool burst into song." Now poets must tramp for days with calloused feet, pick up the sounds of the street, write hymns to the street folk, to students, prostitutes, and salesmen. The poet rejects the past, spitting on the fact that neither Homer nor Ovid invented characters like these. Implicitly comparing himself to John the Baptist, Mayakovsky calls himself the precursor of revolution, which he predicts will come in 1916:

> Where people's eyes stop short
> at the head of hungry hordes,
> in a thorny crown of revolutions
> comes the year 1916.[88]

The Acmeists, also rebels in their own way, were much more restrained in their behavior. One critic ascribes this to the fact that they came from Petersburg. In contrast to the Muscovite Futurists, the Acmeists were "dandies with a certain defiance rather than 'hooligans' with a vengeance."[89]

Ivan Bunin, a poet and writer who refused to join any of these movements, summed up the chaotic kaleidoscope of the Russian literary scene at the time:

> Literally every winter has brought us a new idol. We have experienced decadence, symbolism, neo-naturalism, pornography . . . godfighting, mythmaking, a kind of ystical anarchism, Dionysius and Apollo, "Stages to eternity," sadism, snobbism, "acceptance of the world" and "non-acceptance of the world," cheap imitations of the Russian style, adamism, acmeism—and now we have sunk to the tritest type of hooliganism, tagged by the ridiculous word "futurism." Is this not a Walpurgis night![90]

While Akhmatova was becoming popular as a poet and Gumilyov as a critic, the personal relationship between the two was growing increasingly strained. Akhmatova did not fit the role Gumilyov required of a lifetime companion. Akhmatova herself realized this, and later said that Gumilyov needed a helper, an arms bearer, a faithful companion, and self-sacrificing love, not a jealous, introspective female. The second part of Gumilyov's collection, *Strange Sky*, was devoted to his wife, and contains a poem which reflects the ambiguous feelings he felt for her at this time. The city of Kiev is legendarily connected with the conquering of a serpent by its founder. Here Kiev, the serpent lair, has produced a witch, not a wife:

> From a serpent lair,
> From the city of Kiev,
> I took not a wife, but a sorceress.
> But I thought—she was entertaining
> I surmised . . . she was capricious,
> A merry bird-songstress.
>
> You call out—she frowns
> You embrace her—she bristles,
> And when the moon comes out . . . she languishes,
> And stares, and groans,
> As if she were burying
> Someone—and wants to drown herself.
>
> I assure her: "Christened,
> Right now is the wrong time for me
> To treat you in the ways of the wise.
> You must now carry away languor
> into the Dnieper's whirlpool,
> To the sinful Bald Mountain."
>
> She is silent—just hesitates
> And feels weak and ill
> I pity her, guilty,
> Like a bird shot down
> A birch, roots dug up and dying.
> Over a swamp, cursed by God.[91]

In April 1912, the Gumilyovs left for Switzerland and Italy. It was the last time for many years that Akhmatova would leave Russia. But the trip only exacerbated their difficult relationship. By the end of it Akhmatova was living in Rome and Gumilyov in Florence. Akhmatova was expecting a child, but the pair spent the summer apart after their return. Gumilyov went to Slepnyovo, while Akhmatova went to her mother and cousin Ninochka Zmunchilla on her cousin's estate near the Austrian frontier.[92] When they both returned north, they first rented furnished rooms in Petersburg because the Gumilyov house had been rented for the summer. In the fall they returned to Tsarskoye.[93]

There are various accounts of the birth of Lev Gumilyov. He was born on October 1, 1912. Akhmatova got up very early and felt the labor pains; she plaited her braid and woke Gumilyov, saying, "I think we have to go to Petersburg." They went on foot from the station to the maternity clinic because Gumilyov was so nervous he forgot it was possible to take a horse cab or a tram. At 10:00 A.M.

they reached the clinic on Vasilevsky Island, across the Neva. In the evening, Gumilyov disappeared. The next day, when everyone came to congratulate Akhmatova on the birth of her son, she found out Gumilyov had been out all night and finally reappeared with a "false witness," his cousin Dmitry Kuzmin-Karavayev, a priest. Embarrassed, Gumilyov congratulated her.[94] Makovsky, the editor of *Apollon,* says in his memoirs that Kuzmin-Karavayev had told him that Gumilyov had showed his disdain for the "marriage reins" by wandering around until early in the morning with his cousin, staggering into various bars, not once calling his wife, and drinking in the company of some young girls. His cousin interpreted this as Gumilyov's desire to be different from everyone else, not acting as an ordinary father would be expected to behave.[95] Valeriya Sreznevskaya agrees with the facts but not the interpretation. She says that Gumilyov did indeed spend the night drinking, but he did so to calm his anxiety. It was not customary at this time for fathers to be present at a child's birth, and moreover, holy fathers (i.e., Father Kuzmin-Karavayev) should have known better than to tempt their friends to accompany them to places of entertainment. However, she knows Gumilyov phoned the clinic to find out how his wife was doing, and later picked up Akhmatova and his newborn son and took them to Tsarskoye Selo to a very happy grandmother, where Sreznevskaya and her husband shared supper with them and drank champagne to toast the event.[96]

In a letter to Bryusov written in (1912), Akhmatova said that she had not composed any poems all autumn because of the birth of her child. She enclosed some poems, one of which is a touching tribute to her new son:

> The needles of the wreath burned
> Suddenly around the cloudless brow
> Akh! A smiling nestling
> Was given to me by fate as a gift.[97]

According to Sreznevskaya, Akhmatova nursed Lev herself and stayed home, but "little by little she liberated herself from the role of mother in the sense of really taking care of the infant—for this there was a grandmother and a nurse— and she began to lead her usual life as a literary bohemian."[98] But Akhmatova told a friend in the 1920s that when Lev was born, his grandmother and aunt took him in, saying, "Anechka, you are young and pretty. What do you need a baby for?" She said she protested strongly, but in vain; her husband was on the side of his family and allowed them to take Lev to Slepnyovo. Over the years Akhmatova spent time with her son at Christmas time and during the summers. Her priorities were made clear by young Lev himself, who one day when asked what he was doing, told his aunt: "I am calculating what percentage of time Mama thinks about me."[99]

Gumilyov was attending courses at the university in the fall of 1912, and in order to live closer, he rented an inexpensive room on Tuchkov Street on Vasilevsky

Island, where Akhmatova joined him. They took their meals at a small restaurant nearby. It was around this time that Gumilyov began having an affair with Olga Vysotskaya, who was studying with the famous theater directors Nikolay Yevreinov and Vsevolod Meyerhold. Vysotskaya gave birth to a son, Orest, in October 1913—yet another indication of the serious difficulties of their marriage.[100] A poem published in *Strange Sky* reveals this:

She

I know a woman: silence,
Bitter weariness from words,
Lives in the secret shimmering
Of her dilated pupils.

Her soul is open greedily
Only to the bronze music of poetry,
Before life, fateful and pleasurable
She is haughty and deaf.

Unheard and unhurried,
How strangely floating is her step,
It is impossible to call her beautiful,
But in her lies my happiness.

When I thirst for self-will
And daring and proud—I go to her
To learn about wise, sweet pain
In her languor and delirium.

She is bright in hours of lassitude
And holds lightning in her hand,
And her dreams are clear, like shadows,
On the heavenly burning sand.[101]

By this time Acmeism was becoming an established literary movement. Some attacked it for being eclectic, borrowing from different sources, and having no real program of its own, but the members of the group continued to be enthusiastic and write good poetry. As is often the case, theory followed practice: the two most important articles acting as manifestoes of the movement, written by Gumilyov and Gorodetsky, respectively, did not appear until 1913, when they were published in *Apollon*. In "Symbolism's Legacy and Acmeism," Gumilyov emphasized that the relationship of Acmeism to Symbolism was one of evolution rather than revolution. Both movements faced similar problems but they resolved them differently. He referred to the penchant of Symbolism for mysticism, theosophy, and the occult. In contrast, Acmeism posited that by its very nature, the unknowable cannot be comprehended. The entire sacred significance of the stars relies on the fact that they are infinitely far from the earth, and no human technological inventions such as airplanes will make them come closer. He ends with the injunction: "Always keep in mind the unknowable, but do not offend the thought of it with more or less probable speculation—this is the principle of Acmeism.[102]

Gumilyov stressed that every movement turns to certain poets for inspiration. The Acmeists chose Shakespeare, who showed them the inner world of man; Rabelais, because he portrays the body and its joys; François Villon, who told them about life, not doubting himself while aware of everything—God, vice, death, and immortality—and Théophile Gautier, who found in art worthy garments of irreproachable forms for this life. The hope of the Acmeists was to combine these poets' legacies.

Against this background, Gumilyov departed for his most important trip to Africa in the spring of 1913, accompanied by his nephew Nikolay Sverchkov. This time he went as director of a scholarly expedition to Abyssinia and Somaliland commissioned by the Academy of Sciences. Gumilyov was one of the first Europeans to travel in this part of Africa to study the people, and the materials he gathered would become the foundation of the collection on Africa in the Ethnographic Museum in Petersburg.

Setting out for Africa, Gumilyov wrote a very revealing letter to Akhmatova from Odessa. He noted first how much he respected her as a poet, and how intoxicated he was by his first glimpse of her new work-in-progress, *At the Edge of the Sea*—"so much said so simply." He was convinced that of all the post-Symbolist poets, she would prove to be one of the most significant. He then told Akhmatova explicitly the different roles he expected each of them to play as man and woman:

I know that you do not like it and do not want to understand it, but it is not only pleasant for me but absolutely necessary that, as you depend on me as a woman, I strengthen and foster the man in myself: I never would have been able to guess that hearts can decay hopelessly from joy and fame, but then you would never have been able to concern yourself with research into the country of Gaul or understand seeing the moon that it is the diamond shield of the goddess of the warriors of Pallas.[103]

At this point he recalls his new son: "Kiss Lyova for me. (Strange, I am writing his name for the first time) and teach him to say Pappa."

Gumilyov left Petersburg on April 7, 1913, and did not return until September. Excerpts from his diary reveal the deep meaning Africa had for him: a place of primeval beauty where surreal dreams that arose in his subconscious would later have an important influence on his radically different last—and most important—poetic period. In this passage from his African diary, Gumilyov anticipates the guilt felt by Akhmatova for her generation's indifference to suffering. The dream

Gumilyov describes here resembles the nightmarish embodiment of the revolution in a later poem, "The Wayward Tram":

> At night I thought for a long time about why I did not feel any pangs of conscience when I had killed beasts for amusement and why my blood bond with the world only grew stronger for these killings. But at night I dreamt that for participating in some kind of Abyssinian palace revolution, my head was cut off and I, flowing with blood, applauded the skill of the executioner and was glad how simple this all was, good and not painful.[104]

While Gumilyov was away, his mother asked Akhmatova to sort out the papers in his desk drawer. There she found a letter from one of Gumilyov's mistresses. She did not expect this and says it was the first time she found out about his infidelity. She did not write a single letter to her husband while he was away, and upon his return handed the letters to him with a theatrical gesture. He smiled, embarrassed.[105]

Gumilyov wrote a poem about his marriage, "Iambic Pentameter," published in 1913 in *Apollon:*

> I was young, was desirous and sore,
> But the spirit of the earth was silent, arrogant,
> And drowsing dreams died,
> As birds and flowers die.
> Now my voice is slow and measured,
> I know, life has not worked out—And you,
>
> You, for whom I searched in the Levant
> For the unfading purple of royal mantles,
> I gambled you away, as mad Nealla
> Once gambled away Damayanti.
> The dice flew up, ringing, like steel,
> The dice fell—and there was sorrow.
>
> You said, pondering, severely:
> "I had faith, I loved too much,
> I am leaving, no longer having faith, no longer loving
> And before the all-seeing face of God,
> Perhaps destroying my very self,
> I am renouncing you forever."
>
> I did not dare kiss your hair
> Nor even press your cold, slender hands.
> I found myself repulsive, like a spider,

Every sound frightened and tormented me,
And you left, in a simple and dark dress,
Resembling an ancient Crucifix.[106]

While Gumilyov was away, Akhmatova spent the summer in Slepnyovo; when he returned in September, she went back to Tsarskoye, where she lived part of the time, and the rest of the time with Gumilyov in his rented room on Tuchkov Street in Petersburg.[107] Gumilyov began an affair with Tanya Adamovicha, whose brother Georgy had recently joined the Poets' Guild. Sreznevskaya says Gumilyov had two categories for his women—the first was for true love: Akhmatova, Masha Kuzmina-Karavayeva, for his later affair with Yelena Dubouchet ("Blue Star"). The second category consisted of girls between the ages of twenty and twenty-one. "The romance with Tanya belonged to the latter. It lasted three years and he did not try to hide it from Anna."[108] Tanya wanted to marry Gumilyov, and he asked Akhmatova for a divorce. She told a friend she immediately agreed. But when she informed Gumilyov's mother, she was shocked and remonstrated, "Why? What for?" Akhmatova told her it was Gumilyov who had suggested the idea. One of the conditions for the divorce, however, was that Akhmatova would keep Lev. Gumilyov's mother sent for her son and said to him, "I must tell you the truth. I love Lyova more than Anna and more than you." So the couple remained legally married. But Gumilyov devoted his next collection of poems, *Quiver* (1916), to Tanya.

A further strain on their marriage was Akhmatova's increasing popularity. For a long time Gumilyov was mistrusted and even mocked by the general public, while in the narrow literary circles where he was honored, he was not loved. "His fate was entirely different from Akhmatova's," says Chukovsky. "Critics recognized her immediately, began to devote not only articles but whole books to her. This made him very bitter, and for a long time he was enveloped in a gloating silence." Chukovsky believed that Gumilyov's arrogance, which made it difficult to get close to him, originated not from conceit or pride but from an awareness of his participation in the greatest of all the arts and his conviction that poetry was the highest peak of spiritual and creative life that a person could achieve.[109]

Around this time Akhmatova was visited by a shy young man who contributed articles on art to *Apollon* and was later to become important in her life, Nikolay Punin. Punin made a note of this visit in the autumn of 1914:

I was at Akhmatova's. She was not feeling very well and was lying on the couch. I bragged about my success with women and generally uttered absolute nonsense, mainly because I was so shy. Akhmatova was condescending and regal. Soon I began to attend meetings of the Guild in Gumilyov's house. My poems were published in *Hyperborean*. I got to know Mandelstam in the Guild, one of the best poets of my generation.[110]

Many portraits were made of Akhmatova, showing her characteristic hairstyle with the bangs and her classic shawl.[111] It was the fashion in Russia to turn poets into cult figures, and Blok and Akhmatova were no exception. Often readers did not distinguish between the persona portrayed in the poetry and the poet. One critic even suggested that "The private person had been totally absorbed into the poetic mask; the distance between life and work had been eliminated."[112]

While the literary salons were arguing over style, Blok perceived what they refused to hear—the melody of revolution, resounding in ever stronger tones. In October 1913, he warned that the 1905 Revolution was perhaps only a prelude to what was yet to come: "Not everything can be foretold and foreseen. Blood and fire can give voice when no one expects them to. There is Russia which, having broken free from one revolution, is eagerly staring into the eyes of another and perhaps more terrible one."[113]

But artists chose instead to descend into the cellar cabarets and drown out the sound of impending war and revolution. The favorite in Petersburg was the "Stray Dog." It was in the abandoned cellar of a wineshop in the old Dashkov mansion on Mikhailovsky Square. Its very name symbolized the patrons who came there, stray members of the bohemian set who led irregular family lives and found refuge there.

The Stray Dog was opened on December 31, 1911, by Boris Pronin, a former associate of the avant-garde director Vsevolod Meyerhold. The cabaret had two narrow, brightly painted rooms, a buffet to the side, a small stage, little tables, benches, a fireplace, and colored lanterns.[114] Benedikt Livshits, the poet, described the audience as "divided into two unequal categories: the representatives of art and the 'pharmacists,' " a term used to describe all the others, no matter what their occupation. He goes on to say that "the program varied, from . . . Pyast's 'On the Theater of the Word and the Theater of Movement' to 'Musical Mondays,' Karsavina's dancing or a banquet in honor of the Moscow Art Theater . . . the main substance, however, was not the planned part of the program but the unscheduled happenings which lasted all night."[115] Pyast said many began to imagine the entire world was concentrated in the Stray Dog.

Sergey Sudeikin, the artist who painted the cabaret walls and designed sets for the performances, describes one unforgettable evening when Tamara Karsavina, prima ballerina of the Ballets Russes, came to the Stray Dog: "The evening of Karsavina, goddess of the air, the eighteenth century . . . the music of Couperin . . . our trio on old instruments. The stage in the middle of the hall with real wooden cupids from the eighteenth century standing on a marvelous light blue rug from that epoch with candelabra. . . . Fifty balletomanes (at 50 rubles a seat) watched holding their breath as Karsavina let out a live child-amour from a cage made of real roses."[116]

Akhmatova was one of the many poets who read at the cabaret. Although there is no evidence he ever attended, the works of Blok were read by his wife, Lyubov. Kuzmin spent many nights there accompanying himself on the piano to poems he had composed. Andrey Levinson, a ballet critic, left a romantic description of the poets: "On a precarious stage in the middle of a smoke-filled room loomed . . . the supple specter of the Tatar princess—Akhmatova—the shaggy poet Mandelstam with the rhythmic howl of bronze verses, the unsociable Gumilyov with the sharp skull of a Pericles of the decadent period."[117]

Livshits described one of Akhmatova's "entrances": "When Akhmatova sailed in, in a tight-fitting black silk dress, with a large oval cameo on her belt, she had to pause by the entrance in order to write her latest poems in the pigskin-bound book handed her by the insistent Pronin."[118] Adamovich recalled admiring Akhmatova when he visited the cabaret in 1912:

> They now sometimes refer to her in memoirs as a great beauty. That she wasn't. She was more than beautiful, something better. I have never seen another woman so expressive, her ability to capture attention. . . . Later something of the tragic appeared in her. Rachel in *Phaedra,* as Mandelstam said in his famous poem after one of her readings at the Stray Dog, when she seemed to ennoble and exalt everything around her . . . but my first impression was different. She smiled, laughed, was merry, slyly whispering to her neighbor. But then she was asked to read something, and she suddenly changed, as if turning pale, and in the "mocker," and "gay little sinner of Tsarskoye Selo" [as Akhmatova later characterized herself in *Requiem*] flashed the future Phaedra.[119]

The "famous poem" that Adamovich refers to is one of the loveliest ever devoted to Akhmatova, Mandelstam's "Akhmatova," written in 1914:

> Half-turned, oh grief,
> She gazed at those indifferent.
> Falling off a shoulder
> The neo-classical shawl turned to stone.
>
> Ominous voice—bitter intoxication—
> The soul unfetters one's entrails
> Thus—Rachel once stood—
> As indignant Phaedra.[120]

Vladimir Shileiko was a member of the bohemian crowd that frequented the Stray Dog. He was a noted Assyriologist who translated Babylonian tablets, and also a poet. One evening Shileiko attacked the famous critic Viktor Shklovsky for his talk on Futurism, and accused the entire movement of resembling black magic. In the cabaret, Shileiko's name was associated with a form of satirical improvisation he invented called "Zhora"—every line had to include a combination of the syllables *zho-ra;* the rest was up to the taste of the author.[121] Shileiko was courting Akhmatova at the time: he was enthusiastic about everything she wrote and never stopped talking about her poems. "He was studying Eastern languages," commented another contemporary, Vera Garteveld. "I recall his tall, emaciated figure in a student uniform with large volumes of Persian poetry under his arm, which he brought for Akhmatova. He made me think of Dr. Faustus."[122]

The central figure of the cabaret was the famous actress, dancer, and singer Olga Glebova-Sudeikina, wife of the artist Sergey Sudeikin, and for many years Akhmatova's closest friend. "Elegant, charmingly feminine, always surrounded by hordes of admirers," Chukovsky said of Sudeikina, "she was the living embodiment of her desperate and piquant epoch."[123] She appeared at Ivanov's with Blok, although there was never any indication of any romance between them (which is suggested in Akhmatova's work). Arthur Lourie, who lived with her and Akhmatova in the early 1920s, compared Sudeikina to Debussy's "Girl with the Flaxen Hair," and called her a Petersburg beauty, gray-green eyes like sparkling opals.[124]

Olga Glebova was born on May 7, 1886, in Petersburg, and had a pathetic childhood; often she had to search for her father in pubs and lead him home. After leaving school, she appeared in plays directed by Vera Kommisarzhevskaya and danced in *Swan Lake* at the Maly Theater. She played the role of Columbine in Meyerhold's *Columbine's Scarf* at his experimental studio. One of her most popular roles was Confusion in Yury Belyaev's play of that name, and it is in this role that she appears in the famous painting by her husband. In the 1912–13 season she appeared in a new play by Belyaev, *Psyche*. At the Stray Dog, Sudeikina danced, sang, and recited also great poetry—the works of Russian poets, and of Baudelaire and Mallarmé. Her apartment contained furniture of Karelian birch from the mid-eighteenth century, a clavier, Venetian mirror, Russian glass, porcelain, and embroidery, some of which Akhmatova later inherited when Sudeikina emigrated to Paris.

One episode to which Akhmatova alludes in *Poem Without a Hero* took place on Twelfth Night, January 6, 1913. Sudeikina was playing the Madonna in Kuzmin's version of a nativity play, directed by Nikolay Yevreinov with sets and costumes by Sudeikin. Sergey Diaghilev was present in the audience. The backdrop was dark blue, depicting a battle between angels and devils. In front was a red couch on which Herod sat dressed in a black wool wig tinged with gold; and in the corner, a brown grotto lit by candles and covered with gold foil. The nativity story was enacted on stage, with the birth of Christ and Herod's killing of the innocents, while twenty children from an orphanage wearing gold wigs and silver wings sang in thin voices and walked among the tables with lit candles.[125]

Poem Without a Hero also alludes to another episode that occurred on April 1, 1913, one of the musical Mondays. That night Olga appeared as a bacchante in a nightmarish scene from a piece called *The Goat-legged Nymph,* with grotesque piano music by Ilya Sats. Sudeikina's gorgeous costumes, her frenzied dance, choreographed by Boris Romanov, and her unconsciously expressive movements all added to the bizarre effect.[126]

One evening Akhmatova was reciting with the Acmeists when suddenly an old man, Radetsky, shook his fists and shouted, "These Adams and the slender Eve!" That same evening the peasant poet, Nikolay Klyuev, renounced the Acmeists. He had been corresponding with Blok for several years, who found this a way to make contact "with the people." Klyuev had come to Petersburg in 1911 from the village and had taken part in the Poets' Guild. But he soon found he had little in common with them and that evening, February 15, 1913, in the Stray Dog he made his public renunciation. When Gumilyov inquired what this meant, Klyuev enigmatically replied, "A fish seeks where it is deeper and where it is better."[127] Apparently Klyuev had had enough of the elitist Acmeists and sought out those who wrote politically engaged poetry like his own. In March he left Petersburg; although he still sent his work to Gumilyov, *Apollon* refused to review it. Klyuev would enter Akhmatova's life again a few years later with his new companion, Sergey Yesenin.

Khlebnikov also appeared at the Stray Dog, sitting silently, his head lowered, and as Adamovich describes him, "all immersed in his secret musings of dreams. His presence radiated a certain incomprehensible importance." Mandelstam might be saying something in a cheerful, lively manner, then would suddenly look around and say, "No, I cannot speak while Khlebnikov is sitting over there in total silence."[128]

Mayakovsky, who came from Moscow, was a frequent visitor at the Stray Dog. Livshits describes a typical pose: "Mayakovsky was half-lying in the position of a wounded gladiator, on a Turkish drum which he banged every time the figure of a stray Futurist showed itself in the doorway."[129] Mandelstam introduced Akhmatova to Mayakovsky, and she recounts an amusing incident between the frail Mandelstam and the stalwart Mayakovsky: "Once when everyone was eating and dishes were rattling, Mayakovsky decided to read his poetry. Mandelstam went up to him and said: 'Mayakovsky, stop reading poetry. You're not a Rumanian orchestra!' "[130]

Adamovich described another encounter. Holding Akhmatova's slender, refined hand in his huge paw, Mayakovsky said with mocking enthusiasm: "*Palchiki-to, palchiki-to, Bozhe ty moi!* (These fingers, oh, these fingers, my God!). She frowned and turned away."[131] Lily Brik, Mayakovsky's mistress for many years, said that whenever Mayakovsky was in love, he read Akhmatova, quoting her poetry from morning until night constantly, while he suffered.

Mayakovsky would note her entrance by rising up from behind his drum and making a grand gesture with a wide sweep of his arm. He was always attentive and friendly to her. Akhmatova said, "In his powerful, somewhat cracked voice, one always heard a certain pain." One time when she was posing for the artist Alexandra Exter, he came to the studio, found Akhmatova there, and they exchanged a few words.[132] It was only in chance encounters like this, however, or at the Stray Dog that they met. They were never close friends. Although so different from her own, Akhmatova found his verse before the Revolution interesting, acknowledging, "He was a new voice. He was a real poet."[133] But she did not admire what he wrote as the poet laureate of the Revolution, and in her poem to him written in 1940, "Mayakovsky in 1913," she returned to his early period, saying, "I didn't know you in your glory,/I only remember your stormy dawn."

The music evenings included contemporary works by Debussy, Ravel, Schoenberg, Richard Strauss, and Max Reger. Sudeikin made special decorative panels as backdrops for these concerts. Famous opera singers would show up, future professors of the Conservatory performed, and sometimes music was combined with poetry or ballet. One English journalist even reported hearing ragtime at the Stray Dog.[134]

Another featured performer who combined a rare talent for music and poetry was Mikhail Kuzmin. Born in 1872 in Yaroslavl, he first studied composition, then became one of Russia's leading decadent poets, celebrating homosexuality and practicing the life of a refined aesthete. His poetry is erudite and the themes range from ancient Greece and Alexandria to modern-day Petersburg. Although he and Akhmatova were friends at this time and Kuzmin wrote a very complimentary introduction to *Evening,* she later characterized him as the "only one who practiced evil for evil's sake."[135] (He became the Mephistophelean figure in *Poem Without a Hero.*)

A contemporary described Kuzmin at the Stray Dog:

Onto the stage with tiny, quick steps climbed an amazing imaginary creature who appeared to have been drawn by the capricious pencil of a visionary artist. Short, slender, frail, he had a face that sometimes resembled a faun's and other times a young satyr as portrayed in Pompeian frescoes. His black shiny hair, looking as if it had been varnished with lacquer, was combed forward at the temples, and his narrow beard seemed to have been painted on, emphasizing his unnaturally rosy cheeks. His large, protruding eyes seemed to be alive, but they had seen too much, much too much, and were enhanced by long, almost feminine eyelashes. He smiles and bows, as if made of wax, like an automaton brought to life by Hoffmann's *Coppelius.* He sits down at the piano. What long, pale, sharp fingers he has. Banal modulations merge with the tremolo of his velvet voice. Through a joke, one discerns great longing, through laughter—tears.[136]

The Stray Dog was the scene of numerous personal dramas. Gumilyov never neglected to pay attention to the very beautiful women, which hurt Akhmatova. Akhmatova, however, was caught up in her own relationships.[137] She met the composer Arthur Lourie there, and they had a brief rendezvous, then parted.

Almost no one knew about it. Lourie was born in 1892 in the Mogilev province and came to Petersburg in 1908.[138] Two years later he entered the Petersburg Conservatory, where he came under the influence of the avant-garde. Lourie considered his work the musical version of Russian Futurism. He began to experiment with twelve-tone music, but also with pieces based on quarter and eighth tones. In 1913, he converted from Judaism to Catholicism, and later, when he became part of émigré circles in Paris, he became involved with Jacques Maritain and his group. The first stanza of a poem by Alexander Kron on Lourie describes the impression he made:

> On a gold chain a golden lorgnette,
> Fastidious, arrogantly compressed lips.
> The soul of satyr or incubus
> Conceals a melancholy vision of forgotten orgies.[139]

When the Italian Futurist poet and dramatist Marinetti came to the Stray Dog in 1914, Lourie gave a lecture on the "art of noise," and when Richard Strauss visited, Lourie played a Gluck gavotte in his own modern arrangement, after which Strauss got up and went over to the piano to compliment Lourie.[140]

Those who frequented the Stray Dog also witnessed a change in Akhmatova over the years. At first lighthearted and witty, as Adamovich noted, she became more restrained, perhaps because she felt people were staring at her with curiosity, or perhaps because "little by little something began to change in her character, in her general make-up. Famous and little-known people would come up to her, half-flattering, half-lazily, and touch her hand. It often happened that a man to whom she had just been introduced would declare his love to her."[141]

By the middle of 1913, the Poets' Guild was beginning to suffer a rift among its members. Their enthusiastic turn from Symbolism seemed at first enough to keep them going, but the lack of a unified program soon led to dissension. Vasily Gippius describes what happened: "Having pushed off from the shore of Symbolism and mysticism, the Acmeists did not know where to pull into shore . . . and found themselves in the open seas. One thing was left to them—to give themselves up to the waves, and that's what happened."[142] Both Akhmatova and Mandelstam began to feel the Guild to be a burden. In the winter of 1913 as a joke she and Mandelstam wrote on a piece of paper: "We would like to request that the Guild shut down. We can no longer bear it, and we are going to die." Laughing, she showed it to Gumilyov, who also laughed, then to Gorodetsky, who smiled, but in fact was quite upset. He said, "To all members of the Guild, the verdict: Hang everyone and drown Akhmatova!"[143]

By 1914 it became clear that there was total disharmony between Gorodetsky and Gumilyov. Akhmatova said it was hardly surprising that two poets with such different world views would finally quarrel. Gorodetsky was irritated by Gumilyov's "refinement," his scrupulousness, his elevated claims for form. In the summer of 1914 the group finally disbanded and left the city. And then the war began, putting an end for good to the meetings of the Guild and catching them all up in the whirlwind of history.

In May 1914, Akhmatova and Gumilyov, and Lev went to Slepnyovo. Akhmatova remained there throughout the summer, while Gumilyov left at the end of June for Vilnius, where Tanya Adamovich was living, then returned to Petersburg, where he lived on Vasilevsky Island with Vladimir Shileiko. In her letters Akhmatova complained how boring it was at Slepnyovo, and that she spent most of her time lying on a couch and writing poetry. One of the poems on which she was working was *At the Edge of the Sea,* a long romantic poem. She wrote to Gumilyov that she was worried about their financial situation: "I think we're going to have financial problems in the fall. I have nothing, and you probably don't either. And by August we'll need several hundred rubles. Please don't forget what has been pawned. If possible, redeem it." And she mentioned that Lev was learning to talk: "Lyovushka is healthy and knows how to say everything." In a letter to Georgy Chulkov, she said she was thinking of going to Switzerland to join her brother, who was convalescing there.[144]

Akhmatova's second volume of poetry, *Rosary (Chyotki),* had been published in March. New religious motifs appeared in the collection. At times these images function as sincere quests by Akhmatova to find comfort and solace by turning to God. Elsewhere, she uses religion as an aesthetic device—as part of her cultural heritage, with its inbuilt associations—to express the many nuances of the heroine's relationship with her lover. Several critics have emphasized her use of religious motifs as only one treatment of the theme of love. A. Gizetti goes so far as to see this as decadence.[145] Sam Driver believes the subthemes of old Russia, Russian Orthodoxy, the Russian folk, ancient cities, and the Russian countryside all reflect Akhmatova's cultural heritage. She does not employ mystical words, but ordinary ones known to any Russian Orthodox believer: *epitrakhil* (the long stole of the Orthodox priest), for example, or *emalevyi obrazok* (an enamel icon). These religious artifacts "are as much part of the tradition in which Akhmatova was nurtured as were the literary soirées and prerevolutionary intelligentsia society of St. Petersburg."[146] Yet this combination of religious themes with the dominant motif of passionate, earthly love led the critic Boris Eikhenbaum at the time to call Akhmatova "half nun, half whore," a phrase that would be used by the authorities against her much later in her career.[147]

Other critics argue that the religion in these poems adds a dimension to her earlier work, showing her suffering to be not merely personal but part of the Christian experience. Chukovsky went further, saying her world view was not only Christian but particularly Russian Orthodox, with typical motifs of self-abnegation, resignation, martyrdom, meekness, and poverty.[148] Mandelstam said that the heroine depicted in these verses has a hieratic dignity and religious simplicity that distinguishes her from the conventional stereotype of weak, sentimental women who appeared in most verse by female poets. "There has been a turn toward hieratic stateliness, a religious simplicity and solemnity. . . . The voice of renunciation grows stronger all the time in her verse, and at the moment her poetry bids fair to become a symbol of Russian grandeur."[149]

Another prominent motif in *Rosary* is the city of Petersburg, which Akhmatova, unlike her Symbolist and Futurist contemporaries, celebrates in its historic beauty. The Symbolists were drawn to a city's ugliness and depravity, while the Futurists were attracted to street language and technological wonders. Akhmatova's view was more typical of the World of Art group, who in their paintings and journals depicted the Petersburg of the eighteenth century and the time of Pushkin. They called this admiration for Petersburg's past "Retrospectivism," which they considered part of the Russian revival that began in the latter part of the nineteenth century. Muscovite revivalists turned mainly to famous medieval cities, but the Petersburg group focused on the art and architecture of their own city, seeing this as an important reflection of their reverence for Russia's past and its traditions. The lovely paintings by Alexander Benois and Konstantin Somov are typical of this movement.[150]

Akhmatova also used the city metaphorically and metonymically to reveal emotional states, as she had used aspects of her environment in her earlier works. Her appreciation of the solid, enduring nature of architecture has been contrasted with her observations about the frailty of the human condition:

It is as if the poet is saying to us: how much elegance, self-assurance, beauty, and strength is in these towers, arches, cupolas erected by the human hand—and what vacillation, ephemeralness, bitterness, and sorrow in these flashing human shadows, with their eternal mutual misunderstandings, fatal disagreements, and fleeting change of feeling. How heavy and sad is this fatal contrast between the world and life: the imperious charm of human construction and the insulting imperfection of its vacillating feelings and shy passions.[151]

"My heart beats calmly . . . " (1913) is a perfect example of the subtle interrelationship between personal experience and the cityscape:

My heart beats calmly, steadily,
What are the long years to me!
Under the Galernaya arch,
Our shadows, for eternity.

Through lowered eyelids
I see, I see, you with me,
And held forever in your hand,
My unopened fan.

Because we were standing side by side
In that blissful miraculous moment,
The moment of the resurrection of the rose-colored moon
Over the Summer Garden—

I don't need the waiting
At some hateful window.
Or the agonizing meetings—
All my love is satisfied.

You are free, I am free,
Tomorrow will be better than yesterday—
Over the Neva's dark waters,
Under the cold smile
Of Emperor Peter.

(I, p. 355)

The poem begins under the Galernaya Arch, spanning the street between the Senate and the Synod, from which the famous equestrian statue of Peter the Great is visible. Ephemeral moments become eternal—shadows thrown by lovers under the arch, the lover's hand holding her unopened fan. We then move to the Summer Garden by the Summer Palace, with a small lake, ancient statues, and elegant lawns, where the people of Petersburg love to stroll. Everything seems to be perfect—until the fifth stanza, when the speaker "protests too much," asserting that they are both free, but freedom implies freedom to leave as well, and relationships are fragile and break easily. When she says, "Tomorrow will be better than yesterday," it seems more like a wish than a belief, and this is confirmed by the last image, "the cold smile/ Of Emperor Peter," referring to the famous statue by Falconet that became immortalized in Pushkin's *The Bronze Horseman* as the symbol of authority and the state, which stands high above, peering down at the ordinary people and the dark waters of the Neva.

Tsarskoye Selo continued to appear in Akhmatova's poems. In "With my pencil case . . . " (1912), its swans have become associated with this beautiful spot, and Akhmatova employs them as metonymic symbols to refer to Gumilyov. The "little gray cygnet," whom she first met as a schoolgirl, grew into a "haughty swan" and brought a "ray of sorrow" into her life, which causes her voice to cease making music.

One series of poems in *Rosary* depicts the male as victim as he tries to deal with "first love's bitter pain." The pity of the woman who hurt him comes too late. Akhmatova may be assuming the persona of a woman who rejects her young admirer, or she may be portraying an actual affair she had with a young man. She did say that a "handsome young man," one of the Kuzmin-Karavayev brothers living on the estate near Slepnyovo, attempted suicide over her.[152] In "The boy said to me . . . " (1913), Akhmatova typically selects a few details to reveal the relationship between a couple: a gesture—the young man ardently stroking his lover's hands—reveals his passion, while the coldness of her hands reflects her indifference. In "The Voice of Memory" (June 18, 1913), the dedication to Sudeikina indicates that the speaker is alluding to the suicide of Knyazev, a young soldier and poet, once the lover of Mikhail Kuzmin and then the rejected lover of Sudeikina. The poem condemns the heroine for her indifference.

> *The Voice of Memory*
>
> What are you looking at, staring dully at the wall,
> In the hour when the sunset lingers in the sky?
>
> A seagull on the blue tablecloth of the sea,
> Or Florentine gardens?
>
> Or the enormous park at Tsarskoye Selo,
> Where desperation crossed your path?
>
> Or do you see him at your knees,
> The one who broke your spell for white death?
>
> No, I see only the wall—and on it
> The gleam of the guttering heavenly flame.
>
> (I, p. 327)

The motif serves a moral function: forgetting one's past sins is self-deceit; but consciously remembering and atoning for them leads to salvation. It is easier to forget, as the heroine does here.

A poem on the Stray Dog (January 1, 1913) exemplifies the vast difference between her work and that of Alexander Blok, whose poem "The Stranger" was set in a similar environment. Whereas Blok found revelation in the eyes of the celebrants and creative intuition in wine, Akhmatova sees unhappy carousers shut up in a cellar, making merry, hiding from the storm outside—which may signify the increasing political chaos leading to the Revolution. The same cast of characters, including the poet, would show up later in *Poem Without a Hero*. Both poets' works are reminiscent of Pushkin's small tragedy, *The Feast During the Time of the Plague,* in which the aristocracy revels when death is near instead of helping those in need.[153]

Over the course of her life, Akhmatova wrote several poems to Blok. One of the most famous, "I visited the poet," was written in January 1914:

> I visited the poet.
> Precisely at noon. Sunday.

It was quiet in the spacious room,
And beyond the windows, intense cold

And a raspberry sun
Above shaggy, bluish smoke . . .
How keenly my taciturn host
Regarded me!

He had the kind of eyes
That everyone must recall,
It was better for me to be careful,
And not look at them at all.

But I will recall the conversation,
The smoke noon, Sunday
In the tall, gray house
By the sea gates of the Neva.

(I, p. 363)

It is simple and straightforward; no theatrical gestures, just the kind of eyes that would attract a woman like Akhmatova. The contrast between the intense cold and the raspberry sun perhaps reflects the restraint of characters who hide their strong feelings beneath the surface.

This is very different from Blok's poem, which transforms the quiet, regal Akhmatova into the Carmen figure of Blok's mistress, the singer Lyubov Delmas.

"Beauty is terrible," they'll tell you—
You'll lazily throw
The Spanish shawl over your shoulders
A red rose—in your hair.

"Beauty is simple," they'll tell you—
Awkwardly with your colorful shawl
You'll cover the baby,
The red rose—on the floor.

But, distracted, listening
To every word around you,
You'll muse sadly
And say to yourself:

"Not terrible nor simple am I;
I'm not so terribly simple
To kill; not so simple am I
Not to know how terrifying life is."[154]

In her memoirs, Akhmatova describes a visit to Blok at his home on Ofitserskaya Street on December 15, 1913:

> I brought Blok his books so he could inscribe them. . . . In the third volume he wrote a madrigal devoted to me. . . . I never had a Spanish shawl . . . but at this time Blok was raving about Carmen and Spanish-cized me. I also, of course, never wore a red rose in my hair. It makes sense that he wrote in the Spanish form of a *romancero*. At our last meeting behind the wings of the Bolshoy Theater in spring 1921, Blok came up to me and asked: "And where is your Spanish shawl?" Those were the last words I heard from his lips.[155]

According to Viktor Zhirmunsky, the incident was more complicated than Akhmatova's version. Blok's inscription was not spontaneous. He knew she was coming to visit and wanted to have an inscription ready. But he had written the madrigal the evening before, experimenting with various forms before settling on the Spanish one.[156]

Akhmatova's poem contrasts with Blok's romantic portrayal of her, replacing the Spanish exotica with a realistic picture of the Russian winter and the poet himself. The two poems were published in the March 1914 issue of the journal *Love for Three Oranges,* for which Blok was poetry editor. Akhmatova sent Blok a copy of *Rosary* in March 1914, inscribing on the title page:

> From you came uneasiness
> And the ability to write verse.
> (II, p. 535)

Many of the poems in *Rosary* further explore the theme of unrequited love that had characterized *Evening*. Here, too, Akhmatova selects a gesture to reveal the nature of a relationship, as in one of her most often quoted verses, "One would not mistake true tenderness" (1913). True tenderness is quiet, not expressed through demonstrative behavior. And actions, without sincere feeling behind them, cannot fool a woman in love: the suitor, to whom she addresses this poem, wraps her in furs, utters respectful words about first love, but all this means nothing—his eyes reveal his indifference.

> One would not mistake true tenderness
> With anything else, and it is quiet.
> In vain you carefully wrap
> My shoulders and breast in furs.
> And in vain you utter respectful words
> About the first love.

How well I know those persistent,
Insatiable glances of yours![157]

Several poems continue another earlier theme: the price a poet must pay for her gift is disappointment in love. In "How many demands the beloved can make!" (1913), fame has become bitter because the protagonist can find neither love nor peace. The motionless water reflects the numb state of calm she has achieved. All she can now ask of life is that future generations will read her work.

How many demands the beloved can make!
The woman discarded, none.
How glad I am that today the water
Under the colorless ice is motionless.

And I stand—Christ help me!—
On this shroud that is brittle and bright,
But save my letters
So that our descendant can decide.

So that you, courageous and wise,
Will be seen by them with greater clarity.
Perhaps we may leave some gaps
In your glorious biography?

Too sweet is earthly drink,
Too tight the nets of love
Sometimes let the children read
My name in their lesson book.

(I, p. 317)

But "We met for the last time" (1914) again illustrates the danger of confusing Akhmatova's poetry with her life. Here a woman's creativity is ridiculed by the lover who is about to leave her forever. Instead of despairing, she becomes inspired by the beauty of Petersburg, by the famous Peter and Paul Fortress and the Tsar's Palace, and creates her "latest" song:

We met for the last time
On the embankment, where we had always met.
The Neva was high
And they were afraid the city would flood.

He spoke of the summer, and he also said
That for a woman to be a poet was—absurd.
I can still see the tsar's tall palace
And the Peter and Paul fortress!—

Because the air was not ours at all,
But like a gift from God—so miraculous.
And at that moment was given to me
The latest of all my mad songs.

(I, p. 319)

Akhmatova said explicitly that this poem did not refer to Gumilyov. "One doesn't meet one's husband by the river but at home, at breakfast." Reviewing *Rosary* in *Apollon* (no. 5, 1914), Gumilyov had nothing but praise for his wife's work: "As with most young poets, in Anna Akhmatova one frequently finds the words pain, sorrow, death. This youthful pessimism, so natural and therefore so beautiful, has been the property of 'pentesters' until now, but in her verse it has attained a place in poetry for the first time. Women in love, sly, dreamy, and rapturous, at last speak their own genuine and at the same time artistically convincing language."[158] In his letters during these years, Gumilyov continually asked her for poems and frequently praised those he received.

"You gave me a difficult youth" (1912) reflects the Orthodox belief that suffering is part of being human, and that only by living through it and overcoming it do we become truly moral human beings. The poem begins with a reproach to God for making the speaker's life so difficult, but then asks how she can please the Lord. Instead of anger or rebellion, the poet meekly says she is negligent and not even worthy of being a rose or a blade of grass in heaven:

You gave me a difficult youth.
So much sadness in my path.
How can such a barren soul
Bear gifts to You?
Flattering fate
Sings a long song of praise.
Lord! I am negligent,
Your stingy servant.
Neither a rose nor a blade of grass
Will I be in my Father's garden.
I tremble at every mote of dust,
Before the words of any dunce.

(I, p. 339)

Wendy Rosslyn, discussing this poem in her book on religion in Akhmatova's poetry, cites William James's definition of the difference between morality and religion. Morality accepts the existence of a law of nature and obeys it reluctantly, while in religion service to the highest is never manifested in the form of submission but in the form of welcome. Rosslyn maintains that this poem describes a belief that obedience to the divine arises from love of the divine: "The religious man, admitting his weakness, submits, casts himself upon the divine love and mercy. . . . The keynotes of the religious attitude . . . are a relation of willing helplessness before the divine, willing dependence on the divine mercy, and willing renunciation of minor happiness in the name of a higher one."[159]

Akhmatova's collection was greeted enthusiastically. Vasily Gippius noted that he was afraid the success of *Evening* would quickly spoil Akhmatova and she might repeat successful formulas in her new works, but to his great delight, *Rosary* proved him wrong. He was among those who had welcomed her first volume. "In my welcome was fear that the poet, having been tempted by intoxicating praise, would forget her 'great theme' for effective trifles that would succeed. This danger did not occur—the 'great' lyric theme grew stronger in . . . *Rosary.*"[160]

Gumilyov's review focused on the important stylistic innovations. Akhmatova never explained, she showed: form itself reveals a state of mind. "A faintness and shortness of breath is typical of her rhythms." However, he advised her patronizingly to develop her thought and write longer poems—"the poetess must elaborate upon her stanza if she wishes to master composition. A single spontaneous transport cannot serve as the basis for composition." *Rosary* represented a great step forward from *Evening,* he noted. Yet he chastised the poet for the very quality that made *Evening* so experimental, taking its place among modern masters of stream-of-consciousness writing. To Gumilyov, her leaps in thought reflected a failure to represent a logical flow of images: "Incoherence of thought has vanished, the incoherence so typical of *Evening* and comprising more a psychological curiosity than a poetic quality." He is correct that the use of stream-of-consciousness images is not as pervasive as in her earlier collection; however, they are still very much present and contribute to the brilliance of the verse. It was a technique Gumilyov himself would later use in "The Wayward Tram," to reflect the way the mind works when confronted with crisis and chaos.[161]

The tremendous impression Akhmatova's verses made is clear from the memoirs of one of her readers. He says he first encountered her poems in 1914 when he was living in Archangel. He had been reading widely, from Tolstoy and Chekhov to Strindberg, Ivanov and Bryusov, and the Futurists. One day he found a small volume of Akhmatova's verses on the table of a friend, read one poem, and said, "What a naive and cheerful soul Akhmatova has." His friends laughed and told him to read it again. Upon rereading it, he realized that the words "difficult, heavy, tormented" would more aptly describe Akhmatova's soul.[162]

The Twilight of Imperial Russia: 1914–1917

Fearful times are drawing near. Soon
Fresh graves will be everywhere.
There will be famine, earthquakes, widespread death,
And the eclipse of the sun and the moon.
　　—AKHMATOVA (II, p. 429)

In 1914, World War I began and Petersburg was transformed into Petrograd.[1] For Akhmatova, this marked the true beginning of the twentieth century:

Rosary came out March 15, 1914, and had a life span of six weeks. At the beginning of May the Petersburg season began to fade, and everyone left. This time they left Petersburg forever. We returned not to Petersburg but to Petrograd. We fell from the nineteenth into the twentieth century. Everything became different, beginning with the appearance of the city.[2]

As a result of two Balkan wars in 1912 and 1913, Serbia and other Balkan countries were fighting over portions of Albania. Austria was against Serbian acquisition of land along the Adriatic coast, although Austria had exhibited its own imperialist aims by annexing Bosnia and Herzegovina. On June 28, 1914, the heir to the Austrian throne was assassinated in Sarajevo by a Serbian patriot. Austria-Hungary issued an ultimatum demanding satisfaction for the murder and various concessions. The Serbs rejected the demands, and Austria declared war on July 28. When the Russians began to mobilize in support for Serbia, the Germans declared war against the Russians on August 1 (July 19, Old Style). Initially there was great patriotic fervor. The Russians felt a bond with Serbians, who were fellow Slavs and shared the Orthodox religion. Russia also hoped to gain the Turkish straits.

The war was a disaster for Russia and helped bring down the Romanov regime. Tsar Nicholas had grossly overestimated the capacity of the Russians to fight a global battle. France demanded that Russia invade East Prussia to ease the burden on the Western front, which led to catastrophic defeats in the battles of Tannenberg and the Masurian Lakes. In 1916, again in response to Allied requests to draw pressure away from the Western front, Russia launched offensives and was soon repelled. Often Russian soldiers were sent to the front unarmed. The Russians suffered greater casualties than the armed forces of any other country involved in the struggle; their weapons were inferior, their ammunition in short supply, transportation often broke down, food and fuel shortages plagued the urban population, speculators used the war to make a profit, and inflation was rampant. Moreover, Nicholas made the mistake of assuming the role of commander-in-chief, a duty for which he was ill prepared and which left the capital to the empress. With her was Rasputin, the fanatic religious healer who was able to stop the bleeding of her hemophiliac son Alexey, heir to the throne. Rasputin controlled her will—and the fate of the country—until his assassination in December 1916. The historian Richard Charques sums up the war's effect: "For none of the belligerents was the First World War so catastrophic or so costly as it was for Russia."[3]

The twentieth century, said Akhmatova, began in 1914 when war broke out—just as the nineteenth century had begun with the Vienna Congress, after Napoleon's banishment to Elba. "Calendrical dates have no meaning. In essence no one knows what epoch he lives in. We also did not know at the beginning of the 1910s that we lived on the eve of the first European war and the October Revolution," she wrote in her memoirs.[4]

On the day after Germany declared war on Russia, a patriotic demonstration was held in Palace Square by the Winter Palace. Flags, icons, and portraits of the tsar were carried by a fervent crowd, and as they kneeled, they sang the national anthem. Three years later a similar crowd would call for the tsar to abdicate his throne.

Gumilyov enlisted immediately. In war he could prove his love for his homeland and play out the role of the conquistador heroes of his own works. It was also a realization of his Nietzschean philosophy, for like his trips to Africa, war provided a life-threatening situation, which presented him with the opportunity to show his courage. It was Nietzsche's Zarathustra who urged: "War and courage have done more great things than charity. Not your sympathy, but your bravery hath hitherto saved the victims."[5] Whereas Akhmatova wrote poems expressing the horrors of war, Gumilyov wrote poems about its exhilarating effect on him.

Akhmatova greeted the war in Slepnyovo and she spent the last summer there in 1917.[6] However, the summer of 1914 began quite peacefully. After two weeks at Slepnyovo she soon returned to Petersburg to be with her father. It is difficult to learn how close Akhmatova might have been with her father at this time. There is little mention of him in her friends' memoirs or diary entries relating their conversations with her, only that she sometimes visited him and was with him at his death. He lived in Petersburg and she could possibly have seen him often, but her lack of mention indicates he played an insignificant role in her life after she married and came back north. Her closeness to her mother, however, is revealed by how often she visited Kiev to see her. After visiting her father in the summer of 1914, Akhmatova went to Darnitsa near Kiev, where her mother was living. She visited Moscow, then returned to Slepnyovo, where Gumilyov had come to say good-bye to his family. As a young man in 1907 he had been freed from military duty because of a bad eye, but now in World War I he was accepted, sent to the cavalry, and moved to Novgorod for training.[7] A contemporary, Andrey Levinson, said Gumilyov accepted the war very simply and directly. He was one of those few people in Russia whose soul was prepared for war. "Patriotism was as unconditional as his religious faith. I never saw a person whose nature was more alien to doubt, just as humor was alien to him. His mind, dogmatic and straightforward, possessed no ambiguity."[8] At the end of September, Gumilyov was appointed to Her Majesty's light guard Uhlan troops and sent to the border with East Prussia.

Other poets reacted differently. At the beginning of the war, Blok was helping the families of the mobilized. Akhmatova tells how on August 5, 1914, she and Gumilyov encountered him unexpectedly at the Tsarskoye Selo train station. Gumilyov was already in uniform. When Blok left, Gumilyov commented: "Are they really sending him to the front? That's like roasting nightingales."[9]

Mayakovsky was initially enthusiastic about the war: "I received the news with excitement. To start with, only because of its decorative, noisy aspects. Posters to order, fully warlike, of course." However, the army refused to take him because of his politically suspect background. Instead, his artistic talents were set to work in the draftsman's office of an automobile school. His poem "To You" ridiculed the bourgeoisie for their failing to fight:

To you, living through orgy after orgy
Who have bathtubs and warm toilets!
Aren't you ashamed to read in newspaper columns
about the presentation of St. George crosses?

Do you know, you hundreds of untalented fools,
while thinking of how best to stuff yourselves . . .

perhaps right now a bomb
has shot off Lieutenant Petrov's leg? . . .

If only he had been led off for execution,
wounded, he would suddenly see
how with your lips soiled by a greasy cutlet
you lewdly hum [a poem by] Severyanin.

To please you, loving vulgar women and good food,
Would I give my life?!
I would rather serve pineapple water
to whores at the bar![10]

When Mayakovsky read the poem at the Stray Dog in 1915, a scandal ensued. The women, obviously upset, sighed, "Ai, oi!" A very elegantly dressed lady sitting on a high stool shouted: "So young and healthy . . . and writing such horrible things. He should go to the front." Mayakovsky retorted: "Recently in France a famous writer expressed the desire to go to the front. They sent him a gold pen and the command: 'Stay, your pen is needed more by your country than a bayonet.' " The lady shouted back: "Your pen is needed by no one, absolutely no one."[11]

Mayakovsky soon became disillusioned with the war, writing in his autobiography: "I have been called to the army, and shaved. Now I do not want to go to the front. I am pretending to be a draftsman. . . . Soldiering. Rotten time. I paint (still evading) portraits of the commanding officer."[12] He composed anti-war poems like "Mother and the Evening Killed by the Germans": "The air is paved with the stone, roaring with bombs./And the bloodshot eye of the new moon looked/at the dead fist still holding cartridge cases."

Mandelstam was not drafted, but was sent to the Crimea in 1916. He felt a fear in the face of history, and at this point believed that instead of living in a world of spiritual values, man had been reduced to mere biological survival: "When the First World War broke out, Mandelstam, like the majority of representatives of the enlightened intelligentsia, understood that this time the existence of the tsarist autocracy was truly coming to a close, and without hesitation he surrendered himself, his loved ones, and his beloved city to the power of death."[13] Petersburg, renamed Petrograd, was now transformed for the poet into Petropolis, its Greek name, thereby raising it to the level of myth. It was not wisdom, Athena, who reigned there, but death—Proserpine, spouse of the king of Hades.

We shall die in transparent Petropolis
Where Proserpine rules over us.
In every breath we drink mortal air,
And every hour is our hour of death.
Goddess of the sea, dreadful Athena,
Remove your mighty, stone helmet.

We shall die in transparent Petropolis,
Where it is not you who reigns, but Proserpine.[14]

Akhmatova for her part interpreted the war as a spiritual event. She saw it as a portent of things to come, as God's way of showing His displeasure with the Russian people. She became increasingly convinced of this as she grew older. Indeed, in *Poem Without a Hero,* she would express the belief that war and revolution came to Russia as retribution for the indifference shown by the intelligentsia and upper classes toward the suffering of the people. In "July 1914" (the war began on July 19 on the old calendar in Russia), she remained secure in her belief that Russia would live through a terrible period, but that in the end the Madonna would protect them all, spreading her mantle over them as she had in earlier times, playing the ancient role of woman as intercessor between humanity and the divine:

It smells of burning. For four weeks
The dry peat bog has been burning.
The birds have not even sung today,
And the aspen has stopped quaking.

The sun has become God's displeasure,
Rain has not sprinkled the fields since Easter.
A one-legged stranger came along
And all alone in the courtyard he said:

"Fearful times are drawing near. Soon
Fresh graves will be everywhere.
There will be famine, earthquakes, widespread death,
And the eclipse of the sun and the moon.

But the enemy will not divide
Our land at will, for himself:
The Mother of God will spread her white mantle
Over this enormous grief."

(I, 427)

In an undated letter from the early days of the war to Akhmatova, Gumilyov said that he was sitting in a Polish hut, and so far everything was quite comfortable. "In general the war reminds me very much of my Abyssinian journey. It is almost completely similar: the lack of exotica is hidden by stronger impressions. The only sad thing is that the initiative is not in my hands, and you know how I am used to that." He yearned for more frequent battles, saying the Russian soldiers were far superior as fighters to either the Austrians or the Germans. He continued to maintain this belief throughout the war, even though it became clear to so many others that the situation was desperate. On January 13, 1915, Gumilyov was awarded a St. George Cross for his bravery.[15]

At the end of January 1915, when Gumilyov was sent on a mission to Petrograd, his friends arranged a special evening at the Stray Dog. It was the last time Akhmatova was to go there. She said it was a magical evening: while a snowstorm raged outside, Gumilyov read his verse in the beloved cellar, enveloped in the light blue circles of cigar smoke and listening to the quiet clinking of wineglasses. Gumilyov returned to the front, although he soon became very ill and had to be sent back to Petrograd to a clinic for two months to recover.[16]

At this period Gumilyov began a column called "Notes of a Cavalry Officer" in the morning edition of *Birzhevye vedomosti (Stock Market News)*. There were twelve in the series, over the course of the year. He did not write many war poems. The most famous is "The Worker," in which he portrays an old man on the side of the enemy, doing his day's work, which turns out to be the casting of a bullet that will deprive the poet of his life.

The bullet cast by him will whistle
Above the grey foam of the Dvina,
The bullet cast by him will seek
My breast, it has pursued me.

I will fall, mortally anguishing,
I will see past reality as it was,
My blood will pour like a spring on the dry,
Dusty and trampled grass.

And the Lord will reward me in full measure
For my brief and bitter epoch.
This is what was done by the small old man
In a light grey blouse.[17]

Gumilyov found the war exhilarating—the kind of ultimate experience he felt was necessary in order to be truly creative. He wrote vividly of life at the front: "I did not sleep the whole night. The attacks were so strong that I felt in good spirits. I think that at the dawn of humanity, people also lived anxiously, created a lot and died early. It is difficult for me to believe that someone who eats lunch every day and sleeps every night can introduce something into the treasure house of the culture of the spirit. Only fasting and vigil, even if involuntary, creates a special energy in man which had been sleeping, awakens forces which had been slumbering."[18]

Gumilyov's attitude was in sharp contrast to that of Blok, who soon became disillusioned, writing that "War is a stupid, rotten thing. Today it became perfectly clear to me that the distinguishing feature of this war is that there is nothing great about it. . . . And this is the reason it is impossible to fan our patriotism, and the deceit specially devised for us little people."[19]

The year 1915 saw the publication of Akhmatova's long poem *At the Edge of the Sea,* which had been completed early in 1914. It is about the poet's youth, and is related to "The Gray-Eyed King." A woman longs for extraordinary reality with a prince, and instead lives with a more ordinary mate. Amanda Haight interprets the boy who wants to take the heroine north and the tsar as doubles for Gumilyov, saying, "The two could be said to stand for two different kinds of love, the one spiritual, the other the ordinary day-to-day relationship."[20] However, there is little evidence that Akhmatova ever thought of Gumilyov as the romantic prince. On the contrary, she rejected him for several years. The poem portrays the poet looking back at a carefree childhood, when the heroine is thirteen and does not yet understand the complexities of life. It is the childhood of a very special person, with the gift of spiritual perception, one "touched by God," with an inner freedom independent of external circumstances. She is a dreamer, who would carry with her for her entire life those memories of a carefree youth by the Black Sea.

The magic of the poem lies in Akhmatova's ability to conjure up a period of unconscious sensual awareness of beauty, the sails billowing on the horizon, the fish and gulls, "completely unaware that this was happiness." The child can divine water, gather cartridges and remnants of shrapnel in her skirt "like mushrooms or blackberries" in total innocence of them as symbols of devastation and ruin. Instead, she weaves tales around them: "When I become the tsarina, I will build six battleships." She must reject the tall boy from the north if her dreams are to come true and she does indeed become the tsarina. When the gypsy prophesies that a distinguished guest will come, whom the child will attract with her song, her life changes. She becomes anxious and her Muse arrives to comfort her. But when the tsarevich finally arrives at Easter in the spring, the prophecy is realized in the form of death. He is the captain of a yacht, drowned. Perhaps he represents the end of the poet's childhood, the end of her carefree life in the south, but also the end of instinctive awareness of the world. What has replaced her carefree, sensuous perception is a higher wisdom, gained through the knowledge of death and suffering, and thus the poem witnesses the child's bittersweet transition to adulthood.

The poet Marietta Shaginyan wrote in 1922 about what this poem meant to her generation and the one following the Revolution:

Now that the old editions have disappeared, many (especially contemporary adolescent readers) have not read this poem. For them it will be a discovery, for us it was a revelation. Can it be that the real aesthetic charm, which at first was hidden from us, now suddenly has become a classical work? The rhythm, which seems broken, reflected a profound similarity to Russian folk song. The images, which at that time seemed mannered, now have become simply a drawing, true and eternal in its absolute truth. . . . The entire poem seems like a marvelous seashell full of the sound of the sea and the wind, just as when you put a shell to your ear. The mannered Petersburg lady, foster child of the once fashionable Acmeism—as fashionable as the poet herself—is concealed behind this personal and most wonderfully simple lyric.[21]

By 1915, Akhmatova's fame and place in Russian literature had become secure. The critics not only acknowledged her stylistic innovations but recognized that her *Weltanschauung,* her view of life and human relations, marked an important departure from Symbolist poetry, and also, in fact, from that of Gumilyov, whose style may have developed into the clearer forms of Acmeism, but who was still under the spell of a Nietzschean worldview. Critics contrasted Akhmatova to Bryusov, who represented the idea of the elect as being beyond good and evil, looking at all of life merely as material to be transformed into works of art. Referring to a poem by Bryusov in which he employs an image about sailing "to all seas and piers"—meaning experiencing all aspects of life, good as well as evil— one critic noted that in spite of apparent connection with the Symbolists, Akhmatova was not an irresponsible experimenter, and that for her poetry was much more than just a meaningless sailing from sea to sea and pier to pier—"it is a mysterious and magical activity which has *obligations.*" Another commented, "Once a magician of the word, Valery Bryusov said, 'Perhaps everything in life is only a means for poetry, and from merciless childhood you seek a combination of words.' How inapplicable this is to Akhmatova. For her the word is no less valuable than for Bryusov, but it is not an aim in itself."[22]

In 1913, Akhmatova had met Nikolay Nedobrovo, a man who was going to play an important role in her life, even though their intimacy lasted only a few years. She told friends later that it was he who educated her in the ways of society and had insights no one else had into her own poetry and how it would develop in the future. Noted for his handsome features and fine manners, Nedobrovo had a slender figure, and narrow, expressive hands. He seemed to have come from the nineteenth century, "so refined and fragile," as one friend described him. He was a dandy, always elegantly dressed.[23] His external restraint made him appear cold, but he did form deep friendships. Yuliya Sazonova-Slonimskaya, a literary critic, historian of theater and ballet, and close friend of Nedobrovo and Akhmatova, says: "Nedobrovo appeared haughty and cold, but was actually bitter and lonely. He was a person who craved tenderness, loyalty, and understanding."[24]

Nedobrovo was born in 1884 to an old noble family. He grew up on his parents' estate in Kharkov and attended the gymnasium there, where he met Boris Anrep (who would also play a key role in Akhmatova's life). When Akhmatova met him, Nedobrovo was spending the summer in 1913 in Pavlovsk, and they saw each other frequently. According to Mikhail Kralin, Nedobrovo was not so important for his own poetic works, which had been published rarely, but for his role as an "arbiter of artistic taste." He valued Pushkin as the god of Russian writers because of his pure, clear style, which had become clouded by the vagueness and imprecision of subsequent Russian writers. Other young writers considered him their teacher.[25] A contemporary poet, Alexander Kondratov, noted the broad erudition of Nedobrovo, and said that writers who had already made their mark also turned to Nedobrovo for advice. Perhaps this was what Akhmatova had in mind as the prototype, in the passage on the poet, in *Poem Without a Hero* that compares him with other "lawgivers" of the past:

> Ancient interlocutor of the moon.
> Your feigned groans don't deceive us,
> You write iron laws,
> Hammurabi, Lycurgus, Solon
> Could learn a lot from you.
>
> (II, p. 419)

Nedobrovo had achieved the inner peace that soon became a feature of Akhmatova herself, enabling her to endure the horror of external events. That was why, said Yuliya Sazonova-Slonimskaya, war and revolution could destroy him physically but not spiritually. His feelings for Russia also help explain Akhmatova's own feelings for her native land. For Nedobrovo, Russia was not only the homeland where he happened to be born, but a set of ideas, a spiritual location where a person could learn his true nature and find answers to his spiritual quests. The war was a terrible shock for him, Sazonova says, and he was very ill during this period.

His friend Anrep wrote about how Nedobrovo inspired a feeling of religious awe in Anrep himself—who was an atheist—for which he was grateful his entire life. Once they were walking along the Neva, on the embankment near the Winter Palace, and Anrep asked Nedobrovo whether he believed in God. Nedobrovo replied that he looked on religion as a way of thinking similar to that in the early period of scientific knowledge, when people "thought in images"; but he respected it because, he said, so much of art and literature owed its very existence to this early philosophy. Anrep said Nedobrovo taught him that religious art and music are the highest expressions of the human spirit.[26]

Nedobrovo had married Lyubov Olkhina, whom Anrep describes as a beautiful and spiritual woman, totally devoted to her husband. She had a passion for the Renaissance, and filled her apartment with furniture from that period. At costume balls she appeared in Renaissance dress.[27] Akhmatova told Znamenskaya that Nedobrovo's wife took Akhmatova's relationship with her husband very hard. Akhmatova treated her very condescendingly, once commenting to Znamenskaya that she found the relationship between Nedobrovo and his wife incomprehensible, since his wife's appreciation of poetry was so limited.[28] These remarks are similar to those she made about Pushkin's wife. It seems she either failed to understand or deliberately did not acknowledge that emotional relationships are often built on much more than shared artistic and intellectual interests.

Nedobrovo's wife had good reason to be jealous, since Akhmatova says Nedobrovo moved to Tsarskoye Selo to be near her.[29] He not only admired her poetry but was much attached to her and loved her deeply. In a letter to Anrep dated April 27, 1914, he said it was impossible to call Akhmatova beautiful, but she was so striking that a Leonardo drawing or a Gainsborough portrait should be made of her. In another letter the same year, on May 12, he said he was writing material to amuse Akhmatova in her "Tver solitude."[30]

Nedobrovo could be witty. He wrote a delightful parody of Akhmatova's poem "One would not mistake true tenderness," which shows that polite external action cannot fool the heroine's intuition that her beloved does not really care for her. Akhmatova's version, written in December 1913, reads:

> One would not mistake true tenderness
> With anything else, and it is quiet.
> In vain you carefully wrap
> My shoulders and breast in furs.
> And in vain you utter respectful words
> About the first love.
> How well I know those persistent,
> Insatiable glances of yours!
>
> (I, p. 313)

Nedobrovo's version is a gentle satire:

> Not in vain your breast and shoulders
> Were wrapped in fur by the prankster
> And he repeated the learned words . . .
> But was his fate terrible!
> He gained immortality without chemicals,
> At times annoying you:
> Your song is incomparable balsam
> For the preparation of a mummy.[31]

Nedobrovo's true feelings for Akhmatova were expressed in another poem which contains the following lines:

> How you sing in response to our hearts,
> And, as you open your lips, you breathe life into our souls;
> At the approach of every person
> You hear the song of panpipes in your blood![32]

In the spring of 1913 Nedobrovo founded the Society of Poets, and at the first meeting on April 4, Blok read his new play, *The Rose and the Cross*. Akh-

matova regularly took part in meetings of the Society.[33] Nedobrovo developed
tuberculosis in 1915 and spent his last years in the Crimea. Akhmatova saw him
for the last time in Bakhchisaray in 1916. He died in 1919 in Yalta.

Nedobrovo's article on Akhmatova's poems appeared in 1915 in *Russkaya
mysl (Russian Thought)*. "Based on the evidence of only the first two books,"
notes one critic, "he was able to discern the steel backbone within the elegantly
languid poetess." Akhmatova herself comments that this was "an amazing article,
prophetic. . . . How could he guess the firmness and fortitude in advance! How
did he know this? It's a miracle. Actually, at that time everyone thought all those
poems were sentimental, tearful, capricious. . . . But Nedobrovo understood my
path, my future; he guessed and predicted it because he knew me so well."[34]

Nedobrovo discussed many aspects of Akhmatova's verse. He noted that while
she had mastered all the formal innovations of recent poetry, she was still sensitive
to the poetic heritage of the past. She carefully selected those stylistic devices in
each particular poem that were necessary for the theme. Until Akhmatova, love
had almost always been portrayed from a male point of view: "The poetics of
male desire and attraction to the female have been explored in art to the limits,
whereas feminine emotion and masculine charm is almost unexplored territory.
There are no male counterparts to the Eternal Feminine. . . . There is a feminine
yearning for the Eternal Masculine." Thus, just as great poets like Goethe and
Pushkin sought certain ideal aspects that they associated with the perfect feminine
being, so now the woman poet should be inspired by such an ideal male
counterpart.

"Akhmatova's voice, firm, even self-confident, her very calmness in confessing
pain and weakness," Nedobrovo went on, "the very abundance of anguish, po-
etically refined—all bear witness not to tears over life's trivialities, but to a lyrical
soul, rather harsh than soft, cruel than tearful, and clearly in control rather than
downtrodden." Akhmatova belonged to those special human beings who walk on
the edge of the world, not among more ordinary people. Others who do not
comprehend their desires regard them as cranks, as tattered pilgrims.

Nedobrovo pointed out that the lives described in Akhmatova's poetry cease
to have merely personal value and are transmitted into a force lifting the spirit
of all those capable of responding to the poet. In reading her verses, we see our
own lives as more valuable. She respects her protagonists, showing them in a
heroic light, bestowing dignity upon them. We listen to her as to a prophet. He
also wished that critics would not urge her to broaden her themes: her vocation
lay not in breadth but in the uncovering of deeper layers of the spirit. Only in
the latter case was he wrong, for not only would Akhmatova develop her gift for
discerning the human spirit, but she would attempt to solve the enigmas of history,
of her country and her people.[35]

Although to some it appeared the marriage of Akhmatova and Gumilyov had
dissolved, they continued to see each other. Chulkov reported that in 1915, when
he and his wife returned from Switzerland, they moved to Malaya Street in Tsar-

skoye Selo where the Gumilyovs were living: "She had already separated from her husband. . . . She lived in her mother-in-law's house with her little three-year-old boy. She came to visit us with this little boy—Lyova. She also came alone and read us her poems. Once when I praised a poem I particularly liked, she suggested dedicating it to me, and that made me very happy."[36] This passage is problematic, since no sources indicate Lev was staying permanently with Akhmatova; he continued to live with his grandmother and aunt in Slepnyovo. Perhaps he was visiting Akhmatova at this time.

Akhmatova herself says that on December 24, 1914, she went with Gumilyov to Vilnius, then went alone to visit her mother in Kiev, returning to Tsarskoye Selo at the beginning of January 1915. At the end of the month she gave a reading of Gumilyov's poems in the Duma (Parliament). In the spring, she says, they moved to Petrograd, where they lived in a dark, gray room. She became very ill with tuberculosis and bronchitis. Around June she left for Slepnyovo, but the tuberculosis worsened.[37]

Throughout the war, Akhmatova along with other poets appeared at fundraisers for the wounded. On April 18, 1915, there was an evening of Petrograd poets who recited at the Tenishev Institute to raise money for an infirmary. Akhmatova appeared with Blok, Kuzmin, and Mandelstam, among others, and Sudeikina danced. The evening was also a tribute to Scriabin, who had died on April 14.[38]

That summer Akhmatova went as usual to Slepnyovo, but then returned to Tsarskoye Selo to be with Gumilyov. She arrived in Petrograd the day Warsaw was taken. She and Gumilyov lived in one wing of their house, since the main part had been rented out for the summer. Gumilyov then left for the front. In a letter to Akhmatova dated July 6, he asked to see some of her poems. He was reading the *Iliad:* "It is amazingly appropriate reading. The Greeks also had trenches and barricades and reconnaissance. And some descriptions, comparisons and remarks would do credit to any modernist."[39] He continued to write a column entitled "Letters About Russian Poetry" for *Apollon* when he was on leave, and in 1915 he wrote a marionette drama, *The Child of Allah,* for which Arthur Lourie composed the music. It was not produced because of the war, but it was printed in *Apollon.*

Akhmatova wrote that she was very sick that summer with tuberculosis and stayed in bed six hours a day on doctor's orders. However, when she received a telegram saying that her father was extremely ill, she went to be with him on Krestovsky Island in Petrograd. For twelve days she took care of him, along with Yelena Strannolyubskaya, the woman with whom he had been living for many years. Akhmatova's brother Viktor had been sent on maneuvers in the Pacific, but was supposed to return to Petrograd any day. Her father often woke up at night and asked Akhmatova to call the navy and find out if Viktor had returned. She would go into the next room as though to telephone, telling her father that Viktor would soon arrive. But on August 25 her father died.[40]

In the fall Gumilyov came to Petrograd and spent some time in Tsarskoye waiting for a transfer to the Aleksandriisky Hussars. Around October, Akhmatova entered a sanatorium, Huvinkka, in Finland, where she spent three weeks; Gumilyov came twice to visit her. At Huvinkka she met Russian generals, ensigns of the tsar, and the director of the Petrograd railway.[41]

On Christmas Day, Akhmatova was visited by the famous peasant poet Sergey Yesenin, accompanied by Klyuev. Akhmatova never liked Yesenin or his poetry. She later said he was at times totally illiterate. "I don't understand why they make such a fuss over him. There's nothing to him—but a petty poet. Sometimes there's passion, but how vulgar. He was once a nice little boy . . . now—what's he like! Vulgar. Not a single idea. And what nasty spite. Envy. He envies everyone. He lies about everyone."[42]

When Yesenin first came to Petrograd from the country, he was the darling of the intellectuals, admired for his wonderful freshness and half-shy, half-insolent youth. He represented the distant Russian village, which seemed so wholesome to the intelligentsia, with their decadent cabarets and sophisticated salons. But soon Yesenin set aside his simple, peasant garb and wore more fashionable attire— magnificent shiny leather boots, a blue silk peasant blouse slung with a golden belt, to which a little comb was attached. He would run this comb through his long golden curls, which he had let grow down to his shoulders. But behind the peasant facade was the creative mind of a great poet. Yesenin's early works were exuberant, fondly recalling village life, as in "With the Crimson Juice of Berries":

With the crimson juice of berries on your skin,
Tender, beautiful you were.
You resembled a rosy sunset
And, like snow, you were radiant and bright.

The seeds of your eyes fell, wilted,
Your slender name has melted like a sound,
But what remained in the folds of a rumpled shawl
Is the smell of honey from innocent hands.[43]

Akhmatova recalled the impression Yesenin made on her: "He was somewhat shy, fair, curly-haired, with light blue eyes, and impossibly naive. Yesenin positively shone, holding the newspaper *Birzhevye vedomosti* in his hand, where his poems appeared alongside those of Klyuev, Balmont, Blok, Voloshin and Gippius. At first I could not understand the source of this radiance, but his 'eternal companion' Klyuev helped me understand: 'Well, my highly esteemed Anna Andreyevna,' he broke into a smile and his walrus mustache bristled, his eyes dimming. 'My Seryozhenka [Sergey Yesenin] is here, along with all the famous printed poets, and I'm honored!' "[44]

By the end of 1915, Russia faced a crisis. That November, Blok wrote of the "impenetrable darkness all around; exasperation is written on the faces of all the common people, and the higher circles are disintegrating and becoming de-civilized. The young people as a whole are rude and vulgarly smug and not concerned with politics. . . . They don't want victory, they don't want peace. Where and when will the answer come?"[45] In 1916, Blok was called to active duty as a timekeeper on a bridge in Pinsk near the front. He remained there until March 1917. The brigade lived in the mansion of Prince Drutsky-Lubetsky, which was surrounded by marshes, fields, and woods. The old prince and his wife continued to live there throughout the war, and once in a while the prince would display his family's deeds and charters signed by Polish kings, and by Peter the Great and Catherine the Great. Blok hated the war, which only confirmed his feelings of imminent catastrophe. His brigade included the poet Wlodzimierz Przedpelski, who wrote that the night skies were lit up by rockets, planes flew overhead, and the earth moaned from artillery fire. He said that to his colleagues, Blok was like a demigod. He would talk to them of Rome and Paris, of Napoleon and the eighteenth century, and recite his poems. He did not lose his charm in these fairly pedestrian surroundings. When they asked him if he thought the situation was hopeless, Blok replied no, but it had been easier to deal with difficult situations when he was younger. He said the middle of life was the most difficult— by old age it gets easy again. One evening Przedpelski and Blok went on a troika ride in the snow. Przedpelski was struck by the joy he saw shining on Blok's face, the clear illumination of a soul momentarily freed from grief.[46]

Gumilyov's experience of the war was very different, as was his attitude toward it. A fellow soldier, Yuri Toporkov, relates that Gumilyov relished battle as an opportunity to test his courage. When two officers, under fire in an open field, jumped hastily into the trenches, Gumilyov remained standing and lit a cigarette. As the firing continued he finally also jumped into the trenches, where the squadron commander scolded him for his unnecessary bravado.[47]

Gumilyov spent the winter of 1915–16 in Petrograd, awaiting his assignment to another squadron. He read many religious books, especially works by Pavel Florensky, and often went to church. At the end of March 1916 he became a member of the Aleksandriisky Hussars. But that spring he contracted bronchitis and was sent to Tsarskoye Selo to a clinic, where he met Olga Arbenina, an actress from the Alexandriinsky Theater, later to be courted by both Gumilyov and Mandelstam. Gumilyov also met his future wife, Anna Engelhardt, at this time; she was a nurse working at the military hospital. Her brother says she liked to wear her nurse's uniform or a black coat and cap, hold a small volume of Akhmatova's poems in her hand, and walk in the Summer Garden attracting glances. (Later, people would call her "Anna II" after she became Gumilyov's wife.) Gumilyov went for a month to Masandra, then stopped in Sebastopol on the way to the front in the hopes of seeing Akhmatova. He did not find her, so he went to see Anna Engelhardt for three days in Ivanovo-Voznesensk, where Engelhardt and her brother were visiting their aunt and uncle.[48]

In the second half of August, Gumilyov came to Petrograd to take an exam and visit his family briefly at Tsarskoye. However, he did not stay with Akhmatova, but took a room at 31, Liteiny Avenue, in Petrograd, where he remained until the end of October. That summer Adamovich and Georgy Ivanov had organized a second Poets' Guild, and the first meeting was held in September. Akhmatova did not participate, and the meetings paled in comparison with the first Guild. By the autumn of 1917 they had ceased.

Gumilyov continued to have affairs with other women, although Akhmatova did not learn about some of them until later. In the summer of 1916 he had an affair with a strange woman named Margarita Tumpovskaya. She had been attracted to magic, talismans, and the occult since she was a child, and when they met, she was a convinced anthroposophist.[49]

While Tumpovskaya appeared to be a passing attraction, Gumilyov became passionately involved with Larisa Reisner in the fall of 1916. She was quite young at the time, which was consistent with Akhmatova's observation that Gumilyov only found young girls interesting and could not feel anything toward grown women. The two met at the "Comedian's Halt," a new cabaret that had replaced the Stray Dog, closed by the police in March 1915 because of wartime censorship. The Comedian's Halt opened on October 25, in the cellar of the D. I. Rubinshtein house on the Field of Mars, and it had a regular theater. Reisner was a student at the Institute of Psychoneurosis. She came of a line of landowners in Lithuania, but her father had moved to Petersburg to study and practice law. There Reisner was born in 1895. Her family became increasingly involved in revolutionary activity, and after her father got into trouble while occupying a faculty position in Tomsk, the family fled to Berlin and Paris, where they continued to be involved in leftist causes. When the situation became more stable in Russia after 1907, the family returned, and her father became a professor of law at Petersburg University. Reisner wrote fiction and poetry and began a journal, *Rudin,* in 1915, that made satirical attacks on tsarist Russia. In 1918 she joined the Communist Party, becoming a prominent figure after the Revolution.[50]

Reisner liked Gumilyov's poems and even tried to imitate them. They called each other "Lefi" and "Gafiz," and wrote to each other while separated by the war. On December 8, 1916, he wrote to say how much he missed her:

> Everything I know and love, I want to see as if through colored glass, through your soul, because it has a special color. . . . I do not believe in the transmigration of souls, but I think that in your former transmigrations you were the kidnapped Helen of Sparta, Angelina of Orlando Furioso, etc. I want to take you away. I wrote you a crazy letter because I love you. . . . I remember your every word, every nuance, every movement, but it's not enough. I want more. Yours, Gafiz.[51]

When a friend asked Akhmatova what Reisner was like, Akhmatova replied acidly, "I don't know—I know the poetry she wrote was totally tasteless. But she was smart enough to stop writing."[52] Akhmatova says she was at the Comedian's

Halt only once, at a general rehearsal of a puppet show.[53] She was on her way out when she encountered Reisner for the first time.

> I walked through the door through an empty room, and Larissa was sitting there. I said goodbye to her and gave her my hand. . . . I don't remember who was helping me on with my coat . . . when suddenly in comes Larissa, two guilty tears on her cheeks. "Thank you! You're absolutely marvelous. I'll never forget that you were the first to give me your hand!" What was this all about? A beautiful young woman, what was this all about humiliation? How could I have known then that she was having an affair with Gumilyov? And even if I had known—why wouldn't I have given her my hand?[54]

Reisner later told Akhmatova that Gumilyov had proposed to her, but that Reisner admired Akhmatova too much to hurt her. It is possible that as part of the decorum expected in her society, Akhmatova would have made the gesture of extending her hand to Reisner. However, it is also quite possible that by this time she did not care anymore whether Gumilyov was faithful or not. While spending some time together during this period, each remained absorbed in their own affairs.

Marina Tsvetayeva, the other most famous Russian woman poet of the twentieth century, was an emotional Muscovite both in temperament and in her poetry. Her father was a well-known professor who held important administrative positions in the world of art. Born in 1892, she spent part of her childhood abroad, becoming familiar with Western culture directly. Her first collection of poetry appeared in 1910. After marrying Sergey Efron in 1912, she had a lesbian affair with the poet Sophia Parnok between 1914 and 1916. At the end of December 1915, she came to Petrograd. In her memoir, *An Otherworldly Evening,* Tsvetayeva describes her recitation of poems at one of the literary centers of Petrograd, the home of the naval architect Akim Kannegiser. It was here she met Osip Mandelstam, and they had a brief affair. She had hoped desperately that Akhmatova would be present at this evening, but she was missing. Tsvetayeva wrote in her memoir:

> All of Petersburg was there except Akhmatova, who was in the Crimea, and Gumilyov, who was in the war. The beginning of January 1916 was the beginning of the last year of the old world. It was in the full swing of war. Dark forces. We sat and read poems. For the entire evening the word "front" was not mentioned by anyone, nor the name of Rasputin. . . . Tomorrow Akhmatova will lose everyone—and Gumilyov his life. But this evening was ours! The "Feast During the Time of the Plague"? But those feasting with wine and roses were already specters

of Hades. "Atone?" No . . . But everyone paid . . . Gumilyov with his life; Yesenin with his life; Kuzmin, Akhmatova, and I with life imprisonment within ourselves.[55]

It was at this time that Tsvetayeva wrote a series of poems about Akhmatova, although she was not to meet her until 1940. One of these poems was set to music by Shostakovich.

O, Muse of lament, most lovely of muses!
O you, shawled child of the white night!
You sent a black snowstorm to Rus,
And your howls penetrate us, like arrows.
. . .

In my singing city the cupolas burn
And the bright Saviour is glorified by a wandering blind man
And I give you as a gift my belled city,
—Akhmatova!—and my heart as well.[56]

In *An Otherworldly Evening,* Tsvetayeva says that Mandelstam told her Akhmatova never parted with Tsvetayeva's poems to her and carried them in her purse so long that only shreds remained. However, when Lydia Chukovskaya read this passage from Tsvetayeva's memoirs to Akhmatova much later, in 1958, Akhmatova replied that none of it had happened—"neither the poems in my purse nor the shreds."

Not everyone, however, idolized Akhmatova. Ivan Bunin, the author and poet, wrote a famous parody of Akhmatova's poetry:

Large muff, pale cheek
Pressed against it langorously, and lovingly,
Crossed knees, narrow hand . . .
Nervous, affected and bloodless.[57]

Many poems in Akhmatova's next collection, *White Flock (Belaya staya)* (1917), were devoted to Boris Anrep, who soon replaced Nedobrovo in Akhmatova's heart. He was a larger-than-life character, a romantic figure descended from the medieval Teutonic Knights and a general in the service of the Swedish king, Charles XII, who was taken captive by Peter the Great and remained in the Russian court. Anrep also traced his ancestry to an illegitimate daughter of Catherine the Great. Born in Petersburg on September 28, 1883, he grew up in Kharkov in the Ukraine, where he went to the same gymnasium as Nedobrovo. His family also had an estate in Yaroslavl in the north—Akhmatova refers to this in one of her poems. From 1902 to 1905 Anrep went to law school in Petersburg, where he renewed his friendship with Nedobrovo; in 1908 he married Yuniya Khitrovo, then went to Paris to study art. In England he met members of the Bloomsbury Group. There he helped arrange the Russian section of the Second Post-Impressionist Exhibition, directed by Roger Fry, and his review of the exhibition appeared in *Apollon* in 1912. In 1911 he began an affair with Helen Maitland, a member of the English intelligentsia, with whom he had two children. It is not clear whether Akhmatova knew about Anrep's affair with Maitland, which was going on while he made trips back to Russia. But she never mentioned it to those who wrote down her conversations.[58]

Anrep charmed many of the notable figures of the day, including Lady Ottoline Morrell, the mistress of Bertrand Russell. Morrell's salon was the gathering place for artistic and literary figures. She was quite favorably impressed by Anrep when she first met him, writing, "Lamb's friend, Boris von Anrep, arrived from Paris, clever, fat, good-hearted, sensual, but full of youthful vitality and Russian gaiety."[59] However, when he returned to England during the war, she had a very different response—he appeared rather brutal, and pompously impressed with his rank as captain. He made an equally negative impression on Aldous Huxley, who met him six months later.[60]

At the outbreak of the war, Anrep served in Galicia and then was posted in England, working for the Russian State Commission. He returned to Russia as an officer in 1914 and visited Nedobrovo in Tsarskoye Selo, where he saw Akhmatova and said, "I immediately understood I was in the presence of a remarkable woman and poet, and Nedobrovo's acquaintance with her was the high point of his life."[61]

Anrep said his interest in Akhmatova soon turned to adoration. His conversations with Nedobrovo began to be devoted to one theme: Anna Akhmatova, her poetry and personality. It was then, in 1914, that Anrep's estranged wife Yuniya returned to Russia. Akhmatova said she was attracted to Anrep much more strongly than she had ever been to Nedobrovo, which made her feel guilty, because she had a very tender feeling for Nedobrovo and knew how much she meant to him.[62] In the summer of 1915 Nedobrovo's friend Vera Znamenskaya received a letter from him from the Crimea reporting his unexpected grief because of the change in Akhmatova's feelings for him—presumably because of the place Anrep had assumed in her life.[63] During 1915, Anrep saw Akhmatova frequently when he was back in Russia. He gave her a copy of his poem "Fizy," which she sewed into a silken purse and said she would keep as a sacred relic. They went sleighing, dined out at restaurants, and he listened to her reciting her poems, smiling and singing them in a quiet voice. "Often we were silent and listened to the sounds around us."[64]

In a letter to the Russian émigré scholar Gleb Struve—which Anrep asked Struve not to publish until after his death, since apparently he did not want the details of his relationship with Akhmatova known while he was still alive—Anrep explained the story of Akhmatova's poem "The Tale of the Black Ring," which appears in the collection *Anno Domini MCMXXI* (1921–22). The heroine says her Tatar grandmother gave the ring to her, bequeathing it to her before her death, and the heroine gave it to her true love secretly under the table at dinner. Anrep tells a slightly different story. While in Petrograd in 1916, he was invited to Nedobrovo's home in Tsarskoye Selo, where on February 13 he went to hear Nedobrovo read his recently completed tragedy *Judith*. "Anna Akhmatova will be there," Nedobrovo added. Anrep describes the incident:

> For me to come from the front and find myself in the refined atmosphere of Nedobrovo's Tsarskoye Selo home, hear *Judith* . . . and see Anna Akhmatova was very attractive. I entered and saw Akhmatova sitting on a small couch, and as I went up to her, a secret anxiety came over me, an incomprehensible sick feeling which I always felt wherever I met her or even thought about her. I sat down beside her and Nedobrovo opened the manuscript sitting behind a lovely Italian Renaissance desk and began to read . . . In spite of his impeccable verse, I listened without hearing and tried to concentrate. . . . I closed my eyes and put my hand on the seat of the couch. Suddenly something fell into my hand; it was the black ring. "Take it," whispered Akhmatova. "It's for you." I wanted to say something. My heart was beating. I looked questioningly at her face, but she looked silently ahead. I pressed my hand into a fist and Nedobrovo continued reading. Finally it was over. . . . I rushed to leave and Akhmatova stayed on. In a few days I had to leave for England.[65]

The day before his departure for England, Anrep received a copy of Akhmatova's book *Evening* with the inscription: "To Boris Anrep—One less hope becomes one more song. February 13, 1916. Tsarskoye Selo." This line is taken from a poem dated April 1915, in which Akhmatova expresses a major theme— the transformation of her grief into a work of art:

> I no longer smile,
> A freezing wind chills my lips,
> One less hope becomes
> One more song.
> And this song, against my will,
> I devote to desecration and mockery,
> Because it is unbearably painful
> For the soul to love silently.
>
> (I, p. 387)

Earlier Anrep had given Akhmatova a very beautiful, carved wooden cross he had taken from an abandoned church in the Carpathian Mountains of Galicia. He had written a four-line poem about it:

I forgot the words and didn't say a vow.
Idiot, I put my hands on the helpless maiden
To guard her from the goblet and torment of crucifixion
Which I myself, as a sign of friendship, had given her.[66]

Her response was bitter then as well, for she saw him rarely, and always knew he would soon leave, either to go abroad on duty, or in the end to leave Russia forever. She wrote the poem "When, in the gloomiest of capitals . . ." in August 1916, when she left Petrograd for the south, for Pesochnaya Bay.

. . .

I took with me only the cross
You gave me on the day of betrayal—
So that the steppe wormwood might bloom
And the winds, like sirens, sing.

And here, on the bare wall,
It protects me from bitter fantasies,
And nothing is too terrible for me
To recall—not even the final day.

(I, p. 477)

Anrep left for London in February 1916, hoping to return in six weeks. However, he did not come back until the end of the year, for a short period. His crucifix did not guard Akhmatova from the torment she felt after his final departure in 1917, which she expressed strongly in several poems throughout her life.

In May of 1916 Akhmatova was in Slepnyovo; then at the end of the summer she went south to see her family. In December 1916, she stayed in Sebastopol with Boris Anrep's wife Yuniya, whom she might have encountered through Nedobrovo, since Anrep was later surprised to learn they had ever met.

White Flock was published in 1917. The title comes from a poem in which she addresses her lost lover:

Everything is for you: my daily prayer
And the thrilling fever of the insomniac,
And the blue fire of my eyes,
And my poems, that white flock.

(I, p. 461)

Many of the poems are about the war. They reveal a new consciousness of Akhmatova's place in the world. No longer is she only the voice of women crying out in pain at personal suffering, or asking God why the world is often so cruel.

She is speaking now for her country and her people, a sibyl, a prophetess like Cassandra, who sees a world changing and foresees what those changes will bring—the Apocalypse Blok felt was imminent had finally come, and whether the loss of life meant loss of hope as well remained to be seen. Unlike Gumilyov, Akhmatova did not glorify war. Her patriotism took the form of compassion for those facing death fighting for their land, rather than a rhetorical celebration of heroism. In some poems she uses a parallelism typical of folk poetry, juxtaposing a human or philosophical condition with a scene from nature. In "May Snow," for example, the spring snow that kills the swelling buds—bringing death during the time of hope and renewal—evokes young soldiers dying before their time. She dates the poem "Prayer" for a holiday, Pentecost (May 1915), and offers to suffer—to give up child and lover, and even her gift of song—if only Russia may be saved.

> Give me bitter years of sickness,
> Suffocation, insomnia, fever,
> Take my child and my lover,
> And my mysterious gift of song—
> This I pray at your liturgy
> After so many tormented days,
> So that the stormcloud over darkened Russia
> Might become a cloud of glorious rays.
>   (I, p. 435)

Even before the war, during the winter of 1913, in "Oh, it was a cold day," Akhmatova had begun to portray the poet as prophet:

> Oh, it was a cold day
> In Peter's miraculous city!
> Like a crimson fire the sunset lay,
> And slowly the shadow thickened.
>
> Let him not desire my eyes,
> Prophetic and fixed,
> He will get a whole lifetime of poems,
> The prayer of my arrogant lips.
>   (I, p. 389)

In this poem the heroine reminds us both of Cassandra, the Greek prophetess, and of a *klikusha* (screamer), the Russian female counterpart of the "holy fool," who, though considered mad, is treated with respect since she is believed to be endowed by God with the gift of insight and prophecy. The theme of prophecy continues in "This was my prayer . . . ," written in 1913:

. . .
So I, Lord, am prostrate:
Will the heavenly flame touch
My sealed eyelashes
And my astonishing muteness?
(I, p. 391)

This recalls Pushkin's famous poem "The Prophet," in which the poet receives
the gift of prophetic insight from an angel, who tears out his sinful tongue and
inserts the forked tongue of a wise serpent.

And the voice of God called out to me:
"Arise, O Prophet, see and hear,
Be filled with my will,
Go forth over land and sea
And set the hearts of men on fire with your word."[67]

In one of her early poems about the war—as in the *Igor Tale,* Russia's great
epic—nature reflects the doom over the Russian land:

The sweet smell of juniper
Flies from the burning woods.
Soldiers' wives are wailing for the boys,
The widow's lament keens over the countryside.

The public prayers were not in vain,
The earth was yearning for rain!
Warm red liquid sprinkled
The trampled fields.

Low, low hangs the empty sky
And a praying voice quietly intones:
"They are wounding your sacred body,
They are casting lots for your robes."
(I, p. 427)

Akhmatova provides a parallel between the human condition and nature, but
here it is not a young girl grieving for her lost love, as in so many Russian folk
songs, but wives and widows lamenting their wounded or dead husbands. In the
Igor Tale there is also lament—by Igor's wife: "On the Danube Yaroslavna's voice
is heard; like a desolate cuckoo she cries early in the morning." There is too an
empathy between nature and the terrible events that are taking place—the birds
in the oak trees lie in wait for misfortune, the wolves stir up a storm in the ravines,
the eagles screech and the foxes yelp at the scarlet shields. A passage in Akhmatova's poem describing the dry earth watered by blood and the field ploughed

by the trampling of soldiers' boots recalls a similar passage in the epic describing the battlefield: "The black earth beneath the hooves was sown with bones and watered with blood: a harvest of sorrow came up over the land of Rus."[68] The blood called forth by the soldiers' pricking the body of Christ on the Cross and their blasphemous casting of lots for his robes remind us that Christ suffered to redeem man for his sins. If Russia has sinned, it can atone—there is still hope of redemption.

By 1916, patriotic fervor had been replaced by despair in the minds of many Russians, including Akhmatova. The war began to have an important effect on Akhmatova's life and work. Her poem "In Memoriam, July 19, 1914" (August 1, New Style), written in the summer of 1916, expresses her feelings of this time. Just as the quiet summer was being interrupted by war, so now she will no longer sing only of passion but of the suffering she has been forced to witness. This transition has been ordained not by the blind fate of some vague historical force, but by the will of God.

> We aged a hundred years, and this
> Happened in a single hour:
> The short summer had already died,
> The body of the ploughed plains soaked.
>
> Suddenly the quiet road burst into color,
> A lament flew up, ringing, silver . . .
> Covering my face, I implored God
> Before the first battle to strike me dead.
>
> Like a burden henceforth unnecessary,
> The shadows of passion and songs vanished from my memory.
> The Most High ordered it—emptied—
> To become a grim book of calamity.
>
> (I, p. 449)

Akhmatova's Muse has changed just as Akhmatova has. Now the Muse is experiencing "youthful anguish," for the poet was still in her mid-twenties when she wrote these poems of the grief brought by love and war.

> Why do you pretend to be
> Now a branch, now a stone, now a bird?
> Why do you smile at me
> Like sudden summer lightning from the sky?
>
> Don't torment me anymore, don't touch me!
> Leave me to my prophetic woes . . .
> A drunken flame staggers
> Across the dried up, grayish bog.

And the Muse, in a ragged dress,
Sings despondently and at length.
In hard and youthful anguish
Is her miraculous strength.

(I, p. 425)

In "Somewhere there is a simple life . . ." (1915), Petersburg symbolizes the alienation that fame brings, the price paid by those who live in the capital. And yet they would not choose to live anywhere else:

Somewhere there is a simple life and a world,
Transparent, warm and joyful . . .
There at evening a neighbor talks with a girl
Across the fence, and only the bees can hear
This most tender murmuring of all.

But we live ceremoniously and with difficulty
And we observe the rites of our bitter meetings,
And when suddenly the reckless wind
Breaks off a sentence just begun—

But not for anything would we exchange this splendid
Granite city of fame and calamity,
The wide rivers of glistening ice,
The sunless, gloomy gardens,
And, barely audible, the Muse's voice.

(I, p. 411)

"No, tsarevich, I am not the one" (July 10, 1915) combines the twin motifs of the prophet and the price of fame. Fame is a trap, and her lips no longer kiss but prophesy:

No, tsarevich, I am not the one
You want me to be.
And no longer do my lips
Kiss—they prophesy.

. . . .

Do you want fame?—then you
Should ask me for advice,
Only—it's a trap
Where there is neither joy nor light.

(I, p. 461)

White Flock includes poems about other cities that played an important role in Akhmatova's life. In "Kiev" (summer 1914), she connects her own personal life with the ancient city of Kiev, now the capital of the Ukraine, once the center of the Land of Rus before it was divided, and the place where the Grand Prince Vladimir baptized his people in 988. A statue now stands in his honor overlooking the Dnieper. It is a beautiful city, full of elegant parks, monasteries, and churches with golden cupolas, boulevards lined with chestnut trees, the famous Baroque church, St. Andrew's, built by Rastrelli in honor of the empress Elizabeth's lover Razoumovsky, and later buildings painted in pastel colors.

Kiev

The ancient city seems deserted,
My arrival is strange.
Over its river, Vladimir
Raised a black cross.

The rustling lindens and the elms
Along the gardens are dark,
And the diamond needles of the stars
Are lifted out toward God.

My sacrificial and glorious journey
I will finish here,
And with me only you, my equal
And my lover.

                                              (I, p. 401)

Two poems are devoted to the ancient town of Novgorod, once a great city-state based on trade with the Hanseatic League, with ties to Western Europe. Its citizens had more control over their government than in most Russian cities: they elected their prince and had a town council. Akhmatova's ancestors were wealthy until Ivan III captured the city in his drive to form a centralized government with Moscow as the center and to establish his own clan as the ruling dynasty. Akhmatova was visiting Gumilyov there during his basic training in 1914.

I will go there and weariness will fly away.
The cool of early morning pleases me.
There are villages mysterious and dark—
Storehouses of prayer and work.

My tranquil and trusting love
Of this place will never be conquered:
There's a crop of Novgorod blood
In me—like a shard of ice in frothy wine.

And this can never be remedied,
Great heat will not melt it,
And no matter what I begin to praise—
You, silent, shine before me.

(I, p. 449)

Akhmatova pays homage to Tsarskoye Selo through the beautiful statue of Pierrette, the heroine of a La Fontaine fable, "The Broken Pitcher." The statue also was the subject of a poem by Pushkin written in 1830, "Having dropped the urn . . . ," which reflects a frozen moment captured eternally in this work of art, as in Keats's "Ode on a Grecian Urn." In the Akhmatova poem—written in autumn 1916 and dedicated to Nedobrovo—the speaker is humorously jealous of the ability of the statue to capture her lover's attention:

Already the maple leaves
Are falling on the swan pond,
And on the blood-stained bushes
Of late-ripening mountain ash.

And, dazzlingly slender,
Crossed legs impervious to cold,
She sits on the northern stone
Gazing down along the roads.

I felt uneasy
Before this celebrated maid.
On her shoulders
Beams of fading light played.

And how could I forgive her
The delight of your enamoured praise.
You see, for her, so fashionably nude,
It's fun to be sad.

(I, p. 417)

Akhmatova's poems, like those of Gumilyov at this time, reveal the inevitable disintegration of their marriage. "I don't need much happiness" (May 1914) portrays a woman seeing her husband off to his sweetheart's. She prays to the Madonna for comfort. However, in "Ah! It's you again . . ." (July 1916), it is the wife who has betrayed her husband and now asks for forgiveness, which will not be easily forthcoming. The youth who fell in love with her has turned into a stern and unforgiving husband. Akhmatova continues to employ the technique of juxtaposing nature with a human situation. The autumn landscape, the eerie cries of cranes, and the leafless garden evoke a time of dying and sorrow, reflecting the emotional atmosphere and the feelings of the heroine.

Ah! It's you again. Not as an enamoured youth
But as a husband, daring, stern, inflexible,
You enter this house and look at me.
My soul is frightened by the lull before the storm.
You ask what I have done with you,
Entrusted to me forever by love and fate.
I have betrayed you. And to have to repeat—
Oh, if only you'd get tired of it!
This is how a dead man speaks, disturbing his murderer's sleep,
This is how the angel of death waits by the bed of the dying.
Forgive me now. The Lord has taught us to forgive.
My flesh is tormented by piteous disease,
And my free spirit already rests, serene.
I remember only the garden, tender, leafless, autumnal,
And the black fields and the cry of the cranes . . .
Oh, how sweet was the earth for me with you!

(I, p. 385)

"Under an oaken slab . . ." (1915) may reveal the guilt Akhmatova felt as a mother, for she apparently saw her son only a few months of each year when she visited him on her mother-in-law's estate in Tver.

Under an oaken slab in the churchyard
I will sleep quietly,
You, darling, will come running
To visit Mama on Sunday—
Across the stream and along the rise,
Leaving the grownups far behind,
From far away, my sharp-sighted boy,
You will recognize my cross.
I know you won't be able
To remember much about me, little one:
I didn't scold you, I didn't hold you,
I didn't take you to Communion.

(I, p. 447)

Here Akhmatova employs a device that would become more typical in her later verse—the "non-event," those things which should have happened but did not. In this poem the mother did not scold her child, did not hold him, and did not take him to Communion—the things a mother is normally expected to do, as she helps her child grow up. She is a "non-mother." A related poem is "Tall woman, where is your little gypsy," in which the gypsy wanders in the springtime, longing for her missing burden, her child. Akhmatova's arms too were empty.

A beautiful lyric dedicated to Nedobrovo, written in May 1915, demonstrates her great insight into human relationships. No matter how close and intimate two people may become, they always keep a part of themselves hidden:

There is a sacred boundary between those who are close,
And it cannot be crossed by passion or love—
Though lips fuse in dreadful silence
And the heart shatters to pieces with love.

Friendship is helpless here, and years
Of exalted and ardent happiness,
When the soul is free and a stranger
To the slow languor of voluptuousness.

Those who strive to reach it are mad, and those
Who reach it stricken by grief . . .
Now you understand why my heart
Does not beat faster under your hand.

(I, p. 391)

Critics noted a maturing in the poems collected in *White Flock*. Vasily Gippius wrote that "Her lyricism has developed and broadened and deepened to include a religious feeling for her homeland."[69] In an article on Akhmatova in 1919, the critic and husband of Akhmatova's friend Salomea Andronikova, Sergey Rafalovich, maintained that Akhmatova had moved from themes of dream to those of high tragedy:

She has developed into a great poet. . . . She has not changed the former thread or broken it, she has remained herself, but she has matured. Now the most cultured contemporary scholars and critics listen to her verse with great sensitivity and recognize her as a great poet. Before they said hers was a narrow circle but great. . . . She has broadened her range to include more universal themes, but has not perceived them on a lofty scale, but the same scale of theme from ordinary, everyday life. They reveal the personal and artistic maturity of the poet. . . . It is not external circumstances, the accidents of life, a failure in love or meetings that did not take place with one who was predestined by fate, that creates her tragedy. All this can be called merely drama. Tragedy is inevitability, inescapability, the fatal guilt of an innocent soul. Everyone is able to live through drama. Tragedy is the fate of the strong personality, and one cannot be saved from it by a "mysterious gift of song" or fame or beauty or love—it is impossible to be saved from tragedy.[70]

Rafalovich wrote this in 1919 when Akhmatova's life was relatively peaceful. He could not have known then how prophetic his words would become.

The Revolutionary Years: 1917–1922

Venice rotting with gold, and even eternal Rome
turned pale before the grandness of dying Petersburg.
　—GEORGY FEDOTOV

Akhmatova described the winter in Slepnyovo on the eve of the Revolution:

> Once I was at Slepnyovo in the winter. It was wonderful. Everything
> seemed to go back to the nineteenth century, to Pushkin's time. Sleighs,
> felt boots, bear lap rugs, huge fur coats, gaping silence, snowdrift, dia-
> mond snow. It was there I met and welcomed 1917. After the gloomy
> military Sebastopol where I had been suffering from asthma and was
> freezing in a cold rented room, it was as if I had come upon some kind
> of promised land. In Petersburg Rasputin had already been killed, and
> they were awaiting the revolution.[1]

And the Revolution came. Power was rapidly slipping out of the tsar's hands;
soon he was forced to abdicate when, at the end of February 1917, a revolutionary
crowd took over the city and the situation in the country as a whole deteriorated.
A new government was quickly formed, with the intention that a more permanent

government would eventually be put in its place by a Constituent Assembly. However, its temporary nature was emphasized by its name, the Provisional Government. The government continued the war, totally disregarding the low morale, the lack of ammunition and food, and the thousands deserting because they thought they were fighting for a futile cause. Sympathy and compassion disappeared. The war brought out the worst in everybody. No one believed in victory any more and no one wanted to risk his life in the name of national pride. As a friend of Akhmatova's said, "Words which had once been so significant for us: 'Homeland, Honor, Courage'—lost all meaning. . . . The war had destroyed everything human in us."[2]

Parallel to the government in power another authority arose, the soviets, or councils of workers and soldiers, whose influence over the masses was enormous. Lenin arrived from abroad in April in a sealed train, calling for an end to the war. Forced to flee Russia in August, from his hiding place in Finland Lenin urged the Bolsheviks to prepare for revolution. He returned in October, and the revolution he had hoped for was realized on October 25 (November 7, New Style). The capital was moved to Moscow, which had a major effect on the position of Petrograd. Very soon Moscow became not only the political but cultural center, and Petrograd in its new guise as Leningrad was forced to become peripheral. The war with Germany was over after the new Soviet government signed a peace treaty in March 1918, but within the country the fighting continued. For three years the new Soviet government waged a bloody civil war against the counterrevolutionaries, while at the same time the Bolsheviks were vying for power in a brutal struggle against other leftist groups like the Social Revolutionaries.[3]

Akhmatova was living in Petrograd with her friends the Sreznevskys when the February Revolution occurred. She had come to stay with them in January and remained there until the autumn of 1918. Sreznevskaya's husband was the chief doctor of a mental hospital. They lived on 9, Botkinskaya Street, in the Vyborg district across the Neva, which could be reached by going across the Liteiny Bridge.

When the Revolution began on February 25, Akhmatova was spending the morning at the dressmaker's, totally oblivious to what was occurring. When she attempted to go home in a horse cab to the Vyborg side of the Neva, however, the cabby nervously replied, "Lady, I'm not going over there. They're shooting and I have a family. . . ."[4] So Akhmatova roamed the city alone. She saw the revolutionary manifestoes, troops, and fires set by the tsarist secret police, trying to keep the masses inside and off the streets. Heedless of danger and absorbing impressions she would never forget, Akhmatova just kept wandering, though there was shooting everywhere.

In the evening, when the Revolution was in full swing, Akhmatova went with Anrep to the dress rehearsal of Meyerhold's famous production of Lermontov's *Masquerade*. It was the last act of the tragedy of the old regime, when the Petersburg elite went to enjoy themselves at this splendidly luxurious production in

the midst of all the chaos and confusion. Alexander Kugel, a theater critic, caught
the atmosphere:

> In the streets . . . there was firing. The trolleys stopped running, the
> street lamps burned dimly. . . . Scarce cabdrivers demanded incredible
> sums. Cries could be heard and crowds with flags were gathering. There
> were no people on the streets, and it was eerie. The theater, however,
> was packed—and at what prices! . . . At the theater entrance there was
> a solid black row of automobiles. All the wealth, all the nobility, all of
> Petrograd's enormous pluto-bureau-and-behind-the-front-lines-ocracy
> had turned out.[5]

Describing that amazing night, the Meyerhold scholar Konstantin Rudnitsky
felt that this particular production was totally appropriate:

> Autocratic Russia was collapsing before everyone's eyes. Its imperial
> grandeur became a phantom and everything smelled of decay. . . . The
> entire solemn ritual of the Court, the magnificent uniforms, the bewitch-
> ing power of rank, the strict etiquette, the indestructible preeminence of
> tradition, the arrogance of the nobility, heraldry, orders, epaulettes, re-
> view parades—it was as if they had been licked off by a cow's tongue.
> Everything was disappearing or had disappeared. Everything that had
> been indubitable, substantial, and weighty reality became mystically
> ephemeral, dubious: everything was in question. It was all drowning in
> the Rasputin business, reverses on the front, in corruption, bribery, es-
> pionage mania, in the loud spasmodic patriotism of the newspapers, in
> drunkenness. . . . At this same moment Meyerhold and Golovin showed
> worn-out, perishing Imperial Petrograd a splendid and fearful vision, at
> once opulent and tragic. . . . The spectacle prophesied disaster and the
> end of the world. It was called the "sunset of the Empire," "the last
> spectacle of Tsarist Russia."[6]

Baron Nicholas Drizen's recollection vividly illustrates how feudal Russia was
literally snatched into the modern world by the Revolution. He describes an event
that took place at the Sheremetev Palace, which was soon to become Akhmatova's
home. He says the street was like a carnival celebration, for he found himself in
the midst of young people in chain mail with curved Turkish swords and a sailor
armed to the teeth. He later found out that while looking for arms, this group
had ended up at the palace of Count Sheremetev on the Fontanka Canal. They
were greeted by the owner himself. "Arms?" he asked. "You need arms? Please,
my axes and picks from the sixteenth century are at your service."[7]

Akhmatova said that from the time of the Revolution her attitude toward
blood and death changed radically. The word "blood" now evoked memories of

blood flowing on the snow and stones, and a disgusting smell. "Blood is good only when alive, when flowing in one's veins, but it is absolutely horrible and repulsive in all other cases."[8]

By the summer of 1917 Akhmatova was back in Slepnyovo. In a series of ironic letters to Mikhail Lozinsky, Akhmatova expressed her increasing anxiety as the situation worsened. The village was a "real paradise." "The peasants swear that our house is standing on their bones. . . . Also Socialists! Deserters keep coming, saying that the war is going splendidly, and the peasants believe them." On July 31, she wrote that she wanted to come to Petersburg to spend some time at *Apollon,* but the peasants were promising to destroy Slepnyovo on August 6 because there was a local holiday and "guests" would be coming. "Not a bad way to entertain the guests. I'm going to pull flax and write some bad poetry." Then on August 16 she wrote to say that she had just received a letter from Valya Sreznevskaya, who said the slaughter was getting worse. Akhmatova hoped either to go to Paris in the winter or to remain at Slepnyovo, but either choice was unpleasant, because the only place she really breathed easily was in Petersburg. "But since there is a new custom of flooding the sidewalks with the citizens' blood every month, it has lost its charm in my eyes."[9]

In fact, she was back in Petrograd when the October Revolution took place. On October 23, Lenin returned incognito from Finland, and with the assistance of Leon Trotsky, they staged the Bolsheviks' seizure of power:

The revolution succeeded with little opposition. On November 7– October 25, Old Style . . . Red troops occupied various strategic points in the capital. In the early night hours of November 8, the Bolshevik-led soldiers of the Petrograd garrison, sailors from Kronstadt, and the work- ers' Red Guards stormed the Winter Palace, weakly defended by young- sters from military schools and even by a women's battalion, and arrested members of the Provisional Government. Kerensky himself had managed to escape some hours earlier. Soviet government was established in Pe- trograd and in Russia.[10]

Akhmatova said she remembered the day the Winter Palace was taken. The bridge to the Vyborg district had been raised to disrupt traffic. It was a poignant moment later conveyed by Eisenstein in his film on the Revolution, *October.* Akhmatova says, "I stood on the Liteiny Bridge when it was suddenly raised in broad daylight in order to let the torpedo boats through to the Smolny to support the Bolsheviks. It was the first time I saw the bridge separated during the day. Trucks, trams, people—everything hanging over the suddenly gaping bridge. Under the bridge were torpedo boats."[11]

Boris Anrep described his last visit with Akhmatova in the midst of all the chaos in January 1918:

The streets of Petrograd were full of people. Shots were heard everywhere. I was not spending much time thinking about the revolution. I had only one thought, one desire: to see Akhmatova. At that time she was living in Professor Sreznevsky's apartment on the other side of the Neva. I crossed the ice of the Neva in order to avoid the barricades near the bridges. I reached the house and rang the bell. The door opened and Akhmatova said, "Oh, it's you? On a day like this? They're grabbing officers on the street." She was visibly touched. . . . For some time we spoke about the meaning of the revolution. She was excited and said we must expect more changes in our lives. "The same thing's going to happen that occurred in France during the Revolution, but maybe even worse." We became silent, and she dropped her head. "We won't see each other any more. You're leaving." "I'll come back. Look: your ring." I unfastened my jacket and showed her the black ring on the chain around my neck. She touched the ring. "That's good, it'll save you. It's a sacred object," she whispered. Something eternally feminine clouded her eyes as she held out her arms to me. I felt ecstatic, kissed her hands and got up. Akhmatova smiled tenderly. "It's better this way," she said. I left for England on the first train.[12]

Akhmatova's poem "Prayer" appeared in the newspaper *Pravo naroda* (*The Right of the People*) on November 26 (December 9, New Style), published by the cooperative unions. The poem had originally been written as a prayer in 1915 in the context of the war. The poet says she will take on all kinds of suffering from the Lord, "So that the stormcloud over darkened Russia/Might become a cloud of glorious rays." In this context the poem can be read as a denunciation of the Bolsheviks, whom no one thought would stay in power at the time, and the "glorious rays" of hope become interpreted as the Constituent Assembly, which was to be the first freely elected Russian parliament.[13] The poem was featured with articles clearly directed against the Bolsheviks: "The Bolsheviks have had their say, now it is the turn of the people; the whole nation must demand a Constituent Assembly." On November 28, a reading took place organized by the Union of Russian Writers, where Akhmatova read "Prayer." The Bolsheviks had arrested the Commissioner of Elections on November 23, and then on November 27 they arrested important political figures who were to participate in the elections. When the elections were held the next day, the Bolsheviks turned out to be in the minority. The Constituent Assembly met in January 1918 with the Socialist Revolutionaries—who hoped to turn over the country to the peasants—in the majority. Acting quickly, Lenin sent troops to disperse the Assembly, and he succeeded without any major opposition.[14]

Soon after the disbanding of the Constituent Assembly, on January 22, 1918, at a fundraiser for the Red Cross, Akhmatova read her poems, Arthur Lourie played the piano, and Sudeikina danced. The meeting, which was entitled "Oh,

Russia," became like a protest against the disbanding of the Constituent Assembly in the wake of the punishment of leading political figures. The Symbolists Dmitry Merezhkovsky and his wife Zinaida Gippius also participated in this event. Merezhkovsky said he saw hope for the homeland, whereas Gippius said she expected nothing good to come of the Revolution. The meeting ended with Akhmatova reading "Your spirit is clouded with arrogance" (dated January 1, 1917).

Your spirit is clouded by arrogance,
And that's why you can't see the light.
You say that our faith is—a dream,
And a mirage—this capital.

You say my country is sinful,
And I say your country is godless.
If the blame were ours—
everything could be redeemed and repaired.

All around—water and flowers.
Why bother with this poor sinner then?
I know why you are so terribly sick:
You are seeking death and you fear the end.

(I, p. 447)

The poem was originally meant for Anrep, when it became clear he was leaving Russia for England. However, as Dmitri Segal points out, it was one thing for Akhmatova to call her country sinful in the context of Rasputin and her own decadent generation, and another in that of early 1918, when sin and godlessness were connected with the Bolsheviks. Bolshevik ideology was against any manifestation of religion: in the eyes of the believers, the Bolsheviks were out to destroy the Orthodox soul. Akhmatova certainly must have understood the implications and the new interpretation given to her verses once they appeared in a consciously anti-Bolshevik context, and that she had begun to speak in the language of angry political denunciation. She now began taking on the role which Mandelstam predicted for her, that of Cassandra, whose tragic fate was that she could see the future, but no one would pay attention to her. Mandelstam's powerful poem, written in December 1917, specifically assigns this role to Akhmatova:

I did not see in the blossoming moments
Your lips, Cassandra, your eyes, Cassandra
But in December a solemn vigil—
Memory torments us!

And in December of the 17th year
We lost everything, loving:

One as plundered by the will of the people
Another plundered by himself. . . .[15]

Until the "Oh, Russia" fundraiser, Akhmatova and Gippius—two of the most important women poets in Russia during this period—had never met. Akhmatova said that Gippius appeared for the reading in a red wig, her face heavily powdered, and wearing a Parisian gown. Gippius invited her to visit, but Akhmatova refused, noting, "They [Gippius and Merezhkovsky] were evil—in the simplest, most elementary meaning of the word." Akhmatova said the problem was they never did anything simply. In 1917 Gippius suddenly began phoning Akhmatova and inviting her over, but she would not go. "For some reason she needed me."[16]

Akhmatova, like many of her generation, was anxious, wondering what role, if any, they and their art would play in the new world in which they suddenly found themselves—the new Soviet State, the "Great Experiment," the first country in the world to attempt to realize the ideas of Marx. The actress Lydia Ilyashenko-Pankratova recalled an evening spent with Akhmatova after the Revolution listening to a boy's choir perform Mozart's *Requiem*. Still under the powerful impression of the music, they went out and encountered a religious procession—led by an old priest, followed by people carrying icons and religious banners, and then finally a small, pitiful choir. Akhmatova said: "This is a continuation of *Requiem*." There was a feeling of overwhelming sadness. "Let's stop worrying about art," said Akhmatova. "No one needs art. Let's open a tobacco shop."[17]

Many of the intellectuals fled to Tbilisi, Georgia, right after the Revolution. For several years it remained independent of the Bolsheviks and refugees from the art world, including composers like Nicholay and his son Alexander Tcherepnin, were able to work there under the Mensheviks. Akhmatova and her poetry was frequently mentioned in these circles. The Futurist poet Alexander Kruchyonykh gave a talk in November 1917, citing lines by her, and saying he welcomed the appearance of a contemporary heroine in poetry who replaced the traditional notion of woman as a magic vision. His earlier lecture (June 1918) "On Women's Poetry" had analyzed Akhmatova's work. Sergey Rafalovich wrote in an article entitled "Young Poetry" (1919) that the poets in Tbilisi should follow the lines of Kuzmin and Akhmatova, and he devoted a special article to her in the journal *Ars*.[18]

However, immediately after the Revolution many members of artistic circles remained in Petrograd and Moscow, where some manifested radical changes in their political beliefs. One night Chulkov went to the Comedian's Halt and encountered Kuzmin, who had been transformed from an effete aesthetic into a supporter of the Bolshevik regime. Life in the cabaret was unlike everything else around—unlike the soviets, the unions, the chaos on the streets and at the Winter Palace. By this time Chulkov had become weary of the endless conversations about the collapse of the army and the fate of Kerensky, and he decided to escape to the cabaret and listen to some songs. He describes the shock at seeing what appeared to be a facsimile of Sudeikina, but as a ghost from the past: "There on the familiar little stage was a frail, immodest actress, intellectual and tender, dancing an immodest dance—But my God! How the face of this favorite of the Petersburg aesthetes had changed! She smiled, but what a horrible, gruesome smile!"

Soon everyone left but the regulars. Kuzmin came over. His songs, which had been sung on stages and in elegant salons, were now being drowned out by the sounds of revolutionary marches and shouts about the equality of everyone and everything. Chulkov was amazed, recalling Kuzmin's poems, in which he sang of the sword of the Archangel Michael, then of a marquis in the taste of Watteau, or about sweet little boys and Alexandrian courtesans. "Oh, how this poet loved the autocratic monarchy! He had a passion for the old order and squeamishly turned away from the revolution and hid in the cellar." Chulkov inquired which party Kuzmin belonged to, and smiling, Kuzmin replied, "I am, of course, a Bolshevik." He said there was no point in continuing to fight. "In the twentieth century it is repulsive to fight." And he looked at Chulkov with his large round eyes, his lips still curved in a smile: "I must admit, I like Lenin better than all these liberals of ours who keep shouting about the defense of the fatherland." Chulkov said ironically, "I did not think you had become a Tolstoyan," meaning Kuzmin had embraced the pacifist ideology of Tolstoy. "I'm not," Kuzmin corrected him. "It's just that I cannot endure the English. Understand? And now England is fighting with Germany. We must make peace with the Germans— that's all." Chulkov pointed out how much Kuzmin had professed to love Russia. "It's probably very painful for you that it has been humiliated, plundered and ruined . . ." "Ah, why is that a misfortune?" Kuzmin replied. "Let's give up Petersburg. We have so much land. . . ." And what was the aesthete's attitude toward socialism, Chulkov asked Kuzmin, looking into his empty, innocently depraved round eyes. "I have nothing against it. I really don't care," Kuzmin muttered.[19]

Arthur Lourie, who was also an aesthete rather than a politically engaged artist before the Revolution, became Commissar of Music. He explains his own transformation:

When I was young, my idol was Alexander Blok. I considered him one of the most perfect human beings in the history of the world of art. He had a great influence on me, and taught by him, I heard the music of the revolution. Like my friends, the avant-garde youth—artists and poets—I believed in the October Revolution and immediately joined it. Because the fanatics said we could now realize their dreams . . . we were given full freedom to pursue whatever we were interested in that was in our sphere. Nothing like this had ever happened before . . . during the revolution all fences, walls of buildings were decorated with unbelievable images. It was a fantastic and improbable time.[20]

Lourie is referring here to events like the first anniversary of the October Revolution, for which artists all over the country volunteered to contribute their talents. Nathan Altman, who painted Akhmatova's most famous portrait, planned the Petrograd festival in front of the Winter Palace, putting up Cubist and Futurist designs all around the square. Two years later, on November 7, 1920, in the courtyard of the Winter Palace in Petrograd, he worked with the famous director Nikolay Yevreinov to stage a reenactment of the storming of the Winter Palace, using thousands of Petrograd citizens. Giant arc lights projected against the sky illuminated Altman's abstract designs. There were two platforms, one for the Reds and one for the Whites, and sectors were roped off on either side of the Alexander Column in the courtyard of the palace for the spectators. Twenty-five identical "Kerensky" puppetlike dancers were placed on a rostrum, performing identical gestures, as the Red Army on the right gradually drove the White Army away. The capitalists were portrayed in tall hats, with enormous money bags, while workers were represented as blacksmiths, with hammers in hand. The overthrow of the White Army was followed by the triumphant surge of two thousand spectators noisily proclaiming the triumph of the Revolution.

This performance was only one of many reflecting the enthusiasm of the artists for the Revolution. As Camilla Gray, an authority on Russian avant-garde art, points out, "heroic revolutionary" plays were organized all over the country: Tatlin, Annenkov and Meyerhold designed sets while factory siren symphonies took place under Mayakovsky's supervision in his drive towards "making the streets his brushes and the squares his palette." Trains decorated with Revolutionary themes were sent to the front carrying news of the Revolution—both political and artistic—to every corner of the country. There seemed to be no limit to the ingenuity with which these artists made propaganda for the Revolution.[21]

Mandelstam often came to visit Akhmatova in the early days after the Revolution. She says, "We drove in horse-drawn cabs over the incredible ruts in the roads that winter of the revolution, between the famous bonfires that burnt almost until May, to the rumble of guns carried from somewhere unknown. We drove like this to poetry recitals at the Academy of Arts, where there were evenings in aid of the wounded and where we both recited several times." But Mandelstam's attention became too much for her and went way beyond her sense of decorum. "I had to explain to Osip that we should not meet so frequently, that it would provide material for a negative interpretation of the nature of our relationship. After this, around March, Mandelstam disappeared." Akhmatova writes in her memoir of Mandelstam that he was totally absorbed by the events taking place: "Mandelstam was one of the first to write poems on civic themes. The Revolution was a tremendous event for him, and it is clear why the phrase 'the people' appears in his poetry."[22]

In spite of his enthusiasm, however, he found the vast changes occurring so quickly somewhat unsettling. Lourie says that Mandelstam was afraid of any manifestation of disorder or chaos. "He had a genuine prophetic feeling for the old world as doomed and a new one hoped for but still unrealized." Somehow he had received a room in the Hotel Astoria and took baths several times a day, drank the milk which they brought him by mistake, and went to the famous restaurant Donon's, where the owner, who had lost his head in these dizzy times, gave everyone credit.[23]

Mandelstam's apocalyptic view of history was expressed in a 1918 poem to the city Petrograd, which he continued to call Petropolis. Petropolis, his beloved city, is dying, and there is no indication of what might take its place:

On a terrible height a wandering fire,
But is that really how a star glimmers?
Transparent star, wandering fire,
Your brother, Petropolis, is dying.

On a terrible height earthly dreams burn,
The green star glimmers,
O, if you are a star—brother of water and sky,
Your brother, Petropolis, is dying.

A monstrous ship on a terrible height
Sails along, straightening its wings—
Green star, in magnificent poverty
Your brother, Petropolis, is dying.

Transparent spring above the black Neva
Has shattered, the wax of immortality is melting.
O, if you are a star—Petropolis your city,
Your brother, Petropolis, is dying.[24]

In another poem, written in 1920, Mandelstam summons his friends to leave, friends like Akhmatova and Gumilyov; but it is a city that has buried its past:

We shall gather again in Petersburg
As if we had buried the sun there. . . .[25]

G. P. Makogonenko, a friend of Akhmatova's, a literary scholar and husband of Olga Berggolts, describes the transformation of Petersburg:

It is thanks to Pushkin that Petersburg appeared in literature as the image of the Petrine period of Russian history. Then another Petersburg replaced that of Pushkin in literature, whose sovereign beauty and human individuality were smothered—the city of Gogol, Nekrasov, Dostoyevsky, Blok and Mayakovsky. And the revolution began here, in Petrograd, in the city which after Peter, history again chose as the site of its culmination and crisis. The poets of the first years of the revolution had the honor of publishing a new image of the city and relating the great heights of its conquest by man. . . . After the revolution, the conception of Petersburg changes in poetry.[26]

After having failed his exam in fortifications in October 1916, Gumilyov returned to his squadron at the front until the end of January 1917. He was not in Petrograd during the February Revolution, but was stationed in Okulovka nearby until the middle of March. The February Revolution essentially passed him by—in Akhmatova's words, he "did not notice." He was not interested in politics, but came to Petrograd whenever he was free. In the spring he went to a clinic there because he was having trouble with his lungs, then moved in with Mikhail Lozinsky, and finally into some furnished rooms. It was quite clear he and Akhmatova preferred to live apart. He decided to join the Southern front in Salonika, believing he would not find there the lack of discipline and disorder of the Russian Army which disturbed him so much. Meanwhile, he set off for Paris, hoping to become a foreign correspondent on the *Russkaya volya* through his contacts with his friend Mikhail Struve.[27] His last meeting with Larisa Reisner took place in April 1917. In her final letter to him, Reisner credited him with deepening her feelings about poetry: "I often think we will meet somewhere once again, and once again you will take everything and leave it behind. This cannot be and could not be. Bless you, your poems and your deeds. May you encounter miracles, create them yourself. My darling, my beloved . . . and be purer and better than before. Because there really is a God. Yours, Leri."[28]

Gumilyov never wrote her any more letters, but he sent two postcards. The last one was from Sweden, on his way to London and Paris. "Have a good time. Don't get involved in politics," which was an interesting piece of advice to a future Bolshevik commissar. When he arrived in London, he looked up Anrep, who helped him find a place to stay and introduced him to members of the Bloomsbury Group, including G. K. Chesterton and Roger Fry, whose articles had been published in *Apollon*.

While Gumilyov was in London, an interview with him appeared in print on June 28, 1917. In it Gumilyov condemned the Futurists, especially their contempt for the past, and suddenly expressed a new interest in the spiritual and mysticism. Looking to Paul Claudel in France, Gumilyov said he was awaiting a resurgence of mystical poetry in Russia. He distinguished between drama, which he said reflected man's responsibility to the world, and prayer: "But when he thinks of the final fate of mankind and of life beyond the grave, then he will turn at last to mystic prayer," which, as Rusinko points out, are strange words from the poet who, in 1913, so ardently distinguished between poetic themes that treated what man could know and those he could only intuit as mystery. This change was soon reflected in Gumilyov's own works.[29]

Aldous Huxley mentions meeting Gumilyov in London in a letter (June 1917): "I have been meeting a distinguished Russian poet, Goumilov [sic]. . . . We talked to each other with great difficulty in French, which he speaks rather haltingly and which I always stumble and trip in most fearfully. But he seemed quite interesting and pleasant." He probably visited Lady Ottoline Morrell on June 17, when Katherine Mansfield and Virginia Woolf were attending her salon. Gumilyov met many of the writers connected with *The New Age,* which supported progressive movements in art and politics, and became associated with the poetry movement of which Ezra Pound was a member, Imagism. Russia was generally popular in London during the war, and translations of Russian literature and articles appeared.

When Gumilyov arrived in Paris, the job on the newspaper fell through, but he stayed, working on military missions for the Russian Provisional Government. He frequently visited the avant-garde artists Mikhail Larionov and Natalya Goncharova, who had designed sets for Diaghilev's Ballets Russes.[30]

In Paris, Gumilyov fell in love with Yelena Dubouchet, half Russian and half French, whose father was a famous surgeon. He had met her in 1916 in Petrograd. Larionov did not think Gumilyov was very deeply involved with her and suggested that in general Gumilyov needed to be in love—it inspired him. Because Dubouchet was engaged to somebody else at the time, it provided him with new experience for his creative work. He stayed in Paris from June 1917 to January 1918. After the October Revolution, the new government refused to attack in the Aegean and the Salonika front was liquidated. The Russian Military Committee in Paris was restructured, and Gumilyov asked for a commission in England. He was transferred to London in January 1918, but was given a commission only until April.

In London, he met some of the leading literary and artistic figures of the time.[31] Before he returned to Russia, he went one more time to Paris, taking a stroll every evening with Larionov in the Jardin des Tuileries. On a little path stood a statue with her arms raised over her head, forming an oval. From one angle a star could be seen in the center of the oval. Gumilyov said this was the inspiration for the title of the collection of poems he was writing—*Blue Star,* his name for Yelena Dubouchet. He left for Russia in April 1918. Boris Anrep remembered the day of Gumilyov's departure well. Anrep wanted to send a small gift with him for Akhmatova; presumably Gumilyov knew about their relationship. In his memoirs, Anrep recalls his conversation with Gumilyov:

When he had already packed his trunk, I gave him a rare silver coin with the head of Alexander the Great and some yards of silk for Akhmatova. He stepped back with a theatrical gesture and said, "Boris Vasilyevich, how can you ask this, she is, after all, my wife!" I laughed. "Don't take my request in the wrong way. It's simply a friendly gesture." I don't know if he ever gave it to her, since I never heard anything about it. However, we talked a lot about her poetry. He said he respected her poetry very much, but only someone who understood the "depths of her beautiful soul" could appreciate the real beauty of it. Whether he understood all the "beauty of her soul" or not remained a question for me.[32]

In a perceptive article about Gumilyov, the Russian scholar Vyacheslav Ivanov attempted to explain why Gumilyov, who seemed to represent in all his beliefs and actions the former aristocratic regime, returned to live in the new Soviet State. "A great poet always shares the fate of his nation, regardless of what political program he supports. André Chenier [the French poet guillotined during the French Revolution] published during the revolution. . . . The soaring of his [Gumilyov's] poetry during the last three years of his life is not accidental. . . . Arguing with his time and opposing himself to it, he remained its son, as any great artist does. He was a component part of the elevating spiritual ascent which began in 1910, continued to the beginning of the 1920s, and encompassed the most varied aspects of culture."[33]

When Gumilyov returned to Petrograd in 1918, Akhmatova asked him for a divorce. Upon his arrival, he phoned the Sreznevskys, and they told him she was visiting Viktor Shileiko, the brilliant and eccentric Babylonian scholar who was a member of the Stray Dog crowd and had adored Akhmatova for many years, but who was also a friend of Gumilyov's. Not suspecting anything, Gumilyov went there, and they all sat together, drinking tea and chatting. Then Akhmatova came alone to see him in the furnished room where he was staying. She remained there until morning, then left for the Sreznevskys'. When Gumilyov came to see her, she called him into a separate room and said, "Give me a divorce." He turned pale and left, without asking anything, except if she was getting married, if she was in love with someone else. When she said yes, he asked who it was. "Shileiko," she replied. Gumilyov could not believe it. "That's absolutely impossible," he said. "You're hiding something." Soon after this, Akhmatova accompanied him to Slepnyovo. The whole time Gumilyov was characteristically restrained, sometimes getting angry, but never losing his control. Only once when they were sitting in a room with Lev playing did he suddenly kiss Akhmatova's hand and entreat her, "Why have you made this up? There is no need for a divorce."

The divorce itself was very peaceful. Akhmatova thought he would be glad about it, especially considering his history of affairs, most recently with the "Blue Star" in Paris. But Gumilyov took it hard. Akhmatova wrote that "I lived with Nikolay seven years. We were friendly and inwardly beholden to each other. But I told him we must divorce. He didn't object but I saw he was insulted. . . . He had just returned from Paris after his unsuccessful love affair with Yelena, the Blue Star. He was full of her, but still my desire to leave him insulted him. . . . We went together to Bezhetsk to see Lev. We sat on the couch, and Levushka played between us. Kolya said, 'And why are you doing this?' And that was all."[34]

Akhmatova said Gumilyov's reaction was probably caused by the insult to his pride, and she felt guilty that all his subsequent failures, including his unsuccessful marriage to Anna Engelhardt, could be ascribed to this event. Akhmatova told Luknitsky, "Divorce in general is a very difficult thing." She even felt guilty about Gumilyov's death, as if somehow the divorce were responsible for it, although clearly it had nothing to do with it. After his death, she grieved over him and often felt like punishing herself. A scholar who has written much on Akhmatova, and was a good friend of hers, Lev Ozerov, believed Akhmatova never really understood how much Gumilyov meant to her until after he died.[35] This is corroborated by the poignant poems she wrote right after his death. Other friends have commented that while Gumilyov had his affairs, no one would ever play the same role in his life as Akhmatova. She had a special place that no one could take, and when she left him, it was devastating for him.

Gumilyov did not reveal to others how upset he was by the divorce, and continued to work as well as to play an important role in the new cultural life of the Soviet Union. He moved to Ivanovsky Street, to the apartment of Makovsky, the editor of *Apollon,* who at that time was living in the Crimea.

Akhmatova's relationship with Shileiko was not easy, but it was certainly interesting. He was witty, ironic, and spent most of his waking hours working with his Babylonian clay tablets and cuneiform, the yellowing pages of ancient epics. Someone once described him as "somehow not of this world."[36] Akhmatova said he was incredibly handsome and a genius.[37] It was her idea to go to Shileiko, and she explained why: "I felt so filthy, I thought it would be like a cleansing, like going to a convent, knowing you are going to lose your freedom."[38]

Sreznevskaya describes Akhmatova just before she married Shileiko, when he was ill and she was caring for him at the Sheremetev Palace, where he was living.

The labyrinth of the Sheremetev Palace—the inner courtyard, passageways, staircases leading through corridors—cold, dark, hunting trophies on the walls, finally a door. I entered. An oblong room, bed, couch, a large round table, everything strange and gloomy. A lamp on the table burning oil, leaving the corners of the large room in shadow. By the table sat a man in a soldier's coat, his face very thin, an unwholesome look on his face, a wry grin, caustic conversation, erudite, interesting. He spoke quietly, with his head bent slightly to one side. He talked about Egypt, Babylonia, Assyria, he read tablets from Assyrian by heart. I listened, excited, but noticed his great egotism. I went home with Anya. I saw she was tired, pale. "You know, he didn't sleep all night. He was analyzing his tablets and drinking tea." "And you got up and warmed it and poured it for him." "Well, of course, he is very nervous, very suspicious, and demands undivided attention. All my other relationships and feelings must be excluded." We parted. How long will this be enough for the freedom-loving, independent Anya? When will she have enough of this sacrifice?[39]

Shileiko was born in Peterhof, one of the summer residences of the tsar, and attended Petersburg University. While he was still a student of ancient Middle Eastern archeology, he received a postcard from a French scholar: "We must soon study Russian so we can read your work." In 1913 Shileiko began working in the research section of the Hermitage; he was drafted into the army in January 1917, where he remained until August. But he kept his military overcoat, which he wore all the time after the Revolution and also used as a blanket for the next several years. In 1918 he was on the boards of several important committees for the preservation of great works of art and architecture that were part of the national heritage, and in 1919 he headed the Department of Archeology and Ancient Eastern Art in the Russian Academy. He had worked as a tutor of the Sheremetev family before the Revolution, and because of his position at the Russian Academy he was able to obtain a room in the palace. He was also a professor at the Petrograd Archeological Institute. Shileiko worked for Gorky's World Literature publishing project as one of the directors of the translating section, and prepared translations of Babylonian literature.[40]

Akhmatova's divorce came through in August 1918. She married Shileiko that December. They formalized their marriage at a notary's office, which was the procedure at the time.[41] Shileiko had to work in Moscow, so they moved there, to a street called Third Zachatyevsky. Akhmatova said it was horribly cold, and like most people at this time, they had little to eat. There was a church nearby with bells ringing all the time.[42] Then they moved back to Petrograd, to the Sheremetev Palace. Akhmatova called the palace the "House on the Fontanka" (it was located on the Fontanka Canal). It is a superb eighteenth-century palace, bearing the motto of the family's coat of arms, *"Deus conservat omnia"* (God conserves everything). Mentioned in one of the versions of *Poem Without a Hero* is the beautiful singer, Parasha Zhemchugova, a serf actress who married one of the Sheremetevs and died in childbirth. The poem begins with a vision in the White Hall of the palace where the tsar, Paul I, used to hide and eavesdrop on what guests at the balls were saying about him.

There was never enough wood, and Shileiko was just as incapable as Akhmatova of dealing with the ordinary problems of everyday life. However, Akhmatova did learn to heat the oven, and she stood in line for rations which they gave out at the House of Scholars (which helped scholars and academicians) on Millionnaya Street. Akhmatova says she wrote only about two poems during this period, "Petrograd 1919" and "Apparition," the latter a moving piece about the late tsar.

The round, hanging lanterns,
Lit early, are squeaking,
Ever more festively, ever brighter,
The flying snowflakes glitter.

And, quickening their steady gait,
As if sensing some pursuit,
Through the softly falling snow
Under a dark blue net, the horses race.

And the gilded footman
Stands motionless behind the sleigh,
And the tsar looks around strangely
With light, empty eyes.

(II, 609)

Eventually Akhmatova and Shileiko moved into a different palace, the Marble Palace, where he had received two rooms, which were spacious but cold. The living quarters looked out onto the Field of Mars, which had been used as a parade ground, and the statue of General Suvorov, the brilliant general under Catherine the Great. The beautiful neoclassical palace, faced entirely with marble and granite, had been built by Catherine the Great for her lover Grigory Orlov. The couple's room was divided by a plywood screen into a bedroom and a dining room that contained a table with an electric light bulb hanging over it. There was also a tiny kitchen. In the dining room was an old couch with springs sticking out of it, a bookcase, and a china cabinet. Rare books and valuable manuscripts were lying everywhere.[43]

Many years later, the literary scholar Isaak Yeventov went to see the Marble Palace. The former gardener, who had been at the palace before the Revolution when Prince Konstantin Romanov lived there (he died in 1915), was now supervisor. He showed Yeventov a beautiful formal staircase and marble hall built by the Italian architect Rinaldi and rebuilt by Karl Bryullov in a pseudo-Gothic style. The room was filled with the aroma of rare foreign tobacco used by the prince. They then arrived at the servants' wing, where scholars had been housed, including Shileiko and Akhmatova. According to Akhmatova, they avoided this room because they did not want to be tempted by the fragrance of Turkish and other tobaccos, which they craved but could not afford.[44] "Three years of hunger," she said. "I left the Gumilyovs without taking anything with me. Vladimir was ill. He could do without everything except tea and cigarettes. We had to borrow pans from our neighbors. I had neither forks, spoons, nor pans."[45] She was only able to get a reprieve from the deprivation and cold of the Marble Palace during the summer months, when she went to visit friends at Tsarskoye Selo, where she wrote most of her new poems. Akhmatova maintained that many of the works written during those years were thrown away, which makes it difficult to judge whether she was writing little poetry while she was with Shileiko or whether for one reason or another she destroyed what she had written.[46]

It was a very trying time for both of them. The difficulties of the post-Revolutionary years only exacerbated the problems of two creative and sensitive people. Akhmatova told one friend that Shileiko tormented her, he kept her prisoner, and would not let her out. She also said he forced her to burn all her letters.[47] Amanda Haight relies on evidence from poems written by Akhmatova alluding to Shileiko and interprets the relationship as hostile.[48] However, Tamara Shileiko, who is married to Shileiko's son Alexey, argues otherwise, based on an impressive personal family archive. In a long article depicting Shileiko as both an internationally known scholar and a deeply caring individual, she notes how much affection he felt for Akhmatova, which is shown through the correspondence between them even after they separated. Nayman says that Akhmatova spoke about her marriage as a sad misunderstanding, but without any shade of the resentment or anger reflected in the poems addressed to Shileiko. While some reproached Shileiko for making Akhmatova stand in long lines to get rations and food, as both Tamara and her husband have pointed out, Shileiko had to work hard for those rations, and at least they were both able to survive. In 1925, when her friend Luknitsky said Sreznevskaya had a rather negative opinion of Shileiko, Akhmatova replied that he was often difficult with other people, had the temperament of a scholar, but that he was witty and cheerful, a good person.[49]

Although Akhmatova's poems about the relationship speak of the pain inflicted on her by Shileiko, in general they seemed to have had a great affection for one another and genuinely respected each other's poetry. Certainly Shileiko admired Akhmatova as a poet for many years, when they were together at the Stray Dog and read each other's work. In 1919, he published the following poem in *The Siren,* a Voronezh publication:

In those embittered hardened times
You were the last exalted wound,
You were the swan's short farewell song,
You were the one remaining star.

You were above the poisoned cup,
In harmony with bitter fate,
All that was left: my little dove—
And he, still yearning after you.[50]

Akhmatova showed her devotion to Shileiko by transcribing his dictated translations. They would take a walk for an hour, then return and work until four in the morning, just so they could buy some bread and potatoes the next day.[51] Akhmatova was fascinated by Shileiko's stories about the Near East and loved to listen to him recite Egyptian and Babylonian texts, appreciating the music of ancient speech. He told her about gods and kings, and read her fables in the original languages, then translated them for her into Russian.[52]

One of their constant companions was a St. Bernard, Tapa. At that time in Petrograd there were many stray dogs. Their masters went abroad, leaving them in the care of servants who, in those hungry years, chased the dogs out onto the street. Shileiko found the St. Bernard, hungry and sick, and brought it home. The dog worshipped its new master, and later, when Shileiko moved to Moscow, Akhmatova continued to take care of it.[53]

In 1919 a young poet, N. P. Kolpakova, visited Akhmatova and Shileiko at the Sheremetev Palace and observed the affection that was clear between the two. Akhmatova was alone when Kolpakova arrived. Rather than speaking about her own work, she asked Kolpakova to talk of her poems and her translations of Heine. They discussed the new literary studios that had just sprung up; although Akhmatova thought they were useful, she was skeptical about their ability to produce a great poet, which demanded talent, not just rules. Shileiko then arrived, his head characteristically tilted slightly to the left. He came up to Akhmatova, bent over her, and kissed each hand. He did not take off his coat, probably because it was so cold. When she asked if he had given a lecture that day, he said he had not, because only a few odd couples had shown up, but he was happy because he had managed to buy some apples and matches on the street for her.[54]

The conditions under which Akhmatova and Shileiko were living reflected not only the difficulties the country was having but also the transition Petrograd was undergoing from the brilliant capital of the imperial empire to the status of a provincial city. The capital was moved to Moscow in March 1918, so Petrograd was no longer the administrative and commercial center. Georgy Fedotov describes this gradual but very evident change. He also captures the centuries-old dichotomy between the rational Petersburg [now Petrograd], looking to the West, and the more mystical Moscow, looking to the East. It is essential to understand this dichotomy if one is to comprehend Russian culture, and the crucial distinction between Akhmatova, poet of Petersburg, and her counterpart Tsvetayeva, poet of Moscow.

Whoever visited in these horrible, fatal years of 1918–20 saw how eternity stepped across the rot. All at once the "womb" of the capital crumbled. . . . Only palaces and specters remained. Venice rotting with gold, and even eternal Rome paled before the grandness of dying Petersburg. . . . Petersburg embodied the dreams of Palladio near the Arctic Circle, paved swamps with granite. . . . But Petersburg died and will not be resurrected. Something mad predetermined its doom in its very conception. Here a miraculous feat was accomplished over nature. A titan rose up against the earth and hung a granite rock in space. But what is the rock resting on? On a dream? Here a monstrous force overcame nature and the spirit. Petersburg assimilated everything masculine, everything rational and conscious, everything proud and violent in the soul of Russia, but outside there remained Rus—Moscow, wooden, the suffering land, the wife and mother giving birth, bent over in labor, inexhaustible in her tears, not able to lament for her children devoured by the titan. And when the tears had all poured down, she sent out a curse against it. God heard the mother's curse: "May the horse and rider plunge into the sea." . . . The Empire died, the revolution was drowned in blood and filth.

Fedotov asks: "What will Petersburg be now for Russia. Not all its palaces are empty. Life will not be extinguished everywhere. . . . For a long time Petersburg will remain the domain of Russian thought."[55] He was correct, for the theatrical and artistic life of the city continued to flourish. One of the centers was the House of Arts, or DISK (*Dom iskusstv*), which opened in autumn 1918 in an apartment formerly owned by the prominent Moscow businessman Yeliseyev. The apartment took up three floors in a building overlooking the Moika River.[56] Akhmatova served on the board, along with Gumilyov, Chukovsky, the critic Boris Eikhenbaum, author of one of the most important books on Akhmatova's poetry, Kuzma Petrov-Vodkin, an artist who made some sensitive portraits of her, and the satirical writer Mikhail Zoshchenko, who later would be paired with Akhmatova as victims of Stalin's persecution of artists.

The House of Arts, though mainly a center for literary figures, also included many musicians and artists. Membership was carefully controlled, and new candidates had to be nominated and approved. Leading poets, writers, and scholars taught poetry, prose, and translation. DISK also sponsored lectures and concerts, and provided rooms to live in. Many of these were quite lovely, as the poet Vladislav Khodasevich described them. There was a mirrored hall where lectures took place, a light blue parlor with Rodin statues where Chukovsky and Gumilyov had their studios, and an oak-lined dining room with stained-glass windows and a fireplace.[57] Often on Fridays Albert Benois, the artist and brother of the stage designer Alexander Benois, gave in to the requests of the young people present and played Strauss waltzes on the piano, to which they twirled, intoxicated by the music, unashamed of the boots they wore to keep warm.

Another center, the House of Scholars, which was the creation of the Commission for the Improvement of Scholars' Lives, opened in December 1919. Academicians and professors, housed in the former palace of the Grand Duke Vladimir, received rations, clothing, firewood, and medical aid. Here too the public could hear lectures and talks on a number of topics.

While the House of Arts was under Gorky's protection, the House of Writers was not, and he viewed it mainly as a refuge for writers of the previous generation. Poetry recitals and concerts were held there, and five hundred people a day were given meals at reduced rates. For the younger writers, Akhmatova had already become something of a legend. In the evening there would be thin soup in white bowls, crumbs of claylike bread, and endless quarrels around the table. Everyone dressed in whatever they had—a frock coat taken out of mothballs, a military soldier's shirt, or a romantic black cape.

Georgy Adamovich describes one evening when he met Akhmatova at the House of Arts just before he left Russia. Vodka, hors d'oeuvres, and meat-filled tarts were served—a feast for those years. Akhmatova had the same shawl on her shoulders, the same sad, calm glance, the same singular figure. "I went up to her and told her how beautiful she looked. She smiled, and bending over, whispered, 'The dog has become old' [she was about thirty at the time]. Those were the last words I heard from Akhmatova before I left Russia."[58]

Members of a new group, the Serapian Brothers—named after a group in the tales of E. T. A. Hoffmann—wrote experimental novels and short stories. Zoshchenko said that when the meetings went on too late, he would sometimes put three chairs together and use them as a bed.[59]

Although he plunged into the new life after the Revolution upon his return, Gumilyov still retained his aristocratic ways. Vladislav Khodasevich came from Moscow to Petersburg in 1918. Gumilyov "greeted me," says Khodasevich,

> as if it were the meeting of two monarchs. . . . In his solemn politeness there was something so unnatural that at first I thought he was joking. . . . In deserted, famished Petersburg, cultivated by roaches, both starving, thin, in threadbare coats, surrounded by torn books in the middle of an unheated room, we sat and talked with great importance, in Makovsky's apartment. When I was leaving, in came a slender, pale boy with the same long face as Gumilyov's, in a dirty Russian peasant shirt and felt boots. He had an Uhlan helmet in his hand and brandished a toy saber and was screaming something. Gumilyov immediately sent him away in the tone of a king sending his heir to the governess.[60]

Akhmatova said that just as in the days of the Revolution, Gumilyov ignored the impact of politics on his present situation, because he could work as he wished. In the summer of 1918, Gumilyov became a member of the new publishing house under Maxim Gorky, World Literature. Its aim was to make world classics available to the masses in Russian, as well as to provide a means of sustenance for Russia's great writers and scholars. It was housed in the splendid apartments of the Duchess of Leuchtenberg on Mokhovaya Street. (By the time Gorky left the Soviet Union, World Literature had put out forty-nine volumes. It finally closed in 1924, but by then it had saved the lives of many literary figures by providing them with much-needed work.)

In June, three new sections of World Literature opened offices on 24, Liteiny Avenue, in the Muruzi House: poetry under Gumilyov and Lozinsky; prose under Shklovsky and Zamyatin; and critical theory under Chukovsky and Eikhenbaum. Gumilyov also continued to lead workshops sponsored by the House of Arts.

Gumilyov's marriage to Anna Engelhardt turned out to be another "sad misunderstanding," the phrase Akhmatova would use to describe her own marriage to Shileiko. He seemed to find it easier to relate to very young women—his relationship with Akhmatova was happiest when she was young—and problems occurred as the women matured. And like Akhmatova, he does not seem to have found it easy to be married. Akhmatova's sarcastic sense of humor, which so many of her friends loved and which never appeared in her poetry, shows through in her analysis of Gumilyov's relationship with his new wife. Akhmatova told her friend Luknitsky: "His second marriage was also a failure. He imagined Anna Engelhardt was wax and she turned out to be—a tank. Have you seen her?" Luknitsky replied that he thought she was very nice, with her meek, gentle face and the pink ribbon in her hair. "Yes, that's true—a tender little face, a pink ribbon, but still, a tank. Gumilyov lived with her for three months and then sent her off to his relatives. She didn't like it and demanded he bring her back. He brought her back—and he went off to the Crimea. She is a mean, nasty woman, and he was counting on finally finding someone meek and submissive."[61]

Akhmatova told another friend that when she was young she was difficult to live with, being very independent and spoiled, but even her mother-in-law held her up as an example to Anna Engelhardt. Akhmatova believed the reason Gumilyov married Engelhardt was that he was so upset that Akhmatova had left him, he rushed off to marry a very simple girl out of spite. He thought he could mold her character, "but it was impossible to make a scratch, even a little incision." She believed that in his last years he really did not love anyone, although he had a whole harem among his students, and only very young girls—always his weakness. Moreover, he did not attempt to hide his affairs from his wife.[62]

Akhmatova said she tried to make it as easy as possible for Gumilyov after their divorce, keeping away from literary gatherings and avoiding the homes of mutual acquaintances where she might meet him. She thought he would appreciate her discretion; instead, he reproached her for being so self-absorbed. One of the last times they met he told her, "Your tuberculosis is the result of doing absolutely nothing." She sometimes went to see him on Ivanovskaya Street, where he was living with his mother, his new wife, Lev, and his brother and sister-in-law. Sometimes his stepsister even came to visit from Bezhetsk. In the spring of 1919 Gumilyov moved with his family to a new apartment on Preobrazhenskaya Street, and soon his wife gave birth to a daughter, Yelena.[63]

Gumilyov appeared wherever he was invited—the Baltic Fleet, the Proletcult (a proletarian cultural organization to create art for the masses), clubs, studios. His contemporary Andrey Levinson says, "This 'iron man,' which was what we called him as a joke, brought his poetic teaching unchanged even to these wild auditoriums; he expressed his condemnation of pseudo-proletarian culture openly and did not try to hide his Orthodox faith."[64] No doubt having disciples made Gumilyov feel important and soothed his ego. But he truly enjoyed conveying his enthusiasm for poetry to others and arousing in them a feeling for good literature.

He himself said his workshops were very important because in this "most cruel of historical moments, poetry and art help keep people from becoming callous, from losing their dignity, from falling into despair." He never spared himself or tried to conserve his energy for his own work, which was probably why he attracted so many students. In his teaching, Gumilyov recognized the ultimate importance of talent, but also stressed the necessity for learning the rules of poetry. He never promised his students that they could actually become poets, but what he could do was train sensitive readers.

One of the most loving testimonials to Gumilyov has been left by one of his students, Ida Nappelbaum, daughter of the famous photographer Moisei Nappelbaum, whose elegant portraits of famous figures of his time, including Akhmatova, were an artistic record of the period. She said, "Gumilyov dreamt of making poetry into an exact science, a type of mathematics . . . no mysticism or Futurist transrational language. There is the material—the words. Find the best form for them, put them into this form like molten steel. These lessons would be followed by games, charades, singing. These were difficult years, chaotic years, years of semi-starvation—but for us they were unique."[65]

Nikolay Otsup, another student of Gumilyov's and a great admirer, says no Petersburg citizen at the time could ever forget the impression Gumilyov made walking the streets in his strange Laplander fur coat and hat with ear flaps and large boots from the Commission for the Improvement of Scholars' Lives. He looked friendly but very important, usually surrounded by students. Like everyone else, he would lecture without taking off his coat, steam pouring out of his mouth, his hands turning blue. He would read something about modern poetry—the French Symbolists—then teach on the art of translation or how to write poetry. "He was not doing this only to feed himself and his family but because he loved poetry with all his heart and soul and believed one must use poetry to help people make it easier when they could not answer the question, 'Why am I alive?' He taught people with little talent not because he wanted to make poets of them, which obviously was out of the question, because poets are born, but because he wanted to make them better human beings."[66]

Akhmatova and Gumilyov were now taking on a new role as part of the "older generation," as the next generation of young, admiring students looked up to them as famous poets, surrounded by a romantic aura. Otsup recalls how much he enjoyed the privilege as a young student of being invited to Gumilyov's apartment in 1918, looking at the wall hung with Persian miniatures, a panther skin, and an Arab rifle. And Otsup loved to hear Gumilyov reciting his poetry, drinking in the atmosphere.[67]

However, fate was catching up with Gumilyov, and with all of the prerevolutionary intelligentsia. Although the regime still exhibited a certain tolerance toward experimentation in the arts, this was not true in the political sphere, and the attacks against intellectuals and those younger members of the art world who did not adhere to the Party line became more strident each year. On September 5,

1918, the Soviet of the People's Commissars made a resolution to shoot "all persons connected with White Army organizations, plots, and uprisings." One Party hack, in an article entitled "Attempts at Restoration" in *Iskusstvo kommuny (Art of the Commune)*, no. 1, declared, "With what great effort, and thanks only to the powerful Communist movement, have we been able this last year finally to escape from the years of oppression of bourgeois aesthetics. I must admit I personally feel very good, partly because certain critics have stopped writing or, at least, are no longer being printed, and several poets are no longer read (Gumilyov, for example). They have not changed, not a single iota. The same mincing mannerisms, stylized flourishes, etc. They have only become more colorless and timid."[68] This was the first intimation of the Red Terror.

On a more immediate level, 1919 meant one more cold, hungry year, and one question tormented everybody: how to survive.[69] Otsup says, "We will never forget Petersburg in the period of desolation and defeat, when it was impossible to go out after 9:00 P.M., when the sound of a motor outside your window at night made you terrified: who were they coming for? When it was no longer necessary to remove carrion from the streets—dogs grew thin tearing it apart, and people growing thinner would pull it apart. For us, the dying Petersburg was sad and beautiful, like someone we loved on his deathbed."[70]

Akhmatova describes these years vividly in her memoirs:

The old Petersburg signboards were still in place, but behind them there was nothing but dust, darkness, and yawning emptiness. Typhus, hunger, execution by firing squad, dark apartments, damp wood, and people swollen beyond recognition. You could pick a large bouquet of wildflowers in Gostinny Dvor [the large department store]. The famous Petersburg wooden pavement was rotting. The smell of chocolate still wafted from the basement windows of Kraft. All the cemeteries had been pillaged. The city had not just changed, it had turned into its exact opposite. But people still loved poetry.[71]

Nedobrovo died in 1919. That was the year he began to say with despair that Russia had lost its spirit, and he lost his will to live. He had once thought that since the West had lost its spiritual values, Russia would be the new center of spiritual illumination; but the Bolshevik regime turned his dream into a nightmare. Boris Anrep noted: "Just before he [Nedobrovo] died I wrote him a wild letter from which I remember one stupid but sincere line: 'Dear Nikolay, Please don't die. You and Anna Akhmatova are the only thing left of Russia that I have.'"[72]

It was Mandelstam who told Akhmatova about Nedobrovo's death when he returned in 1920 from the Crimea. He had left Petrograd in 1919 for Kiev, had been arrested by the Whites in the Crimea but managed to avoid execution, went to visit Voloshin, who was hunting eagles on mountain peaks in order to feed his old mother, then carried concealed papers for the Bolsheviks to the north, traveling through Menshevik Georgia to Moscow.[73]

In the spring of 1919, Akhmatova saw Gumilyov frequently. He would visit her with Lev, and when his family left the city, he came alone and ate with her and Shileiko, whom Gumilyov had urged to come to work at World Literature, where he did translations of ancient texts in 1919–20. Shileiko told Pavel Luknitsky that Gumilyov had dragged him there and was like his patron: "For about a year I was his man."[74] Thus, although Gumilyov was bitter about his divorce, he seemed ready not only to forgive but to help Akhmatova and Shileiko at a time of dire stress. He also made it possible for Akhmatova to see Lev. It would have been extremely difficult for her to have taken him in under the circumstances, since the rations Shileiko was getting were barely enough for the two of them.

By 1920, Akhmatova and Shileiko were in a crisis. Shileiko was not receiving anything from World Literature and they had no food. Someone came to visit Akhmatova, bringing a bag of rice from Larisa Reisner, who wanted to see her. Larisa had taken an active part in the Revolution, had joined the Bolshevik Party, and was fighting for their cause in the Civil War, even participating in the campaign to drive the British out of Persia. She became the Red Army's first woman political commissar. She was now living in Petrograd—in the cold luxury of the old Admiralty Building—with her husband Fyodor Raskolnikov, who had a high post in the navy, and she took an active part in the cultural life of the city. Akhmatova shared the rice with her neighbors in the Sheremetev Palace, who were all suffering from dysentery, and agreed to see Reisner. When they met, Larisa was bitter and complained about Gumilyov, saying that she was a virgin when she met him, that she had loved him and he had taken advantage of her. Reisner was shocked at the state of the apartment and how the couple was living. Shileiko was suffering from sciatica. Reisner left, but she returned late that same night with a basket of food and told Shileiko he should go to the hospital.

Akhmatova said Reisner also spoke about Gumilyov with great bitterness, like a wounded animal. She had loved Gumilyov very much until she found out about his affair with Anna Engelhardt in 1916, which was going on at the same time as her own affair. On the insistence of Reisner, Gumilyov was deprived of rations given to him by the Baltic Fleet, for whom Reisner worked.[75]

Akhmatova found it humiliating for Reisner to see her now, and was not eager to have to receive her charity. Reisner was going to take her revenge by telling Akhmatova about her affair and making Gumilyov's life more difficult than it already was. The disparity between the lifestyle of the two is emphasized in Akhmatova's own version of the event, which Lydia Chukovskaya records: "She [Larisa] came to confess to me. I was a beggar then, hungry, I was sleeping on boards—a real Job. . . . Then I was at her place once on business. She was living at that time in the Admiralty: three windows overlooking the *Bronze Horseman,* three—on the Neva. She drove me home in her horse cab. On the way she said, 'I would give everything, absolutely everything, to be Anna Akhmatova!' Stupid words, aren't they? What does that mean—everything? Three windows on the Neva?"[76]

Akhmatova predicted that historians—who think that all women are alike, and all women poets are even more alike—would lump her, Reisner, and Zinaida Gippius together in one group. "They will find all of us—Larisa and Gippius— we will all be called 'women of the time.' They will certainly find a common style among us."[77]

Akhmatova's relationship with Shileiko was growing increasingly difficult. In a letter to his wife dated August 12, 1920, Chulkov describes Akhmatova as a "horrible skeleton, dressed in rags. . . . According to rumor, she is in some kind of strange seclusion at Shileiko's. Both have TB and are living in horrible poverty."[78]

Arthur Lourie decided to help her. He not only admired her work and was attracted to her as a woman—according to Lourie's friend Irina Graham—but thought of her as one of the "insulted and injured" of Dostoyevsky. Graham says Akhmatova came to Lourie herself and their relationship was renewed. Lourie said he "decided to tear her out of the prison created by Shileiko." Under the pretense of needing to cure his sciatica, Shileiko was taken in an ambulance to the hospital; they kept him there for a month. Akhmatova got a job in the library of the Agronomy Institute and received a public apartment on 7, Sergiyevskaya, where she lived from 1920 to 1921. She told Luknitsky that when Shileiko came out of the hospital, he cried, "You have abandoned me! I am poor, sick." She replied that he could move in with her. He refused, since now things were different—the room, everything, in fact, was hers. But he ended up spending the whole winter there.[79]

On December 11, 1920, Bryusov arranged an evening of readings by women poets in Moscow. There were nine women, including Tsvetayeva, who, dressed in "a garment that resembled a priest's cassock, with her usual leather belt and officer's field pouch and a pair of gray felt boots," read poems eulogizing the White Army to an audience of Red Army soldiers and revolutionary students.

The evening is described by Tsvetayeva in her memoirs. By this time Bryusov had given up his ideas about the autonomy of art, "art for art's sake," and had taken up the Communist Party line of defending art for the people. He pretended to have forgotten Akhmatova's name and then berated her for not writing politically engaged poetry. It was one of the first of the criticisms that her work was not relevant to the new Soviet State, and it was particularly insulting coming from someone who for so many years had written poetry that was totally politically irrelevant, and who was clearly using Akhmatova as a scapegoat to prove his own loyalty to the new regime. Tsvetayeva quotes his speech:

"Well, woman: love, passion . . . the best example of such onesidedness of women's work is" (pause) "is . . . comrades, you know . . . is the famous poetess. Comrades, the most famous poetess of our time . . . is the poetess." Behind his back, whispering "Lvova?" He shrugged his shoulders and almost shouting: "Akhmatova! Is the poetess Anna Akhmatova. Let us hope that the social revolution that is going on all over the world and which has already been accomplished in Russia will be reflected in women's works. But meanwhile, I confirm that it has not yet been reflected, and women are still writing about love and passion."[80]

That winter Gumilyov sent his family—his wife, their daughter, his son Lev, and his mother—to Bezhetsk. He continued his lectures and workshops at the House of Arts. He lived alone at 5, Preobrazhenskaya Street, until the end of May 1921, but it was becoming increasingly difficult to survive. The studios at World Literature that had provided income and rations had ceased to exist, and he had to keep sending money to his family. He began eating at the House of Writers on Basseinaya Street.[81] There were rumors he was having an affair with the actress Olga Arbenina. He and Mandelstam quarreled over her, but she soon married Kuzmin's lover, Yury Yurkun. Akhmatova says that another woman played an important role in Gumilyov's life at this time. Nina Shishkina was a gypsy, and she would serve as Gumilyov's "refuge" and solace the last years of his life. He dedicated his poem "Gypsy Camp" to her. "She was his secret refuge in the noisy, angry world," wrote Akhmatova. "Restrained and exhausted, he was able to relax with her. In those difficult times he felt comfortable only with her. Not demanding anything, she always calmed him down with tenderness and patience, and sang to him. She composed music to his verses."[82]

At this time Gumilyov wrote a remarkable poem, "The Wayward Tram," expressing his horror at what Russia had become after the Revolution. No longer was he indifferent. The radical change in his style—from the restrained, cool verses of a craftsman to the experimental shifts in time and excited, almost frantic stream-of-consciousness imagery—shows he had matured as a poet, one who was finally willing to go beyond the measured canonical forms in which he had previously chosen to express himself. Vyacheslav Ivanov says the development of Gumilyov's talent recalls the explosion of a star just before it dies, when a sudden stream of light flames into the space surrounding it.[83]

The central image of the poem is of a tram that has jumped the track of chronological time and passes freely between past, present, and future. The poet remembers presenting himself in a powdered wig to the empress in the eighteenth century, then recalls Mashenka, a simple girl from that period who was his ideal love, living on a side street in Petersburg. In one of his most grotesque visions, Gumilyov speaks of signboards written in letters of blood and human heads being sold at the grocer's instead of cabbages. At the end he turns to religion to give him solace in a world that is too horrible and confused for him to understand:

Where am I? So languidly and apprehensively
My heart beats in reply:

"Do you see the station at which you can
Buy a ticket for the India of the Spirit?"

A signboard . . . letters poured with blood
Spell—greengrocer—I know, there
Instead of cabbages, instead of radishes,
They sell dead heads.

. . .

Like a true fortress of Orthodoxy,
St. Isaac's dome is etched on high,
There I will have a service of intercession
For Mashenka's health, and a requiem for myself.

But still forever is my heart mournful,
And it is difficult to breathe, and painful to live . . .
Mashenka, I never thought
It was possible to love and grieve so much.[84]

Another subtheme of the post-Revolutionary days was the hostility between those who chose to leave Russia and those who remained behind. This is exemplified in an incident involving Merezhkovsky and Gippius after they left for Paris in 1920. Merezhkovsky wrote a letter to a Paris newspaper insinuating that the scholars working for World Literature were traitors because they found it to their advantage to work for the new Soviet State. Andrey Levinson recalls a copy of this letter being brought to a meeting of the World Literature editorial board:

What we called a "board" was really a group of writers and scholars, hungry, poor, without any rights, cut off from readers and from research sources, from the future, some of whom had been touched by death, writers who were denounced by informers and could only weakly defend themselves from the increasing attacks by the authorities, but who were totally loyal to literature and scholarship. And now in this letter, this perhaps fanatic, perhaps hopeless, but lofty, unselfish effort was being attacked with two words, "shameless speculation." . . . Gumilyov, the "iron man" as he was jokingly called, was insulted, mortally offended. He wanted to reply to the foreign press. But how could he prove the purity of his actions as a writer, the full measure of his spiritual independence from the regime? . . . The critic spoke about the ignorance of his colleagues and the improper role they were playing. The first [accusation] was, of course, beneath our dignity to answer. Anyone who calls dozens of professors, academics, and writers ignorant, counting the number of volumes they produced, does not deserve a reply. The second attack was based on a misunderstanding. World Literature was not political. Gorky gave complete freedom to his colleagues. . . . People of the most varied convictions were on the board, and not a single one was a member of the Communist Party. But they were all convinced that in these difficult and horrible times the salvation of the spiritual culture of the country was possible only if each person worked in the area that he had freely chosen for himself. The publisher was not responsible for the difficult conditions under which they had to work. . . . The only people who would laugh at this are those who either are unaware of what they are doing or have no self-respect.[85]

The brutal Civil War that the Soviets had been fighting against the counter-revolutionaries finally ended in 1921. The state was in economic turmoil. Lenin realized he lacked trained managers to run the new Socialist society, so he introduced the New Economic Policy (NEP), with the state retaining large industrial plants, transportation, big banks, and trade, while private enterprise on a small scale was permitted. Although this policy helped industry and agriculture meet the basic needs of the population, it encouraged large-scale corruption and speculation among a new breed spawned by this period, the NEP man.[86]

"When the NEP began," Akhmatova recalls, "everything started to look as before—restaurants, smart cabmen, beautiful young women in furs and diamonds. But it was all pretend—it was only pretending to be like it had been before. It was all spurious. The past had disappeared irrevocably. Its spirit, its people—the new was only an imitation of the old."[87]

The year 1921 began as 1920 had begun—with cold and famine. But it was also a year of death for Akhmatova. Two of the people who meant the most to her—Alexander Blok and Nikolay Gumilyov—died that year, and so did her friend from the past, Amedeo Modigliani:

At the beginning of NEP, when I was a member of the board of the Writers' Union, we often met in the office of Alexander Tikhonov at World Literature publishing house. Tikhonov received many foreign books and magazines. Someone handed me an issue of a French art magazine. I opened it and there was a photo of Modigliani—across from an obituary. From it I learned he was a great twentieth-century artist, and he was compared to Botticelli.[88]

During these difficult years, Akhmatova's innate generosity did not waver. Chukovsky mentions several times when she helped his young daughter. On February 3, 1921, he noted in his diary that he encountered Akhmatova in the vestibule of the House of Scholars, and she told him to come over so she could give him some milk for his daughter. "I ran over to see her in the evening and she gave it to me! Imagine in February 1921 someone offering another person a bottle of milk!"[89]

Akhmatova continued to be popular during these early post-Revolutionary years. The city in 1921 was vibrant with literary life, with posters of recitations by poets plastered everywhere. One evening in the hall of the State Parliament there was a program that included Akhmatova and Kuzmin. Chukovsky went to see Akhmatova, and assumed many others did so as well, because the empty hall filled up in the second half when she appeared. They all knew her and worshipped her books, which were appearing one after another and quickly sold out in all the bookstores. She was then thirty-four, in the bloom of her talent and strength.

Gumilyov was also involved in the rich, vibrant intellectual life. He played an increasingly major role in the administration of the arts in Petrograd. Blok had been head of the Petrograd branch of the All-Russian Union of Poets, but hated the bureaucratic detail, and Gumilyov took his place, thriving on organizing meetings, arranging for wood, clothing, and apartments for members, and solving problems about publications.[90]

In March 1921, Akhmatova did turn to Gumilyov in his capacity as administrator. She went to World Literature to get her membership card in the Writers' Union, which she needed for identification. The secretary wrote out a card and sent for Gumilyov, but he was busy, and she told Akhmatova to wait. Akhmatova sat down on a couch and waited for about ten minutes. Then the door to A. N. Tikhonov's office opened and Akhmatova saw that Gumilyov and Blok were having a lively discussion. When Gumilyov finally greeted her and asked her to forgive him for making her wait, Akhmatova answered, "Never mind . . . I'm used to waiting!" "For me?" "No, in lines." Gumilyov signed the card, coldly kissed her hand, then withdrew.[91]

Gumilyov started yet another version of the Poets' Guild and published a journal, *New Hyperborea,* another weak imitation of the first Guild. As with the second version, Akhmatova had nothing to do with this one. Gumilyov also began a literary circle called the Resonant Shell, which met in the large, cold apartment of the famous photographer Moisey Nappelbaum on Nevsky Avenue. However, Nappelbaum was at the center too of another literary gathering, which Akhmatova did attend. Ida Nappelbaum describes it as one large room with a wide bay window in the middle, pillows and a sheepskin rug on the floor, and a light blue Japanese mural of a golden dragon on the wall. The poets of Petrograd and Moscow lounged on pillows and couches, or stood along the walls—the Serapian Brothers with their girlfriends, those who loved poetry and those who came to hear the latest poems. They would go around the room, each taking turns to read their poems, reciting from wherever he or she happened to be sitting or standing. At the end of the evening tea was served with pieces of black bread. "And everyone was there! The magnificent Anna Akhmatova, the elegant Mikhail Kuzmin, the wonderful Benedikt Livshits, the noble Mikhail Lozinsky, and the master of the 'Resounding Shell,' Nikolay Gumilyov, with friends from the Poets' Guild." Vladimir Mayakovsky was there and Sergey Yesenin came from Moscow. Actors and directors would come by after the theater.[92]

Some of the societies which existed at the time were satirical, such as the Grand and Free Palace of the Apes, founded by the writer Aleksey Remizov in 1908. Remizov was "otherworldly," immersed in medieval Russian antiquity and folklore. He made Akhmatova a member and gave her a Charter of the Apes, "as a sign of raising her to the level of cavaliers of the sign of the apes of the first degree with a squirrel's paw." It was dated August 5, 1921, two days before Remizov's departure from Russia. Gorky mentions this odd society in his memoirs: "His [Remizov's] weird sense of humor and historical attempt to bring some laughter into what he saw as an essentially unjust and cruel world is reflected in the secret society he founded in 1908, the Grand and Free Palace of the Apes. Remizov was the clerk of the federation and issued charters signed by the tail of King Assyka I. These charters were based on medieval models done in ornate calligraphy."[93]

Many of the activities during these years took place at the House of Arts where Mandelstam was living, and where Gumilyov moved in May 1920. Vladislav Khodasevich came to the city in 1920 and moved into the House of Arts. He was shocked by what Petersburg had become:

The society of old Petersburg had outlived the period of its bloom. The more life forged ahead, the more sharply members of the society felt the inevitable separation with the past, and this was the reason they so much wanted to preserve a memory of it. . . . At that time Petersburg became more lovely than it had ever been and might ever be again. Even the most ordinary houses took on a severity and grandeur that only the palaces used to have. Petersburg had been depopulated, trams had stopped running, only rarely would the sound of hooves or cars honking be heard—but the absence of movement was more suitable to Petersburg than motion. There are some people who look better in their coffin—so it was with Petersburg. This was a beauty that was ephemeral. Right afterwards came the horrible ugliness of the end. Right in front of our eyes decay began to touch Petersburg: the sidewalks collapsed, plaster crumbled . . . hands broke off statues. But even this barely perceptible decay was beautiful. Nightingales sang at night in Alexander Square and on the Moika.[94]

Khodasevich describes what it was like as he watched the members of the old world attempting to adjust to the new. The House of Arts housed such well-known figures as Osip Mandelstam; his weakness was *pirozhki* [meat-filled tarts]. "Then, with befitting lateness, Gumilyov appeared with a lady on his arm; she was shivering in a black dress with a deep slit. He walked, tall and arrogant in his frock coat, passing through the hall. He was trembling from the cold, but he bowed magnificently and politely to the right and left and conversed with acquaintances in worldly tone. . . . His entire appearance said: 'Nothing's happened. The Revolution? I haven't heard anything about it.' "[95]

However, Gumilyov could not continue to ignore the increasing conflicts in his personal and professional life. He made his last trip to Bezhetsk on May 18, 1921. His mother told Akhmatova that Gumilyov's wife had sent him horrible letters informing him she would hang or poison herself if she had to stay there any longer. Gumilyov came and took her and his daughter to Pargolovo, to put Yelena in an orphanage, since Gumilyov's mother said it was too difficult for her now to look after his daughter—probably because his mother was quite old by this time and no longer had the energy to devote to her granddaughter that she had so lovingly given her grandson Lev. His wife was obviously not interested in looking after her little girl, but wanted to take part in life in the city.[96] There is no material available that tells how Gumilyov felt, but since he apparently did not protest when Lev was not raised by Akhmatova, perhaps he did not object to this arrangement, given the difficulties of post-Revolutionary Petrograd. Perhaps, too, he did not have strong parental feelings and, like Akhmatova, had been satisfied to see his son at Christmas and in the summer months.

At the end of May, V. A. Pavlov, who occupied a responsible post with the Black Sea Fleet, invited Gumilyov to accompany him to Sebastopol. Gumilyov spent a month on the trip, during which his new collection of poems, *Tent,* was published by the printers of the military fleet. Pavlov, with his usual aggressiveness, was able to convince the printers to produce fifty copies in one night.

On his return, Gumilyov stopped in Moscow, where he gave a reading at the Poets' Café, a strong contrast to the elegant, aesthetic atmosphere of the Stray Dog. The writer Ilya Ehrenburg recalls the café:

> The walls were covered with paintings that must have looked very strange to the public, and with sentences no less strange. "I like watching children die"—that line from Mayakovsky's early, prerevolutionary poem—was on the wall in order to shock those who entered. . . . No one talked art here, there were no discussions, no heart searchings: those present were divided into actors and spectators. The audience consisted of the remnants of the bourgeoisie—profiteers, writers, philistines in search of entertainment. . . . David Burlyuk would mount the platform, his face heavily powdered, lorgnette in hand, and recite: "I like pregnant men."[97]

Composers, musicians, and actors also appeared at the café. The poet Vasily Kamensky recounts the time a young composer, Sergey Prokofiev, played his new work, *Possession.* "While Prokofiev was playing, Volodya [Mayakovsky] sketched an excellent portrait of the composer at the piano and wrote in the album, 'Sergei Sergeievich is playing on the soft, sensitive nerves of Vladimir Vladimirovich.' " One evening several anarchists showed up, led by a certain "Guido," a handsome, dark-haired man in a black velvet tunic, with jewels around his neck and numerous rings on his fingers, rings that had probably once adorned the window of a jewelry store on Moscow's fashionable street, Kuznetsky Most. Two pistols were stuck in his wide belt and he was accompanied by bodyguards. The anarchists had brought a cabaret singer with them, who, very drunk, mounted the platform and began to utter nonsense. Furious, Mayakovsky rushed up and pushed the singer aside. The anarchists yelled, and Guido made his way to the platform waving a revolver. Members of the Red Guard were also present; rattling their rifles, they rose from their seats and marched menacingly on the anarchists, who prudently decided to withdraw.[98]

The strange mixture of types that showed up at the café were present when Gumilyov gave a poetry reading there in July 1921. After he finished, a voice was heard repeating the poetic verses. One of those present described what happened next.

Gumilyov's poems were being recited not by some pale young man, or a literary dandy, or some young girl exhausted by evening vigils. A man in a leather jacket . . . was drunk on the verses of Gumilyov. He had bold features, framed by a black beard, and his face looked biblical. "What Samson is this?" Gumilyov burst out. "Are you surprised that I'm reciting your poems?" asked the stranger. "No," Gumilyov replied politely. "I've memorized all your poems," said the stranger, bursting out in a smile. "That makes me very happy," said Gumilyov, and he gave the stranger his hand. Just as straightforward as before, the man shook his hand and said, "And I'm Blyumkin." Gumilyov's solemn arrogance melted. Like a teenager, he exclaimed: "Are you really Blyumkin?" "Yes—the same," and shaking his hand, Gumilyov said, "I'm happy when my poems are read by warriors and people of great strength."

Yakov Blyumkin worked for the Cheka, the Soviet secret police, and was head of Trotsky's personal bodyguard. On July 6, 1918, he had killed the German ambassador, Mirbach. He himself was later executed, in 1929. Gumilyov wrote some lines on the event:

> The man amidst the crowd
> Who shot the imperial ambassador
> Came up to me to shake my hand
> And thank me for my verses

—the meeting of two men marked for death.[99]

Gumilyov and Alexander Blok, whose strained personal relations mirrored the differences in their philosophies of art and life, ironically would both meet a tragic fate in August 1921. As Khodasevich points out, although Blok was only six years older than Gumilyov, he belonged to a different poetic generation. While he sometimes rebelled against Symbolism, Blok was one of the purest examples of the movement; Gumilyov, however, who never totally threw off the influence of Bryusov, still considered himself a profound enemy of Symbolism. Blok was a mystic, who first worshipped the Eternal Feminine and later wrote blasphemous verses profaning her, while Gumilyov had always crossed himself in front of a church, but seemed totally indifferent to what religion really meant. For Blok, poetry was a spiritual act; for Gumilyov, it was a form of literary activity. "And they could not endure each other." Gleb Struve says Blok was like a poet possessed—a passive poet, who was the instrument of an outside force—and the act of poetic creation was torture for him, while Gumilyov was an active poet, who possessed his material, a craftsman rather than a soothsayer or prophet.[100]

In April 1921, Blok wrote a vicious attack against Gumilyov and Acmeism entitled "Without Divinity, Without Inspiration," which was published after his death in 1925. Although he excluded Akhmatova, his critique of her poetry was not very complimentary: he calls her verse weary, morbid, feminine, and self-absorbed. But it is Gumilyov and the Acmeists who are drowning in soulless theories, in Formalism, who have no understanding of Russian life in general: "They hush up what is most important, the only thing of real value—the soul." If only they would let go, just for a moment become uncouth and awkward, even ugly, so that they would resemble their poor motherland, mutilated, burnt, and devastated, there would be some hope. But, according to Blok, they have no desire to do this and could not even if they tried. He divided the world into those, like Dostoyevsky's heroines, who act on their emotions and intuition, and those whose behavior is based on carefully reasoned thought, who are sensible, practical, like the heroes of Tolstoy and Turgenev. Blok says his own poems are explosive and contradictory, like Dostoyevsky's heroines, whereas Gumilyov solves a poem like a theorem.[101]

Blok had been one of the first to greet the changes in Russian society with great enthusiasm, but he was now growing increasingly disillusioned with the Revolution. As so often, he expressed what he felt through the medium of music. In February 1921, he characterized the Revolution as experiencing a "moment of deceleration . . . a moment of reflection, weariness, a sense of being deserted by the spirit of music. The old music is no more, and as yet there is no new music. It's dull."[102]

One of Blok's greatest poems, "The Twelve" (1918), is about twelve Red Army soldiers who shoot, loot, and threaten to slit the throats of the bourgeoisie. The old order is pathetic and outmoded, yet his representation of the new regime—the cruel, vulgar soldiers—is horrifying. Still, his optimism asserts itself at the end, as the soldiers are led by the figure of Christ wearing a wreath of white roses—perhaps an image of Blok's hope that after a moral cleansing the nation would be purified and the promise of peace on earth and goodwill to men would finally become a reality.

However, by 1921 Blok was convinced, or felt instinctively, that this dream would not come true for a long time, if ever. A young writer who admired Blok described him when he was deathly ill that year: "I have never seen such dead, empty eyes. I never thought that a face could express such utter indifference and melancholy."[103]

Blok helped commemorate the eighty-fourth anniversary of Pushkin's death in 1921. On February 11 at the House of Writers, Blok stood at the back of the hall, and when he was announced, he walked slowly to the stage without looking at anyone. He wore a simple black suit and white sweater, and his message was just as somber: "The poet is entrusted with a task—to free sounds from their native anarchic element; to bring these sounds into harmony and give them form; to introduce this harmony into the outside world." He spoke of the poet's inner freedom, which he characterized as a creative rather than an external peace. In his poem "To Pushkin House" (the Institute devoted to the study of Pushkin), he entreats the great poet for guidance:

> Pushkin! Following in your steps
> We sang of secret freedom!
> Give us your hand in these troubled times,
> Help us in our silent struggle![104]

Blok said a poet dies because he can no longer breathe, because life has lost its meaning. And life had, indeed, lost its meaning for this great poet. He once told Gorky, "God and I are the only mainstays of life and faith. But we became too clever to believe in God, and not strong enough to believe only in ourselves."[105]

Vitaly Vilenkin describes the last time Akhmatova saw Blok—at the Bolshoi Theater in April 1921:

> That evening all the Petrograd literary and artistic intelligentsia arrived. They came by foot from everywhere—there were no trams. Everyone dressed poorly. They were hungry. Akhmatova sat with Khodasevich in a box. Everyone asked Blok to keep reading. It was obvious how tired he was. "If only they would leave him alone!"—she whispered in Khodasevich's ear. They met in the wings. Blok raised his eyes to her and greeted her. "But where's your Spanish shawl?" They never saw each other again.[106]

A month later Chukovsky wrote: "I was sitting backstage with him [Blok]. On stage some 'orator' . . . was cheerfully demonstrating to the crowd that, as a poet, Blok was already dead. 'These verses are just dead rubbish written by a corpse.' Blok leaned over to me and said, 'That's true, he's telling the truth. I'm dead.' " When Chukovsky asked why he did not write poetry anymore, Blok always gave the same reply: "All sounds have stopped. Can't you hear that here there are no longer any sounds?"[107]

Blok died on Sunday, August 7, exhausted and disillusioned. A contemporary described how moved she was when she saw Akhmatova at the funeral on August 10. Akhmatova, who normally disliked showing her emotions in public, cried helplessly.

> His coffin was carried from Ofitserskaya Street to the Smolensk Cemetery on the arms of famous poets, scholars, and actors. His wife and mother were in deep mourning, crying terribly. In the distance in the crowd I suddenly saw a young woman crying bitterly and praying. Her face was so unusual and captivating, I could not tear my eyes away from her. A lovely face, very beautiful—but quite unusual, different from ordinary, worldly beauty. . . . I recognized her, though I had never seen her before. It was Anna Akhmatova. When she came up to the coffin, she bowed over him and crossed herself. Her tears flowed without restraint, although she was covered by a veil. She was wearing a simple gray dress and an unfashionable large hat with a veil—I saw her among thousands in the crowd, and she left a remarkable impression. . . . I thought for the first time in my life I had seen real beauty—and that such beauty really "could save the world."[108]

Akhmatova expressed her grief in a lyrical poem to Blok. His burial took place on the day the Russian Orthodox Church celebrates Our Lady of Smolensk, and she combined these themes:

> Today is the nameday of Our Lady of Smolensk,
> . . .
> We have brought to the Holy Mother of God,
> In our hands in a silver coffin
> Our sun, extinguished in torment—
> Alexander, pure swan.
>
> (I, p. 595)

Chukovsky was in Pskov, far from Petrograd, when he found out about Blok's death. He and the artist Mstislav Dobuzhinsky were on the estate of Prince Gagarin, where they had established a colony of artists and writers under the auspices of the House of Arts. On August 8, Yevgeny Zamyatin wrote him: "Never in my life have I been so sad. Yesterday at 10:30 A.M. Blok died. . . . August 7, 1921, is just as unbelievable as the day in 1837 when they found out Pushkin had been killed." Chukovsky replied: "It was as if I had come there young and happy and was returning an old man, worn out, exhausted. It was as if every house was shouting out, 'Blok is no more. And we don't need Blok. It's just fine without Blok.' But I don't know what comes after Blok. . . . For twenty years, from 1898 to 1918, an endless song streamed through him, and then he stopped—and immediately began to die. His song was his life. The song ended and he was finished."[109]

Larisa Reisner wrote Akhmatova from Kabul, where she was with her husband on a diplomatic mission, begging Akhmatova not to "die while still alive" as Blok had done and stop writing poetry:

> The newspaper came 9,000 versts with the news about the death of Blok. And for some reason it was only to you that I wished to express how bitter and absurd this all is. Only to you—right beside you a column fell, as slender, white, and confused as you. Now, when he no longer exists, your equal, your only spiritual brother—it is even more obvious what you are, that you breathe, are tormented. . . . Most tender poet, are you writing poems? There is nothing more exalted than this; for one line of yours people would forgive the entire horrible, hopeless period. Your art is the entire meaning and justification for everything. . . . You are . . . the bright soul of everyone who lived wrongly, choking with filth, who died from grief. Only don't be silent—do not die while still alive.[110]

Akhmatova needed such encouragement, for Blok's was not the only horrible death she had to experience that year. The last time she saw Gumilyov was in July, while Shileiko was in Tsarskoye in a sanatorium. Gumilyov and Georgy Ivanov visited her at her second-floor apartment on Sergiyevskaya Street. Gumilyov had just come back from the Crimea: he had seen her mother and sister, but brought tragic news of the death of her brother Andrey who had committed suicide in Greece. According to Akhmatova, Gumilyov treated her very coldly. When Gumilyov and Ivanov left, she led them down a winding staircase, from which it was possible to get from her apartment directly to the street, rather than going through the third-floor corridor. The staircase was quite dark, and as Gumilyov began to descend, Akhmatova said, "You go down a staircase like this only to your execution."[111] Again Akhmatova was acting the role of prophetess, though she could have had no idea what lay in store for Gumilyov.

Gumilyov had invited her to come to the Muruzi House and recite at a literary evening there, but she refused, saying she did not feel like going to an event where people would be having a good time, after learning about her brother's death. She was upset that he did not have the sensitivity to understand what a blow her brother's death was to her. She said Gumilyov reproached her for never reciting any more. She was insulted that he had come with Georgy Ivanov, although she later thought the reason Gumilyov did not come alone was that he thought Shileiko would be there. But she was touched when she found out later that Gumilyov had attempted to reassure her mother by telling her Akhmatova had married a wonderful scholar who was also a remarkable person and, in general, that everything was just fine.

On August 3, 1921, Gumilyov was arrested for allegedly participating in a counterrevolutionary plot known as the "Tagantsev Affair."[112] Akhmatova heard about his arrest at Blok's funeral. His friends did everything possible to save him, but no one anticipated that events would unfold as quickly as they did. They visited various authorities, trying in vain to effect Gumilyov's release.

Gumilyov never spoke against the Bolsheviks directly, not because he was afraid but, as a contemporary explained, because politics was outside his circle of interests. He had once predicted that he would not die an ordinary death:

> And I will not die in bed,
> At the notary's or at the doctor's.[113]

He had no concept of the danger he was in. Mandelstam remembered his words: "I'm in absolutely no trouble. I tell everyone openly that I'm a monarchist. For them [i.e., the Bolsheviks] that is the most important thing—that everything is clear. They know this and don't touch me." Akhmatova said this was very typical of Gumilyov, since he was not careless over what he said about the regime. Though he never hid his political position, there is no evidence he ever made blatant statements against the Bolsheviks or tried in any way to foment action against them. Akhmatova said he did not want to interfere with reality—he seemed to pass right through it and it did not touch him, or so he thought.[114]

Vladislav Khodasevich visited Gumilyov on the night before his arrest, just before leaving for a vacation in the country. Since they were not intimate friends, he was surprised by Gumilyov's enthusiasm:

> He didn't want me to leave. I stayed until two in the morning. He was unusually cheerful and spoke a lot on various themes. I went the next day to leave something with him and knocked at the door. No one answered. In the dining room the servant Yefim told me Gumilyov had been arrested during the night and had been taken away. Thus, I was the last to see him free. In his exaggerated joy at my arrival there must have been a presentiment that after me he would see no one.[115]

Gumilyov's arrest can be understood in the context of the time. Russia was in chaos: the famine at the end of the Civil War put the final touch on the exhaustion and ruin experienced during that bloody struggle. The government attempted to requisition food and the peasants responded by refusing to till their land. In 1921 there were uprisings in the countryside, strikes and unrest in the cities. The immediate cause of the Tagantsev Affair and Gumilyov's arrest was most probably the Kronstadt uprising in March. The naval base, which had been one of the chief supports of the October Revolution, rose in rebellion against the Bolsheviks. The sailors and other Kronstadt rebels wanted a Constituent Assembly to elect a new government. As the historian Riasanovsky says, "The well-nigh general dissatisfaction with Bolshevik rule could not have been more forcefully expressed."[116]

On a petition from the scholar Dmitry Likhachov, also president of the Soviet Fund for Culture, the prosecutor of the USSR looked over the case of Gumilyov. Much later, in October 1989, Sergey Luknitsky, son of Pavel Luknitsky, wrote that he had looked at files dealing with the case, in which there are over one hundred pages, mostly letters confiscated upon Gumilyov's arrest. None of the letters bore incriminating evidence. A young geography professor Vladimir Tagantsev in typewritten testimony says that once, through Y. P. German and V. G. Shvedov, Gumilyov was asked to cooperate in a plot, to organize officers and members of the intelligentsia in case of an uprising, and for this he was given money and a typewriter ribbon in order to print proclamations. However, Gumilyov did not write any proclamations; but according to the testimony, he did not inform the authorities of the alleged plot, and for this he was punished. In his testimony, Tagantsev said, "Gumilyov was of a Soviet orientation and was not interested in counterrevolutionary affairs. I never turned to him again."

In an article that appeared in *Novyi mir* in 1987, G. A. Terekhov wrote that he had become acquainted with the file while working in the office of the General Prosecutor. He is convinced Gumilyov's only crime was not informing the government of the plot. Sergey Luknitsky points out that the two men who allegedly tried to draw Gumilyov into the plot both died: German, a naval officer, was shot by a frontier guard on May 30, 1921, while attempting to cross the Finnish border; and Shvedov, a lieutenant, was mortally wounded by the secret police during his arrest in Petrograd on August 3, 1921. So neither could have provided evidence that they had actually spoken with Gumilyov. Gumilyov denied everything in the first reports by his interrogator Yakobson, and then admitted everything that was suggested to him, which Sergey Luknitsky also finds odd. Orest Vysotsky, Gumilyov's son by Olga Vysotskaya, apparently believed that there was a plot and his father knew about it but would not inform on the conspirators as a matter of honor.[117]

Right after Gumilyov was arrested, various important institutions—including the Union of Writers, the Poets' Union, and the Proletcult—petitioned the Petrograd Special Commission to have Gumilyov released. Gorky was in Moscow at the time, but his signature was typed in as representing the House of Arts. Whether he could have done something and did not wish to, or whether he thought there would be plenty of time to take care of the situation when he returned to Petrograd, is still not known.[118]

Adamovich describes how he learned of Gumilyov's detention in the prison on the top floor at Cheka headquarters on Gorokhovaya Street. A voice told him on the phone: "You know, *Quiver* has been held up at the printers." At first Adamovich thought perhaps a new edition of Gumilyov's early work was in trouble with the censor, but the trembling voice and the stress on the words "held up" indicated something was seriously wrong. At that time people were using special "telephone language," which could be understood from just a few simple words. Everyone spoke in neutral tones, almost casually, saying things like, "You know, I think it's getting warm," which meant some rumor indicated that a change was imminent. If someone suddenly "got sick," they understood he was "in the hospital," on Gorokhovaya or Shpalernaya, where the Cheka prisons were located. As soon as the news spread that *Quiver* had been "held up," everyone started working to get Gumilyov out as soon as possible. According to Adamovich: "We went to every possible authority, large and small, telegraphed Gorky, who was in Moscow at the time. But it never occurred to anyone that the end would be so quick and fatal. Nobody imagined an execution. There was absolutely no reason for it—even by the Cheka yardstick."[119]

Nikolay Otsup, who had been an admiring student, was one of those who tried to convince the authorities to let Gumilyov go. The explanation was that Gumilyov was in prison for debt. One of the group with Otsup replied that was impossible, but the president of the Petrograd Cheka, Bugchuk Semyonyov, who looked like a "petty shop assistant," did not wish to argue. He said, "Phone on Wednesday. In any case, not a single hair will fall from Gumilyov's head." On Wednesday, Otsup, surrounded by Gumilyov's friends, called. He was informed he would receive information the next day. After the phone call, Otsup and a friend went to the prisons to look for Gumilyov. At Shpalernaya they were able to get into the courtyard, went up the staircase, and asked through a grating where Gumilyov was being held. The guard mistook them for officials and said Gumilyov had been taken the night before to Gorokhovaya, the other prison. A deputation of members of the House of Arts went to see the commissar of the secret police, who not only could not say why Gumilyov had been arrested but did not even know who he was. "What does your Gumilyevich do?" "Not Gumilyevich, Gumilyov!" "Well?" "He's a poet." "Aha, that means he's a writer. . . . Never heard of him. You see, there're a lot of speculators at large. Perhaps Mr. Gumilyov has some debts he didn't pay." "But Gumilyov isn't a businessman!" Solomon Posner says they laughed after this, never realizing that their laughter would soon "turn into bullets and blood."

On August 25, thirty-five years from the day of his birth, Nikolay Gumilyov was executed.[120]

The Petrograd *Pravda* printed the official communication. Sixty-one people were killed without trial. Of Gumilyov it said: "Thirty-five years old, philologist, poet, member of the board of World Literature. He wrote proclamations. He promised to get a group of intellectuals to take part in an uprising. He received money from the organization for technical necessities."[121]

Akhmatova's brother, Viktor, gives a cogent explanation of Gumilyov's execution: "It was wrong to say he was a monarchist—he never was . . . when the Kerensky government collapsed and the Communists took over in Petrograd . . . they couldn't bring a good life to the people of Petrograd but there was another possibility—to frighten them and terrorize them. And on account of this

Lenin appointed Felix Dzerzhinsky. The Cheka! And they started putting people against the wall and shooting them in order to . . . stay in power through terror. That's why they put Gumilyov against the wall and shot him."[122]

A few days after Blok's death, Akhmatova went into a sanatorium in Tsarskoye Selo. Her friends the Rykovs were living in Tsarskoye on a farm and often invited her to come over. While she was there, she received a letter from Shileiko, saying that there was a rumor that Gumilyov had been transferred to Moscow, which everyone thought was a good sign. Manya Rykova had come over to visit Akhmatova one day and was sitting with her on the second-floor balcony when suddenly they saw her father, Viktor Rykov, below. He had just returned from the city and was on his way to the farm. He saw Manya and called up to her. When she went down to see him, he said something to her, and Akhmatova says Manya suddenly clapped her hands in horror and covered her face. Sensing something was wrong, Akhmatova waited, afraid, thinking something terrible had happened to the Rykov family; but when Manya returned, she said only, "Nikolay"—Akhmatova immediately understood.

In the morning she went to the center of town and read *Pravda* on the wall of the train station, the same station where she had seen Gumilyov so often when they were adolescents. Akhmatova says, "From the station I walked on foot to the Marble Palace to see Shileiko, who already knew. We spoke on the telephone with Samuel Alyansky, who said there would be a requiem in Kazan Cathedral. . . . I was at the requiem."[123]

Nine years later, Akhmatova learned where he was buried: "I know about Kolya [Gumilyov]. They shot him near Berngardovka, along the Irininskaya Road. . . . I found out nine years later and went there. Groves, a small curved pine, next to it another huge one, but with torn roots. This was the wall. The earth sank down, dropped, because they had not filled in the graves. Pits. Two fraternal pits for sixty people."[124]

After Gumilyov was shot, the intelligentsia became scared. Rumors flew around Moscow that Akhmatova had committed suicide, had caught cold at Blok's funeral and died, or had been poisoned. Tsvetayeva found out it was not true, and on August 31 (September 13, New Style), she wrote a long letter to Akhmatova reflecting a new attitude toward her, that of an older sister sharing her grief. "A horrible rumor has been floating around about you recently," she wrote, "which gets worse by the moment. . . . I want you to know that your single friend among the poets turns out to be Mayakovsky, who wanders among the tables at the Poets' Café with the look of a slaughtered bull. He is dying of grief." There was even an evening held in memory of Akhmatova in Simferopol on October 28, with a lecture by the scholar N. K. Gudzy, and a recitation of poems spoken and set to music.[125]

Akhmatova's first collection of poetry to be published after the Revolution was *Plantain (Podorozhnik,* 1921). It was literally a small book, six by three inches,

and contained poems written mainly from 1917 to 1919. (*Plantain* was later incorporated into *Anno Domini MCMXXI*.)

One of the dominant themes of the collection is that of Russia itself. In the
summer of 1917 in Slepnyovo, Akhmatova had composed a series of bitter poems
about a man leaving his homeland and his beloved. In one of her most famous
poems, "You are an apostate . . . ," she attacks a man who has left his country
(probably alluding to Boris Anrep), and uses details with profound emotional
associations for all Russians—the beauty of folk songs, the icons that are both
religious and aesthetic, and nature exemplified by pine trees and quiet lakes. The
poem is about the religious sentiments of a believer who warns that the "apostate"
will lose his soul, that he has forfeited grace, for to destroy ties with one's native
land is a mortal sin. The "green island" is England which, according to the
apostate, is "more civilized." But for Akhmatova it was also godless, and would
never bring real peace to the "Orthodox soul."

> You are an apostate: for a green island
> You betrayed, betrayed your native land,
> Our songs and our icons
> And the pine above the quiet lake.
>
> Why, dashing man of Yaroslavl,
> Unless you've been deprived of reason,
> Are you lost in admiration
> For red-haired beauties and those splendid houses?
>
> So now, blaspheme and swagger,
> Destroy your Orthodox soul,
> Stay in the city of royalty
> And rejoice that you are free.
>
> Why do you appear and groan
> Under my high window?
> You know yourself that even in the sea you won't drown,
> And from mortal combat you'll emerge unharmed.
>
> Yes, neither battles nor the sea terrify
> One who has forfeited grace.
> Because of that you beg to be
> Remembered when we pray.

(I, p. 497)

In an earlier poem, "Like the angel . . ." (February 1916), she also refers to
Anrep, one of several that depict the range of emotions she felt for him over the
course of their relationship. The speaker recalls a ring she has given her friend
as a token of her love, and in thanks for the strength and freedom he bestowed

upon her; but that love is now only a remembrance. In "When he finally hears the news . . ." (1917), she projects her death and reproaches her friend over how he has broken his promise "to look after his friend from the east." "All week I don't say a word . . . ," written in Sebastopol in the autumn of 1916, plays with the idea of expectation. Here a ring is given to the poet by her friend, not to remember him by, or to remember their joy together, but to protect her from love, implying that love in the end brings only grief.

Akhmatova's most damning poem against those who discredited Russia is "When in suicidal anguish"—known for years in Soviet editions as "A voice came to me . . . ," since the first eight lines, in which Russia is compared to a drunken prostitute, were not allowed to be printed. Although dated autumn 1917, the poem was published on April 12, 1918, in *Volya naroda* (the first lines were only first published in the Soviet Union in 1967). Possibly, as in other poems, Akhmatova has given a false date to make it difficult to relate this work to particular events or persons she had in mind. The first lines may refer to the Brest-Litovsk Treaty of March 1918, in which the Bolsheviks capitulated to the Germans. Roman Timenchik suggests that the image of the city as a whore came from Isaiah 1:21: "How is the faithful city become an harlot, she that was full of justice!"[126] Though the speaker is tempted by the voice calling her to leave her suffering country, she remains, not realizing that the horrors she now faces are small in comparison to those she and her companions will have to endure in the future.

> When in suicidal anguish
> The nation awaited its German guests,
> And the stern spirit of Byzantium
> Had fled from the Russian Church,
> When the capital by the Neva,
> Forgetting her greatness,
> Like a drunken prostitute
> Did not know who would take her next,
> A voice came to me. It called out comfortingly,
> It said, "Come here,
> Leave your deaf and sinful land,
> Leave Russia forever.
> I will wash the blood from your hands,
> Root out the black shame from your heart,
> With a new name I will conceal
> The pain of defeats and injuries."
> But calmly and indifferently,
> I covered my ears with my hands,
> So that my sorrowing spirit
> Would not be stained by those shameful words.

(I, p. 529)

Other poems show how the country itself was affected by the Revolution. "And here, left alone . . ." (1917) marks a radical departure from Akhmatova's earlier poems on Tsarskoye Selo. No longer does she portray the elegance of Tsarskoye—her peaceful life there is only a memory. Her solitude contrasts with a time when Tsarskoye was alive with her family and friends. Swans, emblematic of Tsarskoye, now appear as dead or disfigured. One has become a black crow, symbolic of evil in Russian folklore. The poet comes not to rejoice in Tsarskoye's beauty and festivity, but to contemplate the past. The gentle calm associated with the place has become the stillness of death.[127]

Several poems relate to Slepnyovo, which was virtually oblivious to the cataclysmic events that transformed the rest of Russia. In "The river flows . . . ," the inhabitants are totally unaware of what is transpiring during the summer of 1917 between the February and October revolutions. They live in the past, "as in Catherine's days," attending prayer service, awaiting the harvest, and carrying on their love affairs. But that same summer Akhmatova wrote another poem, "And all day . . . ," which reflects a dramatic turn in her perception of what was happening. She does not relate specific events, but evokes the atmosphere of horror and doom hanging over the country:

> And all day, terrified by its own moans,
> The crowd churns in agonized grief.
> And across the river, on funeral banners,
> Sinister skulls laugh.
> And this is why I sang and dreamed,
> They have ripped my heart in half,
> As after a burst of shots, it became still,
> And in the courtyards, death patrols.
>
> (I, p. 529)

In one of Akhmatova's most beautiful nature poems, "I am listening to the orioles' ever mournful voice," written that same summer at Slepnyovo, she conjures up nature's songs of imminent death—the voice of the orioles is mournful, summer is in decline, and although the vision of the slender reapers is quite lovely, still the premonition of inevitable darkness hangs in the air. She beckons her partner to come with her to gaze at this paradise, "where together/We were innocent and blessed," before the end to this peaceful idyll finally arrives.

> I am listening to the orioles' ever mournful voice,
> And saluting the splendid summer's decline
> And through grain pressed tightly, ear to ear,
> The sickle, with its snake's hiss, slices.

And the short skirts of the slender reapers
Fly in the wind, like flags on a holiday.
The jingling of bells would be jolly now,
And through dusty lashes, a long, slow gaze.

It's not caresses I await, nor lover's adulation,
The premonition of inevitable darkness,
But come with me to gaze at paradise, where together
We were innocent and blessed.

(I, p. 513)

Boris Eikhenbaum, who would soon write one of the first important books on Akhmatova, said of *Plantain*:

> The new collection . . . is an unexpected spring gift. We haven't heard her voice since *White Flock* in 1919. A voice sometimes prayerful and severe, other times folkloric and hysterical. There is no need to look for new paths for her—she can and must develop what she has already found. The poetry of Akhmatova is a lyrical novel. We follow the development of narrative lines, we can speak about the composition, the way individual characters are related. In *Rosary* the material was arranged like chapters. *Plantain* is a new chapter of this novel. It is not simply a collection of lyric novellas but a novel with parallel and interweaving lines, with digressions and consistent characters.[128]

Her next volume of poetry, *Anno Domini MCMXXI*, which appeared in 1922, contained poems relating to the changes in her life in 1921. Arthur Lourie, who was living with Olga Sudeikina, was so upset watching Akhmatova, sick and hungry, working in the library of the Agronomy Institute, that he said if she did not quit he would create a scandal. Although she continued to work there until February 1922, Akhmatova did move in with him and Olga in the autumn of 1921. They had a maid who slept with an ax under her pillow, and in spite of the Revolution, still must have adored the monarchy, since under her mattress lay a copy of *Three Hundred Years of the House of the Romanovs*. Akhmatova was back now on the beautiful Fontanka River, for the address was 18, Fontanka, near Nevsky Avenue. She stayed there until February 1923.[129]

On December 24, 1921, Chukovsky visited Akhmatova in this apartment, where she had a small room with a large bed and a table.

> We talked for a long time. The old female servant came in and said there was no wood for tomorrow. "Never mind," said Akhmatova. "Tomorrow I'll bring a saw and we'll saw together." She put down some large pieces of paper on the table. "This is the ballet *Snow Mask* based on Blok.

Please pay attention to the style. I don't know how to write prose," and she began to read her libretto to me, which was like a beautiful, elegant commentary to *Snow Mask*. She was writing for Arthur Lourie. "Perhaps Diaghilev will produce it in Paris." Then she began to read me her poems, and when she read the one about Blok (about his death in 1921) I began to sob and ran out.[130]

The artist Yury Annenkov, who did several memorable portraits of Akhmatova before emigrating to Paris, recounts a lighter side. After an evening at a poetry reading in late autumn, he accompanied Sudeikina home. It was raining, and Olga suggested he sleep on the couch, since he had no umbrella. In the morning, Akhmatova knocked and came in wearing a dark dress and striped apron, carrying a tray with cups, tea, and black bread. "I've brought the children something to eat," she smiled. "What could have been more humble or comfortable than this scene," Annenkov writes. "I must admit the tea and sugar that day tasted better than the most elegant dish somewhere at the Tour d'Argent or Maxim's."[131]

In his diary Chukovsky noted that he visited Akhmatova and Shileiko on January 19, 1920. He says their room was damp and cold, and books were lying all over the floor. "She is tender toward Shileiko," he remarked. "With pride she tells me how he translates poems." Akhmatova impressed Chukovsky with her vast knowledge of Pushkin; she knew his poems by heart, as well as details of his biography, his letters, variants of his texts. She had already begun the research that would provide the insights of one great poet into another. However, there was a second side to the Akhmatova of that period, a side she would soon abandon. "Today she is like a woman of the world, speaking about the latest fashion in Europe and how Russia was behind."[132]

In March, Chukovsky saw her again and noted someone had brought her some dresses. For days the publisher Grzhebin had been phoning Blok, bragging that "I bought Akhmatova," which meant she had given him some poems. Chukovsky told the story behind this. Someone had brought her some dresses to look at that she really wanted, dresses she had been dreaming about for a long time, and she immediately went to see Grzhebin and sold him a book of poetry for a good sum.[133]

Not only did Akhmatova have to watch her beloved Petersburg undergo a slow death, but Tsarskoye Selo also changed drastically. She describes what it was like—all the fences had burnt down, streets were overgrown with grass, roosters of all colors, and goats—for some reason all named Tamara—strolled the streets, bleating. "Shirokaya Street smelled just as strongly of the oaks in autumn, the witness of my childhood, and the crows on church crosses cawed the same way as I had heard them when I walked across Cathedral Square to the gymnasium, and the statues in the park looked as they had in the 1910s. In the horrible, ragged figures passing by, I sometimes recognized residents of Tsarskoye Selo."[134]

After her secluded life with Shileiko, Akhmatova now began appearing at literary evenings, maintaining her popularity, even among members of the new generation. A journalist in Riga reported one such evening in November 1921 at the House of Writers: "And this entire human mass nervously, excitedly, and I would say respectfully restrained, muttered—impatiently awaiting the entrance of the poetess. The public consisted mainly of young people."[135]

A former member of her literary circle before the Revolution, Mikhail Zenkevich, visited Akhmatova at this time in the library, sharing the grief of her losses: "Anna Akhmatova worked as a librarian in the Agronomy Institute (they intend to keep her as a treasure of the state). . . . It was a small, cold room. There was a cluster of people—evidently librarians. I asked where I could find Anna Akhmatova. Suddenly a tall woman came over out of the gloomy group of librarians, and with a smile, gave me her hand—Anna Akhmatova." He describes how a young woman heated the fireplace for Akhmatova and brought some cocoa, as others later would do things for her because they loved her poems. They both sat in their coats, their breath steaming. She said: "I've been living among the dead for the past few months. Kolya [Nikolay Gumilyov] died, my brother died, and Blok. I don't know how much more I can bear." Zenkevich said he had heard a rumor that she wanted to go abroad. "And what will I do there? They have all gone out of their minds there and don't understand anything."

They spoke of Gumilyov. "It was so unexpected," she said. "He was so remote from politics. But he continued to maintain contacts with his old friends in the army, and they might have dragged him into some kind of plot. . . . But let's read some poetry. I'll read some poems about Blok's death. [Arthur] Lourie has written music to them and one will soon be performed at an evening in memory of Blok." And against the white wall appeared the sharply chiseled, severe, Dantean profile of Akhmatova. While she read, fragments of memories rose up before Zenkevich. He recalled how when Gumilyov was in Abyssinia, Akhmatova had read her poems at the offices of *Apollon,* and how Ivanov in a fatherly way took her to task. He recalled the Smolensk Cemetery and saw Akhmatova rise up after falling in tears on the grave of Blok after the funeral. The flame in the fireplace died out, the cups of cocoa turned cold, it was twilight outside. Time to go. He kissed her hand. How she had matured, he thought to himself. Instead of her former feminine vanity, she now reflected a kind of calm wisdom. No matter how much critics attempted to vulgarize her, she still remained Anna Akhmatova.[136]

Ida Nappelbaum remembers when Akhmatova was living with Olga and Lourie and would come to the Monday literary evenings at her father's apartment, sometimes appearing with an escort—Lozinsky or Nikolay Punin—but most often attended by the composer Arthur Lourie. They would come not only to the "Mondays," but also to visit the Nappelbaum family. Sometimes Akhmatova would arrive with Sudeikina. "The two women complemented each other beautifully! At this time Olga was making dolls for a marionette theater—they were of colored silk with embroidered hair. She also made porcelain statuettes of elegant dancers." Nikolay Punin had become head of the Imperial Porcelain Factory and was commissioning Olga to make the statuettes. Ida remembers how Akhmatova and Olga loved these dolls, and created roles for them, brought them to the studio and even had them photographed. Ida said Sudeikina herself was like a living doll, sweet and tender.[137]

At this time the population was still living on rations. Khodasevich tells of another incident in the spring of 1922. Once a week he went with a burlap bag to Millionnaya Street to the House of Scholars for his writer's ration. The most famous scholars and writers could be seen in these lines. Sometimes certain items such as butter and sugar were not given out for several weeks and something else was substituted. Once herring arrived instead, and they had to sell it so they could use the money to buy butter. Two days after this, he set out for the marketplace. He chose a good spot, put his bag of herring down, and waited for customers, thinking he must shout something like: "Here now! Dutch herring! Here they are!" but he just could not make himself do it. "People kept passing by without stopping. Looking off to the side in total despair about twenty steps from me, I saw a tall, elegant woman also standing in front of the same kind of bag. It was Anna Akhmatova. I was just about to ask her if we could sell together so it would not be so boring, but then a customer came up, and another and a third—and soon I sold everything I had. My herring turned out to be first class. . . . After I sold everything, I bought some butter and no longer found Akhmatova at the former spot and went home."[138]

Velemir Khlebnikov also came to visit Olga's. In a delightful memoir, Lourie describes him as one of the only three adults who qualify as "Children of Paradise," the other two being Gérard de Nerval, the nineteenth-century French Romantic poet, and Mandelstam. "All three were madmen. Mandelstam was the most normal of these eccentrics, and it was only when he was in touch with poetry that he fell into the exalted category of holy madness."[139]

Khlebnikov had spent part of the war with his family in Astrakhan, then was drafted into the army, which he detested. He was in Petrograd to witness the October Revolution, then traveled extensively, to the Ukraine and Caucasus, and spent time in hospitals, suffering from typhus and nervous disorders. In 1921 he accompanied the Red Army as a journalist to Iran. It was during the most difficult period of the Civil War, however, that he produced prophetic visions of a technological future. He went with his friend, the artist Peter Miturich, to Novgorod province, where, weakened by malnutrition and bouts with typhus and malaria, he died on June 28, 1922.

Khlebnikov was hopelessly in love with Olga, but never revealed it. Olga, who understood his poems and loved them, was very sweet to Khlebnikov and sometimes invited him to tea. In Lourie's words:

This Petersburg fairy doll, dressed in a luxurious floating light blue silk gown, sat at a table set with old porcelain, smiled and poured tea. I remember all the magnificence of his [Khlebnikov's] sacred poverty; he was dressed in a long frock coat, probably someone else's, with short sleeves, his slender, ascetic arms protruding. He did not wear cuffs. He sat sullen as an owl, serious and stern, drinking the tea silently with the pastry and only rarely dropping a word. He had achieved a certain high degree of madness. There is no egocentricity in people like this. It is a very Russian feature, which is a manifestation of purity and spiritual freedom. . . . He actually could be very decisive, sarcastic, but always only on the level of ideas, when talking about creative things, not in ordinary, everyday matters. . . . In his writings, there was also a certain childlikeness and genuine, profound purity. He was magnificent and solemn, as if he were celebrating the ritual of life and poetry.[140]

Khlebnikov had written a poem to Akhmatova in 1921 that shows the depth of his despair:

And while over Tsarskoye Selo
The foam and tears of Akhmatova were pouring
I, the hammer of the enchantress uncoiling,
Like a sleepy corpse, dragged myself through the desert,
Where impossibility, a tired actor,
Was dying,
Stopping at nothing.[141]

He captures the plight of social planners attempting to make the dreams of a Utopia come true in the midst of hunger and starvation:

Hunger herded humanity.
Men, women, children,
fill the ravine
rushing to find the holy dirt
that substitutes for bread.
Dirt, our silent saviour
beneath the roots of age-old pines.
And at that very moment scientists' minds
were striving toward other worlds,
seeking to fashion a dream of life
out of earths made fertilized by thought.[142]

The famine finally caught up with Khlebnikov himself when he was traveling. This gentle creature, this brilliant "holy fool," beloved by so many, died of malnutrition and disease.

Lourie had been active as the Commissar of Music from 1918 to 1920; he organized concerts, established a network of music schools, created an orchestra that eventually became the Leningrad Philharmonic and a choral academy. He also wrote popular brochures on music and was involved in music publishing, including the works of Prokofiev. Leonid Sabaneyev, the music critic, admired Lourie for his organizing abilities, saying he was "an advocate of extreme directions in music [and] facilitated a fresh and bold enlightened spirit of reality. In spite of the terrible cold in the concert halls, in spite of the need and hunger of musicians, nevertheless by some miracle musical performances blossomed, concerts were numerous and huge audiences attended." Monumental works from both the past and present, which were difficult to understand, were performed. Lourie's hope was to transform the masses through music. However, he was having increasing problems carrying out his work, and in 1921 he was relieved of his position; he became a member of the faculty of the Petrograd Institute of the History of Arts, which included prominent musicologists. In 1922, Lourie left Russia, perhaps because he thought he would be more successful abroad, perhaps because of material difficulties. He supposedly was on a business trip to Berlin, but after a short stay there, he went on to Wiesbaden, then settled in Paris. In 1941, he went to the United States.

On August 17, 1922, Arthur Lourie left on the same boat as Boris Pasternak and his wife, who were also on their way to Berlin. The Pasternaks had visited with Akhmatova and Lourie in Petrograd the week before they left. Yevgenya Pasternak said she would always remember how surprised she was when she spotted Akhmatova's profile in the crowd as she came to say farewell to Lourie.[143]

Some of Akhmatova's most beautiful love poems were written to Lourie. In December 1921, she wrote:

Why do you wander restlessly?
Why do you stare breathlessly?
Surely you comprehend: our two souls
Have been firmly welded into one.

You will be, you will be comforted by me
In a way no one could dream,
And when you wound with an angry word—
You yourself will feel the pain.

(I, p. 555)

Akhmatova was clearly upset when Lourie left, although she told Luknitsky she took it calmly. In fact, she used her restraint as a weapon to infuriate Lourie. "It was my calmness that finished him. . . . When he left . . . it became easy! . . . I walked around with the lightness of a song . . . he wrote fourteen letters and I did not answer a single one."[144] The sentiments expressed in the poem "Separation," dated August 1921, contradict Akhmatova's assertion of "calm." As so often in her life, the outward calm was a facade, an armor hiding the deep pain that she preferred to reveal only in her poetry. She compares her torment at Lourie's leaving to the Passion of Christ:

> I accept separation as a gift,
> And oblivion as a blessing.
> But tell me, would you dare send someone else
> On this way of the Cross?
>
> (I, p. 589)[145]

Apparently Akhmatova remembered this incident wrongly, for the poem was written and published in 1921. It is a good example of how one "creates one's own biography," remembering an episode in an even more dramatic manner than the way it actually occurred.

Akhmatova had other losses to bear in 1922 as well. Her sister Iya died that year of tuberculosis. Her mother was living with her sister (Akhmatova's aunt) Anna Vakar, on a pension given by the tsarist government after Akhmatova's father died, but it was taken away by the Bolshevik government. Whenever Akhmatova had any money, as when she got paid for *White Flock,* she sent some off. Akhmatova's brother Viktor by this time knew he had no future in the Black Sea Fleet after the Bolsheviks took over, and remembering his grandfather, who had made a good living selling furs in Siberia, he went to the island of Sakhalin, where murderers and robbers had been exiled. He said as a twenty-year-old he had a choice between the Cheka, the Soviet secret police, or Sakhalin bandits. He finally made some money and sent for his mother in 1925.[146]

Chukovsky visited Akhmatova at Olga's on December 15, 1922, and recounted in his diary the disparity between her fame and her surroundings. Apparently she was now making small talk rather than engaging in intellectual conversation. He believed this was a facade she had adopted to protect herself from the increasing pain she was encountering.

She was not at home when he arrived, but she soon came in with Punin. Chukovsky describes her surroundings: "Small rooms, a corridor through the kitchen. . . . Who would have said this is that same Anna Akhmatova who— alone in Russian literature—replaced Gorky, Lev Tolstoy, and Leonid Andreyev . . . about whom dozens of articles and books have been written. . . . Behind all these glances you still feel the genuine Akhmatova, for whom it appears awkward to be herself with people, and because she is shy, she has adopted a trivial facade involuntarily, but it is only a shield in order to remain inviolable."[147]

In 1922, Akhmatova's popularity was at its height, perhaps second only to Blok's. Chukovsky noted: "If you sit down three or four times in a bookstore you will see customers coming in and asking, 'Is there any Blok?' 'No.' 'And the "Twelve"?' 'No!' 'Well, then, give me Anna Akhmatova.' "[148]

That year Akhmatova published the large collection of her works entitled *Anno Domini MCMXXI (In the Year of Our Lord 1921).* With a few exceptions, all her new poems were written in 1921, a very productive year for Akhmatova.

Many of these poems refer to her husbands, Gumilyov and Shileiko. Gumilyov's death was shattering to Akhmatova, and she grieved for many years. She somehow felt responsible for his death—even guilty. In "That August was like . . ." (1915), she portrays the two of them as "a soldier and a maid." The change in the life of the capital becomes a metaphor for the change in their own lives.

. . .

What had happened to the capital?
Who had lowered the sun to the earth?
The black eagle on its standard
Seemed like a bird in flight.

This city of splendid vistas
Began to resemble a savage camp,
The eyes of the strollers were dazzled
By the glint of bayonet and lance.
(I, p. 607)

Like her other poems about the war, the tragedy is internalized as her own pain, which in turn gives voice to the grief and sorrow of others. The image she uses is a simple domestic one. The soldier tells the maid:

Now you alone must preserve
Our sorrows and our joys.
It was as if he were leaving the keys
With the housekeeper of his country house.
(I, p. 607)

Those keys were her songs, her poems, and she observed the war through her own eyes, immortalizing the suffering of the soldiers and the people waiting for them to return.

In "The voice of another . . ." (December 1921), the first of a two-poem cycle, the speaker is a dead husband or lover addressing the poet from beyond. While he apologizes for leaving her behind to suffer, one detail reveals that their relationship was not a happy one, for she praises his bitter name. In the second poem, "In that year . . . ," also with a male persona as speaker, the woman reveals that not only did she make their relationship difficult by her infidelity, but she asked her lover for impossible promises. He says to her:

But the hour came for you to stare
Into green eyes, to beg those cruel lips
In vain for the sweetest gift

And for promises such as you'd never heard,
Such as no one had ever uttered.

(I, p. 543)

The poem is a rare example of Akhmatova's use of a Homeric simile: the simile becomes a story in itself—those promises the poet sought which poisoned the speaker's life because he could not fulfill them are compared to someone poisoning a desert spring. Another person coming later would himself get lost, and in the dark would return to this same spring and drink of death.

In an earlier poem written on August 27/28, 1921, right after Gumilyov's execution, Akhmatova personifies the abstract feeling of terror, which leads "the moonbeam to an ax." Akhmatova accumulates details, each of which by itself is not ominous, but together they create the awareness of some indefinable horror lurking. It would be better to be executed by rifle or hung on the scaffold than to have to endure the psychological terror of fear, imminent death, or the pain of someone you love dying. Elsewhere Akhmatova noted that the poem was actually written on the night of August 25, 1921, and that the line about the odor of decay being sickeningly sweet was written in connection with Blok's funeral. Timenchik suggests that the "things in the dark" are Olga's things in the apartment in which she and Akhmatova were living.[149]

Terror, fingering things in the dark,
Leads the moonbeam to an ax.
Behind the wall there's an ominous knock—
What's there, a ghost, a thief, rats?

In the sweltering kitchen, water drips,
Counting the rickety floorboards.
Someone with a glossy black beard
Flashes by the attic window—

And becomes still. How cunning he is and evil,
He hid the matches and blew out the candle.
How much better would be the gleam of the barrels
Of rifles leveled at my breast.

Better, in the grassy square,
To be flattened on the raw wood scaffold
And, amid cries of joy and moans,
Pour out my life's blood there.

I press the smooth cross to my heart:
Go, restore peace to my soul.
The odor of decay, sickeningly sweet,
Rises from clammy sheets.

(I, p. 585)

Although "You are no longer among the living" is dated August 16, 1921, Akhmatova may have purposely dated it before Gumilyov's death, not wishing to call the censor's attention to it. Even so, it is surprising the censor allowed it to be printed.

You are no longer among the living,
You cannot rise from the snow.
Twenty-eight bayonets,
Five bullets.

A bitter new shirt
For my beloved I sewed.
The Russian earth loves, loves
Droplets of blood.

(I, p. 595)

The most poignant of Akhmatova's poems on the theme of Gumilyov's death is "The tear-stained autumn . . ." (September 15, 1921). Here she draws a parallel between nature and the human condition. What is unique about the poem is that instead of the human state being compared to nature, it is the other way around: autumn is compared to a widow in black weeds. Those who know the background of the poem, however, are powerfully touched by the widow's grief.[150]

The tear-stained autumn, like a widow
In black weeds, clouds every heart . . .
Recalling her husband's words,
She sobs without ceasing.
And thus it will be, until the most quiet snow
Takes pity on the sorrowful and weary one . . .
Oblivion of pain and oblivion of bliss—
To give up life for this is no small thing.

(I, p. 603)

A poem about the ancient cathedral of St. Sophia in Kiev opens the section entitled "The Voice of Memory."[151] Akhmatova wrote it on September 15, 1921, soon after she heard that Gumilyov had been executed. Like her predecessors in Russian history, now that Akhmatova was beginning to write on politically sensitive issues, she was learning to use *tainopis* or "secret writing," pretending to discuss one thing while really referring to something that was politically untouchable. It was a favorite device of Pushkin's, which Akhmatova later discussed in her essays on him. Here she speaks of the tolling of the "bell of Mazepa," thundering inexorably as if heretics were being executed. Mazepa was the fearless Ukrainian leader who fought for freedom against the state when battling Peter the Great for Ukrainian independence. The mention of Mazepa may therefore be a covert allusion to Gumilyov's problem with the authorities; the reference to the execution of heretics reinforces this impression.

> The gates are thrown wide open,
> The lindens are naked beggars,
> And there is dark dried gilding
> On the impregnable, concave wall.
>
> The altars and crypts are rumbling,
> And beyond the Dnieper the wide sound rolls.
> Thus the heavy bell of Mazepa
> Over Sophia Square tolls.
>
> Ever more dreadful it thunders, inexorable,
> As if they were executing heretics here,
> And in the woods across the river, mollified,
> It amuses the fluffy young foxes.

On May 8, 1922 (April 25, Old Style), the anniversary of her marriage to Gumilyov, Akhmatova wrote "Prophecy," referring to the "crown of hammered gold" that is worn by bride and groom in a Russian Orthodox ceremony. But her crown is like a crown of thorns, and the dew that will refresh her brow is of blood.

> I saw that crown of hammered gold . . .
> Don't envy such a crown!
> Because it is stolen
> And it wouldn't become you.
> Like a twisted branch of blackthorn,
> My crown will begin to glow on you.
> Never mind that it refreshes
> The delicate brow with crimson dew.
>
> (I, p. 541)

Shileiko is the subject of another group of poems, the cycle called *Dark Dreams,* where Akhmatova expresses her frustrations with their relationship. It opens with a poem written in 1913, when they and their bohemian crowd attended the Stray Dog cabaret. Tamara Shileiko, his daughter-in-law, has suggested that Akhmatova's poem "Praising me inarticulately . . ." was a response to a poem written by Shileiko to Akhmatova that same year. (Like others at the time, Shileiko noted the prophetic and otherworldly aura that set her off from ordinary people.)

. . .
You ascend again
The penitential steps
To unbind before the heart of God
Burdens of imaginary crimes.

Your closed eyes
Are carried away beyond the earthly sphere,
And on your lips burns the thunder
Of words not yet found.

And for a long time you speak slowly, dead . . .
But in prophetic light, in the light smoke
Words numbed with cold
Again come alive—

But barely breathing I hear
How the trembling in your heart increases,
How the soul on soft wings
Flies into this world.[152]

In the five poems that follow in this cycle, the poet has no kind words for her husband; she portrays him as a dragon who forbids her to sing, who wants no children with her, and does not like her poetry. It has been suggested that the last poem is about Arthur Lourie, who asked her to come live with him and Olga Sudeikina. This interpretation seems accurate, since she says her husband's home is a prison and thanks the addressee for letting "this pilgrim" into his home.[153] If this is indeed the case, the poet is asserting that she is not about to enter into another relationship that will bring her pain. She will no longer be submissive, and if she comes to him, it will be of her own accord.

Submissive to you? You're out of your mind!
I submit only to the will of the Lord.
I want neither thrills nor pain,
My husband—is a hangman, and his home—prison.

Well, look here! I came of my own accord . . .
It was already December, the winds were abroad,
And it was so bright in your bondage,
But outside the window, darkness stood guard.

Thus in the wintry blast, a bird
Beats its whole body against the clear glass,
And blood stains its white wing.

Now I have peace and good fortune.
Goodbye, you are dear to me forever, gentle one,
Because you let this pilgrim into your home.

(I, p. 553)

The other poems in the cycle refer to the period when Akhmatova and Shileiko lived together. Cold, famine, and war increased the tensions that developed between them as the years wore on. In "You are always novel and mysterious . . ." (1917), the poet accuses her spouse of smothering her voice, for she can no longer pray or sing. If the dating is correct, it is unclear why this poem was included in the cycle, since Akhmatova did not marry Shileiko until the autumn of 1918, and no biographical data indicates any prior intimacy between them. Later, Akhmatova included the poem "Third Zachatevsky Street" (1940) because it also is associated with Shileiko. It refers to the street in Moscow where they lived briefly before moving to Petrograd. Images associated with decay and grief—a vacant lot, groans at night, a rotting lamppost—reinforce the mood established by the opening simile, which compares the street to a noose around the lover's neck. It is the atmosphere she remembers in the apartment during that difficult period.

The short cycle titled *Biblical Verses* consists of the earliest of the lyrical portraits Akhmatova created at various points in her career. The first, "Rachel," recounts the story of Jacob's hardship in winning Rachel for his bride. The second, "Lot's Wife" (1924), was added later to *Anno Domini*, as was "Michal" (1959–61), when the book was included in *Flight of Time (Beg vremeni)*. The poem on Lot's wife is one of Akhmatova's most famous, and has been cited by critics as an example of how she expressed through allusion to history and myth what she herself cannot say openly. Knowing it is a sin to look back, Lot's wife perishes as she glances back at what is dear to her—simple things such as the square where she sang, the courtyard where she spun, the tall house where she bore children. Similarly, Akhmatova knew when she wrote the poem in 1924 how many simple things that she had taken for granted were now lost forever in the new Soviet world in which she was living.[154]

During this period harsh critics, including friends of her youth such as Kuzmin, were beginning to dismiss Akhmatova as an anachronism, a relic of the past. "Slander" (1922), written in direct reaction to this negative criticism, depicts Slander as an allegorical figure pursuing the poet. (By 1925, Akhmatova was no longer allowed to publish.) In the poem, she says all will hear the shameful ravings of Slander:

And her shameful raving will reach everyone,
So that neighbors will avoid each other's eyes,
So that my body will be abandoned in a terrible void.

(I, p. 601)

As in other poems touching on political events, Akhmatova's poems at this time about the Revolution do not mention it directly. Instead, she speaks of grief and devastation taking over the land. "Everything has been plundered . . ." (June 1921) is reminiscent of Blok's famous poem "The Twelve." While now all one sees is chaos and ruin, there is a belief in the future, an intuitive feeling that this stage of great suffering will lead to a glorious dawn, symbolized in Blok's work by Christ and in Akhmatova's by "the miraculous," which is drawing near.

> Everything has been plundered, betrayed, sold out,
> The wing of black death has flashed,
> Everything has been devoured by starving anguish,
> Why, then, is it so bright?
>
> The fantastic woods near the town
> Waft the scent of cherry blossoms by day,
> At night new constellations shine
> In the transparent depth of the skies of July—
>
> And how near the miraculous draws
> To the dirty, tumbledown huts . . .
> No one, no one knows what it is,
> But for centuries we have longed for it.
>
> (I, p. 579)

In "Lamentation" (May 1922), Akhmatova treats another consequence of the Revolution, the removal of church relics, icons, and vestments in 1922. Leaning on crutches, the saints leave their icon frames, and wrapping her son in a shawl, the Mother of God, the Madonna herself, drops down by an old beggar woman on the front steps of the church.

Memory now begins to take on the role of a major theme in Akhmatova's works. Earlier primarily a private domain, filled with happy or unhappy personal experiences with friends or lovers, memory now for Akhmatova is replete with the tragic deaths of those she loved and admired, with visions of war and revolution, with the smell of blood and corpses rotting. She does not want to remember, she wants to "slam the terrible door" to her memory; but, as her works will show, memory for Akhmatova has become a moral imperative, and it is a sin to forget.

December 1921 was the first Christmas Akhmatova spent in Bezhetsk without Gumilyov. At first glance everything seemed to be the same; but it was an illusion:

Bezhetsk

> There are white churches there, and booming, luminous ice.
> There the cornflower blue eyes of my dear son are blooming.
> Over the ancient town are Russia's diamond nights,

And the sickle of the skies, yellower than the linden's honey.
There blizzards soar from the fields beyond the river,
And the people, like angels rejoicing in God's feast day,
Put the front room in order and lit the lamps in the icon corner,
And on the oaken table the Good Book lay.
There stern memory, so miserly now,
Opened her tower rooms to me with a deep bow;
But I didn't enter, I slammed the terrible door,
And the town was full of merry Christmas sounds.

(I, p. 541)

In July 1922, Akhmatova wrote one of her most famous poems, "I am not with those . . ." Once again she turns to the theme of the tensions between those dear to her who abandoned Russia, like Anrep and Lourie, and those who chose to stay, such as herself. In the 1960s, at the end of both their lives, Lourie wrote Akhmatova after he had left Paris for America that she was right, "foreign bread smells like wormwood."[155]

I am not with those who abandoned their land
To the lacerations of the enemy.
I am deaf to their coarse flattery,
I won't give them my songs.

But to me the exile is forever pitiful,
Like a prisoner, like someone ill.
Dark is your road, wanderer,
Like wormwood smells the bread of strangers.

But here, in the blinding smoke of the conflagration
Destroying what's left of youth,
We have not deflected from ourselves
One single stroke.

And we know that in the final accounting,
Each hour will be justified . . .
But there is no people on earth more tearless
More simple and more full of pride.

(I, p. 547)

Akhmatova was "not with those who abandoned their land," and in another memorable poem, "To the Many," she proudly declared to her people, "I—am your voice." Now she was not only a prophetess who foretold suffering, but a poet of the spiritual; not only a mystic seer like the Symbolist priest, but an artist willing to take on the suffering of others.

The Great Experiment: 1922–1930

The chamber intimacy of Anna Akhmatova, the mystical verses of Vyacheslav Ivanov and his Hellenic motif—what meaning do they have for our harsh, iron age?
   —MAYAKOVSKY, 1922

The early years of the Soviet regime have been called the "Great Experiment." Early in the decade the avant-garde was given free rein to explore new themes and techniques in the world of the arts, as long as the subject matter in some way supported the new Soviet State. The Bolsheviks had consolidated their power and achieved a stable form of government under the New Economic Policy: private business on a small scale was allowed, the stores were again filled with goods, speculators and the black market flourished, and there was an utter fascination with so-called Western decadent bourgeois culture, including jazz, flapper dresses, and whiskey. Akhmatova continued to be popular in the early 1920s, when Eisenstein was producing his first works that changed film history, and Meyerhold had been transformed from an elegant aesthete into a radical theater director, dressed in a leather jacket and worker's cap.

However, in 1924, Lenin died. Petrograd became Leningrad, and Stalin started his bid for power. As the decade progressed and Stalin consolidated his position, it became increasingly difficult for artists like Akhmatova, who had been popular before the Revolution, to find a place in the new Soviet State. Even while there was still some freedom in the arts, at the very beginning under Lenin suppression of thought, arrests, exile, and executions were common.[1] In 1922, the philosopher Nikolay Berdyaev was arrested, along with over a hundred other intellectuals. As a former Marxist, Berdyaev knew the doctrine well, and he was now struggling against the oppression of the individual will, of one's "inner freedom." He believed social equality could be achieved only by one's own individual desire to help one's fellow man, not by the imposition of an outside political force. In his autobiography, he characterized the basic error of communism as the rejection of the freedom and dignity of the human personality.

> Communism, as it was revealed in the Russian Revolution, rejected freedom, rejected personality, rejected the spirit. It is in this and not in its social system that the demonic evil of Communism can be observed. . . . This does not mean I reject socialism, but my socialism is personal and not authoritarian, and does not allow the dominance of society over the human personality, which arises from the spiritual nature of each person because he is a free spirit; the personality is the image of God. I am not collectivist because I do not allow the exteriorization of the human conscience, transferring it to the collective. . . . The idol of the collective is just as repugnant as the idol of the state, race, and class to which it is connected.[2]

On the eve of Berdyaev's arrest, he and his sister-in-law, E. Y. Rapp, were sent to perform forced labor. Berdyaev was sick with fever but forced to get up at five in the morning. It was freezing cold. The prisoners, the so-called bourgeoisie, all with pale, grim faces and dressed in shabby clothes, gathered together in the gloomy morning air, trembling from the cold. Only the glint of rifles and the shouts of the commander pierced the curtain of darkness. It was reminiscent of Dante's Hell. After everyone arrived, the prisoners were sent outside the city to clear railroad tracks of snow. The men chopped ice with heavy shovels while the women piled it up on wagons. Barely able to stand on his own two legs, Berdyaev kept working without eating all day long, but was given a piece of black bread after work.

After he was allowed to return home, Berdyaev chopped up the oak table and armchair from his mother's estate to heat the oven. And then the horrible knock came—that knock that was later to become one of the most feared and frequent sounds of the 1930s:

> Midnight—a horrible knock. Soldiers from the Cheka. Our rooms were searched. Berdyaev said calmly, "It's no use making a search. I'm a declared opponent of Bolshevism and have never hidden it." This did

not help. The Cheka went through all his papers; the search continued until dawn. He was allowed to take a few warm things, and sick, exhausted, he was forced to go on foot to the prison—to Lubyanka.[3]

In September 1922, Berdyaev and other intellectuals were exiled abroad. He went first to Berlin, then to Paris, where he was to spend the rest of his life—always aware of what was occurring in his homeland, and hoping in vain something would change to make it possible to return and lead a peaceful life there based on spiritual choice rather than external coercion.

The fate of other intellectuals also soon became more difficult. After Mandelstam had initially accepted the Revolution with enthusiasm, in 1921 he questioned the poet's serving the state before humanity in general in a moving essay entitled "Word and Culture":

> Today the State has a unique relationship to culture that is best expressed by the term tolerance. But at the same time a new type of organic intellectual is beginning to appear . . . cultural values ornament the State. . . . Inscriptions on state buildings, tombs, and gateways ensure the State against the ravages of time . . . He [the modern poet] sings of ideas, systems of knowledge and State theories, just as his predecessors sang of nightingales and roses.[4]

Mandelstam developed this idea further—and articulated his own philosophy of the role of poetry in post-Revolutionary Russia—in another essay, "On the Nature of the Word," in which he ascribed social and artistic aims to Acmeism. He cited Bryusov's famous lines about "beyond good and evil" (Nietzsche's concept) as the Symbolist credo that Acmeism had to overcome: "I want my free boat to sail in every direction;/And I shall praise the Lord and Devil equally." Mandelstam found this a form of bankrupt "nihilism" that must never be repeated in Russian poetry. Poetry's social role not only must be to educate citizens of the state, but to address all humanity: "Until now the social inspiration of Russian poetry has reached no further than the idea of 'citizen,' but there is a loftier principle than 'citizen,' there is the concept of 'Man.' As opposed to the civic poetry of the past, modern Russian poetry must educate not merely citizens, but men."[5]

In 1923, Mandelstam published his poem "The Age," damning the new era. As Vladimir Markov remarks, only the nearsightedness of the censor allowed it to be published, perhaps because he did not fully grasp its implications.

> My age, my beast, who will be able
> To look in the pupils of your eyes
> And with his blood glue together
> The vertebrae of two centuries?

Blood-builder gushes
from a throat out of earthly things,
The parasite only trembles
On the threshold of new days.

The creature, while it has enough life
Must carry the backbone to the end
And a wave plays
On the invisible spine.
As though it were a child's tender cartilage—
The age of earth's infancy
Again like a lamb, life's vertex
Has been brought in sacrifice.

In order to tear life from captivity,
In order to start a new world,
The knees of gnarled days
Must be connected by a flute,
This is the age which rocks the wave
With human anxiety,
And in the grass a viper breathes.

And the buds will swell once more,
The verdure of shoots will splash forth,
But your spine has been smashed,
My pretty, pitiful age.
And with a crazed smile
Again you look back, cruel and weak,
Like a beast once supple,
At the tracks of your own paws.[6]

Clearly poetry was taking a precipitous turn in the new Soviet State, as
Anatoly Nayman describes:

> When a poet is universal, like Pushkin, his personal poems acquire the
> right to represent "everyone." . . . The new arrangement—speaking "on
> behalf of the people," "for everyone"—redirected the poet's view, which
> now had to look outward and not inward. . . . [A]ny subject and themes,
> those described as outdated or intimate, and which were therefore
> mocked, became officially taboo. . . . It was not a question of the private
> becoming generalised, in so far as that was feasible; the general had to
> be adopted as one's own, in accordance with a given scheme.[7]

The literary critic Wladimir Weidle met Akhmatova in the 1920s and saw her
often until 1924. He says that she learned to endure everything—the corpses, the

crows, hunger, paupers, the dullness of the new hosts, Blok's fate, Gumilyov's
fate, the profanation of saints, lies everywhere. He said that before his departure
for France, she asked him to look over a Russian gymnasium in Paris and see if
they would accept her son if she decided to emigrate. Weidle said he did not do
it because he did not believe Akhmatova was serious. One after another of her
friends left and tried to persuade her to follow them, but she would not.

> I felt she must stay—her as-yet unborn poems could be born only from
> a life interwoven with others, with all the lives in the country which for
> her continued to be called Russia. She was about thirty-five, often sick,
> thin, living in poverty, dressing modestly. Some old lady had given her
> money, thinking she was a beggar, but she must have been half blind,
> since this "beggar" acted like a queen. Not only her face but her whole
> figure was unique. She always served me a cup of coffee and some dessert,
> and never spoke about herself.[8]

At the beginning of the 1920s, several major critics began to seek an answer
to the question of what path the new literature of the Soviet State should take.
Should it build on the traditions of the past, or, like the Futurists, throw tradition
overboard and attempt to build something totally new? It was inevitable that
Akhmatova would become the center of this controversy.

In February 1922, Chukovsky noted in his diary: "Her fame was at its peak.
The Philosophical Association arranged an evening of her poetry, and editors
from various journals were calling her day and night: 'Please give us something!' "
But on March 26 he visited her and found her very upset. They went into her
narrow room, most of which was occupied by a double bed. It was very cold.
"Have you read the editorial?" She handed him the journal *Novaya Rossiya (New
Russia)*. "It's about me. They're making fun of me!" "Do you have any money
now?" asked Chukovsky. She said she had just received a payment for *White
Flock*. "I was able to sew a dress for myself; I sent Lyovushka [her son Lev]
something and wanted to send something to my mother in the Crimea. I'm very
upset. I know they're in great trouble, but I can't send anything. Mama writes
not to send anything."[9]

In one of the first books written on Akhmatova's poetry (1922), Boris Eikhenbaum addressed the issue of the relevance of her works to the new age:

> Akhmatova's poetry is not the same for the younger generation as it was
> for us. We were puzzled, amazed, ecstatic. They [the new generation]
> were not surprised because they came later. . . . This book [Eikhen-
> baum's] thank God is not a memorial, and we are not grandfathers buried
> in our memories. . . . Will we understand each other? History put the
> revolution's line of fire between us, but perhaps it will fuse us in an
> explosion toward creation. . . . The poetry of the Symbolists has re-

mained behind. . . . Before us on one side are Akhmatova and Mandelstam, on the other the Futurists and the Imagists. The fate of our poetry will be decided in the struggle.[10]

Eikhenbaum's book provides insightful analysis of many aspects of Akhmatova's poetry, but it also contains a concept of the heroine of her poems which was to haunt Eikhenbaum when it was used in the Stalinist attacks against Akhmatova later: "Here already we can see the beginnings of the paradoxical, or more correctly, contradictory, double image of the heroine—half 'harlot' burning with passion, half 'nun' able to pray to God for forgiveness."[11] Surely Eikhenbaum should have understood the difference between the normal passion of a woman who felt life deeply, and the decadent eroticism more typical of the Symbolists, such as Gippius. As the artist Yury Annenkov says of this characterization of Akhmatova's poems, " 'Erotic motives'—I never felt them in the poetry of Akhmatova. Love—yes. About love she has written a lot. But Pushkin also wrote a lot about love."[12]

Korney Chukovsky's 1922 article, "Akhmatova and Mayakovsky," was the definitive statement on the future of Russian poetry. Akhmatova and Mayakovsky, he maintained, represented the two possible routes that Russian poetry could take. He saw glorification of pain as a form of Christian humiliation, and Akhmatova as "the last poet of Orthodoxy. . . . Never mind that Akhmatova sometimes talks about Paris, automobiles, literary cafés, this only lends stronger nuance to her real old-Russian soul." Chukovsky focused on her style, what he called the "unsimple simplicity" (*neprostaya prostota*) accessible only to great masters. "Next to her, other poets seem like bombastic rhetoricians." He then contrasted her to Mayakovsky, who was eternally shouting and raging. While Akhmatova speaks kindly of angels, the Madonna, and God, Mayakovsky cannot pass God without threatening Him with a jackknife. Chukovsky ended his long essay noting that all of Russia seemed to be divided between the Akhmatovas and the Mayakovskys. Akhmatova was heir to all that was most valuable in pre-Revolutionary Russian letters, while Mayakovsky had no predecessors and focused only on the future. Chukovsky believed that for literature, "they are both equally necessary. In the future they must exist only as a synthesis, otherwise each of them will inevitably perish."[13]

In the context of the early 1920s, Chukovsky's admiring view of Akhmatova's work ironically became a source for attacking her as a representative of a dead past, of precisely what modern Soviet poetry should not be like, as lesser critics totally distorted Chukovsky's sensitive analysis. Anatoly Lunacharsky, Minister of Culture, who normally was more tolerant, was one who used Chukovsky's article to attack Akhmatova: "One can consider the recluse Akhmatova as the most typical representative of the old world. Chukovsky captured her essence in discussing the small range of her world. I protest against old Russia with . . . the quiet and elegant Akhmatova opposed to Mayakovsky."[14]

In 1923, Mikhail Kuzmin, once Akhmatova's friend and nightly companion at the Stray Dog, wrote that Akhmatova had outlived her role as a poet in Russian society and was important only as a relic of the past. He warned both Mayakovsky and Akhmatova that their very popularity was a danger, that they might easily just continue repeating themselves, since they had found styles that were popular with the public. As soon as the suspicion of stagnation appears, the artist must plunge into the very depths of his soul and call forth a new source—or keep silent.[15] Turning to Chukovsky's article, Kuzmin found common ground between Akhmatova and Mayakovsky, both of whom, he said, were standing at a cross-roads. They must choose either popularity or future creativity. "I love them too much to wish them a creative path and not peaceful and deserved popularity."[16] Kuzmin apparently had not read Akhmatova's many poems on war and revolution, the poems of a woman no longer lamenting only unrequited love but those she loved deeply who were now dead, like Gumilyov and Blok. The maturity and depth of these poems reveal her growth and development as an artist. She did not require Kuzmin to tell her in condescending tones how to become a better poet. At this time Akhmatova was expressing her intense dislike of Kuzmin to friends, and he would become the prototype for Mephistopheles in *Poem Without a Hero.*

Mayakovsky, however, believed that Futurist poetry should be the main model for the new generation. He viewed Akhmatova as a relic who had not adapted to the new age. At an evening entitled "The Purge of Contemporary Poetry" on January 9, 1922, he claimed that the Futurists could best express the rich harmony of new ideas and emotions, and cited Akhmatova among the poets to be "purged." The real task of the artist, according to Mayakovsky, was to convey the contemporary age in artistic images, and "participate actively in the creation of a new kingdom."

When we approach poets of the contemporary period with this criterion, many remain overboard; they cannot be called poets in the real sense of this word: the chamber intimacy of Anna Akhmatova, the mystical verses of Vyacheslav Ivanov and his Hellenic motifs—what meaning do they have for our harsh, iron age? And yet, should we suddenly count Ivanov and Akhmatova as zero? Of course, as literary milestones, as the lastborn child of a collapsing structure, they find their place on the pages of literary history; but for us, for our epoch—these are insignificant, pathetic, and laughable anachronisms.[17]

Was Mayakovsky aware of how dangerous such accusations against Akhmatova were at a time when pre-Revolutionary intellectuals were already considered suspect, and were being arrested and sent into exile? In this context, his words were more than a form of literary criticism; they were dangerous words, which could have been interpreted as a sentence to exile or death. Ironically, Mayakovsky himself was soon to be described as an "insignificant, pathetic, and laughable anachronism," and would later commit suicide, unable to endure the very purges he helped perpetrate against others.

Akhmatova admired the Mayakovsky of the pre-Revolutionary years, but not the poet laureate of the early Soviet period. When many years later a friend remarked that Mayakovsky must have found things difficult among the Briks and their literary salon, which included members of the secret police, Akhmatova replied: "You're making a mistake separating Mayakovsky from the Briks. This was his house, his love, his friendship; he liked everything he found there. It was his level of education, his feeling of comradeship. . . . He loved them until the very end."[18] Even so, she said, his talent set him apart, and he was truly one of the great poets of the twentieth century.

While Akhmatova could not depend on former friends, she found new admirers among the younger generation. Alexandra Kollontay, one of the leading female revolutionaries, claimed that Akhmatova's poetry was "the entire novel of a woman's soul, the poetic expression of the battle of a woman enslaved by bourgeois society, struggling for her human personality. She is not alien; her verses reflect the soul of a woman of a transitional epoch, an epoch marked by a break in human psychology, the mortal struggle of two cultures, two ideologies—bourgeois and proletariat. Akhmatova is not on the side of an outlived ideology but one that is creative."[19]

Nikolay Osinsky, an activist in the October Revolution, who reviewed Akhmatova favorably in *Pravda (Truth)* (July 4, 1922), noted Akhmatova's refusal to leave her country: "Although we are dealing with a person not of our way of life, she has what is most important, most necessary to a poet—an honorable soul and civic consciousness. She refuses to leave not for revolutionary reasons, but for nationalistic ones." He also stated that since the death of Blok, Akhmatova was the greatest living poet of the time.[20]

However, the tide of critical opinion was clearly running against Akhmatova—and even against her supporters. In *Molodaya Guardiya (Young Guard)*, V. Arvatov attacked Alexandra Kollontay, saying Akhmatova's poems developed the neurotic emotions of the submissive martyr in young working women.[21] He denounced Akhmatova for being too narrow, reeking of the boudoir, home, and the family. P. Vinogradskaya in *Krasnaya Nov (Red Virgin Soil)* (1923) asserted that Akhmatova represented capricious women, who served only as toys in the hands of men and in no way reflected the contemporary working woman.[22] And G. Lelevich, in a harsh article that appeared in *Na postu (On Guard)* (1923), described Akhmatova's poetry as "a small and beautiful fragment of aristocratic culture. . . . The circle of emotions open to the poet is exceptionally limited. She has responded to social upheavals, basically the most important phenomena of our time, in a feeble and hostile manner."[23] This last was a particularly important article in the study of the relationship of Marxist critics to Akhmatova's work, since it employed many of the methods that would be used against her for the next several decades—an attack against her aristocratic origins, and a distortion of her works, which go far beyond the circle of "intimate personal lyrics." Employing the methods of Marxist literary criticism, which looks for explanations of an author's style in his or her class origins, Lelevich declared that Akhmatova was typical of a hothouse flower growing up on a noble estate—failing to note that although of upper-class origins, Akhmatova actually grew up in a rather ordinary house in Tsarskoye Selo. Lelevich rejected her patriotic verse, saying it was full of mysticism. He was one of the first to pick up on Eikhenbaum's damning phrase "half-nun, half-harlot," employing it in his attack against her.

Even Leon Trotsky embroiled himself in the debate about Russian poetry and Akhmatova's place in it, writing in *Literature and Revolution:*

One reads with dismay most of the poetic collections, especially those of the women. Here, indeed, one cannot take a step without God. The lyric circle of Akhmatova, Tsvetaeva, Radlova . . . is very small. He [God] is a very convenient and portable third person, quite domestic, a friend of the family who fulfills from time to time the duties of a doctor of female ailments. How this individual, no longer young, burdened with the personal and too often bothersome errands of Akhmatova, Tsvetaeva, and others, can manage in his spare time to direct the destinies of the universe, is simply incomprehensible.[24]

Trotsky's book did not appear until 1923, but chapters were published in September and October 1922 in *Pravda,* two weeks after the government regulation exiling the "most active counterrevolutionary elements from among the milieu of professors, doctors, agronomists, and literary figures from the country." The intelligentsia interpreted these chapters as a clear warning. Nikolay Punin, who would soon become an important figure in Akhmatova's life, published a reply to Trotsky, saying that as a political figure rather than a literary critic, Trotsky did not know what the new culture should be like or how it should develop. "To us, Anna Akhmatova is the most original poet of the preceding generation." "What if," he asked, "Akhmatova put on a leather jacket or Red Army star, would she then be relevant to October [the Revolution]? If so, this would be absolutely terrible." He warned Trotsky not to judge literature on content alone, a practice that had caused earlier Russian critics in the nineteenth century like Pisarev to prefer journalism to Pushkin. Moreover, Trotsky did not reject Russian literature of the past because it did not depict the proletariat and the Revolution. "Why allow works by Bach or the miniatures of Fouquet but not Akhmatova? It is impossible to do any work if there is no feeling for the culture of the past— creating artistic life is different from creating an army or factory."[25]

Akhmatova's friends give us some insight into how she lived during those years of privation. She moved to 3, Kazanskaya Street in 1923, renting two rooms from friends, and then in 1924 to a new apartment on the Fontanka Canal, in an enormous building which had served as the laundry for the court. When Chukovsky went to see her on May 6, 1924, he found her sitting in front of the fireplace, and although it was during the day, there was a candle burning on the mantel of the fireplace. Akhmatova told him there were no matches and she could not light the hotplate. Typically, Akhmatova seemed incapable of solving the more mundane but necessary aspects of life. Chukovsky went to some painters working next door and bought matches for her.[26]

Another friend, Nadezhda Chulkova, wife of the writer Georgy Chulkov, describes how Akhmatova attempted to cope with her situation. Akhmatova treated Nadezhda to some cookies she had baked. "It was impossible to expect any special culinary abilities from Anna Akhmatova—that's why it was even more touching to see her prepare delicious cookies with her own hands from rather suspect material (real flour was rare at that time)."[27]

Akhmatova's pride and dignity prevented her from lowering herself to commercial attempts to exploit her name. In 1924, for example, two entrepreneurs suggested that she should go on a tour of eighteen cities. One of them offered to introduce her readings with a Marxist analysis of her poems. She declined.[28]

In 1924, a flood occurred in Leningrad that remained long in the memory of those who experienced it. It was one hundred years since the last catastrophic flood in the capital, immortalized in Pushkin's narrative poem, *The Bronze Horseman*.[29] Akhmatova and Valentina Shchogoleva were in church at the Smolensk Cemetery at a special service for Alexander Blok. During the peaceful liturgy one could hear the wind slamming against the door, but they remained until the end of the service. Returning on a tram, Akhmatova wanted to go partway on foot. There was a wild wind on the embankment, her shoes were wet, and she ran from lamppost to lamppost, grabbing one after another. In the Summer Garden, the lindens were demolished. But Akhmatova showed no fear.[30]

Akhmatova's personal trials did not prevent her from being a caring friend. She spent the entire summer of 1924 looking after Olga Sudeikina, who had peritonitis and lay in bed, deathly ill, for two months. When Sudeikina recovered, she left for Paris, breaking one of the last links in the chain to Akhmatova's past. Again Akhmatova was invited to go abroad and join her friend, but she declined. Sudeikina was soon writing her letters about how miserable she was living away from Russia. She left some of her things to Akhmatova, who treasured them, carrying them with her wherever she lived over the next decades.

Meanwhile, the attacks on Akhmatova intensified, triggered in part by "Leningrad Today," a literary evening in Moscow devoted to the journal *Russkii sovremennik (Russian Contemporary)* on April 17, 1924. The journal was a literary-artistic publication and Yevgeny Zamyatin and Chukovsky were on the editorial board, which had made an attempt to unify writers outside the official ideology. They published poems by Akhmatova, Blok, Tsvetayeva, Khlebnikov, Klyuev, and Khodasevich, as well as the prose and poetry of Pasternak, and works by Boris Pilnyak, Zamyatin, Chukovsky, and Eikhenbaum. Akhmatova appeared in the first issue with "New Year's Ballad" and "Lot's Wife." The journal was shut down after the fourth issue.[31]

When Akhmatova came to Moscow for the event, she was appalled at the publicity it had received—posters were plastered all over the city announcing her as "coming from Leningrad only once!" Akhmatova was sensitive to the political atmosphere and was afraid so much commotion had been made over the journal that the evening might be interpreted as a counterrevolutionary event. It was clear Akhmatova's popularity was still enormous, for visitors would not leave her alone for a single moment. A half hour before her performance, as she was dressing, she heard a knock at the door—three strange young girls came in to recite their poems. Akhmatova tried to refuse and told them she was getting dressed, but the girls insisted. They read the poems as she dressed.[32]

An account of the event in *Pravda* on April 19, disparagingly entitled "Yesterday's 'Today,' " portrayed Akhmatova as solemn, with a monotonous, sing-song voice, an Old Believer murmuring something about the dead. It said the atmosphere was steeped in cologne, abstract aesthetics and archival dust, frock coats smelling of moth balls. Another article entitled "Non-Contemporary 'Contemporary Bolshevik' " exclaimed, "Could one wish for clearer proof of the anti-revolutionary feelings of Akhmatova? She is obviously an internal émigré." And still another addressed Akhmatova personally. Saying no one expected the poet to reflect the emotion of the Revolution, the author urged her to "run away from reality, hide as a peacock hides its head in its feathers, looking with one eye at God's world—ignoring everything that summons you to life, to the contemporary world, to the Revolution."[33]

The campaign against Akhmatova culminated in 1925, when her poetry was banned by an unofficial Communist Party resolution that was not made public.[34] Akhmatova wrote: "I found out about it only in 1927 after meeting [Marietta] Shaginyan on Nevsky Avenue. Judging by memoirs [of others], I was swallowed up by my 'personal life'—isn't that what you call it now?—and paid no attention. I didn't even know at that time what the Communist Party was."[35]

Nikita Struve maintains that the dramatic decrease in Akhmatova's poetic output was not only a result of not being allowed to publish from 1925 to 1940, but also part of her normal development as a poet. According to Struve, many great poets of Russia, including Pushkin, Blok, Pasternak, and Mandelstam, suffered a crisis around the age of thirty-five years old. In the thirteen years she lived with Punin, Akhmatova wrote some twenty poems; then, after leaving him, in 1940, she wrote twenty lyrics and two long narrative poems, *Way of All Earth* and the first version of *Poem Without a Hero*.[36] What Struve fails to note is that the biological cycle of a poet may indeed influence productivity at different phases of his or her life, but so do the personal circumstances. Her difficult relationship with Punin, the increasing oppression of the Stalinist years, the knowledge that the works she wrote might very probably never be published, and other aspects of her personal life all may have had a tremendous impact on the lack of poetic inspiration. Perhaps for a while Akhmatova lost her ability to transform tragic circumstances into works of great art.

A contemporary said of Akhmatova at this period in her life:

> It is impossible for her to live all the time in this bureaucratic city of St. Petersburg, where you are choked by fog, where there are a few scraggly trees, and where the sun is dim. However, Akhmatova has always been inspired by the classical rhythms of this city of the *Bronze Horseman,* the white nights, and "The Stranger" [Blok's poem]. She reminds me of a nun from some famous hermitage, abandoned by everyone, left alone, with nothing to look forward to.[37]

However, Akhmatova was not entirely alone. By 1924, she was beginning to see Nikolay Punin more frequently. Born in 1888 in Helsingfors (present-day Helsinki), Punin had attended the same gymnasium as Gumilyov in Tsarskoye Selo, then studied in the Faculty of History and Philology at St. Petersburg University. He wrote articles on art and reviews of exhibitions for *Apollon.* His writings reflect a wide range of subjects, from an article on the medieval icon artist Andrey Rublyov, which inspired Gumilyov to write a famous poem, to works on Oriental art. But he is most significant as one of the main champions of the Russian avant-garde and is still remembered today for one of the first important works on Vladimir Tatlin. He was a member of a famous circle of the avant-garde who met at Lev Burni's "Room Number Five," which included Altman, Mandelstam, Klyuev, and Arthur Lourie. And he introduced Russian Formalism to art criticism, focusing on the formal aspects of painting or sculpture—the color, shape, texture, arrangement of forms—and pointing out how themes and emotions were conveyed by the uniqueness of the medium available in each individual art form.

On August 2, 1921, Punin was arrested on unspecified charges; he was released on September 6 at the intercession of Lunacharsky, the Minister of Culture. This was the first, but not the last, time that this major figure, who had done so much for Russian and Soviet culture, was attacked for his artistic beliefs. Punin took active part in establishing the role of art under the new Soviet State. He also became director of the former Imperial Porcelain Factory, and in this post gave commissions to artists (he literally saved Olga Sudeikina's life by giving her commissions to create porcelain dolls before she left for Paris). In 1923, Punin became head of the Institute of Artistic Culture in Petrograd, where such famous avant-garde artists as Malevich and Tatlin worked. He is also remembered as a brilliant pedagogue; from 1926 to 1931 he taught at the State Institute of Art History, and later at other institutions. According to Matthew Frost, "Punin's reviews of the art scene in Petrograd constitute some of the finest contemporary criticism of the Revolutionary period in Russian art. His active support and lucid dissemination of experimental art forms made a significant contribution in the campaign to forge a new role for the creative artist in a Communist society."[38] In 1917, he had married Anna Arens, a doctor and daughter of a former admiral, and they soon had a daughter, Irina.

The year 1924 marked the entrance of another significant person in Akhmatova's life, Pavel Luknitsky, a young man from an old aristocratic family, who was writing a thesis on Nikolay Gumilyov and came to Akhmatova for help. He would provide an important record of her life over the next five years, including an account on her relationship with Punin and recent memories of her life with Gumilyov. At a recent conference in Moscow on the intelligentsia and the Soviet secret police, I have learned from someone who has access to the KGB file on Akhmatova that Luknitsky was submitting reports on her to the Cheka.[39]

Akhmatova was very ill at this time, and Luknitsky brought her medicine as well as food from his mother, ran errands for her, picked up her pension and Shileiko's pay at the Academy when Shileiko was in Moscow, and even wrote letters and telegrams for her (Akhmatova hated writing letters and all her life preferred to send telegrams instead). In return, Akhmatova trusted him and confided many of her most intimate feelings and thoughts to him. Luknitsky's wife says he told her how precious those conversations with Akhmatova were to him, in these early years of his life, and that he was overwhelmed by her amazing memory and enormous erudition.[40]

Luknitsky's reminiscences give us a rare glimpse of the personal side of this very private poet, who hated to reveal herself in public. Although Akhmatova was very ill, she did not like people pitying her or looking after her, and preferred to conceal her needs. At first she may have appeared conceited, proud, and very self-assured; but when one got to know her, she turned out to be sweet and affectionate, friendly and simple, and very vulnerable. She had a clear, serene mind, a great love for the arts, and a complete lack of interest in material comforts. Her great sense of humor and witty, pointed view of a world that was becoming increasingly Kafkaesque do not appear in her work but were attributes often mentioned by her friends throughout her life.[41]

Luknitsky also provides information on Akhmatova's relationship to her son at this time. She had no real permanent place of residence and little to eat, and when Lev came with his aunt (Nikolay Gumilyov's stepsister), he stayed with relatives of Gumilyov's mother, the Kuzmin-Karavaevs. Luknitsky formed a close friendship with Lev and visited him when he came to Leningrad. Lev wrote him letters, sent him plays and poems asking for his advice. When Luknitsky first met Akhmatova, she was living on Shileiko's income, although she eventually got a pension of 40 rubles a month. She took care of picking up Shileiko's salary when he was in Moscow and sent it on to him. She also had a maid, Manya, presumably paid by Shileiko.[42] In January 1926, when Shileiko was in Leningrad, Akhmatova dropped in on Luknitsky. She was carrying a package—food, cheese, and bread—for Shileiko. She told Luknitsky she had shown Shileiko her work the day before. When he finally tore himself away from his own work and looked at it, he told her prophetically: "When they send the honorary mantle from Oxford University, remember me in your prayers." Many years later Akhmatova would receive that "mantle" as he had predicted—but Shileiko was long dead.[43]

In 1925, Akhmatova's increasingly intimate relationship with Punin was not accepted by all her friends. She told Luknitsky that many people did not understand or did not wish to understand. For them, she was still Anna Gumilyova— the widow of Gumilyov—and no one should take his place, even though she had since married Shileiko. Luknitsky noted in his diary that Akhmatova's friends not only did not invite Punin over when they invited her, but often said nasty things about him in front of her, and this hurt Punin. According to Luknitsky, Akhmatova's relationship with Punin's wife, Anna Arens, was a friendly one, and when Akhmatova was sick, Arens would even come visit her, in spite of the fact that she must have known about the affair between Akhmatova and her husband.[44]

In March 1925, Akhmatova's chronic illness took a turn for the worse. Told she must go to Tsarskoye Selo to a sanatorium to recover, Punin found her a *pension*—claiming the sanatorium's regime was too strict, and she would have to share a room with several people. She moved there in April. Punin soon sent a letter for Akhmatova with Luknitsky, to the effect that he could not work without her and hoped they would be able to live together.[45] When Luknitsky arrived on May 5, he found the Mandelstams there. They had arrived just ten days before because Nadezhda Mandelstam, Osip's wife, was also very ill. Akhmatova notes in her memoirs how the two women had first met:

> In the summer of 1924 Osip Mandelstam brought his young wife to see me (at Fontanka 2). Nadyusha was what the French call *laide mais charmante* [ugly but charming]. From that day my friendship with Nadyusha began, and it continues to this day. Osip loved Nadya unbelievably, improbably. When she had her appendix removed in Kiev, he did not leave the hospital guard's room. He would not allow Nadya even a step away from him, would not let her work, was furiously jealous, and asked her advice about every word in his poems. In general, I haven't seen anything like it in all my life. . . . In 1925 I lived on the same corridor with the Mandelstams at Zaitsev's boardinghouse in Tsarskoye Selo. Both Nadya and I were seriously ill, lay in bed, took our temperatures, which were unfailingly high, and, therefore, apparently did not stroll even once in the nearby park.[46]

Like Petersburg, Tsarskoye Selo was undergoing a metamorphosis. It was now called Detskoye Selo ("Children's Village") rather than Tsarskoye Selo ("Tsar's Village"). Akhmatova took Luknitsky to see the Gumilyov house on Malaya Street. With great sadness she looked at the dirty, ruined sidewalks, broken fences, and vacant lots where once pleasant houses stood. "Just think—this city was once the cleanest in all Russia. They took such great care of it! You could not see a single broken fence. . . . It was almost like Versailles. . . . Now there is no Tsarskoye Selo." Luknitsky saw how much pain this visit brought Akhmatova: every stone, every column that she knew so well, was now alien to her.[47]

Punin visited her often. Luknitsky celebrated Easter with her (April 19, 1925), bringing her *kulich,* the tall Russian Easter cake, some wine, and *paskha,* the holiday dessert made of sweetened curd cheese. The Mandelstams had now gone to another *pension,* although they still visited her until the end of April, when they moved to Leningrad.

Akhmatova's friends the Rybakovs, who had lent her money to pay for her stay in Tsarskoye, told her they had received a letter from Olga Sudeikina saying she was awaiting their arrival so she could return with them to Russia, since she found Paris absolutely repulsive and really missed her "Anka."[48] Akhmatova, however, was terrified at the thought of Olga's return, since Olga was utterly incapable of earning an income in the new Soviet State. Before she left she had an apartment and furniture, but she had sold or given away everything. Olga remained in Paris, which was just as well, as her desire to become a fashion designer in Russia—where people were barely able to find enough to eat—showed how out of touch Akhmatova's old friend was with the present reality of her homeland.

Luknitsky reports that Akhmatova was barely surviving financially, living in cold, damp rooms, wearing old clothes, yet she still sent money to her mother, her mother-in-law, and son, among others. She never told her mother her real situation, but pretended she got money from a pension, yet her mother reproached her for sending so little. In order not to worry her, Akhmatova pretended everything was also fine with Olga in a letter to her mother along with some money: "I am sending you twenty rubles, fifteen for you and five for Mama. Sudeikina is inspired and working (sewing) and seems satisfied with her fate. I will be waiting for news from you at Punin's address."[49]

Akhmatova still struggled to stay part of Leningrad's literary life. At the end of December 1924, she appeared at an evening at the Academic Chapel, along with Klyuev, Zoshchenko, Zamyatin, and others, and she appeared there again in February 1925 with Zoshchenko, Klyuev, Alexey Tolstoy, Sologub, and others. However, on May 25, 1925, at an evening of the Union of Soviet Writers, when the crowd shouted, "Give us Akhmatova!" she absolutely refused to come. She explained to Luknitsky that she had never liked to recite; she did not like feeling as if someone were looking at her through binoculars, examining what she was wearing, how she looked. And she complained that she could only be heard in the first few rows—for the others it was like a mime show. Akhmatova then became silent, finally mentioning one other reason—she did not have a dress to wear. "It's no longer 1918, you know," she said poignantly. This still mattered to her.[50]

She continued to maintain her integrity, refusing to accept simple ways to alleviate her poverty by making compromises. She had once gone to see Gorky to see if he could find work for her. He advised her to ask to translate Soviet proclamations into Italian. "Without knowing enough Italian at that time, I could not do it even if I had wanted to," she told Luknitsky. "Just imagine, I would do a translation which would be sent to Italy, which would help put people into prison."[51]

At the end of May she was in the hospital. She returned to the Marble Palace, but by the end of the year she was spending increasingly more time with Punin at the Sheremetev Palace. Sometimes, Shileiko would return and stay for a while in the Marble Palace with her. In 1926 Akhmatova and Shileiko were officially divorced, and he married a woman named Vera Andreyeva; they had a son, Alexey, and lived in Moscow.[52]

In October, Akhmatova received another letter from her mother, saying she had moved to Sakhalin to live with Akhmatova's brother Viktor and his family. She remained there until her death in 1930. Akhmatova also learned that she had become an aunt—Viktor and his wife Hanna had a daughter named Inna.[53]

The suicide of the poet Yesenin on December 27, 1925, was another shock for Akhmatova. He hanged himself in the Hotel Angleterre in Leningrad at the age of thirty, partly because of his disillusionment with the Revolution. He had chosen the wrong Utopia—of peasant origin, he hoped one day Russia would become a land of agricultural communes, of people close to nature, helping each other share the fruits of the earth. But the Social Revolutionaries, who wanted to make this dream come true, lost to the Bolsheviks, who saw the future of the Soviet Union in industrial progress. Yesenin had become increasingly disturbed as he watched the world of the machine encroaching on his beloved Russian countryside. A memorable poem reveals these fears, as a train rushes through the steppes and a little colt hopelessly attempts to overcome it in a desperate race for the future:

> Did you see
> How along the steppes
> Hiding in the misty lakes
> Snorting through its iron nostrils
> On cast iron feet a train dashes by?

> And behind it
> Through the tall grass
> As though in a festival of desperate races
> Flinging its slender legs as high as its head
> A red-maned colt is galloping?[54]

But Yesenin had changed from the innocent, fresh young man who came to Petersburg in the 1910s and, in the words of the poet Vasily Kamensky, "played the country bumpkin," dressed as an elegant version of the picturesque peasant. By the time of his death he had lost all pretense of innocence. He wore city suits and fancy ties, wrote poems about hooligans, had a brief, passionate, but ultimately disastrous marriage with the dancer Isadora Duncan, read Rimbaud and Verlaine, and discussed Picassos he had seen in the avant-garde collection of the Moscow collector Shchukin.[55] At the end it was clear he was at variance with his times, and he died a drunken, broken man.

His suicide was a grievous blow to those who loved him. The poet Nikolay Aseyev says in spite of Yesenin's latest poems, it was possible still to perceive beneath them the face of a dashing boy with wavy blond hair. Aseyev saw "the living, sincere, creative face of a poet, the face washed with cold despair, suddenly revived with the pain and fear of its own reflection. Gone was the insipid color of nationalism. Gone was the convulsive balancing on a tightrope of ambiguous success. Before me stood a man, colleague, poet, seeing his annihilation, clutching at my hand only to feel human warmth. This was the Yesenin I am weeping for."[56] Yesenin's last poem reflects his combination of despair and resignation:

> Farewell, my dearest, farewell
> Friend, you're sticking in my breast
> The promised destinies are weaving
> A thread from parting to meeting.
>
> Farewell, darling, no hand, no word,
> Don't be sad, don't be upset,
> To die—is nothing new in life,
> But nor is it new, of course—to live.[57]

Mayakovsky wrote a rejoinder, saying one must not think of one's personal problems but must build a new life for the masses:

> We must find
>   joy
>   in future days.
> To die—
>   in life
>   is not so difficult
> To create life—
>   is more difficult indeed.[58]

The irony was that Mayakovsky, who was also rapidly reaching the point of ultimate despair, was soon to meet the same fate.

In spite of all her criticism, Akhmatova was extremely upset when Yesenin committed suicide. "He lived horribly and died horribly," she told Luknitsky. "How fragile the peasants are when they are unsuccessful in their contact with civilization—each year another poet dies. . . . It is horrible when a poet dies."[59]

Another death that shook Akhmatova was that of Larisa Reisner, who died of typhus in February 1926. In a distant but implicit way, Reisner's life had touched hers through Gumilyov, and therefore her death moved her more than that of Yesenin. "No one would ever have imagined that I would outlive Larisa!" she said affectionately, and with great sorrow. "Here's yet another death. How people are dying! . . . She wanted so much to live, she was cheerful, healthy, and beautiful. You remember how relatively calmly I took the news of Yesenin's death, because he wanted to die and was seeking death. This—is something quite different. . . . But Larisa!"[60]

In 1925, a large selection of Akhmatova's poems appeared in an enormous anthology of twentieth-century Russian poetry. These were the last of her poems to appear until 1940.[61] Akhmatova's outward calm was beginning to be disturbed by inner turmoil. The years of war and revolution were taking their toll on this fragile, vulnerable woman, who would soon find it impossible to publish her works, which meant that not only could she not commune with others through her verse, but she could not play the role assigned to her by fate—to be the voice of her people.

In November 1925, Luknitsky noted the change reflected in Akhmatova: in the spring she had been cheerful, but her behavior now reflected an inner tension, or in his words, she was "darker." "One feels a slow, engulfing, suffocating fog penetrating Akhmatova's entire being, tormenting her, smothering her, and the more effort she makes to get out of it, the more unsuccessful her attempts to liberate herself from its tentacles. . . . She would make attempts to deceive her friends by appearing unconstrained, laughing, but she did not succeed in fooling them."[62]

By 1926, Akhmatova moved in more or less permanently with the Punins. Luknitsky said this finally gave her a roof over her head, but she was forced to submit to the order of their household. The circle of people close to her narrowed. Akhmatova's friend Natasha Rykova died; Lozinsky almost never visited her. In September, the poet Fyodor Sologub helped her get a pension from the Central Commission for the Improvement of Scholars' Lives: 60 rubles a month, of which, at least when she first moved in, she had to pay the Punins 40 rubles a month for her room.[63] Sologub had written a letter to Anatoly Lunacharsky, urging him to obtain the pension:

We the undersigned workers of culture, art and science turn to you, Anatoly Vasilyevich, as leader of all the republic's cultural activity, with a plea to help reverse the decision of the experts on the Commission for the Improvement of Scholars' Lives. We think we have no need to point out Anna Akhmatova's literary and artistic services. You yourself, Anatoly Vasilyevich, know enough about the evolution of Russian literature to judge Akhmatova's poetic gift and influence.[64]

Akhmatova was still in close touch with Shileiko, and was continuing to take care of Tapa, the St. Bernard who had been with them since their marriage. Shileiko's continual solicitude is shown by his note to his wife about Akhmatova's visit to Moscow in March 1926, when he begged his wife to watch over her: "Dear Vera, here is Anna for you. Please take care of her. I'm very worried about her. Write if she is well. She is too lazy to write."[65]

Under Punin's influence, Akhmatova became more interested in the visual arts, especially the architecture of Petersburg—the old buildings, monuments, iron gates, and bridges. For the rest of her life she would impress people with her knowledge of aspects of the city she loved so much. In spring 1926 she told Luknitsky she had no more time to work with him on his Gumilyov biography since she was spending all her time translating Cézanne for Punin for his lectures at the State Institute of Art History. Punin had expressed his dissatisfaction to Luknitsky about the fact Shileiko still had not left for Moscow, since that prevented Akhmatova from working regularly on Cézanne. She also worked with Punin on preparing material on the French artist David. Once she stayed up all night reading a book about Ingres to prepare Punin for a talk.[66] She thus found herself in the same role she had played with Shileiko, that of an intelligent companion who helped a brilliant man with his work—a man she loved, and who in turn respected her own gifts and talents. It was a role the poet seemed genuinely to enjoy.

In November 1926 Akhmatova received a letter from Tsvetayeva from Belle-vue, near Paris. The life of Tsvetayeva and other leading Russian exiles abroad provides an insight into the fate that might have awaited Akhmatova had she gone abroad. The attitude of the émigrés changed as it became increasingly clear that the Soviet Union, ruled by the Bolsheviks, was there to stay for a long time:

> When the refugees from the October Revolution fled from their country by the hundreds of thousands they expected to stay away for a few years at most. . . . Surely the Russian people would not endure this new tyr-anny indefinitely. . . . But the majority of exiles realized by about 1925, that they were in for a long, perhaps indefinite stay abroad. The reali-zation was reinforced by the gradual ban on importation into the Soviet Union of emigre books and periodicals and by the increasing restrictions on travel abroad by Soviet citizens.[67]

For some reason, Tsvetayeva thought Akhmatova was about to emigrate to Paris and told her: "I'm writing you on the joyous occasion of your arrival." She wanted to know if Akhmatova would be coming alone or with her mother and son. "But no matter how you come," she said, "come bravely." Tsvetayeva would meet her at Bellevue Station.[68]

Lydia Ginzburg was a contemporary of Akhmatova's, who felt that the poet both represented and contradicted her era. Akhmatova had taken upon herself the responsibility for her epoch, for the "memory of the dead and the glory of the living." But arguing whether Akhmatova was part of Soviet culture was futile. "She is a historical fact which is impossible to annul, but we, the humanitarian youth of the twenties, are not a historical fact for her because our history began when her literary history perhaps ended." Ginzburg attributed Akhmatova's powerful impact on those she met, in part, to her bearing and gestures, reflections of her aristocratic past, which were foreign to the new generation growing up under the Soviet regime. In the old system, dress and gestures were signs of social differentiation, reflecting who was in command and who obeyed. In the Soviet period, the head of state was not to be distinguished from any worker, and expressive gestures were forbidden. There were still differences in rank, but those in power and those who were workers were both part of the proletariat, and hence allegedly equal. Akhmatova's very gestures—the movement of her hands, the turn of her head—reflected a system that had disappeared, a certain grandeur that no longer existed.[69]

Ginzburg also notes that sometimes a poet is like his poem—Mayakovsky, for example, whose poetry reflected his speech, his voice. But this was not true of Akhmatova. Her poetry in the 1920s did not in fact reflect her vast knowledge of history and literature, nor her witty, glittering, sometimes merciless wit. But what was similar in her poetic method was the way her mind worked: sober, observant, rational. Her lyrics were never a spontaneous outpouring of feeling but the result of poetic discipline, self-control. "Poetry was a transformation of an inner experience. . . . The personal becomes the universal."[70]

Luknitsky noted Akhmatova's ability at this time to conjure up figures from the past. It could be Pushkin or Dante, but "she always spoke with an intonation . . . as if he were her good friend, with whom she had just spoken, as if he had gone into the next room and would return any moment. . . . There was absolutely no gap in the centuries." She knew not only their works but the important dates of their lives, their jokes, passions, even their moods. "Her ability to cross centuries and time, to penetrate people's souls, was amazing." That was why her home, which at this time few visited, always seemed full of life. Here one could meet Dante "in person," as well as Michelangelo, Rastrelli and Byron, Shelley and Chenier, and most of all, most intimately, Alexander Pushkin.[71]

Pushkin had long been Akhmatova's mentor and spiritual counterpart, ever since she felt his presence as a child in Tsarskoye Selo. She returned to him often, and no doubt in these trying times found comfort and solace in his work. During the 1920s, her work on Pushkin took on a more serious aspect, and as Akhmatova began to write less verse, the poet turned into the poet-scholar, exploring the depths of erudite and personal association in the works of Russia's great writer.

It is clear that many of Pushkin's methods were typical of Akhmatova's own work and that as she analyzed his methods, she was also exploring her own creativity. Borrowing the lines or phrases of other poets is typical of poets of genius as well as those of lesser gifts. The difference lies in how these poetic loans are integrated into their own work. According to Akhmatova, a genius is a usurper who grabs words, similes, images from everywhere, often the simplest, those unnoticed by anyone. But when the genius uses them, they become inimitable, identified only with him or her. She once likened Pushkin's method to a furnace melting down all the material borrowed, out of which something entirely new was produced, something that was peculiarly Pushkin's own. His contemporaries such as Batyushkov, on the other hand, did not transform such material but merely inserted it mechanically into their own work, where it remained the same.

Akhmatova also discussed the burden of tradition, of coming after Pushkin. Difficult as it was for poets working immediately after him, she thought, they also benefited from the new routes Pushkin opened and forced them to follow—that is the role of a genius.

Akhmatova was preparing articles on Pushkin that would soon enter the canon of Pushkin scholarship. She began by reading his sources of inspiration—Dante, Chenier, Byron, and the German Romantic poets—using textbooks, grammars, and dictionaries to comprehend them fully. She also consulted Lozinsky, one of the premier translators of the classics into Russian, and Boris Tomashevsky, one of the leading Pushkin scholars in the Soviet Union; later Tomashevsky, along with his wife, the scholar Irina Medvedeva, would become two of her best friends, supporting her in times of dire need. At first Pushkin scholars treated Akhmatova's work skeptically, but they soon became convinced of her seriousness and were impressed by her vast knowledge. Examining the influence of the French poet Chenier on Pushkin, she perceived that Pushkin only borrowed verses that corresponded to his own credo, and often transformed what he derived into something far more complex. Akhmatova also studied how Pushkin had enriched the Russian language in ways that, while imperceptible to others, were obvious to her as a poet, sensitive to the language she used as her own artistic medium. She made many fascinating discoveries; for example, she was sure a certain page in Pushkin's novel *Eugene Onegin* had been influenced by the Italian Renaissance poet Ariosto. She read Luknitsky passages in Italian and translated them for him, proving her point.[72]

In the minds of many, Akhmatova's literary career as a poet was now over. Her name appears in the *Literary Encyclopedia* for 1929, where she is described as "a poetess of the aristocracy who has not found a new function in capitalist society, but has already lost her old function in feudal society."[73] The article repeats the same clichés about her that had appeared in articles in the early 1920s— her works reflected the culture of the landed gentry—and cited Eikhenbaum's phrase that she was "half nun, half harlot." The article did, however, admit that she was gifted.

The movement against Akhmatova had even claimed some of her closest friends. In 1928, Luknitsky went to the Crimea, and while he was there he saw the Mandelstams. Akhmatova herself had gone south to Kislovodsk briefly in 1927 to regain her health in the warm Caucasian sun. In 1927, when Osip Mandelstam was gathering his articles together for a book, he came across one he had written in the early 1920s against Akhmatova. His wife claims these critical remarks were a concession to the times: "His disavowal of Akhmatova in 1922 was a concession to all the hue and cry about Acmeism, allegations that it was outmoded . . . the logic of the times demanded that Mandelstam part company with Akhmatova. . . . But he very soon came to his senses."[74] How much Akhmatova meant to Mandelstam at this time is clear from a letter he wrote her while Luknitsky was visiting in the Crimea. It is dated August 25, 1928, the anniversary of Gumilyov's death. Mandelstam realized that only Akhmatova was left of the great poets from before the Revolution with whom he was really close, whom he cared for not only as a fellow poet but as a dear and treasured friend.

> Dear Anna Andreyevna,
> . . . I want to go home. I want to see you. You know that I'm able to carry an imaginary conversation only with two people, Nikolay Gumilyov and you. My conversation with Kolya [Gumilyov] has never ceased and will never cease.[75]

At the end of the 1920s Akhmatova was still living with the Punins, she and Punin in his study, while Punin's wife and daughter slept in another room. They had dinner and supper together in the dining room.[76] In 1928, her son Lev, now sixteen, came to live with them in the Sheremetev Palace. He became a student at the school where Punin's brother Alexander was headmaster, and after he graduated, he entered Leningrad University, where he studied Central Asian history. (Later he would become one of the leading scholars on Central Asia in the Soviet Union.)[77]

All through this period Akhmatova's relationship with Shileiko continued. In her own impractical way she was attempting to keep things in order in his apartment at the Marble Palace. However, in 1927 she wrote a frantic letter to him, saying she had found a note that the electricity would be turned off if she did not pay the bill. He also had forgotten to send her the power of attorney for September, and she had no money to pay for the apartment, the electricity, or Tapa's food.[78] Her affection for Shileiko is revealed in a small volume of poetry by François Villon that is in the Shileiko archive. It bears the dedication: "To Vladimir Shileiko from his old friend Akhmatova. Carnival, Sunday 1927." While she may have written that "You forbid singing and smiling" (in her poem "You are always novel and mysterious . . . ," December 1917) early in their relationship, clearly he loved her poetry, and she considered him a sensitive critic and turned to him for advice. On November 26, 1928, Akhmatova wrote him:

> Dear friend,
> I'm sending you my poems. If you have some time this evening, please take a look at them. . . . Please note down on a separate piece of paper

what you don't consider worth printing. I'll come by tomorrow. Please forgive me for disturbing you.

                                                    Your Akhmatova.[79]

Shileiko became very ill in 1929. He was in Leningrad in early December that year when Akhmatova went to see him with Luknitsky. He was pale and coughed up blood; they knew he did not have long to live. Luknitsky said Shileiko's apartment was also dying. He was told to move out of the Marble Palace because the building was being transferred to another department. He asked Akhmatova to take all their things to the Sheremetev Palace. The corridor was filthy, littered with garbage. The next day Akhmatova and Luknitsky came to the apartment and worked from morning until afternoon, separating the various belongings into piles—hers, Shileiko's, and Luknitsky's, as well as the archives of Sudeikina and Arthur Lourie. The place was strewn with rags, empty cigarette packs, bottles, and Babylonian cuneiform tablets. On Saturday, December 7, Shileiko left for Moscow, and Akhmatova said goodbye to him for the last time. Early on Sunday morning Luknitsky and Akhmatova set out to complete the "funeral" of the apartment. Along with other things to be moved was furniture Olga Sudeikina had left behind. Everything was put out on the sidewalk. One woman passing by said sympathetically, "Poor things . . . Where are they being taken . . . to be sold, eh?" Shileiko died the following year, on October 5, 1930.[80]

By 1928, Stalin had consolidated his position and launched one of the most terrifying periods in Soviet history, the era of collectivization, which lasted from 1928 to 1933. The peasants put up an enormous resistance to having their land taken away—burning their own crops and killing their own livestock. The result was famine. Millions of people were deported and resettled. Purges began, although the real Terror and the trials did not start until 1934.

It was becoming increasingly difficult for anyone to publish. In spite of having heard that the government had no intention of ever publishing her works again, Akhmatova still attempted to approach the state publishing houses. She prepared a two-volume collection of her poems, and in 1926 thought the "Petrograd" publishers might print it. Gessen, the publisher, had accepted the manuscript and even asked Akhmatova to correct proofs, but then nothing more happened. Luknitsky thought perhaps it had something to do with censorship. Then in 1927 Luknitsky noted in his diary that the censor would allow only five hundred copies, which was worse than prohibiting it, since no publisher could afford to issue such a limited edition. When the cooperative Publishers of Writers in Leningrad was founded, the galleys of the two-volume collection were transferred there, and publication of the poems was announced, but soon the same story was repeated. In December 1928, the literary critic D. I. Vygodsky wrote in his diary that Zoya Nikitina had brought him the first volume of Akhmatova's work from Gublit. "They threw out eighteen poems. Everything where there is 'God,' 'Prayer,' 'Christ,' etc. Some of the best poems are among them. And this is not all. They promised to throw less out of the second volume. On Thursday they'll return it. Zoya phoned Akhmatova, who said, frightened: 'Eighteen from the first volume alone!'" The next month Luknitsky wrote: "It has been decided by Gublit to print a collection of her poems on the condition that eighteen poems be thrown out of the first volume and forty from the second. In other words, there will be no edition (unless the conditions are changed, which is almost hopeless)." Finally, on February 9, 1929, Luknitsky wrote that it was indeed hopeless. Akhmatova's poems would not be published.[81]

Akhmatova did not give up easily. In 1930 she even went to see one of the poet laureates of the Bolsheviks, Demyan Bedny. The bibliophile E. F. Tsipelzon noted in his diary on July 5, 1930, that he saw this unlikely pair, Akhmatova and Bedny, dining together in the Moskovskaya Hotel. Demyan Bedny (Demyan the Poor) was the pseudonym of Yefim Pridvorov, the illegitimate son of a grand duke and friend of prominent Party members, a trusted bard of the new regime who wrote vulgar propaganda jingles in the style of popular songs. Tsipelzon continues that Akhmatova had apparently come from Leningrad to take care of publishing two of her books that had already been printed but were being held up. The poet Anna Radlova wrote about this strange alliance in a letter to her husband, the famous director Sergey Radlov, on August 28: "Katayev said that in the spring at his *Squaring of the Circle,* there was Akhmatova with Efros and Demyan Bedny, who was showering her with compliments. This is a bridegroom from hell, isn't it?" By the mid-thirties all attempts to publish a collection of her poetry ceased.[82]

Akhmatova was not alone. In August 1929, the infamous attacks against Boris Pilnyak and Yevgeny Zamyatin began. Both authors were considered "fellow travelers" rather than hard-core supporters of the Communist state, and their condemnation was a turning point in the relationship of the intelligentsia and the state. Henceforth the Stalinist line would become harder and criticism of the state was forbidden.

Zamyatin's book *We,* the prototype for George Orwell's *1984* and an anti-Utopian satire predicting the sterile society that would result from a perfectly planned state, was published in Prague in 1927. Pilnyak's *Red Mahogany,* which exposes the disintegration of the revolutionary ideals of the Soviet State and the corruption of the NEP period, was published in Berlin in 1929. Both books had been censored in the Soviet Union, and officials were furious that they managed to appear abroad. In response to the attacks on Zamyatin and Pilnyak and the reorganization of the Union of Writers into the All-Russian Union of Soviet Writers (VSSP), many writers—among them Bulgakov and Pasternak—resigned. Pilnyak was forced to resign as president of the All-Russian Union of Writers (VSP), which was the officials' goal all along. The Leningrad section of VSP entered the new organization, and Luknitsky played an active role in this event. On October 13, 1929, Luknitsky went to a meeting of the Writers' Union. He noted in his diary, "In my pocket was Akhmatova's resignation: 'To the board of the Writers' Union, I declare my resignation from the Writers' Union. October

13, 1929. A. Akhmatova.' " However, Luknitsky never turned it in. Perhaps, knowing better than Akhmatova how dangerous the political situation was, he was protecting her from the possible political repercussions.[83]

By the end of 1929, Luknitsky writes that Akhmatova was living as before, sadly and quietly; it was cold and gloomy in the apartment, and he did not visit there often or for very long. In 1930 he made a trip to Pamir to write a book, and did not see Akhmatova again for many years. But his record of the years he was with her is invaluable.

There was to be one more loss to Russian letters in 1930—yet another poet. The loud voice of Vladimir Mayakovsky was suddenly stilled. His play *The Bedbug,* satirizing the NEP as well as the perfect, scientifically planned Soviet State, received bad reviews despite its brilliant staging by Meyerhold in 1929. Allegedly the working class was not portrayed properly, and when the action was transferred to the future, to the year 1979, the play was supposedly primitive and unprofound. One reviewer said, "Reluctantly we come to the conclusion that life in 1979 [the future], under socialism, is fairly dull," which, of course, was exactly what Mayakovsky was trying to show.[84] Mayakovsky's *The Bathhouse* (1930) got equally bad reviews. Zoshchenko said that "the audience received the play with a killing coldness. I don't recall a single burst of laughter. After the first two acts there was not the slightest applause. I have never seen a more terrible flop."

In February 1930, Mayakovsky organized "Twenty Years' Work," an exhibition of his life's work, at the Press House. Olga Berggolts, a poet and friend of Akhmatova, described how it was boycotted by many writers, and only a handful of people from the young writers' group "Relay" came and spent days there. She says she suffered at the sight of the "tall man with a sad and austere face, arms folded behind him, as he paced the empty rooms."[85] At an evening devoted to this exhibition on March 25, Mayakovsky gave his own epitaph: "All my life I've worked, not just to produce pleasant trifles and cajole the ear, but I have somehow managed to cause unpleasantness to everyone. My main occupation is to chastise, to scoff at what I consider wrong, things that have to be fought against. And the twenty years of my literary work have mainly been a literary bashing of heads, not literally, but in the best sense of the word. . . . It is very hard to do the work I want to do. . . . The task of bringing worker audiences closer to great poetry, to poetry created seriously, without hack writing and without a deliberate lowering of standards."[86]

The final indignity occurred on April 9, when Mayakovsky was taunted at a meeting with students, who said he should prove that in twenty years anyone would read him. His increasing isolation, his rejection by Tatyana Yakovleva (the beautiful Russian he met in Paris who married an American instead of returning with Mayakovsky to the Soviet Union), the negative reviews, and the increasing politicization of literature, which he himself had helped to promote, all contributed to his despair. On April 14, 1930, at 10:25 P.M., Mayakovsky shot himself in his room on Lubyankaya Street with the revolver he had used as a prop twelve years before in the film *Not for Money Born*. His last letter reveals that, like Yesenin, he was ready "to call it quits" with life. This last work is a "letter to everyone":

> To all!
> Do not charge anyone with the responsibility for my death, and please do not gossip. The deceased very much disliked gossip.
> Mother, sisters, friends, forgive me—this is not the way (I do not recommend it to others), but there is no other way out for me . . .

> As they say,
>   a bungled story.
> Love's boat
>   smashed
>   against existence.
> And we are quits
>   with life.
>   So why should we
> idly reproach each other
>   with pain and insults?
> To those who remain—I wish happiness.
>
> Vladimir Mayakovsky[87]

Pasternak describes what it was like to see him at the end:

> He was lying on his side, face to the wall, stern, big, under the sheet reaching up to his chin, with his mouth half-open, as if asleep. Proudly turned away from everyone, even lying here, even asleep thus, he was stubbornly tearing himself away and going somewhere. His face restored the time when he called himself the beautiful twenty-two-year-old, because death had stiffened the facial expression, which hardly ever gets into its clutches. It was the expression with which one begins life, not the one to end it.[88]

The Great Terror: 1930–1939

You should have been shown, you mocker,
Minion of all your friends,
Gay little sinner of Tsarskoye Selo,
What would happen in your life—
How three-hundredth in line, with a parcel,
You would stand by the Kresty prison
> —AKHMATOVA, *Requiem*
>   (II, p. 101)

The 1930s witnessed a new stage in Stalin's purges, the "cleansing," which took the form of "show trials" and increased in scale the number of victims accused of being "enemies of the people." Many Party members lost their jobs during the 1928 collectivization for showing leniency toward the peasants. The year 1933 saw another vast purge. Stalin's Terror had begun, but most people continued to believe all was well with the nation, primarily because, according to Nadezhda Mandelstam, their minimum everyday needs were being met: "We think that everything is going along as it should, and that life continues—but that is only because the trams are running."[1] However, others were under no delusions as to what was happening, and she attempts to explain why such people put up so little resistance against what was happening to them:

> There had been a time when, terrified of chaos, we had all prayed for a strong system, for a powerful hand that would stem the angry human river overflowing its banks. This fear of chaos was perhaps the most permanent of our feelings—we have still not recovered from it, and it is passed on from one generation to another. There is not one of us—either among the old who saw the Revolution or the young and innocent—who does not believe that he would be the first victim if ever the mob got out of hand. . . . What we wanted was for the course of history to be made smooth, all the ruts and potholes to be removed, so there should never again be any unforeseen events and everything should flow along evenly and according to Plan. This longing prepared us, psychologically, for the appearance of the Wise Leaders who would tell us where we were going. And once they were there, we no longer ventured to act without their guidance and looked to them for direct instructions and foolproof pre-scriptions. . . . In our blindness we ourselves struggled to impose una-nimity—because in every disagreement, in every difference of opinion, we saw the beginnings of new anarchy and chaos. And either by silence or consent we ourselves helped the system to gain strength and protect itself against its detractors . . . so we went on, nursing a sense of our own inadequacy, until the moment came for each of us to discover from bitter experience how precarious was his own state of grace.[2]

As Akhmatova put it in her later works, life was a finely woven fabric, consisting of threads intertwining the situation Fate had created and the choices one made within those conditions. The people who had remained behind after the Revolution chose to do so, not knowing what Fate had in store for them. Yet Akhmatova also said later in life that she was not sorry for the choice she had made, and did not regret that she stayed with her country and her people when they suffered the most. How individuals reacted to the Terror which they shared in common revealed the differences between those who attempted to maintain their integrity and those who found the external pressure unbearable and made compromises. No one who has not been faced by the same conditions dare judge their actions. As Dmitry Usov, a philologist, wrote in March 1931:

> You're right—one must live no matter what (and I'm the first to repeat this). But the fact is that if one looks with the eyes with which we are looking at the world now, I'm a dead man. You know I have a feeling of duty and responsibility—but it's more than my strength can bear to see life where there is really only death and destruction for me and those

like me. You look at Anna Akhmatova and say that you don't have the spirit to tell yourself, "Every person chooses his own fate." But there are paths which we do not choose and it is impossible to depart from such paths without parting from life itself.[3]

Akhmatova was no longer published during these long years, nor did she give public readings. However, she had left her seclusion and now appeared at concerts, on walks in the Summer Garden, and at the Lenkublit dining room, where writers had subsidized meals. Nadezhda Rykova wrote that during the years 1930–34 writers were helped by the Commission for the Improvement of Writers' Lives (*Lenkublit*). A dining hall was opened for members of literary organizations, which soon turned into a literary club where everyone ate kasha. Rykova often sat at the same table as Akhmatova. She says that although Akhmatova was rarely printed, no one—especially among young people—forgot her poetry. People frequently came to visit the poet and asked her to read.[4]

It was clear by 1930 that Akhmatova's relationship with Punin was already beginning to become difficult, and her feelings toward him were ambiguous. She said later that by 1930 she wanted to move to the Sreznevskys', but Punin said her staying was a matter of life and death. And yet, she added, "He always made you feel how bored he was with you." Clearly Akhmatova was attached to Punin and somehow hoped things would get better, but they only worsened. In 1933, she was forced to sell her library. She remembered how the books were standing in piles in a large room, many with inscriptions to her. "Punin said this never happened. He remembers what he wants to. I have no books any more."[5]

Akhmatova analyzed the psychological relationship with Punin's wife and child, with whom she was still living. She said that Punin attempted to re-create his own childhood through this situation—a stepmother persecuting her stepchild—but instead Akhmatova took care of Punin's daughter Irina while Punin's wife, Anna Arens, was away because of her medical practice. "I was supposed to persecute Ira," Akhmatova said. "But I didn't. I taught her French. . . . What tender letters the little girl wrote me!"[6] The relationship between Irina and Akhmatova was indeed a complex one, especially after Lev began to live with them; it would become even more difficult when Irina grew up and Akhmatova stayed on after Punin was no longer there.

One of the few testimonies we have about Akhmatova's life during the early thirties is that of the art historian Vsevolod Petrov, who was a young man at the time, working with Punin on various artistic projects. He has left a portrait of Punin which shows why Akhmatova found him so attractive. Petrov said people were fascinated by the excitement Punin generated when speaking, which sometimes was reflected in a nervous tic; he had an absolute mastery of the Russian language and wrote and spoke with great eloquence. Petrov explains why Punin commanded so much respect in the world of art:

There are people who have absolute musical pitch. Many composers and musicians do not have it, and many piano tuners have it. It has little to do with actual musical talent. One can also speak of "absolute vision," when someone sees forms and colors in greater clarity than the ordinary person. This is also not a talent and has little to do with a gift for painting. Punin did not have good eyesight, and that is why he was not drafted to fight in World War I. However, what he did have was the absolute vision of an art historian, a faultless feeling for artistic quality, a refined ability to see a certain harmony in an artistic work. And this was a special talent based not on physical sight but on a certain kind of spirit and intellectual capability. He had a talent for analysis and for scientific synthesis. This unusually strong intuition revealed the very essence of a creative concept in a work of art.[7]

Petrov describes Akhmatova in 1932, when he first met her. She was forty-three—tall, elegant, very thin—and resembled her Altman portrait. Petrov was working on the archives of *Apollon* and the World of Art artists, and his discussions with Akhmatova about his work took her back to the atmosphere of pre-Revolutionary Russia, to the period she called "our epoch." To Petrov, Akhmatova and Punin were two remarkable figures, living embodiments of the spirit of this epoch, which coincided with the years of their youth—a period that would never be repeated in Russian culture. At the time he met them, they seemed a loving couple, almost like newlyweds, although they had been together about ten years. He never heard them quarrel. Their tastes seemed to be similar in many important respects, but temperamentally they were quite different. Akhmatova was not romantic in the traditional way, but more in the classical sense of Pushkin or Goethe. Petrov noted her faultless sense of form, which was reflected in everything she did, from her poems to her restrained manner of speaking and acting. She reflected an inner harmony and tact in the broadest sense of the word. This serenity was in sharp contrast to Punin's chaotic intuitiveness. But in spite of Akhmatova's regal bearing, Petrov says she was beginning to show signs of being affected by the increasingly sinister atmosphere of the 1930s.

Conscious of the turmoil in their homeland, Akhmatova's friends abroad continued to worry about her. Yevgeny Zamyatin, who went to Paris after the vicious attacks on *We,* sent her packages and money, as did Georgy Chulkov.[8]

Like Zamyatin, Yury Olesha was also a member of the Serapian Brothers, the literary group that wrote satires on the NEP period and life under the Soviet regime. He recalled meeting Akhmatova in the early thirties. Because they both came from Odessa in the Ukraine, he felt a common bond with her:

I consider her one of the most talented poets of the Russian constellation of the twentieth century. When I was a schoolboy she was already famous. I had not met her after I had become a well-known writer. I thought a lot of myself at that time, since I had gained a certain amount of recognition. Finally, one night in Leningrad, when I had decided to go to the restaurant in the Hotel Europe, a writer friend asked me if I would like to meet Akhmatova. I did. Perhaps I wanted to show off. In any case, I said to myself, damn it, she must understand who she was speaking with. I sat down at a little table. . . . Suddenly she began to speak. She said that she was translating *Macbeth*. She told me there are lines where the hero says that his homeland is more like a stepmother than a mother, and that people in his homeland are dying more swiftly than the flowers fade in their hats. She liked this, she said, or rather, she did not say it, but her face showed it. Possibly knowing about my fame, she also wanted to let me know who she was. I felt like a little boy, like a schoolboy.[9]

Akhmatova had begun translating *Macbeth* in the early thirties, and worked on Act I, Scene iii, where the witches predict Macbeth will become king. Perhaps she never worked on it further because two translations of the play came out in 1934, one by Sergey Solovyov and another by Anna Radlova.[10] She obviously saw parallels between the murders committed by Macbeth and his wife to gain power and what was occurring in the Soviet Union. Lady Macbeth, the "Scottish queen," appears in a famous poem written in 1933 by Akhmatova evoking the blood spilled by the Bolsheviks:

Wild honey smells like freedom,
Dust—like a ray of sun.
Like violets—a young maid's mouth,
And gold—like nothing.
The flowers of the mignonette smell like water,
And like an apple—love.
But we learned once and for all
That blood only smells like blood.

And in vain the vice-regent of Rome
Washed his hands before all the people,
Urged on by the ominous shouts of the rabble;
And the Scottish queen
In vain washed the spattered red drops
From her slender palms
In the stifling gloom of the king's home . . .

(II, p. 96)

The world was beginning to close in on Akhmatova's friends. Mandelstam was now one of the few poets left of her status from before the Revolution. Even then, they had had a very special relationship of mutual affection and respect.

(Although he had written criticism against her in the early 1920s, he was never to do so again.) As the circumstances around Mandelstam rapidly grew worse during the Terror, Akhmatova proved a loyal friend, and helped him in any way she could. In Nadezhda Mandelstam's words: "The Akhmatova I knew was a fierce and passionate friend, who stood by Mandelstam with an unshakable loyalty, his ally against the savage world in which we spent our lives, a stern, unyielding abbess ready to go to the stake for her faith."[11]

In 1928, Mandelstam published collections of poems, critical essays, and prose. But for four years he had found it difficult to publish his work and had been forced to earn his living writing children's books, doing hack translations and journalism, and any odd jobs he could find in government publishing houses. Ironically, "his standing among connoisseurs of poetry had never been higher, but the Soviet state viewed him with increasing suspicion and malevolence."[12]

Nikolay Bukharin was able to help Mandelstam early in the 1930s when he got into trouble, although Bukharin's own star was soon to fall. Bukharin had been one of the main theoreticians of the Communist Party and disagreed with Stalin that the Soviet Union must embrace rapid industrialization and collectivization. Soon after Stalin took power, in 1929, Bukharin was relieved of his position as head of the Comintern, the international organization of Communists, and was expelled from the Politburo. He was executed in 1938—accused of sabotage, espionage, and a conspiracy to kill Lenin and Stalin as early as 1918. However, when Mandelstam turned to him for help at the beginning of the thirties, Bukharin was still an important figure, and was able to arrange for Mandelstam and his wife to be sent to Armenia on a survey. Upon his return, Mandelstam wrote *Journey to Armenia*, published in 1933, his last work to appear in the Soviet press for three decades.

In the autumn of 1933, the Mandelstams received an apartment in the new writers' house on Nashchokin Street in Moscow. In one room there was almost no furniture, and that was where Akhmatova stayed whenever she came to visit. Mandelstam nicknamed it "the heathen temple." Akhmatova said of this period in his life: "It was constantly necessary to telephone somewhere, expect something to happen, hope for something to happen. But nothing ever came of it."[13]

Sharing the apartment with the Mandelstams was Sergey Klychkov, a peasant poet and novelist who would be arrested in 1937. Nadezhda Mandelstam describes him as "an outlandish but most gentle creature, a gypsy with bright dark blue eyes."[14] He spoke like a Russian peasant, and his whole face was lit from within. Akhmatova's meeting with Klychkov in the apartment was like an encounter between a "peasant" and a "grande dame," but in spite of their differences, they felt a kinship and respected each other.

Klychkov, who had been living with his wife, daughter, and mother-in-law in this communal apartment, gives an insight into the eroding effects of such communal living on one's creativity in his correspondence with the authorities: "Frankly speaking, it is impossible to work in the midst of pots and pans, cooking and cleaning—and exhausted from the horror of all this commotion, I beg you to expel me from the [Soviet] Union [of Writers]. It's better to live under a bus than experience all this humiliation. My God, I'm already an old man and no longer have the strength to put up with all this constantly."[15]

Within a few years Mandelstam aged tremendously. He grew heavy, gray, and began having problems with his breathing. His pension was hardly enough to pay for his apartment and buy his rations, and he had to supplement it by income from "half-translations, half-reviews, half-promises," as Akhmatova puts it in her memoir. But in spite of all this, his poetry at this time improved, and so did his prose.

In 1933, the Mandelstams came to Leningrad. Mandelstam had been invited to recite for two evenings. Yelena Tager, a poet and writer, remembers the event. She said there were no announcements or posters, but the hall was packed, young people stood in the corridors and crowded at the doors. Mandelstam read with ferocious intensity, his head tossed back as usual, "erect—as if a whirlwind was tearing him from the earth and flinging him upward." His hair was thin now, and fatigue and sorrow had furrowed his brow. "He's old!" yelled the crowd. "He's supposed to be young. How shabby he's become." He read about his youth, and everyone listened, holding their breath—then the applause. But there were others in the hall who were dissatisfied.

> Someone threw a note onto the stage. Mandelstam picked it up slowly. It was clearly provocative. It suggested that he talk about contemporary Soviet poetry and explain the significance of the older poets who had come from pre-Revolutionary times. We saw Mandelstam turn pale: he clenched his fists and crumpled the note. . . . He was being subjected to a public interrogation and had no way of getting out of it. There was an uneasy silence. Some were indifferent, some curious, and others turned pale. Mandelstam stepped up to the very edge of the stage, his head thrown back, eyes sparkling. . . . "What do you want from me? What kind of an answer? I am the friend of my friends!" A pause. Then, with an ecstatic, victorious shout: "I am . . . the contemporary of Akhmatova!" And then a storm of applause.[16]

Vladimir Admoni, a scholar of German literature, who later became a good friend of Akhmatova, recalled going with his wife to hear the recitation. "We were shaken by the poems that Mandelstam read—those we already knew and those we heard for the first time. But we were most struck by Mandelstam's image, a combination of pride and doom, strength and fragility. . . . He behaved with such natural assurance, as if there was room within him for the tremendous power of the human spirit, the inexhaustible and deep force of poetry. And yet, in spite of this, his small figure seemed—and was—extremely vulnerable and unprotected." Admoni says the feeling that Mandelstam was a doomed figure was even stronger because on the evening of one of his readings, at the House of Journalists, a whisper rippled from one person to the next—before the evening began, during the reading, and in the pauses between poems—of the news of the arrest of several teachers and students at the university.[17]

Mandelstam also visited Akhmatova on this trip to Leningrad. He had just learned Italian and was raving about Dante, reciting whole passages by heart. Akhmatova too loved Dante, and when they began to talk about *Purgatory,* Akhmatova recited the Canto describing the appearance of Beatrice, and Mandelstam started to weep. "I was frightened," she said. She asked Mandelstam what was wrong; he replied, "No, it's nothing, just those words, and in your voice."[18] Nadezhda said Akhmatova seemed to be at ease and in high spirits at the time, but Punin was very boisterous, laughed a lot, and his tic—the left cheek and eyelid twitching—was worse than ever.[19]

Akhmatova called the early 1930s the "vegetarian years," meaning it was a relatively harmless time in comparison to the "meat-eating" years that were to come. But when visiting the Mandelstams in Moscow, she felt that "in spite of the fact that the time was comparatively vegetarian, the shadow of trouble and doom lay on this house." She recalls a walk she took with Mandelstam along Prechistenka Street in February 1934. "We turned onto Gogol Boulevard and Osip said, 'I'm ready for death.' "[20]

No one is ever really ready for death. When finally arrested, the gentle, sensitive poet was so shocked he slowly went mad. A poem dedicated to Akhmatova, written in 1931, reveals his apprehension:

Keep my words for their aftertaste of misery and smoke,
for the resins of round patience, the honest tar of toil,
the way water in Novgorod wells must be honey-black
so by Christmas you can see, seven-fin star reflected . . .

And in payment, father, friend, tough helper,
I—unacknowledged brother, renegade in the people-family—
I promise to build such thick log-walls
that Tartars could lower princes in them like buckets.

If only those old executioner's blocks loved me!
The way they play croquet in the garden, like striving forward Death
    itself,
oh we'd walk the rest of my life in an iron shirt, for that and
for executions like Peter's, I'd hunt for a huge axe-handle in the
    woods.[21]

The poem that finally got Mandelstam into trouble was a satirical portrayal of Stalin, the "Kremlin's mountaineer," mentioning his "cockroach whiskers" and "fingers fat as worms." He supposedly read it only to a few people, but Emma

Gershtein, a literary scholar who was close to the Mandelstams, to Akhmatova, and had a romantic relationship with her son Lev, said that Mandelstam read it to everyone possible, and Stalin soon found out about it.

We live, deaf to the land below us,
Ten steps away no one hears our speeches,

But where there's so much as half a conversation
The Kremlin's mountaineer will be mentioned.

His fingers are fat as worms
And the words, final as lead weights, fall from his lips
His cockroach whiskers leer
And his boot tops shine.

Around him a crowd of thin-necked leaders—
Fawning half-men for him to play with.

The whinny, purr or whine
As he prances and points a finger.

One by one forging his laws, to be flung
Like horseshoes at the head, the eye or the groin.

And every murder is a treat
For the broad-chested Ossete.[22]

The arrest order was signed by Genrikh Yagoda, head of the secret police. Akhmatova was visiting Mandelstam in May 1934, and was there the actual night of the arrest. It was difficult for her to pay for the trip, but she had come after many pleading telephone calls and telegrams from Mandelstam. She had so little money she had taken along Remizov's document declaring her membership in the Charter of the Apes, that whimsical association of creative people he had invented, and the statuette of herself by Yelena Danko to sell to the literary museum. Akhmatova describes the evening of the arrest in her own words. (The scene's grotesqueness was heightened by the sound of a ukulele heard through the thin walls, played by another member of the communal apartment, the poet Kirsanov.): "The search went on all night. They were looking for poetry, and walked across manuscripts that had been thrown out of the trunk. We all sat in one room. It was very quiet. On the other side of the wall, at Kirsanov's, a ukulele was playing. . . . In farewell he [Mandelstam] kissed me. They took him away at seven in the morning."[23]

Akhmatova sat with Nadezhda Mandelstam in the ransacked apartment. "You must keep your strength up," she told her, meaning that Nadezhda must prepare for her ordeal, since people were often held for a long time before they were exiled or killed. Akhmatova's son Lev had been living with the Mandelstams the winter of 1934–35, but had gone to the Ardovs' in the same building so his mother would have a place to stay. He came over very early in the morning to have tea with them and was told the news as he walked through the door. Nadezhda describes him as he appeared at that moment:

He was still a boy, but so alive with ideas that wherever he appeared in those years he always caused a stir. People sensed the dynamic strength fermenting in him and knew that he was doomed. Now our house had been stricken by the plague and become a death trap for anyone prone to infection. For this reason I was overcome by horror at the sight of Lev. "Go away," I said. "Go away at once. Osip was arrested last night." And he obediently went away. That was the rule among us.[24]

Boris Pasternak went to see Bukharin to intercede for Mandelstam— Bukharin was now editor of *Izvestiya* and still had some power. And Akhmatova went to the Kremlin to see Stalin's old comrade, Avel Yenukidze, who was Secretary of the Central Executive Committee. Akhmatova says it was a miracle to be able to penetrate the Kremlin. However, the actor Ruslanov had arranged for Akhmatova to see Yenukidze through his secretary. Yenukidze was polite enough, she said, but immediately asked, "But perhaps, a few poems?", meaning he knew very well about Mandelstam's satirical attack against Stalin, and other unpublished poems against the regime. Due to the efforts of Akhmatova and Pasternak, the outcome was not as harsh as it might have been. The verdict was three years in Cherdyn, a small town on the River Kama in the Urals.[25]

Fifteen days later, Nadezhda received a phone call saying if she wished to go with her husband, she should be at the Kazan Station in Moscow for the departure. Akhmatova accompanied her to the station, stopping with her on the way at the Lubyanka prison for documents. She could not wait until Mandelstam arrived, because otherwise she would have missed her train to Leningrad, and she always regretted this: "It was very bad that I did not wait, and that he did not see me, because, as a result, in Cherdyn he began to think I had certainly perished."[26] Nadezhda says that walking around Cherdyn, Osip would look for Akhmatova's corpse in the ravines.[27]

In Cherdyn, Mandelstam broke his arm when he threw himself from the window of the hospital because he thought they were coming to take him away to be executed. Nadezhda sent a telegram to the Central Committee. Finally, through Bukharin's help, Mandelstam was able to choose a different place for his exile. Mandelstam's sentence was commuted to "minus twelve," which meant that he could pick out any place to live except twelve major cities. They chose Voronezh, the town where Peter the Great had built his Azov fleet.

The real Terror started after the assassination on December 1, 1934, of Sergey Kirov, Stalin's chief lieutenant in Leningrad, by Leonid Nikolayev, a young Communist. The incident became the excuse for the bloodbath known as the Great Purge that went on for four years. The murder was blamed on foreign powers, on Trotsky, Zinovyev, and others who were opposed to Stalin. (Much later, at the Twentieth Party Congress in 1956, Nikita Khrushchev hinted that Stalin himself was responsible for the crime.) The Central Executive Committee deprived anyone accused of "terrorist acts" of any right of defense, which allowed for mass arrests and the deportation or execution of thousands. Andrey Zhdanov, who would be responsible for Akhmatova's tremendous suffering after the war, took Kirov's place in Leningrad. At a public trial in 1936, sixteen Bolsheviks, major figures in the Communist Party, were accused of working for Trotsky and committing terrorist acts against Stalin and the country and were blamed for Kirov's death. All sixteen were sentenced to death and executed. Nikolay Yezhov replaced Yagoda as head of the secret police. Yagoda himself was arrested in 1937 and executed the following year. On June 11, 1937, there was a trial of Red Army commanders, all of whom were executed: the Red Army lost half its officers, for which Stalin and the country would pay dearly when the Germans attacked in World War II, since there were few officers left with enough experience to put up a proper defense.

The last major show trial took place in March 1938, when twenty-one former members of the opposition to Stalin were condemned. All but three were sentenced and executed, including Bukharin. Merle Fainsod, who conducted interviews with former members of camps, describes this terrible period in Soviet history: "The arrests mounted into the millions; the testimony of the survivors is unanimous regarding crowded prison cells and teeming forced labor camps. Most of the prisoners were utterly bewildered by the fate which had befallen them. . . . Under the zealous and ruthless ministrations of NKVD examiners, millions of innocents were transformed into traitors, terrorists, and enemies of the people."[28]

Olga Freidenberg, an important scholar and a cousin of Pasternak, kept a diary throughout her life. During the thirties she noted:

> Stalin launched a machine of destruction known by the name of Yezhovshchina. Yezhov was the head of the secret police. He was always referred to by such Homeric epithets as "the Iron Commissar" and "Stalin's comrade in arms." A period of dreadful political trials, arrests, and exile began. The revolutionary intelligentsia, the head of the body of the Soviet people, was cut off. Every evening, radio broadcasts telling about a bloody trial would be followed by records of folk dances. My soul has never recovered from the trauma of the prisonlike hell of the Kremlin chimes striking the midnight hour. We had no radio, but the midnight chimes sounded particularly sinister when they followed on the terrible words, "The sentence has been carried out."[29]

An acquaintance of Akhmatova's, Lyubov Yakovleva-Shaporina, described the atmosphere in Leningrad. Every evening before she went to sleep she prepared everything in case of arrest. Everyone was innocent but considered guilty. If one was not shot or exiled, it was only due to happenstance. For many, exile meant death, for the sick had no way of earning money—children and very old people were sent into exile along with everyone else.

The description by Yakovleva-Shaporina of saying farewell to friends is typical of what it was like for millions who were leaving their homes, perhaps forever:

> My heart contracted when I got to the train station. It was terrible. What I saw there is impossible to convey. An enormous crowd on the platform. The air was misty, perhaps it was smoke. It seemed as if the city were burning, as if houses were enveloped in flames and the conflagration had driven thousands of residents out into the streets. They were attempting to save whatever they could of their property, to save it from the fire, as long as their strength remained. On the platform were a piano, cupboards. . . . What were they doing on the platform? Probably they had hoped to put them somewhere on the train but did not have enough strength to do so and left them behind. People brought with them normal, ordinary things with which they were reluctant to part. Things that had been in the family for decades, things they had grown up with . . . Now everything had to be sold for almost nothing. And the tears . . . those who were leaving cried, the ones remaining also cried.[30]

A sword of Damocles hung over Akhmatova's friend Mikhail Lozinsky, the great translator of Dante and Shakespeare. He had been sentenced to leave Leningrad, but Alexey Tolstoy and the Union of Writers intervened, managing to save him at the last minute.

Nadezhda Mandelstam commented:

> We never asked, on hearing about the latest arrest, "What was he arrested for?" but we were exceptional. Most people, crazed by fear, asked this question just to give themselves a little hope: if others were arrested for some reason, then they wouldn't be arrested, because they hadn't done anything wrong. . . . "What for?" Akhmatova would cry indignantly, whenever, infected by the prevailing climate, anyone of our circle asked this question. "What do you mean *what for?* It's time you understood that people are arrested for nothing!"[31]

The Terror was coming closer to Akhmatova herself. She tried to help friends who were affected by it. Yelena Bulgakova, wife of Mikhail Bulgakov, the famous author of *The Master and Margarita,* noted in her diary on April 7, 1935, that she gave lunch to Akhmatova, who had come to Moscow to help one of her acquaintances who had been exiled from Leningrad.[32] Others related how Akhmatova escorted one of her exiled friends to a train station in 1935, where she had to stop every few steps to say hello to acquaintances, many of them members of the aristocracy being sent into exile on the same train.[33]

In 1933, Akhmatova's son Lev was first arrested. Like many others, he was totally innocent of any anti-Soviet agitation. Perhaps it was enough that he was the son of Nikolay Gumilyov and Anna Akhmatova. He describes how many like him, children of parents whom the government considered suspect, were sent into exile on trumped-up charges. He had been visiting a colleague, the Middle Eastern scholar Eberman, to consult him about the translation of an Arabic poem. Suddenly there was the proverbial knock on the door, and a crowd of people rushed in, grabbed them, and brought them to prison. Lev spent nine days in prison, but Eberman was not so lucky; Lev assumed he died in prison in 1949.[34]

The next arrest took place in October 1935. Lev said that students from families of the intelligentsia were being arrested, especially those doing well in their courses. A history department had recently been organized at the university, and just after students had been accepted, the purge began, including Lev himself. Everyone arrested was declared a member of an anti-Soviet organization. At this time they did not torture anyone, simply interrogated them. Punin, supposedly the head of one of these organizations, was also arrested.

Yelena Bulgakova noted in her diary on October 30, 1935: "During the day the doorbell rang. I went out—it was Akhmatova—with a terrible look on her face and so thin neither I nor Misha [Mikhail Bulgakov] could recognize her. It turned out they had arrested both her husband [i.e., Punin] and her son. She had come to deliver a letter to [Stalin]. She was totally distracted, mumbling something to herself."[35]

Akhmatova, along with Punin's wife, burned every document that might appear compromising. She then went for help to the writer Lydia Seifullina, who turned out to be a very good friend. Seifullina phoned officials in the Communist Party and the NKVD, and they told her Akhmatova should deliver a letter to Stalin at the Kutafya Tower of the Kremlin, and that Poskryobyshev (Stalin's secretary) would hand it over to Stalin himself. The next day Akhmatova copied the letter to Stalin by hand and she drove with Boris Pilnyak to the Kremlin. Pilnyak handed over the letter.[36]

Boris Pasternak also helped by writing a letter to Stalin, telling Akhmatova, "Regardless of how much any other person might have begged me to write, I would not have done so, but in your case. . . ." Akhmatova wandered around Moscow in a trance, and then spent some time with the Pasternaks. Trying to take her mind off her problems, they spoke all evening about Annensky, and then they put her to bed. When she awoke the next morning, Zinaida, Pasternak's wife, showed her the telegram from Leningrad from the Punins saying that both Punin and Lev were already home. Poskryobyshev phoned the Pasternaks with the happy news of the release.[37]

The release was so unexpected that Punin was actually upset when they awoke him during the night—he thought it was for another interrogation. He also realized if he left at that moment, there would be no trams, and asked if he could stay the night, to which they replied, "This is not a hotel!"[38]

In his autobiographical novel, the Ukrainian poet Teren Masenko tells us of meeting Akhmatova at Pilnyak's. He describes how nervous she was, but that her pale blue eyes reflected great spiritual strength. Masenko admired Boris Pilnyak's sensitive treatment of Akhmatova—no one but Pilnyak knew what she was going through at this point. Before supper he proposed a toast: "The first toast is to Anna Akhmatova," and then in Ukrainian, "Long live—but who—we alone know!" Masenko looked across at Natasha, Pilnyak's daughter, for an explanation, but only found out later what this meant: "He [Pilnyak] had done something unprecedented. Something one in a hundred thousand would have done. I bow down before him."[39] But in two years' time no one was able to save Pilnyak himself. He was arrested and accused of collaborating with the Japanese and of supporting Trotsky. There were rumors that he was executed in 1938.[40] Akhmatova wrote a moving poem to Pilnyak in gratitude for his help:

All this you alone can guess . . .
When the sleepless darkness seethes,
That sunny, that lily-of-the-valley wedge
Will pierce the December night's gloom.
And along this path I'll come to you.
And you will laugh a carefree laugh.
But the fir tree forest and the rushes in the pond
Answer with a kind of strange echo . . .
Oh, if I'm waking the dead,
Forgive me, I can't do otherwise;
I grieve for you as for my own,
And I envy anyone who weeps,
Who is able to weep in this terrible hour
For the one who lies in the ravine's depth . . .
But the moisture boiled off before it reached my eyes,
My eyes were not refreshed.

(II, p. 92)

Another who perished during the years of the Terror was the peasant poet Nikolay Klyuev: Akhmatova says that when Mandelstam came to Leningrad in 1933, he recited an excerpt from Klyuev's poem "The Revilers of Art":

Akhmatova—a jasmine bush
Adored by the gray asphalt,
Has she lost the path to the caves,

Where Dante went and the air is thick,
And a nymph spins crystal flax?
Amidst Russian women distant Anna
She, like a cloud, appears through
The evening broom bush like a streak of gray![41]

These lines were written in Moscow, where Klyuev had moved at the end of 1931. Gray asphalt symbolizes the city, which Klyuev, the peasant, thought stifled true creativity. Lines from this poem would later appear in the second part of Akhmatova's *Poem Without a Hero*.

Klyuev was arrested in 1934 and sent to Siberia. In 1935, he sent a letter to a friend, saying:

I'm not sorry for myself as a public figure, but for my song-bees, sweet, sunny and golden. My heart is very sad for them. I believe that one day it will be understood that without the salt of Russian song, the poetry under our snowstorm sky, to the noise of weeping Novgorod shores, will be insipid. It is with a great pain in my heart that I sometimes read the poems of superficially famous poets in the newspapers: How gray! How insignificant! Not a word, not an image! Everything in foreign taste. Colors? Pure synthetic, whitewash and soot. Poor Vroubel, poor Picasso, Matisse, Serov, Gauguin, Verlaine, Akhmatova, Verhaeren! Your dawns, lightning, and pearls are of no use to us. Very harmful and pathetic.[42]

In the summer of 1935, Akhmatova saw Pasternak, who had stopped in Leningrad on his way back from the International Congress of Writers in Paris. They took walks together around the city, and he told Akhmatova he was suffering from mental problems. It was a difficult time for him; he had stopped writing poetry and believed his days as a poet were over.[43] Akhmatova was writing little at this time, and Mandelstam had gone through a similar crisis between 1925 and 1930. Nadezhda Mandelstam tried to explain what happened to all three:

"It must be something about the air," said Akhmatova—and there was indeed something in the air: the beginning, perhaps, of that general drowsiness which we still find so hard to shake off. Was it just coincidence that these three active poets were stricken by dumbness for a time? Whatever the differences in their basic attitudes, the fact is that before they could find their voices again, all three had to determine their places in the new world being created before their eyes.[44]

By 1935 Akhmatova felt the same emptiness, that sense that her Muse had forsaken her, which Pasternak had felt a few years before. She told her friend Nina Olshevskaya, "I probably have already written everything [I ever will]. Poems no longer come into my head."[45]

Nina was to become one of Akhmatova's closest friends, especially after the war when Akhmatova came to Moscow and stayed with her for long periods of time. During the thirties Nina was an actress with the Moscow Art Theater and later at the Soviet Army Theater. Her husband, Viktor Ardov, wrote humorous stories, film scenarios, and satirical sketches. At this time they lived on the first floor of the same building as the Mandelstams, and that was where Akhmatova met them. Alexey Batalov, Nina's son by her first marriage and now one of Russia's leading film actors, was also living with them. He has described what it was like to have Akhmatova come visit. Batalov was used to celebrities filling the apartment, who for this six-year-old child were like uncles and aunts. But Akhmatova was different. "Every time a special lady came from Leningrad, she immediately got the couch. . . . Everything about her was Leningrad—her hairdo with the long bangs, her simple, long dress, her slow movements, her quiet voice."[46]

In February 1936, Akhmatova went to visit the Mandelstams in Voronezh. They were finally able to have a short vacation in Zadonsk because Akhmatova and Pasternak each contributed 500 rubles. During his exile Mandelstam was not allowed to publish his own original works, which would have brought in some income. The first winter of his exile his pension was stopped. At first he was given money for some translations, but by 1935 that had ended. After constant pleading, Mandelstam was given work in the local theater as literary director and at a local broadcasting station; he also wrote program notes for concerts. He and Nadezhda lived on cabbage soup and eggs. Then, in the autumn of 1936, after their trip to Zadonsk, they returned to find the radio station and the theater closed. In his typically unrealistic fashion, Mandelstam had the brilliant idea of getting a cow, but suddenly realized they would have to find fodder to feed it. Even so, Mandelstam enjoyed Voronezh, whose population were descendants of outcasts and runaway convicts from the time of Peter the Great, and whose streets bore such colorful names as Strangler's Lane, Embezzler's Street, Counterfeiter's Row.

A young poet named Sergey Rudakov was also exiled to Voronezh and became close to the Mandelstams. He noted that Akhmatova arrived on February 5, 1936. Rudakov and Nadezhda met her at the station and found something nightmarish about her appearance—she seemed so old. But once at the Mandelstams', she was transformed, becoming lively and seemingly ageless. He wrote to his wife how beautiful Akhmatova was. Mandelstam and Akhmatova read Dante together, talked, and joked. Nadezhda describes this special moment in their lives: "When he [Osip] was with Akhmatova, one could always see that their relations went back to the madcap days of their youth. Whenever they met, they both became young again and made each other laugh with words from their private vocabulary."[47]

Akhmatova eventually became close enough to Rudakov to entrust her valuable Gumilyov files to him, hoping he would use them to write about Gumilyov.

Rudakov was killed in World War II, and the files were kept by his wife, Lina. She asked Emma Gershtein to tell Akhmatova that the manuscripts had been accidentally destroyed. Akhmatova, however, was sure Lina had sold them. Apparently she was right, because over the years manuscripts from this archive have appeared in private hands or in Pushkinsky Dom, the institute in Leningrad devoted to literature.[48]

Ryszard Przybylski says Mandelstam could not tolerate complaints about fear. Back in 1910, Mandelstam had written that admiration of one's own suffering weakens the soul. "Even in the lowest circle of hell one is bound to fight against his fate."[49] However, in the end Mandelstam at one point gave in to utter despair. After his first exile, he wrote a poem in praise of Stalin, hoping it would save him, but later characterized what he had done as a sickness. He told Lydia Ginzburg that when they interrogated Joan of Arc, the third time they showed her the bonfire which had been prepared for her, she revoked what she had said. But when she was shown it a fourth time and confirmed her earlier claims, they asked her, "Why did you agree yesterday?" "I'm afraid of fire," she replied. ("J'ai peur du feu.")[50] Similarly Mandelstam lost his nerve and wrote an ode to Stalin, only to regret it later.

In March 1937, Mandelstam wrote a poem indicating he felt his end was near. The poet identifies with Dante and expresses a love of life:

> Don't separate me from life—it dreams
> Of killing and caressing at once,
> So that Florentine yearning may beat
> At the ears, the eyes, and the eyesockets.

Instead of adorning his temples with a laurel wreath, a new ritual is proposed:

> Don't place, don't place
> The sharply caressing laurel on my temples—
> Rather, cut open my heart
> Into the pieces of a blue bell.

The poem ends with the sound of the poet's heart spreading out across the world, becoming the sky, and like an echo of the sky, returning to man:

> And when I die, my service done,
> The lifelong friend of all living things,
> May the response of heaven in my breast
> Respond farther and higher.

Przybylski believes Mandelstam never lost his faith in life and God, despite—or perhaps because of—his suffering. "Despite the ruthlessness and the wild cruelty of the executioners, despite the stupidity and boorishness of the crowd, he remained to the end God's grateful guest."[51]

Mandelstam's term of exile expired in May 1937. When he and Nadezhda returned to Moscow, Akhmatova was the first to visit him, and he read his new poems to her. Nadezhda says, "Mandelstam paced rapidly around the room and recited to Akhmatova. He was giving her an account of what he had written in Voronezh. In return, Akhmatova read him a poem she had written about him in Voronezh."[52]

At first this poem of Akhmatova's appears to be a poetic description of Voronezh in winter, with its reference to the statue of Peter the Great, who built his fleet there, and the Battle of Kulikovo, a landmark in Russian history, fought nearby in 1380, when the Grand Prince Dmitry Donskoy defeated the Tatars after many years of domination. But the idyllic winter scene suddenly becomes grotesque as eternal night descends on the "poet in disgrace." These last four lines were omitted when the poem was first published in 1940:

> And the whole town is encased in ice,
> Trees, walls, snow, as if under glass.
> Timidly, I walk on crystals,
> Gaily painted sleds skid.
> And over the Peter of Voronezh—crows,
> Poplar trees, and the dome, light green,
> Faded, dulled, in sunny haze,
> And the battle of Kulikovo blows from the slopes
> Of the mighty, victorious land.
> The poplars, like cups clashed together,
> Roar over us, stronger and stronger,
> As if our joy were toasted by
> A thousand guests at a wedding feast.
> But in the room of the poet in disgrace,
> Fear and the Muse keep watch by turns.
> And the night comes on
> That knows no dawn.

> (II, p. 87)[53]

The Mandelstams were not allowed to stay long in the capital. People of their status could reside only at points over 100 kilometers from Moscow, and the area accessible by railroad in this belt was crammed with former prisoners and exiles. The couple consulted maps of the Moscow region, settling at last on the small village of Savelovo on the high bank of the Volga, with three streets and a tea room where they could read the local newspaper. From there they made visits to Moscow.[54]

By July 1937 Nadezhda said they were no longer trying to devise plans to save themselves, but only how they could hold out until the fall. Moscow was empty—everyone was on vacation. Mandelstam proposed a trip to Leningrad, where they spent two days, staying with Akhmatova. Nadezhda says Akhmatova seemed at ease and in high spirits, and Punin was boisterous and laughed a lot, but Nadezhda noticed his left cheek and eyelid twitched more than ever. Akhmatova saw the Mandelstams off at the station.[55]

The first visit gave them enough to live on for three months, thanks to friends. They returned in the fall and met with Akhmatova for the last time. She read Mandelstam her poem "A Little Geography" (1937), dedicated to him. The city of Leningrad has become a transit point to exile:

Not like a European capital
With the first prize for beauty—
But like stifling exile to Yeniseysk,
Like a transfer to Chita,
To Ishim, to waterless Irgiz,
To renowned Atbasar,
To the outpost Svobodnyi,
To the corpse stench of rotting banks—
So this city seemed to me
On that midnight, pale blue—
This city, celebrated by the first poet,
By us sinners and you.

(II, p. 573)

In her memoir, Akhmatova describes her last meeting with Mandelstam:

I saw Mandelstam for the last time in the fall of 1937. He and Nadya had come to Leningrad for two days. It was an apocalyptic time. Misfortune was at all our heels. They had absolutely nowhere to live. Osip had great difficulty breathing and gasped at the air with his lips. I went to see them but I don't remember where they were staying. It was all like a terrible dream. Someone who arrived after me said that Osip's father ("Grandpa") didn't have any warm clothing. Osip took off the sweater he was wearing under his jacket, so that it would be given to his father.[56]

The couple returned to Moscow, and then decided to go to Kalinin on the advice of Isaak Babel, the famous author of *Red Cavalry,* stories about the Civil War. In the fall, Vasily Stavsky, secretary of the board of the Soviet Union of Writers, told Mandelstam he should go to a rest home while the question of work for him was being decided. They were issued vouchers for a rest home at Samatikha, which they thought was a hopeful sign—most of the people there were workers from various factories. The Mandelstams were very well looked after and thought the worst was over. On May Day, 1938, they did not go out but could hear the people celebrating. Then, the next morning, they were wakened by the dreaded knock on the door. Two men in military uniform and a doctor entered with a warrant for Mandelstam's arrest. Nadezhda was never to see him again.[57]

Akhmatova says Nadezhda came to Leningrad and told her, "I will not be at peace until I know he is dead." At the beginning of 1939, Akhmatova received a short letter from Emma Gershtein: "Lena's [Osmerkina] friend had a baby girl, but her friend Nadezhda [Mandelstam] has become a widow." That was how Akhmatova learned of Mandelstam's death.[58] The last letter received from Mandelstam was to his brother Alexander. "Where is my Nadinka?" he wrote, and asked for warm clothes. In June 1940, Mandelstam's brother was summoned to the Registry Office and handed Mandelstam's death certificate. His age was given as forty-seven, and the date of his death as December 27, 1938. The cause was listed as "heart failure."[59]

Akhmatova concludes her memoir of Mandelstam with the words: "For me he is not only a great poet but a great human being who, when he found out (probably from Nadya) how bad it was for me in the House on the Fontanka, told me when he was saying goodbye at the Moscow train station in Leningrad: 'Annushka' (which he had never used before), 'Always remember that my house— is yours.' "[60]

Nadezhda tried to answer a question that has been asked many times throughout history: Why did an event like the Terror encounter so little resistance?

> We were all the same: either sheep who went willingly to the slaughter, or respectful assistants to the executioners. Whichever role we played, we were uncannily submissive, stifling all our human instincts. Why did we never try to jump out of windows or give way to unreasoning fear and just run for it—to the forest, the provinces, or simply into a hail of bullets? Why did we stand by meekly as they went through our belongings? Why did M[andelstam] obediently follow the two soldiers, and why didn't I throw myself on them like a wild animal? What had we to lose? Surely we were not afraid of being charged with resisting arrest? The end was the same anyway, so that was nothing to be afraid of. It was not, indeed, a question of fear. It was something quite different: a paralyzing sense of one's own helplessness to which we were all prey, not only those who were killed, but the killers themselves as well. Crushed by the system each one of us had in some way or other helped to build, we were not even capable of passive resistance. Our submissiveness only spurred on those who actively served the system. How can we escape the vicious circle?[61]

Before Mandelstam's death, Nadezhda had experienced what thousands of other women in the Soviet Union endured during those years—hours of waiting in endless lines in front of a prison window. "The only link with a person in prison was the window through which one handed parcels only to be forwarded to him by the authorities." Once a month, after waiting over three hours in line, she would give her package to the man behind the window.[62]

Now it was Akhmatova's turn to stand in line. Lev was arrested again on March 10, 1938. Mandelstam had once told Akhmatova, "It will be difficult to protect him. There is death inside him."[63] Lev said that he was accused of being politically suspect. This time everything was different. They began to torture him. Since he did not wish to confess anything, they continued beating him for eight months. In Leningrad he was sent first to the inner prison of the NKVD on Shpalernaya Street, then to the Kresty (Crosses) prison across the Neva for eighteen months. They then sent him to the White Sea Canal with a ten-year sentence, but soon brought him back to Leningrad, since the verdict was changed to a more severe one—article 58.17 of the Criminal Code: terroristic activity. Lev was condemned to be shot. However, in the interim Yezhov, head of the NKVD, was removed, and although much remained the same, they stopped beating prisoners. Lev's case was sent to the Special Committee (*Osoboye soveshchaniye*), and soon his sentence was commuted to five years (article 58.10–11). He was sent to Norilsk, in Siberia.[64]

Lev's stepbrother Orest Vysotsky had come to visit Lev on the evening of his arrest and rushed to tell Akhmatova of it. "I still remember how strained she was, gripped with fear for Lev. I think this dark fear haunted her throughout her life." Orest had got to know Akhmatova and Lev in 1936, when he came to Leningrad to study at the Forestry Academy. Soon after Lev's arrest, Orest himself was detained with his fellow students for "counterrevolutionary terrorist activities." He spent a year and a half in a cell, but was finally acquitted and reinstated at the Academy.[65]

The last year of the Great Terror provided the backdrop for Lev's arrest. In March 1938 Bukharin was tried, as well as Yagoda, former head of the NKVD. A huge wave of arrests flooded the country. The persecutions of 1937–38 also included the leaders of the Red Army, who were not tried publicly. Possibly the growing disapproval of the show trials prompted Stalin to move against them. In December 1938, Yezhov was relieved of his position as head of the secret police; he was succeeded by Lavrenty Beriya, a Georgian compatriot of Stalin. Little changed—exile and forced labor continued, but now deportation was accomplished without much publicity. The most prominent figures among the persecuted had already been liquidated and public exposure was no longer necessary. Stalin possibly believed that his power was safe only if the Party wiped out the memory of the years of struggle for freedom, the Revolution, and the Civil War. The Terror bred a mass hysteria that one writer likens to the Spanish Inquisition.[66]

Lydia Zhukova, a member of the intelligentsia, stood in one of those long lines in front of the prison, and describes seeing Akhmatova. She says the hours seemed endless: You felt like leaning against the wall or dropping to the ground from fatigue, but somehow you held out and obediently kept waiting until you had the joy of shoving a parcel through the window grating. That was where Zhukova first saw Akhmatova, on Shpalernaya. Akhmatova went up to the little window:

There stood . . . an aloof mannequin; quietly, without compressing her lips, in her particular Akhmatovian whisper, she said: "Akhmatova—for Gumilyov." Then I noticed her manner of speaking, barely moving her lips . . . and these names would reverberate up and down the frozen line. Lev Gumilyov, son of two poets, punished for the sins of the fathers, perhaps only because they were poets. . . . Wearing something long, dark, and heavy, she appeared to me like a phantom from the past, and it never entered my mind that this old-fashioned lady in an ancient coat and hat would still write so many more brilliant new poems.[67]

Indeed, Akhmatova had begun to write brilliant poems again. Her "mute" period was over, as the impressions of the many years of quiet suffering finally rose to the surface. Philosophical themes, such as humanity's place in the universe and the role of suffering in the life of those who believe in a benevolent God, now began to play a more dominant role in her work. "In 1936 I began to write again, but my handwriting changed, my voice sounded different, and my life passed under the reins of a Pegasus which somehow reminds one of the apocalyptic White Horse or Black Horse of poems that were yet to be born—a return to my first style is impossible. Whether it is better or worse one cannot judge."[68]

When her creative powers returned, Akhmatova wrote the cycle of poems about the Great Terror that have since made her world-famous—*Requiem* (1935–40). Anatoly Naiman, Akhmatova's literary secretary at the end of her life, points out how very personal this work is:

The hero of this poetry is the people. Not a larger or smaller plurality of individuals called "the people" for political, nationalist, or other ideological reasons, but the whole people, every single one of whom participates in what is happening on one side or the other. . . . What differentiates it from, and thus contrasts it to, even ideal Soviet poetry is the fact that it is personal, just as profoundly personal. . . . The personal attitude is not a rejection of anything; it is an affirmation which is

manifest in every word of *Requiem*. This is what makes *Requiem* poetry—
not Soviet poetry, but simply poetry: it could be personal only if it dealt
with individuals, their loves, their moods, and their selves in accordance
with the officially sanctioned formula of "joys and sorrows."[69]

Another critic maintains that the cycle places the suffering heroine in the
context of important literary works on the suffering of mothers and wives, such
as Nekrasov's portrayal of the wives of Decembrists who followed their husbands
into exile at the beginning of the nineteenth century, poems Akhmatova heard
as a child. Earlier examples are the heroines of Euripides—Andromache, Hecuba,
the Trojan women. All of them share a similar range of emotions: hope, the threat
of death, madness, indifference, and a readiness to accept death.[70]

The portrayal of intense suffering does not mean that the poet has lost her
faith. Inherent in the works of great Russian writers like Dostoyevsky and Berdyaev is the Orthodox belief that suffering is an important aspect of life, by which
one's faith is tested. One has three choices: to overcome one's doubt and accept
the idea that suffering is part of a divine plan, whose meaning is known to a
benevolent God; to become immoral, give up one's faith, and turn to demonic
forces; or to become totally amoral, in the belief that the individual is the sole
arbiter of his or her own destiny. Never in any of Akhmatova's writings or conversations with trusted friends did she admit to doubt or lack of faith in the
mysterious and often incomprehensible ways of a Divine Creator. She would not
agree with Albert Camus's philosophy of the absurd. In his *Myth of Sisyphus,*
Camus finds no way out of his metaphysical dilemma—either we are not free and
almighty God is responsible for evil; or we are free and responsible, but God is
not omniscient, all-powerful. Camus prefers to accept a world without God, an
essentially amoral universe where good and evil coexist without aim or meaning.
But there is another answer—that it is possible to believe in a God who created
a universe containing both good and evil, and the individual has the freedom to
choose between the two. Only in such a universe, rather than one in which one's
fate is predestined, can people be judged as moral human beings who will ultimately be rewarded for their actions.

The poet Joseph Brodsky saw the text of *Requiem* itself as a confirmation of
Akhmatova's faith, saying:

The degree of compassion with which the various voices of *Requiem* are
rendered can be explained only by the author's Orthodox faith; the degree
of understanding and forgiveness which account for this work's piercing,
almost unbearable lyricism, only by the uniqueness of her heart, herself,
and this self's sense of time. No creed would help to understand, much
less forgive, let alone survive this double widowhood at the hands of the
regime, this fate of her son, these forty years of being silenced and
ostracized.[71]

Akhmatova did not foresee the Terror, but by 1930 she certainly knew what probably lay ahead, considering all that had already occurred to her and to millions of others under the Soviet regime. Yet she chose to stay and suffer with her people. This is made clear in the epigraph to *Requiem,* which was added in 1961, from the poem "No, we didn't suffer together in vain" (1961), not published in the Soviet Union until after her death:

> No, not under the vault of alien skies,
> And not under the shelter of alien wings—
> I was with my people then,
> There, where my people, unfortunately, were.
>   (II, p. 95)[72]

The epigraph does not ground the poem in any particular historical context, hence the theme becomes universal. In typical Akhmatova fashion, much is said in few words. Through the metaphor of a sheltering wing, the first two lines convey the idea that no matter where the foreign land may be, it promises comfort, refuge. One word, "unfortunately," in the last line, is enough to let the reader imagine that in the poet's own land the situation is grimmer; but this situation is unspecific and therefore universal—it could be war, natural catastrophe, or (as is implicit in the cycle) political oppression.

"Instead of a Preface," a short prose piece, introduces the cycle:

> In the terrible years of the Yezhov terror, I spent seventeen months in the prison lines of Leningrad. Once, someone "recognized" me. Then a woman with bluish lips standing behind me, who, of course, had never heard me called by name before, woke up from the stupor to which everyone had succumbed and whispered in my ear (everyone spoke in whispers there): "Can you describe this?" And I answered: "Yes, I can." Then something that looked like a smile passed over what had once been her face. (I, p. 95)

Now Akhmatova fulfills her destiny as the voice of her people, taking on the persona of the village Wailer and the Madonna—the religious prototype for all mothers who must watch helplessly while their children suffer, somehow fulfilling an incomprehensible destiny. The mother can only provide comfort and prayer so that the pain and agony may be somehow alleviated.

The "Dedication" was written in March 1940, introducing the theme of "mortal woe" that permeates the cycle:

> Mountains bow down to this grief,
> Mighty rivers cease to flow,
> But the prison gates hold firm,

And behind them are the "prisoners' burrows"
And mortal woe.
For someone a fresh breeze blows,
For someone the sunset luxuriates—
We wouldn't know, we are those who everywhere
Hear only the rasp of the hateful key
And the soldiers' heavy tread.
We rose as if for an early service,
Trudged through the savaged capital
And met there, more lifeless than the dead;
The sun is lower and the Neva mistier,
But hope keeps singing from afar.
The verdict . . . And her tears gush forth,
Already she is cut off from the rest,
As if they painfully wrenched life from her heart,
As if they brutally knocked her flat,
But she goes on . . . Staggering . . . Alone . . .
Where now are my chance friends
Of those two diabolical years?
What do they imagine is in Siberia's storms,
What appears to them dimly in the circle of the moon?
I am sending my farewell greeting to them.

(II, p. 97)

As Michael Basker has shown, the opening reveals that the natural order has been disrupted, part of a general pattern in the entire poetic cycle reflecting a disruption of the universe caused by the Terror.[73] The early lines evoking nature mourning in sympathy recall Akhmatova's earlier poem "July 1914," part of a two-poem cycle, about another catastrophe, World War I:

July 1914
1

It smells of burning. For four weeks
The dry peat bog has been burning.
The birds have not even sung today,
And the aspen has stopped quaking. . . .

(I, p. 427)

Both reach back to the famous medieval Russian epic the *Igor Tale*. On the day of battle black clouds come in from the sea, streaks of blue lightning quiver within them, the birds in the oak trees lie in wait for misfortune, eagles screech and foxes yelp.[74]

Through literary allusion Akhmatova adds implicit interpretations to the text. The phrase "prisoners' burrows" refers to Pushkin's poem "Message to Siberia," where the poet encourages his exiled friends who participated in the Decembrist rebellion to have hope, "his free music pours round their prisoners' burrows," giving them faith. But Akhmatova's lines are bitterly ironic, for here "the prison gates hold firm," and hope is distant, "singing from afar."

Akhmatova progresses from seeing herself at first as one with the other women through most of the poem, to feeling cut off from them while still physically among them, to becoming totally detached, separate: "But she goes on . . . Staggering . . . Alone." The last lines bring us to the present (1940), as the poet asks where those friends are who came together not out of choice but by chance, because they shared one thing in common—they had come to communicate with loved ones in prison through the package they shoved through the little prison window.

The Prologue makes no direct allusion to the poet herself, but to all women:

Prologue

That was when the ones who smiled
Were the dead, glad to be at rest.
And like a useless appendage, Leningrad
Swung from its prisons.
And when, senseless from torment,
Regiments of convicts marched,
And the short songs of farewell
Were sung by locomotive whistles.
The stars of death stood above us
And innocent Rus writhed
Under bloody boots
And under the tires of the Black Marusyas.

(II, p. 99)

The first line leads us to believe a happy event is being described, but we soon learn that the only ones smiling are the dead. Implicit is the idea that those alive in this situation are going through an unbearable hell, while peace and rest come only to those already beyond. Although rare in Akhmatova's poetry, when simile is used it is a powerful device. Leningrad as a useless appendage becomes a city no longer fulfilling a useful function in life: it has become a city of the dead. Short songs of farewell become a simple, everyday symbol of the thousands leaving Leningrad for exile, for the trip the passengers are taking leads them to Siberia and the camps. Basker perceptively interprets the "stars of death" as the red stars above the Kremlin.

Instead of "Russia," Akhmatova purposely uses the term "Rus"—the medieval name for the territory which included parts of present-day Russia, Ukraine, and Belorussia. It was composed of wealthy city-states equaling Florence and Venice in power and beauty. In this way the poem is transformed from a description of one particular city during the Terror to a symbol of the entire land in historical and mythical time. This ancient land is now writhing under the boots and tires of the modern Soviet police state, conveyed by the metonymic image of the police vans called *chyrnaya Marusya* or the Black Marusya, taking prisoners away. This was not the big, black van known as *chyrnyi voron* ("black raven") which every Russian would recognize, similar to the American Black Maria, but a regular delivery truck carrying bread, milk, and other ordinary products.[75] The name "Marusya" is the village version of Maria, and lacks the more elevated overtones of Maria the Madonna, although the allusion to the Madonna is clear—the Black Marusya is a religious inversion. The Madonna is holy, with the ability to intercede between man and God, to bring comfort and solace to humanity; but the Black Marusya strikes terror and fear in the hearts of men and carries out the dark work of the forces of evil.

In Poem #1 (1935), the poet compares herself to a peasant woman performing the ancient Russian ritual of *vynos*—the carrying out of the dead from the house to the vehicle that will take the body to the cemetery. Instead of a dead body, however, this time it is a live prisoner, someone beloved, perhaps on the biographical level Punin or Mandelstam.[76]

> They led you away at dawn,
> I followed you, like a mourner,
> In the dark front room the children were crying,
> By the icon shelf the candle was dying.
> On your lips was the icon's chill.
> The deathly sweat on your brow . . . Unforgettable!
> I will be like the wives of the *Streltsy,*
> Howling under the Kremlin towers.
>
> (II, p. 99)

The *vynos* is one of several episodes in the funeral rite, which is accompanied by laments, usually sung by a professional wailer from the village, the *prichitalnitsa.* The laments are improvised recitatives, incorporating traditional stock phrases adapted by the lamenter to the person who has died and the woman who is grieving.

The clue that the speaker is from the peasant milieu is provided by the reference to the *gornitsa,* a special room where rich peasants received guests. The religious associations are conveyed through motifs such as icons, the sacred images painted on wood to which the Orthodox pray, and the *bozhnitsa* or icon shelf, placed in a special corner of the house where meals are held and rituals like matchmaking take place.

In the end the poet compares herself to the wives of the *Streltsy,* or Archers, the elite military corps employed by Sophia, Peter the Great's half sister. They supported Sophia in her fight for the throne in 1798 because they believed Peter was godless, the Anti-Christ who would destroy Russia. Their wives lamented for them under the Kremlin towers, and the event was immortalized in Vasily Surikov's famous nineteenth-century painting, *The Morning of the Execution of the Streltsy.*

In Poem #2 a playful moon is contrasted with the lone figure of the suffering woman:

> Quietly flows the quiet Don,
> Yellow moon slips into a home.
>
> He slips in with cap askew,
> He sees a shadow, yellow moon.
>
> This woman is ill,
> This woman is alone,
>
> Husband in the grave, son in prison,
> say a prayer for me.
>   (II, p. 101)

The poem sounds like a nursery rhyme or lullaby—a Cossack lullaby because of the reference to the Don, where Cossacks lived. The phrase "quiet Don" connotes folklore since it is used in numerous historical songs.[77] For example, there is a famous soldiers' song in which the land has been ploughed with horses' hooves, sown with Cossack heads, and blossomed with orphans. It ends:

> What are the waves of the glorious quiet Don filled with?
> The waves of the quiet Don are filled with fathers' and mothers'
> tears.[78]

Cossack sons were constantly exposed to danger, which meant the women were subject to loss, to the pain of a "Husband in the grave, a son in prison." A "Husband in the grave" may refer to Gumilyov. The deceptively simple structure of the poem accounts for the shock that occurs when we learn only in the last line that the woman ill and alone is the poet herself. Suddenly the objective narrative is transformed into vividly personal perceptions.

Poem #3 (1940) again shows how Akhmatova's use of structure influences the meaning and impact of a poem:

> No, it is not I, it is somebody else who is suffering.
> I would not have been able to bear what happened,
> Let them shroud it in black,

And let them carry off the lanterns . . .
Night.

(II, p. 101)

Basker has explained that the regular structure of meter and rhyme in Russian is
abandoned to represent the disintegration of the self. He adds that "The fourth
line tails off with suspension points, and all development is halted by the single
disruptive monosyllable of the fifth: *Noch* [Night]. The poem breaks off into
another premature silence, the formal counterpart of unutterable darkness."[79]

The next poem, #4 (no date), articulates the theme underlying *Poem Without
a Hero*, that the "gay little sinner" and her whole generation would pay for their
indifference to the sufferings of their land and their people:

You should have been shown, you mocker,
Minion of all your friends,
Gay little sinner of Tsarskoye Selo,
What would happen in your life—
How three-hundredth in line, with a parcel,
You would stand by the Kresty prison,
Your tempestuous tears
Burning through the New Year's ice.
Over there the prison poplar bends,
And there's no sound—and over there how many
Innocent lives are ending now . . .

(II, p. 101)

The poet herself pays by standing three-hundredth in line with her parcel by the
Kresty [Crosses] prison. The name as well as the cross-shape of the prison evokes
the Christian symbolism of the Cross, standing for atonement and redemption.

The poems #5–#9 (1939–40) trace the poet's state of mind, moving from a
wish for death to being overcome by madness, which she welcomes because she
hopes it will help her achieve oblivion, total forgetfulness. In #8, "To Death"
(1939), the speaker no longer wishes to reconcile herself to the situation and only
begs for death to bring her comfort. It is a theme that has a long tradition in
Russian literature. In Mussorgsky's song cycle *Songs and Dances of Death*, death
brings peace to a soldier on the battlefield, to a sick child whose mother is grieving;
and in Nekrasov's poem "Grandfather Frost," the cold brings comforting death
to a poor peasant woman who has just buried her husband.

To Death

You will come in any case—so why not now?
I am waiting for you—I can't stand much more.

I've put out the light and opened the door
For you, so simple and miraculous.
So come in any form you please,
Burst in as a gas shell
Or, like a gangster, steal in with a length of pipe,
Or poison me with typhus fumes.
Or be that fairy tale you've dreamed up—
So sickeningly familiar to everyone—
In which I glimpse the top of a pale blue cap
And the house attendant white with fear.
Now it doesn't matter anymore. The Yenisey swirls,
The North Star shines.
And the final horror dims
The blue luster of beloved eyes.

(II, p. 107)

The fairy tale that death may bring is not a harmless piece of fantasy, but what has by now become an "old story"—the search, arrest, exile, and perhaps death. The secret police wore light blue caps, and a house attendant had to be present at an arrest. The reference to the Yenisey River is not a stereotyped cliché of time being compared to a rolling river, but is directly associated with the Great Terror—the Yenisey is the site of many prison camps in Siberia, including Norilsk, where her son was exiled. As Etkind points out, this recalls a Mandelstam poem from the same period, "Beyond the thundering voice of future centuries" (1931):

Lead me way into the night, where the Yenisey flows
And the pine reaches to the stars
Because I am not a wolf by blood
And only someone my equal will be the death of me.[80]

The real subject of Akhmatova's poem is probably Mandelstam, especially since in 1939 she received the news that he had died.[81]

The cycle reaches its culmination in #10, "Crucifixion," consisting of two poems. The first was written in 1940:

Crucifixion

1

"Do not weep for Me, Mother,
I am in the grave."

A choir of angels sang the praises of that momentous hour,
And the heavens dissolved in fire.

To his Father He said: "Why hast Thou forsaken me!"
And to his Mother: "Oh, do not weep for Me . . ."

(II, p. 109)

The epigraph is in Church Slavonic, the sacred language of the Orthodox Slavs. It is based on lines from the ninth chant of the Holy Week service, which are "Do not weep for Me, Mother, as you gaze upon the tomb."[82] On the Cross, first expressing his human aspect, Christ addresses God the Father, asking why he has been abandoned and forced to experience the suffering of an ordinary man: "Eloi, Eloi, lama sabachthani" (My God, my God, why hast thou forsaken me? [Mark 15:34]). But to his Mother he says, "Oh, do not weep for Me," because he knows he is divine and will be resurrected. Christ must feel human pain, or his sacrifice is meaningless, but he suffers as part of a divine destiny in order to bring salvation to humanity—therefore his mother should not weep. In the Annunciation, Mary received the message that her son would have a unique destiny when she was told he would reign over the house of Jacob forever, "and of his kingdom there shall be no end" (Luke 1:33).

Amanda Haight suggests that the cycle's second poem (1943) illustrates different kinds of suffering: Magdalene, the suffering of rebellion, John, the silent suffering of one trying to kill memory and feeling; but the Mother's suffering is so great no one can bear to look at her.[83]

2

Mary Magdalene beat her breast and sobbed,
The beloved disciple turned to stone,
But where the silent Mother stood, there
No one glanced and no one would have dared.

(II, p. 111)

Akhmatova is faithful to the original description of the apostle in John 19:26–27, where no specific person is named: "When Jesus therefore saw his mother, and the disciple standing by, whom he loved, he saith unto his mother, 'Woman, behold thy son!' Then saith he to the disciple, 'Behold thy mother!' And from that hour that disciple took her unto his own home." Over the centuries in depictions of the Crucifixion the disciple has been portrayed as John. Akhmatova's version differs dramatically from the original. Here the disciple, rather than acting as a comforter, himself becomes helpless, and the mother remains alone and unprotected.

In "Epilogue I," the poet reconfirms that hers is the voice of all those who have experienced what she has. The cycle ends with "Epilogue II," whose theme is "remembrance," which would become a major motif in Akhmatova's later works. Memory becomes a moral imperative, for the indifference of her own generation to the sufferings of the people, the years of Terror, is a sin.

In the Orthodox ritual, Remembrance Day marks the anniversary of the death of a member of the Orthodox Church, and a service is held in his honor.[84] If the poet is to be remembered by her country, she asks that it not be near the sea, the scene of her childhood (Akhmatova was born by the Black Sea and spent many of her childhood summers there), nor near the pine stump in the tsar's garden. Presumably this refers to Tsarskoye Selo, where Akhmatova grew up and spent her early married years. Further, an allusion to a tree stump also appears in her poem "Willow," written in 1940, the same year as this poem, contrasting the tranquillity enveloping her in the peaceful environment of Tsarskoye, of which the silver willow is a symbol, and her later years, when the tree is nothing but a stump—like the dead willow, the tranquillity of Tsarskoye Selo has disappeared. Instead of these happy allusions, though, the poet wishes her monument to be where she stood for three hundred hours—in front of the prison.

In the fifth stanza, she says she will weave a *pokrov* (mantle) to protect the women who waited in line with her:

> I have woven a wide mantle for them
> From their meager, overheard words.
>
> I will remember them always and everywhere,
> I will never forget them no matter what comes.
>
> And if they gag my exhausted mouth
> Through which a hundred million scream,
>
> Then may the people remember me
> On the eve of my remembrance day.
>
> (II, p. 113)

The word *pokrov* evokes a network of associations in Russian culture. It is connected with the holiday of Intercession celebrated on October 1, the feast day commemorating Andrew, a "holy fool," gifted by madness and prophecy, who had a vision of the Madonna in a Byzantine church in Constantinople. The holiday is the subject of many icons and the name of numerous Russian churches. The Madonna took off her mantle and laid it over the congregation as a sign of her intercession between humanity and heaven, a gesture symbolizing her role as protector of the people. In the context of *Requiem*, the word *pokrov* associates the poet with the Madonna—Akhmatova becomes an intercessor and voice of her people, although her mantle will be "woven of words."

In the last stanza there is another covert biblical reference, this time an ironic allusion to the dove. Since the time of Noah, the dove has been associated with peace and renewal of life; but in this poem we hear a "*prison* dove" cooing in the distance, caught like the prisoners in the nightmarish world of the Terror, while boats quietly sail on the Neva River, symbolic of people in the outside world who remain totally indifferent to the suffering of those inside Russia and inside the prison walls.

Akhmatova was afraid to write *Requiem* down. Lydia Chukovskaya, an author and daughter of the eminent critic Korney Chukovsky, was one of the few people to whom the poet recited the work when it was first composed, and who committed it to memory. Akhmatova would visit her and read her the poems in a whisper, but when Chukovskaya came to see her in her own apartment, Akhmatova would stop suddenly in the midst of a conversation and glance up at the ceiling and walls, where she assumed there were hidden microphones. Then she would say something quite ordinary like, "Would you like a cup of tea?", while scribbling swiftly on a piece of paper and handing it over. "Autumn is so early this year," Akhmatova would say, and after Chukovskaya had memorized the lines, Akhmatova would light a match and burn the paper in an ashtray.[85]

Chukovskaya first came to visit Akhmatova because her own husband, the brilliant physicist Matthew Bronstein, had been exiled, and Chukovskaya had heard about Akhmatova's letter to Stalin which resulted in the release of Punin and her son. She thought Akhmatova could give her good advice. However, times were different, and Akhmatova could no longer even help her own son.[86]

Chukovskaya kept a diary of her conversations with Akhmatova from 1939 to 1942, when they quarreled. In 1952, they became friends again and Chukovskaya continued her diary until Akhmatova's death in 1966. In her preface to the diaries, Chukovskaya mentions what an important role Akhmatova played in her own life:

> I felt drawn to write about her because she herself, her words and deeds, her head, shoulders and movements, her hands, possessed a perfection usually found in this world only in great works of art. The fate of Akhmatova—something more than her own particular personality—carved before my very eyes a statue of grief, orphanhood, pride and courage out of this famous and abandoned, strong and helpless woman. I had known Akhmatova's earlier poems by heart since childhood, but the new ones, together with the movements of her hands burning the paper above the ashtray, together with the aquiline profile standing out like a blue shadow on the white wall of the deportation prison, entered my life as naturally as long ago the bridge, St. Isaac's Cathedral, the Summer Garden or the Embankment had done.[87]

By this time Akhmatova perceived her relationship with Punin as disintegrating rapidly. In a poem written in 1936, she likens herself to a domesticated animal in his house:

> I hid my heart from you
> As if I had hurled it into the Neva.
> Wingless and domesticated,

I live here in your home.
Only . . . at night I hear creaking.
What's there—in the strange gloom?
The Sheremetev lindens . . .
The roll call of the spirits of the house . . .
Approaching cautiously,
Like gurgling water,
Misfortune's black whisper
Nestles warmly to my ear—
And murmurs, as if this were
Its business for the night:
"You wanted comfort,
Do you know where it is—your comfort?"
(II, p. 83)

According to Chukovskaya, Akhmatova finally left Punin on September 19, 1938. She said they had lived together for sixteen years.

At the end of the 1930s another important person entered Akhmatova's life: Vladimir Garshin, the last of the men Akhmatova hoped would become a lifetime companion. He was a doctor and professor, a member of the Academy of Medical Sciences, and nephew of the famous nineteenth-century Russian writer Vsevolod Garshin. He shared many interests with Akhmatova, including her love of art and poetry. Garshin was a serious coin collector; he had a large library of books on art, loved Russian poetry, and wrote verse himself. He retained the polite, old-fashioned manners of those brought up before the Revolution. Zoya Tomashevskaya says he was strikingly handsome.[88]

Akhmatova had met Garshin when she was a patient in the Kuibyshev Hospital, and he began to visit her at the House on the Fontanka (as the Sheremetev Palace was called). Garshin was married at the time (his wife died during World War II), but he helped Akhmatova get through this very difficult period when her son had been imprisoned and her relationship with Punin had disintegrated. He appears constantly in the pages of Chukovskaya's diary, watching over the poet like a guardian angel. He was with her on the day she went to the prison for the last time to give her son a package before he was sent into exile.[89]

Lev left Leningrad for exile in mid-August 1939. On August 14, Chukovskaya got an urgent call from Akhmatova, who spoke in an unrecognizable voice: "Come." When Chukovskaya arrived, Akhmatova told her that Lev was being sent north and asked her to help get some warm clothes for him. Chukovskaya made some phone calls and found one person with a cap, another with a scarf, and still another with a sweater to spare. Before she even asked, when she called, everyone immediately understood. "A hat? No hat, but won't he need gloves?" Boots, said Akhmatova, were essential. It was important for them to reach Lev's friend, the biology student Kolya Davidenkov, who, she said, would give them a pair of boots. However, Akhmatova was so distracted she could not explain to Chukovskaya how to reach this place, and they spent a long time riding the trolleybus before Akhmatova remembered the way. Kolya had been arrested and had been in prison with Lev, but by a quirk of fate, in 1939, along with a group of other students, he had been released.

When they arrived, they learned that Kolya's boots were being repaired, but he promised to get them back immediately from the shoemaker and declared he would come to Akhmatova's house by eight o'clock the following morning. On the way home, Akhmatova told Chukovskaya: "August is always a terrible month for me. . . . My whole life." August was the month both Gumilyov and Alexander Blok had died.

The next day, at eight o'clock precisely, a panting Kolya arrived at Chukovskaya's house and then accompanied her to the prison courtyard to deliver the packages. It was desperately hot, and the day seemed to last forever. Sometimes Chukovskaya or Kolya would take Akhmatova's place in line, so she could sink down on a stone or log and rest. Chukovskaya said as she looked at the people standing in line, Akhmatova's clear profile stood out strongly amid a blur of indistinct faces.[90]

Akhmatova had begun making public appearances again. She had been invited to recite at an evening devoted to the memory of Blok on November 10, 1938, at the House of Literature. She read her poem "Today is the nameday . . . ," the poem she had written in 1921 after Blok's death, then immediately left. But Chukovskaya noted the great impression she made: "I was struck by her bearing, her azure shawl, her distracted glance and her voice. It was impossible to believe she was just like the rest of us."[91]

Chukovskaya described the neglected and disorganized state of the room in which Akhmatova now lived. A ragged armchair, missing one leg and with springs protruding, stood beside the oven, and the floor was unswept. Akhmatova had some pretty things: a carved stool, a mirror in a bronze frame, prints on the walls; but Chukovskaya suggests that instead of enhancing the room, these objects only emphasized the wretchedness of it all. And yet on February 8, 1940, Chukovskaya noted that Akhmatova served her wine in crystal glasses, and they ate pastry from elegant plates. Akhmatova told her, "They say we should not eat on these plates, we must save them, but I don't like saving things. . . . They're lovely, aren't they? Drawings in the style of David." When Garshin gave her a beautiful compact and cigarette lighter made of lapis lazuli, Akhmatova told Chukovskaya, "I like these new things from the present. But we all live among things from long ago."[92]

Akhmatova continued to show her generosity throughout these terrible years. In September 1936, the newspaper *Literaturnyi Leningrad (Literary Leningrad)* published her translation of a poem by E. Khrenets with a note that read: "The honorarium for the translation of this poem I wish to be conveyed to the fund for the aid of wives and children of the heroic Spanish people, fighting for the freedom and independence of their country."[93]

Akhmatova was still subject to small but painful indignities, as people forgot or did not bother to read her poetry. She told Chukovskaya she was required to verify her signature on a new pension book. The house manager said she first had to write her name down on a separate piece of paper. "What for? Does he think the signature in my book is false? I was furious. I was insulted. I wrote my name on a piece of paper and said: 'Apparently you want to sell my autograph to *Literaturnaya Moskva (Literary Moscow)*? You're right, they'll give you fifteen rubles for it.' He got embarrassed and tore it up, then asked, 'Apparently you once were a writer?' "[94]

The 1930s had witnessed a hardening of the Party line on the arts. The Great Experiment was over, and Anatoly Lunacharsky, who had presided as the Minister of Culture, was relieved of his position. A new Union of Soviet Writers was formed in 1932; publishing houses, journals, newspapers, and the censors were now under the strict control of the Communist Party. In 1934, Andrey Zhdanov demanded that the Union of Soviet Writers accept Socialist Realism as the doctrine that was to guide the arts. Now writers had to portray contemporary reality not as it was but as it should be in an ideal Socialist State, in a style that was simple and accessible.[95]

In this oppressive atmosphere Akhmatova turned to literary scholarship and now began to publish papers and give lectures on Pushkin, based on the research she had begun in the 1920s. In 1930, the scholar Boris Eikhenbaum wrote Nikolay Khardzhiyev, another scholar, "Akhmatova was visiting. Intense but intelligent. . . . Her observations about Pushkin are very interesting."[96] In February 1933, she presented a paper on Pushkin's verse tale, *The Golden Cockerel,* on which she had been working with Khardzhiyev for two years. Her talk took place before some of the most famous Pushkin scholars in the country, at Pushkinsky Dom, an institute and archives devoted to the study of literature. She was also appointed a member of the Pushkin Commission, which was preparing the edition of Pushkin celebrating the one-hundredth anniversary of his death. In 1936 Akhmatova said: "I am now working on a commentary for the third volume of the Academy edition of Pushkin (to *The Golden Cockerel*). This work is devouring all my time. For the first volume I translated all his French poems printed in the commentaries and also Pushkin's French verse." She also contributed the notes to *The Golden Cockerel* for an album of drawings edited by the Pushkin scholar S. M. Bondi, which appeared in 1939.[97]

Akhmatova's first article on Pushkin was entitled "The Last Fairy Tale of Pushkin," and it appeared in the journal *Zvezda (The Star)* in 1933. Little had been written by any scholar on this splendid satirical tale, in which Pushkin attacks lazy and incompetent rulers. It was Akhmatova who made the discovery that *The Golden Cockerel* was not based on a Russian folk tale but was derived from Washington Irving's story, "The Legend of the Arabian Astrologer," in *The Alhambra* (1832).

This tale is about an old ruler, Dadon, who asks a seer for help against continually invading neighbors. The seer gives him a golden rooster, the "golden cockerel," who sits atop a spire and warns when there is threat of invasion, but says one day he will come to get a reward for his gift. During one battle the tsar encounters a beautiful queen and comes under her spell. The wise man appears, asking Dadon for the queen, as his reward, but the tsar refuses and kills the seer. The golden cockerel flies down off the spire and pecks Dadon, who falls off his chariot and dies, and the queen disappears.

Akhmatova proves to be a master of rigid scholarly analysis. She begins by discussing the availability of Irving's writings in Russia when Pushkin wrote his work, referring to publications in Russian and French as well as reviews in Russian journals. She also checks Modzalevsky's *Biblioteka Pushkina* (*Pushkin's Library*) to see if Pushkin had a copy of Irving's work in his library. Then she focuses on the polemics surrounding Irving's tale and the possible sources for this literary hoax.

The second section is devoted to a detailed account of the differences between the two texts. Akhmatova points out that the variations in treatment are an important means for discovering differences in the two authors' attitudes toward their theme. She discovers that the lexicon in Pushkin is much more typical of the Russian folk tale than the more elegant English style employed by Irving; perhaps—she notes—this is because the work is supposed to be related to other imitation folk tales by Pushkin that he was writing at the time. Moreover, there is a general pattern in the changes Pushkin makes—his work is much more satirical, and he clearly has the Russian tsar in mind. She believes the work is really a form of *tainopis,* or "secret writing," in which Pushkin pretends to be telling a simple tale but is in fact making moral judgments or satirical attacks against the status quo. This was a typical device of Pushkin's in other works.

This leads to Akhmatova's examination of facts in Pushkin's own life. Nicholas had made him accept the lowly position of chamberlain at court, usually awarded to young boys. He was not allowed to publish many of his important works and was refused access to archives to continue his research on the rebel Pugachov. The tale becomes a form of defiant revenge against the tsar.

Akhmatova shows how Pushkin used the tale of the Golden Cockerel to express problems in his own life that he could not discuss openly without incurring the wrath of the censors and the tsar. But the article also reflects the way Akhmatova herself was coping at this time with censorship and the increasing oppression of the Stalinist regime. Her writings on Pushkin are thus also a form of secret writing—in discussing Pushkin's defiance of authority, she manages covertly to demonstrate her own.

In 1936, Akhmatova published another article entitled "*Adolphe* by Benjamin Constant in the Work of Pushkin." Akhmatova perceptively points out that this novel, *Adolphe,* was important in Pushkin's life because it helped him solve a series of problems at the end of the 1820s. Pushkin himself considered it a significant prototype of the psychological novel both for him and for his contemporaries. Akhmatova provides an exhaustive analysis of traces of the novel found in Pushkin's various works. Not only was the subject matter important for Pushkin, as Akhmatova points out, but also the *language* of Vyazemsky's translation, which provided modern Russian writers with the literary means to convey psychological thought processes, describing the conscious and the subconscious, the rational and irrational forces governing our actions.

The novel served Pushkin as a model for transforming events in one's own life into literary form. In turn, Pushkin's works had already served as a model for Akhmatova to transform events in her personal life into great poetry.

Akhmatova continued to stay close to Pushkin scholars, and when Dmitry Yakubovich, president of the Pushkin Commission, died on May 30, 1940, she went to his funeral. As the coffin was being carried down the stairs, the clock on the landing chimed and chrysanthemums fell all over the stairs beneath the feet of the bearers—a powerful image that Akhmatova included in *Poem Without a Hero*.[98]

Akhmatova's life in the communal apartment in the Sheremetev Palace during the late thirties is described as exceedingly depressing. Korney Chukovsky gave his impression of the "cursed walls," where "the roar of the gramophone never stopped from behind the doors of polite neighbors." Akhmatova spent hours caring for her neighbors' children, the Smirnov boys, treating them with sweets and reading them books—Walter Scott for the older one and for the younger, *The Golden Cockerel*. Chukovsky cites a young woman who knew Akhmatova at that time: "I often noted that with a child in her arms, she resembled a statue of the Madonna, not only her face but her entire being, with a certain mournful and humble grandeur."[99] But her attachment to these children also brought her grief. They were beaten often by their drunken father and their hysterical mother. In August 1940, Chukovskaya recorded that Akhmatova told her she could not stand to hear her neighbors beating their young son. The day before, she had gone to the door and hammered on it with her fists.[100] Thus Akhmatova had the experience of taking care of small children, as she did Punin's daughter Irina, as well as Irina's own daughter, Anna Kaminskaya, an experience she had missed with her own child, Lev.

By this time Punin was having an affair with one of his assistants, Marta Golubeva, who never actually lived with him at the apartment, but from Chukovskaya's notes, her voice could sometimes be heard behind the wall. Chukovskaya also records that in September 1939 Akhmatova was complaining about Punin's stinginess—shown earlier while Lev had been living with them, when he would humiliate Lev at the dinner table, saying the butter was only for his own daughter, Irina.[101]

Despite the difficulties of this household, Akhmatova preferred it to the unknown. On January 13, 1940, Akhmatova told Chukovskaya that her pension had been raised to 750 rubles a month, and that Zoshchenko had gone to the official City Council, Lensovet, to ask for an apartment for her. But Akhmatova did not want to move. Instead, she hoped the Smirnovs would move to a new room in the communal apartment and give her theirs. "A known communal apartment is better than an unknown one. I've grown used to everything here. And when Lyova returns, he will have a room. And he will return one day."[102]

Akhmatova's mental state is reflected in the anxiety she caused in Garshin, who was worried about her. He mentions Akhmatova's friend, Valeriya Sreznevskaya, whose mental condition also was rapidly deteriorating. He complained to Chukovskaya on July 9, 1940: "The problem is that she [Akhmatova] does not want to undertake anything new. The most important thing is for her to leave here, leave this apartment. There are traumas here from both sides, from both neighbors. But she won't leave. Why? Because she's afraid of the new. And endless thought about her madness: she saw her sick friend Sreznevskaya and is now looking for the same symptoms in herself. Have you noticed, she always takes some fact which is debatable and makes conclusions from it with iron logic. And this horrible intensity of spiritual and emotional life is burning her up!"[103]

In August, Chukovskaya spoke with Garshin again; he had just returned from a summer holiday and had found Akhmatova on the verge of madness. Because Akhmatova suspected she was under police observation, she had put a hair in her poetry notebook, and it had disappeared. She was sure they had made a search in her absence. Then Garshin suddenly became upset. Chukovskaya went to the kitchen and made him some tea, asking him what was wrong. Was it Akhmatova's state of mind, her anger? "No," he answered. "It's me. I understand I must be with her, only with her. She will not fight with her psychosis, she won't try to overcome it," he sobbed.[104]

It must have increased Akhmatova's extremely fragile state of mind at this time to watch her dear friend from childhood slowly going mad. The years of Terror had been too much for Valeriya Sreznevskaya. Akhmatova told Chukovskaya in November that she had been with Valeriya for three days, before she was finally taken to the hospital. She lay on her bed in a torn blouse, hair disheveled, and said, "You know, Anya, Hitler is Feuchtwanger and Ribbentrop is the man who, you remember, courted me in Tsarskoye Selo. You'll see." Akhmatova said, "I've known Valya since I was twelve years old, but only now do I understand her completely. She is a woman of unusual strength and pride. I understand from only a few words she uttered in her delirium that all her life she's been tormented by pride. . . . When they came for her, there was no delirium—just calm, normal conversation. She now considers me a traitor." Then Akhmatova took down a small volume from the bookcase, the *Divine Comedy,* and handed it to Chukovskaya. "She gave this to me as a gift recently. Look at the inscription." Chukovskaya read it: "To dear Anya on the threshold of hell. V.S."[105]

For many years there had been someone to look after household matters in Akhmatova's life. When she lived with Olga Sudeikina and Arthur Lourie, there was a maid, and at some point in her life with Shileiko, there was Manya, the maid at his apartment in the Marble Palace.[106] When she moved in with the Punins, they also had domestic help. Chukovskaya's diary entries in 1940 indicate, however, that Akhmatova's situation had become much harder. In July 1940, she noted that Akhmatova looked thin, that her face was gray and her feet swollen. She never left the house. Sarra Arens, sister-in-law of Anna Arens, Punin's wife, helped Akhmatova by washing her clothes and getting something for her to eat, as did Olga Vysotskaya, who was now living in Leningrad. In September, Akhmatova described her living conditions to Chukovskaya. Tanya Smirnova, her neighbor with the two sons, had left for Vyborg without leaving Akhmatova anything to eat, she said Punin would not allow his maid to do anything for her, and the dining hall of the House of Writers was closed. "Soon they will put me in the hospital, and at least there I will eat three times a day."[107]

Lydia Ginzburg says a new generation was growing up in the 1930s, born during the Soviet period. For them, the Russian classics were lost, the very literature young people of her generation had loved from childhood—Pushkin, Lermontov, Nekrasov. As teenagers or even children, they had felt every line of Blok, Akhmatova, and Mandelstam. "I remember as a twelve-year-old, I and Zhenya Lunts would hide . . . and read Blok's 'Stranger' aloud to each other, 'Nightingale Garden,' 'By the Sea.' Today's young people could not reach the classics because there is only one path to them—through contemporary poetry—and there is no contemporary poetry, so the route is sealed."[108]

However, Akhmatova was not entirely forgotten. The poet Vadim Shefner wrote that students continued to read her poetry in spite of the difficulty of obtaining copies of her work. Akhmatova was never mentioned in school, but Sheffner had managed to find her verses and learn them by heart, remarking, "The official ban against Blok, Yesenin, and Akhmatova made them even more interesting to us." At the end of 1938 a group of young Leningrad writers, of which he was a member, invited Akhmatova to a meeting. She listened carefully to the recitation of one poet, then instead of the more merciless criticism of his peers, she gave him a gentle but helpful critique, speaking very directly as one poet to another.[109]

The only available poems by Akhmatova were those that had been printed long ago. However, in February 1939, at a literary gathering, Stalin suddenly remembered her and asked, "Where is Akhmatova?" He was told she was in Leningrad. "Why isn't she writing?" he asked. They tried to explain, mentioning her appearance at one evening in 1924 that had been a great success. Akhmatova believed someone "high up" had been present that evening and did not like the poems, and as a result the publication of her works ceased. "Give her permission to publish," Stalin ordered. And so in 1939 Akhmatova's works appeared once again. Poems came out in journals, and she was allowed to prepare a new edition, entitled *From Six Books* (*Iz shesti knig*), which appeared in the summer of 1940. On the day it came out there was a long line in front of the Moscow bookstore selling it on the street Kuznetsky Most. There was a rumor that Stalin gave orders to print it because his daughter Svetlana loved Akhmatova's poetry, and the collection was swiftly nicknamed "Papa's gift to Svetlana."

The influential novelist Mikhail Sholokhov suggested the collection be nominated for a Stalin Prize in 1940, and Alexey Tolstoy and Nemirovich-Danchenko, literary director of the Moscow Art Theater, supported the idea.[110] V. Pertsov published a review of the book in *Literaturnaya gazeta* (*Literary Gazette*) when it came out, saying that Akhmatova's poetry had been "drowned for many years, although she continued to write." He referred to the years when none of her poetry appeared as the "geological period," and said she was now writing even better than before. "The master is not exhausted." She had not grown old, he said, in spite of so many years of solitude; on the contrary, she had gained in maturity. He noted a development toward more objective themes, as in "Lot's Wife," "Dante," and "Cleopatra." Pertsov even praised her early love poems, saying they were much better than the "fashionable" lyrics on this subject written by other poets at the time. Employing Marxist criticism, he noted that Akhmatova was a product of her class and time, and could not have written otherwise. Her early verses were composed during the "bourgeois disintegration of the family," which accounted for themes that did not reflect "the ideal contemporary [meaning Communist] woman or the women one encounters in Pushkin and Nekrasov."[111] (This criticism fails to note the total collapse of family life portrayed as a positive feature in the new Communist state in such works as Gladkov's novel *Cement*.) In other words, Pertsov was saying that Akhmatova was a typical product of her times, predestined by economic circumstances and the period in which she lived to write in a certain manner. Pertsov ended by admitting Akhmatova was a great poet, but criticized her for the narrowness of her themes. In spite of its reservations about Akhmatova's poetry, this article marked a major change in direction by Soviet critics toward her work. Timenchik even interprets it as a slight "thaw" before a similar easing of restrictions during the Khrushchev era.

However, a few months after publication, when the book fell into Stalin's hands, he decided he did not like one of the poems, "Slander," paying no attention to the fact it was written in 1922, and assuming it was directed against the Stalinist regime (many of the poems were undated in this collection). The book was withdrawn from bookshops and libraries, and Stalin again forbade her poetry to be printed.

In 1940, Akhmatova became a member of the Union of Soviet Writers. In protest against the treatment of Zamyatin and Pilnyak, she had refused in 1934 to fill out a questionnaire that was necessary to become a member of the Union, but now she accepted membership in the organization. On January 5, 1940, there was a solemn ceremony initiating her. Her old friend Mikhail Lozinsky, now secretary of the Union, said her poetry would live as long as the Russian language existed: her poems would be collected just as the lines of the Roman poet Catullus had been. Many people attended the ceremony. Several of her poems were published in the journal *Leningrad* this year.

Boris Pasternak sent Akhmatova a long letter praising *From Six Books* when it appeared that summer, saying:

Your name is once more *Akhmatova* in the same way when that name stood for the best part of the Petersburg you described. It has its previous power to recall the time when I would not have dared believe that I would ever know you, or have the honor and good fortune to write you a letter. This summer it stands for all it stood for then and, as well, for something new and extremely great, which I have observed lately but have never before connected with the former.[112]

Pasternak noted certain passages he particularly liked and commented on changes he noticed in her work. While Akhmatova may have been flattered, she suspected he had not read much of her earlier poetry: "The poems he mentions were mainly from *Rosary* and *Anno Domini*," she told Chukovskaya, "that is, the ones everyone has known for ages by heart. I'll explain. He's simply reading my poetry for the first time. When I began, he was in Centrifuge [the avant-garde literary group] and was hostile toward me and simply had not read my poems. Now he's reading them for the first time and suddenly making a discovery. Dear, naive, beloved Boris."[113]

Later, in 1956, Akhmatova again suggested to Chukovskaya that in 1940 Pasternak was reading her for the first time. However, this is not true. In his autobiography, Pasternak mentions how in 1910–20 he was struck by the beauty of her writing. There was never any indication that he was hostile to her or her work; in fact, many of his innovations in turning from the erudite themes of Symbolism to the more psychological themes of everyday life are similar to her own. Indeed, he ended his letter by admitting how much influence she had not only on him but on Mayakovsky as well:

Once more one is convinced that except for Blok, no one has had such power of eloquence about the particular; like the early Pushkin you are altogether unique. It is likely that I, Severyanin, and Mayakovsky are infinitely far more indebted to you than one normally assumes, and this indebtedness goes far deeper than any of us recognizes, because it is unconscious. How much all this imprinted itself on our imagination has been shown by how often it has been echoed and imitated! What examples of refined painting in words and precise accuracy![114]

Chukovskaya noted Pasternak's early homage to Akhmatova in 1929, when he alluded to her poem "Lot's Wife," in which Akhmatova expressed the fear of looking back. He also accurately characterized the relationship of her work to prose, which Mandelstam too had noted—her ability to capture psychological relationships typical of the nineteenth-century novel within a few lines of verse, "Where crumbs of unremitting prose grew strong."

To Anna Akhmatova

It seems I'm choosing what is essential
That I can compare to your special power.
And if I am mistaken, I do not care,
For I shall cling to all my errors still.

I hear the continual patter on wet roofs,
That smothered eclogue of wooden pavements.
A certain city appears in every line,
And comes to life in every syllable.

The roads are blocked, despite the tide of spring
Everywhere. Our clients are stingy, cruel.
Bent over piles of work, the sunset burns;
Eyes dull and moist from sewing by a lamp.

. . .

I know that eyes and objects vary greatly
In singleness and sharpness, yet the essence
Of greatest strength, dissolving, is the sky
At night beneath the gaze of polar light.

That's how I recall your face and glance.
It is not the image of that pillar of salt
That, now exalts me, in which five years ago
You set in rhyme our fear of looking back.

But as it appears in all your early work,
Where crumbs of severe prose grew strong,
Everywhere, like wires conducting sparks,
Your work throbs with our remembered past.[115]

In 1936, when Akhmatova became inspired to write again, she dedicated one of her loveliest poems to Pasternak, whom she calls "an eternal child." It is based on motifs from poems and biography. "Daryal gravestone" refers to his trips to Georgia, his great love of Georgian culture, and his admiration for the poets Paolo Yashvili and Titsian Tabidze, both of whom perished in the purges. Pasternak's reverence of nature and everyday reality are reflected in this poem.

The Poet

He who compared himself to the eye of a horse,
He glances sideways, looks, sees, recognizes,

And instantly puddles shine
As melted diamonds, ice pines.

. . .

He was rewarded with a kind of eternal childhood,
His generosity and keen-sightedness shone,
The whole earth was his inheritance,
And he shared it with everyone.

(II, p. 85)

On March 9, 1940, Chukovskaya noted that Pasternak had given Akhmatova a book of his poems with the inscription "After an argument." He had come to Leningrad and had given one of their mutual friends 500 rubles for her. (Akhmatova was sick and could not see him.) When she got well, she went to Moscow, sold some manuscripts to scholar Vladimir Bonch-Bruyevich for the Literary Museum, and took the money to Pasternak. He refused to accept it, screaming: "I did not expect this of you. I gave it to you with the purest of motives." "I also sold my manuscripts with the purest of motives," Akhmatova replied.[116]

In January 1940 the Leningrad Executive Committee decided to form a commission to celebrate the tenth anniversary of the death of Mayakovsky. At one of the last sessions of the committee, it was decided that the focus of the celebration was to be an evening devoted to him at the Academy Chapel, which would be broadcast on the radio. Nikolay Tikhonov, the leading Soviet poet on the commission, said Akhmatova had written a poem to Mayakovsky recently and should be invited to participate. Several members of the committee, such as Dmitry Shostakovich and the poet Vsevolod Rozhdestvensky, supported the idea, and it was approved. The critic Isaak Yeventov was asked to go and attempt to persuade Akhmatova to appear. It was not an easy task, since she rarely forgot anything and was slow to forgive. She recalled very well how Mayakovsky had spoken out against her in the 1920s.

When Yeventov began speaking of Mayakovsky, she interrupted him and said, "You probably know that once he made fun of me publicly, when he read 'The Gray-Eyed King' to the melody of a popular tune, 'The Merchant Went to the Fair'?" There was an awkward pause, since Yeventov did indeed know all about this. He was more worried that Akhmatova would bring up the evening in January 1922 when Mayakovsky called Akhmatova a relic of the past. Someone told Yeventov the reason Mayakovsky scanned "The Gray-Eyed King" to a popular melody was that he had been attempting to illustrate how one could turn a poetic text into rhythmic figures. Lily Brik had repeated to Yeventov that whenever Mayakovsky was in love, he read Akhmatova's poetry. Moreover, if Mayakovsky made fun of an Akhmatova poem, he was really laughing at his own sentiments, which he could not control. Finally, after more persuasion,

Akhmatova agreed to recite at the Academy Chapel. The poem she chose is entitled "Mayakovsky in 1913":

> I didn't know you in your glory,
> I only remember your stormy dawn.
> But perhaps today I have the right
> To recall a day from those far-off years.
> How in your poems sounds hardened,
> New voices swarmed . . .
> Your youthful hands were not lying idle,
> You were constructing formidable scaffolding.
> Everything you touched no longer seemed
> The same as it had been before.
> What you destroyed—was destroyed,
> A verdict beat in every word.
> Lonely and often dissatisfied,
> You rushed your fate impatiently,
> You knew that soon, joyful and free,
> You would begin your great battle.
> And the hum of the rising tide of response
> Was audible as you read to us.
> Rain slanted its eyes wrathfully,
> You quarreled violently with the city.
> And your still unheralded name
> Flew like lightning around the stuffy hall,
> So that today, treasured throughout the land,
> It might ring out like a battle cry.
>
> (II, p. 131)

Yeventov speculated as to why the poem takes place in 1913:

In Akhmatova's memory, the year 1913 was preserved as a very special year in the calendar of her fatherland. This was the last year of pre-war Russia. The chaos and contradictions of former life reached their limit; the country lived with a presentiment of inevitable changes and catastrophes. In the days when she was composing the poem on Mayakovsky, Akhmatova nurtured the idea of a great epic work based on events which—real and imagined—would occur in this very year, 1913. For her this year became the focus of everything that took place in former times, doomed to perish. That is how her *Poem Without a Hero* arose. And Mayakovsky, who with his enormous voice predicted a storm, became the poetic expression of that troubled and doomed prewar Russia.[117]

Akhmatova told Anatoly Naiman that she genuinely liked Mayakovsky's poetry early in the century, even though it was so very different from her own. She
remembered the young Mayakovsky almost with tenderness, and said that if he
had stopped writing poetry before the Revolution, he would have been greater
than anyone else in Russia, "a vivid, tragic poet of genius." But then after the
Revolution he wrote lines like "My militia cares for me," which Akhmatova said
was just going too far. "Can you imagine Tyutchev [a great poet of the nineteenth century] writing, 'My police force cares for me'?" She believed Mayakovsky understood what was really going to happen, unlike Akhmatova and her
friends.[118]

Her poem depicts a gifted man who both created and destroyed, referring to
the Futurist desire to reject the heritage of the past in order to compose great
works of the future. Avoiding mention of his years of suffering and his suicide,
she portrays Mayakovsky in 1913, when his "still unheralded name/Flew like
lightning around the stuffy hall," and notes that in 1940, when she wrote the
poem, his name had become "treasured throughout the land," ringing out like a
battle cry.

In the year 1940 Akhmatova was finally to meet the poet Marina Tsvetayeva, who
had been living abroad, but like so many exiles now returned, was not fully aware
of the Terror. The actual situation had not been reported to the outside world.
After Hitler's assumption of power, the Soviet Union began to look better and
better to many Western intellectuals. The brutality of the Nazi regime was pub-
licized far more widely than what had taken place in Stalin's Russia. "The purges
and show trials in Moscow were written about in the Western press," Simon
Karlinsky points out in his book on Tsvetayeva, "yet thousands of Russian exiles
were returning home during those years from Europe. . . . We now know that
after a year or two, they were all accused of espionage or sabotage and sent to
labor camps or shot."[119]

Early in September 1937, the bullet-riddled corpse of an unknown man was
found on a road near Lausanne in Switzerland: he was an important official
working for the Soviet secret police, who had decided to defect. Tsvetayeva's
husband, Sergey Efron, was implicated; later it was learned he had taken part in
this assassination as well as the murder of Trotsky's son in 1936. Efron fled to
Spain, and from there he made his way to the Soviet Union. Although Tsvetayeva
said she knew nothing about her husband's collaboration with the Soviet regime,
none of the Russian émigré community believed this, and they ostracized her.
She remained in France until the summer of 1939, when she and her son left for
the Soviet Union. They joined her daughter, who had returned to Russia in 1937,
and Efron at a villa near Moscow operated by the NKVD, for agents who had
to flee from the West. Tsvetayeva now was forced to admit the true nature of her
husband's activities. But the regime turned on her and her family as well. In
August, the police arrested her daughter. Then, on the eve of the celebration of

the October Revolution, they came for her husband. Like Akhmatova, Tsvetayeva too stood in line outside the prison. Soon she was evicted and left without money or a place to live. Pasternak helped her find translation work, and she was allowed to stay at a resort at Golitsyn outside of Moscow, which was operated by the Union of Soviet Writers. There, in 1940, she met Viktor Ardov, and she asked him if she could meet Akhmatova when she was visiting Ardov and his wife Nina Olshevskaya at their apartment in Moscow.[120]

Tsvetayeva was disillusioned when she read *From Six Books,* not realizing that censorship had prevented Akhmatova from including many of the new poems that reflected her "new handwriting." Tsvetayeva wrote in her notebook on September 5, 1940, "Yes, yesterday I read and reread almost all of Akhmatova's book . . . old, weak. . . . There were some good lines. . . . But what has she been doing since 1917? Turned inward. This book is an uncorrected blank page. . . . Pity."[121]

The two women were very different: Akhmatova, the poet of the north, was known for her restraint and solemnity; Tsvetayeva, the Muscovite, for the intensity of her emotions. Arthur Lourie once remarked to Akhmatova: "You treat Tsvetayeva the way Chopin treated Schumann—Schumann thanked Chopin, and the latter got out of it with polite, evasive remarks. Tsvetayeva is like Schumann in relation to the golden-mouthed Anna of All Rus."[122]

Viktor Ardov describes the visit. The two poets went into the tiny room where Akhmatova usually stayed when visiting, and remained there for most of the day. Akhmatova never revealed what they discussed. The next day, Tsvetayeva saw Akhmatova at the home of Khardzhiyev, who said, "Tsvetayeva was sparkling. She was full of Paris and talked brilliantly." Akhmatova later told him that she felt dull and bovine in contrast. But Khardzhiyev, on the contrary, seeing her with the quicksilver Tsvetayeva, was struck by what he described as "Akhmatova's complete and utter genuineness."[123]

Akhmatova never wrote about the visit. She said she wished simply to recall these two days "without any legend." However, she realized how different it would have been had Tsvetayeva lived to describe the encounter. She would have conveyed the event in highly emotionally charged language. "It is horrible to think how Marina herself would have described these meetings if she had remained alive and I had died on August 31, 1941. It would have been 'a fragrant legend,' as our grandfather used to say. Perhaps it would have been a lament for a twenty-five-year-old love which turned out to be infatuation, but in any case it would have been magnificent."

Akhmatova had written a poem to Tsvetayeva that March, yet she did not read it to her. She told Chukovskaya later that she decided not to because of the line referring to her family—Tsvetayeva's daughter was still in a camp (she was to remain there for seventeen years) and her husband had by then been shot.[124] The epigraph is taken from a Tsvetayeva poem entitled "To Akhmatova" (1921).

Belated Reply

> *My white-handed one, dark princess.*
> *M. Ts.*

Invisible, double, jester,
You who are hiding in the depths of the bushes,
The one crouching in a starling house,
The one flitting on the crosses of the dead.
The one crying from the Marinka Tower:
"I have come home today.
Native fields, cherish me
Because of what happened to me.
The abyss swallowed my loved ones,
The family home has been plundered."
We are together today, Marina,
Walking through the midnight capital,
And behind us there are millions like us,
And never was a procession more hushed,
Accompanied by funeral bells
And the wild, Moscow moans
Of a snowstorm erasing all traces of us.

(II, p. 583)

Akhmatova prepared a collection of her verse for print, containing poems written between 1924 to 1940. The collection was at first entitled *Reed*; it was never published separately, but appeared in *From Six Books* as *Willow*. Although the poems are few in number, most written after 1936, they indicate that she never completely stopped writing poetry, even during the most difficult times.

Akhmatova explained to Chukovskaya that the title referred to an Eastern legend about two sisters who killed their younger sister on the shore of a river and successfully concealed their deed. However, a reed sprang up on the site of the bloodshed. A shepherd cut a pipe for himself, blew into it, and the reed began to sing of the murder.[125]

The first poem, "Inscription on a Book" (1940), which she wrote in a copy of *Plantain* given to her friend Lozinsky, alludes to this tale. Akhmatova describes herself as "an almost post-Lethean shade," that is, someone who feels as if she has crossed the Lethe in Hades, where souls forget their past life. But there is hope, because she says the reed has revived—her gift of song has returned:

From the dark mist of magic mirrors,
And over pensive Lethe
The reed, revived, might start to sing.

(II, p. 73)

"The Muse," written in 1924, is Akhmatova's most tender tribute to her faithful companion:

The Muse

When at night I await her coming,
It seems that life hangs by a strand.
What are honors, what is youth, what is freedom,
Compared to that dear guest with rustic pipe in hand.
And she entered. Drawing aside her shawl
She gazed attentively at me.
I said to her: "Was it you who dictated to Dante
The pages of *The Inferno?*" She replied: "It was I."

(II, p. 73)

The Muse visits the poet at night, when her unconscious, creative powers are at their height. She comes not when everything is going well, but when "life hangs by a strand." Continuing the theme of renunciation of her early poetry, Akhmatova knows she must give up the "ordinary" things of life—honors, youth, freedom—for the gift of creation. Here she establishes her connection with great poets, symbolized by Dante, who suffer both in their personal lives and in their relationship with the state.

In August 1936, Akhmatova devoted a poem to Dante, emphasizing his role as the archetypal poet in exile, playing the same role as Ovid did in Pushkin's work.[126] Like Akhmatova's Petersburg, Dante's Florence represents a way of life and thought. In his case it will be lost to him because he was exiled for his political beliefs. The poem may also be an indirect allusion to Mandelstam, another poet in exile. Dante was forced to leave his beloved city in 1302 after the victory of the opposing party. Several years later he was offered the possibility of returning under condition of a humiliating public repentance, which he spurned. He refused to walk "with a lighted candle"—the ritual of repentance—even to be able to return to Florence. Unlike Lot's wife, he refused to look back.

Dante

Il mio bel San Giovanni
—Dante

Even after his death he did not return
To his ancient Florence.
To the one who, leaving, did not look back,
To him I sing this song.
Torch, the night, the last embrace,
Beyond the threshold, the wild wail of fate.

Andrey Gorenko, father of
Akhmatova. (courtesy
Moscow collection)

Inna Gorenko, mother of
Akhmatova. (courtesy
Moscow collection)

Valeriya Sreznevskaya (née
Tulpanova) was Akhmatova's
friend in childhood and
remained her confidante later in
life. (courtesy Akhmatova
Museum)

Memorial plaque in memory of Akhmatova in Kiev,
Zankovetskaya, 7 (formerly Meringovskaya). "In this building the
outstanding Russian poetess Anna Akhmatova lived in 1906."
(courtesy Roberta Reeder)

Class of Kiev Fundukleyevskaya Gymnasium. Akhmatova, second from left, second row from bottom. (courtesy Moscow collection)

Inna Gorenko (mother) with Anna, Iya, Andrey, and Viktor (1909). (courtesy Akhmatova Museum)

BELOW: Fundukleyevskaya St. in Kiev on which the Fundukleyevskaya Gymnasium is located, where Akhmatova went to school. (courtesy Akhmatova Museum)

ABOVE: Nikolay Gumilyov (c. 1905). Poet and first husband of Akhmatova. Shot by the Bolsheviks in 1921. (courtesy Akhmatova Museum)

ABOVE: Alexander Blok (1907), the most memorable of the Symbolist poets, who became the prototype for one of the major figures in Akhmatova's great work, *Poem Without a Hero*. (courtesy Akhmatova Museum)

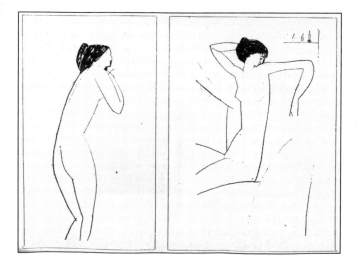

ABOVE: Nikolayevsky church in Nikolska Slobodka on the other side of the Dnieper from Kiev in the Chernigov Province (now part of Kiev). Akhmatova and Gumilyov were married here. (courtesy Akhmatova Museum)

LEFT: Modigliani drawings (1911). Akhmatova had an intimate relationship with Modigliani in Paris when she was visiting in 1911. (courtesy Fonds Mercator Paribas)

UPPER LEFT: Vyacheslav Ivanov, leader of the mystical movement in Symbolist poetry. His apartment, "The Tower," was the center of artistic activity, where Akhmatova met many important figures of the Silver Age and read her own poetry. (courtesy Akhmatova Museum)

UPPER RIGHT: Nikolay Berdyaev, a leading Russian philosopher. His ideas had an important influence on Akhmatova's later work. He was exiled from Russia soon after the Revolution, but his works were known to those who remained. (courtesy Akhmatova Museum)

LOWER RIGHT: Osip Mandelstam (1910s), one of the few of Akhmatova's peers to remain after the Revolution. (courtesy Akhmatova Museum)

LOWER LEFT: Nikolay Nedobrovo (1914), one of the first to perceive how Akhmatova's severe and elegant style differentiated her from other women poets and realized her potential for being placed in the ranks of great poets of the world. (courtesy Moscow collection)

Olga Glebova-Sudeikina. Sang, danced, and acted in the Stray Dog Cabaret and was one of Akhmatova's best friends before the Revolution. (courtesy Moscow collection)

Stray Dog Cabaret (New Year's Eve, 1911). This cabaret became one of the most important meeting points for poets, musicians, and artists in Petersburg during the Silver Age. (courtesy Moscow collection)

Arthur Lourie (1910s), an avant-garde composer who was frequently seen in the Stray Dog. He and Akhmatova lived together briefly with Olga Sudeikina after the revolution when Lourie was First Soviet Commissar of Music. (painting by Saveli Sorin, courtesy Irina Graham)

Vsevolod Knyazev, a young soldier and poet. His love affair with Sudeikina became the background to one of Akhmatova's greatest works, *Poem Without a Hero.* (courtesy Moscow collection)

Mikhail Kuzmin, a refined aesthete, composer, and poet who was one of the leading figures in the Stray Dog Cabaret. He wrote the preface to Akhmatova's first collection, *Evening* (1912). (courtesy Akhmatova Museum)

Vladimir Mayakovsky (1918), the most prominent of the wild Futurists whose poetry and erratic behavior shocked the bourgeosie.

Velimir Khlebnikov (1913), a poet and member of the Futurists. His themes ranged from early pagan Slavic rituals to predicting the future of Russia through mathematical equations and numerology.

Vladimir Shileiko became Akhmatova's husband in 1918. He was a respected Assyriologist and poet. (courtesy Moscow collection)

Boris Anrep, right, was an artist and poet who
became close to Akhmatova during World War I.
Many of her poems from this period are devoted
to him. (courtesy Moscow collection)

Cross given by Anrep to Akhmatova. (courtesy Zoya
Tomashevskaya collection)

Portrait of Akhmatova by Yuri Annenkov done in 1921, when Annenkov was doing a series of portraits of leading artistic figures in Russia. (courtesy Moscow collection)

ABOVE: "Resounding Shell," a group of poets led by Gumilyov after the Revolution. (photo by M. S. Nappelbaum, courtesy Akhmatova Museum)

RIGHT: Akhmatova (1924). (courtesy Akhmatova Museum)

BELOW: Nikolay Gumilyov on left. Alexander Blok on right. After the Revolution. (courtesy Akhmatova Museum)

Akhmatova (1922). (portrait by Kuzma Petrov-Vodkin, courtesy Akhmatova Museum)

Nikolay Punin, famous avant-garde art critic with whom Akhmatova lived for over fifteen years. (courtesy Punin family)

Wing of Sheremetev Palace in which Akhmatova lived with Punin and his family. (courtesy Roberta Reeder)

Gate to Sheremetev Palace, Petersburg. (courtesy Roberta Reeder)

Boris Pasternak (1927). (courtesy Pasternak family archive)

Lev Gumilyov, Akhmatova's son (1930s). (courtesy Moscow collection)

Akhmatova (1930s). (from photo by Lev Gornung, courtesy Moscow collection)

ABOVE LEFT: Nikolay Punin (1930s). (courtesy Punin family)

ABOVE RIGHT: Nadezhda Mandelstam, wife of the poet Osip Mandelstam and close friend of Akhmatova's since 1920s. (courtesy Moscow collection)

BELOW: Akhmatova's collection *From Six Books,* which was allowed to be published by Stalin, who then forbade its distribution. Inscription to Zoya Tomashevskaya, 1956. (courtesy of Zoya Tomashevskaya collection)

Akhmatova (1920s). (photo by M. S. Nappelbaum, courtesy Akhmatova Museum)

From hell he sent her curses
And in paradise he could not forget her—
But barefoot, in a hairshirt,
With a lighted candle he did not walk
Through his Florence—his beloved,
Perfidious, base, longed for . . .

(II, p. 117)

In another of her lyrical portraits, "Cleopatra" (February 1940), Akhmatova again deals with the theme of a great figure facing humiliation. Here she depicts a woman who chooses to end her life rather than submit to authority:

Cleopatra

> *Alexandria's palaces*
> *Were covered with sweet shade.*
> —Pushkin

She had already kissed Antony's dead lips,
And on her knees before Augustus had poured out her tears . . .
And the servants betrayed her. Victorious trumpets blare
Under the Roman eagle, and the mist of evening drifts.
Then enters the last captive of her beauty,
Tall and grave, and he whispers in embarrassment:
"You—like a slave . . . will be led before him in the triumph . . ."
But the swan's neck remains peacefully inclined.

And tomorrow they'll put the children in chains. Oh,
    how little remains
For her to do on earth—joke a little with this boy
And, as if in a valedictory gesture of compassion,
Place the black viper on her dusky breast with an indifferent hand.

(II, p. 119)

While refusing to accept suicide as a solution to her own grief, Akhmatova describes the state of mind of a great queen who does, rather than render unto Caesar what he wishes—her submission. As in many of Akhmatova's poems, there is an implicit "prehistory." Cleopatra is shown at the moment before her death. Antony has been defeated by Augustus Caesar and has committed suicide, and now Caesar wishes the glorious Queen of Egypt to be paraded like a slave before him. In a few telling details, Akhmatova reveals that rather than encounter her self-imposed death with hysteria, Cleopatra greets it with dignified restraint. In antiquity, Cleopatra's suicide was viewed as an act of courage, but for a faithful believer in Christianity, it was not a viable option. Instead, Akhmatova's "inner peace" and strength enabled her to endure.

Tsarskoye Selo appears in several of these poems as a place of memories. In this Akhmatova resembled Pushkin, who also reminisced fondly about Tsarskoye Selo, as the following poem, published in 1823, shows:

Lead, lead me under the linden canopy,
Always kind to my free idleness.
To the shore of the lake, the quiet slope of the hills! . . .
And again I will see the carpet of thick meadows,
And a decrepit handful of trees, and the bright valley,
And the familiar picture of gilded shores.
And in the quiet lake, amidst gleaming ripples,
The proud flock of tranquil swans.[127]

For Akhmatova, however, Tsarskoye Selo begins to take on symbolic overtones as a place of "non-return," representing a way of life that was now over and must be condemned. By 1925 she had already been upset by what her town had become, when she was in a sanatorium there. She had shown Luknitksy—who had come to visit—the dirty, ruined sidewalks and broken fences, and had told him: "Now there is no more Tsarskoye Selo." In 1929, when Akhmatova wrote the poem "This city, beloved by me since childhood," it was called by its new name, Detskoye Selo ("Children's Village"). The poem recalls the time when everything came easily; now death, the "noseless fiddler," plays about this past that will never return. The image of "December silence" reinforces the sense of death; and only for a brief moment does happiness appear, right at the end: "as if an old dear friend/Had just stepped onto the porch with me."

The city, beloved by me since childhood,
Seemed to me today
In its December silence
Like my squandered inheritance.

Everything that came easily,
That was so easy to give away:
Burning emotions, the sound of prayers,
And the blessing of the first song—

Everything flew off like transparent smoke,
Decayed in the depths of mirrors . . .
And then a noseless fiddler began to play
About the irrevocable.

But with a stranger's curiosity,
Captivated by each novelty,
I watched how the sleds skimmed,
And listened to my native tongue.

Then with a freshness wild and strong,
Happiness fanned my face,
As if an old dear friend
Had just stepped onto the porch with me.

(II, p. 77)

"Youth" is from a small 1940 cycle that was supposed to be about her child-hood. The main text was apparently lost in the Siege of Leningrad.[128] The first stanza evokes a cozy picture of Tsarskoye life—a lover's agreement signed among flower kiosks, the sound of the gramophone in the distance. However, disaster is anticipated in the second stanza with the comparison of cherry blossoms to white mourning and the glow of clouds to "bloody Tsushima foam"—a reference to the defeat of the Russian fleet in Japan, a turning point in Russian history. But the residents of Tsarskoye pay no attention—to them life was "like a carnival," the "finale of a *grand gala*":

. . .

And superimposed against the sunset
Was the cherry trees' white mourning,
Which fell as fine,
Dry, sweet-smelling rain . . .
And the clouds glowed
As bloody Tsushima foam,
And smoothly rolled the landaus
of people long since dead . . .

But to us, that evening
Was like a masquerade,
Was like a carnival,
The finale of a *grand gala* . . .

(II, p. 123)

The poem then returns to the present: nothing remains of that house in which she lived, of the hats and shoes that are metaphors for the elegant, aristocratic way of life. The implicit retribution of history has taken its toll for the carnival-like atmosphere in which Akhmatova and her generation enveloped themselves while disaster was imminent.

In January 1940 she wrote a poem, "Willow," about Tsarskoye Selo, in which she referred to the stump that also appears in the second Epilogue of *Requiem*. The willow stump she thought would last forever becomes the subject of philo-sophical contemplation. As an epigraph, she quotes a line from the Pushkin poem about Tsarskoye Selo cited above.

Willow

> *And a decrepit handful of trees*
> —Pushkin

And I grew up in patterned tranquillity
In the cool nursery of the young century
And the voice of man was not dear to me,
But the voice of the wind I could understand
I liked burdocks and nettles,
But best of all the silver willow.
And, obligingly, it lived
With me all my life; its weeping branches
Fanned my insomnia with dreams.
And—strange—I have outlived it.
There the stump stands; with strange voices
Other willows are conversing
Under our, under those skies.
And I am silent . . . As if a brother had died.

(II, p. 121)

The willow, now only a stump, represents the poet's friends who have long since disappeared. Nothing is quite the same in Tsarskoye Selo. This brings to mind a two-line poem, "All the unburied ones . . . ," written much later, and unpublished during her lifetime, in which Akhmatova conjures up the image of Antigone, left behind to bury the dead:

All the unburied ones—I buried them,
I mourned for them all, but who will mourn for me?

(II, p. 653)

One of the most important poems from 1940 is "The Cellar of Memory," because it introduces the idea of memory as a moral imperative:

The Cellar of Memory

But it is pure nonsense, that I live grieving
And that reminiscence gnaws at me.
I don't often visit memory
And it always surprises me
When I descend with a lamp to the cellar,
It seems to me—a landslide
Rumbles again on the narrow stairs.
The lamp smokes, I can't turn back,

And I know that I am going toward the enemy.
And I beg, as if for charity . . . But there
It is dark and quiet. Finished, my holiday!
It is already thirty years since they bid the ladies good-bye,
And that mischievous wag died of old age . . .
I am too late. What a misfortune!
I am forbidden to appear anywhere.
But I am touching the paintings on the walls,
And warming myself by the fireplace. How marvelous!
Through this mold, these fumes and slime,
Flashed two green emeralds.
And the cat mewed. Well, let's go home!

But where is my home and where is my reason?

                                        (II, p. 125)

The poem is one long monologue, almost as if it were spoken in a single breath. The poet makes a distinction between recollection—the conscious choice to think of the past—and remembrance, when reminiscences suddenly flood the mind with often unwelcome memories. She remembers involuntarily, in spite of herself, instead of consciously recalling. The poem becomes a metaphor for delving into one's memory, represented here as a cellar cluttered with images and events the poet wishes to forget. She is being pushed toward "the enemy"—forced to confront her past. For a moment she seems to have found a quiet place of refuge, a home in the cellar of memory. But it is all an illusion—there is no home. "Home" in this context means not only where one lives, but warmth, comfort, emotional support. Without such a "home," one loses one's reason.

Several of the poems in *Reed* may allude to Gumilyov—notably "Incantation," written in April 1936, on the fiftieth anniversary of his birth. In a manuscript version the first line reads, "Through the prison gates." It is Easter, and the poet invites an unnamed addressee to come back from the dead and join her for supper, a motif that reappears later in *Poem Without a Hero:*

Incantation

Through the high gates,
From beyond the Okhta swamps,
By the untraveled path,
Through the unmown meadow,
Across the cordon of night,
To the sound of Easter bells,
Uninvited

Unbetrothed—
Come have supper with me.

(II, p. 81)

In "Thus dark souls take flight . . ." (1940; II, p. 125), although the addressee remains unnamed, Akhmatova again appears to be addressing the spirit of Gumilyov, inviting him to stay a little longer. She recalls when they were in Poland together on their way to Paris in 1910; she hoped he would somehow return, but now no longer cares. This is a stance often assumed by her heroines when life is too difficult to endure and indifference becomes a way of avoiding intense pain. Yet such indifference is only a mask, a self-delusion, just as she pretends in the poem that Troy did not fall and Ebany, the hero of the Babylonian epic *Gilgamesh,* did not die. But Troy did fall, and Ebany did perish, and although she expresses the wish to drowse under a green willow, a ringing in her ears gives her no peace. She will never have peace—it is not her destiny. Fate compels her to continue to be a witness to the sounds of the suffering and joy around her, which she transmutes into magnificent verse.

In a cycle of bitter poems entitled *Parting,* Akhmatova reflects on her feelings about her relationship with Punin. In the first, she talks about the long and dreadful duration of their parting, which took not weeks, not months, but years. Their relationship began in the early 1920s and lasted until the end of the 1930s, but it became increasingly difficult. In the poem Akhmatova says real freedom brings "no more treason, no more betrayals," but it also brings a chill, as the warmth of human feeling is slowly extinguished.

The second poem was written in 1944, after most of the works in the *Reed* collection had appeared in *From Six Books.* It was added later to the cycle when it appeared in the last collection published during Akhmatova's lifetime, *Flight of Time.* The poem marks the moment of final rupture—when one finally knows the time has come to part forever. Precisely at that moment

A bird began to sing in a voice of rapture
About how much we cherished one another.

"The Last Toast," written in 1934, is the most bitter of these three lyrics.

The Last Toast

I drink to the ruined house,
To the evil of my life,
To our shared loneliness
And I drink to you—
To the lie of lips that betrayed me,
To the deadly coldness of the eyes,

To the fact that the world is cruel and depraved,
To the fact that God did not save.

(II, p. 130)

The poem is a toast not to future happiness but to the misery and pain that this relationship brought her. Akhmatova comes up with one of her brilliant, concise encapsulations of a psychological relationship—"shared loneliness"—when two people share the same physical space as lovers or as man and wife but remain psychologically separated.

In 1939, Akhmatova also wrote a beautiful lyric, "Celebrate our latest anniversary," to the man most important in her life at this time, Vladimir Garshin. In her Draft Notebook it is dedicated to him, although it appears in *From Six Books* without any dedication. It is a snowy night, sparkling like diamonds. The lovers have no idea where they are going, but his voice hovers over her shoulder as the snowy powder becomes a warm silver, illuminated by a sudden ray.[129]

Akhmatova's reaction to the purges and suffering took many forms in her unpublished work. One of her most powerful responses to the Terror is "Stanzas," written in 1940. Here she indirectly addresses Stalin, enumerating infamous figures in Russian history who have lived in the Kremlin, and implying that the leader in the Kremlin now lives up to and even surpasses his predecessors in the enormity and extent of his cruel acts. The poet dreams to a "Sagittarius moon," which might place the time of the poem in late November–December (referring to the astrological sign), or it may refer to the *Streltsy* (Archers), the elite military corps punished when they rebelled against Peter the Great, since *Streltsy* is a term for both. Fortunately, the authorities did not discover the poem. It was published for the first time in the Soviet Union in 1989, in *Leningradskaya pravda (Leningrad Truth)* and in *Ogonyok (Little Flame)*.

Stanzas

Sagittarius moon. Beyond the Moscow River. Night.
Like a religious procession the hours of Holy Week go by.
I had a terrible dream. Is it possible
That no one, no one, no one can help me?

You had better not live in the Kremlin, the
                    Preobrazhensky Guard was right;
The germs of the ancient frenzy are still swarming here:
Boris Godunov's wild fear, and all the Ivans' evil spite,
And the Pretender's arrogance—instead of the people's rights.

(II, p. 583)

In another unpublished poem, "Why did you poison the water" (1935), the poet complains that instead of being rewarded for staying in her motherland, she was punished by having her freedom taken away. It was first published in the Soviet Union in 1989 in a Riga journal, *Daugava*.[130]

> Why did you poison the water
> And mix dirt with my bread?
> Why did you turn the last freedom
> Into a den of thieves?
> Because I didn't jeer
> At the bitter death of friends?
> Because I remained true
> To my sorrowing motherland?
> So be it. Without hangman and scaffold
> A poet cannot exist in the world.
> Our lot is to wear the hair shirt,
> To walk with a candle and to wail.
>   (II, p. 573)

Another unpublished work, "Imitation from the Armenian," has been compared by Sonia Ketchian to the original work by H. Tumanjan. In Akhmatova's poem, the speaker projects herself as a black ewe into the dream of the person addressed, who becomes the emperor—the Padishah—and, by indirect allusion, Stalin. She asks him if he found the meal of her children tasty. The original poem, translated by Ketchian, reads:

> In my dream a ewe
> came near me
> up to me
> with a question:
> May God preserve
> keep
> your son
> how was the taste of my child
> infant?

As Ketchian points out, Akhmatova's poem promises no retribution: "The power and good fortune of the ruler are exemplified in the undeserved preservation through the luminous will of a biased Allah as well as by man's might, manifested through the image of holding the universe like a bead."[131]

Imitation from the Armenian

> I will appear in your dreams as a black ewe,
> On withered, unsteady legs

I will approach you, begin to bleat, to howl:
"Padishah, have you supped daintily?
You hold the universe, like a bead,
You are cherished by Allah's radiant will . . .
And was he tasty, my little son?
Did he please you, please your children?"

(II, p. 575)

In another short poem from the 1930s, Akhmatova rejects the role of prophetess, but finds there is one gruesome thing about the times that prevents her from writing verse—the horrible clanking of prison keys:

And I am not at all a prophetess,
My life is as clear as a stream,
But I simply do not feel like singing
To the sound of prison keys.[132]

In "I know I can't move from this place" (1939), the poet identifies with the Boyarynya Morozova—one of the great female figures in Russian history, who was immortalized by Vasily Surikov in a large painting portraying her in chains on a sleigh, being taken into exile (she appears in other poems by Akhmatova as well):

I know I can't move from this place.
Because of the weight of the eyelids of Viy,
Oh, if only I could suddenly throw myself back
Into some sort of seventeenth century.

On Trinity Eve to stand in church
With a fragrant branch of birch,
To drink of sweet mead
With the Princess Morozova.

And then at twilight in the sleigh,
To sink in the dingy snow.
What mad Surikov
Will paint my last journey?

(II, p. 577)

Morozova was a follower of the priest Avvakum in the seventeenth-century schism between him and Patriarch Nikon. The patriarch introduced changes in the Orthodox ritual, attempting to bring the Russian version of Orthodoxy closer to that of the Greeks, from whom the Russians originally received their faith. This caused a great furor among all classes, and Morozova, a noblewoman *(boyarynya)*, supported the schismatics, or Old Believers, as they are called. She was confined in a convent, tortured, and finally incarcerated in the small town of Borovsk, where she died in 1675.

According to Nadezhda Mandelstam, the last two lines of this poem, "What mad Surikov/Will paint my last journey?", originated in a remark made by Punin to Akhmatova in the Tretyakov Gallery: "Now let's go and see how they'll take you to your execution."[133] Akhmatova introduces an allusion to a weird creature, Viy, one of the most horrible creatures in Ukrainian folklore, whose eyelid reaches to the ground, and who appears in a famous tale of that name by Gogol. This adds to the grotesque atmosphere of the poem, and the tragic fate the poet sees ahead.

One of the most memorable lyrics written at this time, "When someone dies" (1940), which was included in *Reed*, is about neither love nor history, but it shows penetrating insight into human nature. Our perception of someone changes after he dies, symbolized here by his portraits—just as our perception of Akhmatova would change after her own death.

When someone dies
His portraits change.
The eyes gaze in a different way and the lips
Smile a different smile.
I noticed it when I returned
From a certain poet's funeral.
And since then I've checked frequently,
And my conjecture has been confirmed.

(II, p. 129)

The War Years: 1939–1945

The hour for courage strikes upon our clocks,
And courage will not desert us.
   —AKHMATOVA, "COURAGE," 1942

The specter of war hung over Europe. In August 1939, Stalin signed the Nazi-Soviet Pact, the "Unholy Alliance." Some thought this gave Stalin the time he needed to prepare his troops against a German invasion, but as Harrison Salisbury has shown in his book on the Siege of Leningrad, *The 900 Days,* when the invasion did occur, the country was unprepared.[1] Other critics maintain that Stalin's reason for signing the pact was to bring about a war between Germany and the West that would destroy both, leaving the Soviet Union in an unchallenged position in Europe.[2] In the agreement, control over Finland, Estonia, Latvia, and Bessarabia was given to the Soviet Union. Although Lithuania was to be given to Germany, after the fall of Poland in September, Germany traded this claim to Russia in return for a share of Poland. Germany now had access to Russian food and raw materials, including petroleum. Hitler traded his stance of the leading anti-Communist in Europe for matters of expediency.

The war between Hitler and the West began on September 1, 1939, when Hitler invaded Poland. Two days later England and France formally declared war on Germany. In accordance with the pact, Soviet forces occupied the eastern region of Poland, which includes areas now part of the Ukraine. The Soviets also moved against Finland, but they encountered more opposition than they had expected. In December 1939 the Soviets invaded, and for three months the Finns fought valiantly; but on March 12, 1940, a peace treaty was signed allowing the Soviet Union to incorporate a large area of Finnish territory, although Finland maintained its independence.[3] In January 1940, Akhmatova wrote an unpublished poem relating to this event. Implicit is the idea that the Soviet leader has thought up new ways to torment the people. Instead of torture chambers, he releases prisoners and sends them off to die in battle—not to defend the fatherland, but to conquer new territory for the Soviet Empire:

To the New Year! To new bitterness!
See how he dances, mischievous child,
Over the smoky Baltic Sea,
Bowlegged, hunchbacked and wild.
What kind of fate has he
For those beyond the torture chamber?
They have gone to the fields to die.
Shine on them, heavenly stars!
Earthly bread, beloved eyes,
Are no longer theirs to see.
(II, p. 577)

Pasternak wrote Akhmatova a moving letter on November 1, 1940, trying to comfort her about the fate of her collection, *From Six Books,* which had been withdrawn from publication that summer, and sharing his anxiety about what was facing Russia with the threat of war:

Dear Anna Andreyevna,
Is there anything I could possibly do to cheer you up a little and bring some interest into your existence in this darkness that has once more descended upon us, the shadow of which I feel over myself as well and shudder every day. . . . How could I remind you adequately that to live and wish to live (not any way but only in your way) is your duty to the living, because conceptions of life are easily destroyed and rarely sustained by anyone, while you are their main creator.

My dear friend and inaccessible model, all this I should have said to you on that grey August day, when we saw each other last and you reminded me how unequivocally dear you were to me.

Pasternak then referred to the attacks on *From Six Books,* and to the attacks on Britain, for his family was now living in Oxford:

I do not read newspapers as you know. Yet recently when I ask people
what is new in the world I discover one encouraging thing and one sad
one: the British are holding out, but Akhmatova is being attacked. I
fondly hoped between these two items of news which affect me equally
closely there could be some kind of osmosis, so that the sweetness of
one could soften the pain of the other.[4]

Akhmatova expressed her deep concern and sympathy for Britain by turning
to Shakespeare. In "To the Londoners" (1940), she notes that Shakespeare had
written twenty-three dramas, but now "Time . . . is writing the twenty-fourth,"
presenting events far more terrifying than those in his plays:

Time, with an impassive hand, is writing
The twenty-fourth drama of Shakespeare.
We, the celebrants at this terrible feast,
Would rather read *Hamlet, Caesar* or *Lear*
There by the leaden river;
We would rather, today, with torches and singing,
Be bearing the dove Juliet to her grave,
Would rather peer in at Macbeth's windows,
Trembling with the hired assassin—
Only not this, not this, not this,
This we don't have the strength to read!

(II, p. 175)

With Hitler's shadow over Europe, Akhmatova also wrote a haunting long
poem called *The Way of All Earth* (1940). It is a meditation on death in the midst
of the turmoil and chaos of war. The heroine tells her own tale. She is a woman
from Kitezh, a medieval city allegedly saved by prayer from the Tatar invasion:
"Some say it [the city] was lifted up to the heavens and its reflection seen on a
lake into which the enemy rushed to their death, others that like other legendary
cities, it sank deep into the lake where its towers can be seen on days when the
water is specially clear."[5] Akmatova said the poet Klyuev had called her *"Kite-
zhanka,"* or "woman from Kitezh." The image of Kitezh had played an increasingly important role in Klyuev's own works, representing an ancient, "genuine"
Rus, which, as Klyuev wished to believe, would rise once again in all its dazzling
beauty. Possibly the memory of Klyuev, who died in a Stalinist camp, was a
stimulus for Akhmatova's work on *The Way of All Earth*.[6] Akhmatova herself
describes how the poem came to her:

In the first half of March 1940 on the margins of my manuscripts, disconnected lines began to appear to me out of nowhere. The meaning of
these lines seemed very dark to me at that time and, if you wish, even

strange. For a rather long time they did not promise to turn into anything whole and seemed to be ordinary meandering lines, until they beat their way through and reached that refinery from which they emerged as you see them now.[7]

The Way of All Earth is a combination of personal biography and allusions to Russian history and culture. The epigraph immediately conjures up mankind's last journey—the journey to death: "Sitting in the sled, setting out on the way of all earth." However, this epigraph not only reflects the poet's own awareness of imminent death but by its allusions elevates this awareness to a universal level. The line is taken from a medieval Russian work, *The Instruction of Vladimir Monomakh for His Children*. Early in the thirteenth century the ruler of the land of Rus, Vladimir Monomakh, left behind his worldly wisdom to his children, as he was about to go "the way of all the earth," to his death. He sits "on the sled," for it was part of Russian tradition to convey the body to the cemetery in a sleigh. The wisdom incorporated in the *Instruction* became part of the heritage of the Russian people. But the epigraph also recalls the biblical phrase, I Kings, 2:1–2: "Now the days of David drew nigh that he should die; and he charged Solomon his son, saying, I go the way of all the earth; be thou strong therefore, and show thyself a man." In this poem, perhaps Akhmatova is taking on the role of teacher— the older, wiser person handing down her wisdom to future generations.

The apocalyptic atmosphere of the time is emphasized by Akhmatova in a second epigraph, which derives from Revelation 10:6, the actual prophecy of the coming Apocalypse: "And [the angel] sware by him that liveth . . . that there should be time no longer." Akhmatova sees the intimations of impending doom and debacle from the period before World War I—the Russian defeat at Tsushima, the Dreyfus Affair, and the Boer War—as stages in an approaching end, when after the Day of Judgment there will be no more time, and life will be eternal.

The poem itself is a lament for Old Europe, of which "only a scrap remains." The heroine has been summoned home across a land filled with soldiers, trenches, bayonets—a world, as in the tales of Hoffmann, where reality turns into the grotesque:

> Right in the face of bullets,
> Thrusting the years aside,
> Through Januarys and Julys,
> I will somehow get there . . .
> No one will notice my wound,
> Nor hear my cry,
> Me, the woman of Kitezh,
> They have summoned home.

(II, p. 375)

What the heroine recalls of Kitezh is not a fairy-tale landscape with palaces and formal gardens, but simple things—an apple orchard, the groan of an old barrel organ, the sights and sounds of everyday life. But they are elusive, she cannot touch them. She cannot go home again. To reach her childhood home, she must first go by way of a crucified capital, Petersburg, the center of pre-Revolutionary Russia, and if she does succeed in returning, she will find the house deserted, "And in a dark heap/A man with his throat cut sleeps." Here she will not find refuge in the past. Although she has reached the threshold of fame, a voice warns her:

> "You will come back here
> You will come back more than once,
> And again you will strike
> Against unyielding diamond.
> You had better pass by,
> You had better go back,
> Defamed, praised,
> To the paternal garden."
>
>   (II, p. 379)

The "paternal garden" is not the little house in Tsarskoye Selo where the poet once lived, but heaven itself, where God the Father resides. There is only one way to "get beyond the ancient crossroad," and that is through death. Like Vladimir Monomakh, the poet says, "I will take my place calmly/In a light sled"; she is ready to be laid to rest in her last dwelling place.

> I waited for the great winter
> A long time,
> Like a white ascetic rite
> I take it on.
> And I will take my place calmly
> In a light sled . . .
> I will return to you before nightfall,
> People of Kitezh.
> There is one way to get beyond.
>
>   (II, p. 383)

> The ancient crossroad . . .
> Now no one accompanies
> This woman of Kitezh,
> Neither brother nor neighbor,
> Nor the first bridegroom—
> Only a branch of pine,
> A sunny rhyme

Dropped by a beggar
And picked up by me . . .
In my last dwelling place
Lay me to rest.

(II, p. 383)

This poem is not about escape from life, but "expresses faith in the most profound sense of the word. Strength here stems from the recognition that the poet has come from God and will one day return to Him, and that she must make her way through time to the place where there will be none."[8]

Early in November 1940, the "Unholy Alliance" between Hitler and Stalin began to unravel. Hitler probably realized that a conflict with Russia was inevitable, and it was wise to attack while German forces were still fresh and strong. Germany also did not like being dependent on Russia for raw materials. Hitler distrusted Russia's aim to absorb surrounding territory, and in turn Stalin did not trust the German troops in the Balkans and Finland. German preparations for "Operation Barbarossa" were ordered to be completed by May 15, 1941. As Dmytryshyn put it, "The incompatible allies parted company."[9]

On June 22, 1941, the German ambassador, Count von der Schulenburg, delivered Hitler's declaration of war to the Soviet Commissar for Foreign Affairs. Hitler's armies rolled into the USSR at dawn that day. The attack should not have been a surprise. Between April and June, Churchill had informed Stalin several times about the regrouping of the German troops, and in May, Soviet military attachés in Berlin conveyed the same information to their superiors in Moscow. But Stalin chose to ignore the situation. He had already accomplished the decimation of his main officer corps through purges. Salisbury analyzes the cause of the poor Soviet performance in the initial attack.

> Stalin could not have had more specific, more detailed, more comprehensive information. Probably no nation ever had been so well informed of an impending enemy attack . . . But the Soviet experience reveals that neither the quantity nor the quality of intelligence reporting and analysis determines whether a national leadership acts in timely and resolute fashion. . . . Unless the leadership is prepared to act upon such reports, regardless of preconceptions, prejudice, past commitments and personal politics, the best intelligence in the world goes to waste—or even worse, is turned into an instrument of self-deceit. This was clearly the case with Stalin.[10]

The attacking troops included not only Germans, but Italians, Rumanians, Hungarians, and Finns. Three million men marched against Russia on a front extending from the Baltic to the Black Sea. The troops advanced under the protection of thousands of planes. The Nazis expected that Russia would fall within a few weeks, but they were wrong. In September Nazi and Finnish troops began the Siege of Leningrad, which lasted for 900 days. Under constant bombardment and near starvation, the population successfully withstood the siege. The fall of Leningrad would have been an important symbolic victory for the Nazis, and would have led to a collapse of morale in the country as a whole. While resulting in great suffering and sacrifice, the preservation of the city of Leningrad in Russian hands meant a moral victory that gave courage to the millions of soldiers and civilians who fought valiantly to save their land and their people.

Andrey Zhdanov, who was in charge of Leningrad, was in the Crimea on vacation, and no one could act without his orders. Stalin was also absent from Moscow, and no major decisions could be made without him. When Stalin returned, he locked himself in his room in a state of nervous collapse.[11] The retreating armies of Leningrad were severely battered. On June 30, the call went out for a People's Volunteer Corps. Dmitry Shostakovich, the composer, wrote on his application: "Up to now I have known only peaceful work. Now I am ready to take up arms. Only by fighting can we save humanity from destruction." He was not accepted, but was assigned to air-raid duty. One of Akhmatova's most loyal friends, Yevgeny Shvarts—a gentle, sickly, nervous satirist and writer of children's fairy tales—also volunteered, although his hands shook so badly from Parkinson's disease that he could hardly sign the application. "How can you hold a rifle?" someone asked. "Never mind," Shvarts replied. "There are other things to do." When Shvarts was rejected, he and Zoshchenko worked night and day for a week and completed a satire, *Under the Lindens of Berlin,* which was performed at the Comedy Theater. After the theater was evacuated in August, Shvarts and his wife refused to leave. They stayed on in Leningrad as members of the defense unit for their house at No. 9, Griboyedov Canal.[12]

One night Shostakovich invited some friends to his apartment, which was littered with sheets of music on which he was writing his Seventh Symphony, the "Leningrad." Shostakovich was at his piano ready to play when suddenly the air-raid sirens sounded and enemy aircraft could be heard. Shostakovich played on. When he had finished the first movement, he sent his wife and children to an air-raid shelter, but asked his friends to remain, as he continued with the second movement to the crashing accompaniment of anti-aircraft guns. The third movement was incomplete. Shostakovich's friends made their way home after the all-clear was sounded. "Shostakovich's music, the roar of the guns, the fires springing up, the bombs, the sirens, the planes—blended into a cacophony in which reality and art were inextricably mingled."[13]

Olga Freidenberg, Pasternak's cousin, noted in her diary in September 1941: "Disaster is approaching." First stores closed down, then the air was filled with deafening gunfire, houses shook, and people rushed about wildly, not knowing where to seek refuge. But the Russian people survived. "It is impossible to get used to such horror, but we did," she wrote. Leningrad was encircled, and the bombardment went on for nine months, day after day, relentlessly. The city was unprepared; there were almost no air-raid shelters, and people ran to cellars. If one of these buildings was hit by bombs, they would be buried alive. By December, the city was without fuel and rations grew short. The less bread there was, the longer the lines. Trolleys stopped running, and people walked in silence for miles, over bridges, over frozen rivers, pulling sleds behind them piled high with boards, logs—anything that could be used for fuel.[14]

To make matters worse, in the middle of the siege eminent scholars were arrested, including Viktor Zhirmunsky, one of the first to predict Akhmatova's greatness, and later editor of the first scholarly edition of her work. No epidemic or bombs could have killed as many people as cold and starvation did during the blockade. "They fell while walking, collapsed while standing in line, the streets were strewn with corpses, and the yardmen gathered them up each morning like trash. It is said that three and a half million people perished that winter in Leningrad. . . . It was forbidden to talk, complain or appeal for help."[15]

Two of the numerous heroic women who risked their lives during the siege were Olga Berggolts, the poet, and Mariya Yudina, the pianist. Berggolts broadcast on the radio every day, trying to encourage the people to keep fighting. She wrote a poem describing how a peaceful area in the countryside, once the site of a children's camp ringing with laughter, was now the front:

> . . .
>
> I know, there is no death: it does not sneak up,
> it does not smother slowly—
> life simply flashes and explodes,
> a full string like a song.
>
> . . .
>
> How quiet it is today here, on the front!
> there amidst the ruins; over the chimney,
> a narrow moon rose on the horizon,
> a young village moon.
>
> And a string rings out, rings out in the fog,
> praying for great joy . . .
> All in blood,
> in grievous, rusty wounds,
> my land, I love, love you.[16]

Mariya Yudina had been expelled from the Leningrad Conservatory because she openly espoused religion. Now she came all the way from Moscow to give concerts in Leningrad. Yudina's courage was exemplary. "One had to have a mighty and unbending spirit to choose to come to our grim city and risk the deadly bombardments and return to her room on the seventh floor of the Astoria Hotel in the pitch blackness of Leningrad nights," says Olga Freidenberg.[17]

In the early months of the war Akhmatova also proved to be heroic. People still remember the inspired speech she gave on the radio addressed to the women of Leningrad. At the end of August 1941, the radio committee received an order from Moscow to begin transmissions about the blockade. Georgy Makogonenko, the literary critic and Olga Berggolts's husband, decided to feature Leningrad soldiers, Party workers, and housewives, all of whom joined the city's Volunteer Corps, on the show. Makogonenko wanted to bolster Leningraders' spirits to resist the Nazis. He asked a famous scholar and a theater director to appear on his show, but both were reluctant. They wanted to know if the program was being transmitted to the entire country, afraid the Fascists might hear them. Then Makogonenko turned to Shostakovich and Akhmatova. The critic explained why he turned to Akhmatova, even though many Russians had not been able to read her poems for years: her works were forbidden, yet her name was forged into history—the history of Russian literature and culture. The very name "Akhmatova" was associated with Leningrad. The poet in turn showed her steadfast love for her city in a new poem, "Vow":

And she who is parting with her sweetheart today—
Let her forge her pain into strength.
By the children we swear, we swear by the graves,
That no one will force us to submit!

(II, p. 181)

This poem became part of the cycle called *The Wind of War,* written in 1941–45.

Makogonenko and Olga Berggolts went to visit Akhmatova. Although she was sick, she said: "I'm grateful for the invitation and certainly will recite. Only it will be difficult to get to Manezhnaya [Street]," where the radio station was. He agreed to tape her in her apartment, and sent Olga with a sound engineer to record her speech. Berggolts recalled how the voice of the poet who had been perceived by Tsvetayeva as the "Muse of Lament" rang out tragically and proudly. "She did not recite then as the Muse of Lament, but as a real and courageous daughter of Russia and Leningrad."

My dear fellow citizens, mothers, wives, and sisters of Leningrad. It is more than a month since the enemy began trying to take our city and has been wounding it heavily. The city of Peter, the city of Lenin, the city of Pushkin, Dostoyevsky, and Blok, this great city of culture and labor, is threatened by the enemy with shame and death. My heart, like those of all the women of Leningrad, sinks at the mere thought that our city, my city, could be destroyed. My whole life has been connected with Leningrad: in Leningrad I became a poet and Leningrad inspired and colored my poetry. I, like all of you at this moment, live only in the unshakeable belief that Leningrad will never fall to the fascists. This belief is strengthened when I see the women of Leningrad simply and courageously defending the city and keeping up their normal way of life. . . . Our descendants will honor every mother who lived at the time of the war, but their gaze will be caught and held fast particularly by the image of the Leningrad woman standing during an air-raid on the roof of a house, with a boat-hook and fire tongs in her hand, protecting the city from fire; the Leningrad girl volunteer giving aid to the wounded among the still smoking ruins of a building. . . . No, a city which has bred women like these cannot be conquered. We, the women of Leningrad, are living through difficult days, but we know that the whole of our country, all its people, are behind us. We feel their alarm for our sakes, their love and help. We thank them and we promise them that we will be ever stoic and brave.[18]

Berggolts also stressed that Akhmatova did her part as an ordinary citizen: "I remember her near the old iron gates of the fence of the House on the Fontanka. . . . Her face at once severe and angry, a gas mask thrown over her shoulder, she took on the fire watch like a regular soldier. She sewed bags for sand which were put on the trenches."[19]

Shostakovich had also readily agreed to speak. On September 16, he talked about his work: "An hour ago I finished the second part of my new symphony. If I am able to finish it, it will be called the Seventh Symphony. . . . I am telling you this, because you should know life in our city is going on as normal. We are all carrying on."[20] On this same day, the headline of *Leningradskaya pravda*, "ENEMY AT THE GATES," was plastered all over the city.

When the bombing began, Akhmatova telephoned Boris Tomashevsky, the famous Pushkin scholar. He immediately went to fetch her to stay with his family at the House of Writers on the Griboyedov Canal. On their way back, on the Square of the Arts (Mikhailovsky Square), the air-raid siren suddenly sounded and everyone ran, seeking shelter. Akhmatova and Tomashevsky rushed into one courtyard, then another, and finally stumbled down a crooked staircase into a cellar. Tomashevsky looked around and said, smiling: "You know, Anna Andreyevna, you've come to the Stray Dog!" Akhmatova replied calmly, "It's always like this with me."

The first few days Akhmatova stayed in Irina Tomashevskaya's (Boris's wife, well known as the scholar Irina Medvedeva) room. Whenever there was an air raid, they all went down to the cellar. Then the superintendent of the building, Moisei Yepishkin, decided to put a couch in his hall, and that was where Akhmatova lived. Yepishkin had vivid red hair and was very quiet and good-natured, never refusing anybody anything. Tomashevsky liked to call this gentle man a philosopher. One day, when Akhmatova asked him to get her a pack of cigarettes, he readily obliged. He went off to the tobacco shop on Zhelyabov Street and never returned. In one of those cruel, "impersonal" acts of war, a shell hit the shop just as he reached it. Akhmatova never forgot that day for the rest of her life.

Garshin came to see Akhmatova at the Tomashevskys'. Zoya Tomashevskaya, their daughter, noted that when he came over, he would immediately go to Akhmatova's room and never drank tea or socialized with the Tomashevskys, although they were always very hospitable. When Akhmatova moved to Yepishkin's couch, Zoya would see Garshin in the courtyard coming every evening to bring Akhmatova food.[21]

On September 28, 1941, Akhmatova reluctantly left for Moscow. Both she and Mikhail Zoshchenko were told by the City Council that they were being evacuated to Central Asia on orders from Alexander Fadeyev, a writer who was high up in the Union of Soviet Writers. And so for the first time the two names—Akhmatova and Zoshchenko—were linked. In fact, the evacuation of many important writers, artists, musicians, and filmmakers to Central Asia saved their lives. Akhmatova would remain in Tashkent until May 1944.

Before departing, Akhmatova saw Pavel Luknitsky after many years. In his diary for September 28, 1941, he noted he had found out that Akhmatova was about to be evacuated and wanted to say goodbye to her. He recorded that she was sick and weak, but sat with him on a bench while they talked. Akhmatova told him it was right that in ancient myths the earth was always the mother, always indestructable. Only the earth could shrug off the terrors of bombardment.[22]

In Moscow, Akhmatova visited her old friend Nadezhda Chulkova, who wrote:

> I treated her to an omelette and coffee with cream. She was surprised I suggested such a treat. . . . At this time people were starving in Leningrad. . . . She had flown from Leningrad to Moscow with the writer Zoshchenko. Their plane was accompanied by an air escort. She said: "We should have left a long time ago. We Leningradians were not thinking when we refused to be evacuated. But at the time it was so warm, everything was fine; there were many flowers and no one believed in the possibility of this horror that everyone is now going through."[23]

Akhmatova told Nadezhda what it had been like to sit with her neighbors in a bomb shelter in the garden, with a child in her arms. Suddenly she'd heard a roaring, shrieking, and whistling, such as she had never before heard in her life—hellish sounds. "And what were you thinking of at the time?" asked Chulkova. "How badly I had lived my life and how I was not ready for death," Akhmatova replied. Chulkova asked if it was possible to repent in one moment and receive forgiveness. "No, you must prepare for death beforehand." Akhmatova also said she was hoping she would be received well by the Tatars, because of her Tatar ancestry.

Toward the spring of 1942 more people were evacuated from Leningrad, and the Tomashevskys received orders to leave for Krasnoyarsk. They did not have a kopeck left or any valuables to sell. Zoya Tomashevskaya said they felt the end had come. However, she remembered that in October 1941 they had received a call from Moscow from Fadeyev. Akhmatova, in despair that she had left them in such dire poverty when she fled to Moscow, begged Fadeyev to give them a permit to live there, but Tomashevsky absolutely refused to leave Leningrad, saying, "Without books I'm a dead man." They dreaded leaving, but still it was only Moscow. There were friends and possible work, and it was a short trip, while it would have taken weeks to get to Krasnoyarsk. And so the family left for Moscow, where they spent the war years. From there they corresponded with Akhmatova in Tashkent.[24]

Margarita Aliger accompanied Akhmatova on the train from Moscow to Central Asia. Pasternak was going to put Akhmatova in his former wife's apartment (she had gone to Chistopol with their son Yevgeny), but she was included among the writers going to Chistopol. Pasternak was part of this group, on his way to join his wife and child, already in Chistopol. Akhmatova and Pasternak sat together, talking quietly, seemingly unaffected by the stress of the moment. "Many of us were upset, anxious about the future, worried about our luggage—which was quite natural at that point; no one could condemn us for that—but these two were outside of everything around them. They were somehow separate from the rest, calmer, freer, more independent, and their presence somehow made it easier for us."[25]

Lydia Chukovskaya was in Moscow early in May, and left for Chistopol, on the Kama River in the Urals, on July 28, 1941. (Writers more favored by the regime were sent to Chistopol, which had good facilities.) There she met Marina Tsvetayeva, who had moved with a group of writers to nearby Yelabuga, a small Tatar town. Tsvetayeva had little money and no hope of work; she applied for the position of a dishwasher at the writers' mess hall but was told there were too many other applicants for the job. When Chukovskaya found out about this, she said: "If Tsvetayeva can be appointed to wash dishes, why not let Akhmatova wash the floors, or hire Alexander Blok, if he were still alive, as the mess hall stoker? That would really make it a writers' mess hall." Chukovskaya and two of her friends, the writer Mikhail Schneider and his wife, helped Tsvetayeva as best they could, and finally she was granted the right to live in Chistopol. However, the humiliation she had to go through to get the permit and the feeling of ultimate despair about her situation were apparently too much for her. On the afternoon of August 31, she was found hanging from a hook inside the entrance to her hut. As Karlinsky says: "Marina Tsvetaeva, one of Russia's greatest poets of this or any century, was buried in Yelabuga in an unmarked common grave whose location is unknown," instead of the grand funeral procession through the streets of Moscow she had predicted in an early poem.[26]

On October 15, Chukovskaya noted that she had received a telegram from her father to say that Pasternak and Akhmatova were on their way to Chistopol. "Akhmatova in Chistopol! This is unimaginable, like seeing the Admiralty spire or the General Staff Building Arch [both in St. Petersburg] in Chistopol!"[27]

One evening when everyone had already gone to bed, there was a knock at the gate of the house where Chukovskaya was staying. The landlady, swearing, went out with a lantern to open it, and Chukovskaya ran after her.

Anna Andreyevna stood at the gate with someone who I could not make out in the dark. The light of the lantern fell on her face: it was desperate . . . wearing someone else's fur coat flung open, a white wool scarf, carefully hugging a bundle to her breast. She kept falling down or screaming. I grabbed the bundle, took her by the hand and led her home across the mud. I gave her some leftovers, then put her into my bed and lay on the floor on a mattress.

On October 21, Chukovskaya recorded her conversation with Akhmatova about Tsvetayeva:

Today I went with Akhmatova along the Kama. I led her across the same swampy meadow across which I had helped Marina two months ago. "It's strange," I said, "the same river and meadow. Two months ago I led Marina Ivanovna across this very spot, this same meadow. And we spoke about you. And now she is no more, and I'm talking about her with you. On this very spot!" Akhmatova did not reply, only stared at me. I did not tell her about our conversation. I had expressed my joy to Tsvetayeva that Akhmatova was not here in Chistopol, in this half Tatar village drowning in mud, cut off from the world. "She'd die here for sure . . . this life would kill her. . . . She doesn't know how to do anything." "And do you think I can?" Tsvetayeva interrupted.[28]

Chukovskaya received papers and money from her father to travel with her children to Tashkent in Uzbekhistan, where he was now living, and Akhmatova went with her. On the way they stopped in Kazan, once the center of a Tatar princedom, then incorporated into the Russian Empire when it was conquered by Ivan the Terrible in the sixteenth century. In the nineteenth century it had one of the major universities in the country, and Tolstoy and Lenin had been students there. However, during the war it was a communications point between European and Asian Russia, as thousands of refugees fled to the East. The Printing House was filled with people coming from Moscow. Akhmatova and Chukovskaya arrived by boat, and made their way to the Printing House, where Akhmatova slept on a table and Chukovskaya on some chairs. Chukovskaya went to see Samuil Marshak, the translator and author of children's books, and he helped them find a place on the train to Tashkent. They waited four hours in the dark on the platform for the train to arrive. Akhmatova sat in silence the whole time—the same restrained silence she had observed while standing in prison lines. Once on the train, Chukovskaya read Akhmatova letters she had brought, sent to her from Leningrad. As she read, she cried, while Akhmatova still remained silent. They were both thinking of Leningrad. Akhmatova read *Alice Through the Looking-Glass,* which Korney Chukovsky had given Chukovskaya to read to the children. "Don't you think," asked Akhmatova, "that we are now beyond the looking-glass?"[29]

On November 8, they finally reached their destination and saw camels in the distance. Akhmatova was excited, spying an eagle and noticing that the river was yellow: they were near Tashkent. Everything was warm and the flowers were in bloom. Korney Chukovsky met them at the station in a car and took the children with him, depositing Chukovskaya and Akhmatova in a hotel.

For the first few weeks Chukovskaya and Akhmatova lived together there. Then Akhmatova was given a room in the Hostel for Writers on 7, Karl Marx Street, while Chukovskaya lived with her children at her parents' house, before moving to another writers' hostel. No matter where she lived, she visited Akhmatova every day, bringing her food from the bazaar, or coal for her stove, or standing in line to get her rations. She also helped edit poems. Chukovskaya once forgot her own birthday, but Akhmatova did not forget—and arranged a surprise party in her honor. When Chukovskaya became sick with typhus, Akhmatova in turn watched over her. But in the late autumn of 1942 Akhmatova began to insult Chukovskaya in front of other people. Once, Akhmatova sent for her, and when Chukovskaya arrived, Akhmatova changed her clothes and left. Chukovskaya says she never understood what had happened between them.[30] She decided then that it was best not to see Akhmatova, and stopped visiting her that December. (She left Tashkent for Moscow in the autumn of 1943 and would not see her friend again until 1952.)

The room under the iron roof that Akhmatova occupied in the hostel was meant to be a temporary home, but she lived there from November 1941 until May 1943, except for a period spent convalescing at Dyurmen, outside the town. She ate in the dining hall at the Union of Writers, and during the warmer months outside, in the spacious courtyard of the building. Akhmatova said in Tashkent there were invalids at every step, and at night you could hear the sound of the knocking of their wooden legs on the sidewalk, "moving on three legs." Opposite where she lived was a hospital: on hot days the wounded crawled out onto the street and sat on the sidewalk, like human stumps.[31]

While Akhmatova enjoyed the beautiful surroundings and the hospitality of the people who lived there, she did not always enjoy her neighbors who had been evacuated from Leningrad and Moscow. Various women were jealous of Akhmatova and constantly gossiped about her, creating "intrigues" to make her life uncomfortable. Akhmatova referred to them as the "knitters"—an allusion to the "furies of the guillotine," as the women portrayed in Dickens's *Tale of Two Cities* were called. They envied her and slandered her. Chukovskaya noted that in Tashkent, as everywhere, Akhmatova was received with honor, respect, and veneration by many, but not all. The women writers especially were irritated by her—by her combination of helplessness and authority, her illness and her fame, her independence and her inability to drag a pail of water and coal, which others did for her willingly. Akhmatova usually responded to the gossip with a smile and a joke, though sometimes she grew angry.[32]

In spite of Punin's earlier treatment of her, Akhmatova was ecstatic to learn that he would be passing through Tashkent and she might see him. At the end of April 1942, she wrote to her friend Nikolay Khardzhiyev, who was living in Alma Alta: "Punin came through Tashkent on the way to Samarkand. He is in bad shape and it is impossible to recognize him."[33] He had been evacuated from Leningrad along with other members of the Institute of Art History to Samarkand. He was with his wife and daughter and her baby, Anya. Later, when Akhmatova came to visit the Tomashevskys in Moscow in May 1944 on her way back to Leningrad, she told them what a sad postcard she had received from Punin in Cherepovets. He wrote that he would barely be able to get to Tashkent and begged her to help him and his family. Zoya says, "At that time Akhmatova never parted from the postcard or the letter from Punin from the Samarkand hospital."[34]

Zoya Tomashevskaya describes how her friend Olga Ivanova told her that in 1942 she had seen Akhmatova waiting one day at the train station. Ivanova had just lost her small daughter, and she tried to escape her grief by spending days at the Tashkent Station in hopes of meeting her husband coming from the front. Once, at the other end of the platform, standing like a statue, was a woman with red carnations in her arms—Akhmatova. She was waiting anxiously for someone. It turned out it was Punin. The Punins stayed for one day, and then Akhmatova saw them off. The letter to which Zoya Tomashevskaya refers was written by Punin after he arrived in Samarkand, revealing the depth of his feelings for Akhmatova:

The realization that I am still alive brings me to a rapturous state and I call this—the feeling of happiness. Moreover when I was dying, that is, knew that I would undoubtedly die . . . I also felt that rapturous happiness. At that time particularly I thought a lot about you. This was because in the intensity of the spiritual experience I was going through there was something . . . akin to the feeling alive in me in the twenties when I was with you. It seemed to me that for the first time I understood you so fully and comprehensively—and it was just because it was so completely unselfish, as I, of course, did not expect ever to see you again. It was really a meeting and farewell with you before death. And it seemed to me then that I knew of no other person whose life was so whole and therefore so perfect as yours, from your first childish poems (the left-hand glove) to the prophetic murmur, and at the same time roar, of the *Poema [Poem Without a Hero]*. . . . You know, many people judge you on account of Lyova [Lev Gumilyov], but then it was so clear that you did the wisest and by far the best thing you could do in the circumstances (I am talking about Bezhetsk), and Lyova would not be the person he is without his Bezhetsk childhood. I also thought a great deal about Lyova, but I'll talk of that another time—I am guilty before him. . . . To die was not something terrible—and I had no pretensions to continuing to live personally or to being preserved after death. I just am not interested in that at all. But that which is immortal exists and of that thing I am a part. It was solemnly splendid. Then you seemed to me, as you do now, to be the highest expression of that which is immortal that I have met with in my life. In the hospital I happened to re-read *The Devils*. Dostoyevsky, as always, seemed heavy and not at all my kind of reading, but at the end of the novel like the golden dawn shining through terrible, incredible gloom, I found these words: "A thought which had been with me continuously about the existence of something infinitely more just and more happy than I, fills me with immeasurable tenderness—and as for glory—whoever I might be, whatever I might have done to anyone, it is far more necessary than to be happy myself to know and believe every minute that somewhere there is perfect and peaceful happiness for everyone and everything." These words were just about a perfect expression of what I felt then. Particularly—"and as for glory"—"peaceful happiness." You seemed then to be the expression of the "peaceful happiness of glory." Dying, I came closer to it.[35]

Tashkent was an extraordinary gathering place for the Russian intelligentsia during the war. Major critics and writers held poetry readings, and concerts were performed. Svetlana Somova, who was living there at the time, said she came to know the value of the old Russian intelligentsia when she met them during the war. They were a special stoical breed, able to retain their feelings of worth under any circumstances, sustained by a world of intellectual values, and capable of sacrificing everything for victory.

Somova describes how she saw Akhmatova walking down the street with Korney Zelinsky and Viktor Zhirmunsky on their way to hear Alexey Tolstoy give a reading of his new play, *Ivan the Terrible*. She says that Khamid Alimadzhan, secretary of the Union of Writers in Tashkent, helped Akhmatova during this period. Akhmatova often read her poems at poetry evenings, in hospitals, or in the auditorium of the Frunze Military Academy. Looking very elegant in a dark dress, she read in a quiet voice. Somova tells how in one large ward a young man lay suffering horribly but silently—he would not answer any questions. Akhmatova immediately went over to him, sat quietly near the bed, then, in a soft voice, began to recite her poems about love. It was difficult, said Somova. No one knew what to read to people half-alive. But it suddenly became very quiet in the ward. The faces of the sick and wounded grew calm. "Someone said that all great women—Sarah Bernhardt, Vera Komissarzhevskaya [a great Russian actress at the turn of the century], Akhmatova—had voices 'with a crack,' which lent them a special charm."[36]

The Tatars in Tashkent recognized that Akhmatova was special, that "the hand of God" was upon her. Uzbeks sold sour milk in clay pots or enamel pails, shouting, "Sour milk, sour milk" in high-pitched voices. One old Uzbek sold his milk in the corridors of the hostel where Akhmatova lived. He was dark, with gray hair bound up in a turban of dirty white rags. The women poured out of their rooms, joking, and the old man began to pinch them, urging them to buy an extra spoonful of milk. There was lots of laughter and lots of noise. Suddenly the Uzbek stopped and said, *"Dzhim* [Quiet] . . . *mullah!"* Akhmatova had opened her door, and this old man from the village immediately recognized someone more elevated, which to him meant a *mullah,* a person of great wisdom.[37]

Often members of the intelligentsia would gather in the evening. Joseph Czapski, a Polish officer who was also an artist who had studied in Russia in his youth, described one such evening at the home of Alexey Tolstoy. Czapski had been captured in September 1939 and was in a prison camp until 1941; then he and other Polish officers were released when Stalin decided to create a Polish squadron to fight the Nazis. In 1942, Czapski was with General Wladyslaw Anders in Tashkent. Later the troops under Anders were sent to Iran under British auspices. According to Chukovskaya, other meetings besides the one Czapski describes took place between him and Akhmatova. However, Czapski had to cooperate with the NKVD officer Sokolovsky, who had been assigned to watch him, so Czapksi kept silent about those meetings in order to protect Akhmatova.[38] "About twelve o'clock we gathered in a large drawing room around a table loaded with wines, some excellent dried fruits and other sweetmeats," says Czapski. " . . . It was cool, and there was a feeling of buoyancy in the air. I can still see Akhmatova, as she sat that evening, silent, with tears in her eyes, while I gave a clumsy translation of that verse of 'Christmas in Warsaw.' " Czapski tells of his difficulties in conveying the beauty of Polish poetry to foreigners, but says that he had never aroused such interest in it as on that night among this "last remaining handful of Russian intellectuals. . . . I realized what a hunger there is among Russians for poetry, genuine poetry." Akhmatova, he writes, wore a simple dress; her hair was lightly touched with gray, kept in place by a colored handkerchief. She spoke little, but when he asked her to read, she recited passages from her *Poem Without a Hero,* which she was working on at the time. "The verses, which she declaimed in a strange sort of chant . . . were devoid of optimistic propaganda. . . . But 'The Poem of Leningrad' is in fact the only work of its kind that has moved me, however briefly, to understand as something *real* the defense of the heroic, half-starved and ruined city."[39] Many years later, in December 1959, Akhmatova would recall that evening in a poem entitled "from the cycle 'Tashkent Pages':"

That night we drove each other crazy,
The ominous darkness shone only for us,
The canals murmured to themselves
And the carnations smelled of Asia.

And we passed through the alien town,
Through midnight heat and smoke song—
Alone under the Serpent constellation,
Not daring to look at each other.

It could have been Istanbul or even Baghdad,
But alas! Neither Warsaw nor Leningrad,
And this bitter difference
Was stifling, like the air of orphanhood.

And I imagined that centuries marched by,
And an invisible hand beat a tambourine,
And sounds, like secret signs,
Circled before us in the darkness.

I was with you in the mysterious gloom,
Walking as if in no-man's-land,
But suddenly the crescent moon
Skimmed like a diamond boat over this meeting-separation . . .

And if that night should return to you
In the course of your hidden fate,
Know that someone dreamt
About this sacred moment.

(II, p. 293)

Zhanna Levina who was a young girl at the time of the war, was living with her uncle's family in Tashkent in the same building as Akhmatova. She describes her as tall, stately, regal. One day Zhanna's teacher asked her to invite Akhmatova to come listen to poems written by the students. Zhanna overcame her shyness and went to ask, and Akhmatova readily agreed. She listened very patiently to the poems, then talked about poetry and poets. Akhmatova also gave English lessons to Zhanna's brother.[40]

One of Akhmatova's closest friends during her stay in Tashkent was the composer and conductor Alexander Kozlovsky. Born in Kiev in 1905, he graduated from the Moscow Conservatory, was a conductor at the Stanislavsky and Nemirovich-Danchenko Theater, and then became a conductor in Tashkent, where he also taught music at the conservatory. Somova implies that the relationship between Akhmatova and Kozlovsky was more than mere friendship.

Kozlovsky had gray eyes, radiant and mocking, and his whole being reflected restrained passion. He did not immediately attract attention, being short, modest, and quiet; but once having seen him one realized there was something special about this man who inhabited his own world—the world of music.[41] Kozlovsky composed music for Akhmatova's drama *Prologue* and for parts of *Poem Without a Hero.* In turn, Akhmatova dedicated a beautiful lyric, "Apparition of the Moon," to him, combining the visual image of a moon of mother-of-pearl and agate with Beethoven's *Moonlight* Sonata:

> From mother-of-pearl and agate,
> From smoked glass,
> So suddenly it slanted
> And so festively if floated—
> As if "Moonlight Sonata"
> Had just crossed our path.
>   (II, p. 201)

Although Akhmatova missed Leningrad, she found Tashkent beautiful and exotic. Her sojourn there is reminiscent of Pushkin's stay in the south of Russia.[42] The Central Asian landscape awoke in her a strange feeling for the sensual beauty of the East and her Tatar heritage. In "I haven't been here . . ." (1944), she evokes that heritage, recalling how her ancestors invaded Russia in the thirteenth century and ruled the land for several hundred years. Not only was Akhmatova part Tatar, she also had the blood of the royal line of Genghis Khan in her veins.

> I haven't been here for seven hundred years,
> But nothing has changed . . .
> In the same way the grace of God still pours
> From unassailable heights,
>
> The same choirs of stars and water,
> The same black vaults of sky,
> And the wind spreads the seed the same way,
> And mother sings the same song.
>
> My Asian house is sound,
> And I can be tranquil . . .
> I will return. And now, fence, bloom!
> New reservoir, fill!
>   (II, p. 201)

Chukovskaya conjures up the atmosphere of Tashkent—its steep, narrow alleys winding from the street down to the bazaar, an Eastern marketplace with vegetables and fruit piled high, sheep carcasses hanging just out of people's reach, flat white loaves of bread offered at staggering prices by hucksters, and sun-blackened women trading in Oriental sweets.[43] Somova describes a city filled with one-story houses, and in each house a garden or courtyard with fruit trees where people lived when it got warm—there they slept, worked in the open air or in the shade of a mulberry tree, and were greeted upon waking by the fragrance of blossoming almond and apricot trees.[44] A later poem, written in May 1945 after Akhmatova had left Tashkent, evokes this heady atmosphere:

> As in a refectory—benches, a table, a window
> With an enormous silver moon.
> We are drinking coffee and red wine
> We are delirious with music . . .
>   It's all the same . . .
> And a branch is beginning to blossom above the wall.
> And in this there was a pungent sweetness,
> An inimitable sweetness, most likely.
> Our native land gave us a harbor
> Of immortal roses, dry grapes.[45]

In April 1942, Akhmatova learned that Valya Smirnov, the little boy she used to take care of in the communal apartment, had died during a bombing raid. Her grief was transformed into a poem:

> Knock with your little fist—I will open.
> I always opened the door to you.
> I am beyond the high mountain now,
> Beyond the desert, beyond the wind and the heat,
> But I will never abandon you . . .
> I didn't hear your groans,
> You never asked me for bread.
> Bring me a twig from the maple tree
> Or simply a little green grass,
> As you did last spring.
> Bring me in your cupped palms
> Some of our cool, pure, Neva water,
> And I will wash the bloody traces
> From your golden hair.
>
> (II, p. 187)

Akmatova's most famous wartime poem, "Courage" (February 1942), was on everyone's lips, and inspired not only the Russian soldiers but those they left behind at home. Here the "Russian word" which the poet uses to provide courage to her people becomes symbolic of Russian culture and the nation as a whole:

Courage

> We know what lies in balance at this moment,
> And what is happening right now.

The hour for courage strikes upon our clocks,
And courage will not desert us.
We're not frightened by a hail of lead,
We're not bitter without a roof overhead—
And we will preserve you, Russian speech,
Mighty Russian word!
We will transmit you to our grandchildren
Free and pure and rescued from captivity
Forever!
(II, p. 185)

The Leningrad theater critic R.W. Benyash, who visited Akhmatova at the end of 1941, said that her spirituality and seeming remoteness did not isolate her from ordinary life. The radio in her bedroom was always on. "When she listened to the regular report, her face seemed like the living embodiment of tragedy. . . . But even in the gloomiest days she reflected deep faith. It was as if she knew what none of the rest of us knew. . . . She not only believed in final victory, she was sure it would come."[46]

In 1942, Akhmatova became very ill with typhus. She once said: "It was in Tashkent that I found out for the first time what a tree's shadow meant in the scorching heat, and the sound of water. And I also discovered what human kindness meant: I was very sick in Tashkent."[47] After being treated in the hospital, she spent some time convalescing at Dyurmen outside the town. There she began to write fragments of an autobiography, which she would continue over the years after the war. In this fragment she recalls hearing her heels clicking in the Tsarskoye Selo arcade as a child on her way to school. The snow around the cathedral was turning dark, ravens crowed, bells tolled, someone was being buried. The skeleton would wait in his coffin for the burial near the cathedral.[48]

Her weariness and delirium are captured in "Typhus," written November 1942:

Somewhere sweet night is young,
Starry, frosty . . .
Oy, worn-out, oy, wasted
Typhus head.

She imagined herself
On the pillow dreaming,
Knowing that she doesn't know, knowing that she doesn't know
That he is responsible for everything,

That beyond the garden, beyond the river,
A nag with a coffin is plodding.

There's no need to put me underground,
I'm only—the storyteller.

(II, p. 607)

When Akhmatova became sick once in 1943, this time with scarlet fever, the Uzbeks again helped her. The Uzbek archives contain the following document: "To Comrade Ivanov. The poet Anna Akhmatova is living and working right now in Tashkent. She is the most important representative of Soviet poetry. Because of illness, the Union of Soviet Writers asks your permission to give Comrade Akhmatova fuel. Secretary SSP UzSSR Kh. Alimadzhan, October 25, 1943."[49]

In 1943, Alexey Tolstoy helped put out Akhmatova's *Selected Poems*. In a letter to Irina Tomashevskaya dated June 21, 1943, Akhmatova said that she had been ill for a long time, but had recovered in May. She describes the new volume: "My book is small, incomplete and strangely put together, but still it's good that it's come out. Very different people are reading it, and in a very different way."[50]

Pasternak wrote an unpublished review of the book:

This is a new and noble occasion for the resurrection of a famous woman writer, her role as an innovator of gigantic proportions. . . . She transformed Blok by her new realism. Used to loss, she was hardly prepared for the trial of immortality. The collection convinces us that the writer was never silent and responded to the questions of the time in spurts. . . . It would be strange to call Akhmatova a poet of war; the predominance of a feeling of threat in the atmosphere of the age has lent her work a certain significance. There are two features—national pride and artistic realism. . . . All her images, whether an image of the forest . . . or the noisy atmosphere of the capital, contain a rare feeling for detail.[51]

Pasternak and Akhmatova had shared the same train on the way to Kazan, and Pasternak took a steamer from there to Chistopol. But instead of going on to Tashkent, he joined his family—and remained in Chistopol. Conditions there were very different from the warm, luxurious atmosphere of Tashkent. In Chistopol it was often freezing, and they had little to eat. However, Pasternak was grateful for the refuge it provided during the war. He spent two winters there with his family, but in the warmer months he lived in his dacha at Peredelkino, from where he made frequent trips to Moscow. During the war years he worked on his famous translations of Shakespeare.[52]

Akhmatova's faith at this period was severely tested by her fear for her son, Lev. He was doing time in Siberia, in Norilsk, then working on a geological expedition near Turukhansk. Many prisoners were released in order to fight in the war. Lev had asked to go to the front, but for a long time he was not granted permission. (Later he was allowed to fight and was at the taking of Berlin in the spring of 1945.) In April 1943 Akhmatova wrote Irina Tomashevskaya that she had just received a letter from Lev. She had not heard from him or had news of him for seven months and told Irina she was going out of her mind with worry.[53] She wrote Khardzhiyev (June 2, 1943) that she had received a telegram from Lev from Novosibirsk, and that he was on a special expedition that would last several months. "Novosibirsk," a city in Siberia, may be a place name used symbolically by Akhmatova for "somewhere remote."[54]

One of Akhmatova's constant companions and sources of comfort in Tashkent was a teenager named Eduard Babayev. In his memoir he recalls returning to Tashkent from a military expedition in Samarkand and hearing an artillery officer on the station platform reading a poem from a small white book to his friends. It was the edition of Akhmatova's *Selected Poems* published in 1943. Without going home, Babayev rushed straight from the station to look for the book, but everywhere he went he was told the same thing: "Sold out, too late." There was one last kiosk, which belonged to a certain Semyonova, on the corner of Pervo-maiskaya Street. If he really wanted this book, Semyonova told him, he would have to go to the Union of Writers and find Tikhonov, the poet who was soon to become the secretary of the Union of Soviet Writers. Tikhonov had just taken one hundred copies from her, everything she had. Babayev ran and found Nikolay Tikhonov, who gave him a copy, then asked him to take some copies to Akhmatova. Babayev was excited and overwhelmed. On the way he met Nailya, a nurse, and when he told her he was going to see Akhmatova, she told him, "Take off your shirt! You look like a dervish! . . . Akhmatova is a European poet, and you have the dust of Asia upon you." Babayev replied, "It doesn't matter, Khamid Alimadzhan said in the East trust only those who have the dust of roads traveled by people on their bashmaks [shoes]." "That may be," said Nailya, "but put on a clean shirt." She found one for him.

Babayev imagined he would find Akhmatova with many guests and would sit in a corner where he could watch her unnoticed. He began to worry about what he would say to her. But it turned out she was alone. When the door opened, he recognized her immediately. She asked him to tell her about himself, and then she laughed quietly. "Now I understand why you have such dirty shoes, but tell me, for God's sake, where did you get such a clean shirt?"

Babayev became Akhmatova's guide around Tashkent, and often accompanied her on her evening walk. He thought she chose him for a companion because he did not pester her with literary conversation. In one of their chats she told Babayev something he would never forget: "The most difficult trial of all— is the trial of fame."

Babayev relates how one time a Lieutenant Krylov came to see Akhmatova. She had met him in the hospital where he was lying wounded. He was from her generation—the "old cavalier," she called him—and had earned a St. George Cross during World War I. Krylov loved Akhmatova's poems and carried *From Six Books* to the front. "I'm flying out tomorrow at six A.M.," he told Akhmatova, "I could not leave without saying goodbye to you."[55]

Years later in Moscow, Babayev began to recall Tashkent, mentioning the poem *"De profundis . . ."* (March 1944) to Akhmatova. She told him: "These poems have been lost. I didn't write them down, and now I can't remember them." But Babayev had written them down and was able to hand them over to the author with a bow. "A star's gift," Akhmatova said. *"De profundis . . ."* begins with the Latin words from the Catholic hymn for the dead. The poem is a lament for her entire generation:

De profundis . . . My generation
Tasted little honey. And now
Only the wind hums in the distance,
Only memory sings about the dead.
Our hours were numbered,
Till of that long-awaited watershed,
Till of that great mountain's peak,
Till of that violent flowering
Remained only one breath . . .
Two wars, my generation,
Lit your terrible path.

(II, p. 609)

On June 2, 1943, Akhmatova wrote Irina Tomashevskaya that almost the entire group evacuated to Tashkent in 1941 had now returned to Russia. About one thousand people left with the Academy of Sciences, and the city was once again a sleepy, foreign provincial town. Akhmatova still did not have a *vyzov* and *propusk* [necessary documents] allowing her to return to Leningrad. No Soviet citizen could live in a particular city or town without them. She also wrote Khard-zhiyev on December 14, 1943, that she had been detained because of her bout with scarlet fever—conveyed in an epigram:

"An inadequate excuse,
You should be on your way."
"And almost left,
But was stopped by scarlet fever."[56]

In May, Akhmatova had moved to a new house, 54, Zhukovskaya Street—it was spacious and isolated, surrounded by enormous poplars. She wrote Khard-zhiyev on June 2 that she had never lived in such an empty house, "although ruins and wasteland are my specialty." Her quarters were right above Nadezhda Mandelstam's. "Nadya has become very kind and compassionate," she said. "She is extremely gentle with me."[57]

Akhmatova had moved into the former room of Yelena Bulgakova, widow of the writer and dramatist Mikhail Bulgakov. She had become friends with them in the early 1930s when they lived in the same building as the Mandelstams in

Moscow. One of Akhmatova's friends, Vitaly Vilenkin, described Yelena as always hospitable, no matter how hard her fate—someone who always believed in people and attracted them by her kindness, her lively mind, and her feminine grace.[58] Yelena gave Akhmatova the manuscript of Bulgakov's novel *The Master and Margarita* to read in Tashkent. His work had been banned in 1930 and he became a literary consultant at the Moscow Art Theater while continuing to work on the novel from 1928 until his death in 1940.

The novel is about the Master, a writer in the 1930s whose own work—the tragedy of Pontius Pilate—is condemned, so that the author too is destined to perish. It moves back and forth between solemn, lyrical passages of the religious story and a rollicking, biting satire on the 1920s, the NEP period, when the devil comes to Moscow to unmask all the corruption. Toward the end of the novel the Master's mistress, Margarita, attends a witch's sabbath. Akhmatova captures these images in her poem to Yelena, written in August 1943:

The Hostess

Before me in this chamber lived
A solitary sorceress:
Her shadow is still visible
On the eve of the new moon.
Her shadow still stands
By the high doorsill,
And sternly and evasively,
She glances at me.
I am not one of those
Subject to other people's spells,
I myself . . . But, by the way,
I don't just give my secrets away.

(II, p. 213)

Akhmatova continued to take part in the literary life of Tashkent. In 1943, there was a celebration in memory of Mayakovsky. Akhmatova read "Mayakovsky 1913" in honor of the occasion.[59]

Svetlana Somova describes one remarkable day in May 1944 when Akhmatova personally experienced Uzbek poetry and culture. She met the legendary poet Gafur Gulyam, known to the people as "Gafur the Magnificent." He said to Akhmatova, "You are called Anna. In Uzbek, 'Anna' means 'Mother.' Come with me to a Kishlak [an Uzbekistan village] where tomorrow they are letting out the first waters into the empty fields." She did not want to go, but he persuaded her, saying, "As a mother you must." She replied that she did not know Uzbek, so he called up Saida Zunnunova, a young poet whose works had been translated into Russian.

In the car on the way, Somova noticed Akhmatova's lips moving silently. Saida also noticed this and became silent, as did Gafur. They sensed something special was taking place. Akhmatova whispered something, then suddenly recited a new poem out loud.

Soon the Uzbek clay hut, its flat roof covered with crimson poppies, appeared at the edge of the desert, along with a pond surrounded by poplars. The host came out and greeted Akhmatova, *"Salyam aleikem, Anakhon"* (Hello, Mother). They were led to the women's half of the house and treated to sweets. The following morning, the festival of letting out the water began. There were bonfires, music, dancing, and songs accompanied by drums, flutes, and huge trumpets. They put a transparent white silk scarf on Akhmatova. To the left lay the bare channel of the new canal, and soon water flowed into it, over the fresh earth, as musicians and dancers performed. Gafur took Akhmatova by the hand and said, "Put your foot in, *Anakhon,*" and with light grace, she took off her shoes and stepped into the canal.

Pilaf was served, amber grains of rice with berries and red pepper. Men and women sat together. Gafur called Akhmatova a *shair-shunka* (poet-eagle): She had flown to them from the fighting city of Leningrad to bring water to their desert. Akhmatova understood that they wished her to recite some poetry. She spoke very slowly, very melodiously, and the peasants, most of whom did not know Russian, rocked their heads quietly in time. Khalima Masyrova, a poet who had just sung his own "nightingale songs," also heard and understood. Akhmatova recited "Everything comes back . . ." (December 1943), and Gafur Gulyam read his famous poem *"Saganysh,"* which means "Pining." Akhmatova's poem mentions Khalima:

> Everything comes back to me again:
> The scorching night and the languor
> (As if Asia were raving in her sleep),
> The nightingale singing of Khalima,
> And the blossoming of Biblical narcissus,
> And the invisible blessing
> Of wind rustling over the land.
>
> (II, p. 199)

The sky turned lilac, and early stars, large and hanging low in the Eastern sky, appeared over the teahouse, their flecks of light playing on the white porcelain drinking bowl which the poet Gafur Gulyam handed Uzbek-style—with two hands—to the poet Anna Akhmatova.[60]

While she was in Tashkent, Akhmatova worked on a play, *Enuma Elish,* about the relationship of the poet to the state. Akhmatova herself, however, said that she burned it on June 11, 1944, in the House on the Fontanka after she returned to Leningrad, but gave no reason why. According to Nadezhda Mandelstam,

Akhmatova burned the play after her son Lev was arrested and taken away in 1949. Nadezhda believed that had the authorities read Akhmatova's play, they would have been tempted to arrest her as well.[61]

The title, *Enuma Elish,* which means *When Above,* derives from the first words of the ancient Babylonian creation epic that includes *Gilgamesh,* and that was part of a New Year's ritual.[62] In her introduction, entitled "Instead of a Preface," Akhmatova wrote:

> When I came out of the hospital after a bout of typhus in Tashkent at the end of 1942, everything for some reason began to seem like a drama, and I wrote *Enuma Elish.* The first and third acts [in prose] were all ready. "Prologue" was left to be done, i.e. the second act. It had to be in verse and represented a passage of the play written by the heroine Enuma Elish-X. In this play the role of the somnambulist was played by X herself. By moonlight she descended the sheer wall of her cave—after wandering in the dark for a time, without waking up, she prayed to God and lay on a goat's skin which served as her couch. In the moonlight a guest from the future appears on the wall dimmed by the smoke of fires. Their dialogue [ensues].[63]

Much later, at the beginning of the 1960s, the poet said, "It thought of returning to me." Akhmatova vainly attempted to recreate the lost text, but never fully succeeded. Shortly before her death, she collected what was finished in an envelope with the inscription: "A. A. Akhmatova. 'Prologue' (Dream Within a Dream). 1965."

The prose parts framing the verse play-within-a-play take us from the stage to the auditorium. It is a grotesque social satire addressed to the "real world," the Philistine public hostile to the poet. The central part—"Dream Within a Dream"—is a verse drama in which the heroine is the author, simultaneously poet and actress playing the main role. Set during the war, the play dramatizes the trial of a poet before a writer's tribunal.

The first part takes place in the theater dressing room, as the maid Frosya helps to wake up the heroine. The actress is in despair because she has come offstage unable to finish the play. A tall woman enters in a *yashmak* (a Muslim veil) carrying a basket of violets. She is the heroine's double: she orders the actress to change clothes with her and go to the square to sell violets, and she will perform in her place.

The second part, "Dream Within a Dream," is performed with an orchestra before an audience on stage. While it is being performed, there are snatches of conversations in the audience and scenes in the wings between the director and his assistant, interrupting the action. A mysterious dream appears to the sleeping heroine, where two lovers—He and She, or the Guest and X—engage in a sado-masochistic discourse. Most of the fragments of this part in the archives allude to events in Akhmatova's life after the war, and therefore could not have been part of the original concept of the verse drama.

The third part returns to prose: it portrays the Kafkaesque trial of the heroine after the failure of her play, and ends with her tragic death. It is a grotesque parody of the many examinations of scholars and writers, forcing them to make "confessions" about the incorrect attitude reflected in their works. Unfortunately, such "trials" actually took place, both before and after the war. Vladimir Admoni discussed the attacks in 1949 against his wife, the scholar of American literature Tamara Silman, who had written the chapter on American Romanticism in a history of American literature. Among other things, it was insinuated that the work appeared in a green cover because green was the color of the American dollar. Silman had to appear on a stage where the tribunal took place and defend her writings.

> Everything had been carefully prepared. The Party Bureau had distributed the roles: who should attack whom, when someone should appear. Everything was subject to attack: words written by the victims, their lectures, how they administered their departments (. . . Silman headed the Department of Foreign Literature). No one was interested in the real facts. Everything was altered, distorted as much as possible. Everything was simply made up. No one paid any attention to the answers of the accused. Moreover, if one attempted to answer correctly, to expose all the lies and misrepresentations against the accused, he would be the victim of even wilder, more grotesque slander. . . . Argument was useless. The only way out for the accused was repentance. Then at least he would not be arrested.[64]

Nadezhda Mandelstam, who read Akhmatova's play in Tashkent, provides a useful commentary. She says as she remembers it, the heroine descended a rickety ladder, after being awakened at an unearthly hour, and appeared before her judges in a nightgown. The writer on trial was forced to answer not only for what she was writing but for what she was thinking. "All the commonplaces of official literature and ideology were reproduced in fantastically concentrated form and with deadly accuracy."[65] (The excerpts in the archives, written later, refer to events and even phrases used in the context of Akhmatova's own grotesque encounter with the authorities after the war.)

In March 1944, Akhmatova was finally expecting permission to return to Leningrad. One of the reasons she wanted so desperately to return was to be with Garshin. After she was evacuated, he had remained behind in Leningrad, becoming chief coroner of a city filled with corpses during and after the terrible siege. It was a time of such privation that there were rumors of cannibalism. By February 1942 as many as 650,000 deaths had been registered—many more were not even noted. Such horrors must have had their effect on Garshin. There was already a history of mental illness in his family—his relative, the famous writer, had been in a mental institution.

Not too long after Akhmatova had left the Tomashevskys in 1941, they received an unexpected visit from Garshin. It was a gloomy November evening and they heard a knock on the door. It was dark, since there was no electricity. Garshin came in and asked permission to sit on "his sofa," the one which had been taken to the superintendent Yepishkin's where Akhmatova stayed before she left for Tashkent, and which now stood by the door in their apartment. He sat silently, and left without saying a word. Afterward he began to visit quite frequently. Around New Year's he brought Irina Tomashevskaya a present, *Lives of the Saints,* twelve volumes bound in beautiful leather, saying that he had received them from Akhmatova. At the end of January 1942 he found everyone in a very bad way. Their ration cards had been lost. It was quite dark and very cold in the room. Garshin sat for a while, silent as usual, then suddenly said: "The horses have already all been fed, but I have some oats left. I could give them to you, if you send someone with me."

As chief coroner of Leningrad, Garshin was allowed horses for funerals and burials. It was horrible, said Zoya Tomashevskaya. He lived in a house on the Fontanka Canal. The curfew was already in force, and the rumors of cannibalism made people afraid to go out. However, Zoya's mother ordered her to go, since she herself was afraid of Garshin, while Zoya was not; to a young girl, he seemed very handsome, like a romantic hero. Garshin gave her a whole bag of oats. She went home alone, trying to run as quickly as possible. Over each stretch of territory she recited poetry—a chapter from *Eugene Onegin,* something from Akhmatova's *Poem Without a Hero*. This bag of oats, which they managed to grind up in a coffee mill, saved them from real disaster. Garshin came more and more rarely. Eventually he moved to his institute and lived there until the end of the war. Later, Zoya's parents gave him a volume of Pushkin's works in gratitude, inscribed:

To Vladimir Garshin
To a real human being even in bestial godforsaken times
With love
From Irina and Boris
Tomashevsky[66]

In October 1942, Garshin's wife collapsed on the street and died. He found her in a morgue and identified her by her clothes—her face had been devoured by rats.[67] Aliger says that Garshin was haunted by this image, and that his memories of it disturbed his relationship with Akhmatova.[68] He wrote to Akhmatova proposing marriage, asking if she would take his name, and she agreed.[69] In a letter to a friend, he wrote: "Don't judge me. I can't live without Anna Akhmatova. I have summoned her to Leningrad. Don't judge me for wanting to be with her so soon after the death of Tatyana."[70] Garshin promised Akhmatova that he would find them a new apartment, since she did not want to return to the communal apartment with the Punins at the Sheremetev Palace. On April 6, 1943, she wrote Khardzhiyev, "I live in mortal fear for Leningrad, for Vladimir Georgiyevich [Garshin]. I've been very sick and have gone totally gray."[71] On April 14, Akhmatova sent a copy of her work so far on *Poem Without a Hero* to Khardzhiyev, asking him to give it to Garshin, and adding: "Vladimir Georgiyevich is in Leningrad working from seven-thirty in the morning to eleven at night with no days off. During the shooting and bombardment he gives lectures and does research. He is behaving like a real hero."[72] Akhmatova had been able to keep in contact with Garshin through the pianist Mariya Yudina. Akhmatova sent messages from Tashkent to the Tomashevskys after they moved to Moscow, and they passed them on to Yudina to give to Garshin when she went to perform in Leningrad.

In a short poem sent in a letter to Garshin, Akhmatova uses the imagery of war to convey her feeling of being cut off from her beloved both physically and psychologically. On the physical level, the three fronts refer to the defenders of Leningrad, the German troops blockading the city, and the Soviet troops holding the Germans in partial encirclement. On the metaphorical level, the poet speaks of a border between her and her beloved where they confront each other, which resembles the border between oneself and the enemy:

> My eyes don't move from the horizon,
> Where the snowstorms dance the czardas.
> Between us, my friend, there are three fronts:
> Ours and the enemy's and then ours again.
>
> (II, p. 601)

In March 1944, Akhmatova was preparing to leave for Leningrad. Garshin sent her a telegram every week saying that she would receive permission to come "any day." At the end of April, she wrote a lyrical poem to Garshin, looking forward to their meeting again. It became part of the cycle *The Wind of War*:

> To the right the vacant lots unfurl,
> There's a strip of dawn as ancient as the world.
>
> To the left, streetlights like gallows trees,
> One, two three . . .
>
> And over everything a jackdaw's cry
> And the moon's pallid face
> Arise completely irrelevantly.
>
> It's—not from its life and not from that one,
> It's—when the golden age will dawn,

It's—when the war is over,
It's—when we meet once more.

(II, p. 191)

Akhmatova started home on May 15, stopping over in Moscow, where she stayed with Nina Olshevskaya, who described this visit to her husband Viktor in a letter:

I just came from the station. I accompanied Anna Andreyevna. I am very sad because she was such a joy for me, just like in her lines: "I know you are my reward for the years of torment and toil . . ." It was so warm and interesting for me with her, and the main thing, intellectual. It's been so long in these years of isolation and solitude that I've got out of the habit of thinking about ideas. It will be very boring now without our nightly vigils, which I was becoming accustomed to these past days.[73]

Akhmatova gave a poetry reading in Moscow. The folklorist Natalya Kolpakova wrote in her diary how moved she was when she heard Akhmatova reciting. The House of Writers had arranged a series of recitations called the "Verbal Almanach," and poets from the blockade and the front as well as the audience participated. The evening on which Akhmatova read took place at the Polytechnic Museum. "Among them all Anna Akhmatova stood out like the sun among the stars," wrote Kolpakova. "She had grown amazingly more beautiful these past years! You could not take your eyes off her. The wonderful face and that unforgettable look—almost gentler, nicer, and more profound than before. And, moreover, even sadder. She read her poems of the past few years. And in the intonation, in her eyes, in the sound of her voice one heard something enormous—suffering—something all our Leningrad poets from the front and the blockade could not put into their own poetry."[74]

One of the reasons Akhmatova looked so young and radiant was that she was looking forward to seeing Garshin again and becoming his wife. She told all her friends in Moscow that she was going to be married. Margarita Aliger commented that she had never seen Akhmatova so happy: she was lively, transformed, young and pretty. Her son was alive and well, her city had been liberated, and people were waiting for her there. Life would begin anew.[75]

But when Garshin met her at the station in Leningrad, something was clearly wrong. Vladimir Admoni had returned on the same train as Akhmatova. He said she and Garshin walked up and down the platform for ten minutes, and when Akhmatova returned, she said calmly: "Everything has changed. I'm going to Rybakova's"—meaning her friend Lydia Rybakova.[76] She stayed with the Rybakovs for several months in a small room, since her room in the Sheremetev wing was in a terrible state.

Akhmatova did not let her Moscow friends know immediately what had happened. Finally, on July 24, Nina Olshevskaya received a telegram. It was a month and a half since Akhmatova had been in Moscow. "I wish good health to all of you. I'm living alone. Thank you for everything. Akhmatova." It was a typical Akhmatova text—concise, yet full of indirect innuendos the reader would have to decipher. The phrase "living alone" put Nina on guard, but it was difficult to guess what the trouble was. Three weeks went by, and then on August 6 another telegram arrived: "Garshin is mentally ill. Separated from me. I'm telling only you. Anna." Right after this came a postcard, written three days later:

> My dear, thank you for the letter—it touched me very much and made me remember you and myself, what I was like in May. Did you receive my telegram, do you know my news? I'm still not on the Fontanka; there is no water there, light or glass [in the windows]. And no one knows when they will appear. I was in Terioki (two days)—I read poems to the wounded. I warmly kiss you and the children. Greetings to your mama; I think about her pain [Olshevskaya's mother had been let out of a camp so she could die in her daughter's arms]. And please have Nikolay Khard-zhiyev write me. Yours, Anna.[77]

"What a restrained postcard and what an ability to sympathize and participate in all the grief and problems of everyone around her," Olshevskaya commented.

At first Garshin visited Akhmatova. He brought her food, and they would talk for a long time in her room. Then after ten days Olga, Rybakova's daughter, heard Akhmatova shriek. Garshin ran out and left, and they never saw each other again. At Akhmatova's request, Rybakova went to Garshin and took back Akhmatova's letters, which Akhmatova destroyed, along with his letters to her. She also removed the dedications she had written to Garshin in *Poem Without a Hero* and other poems. At the end of 1949, Garshin became seriously ill. Rybakova visited him and Olga continued the visits after her mother's death. He often asked about Akhmatova, but she did not want to hear his name mentioned and shut him out of her life completely. He died in 1956.[78]

Yu. I. Budyko has attempted to explain what happened between Akhmatova and Garshin:

> How could it be that two people so close before the war got through the difficult years of the war, met and—without any apparent cause—separated when nothing prevented them any longer from being together? However, it was not really the same two people who met in June 1944 as those who had parted in September 1941. Anna Andreyevna had gone through a lot of difficult times, but as Aliger testifies, she was "animated, transformed, young and lovely." But Garshin, who had lived through the blockade, was very sick at this time and carrying the heavy burden of

psychic trauma. It would take a long time to restore his health, and he did not have this time. And so their paths parted.[79]

However, another important reason why the relationship did not work out was that Garshin had an affair with a woman doctor during the war (not a nurse, as Haight suggests), who was the same age as Akhmatova, and whom he married after the war.

Akhmatova transformed her grief and disappointment into a terrifying poem entitled ". . . And the man who means," written in 1945:

. . . And the man who means
Nothing to me now, but was my concern
And comfort in the bitterest years—
Wanders like a ghost on the outskirts,
The back streets and the back yards of life,
Heavy, typified by insanity,
With a wolfish grin . . .
                    O God, God, God!
In your eyes how grievously I have sinned!
Leave me pity at least . . .
                    (II, p. 261)

When Akhmatova first returned to Leningrad, she was shocked by what the city had become. She tried to express her feelings in prose, though she found it more difficult than verse:

In May 1944 I flew to Moscow, which was already full of joyful hopes and expectations of an approaching victory. On June 1st, I returned to Leningrad. The horrible specter pretending to be my city so struck me that I described my encounter with it in prose. That's when I wrote the studies "Three Lilacs" and "A Visit with Death"—the latter about reciting poetry at the front in Terioki. Prose always seemed very mysterious and tempting. I knew everything about poetry from the very beginning— I never knew anything about prose. Everyone praised my first attempts very highly. Of course, I didn't believe it. I called Zoshchenko. He suggested I rearrange a few things, but basically agreed with the rest. I was very happy.[80]

Lyubov Yakovleva-Shaporina described how much she thought Akhmatova had changed, and what Akhmatova said after she had witnessed the decimation of the city:

I met Anna Andreyevna on the street. She had become heavy, older. . . . "It's horrible here, terrible . . . Two million shades hover

over us, shades dying of hunger. This never should have happened; everyone should have been evacuated in August, in September. . . . There should have been enough provisions. This is some terrible mistake by the authorities . . . There are no heroes here, and if the women endured the hunger more stoically—that is because they have more layers of fat and not because of any heroism. You think I wanted to leave?—I did not. They offered me a plane twice and finally they told me the pilot would come and get me. Everything is absolutely horrible here, horrible."[81]

Akhmatova's accommodations were a catastrophe. Her room in the building on the grounds of the Sheremetev Palace was filthy—the ceiling had gaping holes, and the glass in the windows was smashed. Makogonenko helped her, although it was a real challenge to attempt to renovate anything at this time. He called Vsevolod Marin, a friend of his wife, Olga Berggolts. During the blockade, Marin had worked as deputy director of the Saltykov-Shchedrin State Public Library; the experience transformed this librarian into a master of all trades. Makogonenko explained what was required and who it was for. Marin was insulted that Makogonenko attempted to tell him the significance of Akhmatova. "My good man," Marin replied, "don't take me for a lunatic. I am literate. Let's go. We must have a look at it." After a survey of Akhmatova's quarters, Marin said he would persuade a friend who was a carpenter to do the job, and Makogonenko would pay for it. By the time the carpenter was finished, the room looked like new. The only thing still lacking was glass, but Marin said, "I have no extra glass, but for Akhmatova we must use reserves." In the library warehouse there were some duplicates of portraits of writers, and he took the glass from these pictures, remarking, "I think they will forgive us."

Makogonenko and Olga went to visit Akhmatova after she moved in. It was Spartan: there was hardly any furniture, just a card table, two chairs, a couch, and the Modigliani drawing. They had brought her red roses, which caused Akhmatova to comment: "I love it. Your red bouquet reminds me of visits long ago to Modigliani's apartment. It's as if it were from another century. We often met during my stay in Paris. Once I went to visit him with a bunch of red roses but I could not find him," and then she told them the story of how she threw the roses through the window and how amazed Modigliani was to find them there.[82]

Eventually the Punins also returned to Leningrad, to the communal apartment, but without Anna Arens, Punin's wife, who had died in 1943 in Samarkand. Akhmatova was delightfully surprised that the tiny Anya, Punin's granddaughter, had not forgotten her. When the child saw Akhmatova, she immediately climbed up on her knee and embraced her with her little arms. Using the nickname "Akuma," which Shileiko had given Akhmatova and which the Punins used as well, she whispered in her ear: "Akuma, I dreamt about you," which immediately won the poet's heart.[83] It would take years for the city to recover, but Akhmatova soon began to find peace once more now that she was home again.

The Cold War Begins: 1946–1952

He will come to me in the Fountain Palace
. . .
But it's not the first branch of lilac,
    Not a ring, not the sweetness of prayers—
        It is death that he bears.
    —AKHMATOVA, *Poem Without a Hero* (II, p. 407)

At the beginning of 1945, the war that had cost so many lives and caused so much suffering was finally coming to an end. The date of the official capitulation of the Nazis was celebrated by the Russians on May 9, 1945. The leading powers responsible for winning the war—the United States, Great Britain, and the Soviet Union—divided the world into spheres of influence under their control when their leaders met at Yalta in February 1945 and in July–August in Potsdam. The Soviet Union maintained its power over most of the parts of Eastern Europe that it had gained during the war and also held territory in the Far East.[1]

Akhmatova, along with many others—average citizens as well as leading intellectual and literary figures—would bear the brunt of yet another wave of relentless terror, orchestrated by Stalin in his frenzy both to safeguard Soviet territorial gains and to ensure the subservience of the Russian people.

Events moved quickly to change the friendly relationship among the Allies to a belligerent one, and the relative freedom of expression among the Soviet intelligentsia during the war years to a state of mute silence. On February 9, 1946, Stalin delivered a speech reaffirming the superiority of communism and the fear of imminent capitalist wars, thereby providing a pretext for not transforming a state geared to war production into one with more peaceful goals: no peaceful international order was possible, production of iron and steel, "the basic materials of national defense," must be trebled, and consumer goods "must wait for rearmament." George Kennan, U.S. Chargé d'Affaires in Moscow, sent a telegram to Washington urging a strong resistance to advancing Soviet power. On March 5, Churchill delivered his famous speech at Westminster College in Fulton, Missouri, declaring:

> An iron curtain has descended across the Continent. Behind that lie all the capitals of the ancient states of Central and Eastern Europe. . . . I do not believe that Soviet Russia desires war. What they desire is the fruits of war and the indefinite expansion of their power and doctrines. But what we have to consider here today, while time remains, is the permanent prevention of war and the establishment of conditions of freedom and democracy as rapidly as possible in all countries.

But Churchill called for a good understanding with Russia under the auspices of the United Nations, supported by "the whole strength of the English-speaking world and all its connections." Stalin's reply, in an interview on March 14, focused on Churchill's idea that the world depended mainly on English-speaking countries. "The English racial theories," said Stalin, "have brought Mr. Churchill and his friends to the conclusion that those nations who speak English, as the only full-blooded ones, must rule over the other nations of the world."[2] The Cold War had begun.

The Soviet Union had been laid waste. Millions of soldiers had died fighting or were in prison camps; millions of civilians had been killed or maimed for life. Over a thousand cities had been completely destroyed; factories and farms were ruined. The cities and countryside were full of homeless people wandering through the streets looking for food. It would be many years before the Soviet Union would recover. The nation was on its own, as the Iron Curtain descended in March 1946. Joseph Brodsky describes what Leningrad was like just after the war:

> Gray, pale-green facades with bullet and shrapnel cavities; endless, empty streets, with a few passersby and light traffic; almost a starved look with, as a result, more definite and, if you wish, nobler features. A lean, hard face with the abstract glitter of its river reflected in the eyes of its hollow windows. . . . Those magnificent pockmarked facades behind which— among old pianos, worn-out rugs, dusty paintings in heavy bronze frames,

leftovers of furniture (chairs least of all) consumed by the iron stoves during the siege—a faint life was beginning to glimmer.³

It took time before Stalin's iron hand would be felt again. The months immediately following the war were a period of great popularity for Akhmatova. Her poems were printed in Moscow and Leningrad journals, and a new book of her works was at the typesetters.⁴ She was chosen as a member of the board of the Leningrad section of the Union of Writers, and she appeared at official affairs and sessions on poetry. She was now in her fifties, but rather than betraying weariness or a sense that she had accomplished her life's work, she was soon to write many of the works that would make her immortal.

Nikolay Punin had returned in July 1944, with his daughter Irina and granddaughter Anya. Irina's husband had died during the war, but she had remarried. They moved back to their communal apartment in the building on the grounds of the Sheremetev Palace. In August Akhmatova moved from the Rybakovs' into her small room in the apartment. The Arctic Institute had taken over the Sheremetev Palace, and anyone coming to visit Akhmatova had to show their passport and receive a pass at the entrance. Arrival and departure times were recorded— a convenient way for the secret police to keep track of Akhmatova's guests.

Soon after the war, Akhmatova was once again entertaining, albeit modestly, the artistic elite of Leningrad. One of her first visitors was Tatyana Vecheslova, the ballerina, who came to see her in the autumn of 1944. They both sat in coats in front of an electric stove, since Akhmatova had no wood for the regular oven. Akhmatova's room was bare, just a cot covered with a simple gray blanket and two or three rare antiques. Akhmatova was dressed in simple black; they both sat quietly and chatted.

One evening Akhmatova paid a visit to Vecheslova. The ballerina's apartment was full of artists, actors, dancers, theater people. Everyone had already arrived except Akhmatova, but they would not sit down at the table. Suddenly she appeared at the door and everyone stood up, even the young people who had never seen her and did not recognize her. Vecheslova says, "That was the effect Akhmatova had on people. She was very modest and dignified, very tactful. . . . Can one learn this? Education, erudition, culture—all this helps in any profession. But it is impossible to learn 'to be a poet.' "

The effect of Akhmatova's opinion on Vecheslova herself was reflected when Vecheslova invited Akhmatova to see her dance the role of Kitra in *Don Quixote*. Vecheslova was extremely nervous about what Akhmatova would think of her performance—perhaps she would be disillusioned or find her dancing inadequate. After the performance Akhmatova's good friend, one of the leading actresses of Russia, Faina Ranevskaya, invited Vecheslova, Akhmatova, and others over to her room in the Hotel Astoria where she was living. The dinner was fantastic for the time—endless sandwiches with different spreads, and wine when there was no wine to be had in restaurants. Akhmatova looked young again. She was in a good mood, and instead of criticizing the performance, she made the ballerina feel good too, saying how lovely the theater was and what a joy it must be to dance there.[5]

In February 1945, two artists—A. A. Osmyorkin and Boris Yoganson—dropped by with a bottle of champagne and some crabs. The evening seemed to pass cheerfully and, after they left, Punin returned to help Akhmatova with the dishes. He noted in his diary that she began to cry because Osmyorkin had mentioned that Lev was in a penal brigade (actually by this time Lev had been freed to help fight in the war). Punin had not seen her this depressed for a long time. "What do they want from me, from me and from Lev? . . . What has he done, my boy? . . . He is young, capable, full of strength—they envy him and are using the fact that he is Gumilyov's son. . . . They made Gumilyov's widow out of me."[6] But on November 16, 1945, Punin noted that Lev Gumilyov had returned from the front two days before. Akhmatova came to see Punin in a very excited state and ran around the apartment crying with joy.[7]

Lev returned after having taken part in the capture of Berlin and remained for some months in that city. He was reinstated in the history faculty, and after passing his exams, his diploma was ready to be given to him. However, the events that were soon to overtake Akhmatova swept him up in their path and he did not receive his diploma.[8]

That autumn Akhmatova received another important visitor, the man whom she later said brought her doom instead of lilacs—the distinguished Oxford professor Isaiah Berlin, who would become the prototype for the "Guest from the Future" in *Poem Without a Hero*. Akhmatova even suggested this meeting was a cause of the Cold War. While this was certainly an exaggeration, the events that ensued because of their encounter certainly aggravated the already tense relationship between the West and the Soviet Union.

It all seemed very innocent at first. Berlin had only the best of intentions. He was provisional First Secretary of the British Embassy in Moscow and had come on a visit to Leningrad. While browsing in a bookstore there, he met the well-known literary scholar V. N. Orlov. Berlin began discussing the Siege of Leningrad and inquired what had happened to many of the artists and intellectuals during this time. "You mean Zoshchenko and Akhmatova?" Orlov asked. For Berlin, Akhmatova was a figure from a remote past. He had been born in Riga, Latvia, in 1909, and had not seen Petrograd since he was a boy of ten. Although the city had been so damaged during the war, he says in his memoirs that for him it still remained indescribably beautiful.

Orlov phoned Akhmatova and they went to see her that same afternoon. Berlin describes his first impression of her: "Immensely dignified, with unhurried gestures, a noble head, beautiful, somewhat severe features, and an expression of immense sadness." After conversing for a while, Berlin suddenly heard his name being called. It was Winston Churchill's son Randolph, whom he had known as an undergraduate at Oxford and who had come to Russia as a journalist. Churchill needed an interpreter and had found out from an acquaintance who had accompanied Berlin to the bookstore that Berlin was visiting Akhmatova at the Sheremetev Palace. Since he did not know the exact location of Akhmatova's apartment, as Berlin describes it, "he adopted a method which had served him well during his days in Christ Church [his college at Oxford]," that is, to shout Berlin's name as loudly as he could. Berlin rushed down the stairs and left with Churchill. He realized it was dangerous for any Soviet citizen to meet with a foreigner privately. As Haight points out, "Managed quietly, with tact, a meeting might well have been 'overlooked,' but to have the son of Winston Churchill shouting wildly in one's garden as one entertained another foreigner could hardly pass without notice."[9]

Later Berlin called Akhmatova to apologize, and when he asked if he could see her again, she told him to come at nine that evening. They talked of many things—of how she worshipped Dostoyevsky, despised Turgenev, and condemned Tolstoy for his treatment of Anna Karenina; of friends whom Berlin had met— Arthur Lourie and Salomea Andronikova. Akhmatova recited *Poem Without a Hero* to him, and Berlin later wrote that he realized he was listening to a work of genius. He also heard her read *Requiem*. He wanted to transcribe both works, but she told him they would be published in a book of verse the following February, and she would send him a copy. Akhmatova also spoke of her loneliness and isolation. "Leningrad after the war was for her nothing but a vast cemetery, the graveyard of her friends; it was like the aftermath of a forest fire—the few charred trees made the desolation still more desolate." But she spoke without the slightest trace of self-pity, "like a princess in exile, proud, unhappy, unapproachable, in a calm, even voice, at times in words of moving eloquence."[10]

Berlin believed it was the appearance of Churchill that caused absurd rumors to circulate in Leningrad that a foreign delegation had arrived to persuade Akhmatova to leave Russia, and that Winston Churchill, a lifelong admirer of the poet, was sending a special aircraft to take her to England.[11]

On January 5, 1946, Berlin visited Akhmatova once again on his way back to England. The immediate result of these visits was a cycle of poems, *Cinque*, written between November 26, 1945, and January 11, 1946. They are some of the loveliest and most tragic poems in the Russian language. In one, written on December 20, Akhmatova compares her late-night dialogue with Berlin to inter-laced rainbows:

Sounds die away in the ether,
And darkness overtakes the dusk.
In a world become mute for all time,
There are only two voices: yours and mine.
And to the almost bell-like sound

Of the wind from invisible Lake Ladoga,
That late-night dialogue turned into
The delicate shimmer of interlaced rainbows.

(II, p. 237)

The last poem of the cycle, written on January 11, 1946, was more prophetic than Akhmatova realized:

We hadn't breathed the poppies' somnolence,
And we ourselves don't know our sin.
What was in our stars
That destined us for sorrow?
And what kind of hellish brew
Did the January darkness bring us?
And what kind of invisible glow
Drove us out of our minds before dawn?

(II, p. 239)

Akhmatova told Berlin later that Stalin had found out about the visit and said, "This means our nun is now receiving visits from foreign spies." On the day after he left Leningrad, January 6, people in uniform were posted at the entrance to her staircase, and a microphone was put in the ceiling. However, Akhmatova was still unaware of the political forces swirling around her. During the first months of 1946, she worked very hard. She was preparing a volume of her poems, *Selected Works,* edited by V. N. Orlov, for publication. There were old poems as well as new ones in the sections "Reed" and "Odds." On March 11 a contract was signed, and Irina Punina and Akhmatova went to the publishers to discuss the final copy. She was very excited about it, and Irina remembers that one sunny day at the end of spring they were riding in a taxi doing various errands, and at the end of the trip they were to go to the publisher's to look at a final mock-up of the book. The car was turning from Admiralty Boulevard to Nevsky when suddenly Akhmatova turned to Irina and asked, "What do you think, what kind of cover would be best? What about a gray one?"

At the beginning of March, Olga Berggolts brought a photographer to Akhmatova's room. One of his photos, featuring Akhmatova with Irina's little daughter, Anya Kaminskaya, appeared on March 8 in the newspaper *Vechernii Leningrad (Leningrad Evening)* in a column entitled "Famous Women of Our City."[12]

In April, Akhmatova was invited with a group of other Leningrad poets to go to Moscow to present an evening of poetry at the Writers' Club, and another at the Hall of Columns, Moscow University, which were very successful. Nadezhda Chulkova did not attend, but an acquaintance told her that Akhmatova appeared on April 2 at the Writers' Club, characterizing this as a "real triumph." For a long time they would not let her begin because the applause was so deafening. The scene was repeated on April 3 at the Hall of Columns.[13]

The evening at the Hall of Columns was indeed memorable. Akhmatova and Pasternak appeared together: Akhmatova read at the end of the first half, which was devoted to the Leningrad poets, and Pasternak opened the second half, highlighting the Moscow poets. Afterward, Pasternak invited Akhmatova and other friends to his apartment, where they ate, drank, and recited poetry.

But Akhmatova was frightened by the ovations she received at the Hall of Columns, confiding to a friend, "Like a vampire, an executioner will always find a victim, otherwise he cannot survive. I knew I was doomed the moment a girl ran up to me and dropped down on her knees in the Hall of Columns after I finished reciting my poetry at a special evening there. That night the verdict against me was probably decided, but my punishment came later—along with Zoshchenko's."[14]

Nadezhda Mandelstam noted that Akhmatova was being watched. There was always someone stationed outside the Sheremetev Palace. The weather was cold, and the spy would try to keep warm by stamping his feet and swinging his arms energetically. Then he was replaced by someone less lively. One time a flashbulb went off as Nadezhda and Akhmatova were walking through the courtyard to the poet's apartment.[15]

August had always been an unlucky month for Akhmatova. August 1946 began peacefully enough. On the 8th, Akhmatova appeared at an evening in memory of Blok at the Bolshoi Drama Theater, where she and Mikhail Dudin read poems about Blok. When she appeared on stage, the audience gave her a standing ovation. That night Akhmatova read a poem she had written in June 1946:

He is right—once again streetlight, drugstore,
The Neva, silence, granite . . .
Like a monument to the beginning of the century,
There this man stands—
When he said farewell to the Pushkin House
He waved his hand
And assumed a mortal weariness,
Like an unmerited peace.

(II, p. 301)

Akhmatova was paraphrasing Blok's famous poem written at the beginning of the century, reflecting the boredom he felt about the sameness of everyday life— a meaningless reality symbolized by night, a street, a streetlight, and a drugstore— which will forever be repeated. Akhmatova's poem also speaks of the end of this great poet's life, when he recited his verses written in honor of the anniversary of Pushkin's death on February 11, 1921. This event gave Blok the chance to talk about the poet's suffering. He spoke of Pushkin's "secret freedom," that inner freedom which external events should not be able to destroy, although in the case of Blok, they finally did. His disillusionment with the hopes he had for a revolution that would purge the old Russia of its sins and bring a new, innately pure world in its place was more than he could bear. "Mortal weariness"—the phrase employed by Akhmatova in her poem—beautifully expresses Blok's state of mind during those last months of his life. "The poet dies," he said, "because he can no longer breathe, because life has lost its meaning."[16]

Akhmatova's own "inner freedom" was soon to be severely tested. On August 15, she had to attend to some business at the Union of Soviet Writers and could not imagine why everyone was suddenly avoiding her. On her way home, she bought some herring and ran into Zoshchenko, who said in despair: "Anna Andreyevna, what can we do?" She did not know what he was talking about, but tried to comfort him: "We must be patient, everything will be all right." Only when she unwrapped the fish from the newspaper did she read the Resolution of the Central Committee and realize why Zoshchenko had been so upset.[17]

Totally disregarding the patriotic poetry that Akhmatova had written during the war, her poems about her love for her homeland and her criticism of those who abandoned it, and despite the fact that she had proven a model of courage to the women of her own land, the Central Committee of the Communist Party on August 14, 1946, passed a Resolution condemning the journals *Zvezda* and *Leningrad* for publishing the works of Akhmatova and Zoshchenko. As in the early 1920s, Akhmatova was accused of being a relic of the past, reflecting bourgeois aestheticism and decadence rather than social awareness. Stalin needed a victim, and a famous one, to teach a lesson to his people—that the relative freedom and communication with Westerners granted during the war was now over. And Akhmatova turned out to be the perfect victim. She was still associated in Stalin's mind with pre-Revolutionary Russia; she had been meeting with a foreigner at a time when Stalin was xenophobic and waging a campaign against "cosmopolitanism"; finally Stalin, as the writer Konstantin Simonov points out, also was suspicious of Leningrad, and Akhmatova was eternally and inextricably associated with Leningrad. Simonov interprets the attack on both Akhmatova and Zoshchenko not as an isolated incident, but as a symbol of the relationship between the state and the arts, as well as between the Soviet Union and the West:

I remember at the end of the war and right after in 1946 there was a liberal feeling among the intelligentsia. . . . Communication became simpler between the intelligentsia here and those countries with whom we had fought against a common enemy. I thought communication with foreign correspondents, which had been fairly extensive during the war, would continue, that there would be trips back and forth. American films . . . I think the attack against Akhmatova and Zoshchenko was not concerned so much with them in particular. . . . Apparently Stalin felt something in the air which in his opinion demanded a quick twisting of the screws and suppression of hopes for the future. Stalin was always suspicious of Leningrad, a feeling he had retained since the twenties, a feeling that there had been attempts there to create a spiritual autonomy. The aim was clear—it was carried out quickly, mercilessly; there was a certain carelessness in the selection of who it was addressed to and in the nature of the accusation. . . . I thought then: Why Akhmatova, who had not emigrated, who had recited so many times during the war? . . . It was crude, unjustified. . . . It was a way of showing the intelligentsia its place in society and reminding them that the tasks before them were just as clear as before the war.*[18]

Many years later Akhmatova described the day she found out about the Resolution to her friend Silvia Gitovich. When Akhmatova went to the Writers' Union, she walked up the stairs calmly and everyone greeted her respectfully but timidly, pressing their bodies against the wall to let her pass. Confused employees held their breath and sat numb, their eyes downcast. After she had finished her business, as usual she said goodbye, and without hurrying, headed toward the exit. As soon as the door closed behind her, there was a sad sigh of amazement. Reports about her visit and her self-control spread from room to room. Akhmatova said, "I knew absolutely nothing about it. I had not looked at the morning papers and had not turned on the radio, and apparently no one thought of calling me. So when I talked to them [at the Writers' Union], it was in total ignorance of what had come down upon my head."

Akhmatova's friend Silvia Gitovich says that all the newspapers were full of the names "Zoshchenko" and "Akhmatova." The Resolution was the main topic of conversation. Not everyone understood why the two writers were being attacked. One heartsick old lady standing in line was overheard saying that everyone knew what a rascal Zoshchenko was, what a scoundrel, but why were they accusing his wife Akhmatova? "I know why," answered someone else. "Husbands are scoundrels, and the poor wives always end up paying for them." People were confused, Gitovich says—they did not always get the facts straight, but they also knew Akhmatova was a great poet, and they were upset.[20]

One week later, September 4, 1946, Andrey Zhdanov, Secretary of the Central Committee, attacked Akhmatova at the Leningrad branch of the Union of Soviet Writers, announcing a Regulation expelling her and Zoshchenko from the

---

*The decree was finally lifted on October 20, 1988. An article in *Literaturnaya Rossiya* (no. 44, 1988), entitled "The Serpent's Head Bruised at Last," states that on October 20, 1988, the Politburo of the Central Committee of the Communist Party called the accusation against the journals *Zvezda* and *Leningrad,* and against Akhmatova and Zoshchenko, an error that distorted Lenin's policies regarding the relationship between the state and the artistic intelligentsia. "The works of Anna Akhmatova and Mikhail Zoshchenko have taken their rightful place in the enrichment of the world of the spirit, and the shaping of man's civic position. Their personality and books are restored to us in their true greatness and significance."[19]

Union. But his speech was broader than just an attack on two writers. Its basic thrust was to warn all Soviet writers against the bourgeois culture of the West, and to extoll the superiority of socialism, which was to be demonstrated by the arts. He also warned that Akhmatova's works would harm the morals of the young:

> What positive contribution can Akhmatova's work make to our young people? It can do nothing but harm. It can only sow despondency, spiritual depression, pessimism, and the desire to walk away from the urgent questions of public life—to leave the wide paths of public life and activity for the narrow little world of personal experience. How can we place the education of young people in her hands![21]

He returned to Eikhenbaum's phrase, calling Akhmatova "half nun, half harlot": "The gloomy tones of hopelessness before death, mystic experiences intermingled with eroticism—this is the spiritual world of Akhmatova, a leftover from the old aristocratic culture which has sunk once and for all into the oblivion of 'the good old days of Catherine.' Half nun, half harlot, or rather a harlot-nun whose sin is mixed with prayer." Akhmatova and Zoshchenko were expelled from the Union of Soviet Writers that evening.

Andrey Zhdanov was born in 1896 in Maryupol on the Azov Sea and became a member of the Bolshevik Party at nineteen. During the Civil War he helped conquer the Ural regions for the Bolsheviks and directed the Party in Nizhni Novgorod from 1924 to 1934. He quickly rose to its top ranks and became a member of the Politburo. It was Zhdanov who presented the doctrine of Socialist Realism at the Union of Soviet Writers in 1934 that created a uniform style and thematic repertoire, a doctrine that would suppress the creativity of people in all the arts for years to come.[22] Zhdanov was Party Secretary of Leningrad from 1934 until his death in 1948. He worked very hard to save the city during the siege, when it was sorely neglected by those in power in Moscow. Certainly aware of Akhmatova's important role in the war, he nevertheless was instrumental in having her expelled from the Union of Soviet Writers.

Ida Nappelbaum, who took photos of Akhmatova in the early 1920s, described what it was like sitting in the auditorium at the meeting of the Union of Soviet Writers when they expelled Akhmatova and Zoshchenko:

> A closed page. A hidden page. I can't and don't want to disclose this page. I sat frozen, mute, and they anathematized her. And deathly silence hovered over the White Hall, as if it were empty yet overflowing with living human beings. She was anathematized, and we listened and heard and were silent. And when everything was over, the entire hallful of silent people rose and went out onto the steps of the beautiful ancient building into the warm, dark, quiet night.[23]

The writer Innokenty Basalayev gave more details:

The speaker [Zhdanov] walked to the stage from behind the audience accompanied by many people. He walked calmly, serious and silent, carrying a file. Everyone stood up and began to applaud. He stepped up to the platform. The meeting began at 5 P.M. The presidium sat down. It was quiet. For a few seconds he remained silent and then began to speak. And in a few minutes a strange and weird silence broke out. The hall became totally mute, frozen, turned to ice. . . . His address was astounding. The writer M. Nemerovskaya felt sick and wanted to leave. Pale, she stood up, and staggering, walked between the rows. They helped her. She went out into the corridor toward the exhibit, but she was not allowed out. The enormous white door of the hall was closed tight. It was forbidden to leave. She sat down somewhere in the back. We left the meeting in silence. It was one in the morning. It was already dark in August. The Smolny Garden was in a damp autumn mist, and the electric bulbs of the streetlamps shone dimly. It was quiet in the Summer Garden. . . . The motionless trees seemed to be eavesdropping. Not a word, not a whisper was heard from the steps of the grand formal entrance. Several hundred people left the building slowly and silently. Just as silently they passed along the straight *allée* to the empty square and silently went off to the late trolleys and buses. Everything was unexpected and incomprehensible.[24]

Pasternak, who was a member of the board of the Union of Soviet Writers, refused to go to the meeting denouncing Akhmatova and Zoshchenko. He told them he was suffering from inflammation of the nerves and was too ill to attend. The board expelled him for this, but Pasternak went to see Akhmatova in spite of possible further consequences to himself, and gave her 1,000 rubles.[25]

Irina Punina was in Riga at the time. She and her daughter Anya were standing at a bus stop when Anya suddenly said, "I heard them saying 'Akhmatova and Zoshchenko' on the radio today." The relative they had been visiting bought a paper and they found out what had happened. Irina returned to Leningrad immediately. Akhmatova was in bed refusing to see or speak to anybody. She knew her ration card would be taken away, and Punin told Irina to arrange for Akhmatova to eat with them, although they had been leading more or less separate lives by then.[26]

At the beginning of September, Nina Olshevskaya, who was to become one of Akhmatova's closest friends in the last part of her life, came to see Akhmatova in Leningrad. In August she was on vacation with her sons in Koktebel in the Crimea. She wrote her husband Viktor, asking how Akhmatova was, whether she had already come to Moscow or was thinking of doing so. She received a telegram in response: "Fool, read the newspapers!" She read the decree against Akhmatova and immediately decided to go home, but it took her a while, since it was difficult to get a ticket. Irina Punina says that when Olshevskaya arrived, she and Akhmatova burned her manuscripts. Olshevskaya brought her back to Moscow, and when they walked down the street, they met writers who crossed over to the other side. Alexey Surkov, then editor of *Literaturnaya gazeta* and later secretary of the Union of Soviet Writers, although doing what was necessary in following Party orders to retain his position of power within the literary world, thanked Olshevskaya for taking Akhmatova into her home, and later helped Akhmatova through his influence and connections (although in *Literaturnaya gazeta,* September 7, 1946, he apologized for publishing an interview and portrait of Akhmatova the year before in the section called "Future Books," saying he had lost his keen powers of perception, but now it was clear he had made a grave error). Lev came to Moscow, and then Olshevskaya, Lev, and Akhmatova all returned to Leningrad together.[27]

Ilya Ehrenburg was abroad in France with his wife when the decree was published, in the small town of Vouvray near Tours. One morning he and his wife Lyuba drove to La Bachellerie to the house where Anatole France had lived. Ehrenburg was taking a nap in the hotel when Lyuba woke him. She had read about the condemnation of Akhmatova and Zoshchenko in a Paris newspaper. The first thing Ehrenburg did when he reached Paris was to rush to the embassy and ask for newspapers. In October, when he returned to Moscow, he learned the details:

> I had believed that after the Soviet political victory, the thirties could not repeat themselves, yet everything reminded me of the way things had gone in those days: writers, film directors, and composers were called together . . . every day new names called the list of those censured. . . . I saw Anna Andreyevna in 1947. She was sitting in a small room where her portrait by Modigliani hung on the wall and, sad and majestic as ever, was reading Horace. Misfortunes crashed down on her like avalanches; it needed more than common fortitude to preserve such dignity, composure, and pride.[28]

The attacks against Akhmatova and Zoshchenko marked a new stage in the history of the relationship between the state and the arts in the Soviet Union. Never before had the Central Committee of the Communist Party expressed its opinion directly about cultural life; it had always spoken through organizations like the Union of Writers or the press. Moreover, before, as in the campaign against Pilnyak and Zamyatin in 1929, the campaigns were limited and usually lasted only a few months. But the new purges lasted until Stalin's death and soon were directed against the other arts as well. Like Akhmatova, Shostakovich had been criticized earlier, before the war. On January 28, 1936, an article in *Pravda* entitled "Chaos Instead of Music" had attacked Shostakovich's opera *Lady Macbeth from Mzensk District.* Like Akhmatova, he wrote patriotic works, and his Symphony No. 7, the "Leningrad" Symphony, devoted to the war and liberation, was performed all over the Soviet Union and abroad by such conductors as Sto-kowski, Koussevitsky, and Toscanini. Yet in 1948 both Prokofiev and Shostakovich, among others, were attacked for their incomprehensible music and their Formalism by the same man who attacked Akhmatova and Zoshchenko—Andrey Zhdanov.[29]

On September 4, 1946, the Party Central Committee castigated Soviet film-makers and accused Sergey Eisenstein of portraying the bodyguard of Ivan the Terrible as a degenerate band, resembling the Ku Klux Klan. Eisenstein continued to work on Part II of *Ivan the Terrible,* in which similarities between the cruelty of Ivan and Stalin become clear. The allusions to a leader who became a symbol of man's inhumanity to man were also obvious to Stalin. On February 24, 1947, Eisenstein and Nikolay Cherkasov, the actor playing Ivan, were summoned by Stalin to a midnight meeting at the Kremlin to discuss the issue. Eisenstein was given a chance to revise the film. Referring to another tsar, Boris Godunov, who used force to gain his own ends, Eisenstein told his friend the next day: "Boris Godunov said, 'This is the sixth year of my reign, but there is no happiness in my soul.' I cannot make such a picture without taking into account the great Russian tradition, the tradition of one's conscience. One can attempt to explain force, to legalize it, to substitute it, but it is impossible to justify it. If you are a real human being, then you must repent."[30]

Chukovskaya analyzed Akhmatova's dilemma after the decree:

Zoshchenko and Anna Andreyevna were not arrested and not shot. Both endured another, less cruel but sufficiently difficult verdict. For a year and a half, pages of newspapers and journals cited Zhdanov's speech enriched by new proofs that Akhmatova was an enemy of the people and that Zoshchenko hated them. Every student was taught the August 14th Regulation. It was part of all their textbooks. It was not the poems of Anna Andreyevna about Shakespeare and Dante, the bombing of London, Paris perishing, her native Petersburg, dying Leningrad, not her confessions of love—elevated, pure, passionate—not her poems about Pushkin that our children learned by heart, but Zhdanov's foul language.[31]

Chukovskaya felt certain that the attack was more than an individual, specific event. It was an example of an attempt to reduce the intelligentsia to a state of numbness. She knew that in Russia poetry has a great power over the people's hearts, and the bureaucracy feared it.[32] Akhmatova had become a symbol, and what had happened to her was a foretaste of what was soon to happen to thousands of great artists and thinkers in the Soviet Union.

The critics clearly had a problem in transforming the poet Akhmatova, author of patriotic verses, into a pariah, an outcast from her society. Chukovskaya addresses this issue, saying ironically that during the war Akhmatova had the "impudence" to be recognized as patriotic; in fact, certain of her poems were even praised. Whereas earlier she had been identified once and for all as writing intimate-boudoir, bourgeois poetry, creating verses about her wretched love affairs, critics who knew nothing about Akhmatova's anti-Terror poems and neglected the patriotic verses of World War I and just after the Revolution said that it was quite clear that World War II suddenly awoke a patriotic feeling in her. They praised her for these poems. Now in 1946 it had to be proved that Akhmatova, even during World War II, was indifferent to the fate of her people and her country. The solution was to distort lines and dates. Chukovskaya cites a typical example: Tamara Trifonova, in her article "Poetry Harmful and Alien to the People," which appeared in *Leningradskaya pravda* on September 14, 1948, misdated a prewar poem written in 1941 as 1942, and then claimed that the poem indicated that in the midst of the blockade, Akhmatova was taking strolls around the city admiring the reflection of golden spires in the water of the canals and rivers:

> Oh, is there anything in the world I know better,
> Than the gleam of spires and reflection of these waters!

Meanwhile bombs were bursting everywhere, houses were on fire, people were perishing. Clearly the poet was indifferent to the fate of her fellow citizens. Unbelievably, Trifonova even managed to find something wrong with Akhmatova's most famous wartime poem, "Courage." She focused on its most quoted lines:

> And we will preserve you, Russian speech,
>   Mighty Russian word!
> We will transmit you to our grandchildren
>   Free and pure and rescued from captivity
>   Forever!
>   (II, p. 185)

Trifonova says that when the Nazis had captured half the country, all that Akhmatova was worried about was "saving the Russian word."[33]

On August 30, 1946, I. V. Sergiyevsky's article "About the Anti-National Poetry of A. Akhmatova" appeared. Akhmatova had no right to claim that her muse was the same as Dante's, who passed judgment on his contemporaries and lived with political passion. War was a curse for Russia, but also a great school of experience, whereas in Akhmatova's works it was represented only as a source of pain and suffering. She depicted the defenders of Leningrad as moving blindly toward inevitable death, rather than determining their own fate.[34]

Vs. Vishnevsky, editor of the journal *Znamya* (*Banner*), said in a statement which appeared in *Literaturnaya gazeta* on September 3 that he found Akhmatova's behavior unforgivable. Her reaction to the accusations was silence. He recommended that both she and Zoshchenko be forced to leave the Soviet Union.[35]

Akhmatova was even attacked for her Pushkin articles, on the grounds that she said his fairy tale *The Golden Cockerel* was derived from Washington Irving— a foreigner. In *Literaturnaya gazeta* (June 29, 1947), Viktor Sidelnikov said this was a clear example of groveling before a foreigner and that Akhmatova had accused the great Russian poet of lowering the lexicon. However, if Sidelnikov had read her article more carefully, he would have found that Akhmatova had shown that Pushkin made a conscious attempt to transform the more refined, learned language of Irving into colloquial folk style in order for the work to fit into his cycle of folk tales, and the better to conceal his hidden satirical attacks against Tsar Nicholas I.[36]

Boris Eikhenbaum, who had written one of the first important scholarly books on Akhmatova's work in the early 1920s, but who also was responsible for the phrase in the book characterizing Akhmatova as a nun and a whore, joined the attack on September 25, 1946, saying, "We know that some of our comrades have made terrible mistakes, which the Regulation of Zhdanov has pointed out." He criticized I. S. Yeventov for writing a favorable article on Zoshchenko, and Vladimir Orlov for making a speech on the radio devoted to the poetry of Akhmatova in which Orlov stated that her works were an example of Soviet literature for all. Eikhenbaum then said that he himself had been accused of saying positive things about Akhmatova, but this was clearly a political error. It had never occurred to him to think about Akhmatova's poetry in political terms; but that had been naive on his part. While he found the poems she had written during and after the war significant, he had not realized they remained tragic, but now he certainly recognized his error. He emphasized that what he had said before must be understood as political naivete rather than the result of malicious intent.[37]

Alexander Fadeyev, who had replaced Nikolay Tikhonov as secretary of the Union of Soviet Writers in 1946 after Tikhonov was attacked in the same Regulation directed against Akhmatova and Zoshchenko, presented a paper in Prague to the Czech Society of Cultural Ties with the USSR, which was later published in *Literaturnaya gazeta* (November 16, 1946). In his speech, Fadeyev maintained that Akhmatova's verse was the last trace of decadence, full of pessimism, and had nothing in common with Soviet life.[38]

Lyubov Yakovleva-Shaporina noted in her diary for January 20, 1947, that she met with Akhmatova, and they discussed Fadeyev's speech. Yakovleva-Shaporina herself was upset that someone from the intelligentsia would do such a thing, but Akhmatova replied that she felt only pity for him, since he had been sent for that express purpose. She also knew that her poetry was none the worse for what he had said.

The reaction among the émigrés abroad is reflected in an article by Nikolay Berdyaev, "About Creative Freedom and the Fabrication of Souls," that appeared in *Russkie novosti* (*Russian News*) in Paris on October 4. Berdyaev acknowledged that there had been censorship under Nicholas I (when Pushkin was writing his poetry), but those censors were stupid—a blessing, Berdyaev says, because now they were no longer stupid. There had never been a time in history when genuine literature and art were created on the directives of authorities with demands to carry out a prescribed—and thereby official—point of view. It was absurd to turn works of art into a utilitarian means for building factories and producing arms for possible war. "I fail to see how the lyric poetry of Akhmatova might prevent the building of even one factory," he argued, "or ensure the readiness of one tank. It is also difficult to imagine that she can write poetry that would help increase the number of tanks, and yet it is patriotic verse that she has written." He referred to the period eighty years before, when the Russian critic Pisarev wanted authors to write works based on natural science; now art was being used to popularize Marxism. He pointed out that between the 1860s and the Soviet period there had been a cultural renaissance that confirmed the independent value of art and of spiritual values in general (in contrast to the utilitarian and materialistic view of art).

Berdyaev praised the Soviet Union for the progress that had been made in the education of the masses. But he condemned the lack of freedom: "It is an elementary truth that there is no creative work without freedom. Creativity is an act of freedom. Creative work cannot be organized according to the model of the economic life of a country or of the military barracks." Philosophical thought cannot develop if only the official ideology of dialectical materialism is allowed. There is no such thing as "forced virtue." A person can express the fate of his nation only if he is connected inwardly with it, and not forced by external pressure—"We judge a people above all by its geniuses, its peaks, and not by the ordinary life of the masses, by quality and not by quantity." Berdyaev made sure to note, however, that creative freedom does not mean self-absorption—an indifference to the fate of the world and the nation—hence he would never accept the postwar beliefs of Camus and other Existentialists. However, it is impossible to confuse this inner necessary connection with the life of one's people with "slavery," with an external command to write on certain themes. The basic mistake was the premise that one could fabricate, manufacture souls. "One cannot have a dictatorship over the spirit. It only begets slavery. This is the main tragedy of Russia. Let the government take care of economic needs and the military defense of Russia and not interfere in the spiritual culture."[39]

Berdyaev also warned the Soviet Union that instead of protecting Russia from the West, totalitarianism and isolationism would only increase Western hostility to Soviet Russia. What happened to Akhmatova and Zoshchenko would be transformed into anti-Soviet propaganda, providing a weapon in the hands of the enemy: "Dictatorship over the spirit, over creative work, over thought and the word, is not a necessity, but an evil deriving from a false world view and a will to power. Only slavery results. This is the main tragedy of Russia." And he warned that the Russian people must remain faithful to universalism. An isolating nationalism would be a betrayal of the Russian ideal.[40]

Akhmatova's life was becoming increasingly difficult, but as she told

Yakovleva-Shaporina, men react to such persecution worse than women. Zamyatin found it very hard to live through this period of his life. Zoshchenko got sick and locked himself up in his apartment on the Griboyedov Canal. His friends abandoned him, stopped phoning him, and if he went out into the street, his acquaintances looked the other way. Akhmatova, however, remained stoical. She also had some wonderful, loyal friends who helped her through this very difficult period.

One of the first impacts of the Regulation was on her source of food, already difficult to obtain in the immediate postwar years. Until she had to give up her ration card, Akhmatova received 500 rubles a month, which was good money for that time. As a professor, Punin was only receiving 300 rubles. Irina Punina kept all the cards and bought groceries for Akhmatova separately. Akhmatova had been "feeding" many people, friends and acquaintances. On September 29, a phone call came from the Union of Writers ordering her to give up her card. Irina went with Akhmatova and Lev to their regular store, since the September ration card was still valid, but they were refused any food. There they met Zoshchenko's maid, who was also having problems. They were sent to another store near the Kazan Cathedral. After long and complicated explanations, the manager said they could receive groceries, but only what had been left over from that month, and they would get flour for bread. Tomorrow a new month began. They agreed. Lev grabbed a bag of flour, Irina some groceries, and they said goodbye to Zoshchenko's maid, who told them, "I'm bringing everything to my Zoshchenko." From then on Akhmatova was given one card a month—not to have had one at all would have meant starvation. She continued to eat with the Punins, while Lev ate in a cafeteria.[41]

Yelena Galperina-Osmyorkina, wife of Akhmatova's friend A. A. Osmyorkin, the well-known artist, came to Leningrad about two months after the Zhdanov affair and brought Akhmatova food. Akhmatova laughed as she picked up the basket sitting on her table. Then she noticed ration cards lying under it. "What's this?" asked Osmyorkina, amazed. "They keep sending them to me." "Who?" asked Osmyorkina." "I really don't know," Akhmatova replied, "but they send me cards almost every day." There was not a hint of irritation or anger in her voice. Nina Olshevskaya sent her monthly packages from money collected from Moscow friends, whose names remain unknown, and Irina Tomashevskaya did the same in Leningrad.[42]

Another friend, Silvia Gitovich, reports that eventually the authorities became interested in how Zoshchenko and Akhmatova were doing. The two were summoned to the Smolny and given ration cards. The young secretary, noting the name on Akhmatova's pass when she left the Smolny, looked up at her and quickly whispered: "No matter what, I love your poetry."[43]

The poet Vladimir Kornilov recalls having a conversation with Akhmatova much later, in 1963, in Komarovo about how students of his generation were shocked by the Regulation:

I told her [Akhmatova] how we, then students of the Leningrad Institute, were upset by the Communist Party Regulation of '46 against the journals *Zvezda* and *Leningrad*. For us it was a tragedy: we all loved Akhmatova and knew her by heart. I remember selling bread in order to be able to buy *Rosary* and *Anno Domini* . . . and now this regulation produced a crack in our consciousness. I told this to Akhmatova. She said, "Yes, you know, I wrote a poem. I'll tell you why I wrote it: my granddaughter came and said: 'Akuma, you know what, we studied about you yesterday.' I said, 'Really? What do you mean? Show me.' And she brought her textbook from the ninth grade, and there it was written that Akhmatova and Zoshchenko were unfit and totally worthless." And then Akhmatova wrote a poem and she read it to me later. I immediately memorized it. There are only eight lines in it:

This is neither old nor new
Nothing like a fairy tale.
Just as they cursed Otrepyev and Pugachev,
For thirteen years they have been cursing me.
. . . and cruelly,

Unyielding as granite,
From Libava to Vladivostok
The never-ending anathema rings out.
(II, p. 655)[44]

The poem was written in 1959. Akhmatova compares her fate to that of historic personages. Pugachev was the popular Don Cossack leader of the uprising against Catherine the Great. He pretended he was Peter III, the husband of Catherine and legal ruler of Russia until his assassination by Catherine's followers. The monk Grigory Otrepyev proclaimed that he was Dimitry, the heir to the throne at the end of the sixteenth century. Dimitry was mysteriously killed, presumably by hired assassins of Boris Godunov, who then ascended the throne. Otrepyev gathered support in Poland and took over Russia briefly, alienating the people because of his attempt to introduce Polish culture and the Catholic religion. Just as they were cursed from Libava, a town in Latvia, to Vladivostok, in the east of the Soviet Union—in other words, from the western to the eastern borders— Akhmatova too feels cursed by the Regulation.

Lev Gumilyov claims he was one of those who suffered the most after the August 14 decree against his mother. He was not allowed to get his degree and defend his dissertation, even though it was already written and all his exams had been taken. Instead, a testimonial against his character was written, which declared that he was arrogant and incommunicative, and uninterested in community work, which he supposedly considered a waste of time. This had been invented by Zoya Gorbachyova, secretary of the Party organization where Lev studied. He then went to work in the library of an insane asylum on Vasilyevsky Island on the other side of the Neva. After a while he was able to receive a positive testimonial and was allowed to defend his dissertation on December 28, 1948. However, his success was short-lived, for Lev was soon once again to be a victim of the regime's postwar paranoia.[45]

Another of those condemned in the Regulation was the poet Olga Berggolts, who remained in Leningrad during the siege, speaking every day on the radio, urging her people to keep up their courage. She and her husband, the scholar Georgy Makogonenko, saw Akhmatova often in the years after the Regulation. One night Akhmatova came over to visit them in their apartment on Rubinshtein Street. They had other visitors—Yevgeny Shvarts, the brilliant author of satirical plays against all oppressive regimes, including Nazism and Stalinism, and Yuri German, condemned in the Regulation for his article on Zoshchenko. They were all sitting around a small table with candles. Their conversation was lively, but no one spoke of "the event," which would have been like speaking about the dead. The evening was characterized by typical Russian black humor. Shvarts told Makogonenko that he should feel bad that he had not been included in the Regulation. After all, they had all been attacked, but here sat Makogonenko with no one paying attention to him. Shvarts said the regime had never stopped criticizing his play *The Dragon,* a brilliant satire against Stalin ostensibly based on a Hans Christian Andersen fairy tale. On another evening the same group gathered: it was pouring outside. When Akhmatova arrived, she took off her shoes and warmed her feet by the fire. Makogonenko describes what he felt as he watched her at this moment:

> Her figure made a strange impression. By the fireplace sat a woman no longer young, gray, poorly dressed, without shoes, warming her cold feet. At the same time in her entire figure, in her proudly thrown back head, in the severe features of her face—there was something grand and simple. . . . Poverty only emphasized her dignified impression.[46]

Yuri German poured some cognac and proposed a toast: "To our Anna Andreyevna, to our queen-hobo!", kissing her hand. Her lips barely trembled in a smile as she said "Thank you." Shvarts was very lively that evening, telling stories about how his plays had been forbidden. No one alluded to Akhmatova's present position. But Akhmatova understood the good intentions of her friends—she never could bear pity. She began reciting recent poems in her quiet, deep voice and joined actively in the conversation. And yet, says Makogonenko, there was something that distinguished her from everyone else, a kind of distance. Akhmatova belonged to another world, to the art of the nineteenth century—she lived by it. Poetry was her life and her very being. That was why the blows of fate, poverty, and disorder could never destroy her.[47]

The Regulation also had immediate repercussions on Akhmatova's *Selected*

Poems, edited by Surkov, which had been published in Moscow. It was destroyed, and another collection, *Poems 1909–1945* (published in Moscow and Leningrad, 1946) also was almost completely destroyed.

Makogonenko received a manuscript version of the collection "Odds" (*Nechet*) from Akhmatova, which was to contain works from 1936 to 1946 and was to be her seventh book. It gave a totally new impression of Akhmatova's poetry, and showed her increased interest in history and the role of the poet. On November 24, 1945, an announcement had appeared in "Future Books" in *Literaturnaya gazeta,* of a forthcoming collection of her poems to be published early in 1946 by Goslitizdat, the State Literary Publishing House, in Leningrad. One section, "Odds," would be devoted to poems of the war years. The collection was never published, but Akhmatova gave this section as a birthday present to Makogonenko. Later, when Akhmatova's poems were finally published as *The Flight of Time,* the collection included a section called "Odds," but these poems were different from the ones in the Makogonenko manuscript.[48]

Akhmatova met this latest blow with characteristic Stoicism and resourcefulness. Instead of being crushed at being branded an outcast, she turned to her beloved Pushkin and wrote her most brilliant article on him, "Pushkin's *The Stone Guest,*" which she finished in April 1947. She wrote Nina Olshevskaya on February 19, 1947, about her interest in Pushkin's wonderful, concise plays known as *The Small Tragedies,* of which *The Stone Guest,* about the Don Juan legend, is one of the most impressive: "My Nina, how long it has been since I've heard anything about you. It's boring. I was sick in August and am sick again. I'm studying the *Small Tragedies* and *Tales of Belkin* [Pushkin]."[49]

The fact that Akhmatova's article has clear affinities with her own life is apparent from the start. Akhmatova emphasizes that Pushkin wrote *The Stone Guest* in 1830 at an important turning point in his life, when he was no longer concentrating on the love lyrics and poems with romantic heroes that had made him so popular. Like Akhmatova, his "handwriting" changed when he began addressing more universal issues; but instead of making him more appreciated, this caused the critics to turn against him. As with Akhmatova, they wished to relegate him to his early period and ignore the works of his more mature years, which he considered more important. Pushkin's relationship with his readers, which he describes in the draft of an article (1830), could apply just as well to Akhmatova:

> The concepts, feelings of an eighteen-year-old poet are still close and similar in nature to everyone; young readers understand him and with great enthusiasm recognize their own feelings and thoughts in his works, expressed clearly, vividly, and harmoniously. But the years pass—the young poet grows up, his talent develops, his ideas are on a higher level, his feelings change. His songs are no longer the same. Yet the readers treat all this with a cold heart and are indifferent to the poetry of life.

The poet draws away from them and slowly but surely becomes totally isolated. He creates—for himself—and if he still publishes his works, they are greeted with coldness, neglect, and he finds an echo to his sounds only in the hearts of a few admirers of poetry, as alienated and lost in the world as he is.[50]

Like Akhmatova's poetry, one of the distinctive features of *The Stone Guest* is its "breathtaking conciseness." In a few understated scenes, the traditionally romantic hero is transformed into a poet with deep feelings, who represents a moral idea that is expressed through nuance rather than moralizing speeches.

Also like Akhmatova's poems, the work is based on an extensive prehistory to which the text alludes at various points: Juan's various adventures, love affairs, betrayals, and exile, which the reader is expected to know since by Pushkin's time—especially through Mozart's opera *Don Giovanni,* and the treatments of Molière and Byron—the Don Juan theme had become part of the cultural heritage. In a passage omitted from the article, Akhmatova discusses this important aspect that is also a prerequisite to understanding her poems—how much the poet must trust the reader to fill in gaps and comprehend the text through hints provided by the author. In the early works it is usually the prehistory of a love relationship, since her poems often present a climactic moment in a relationship—frequently when it is almost over. In Akhmatova's later period, the poems become more complex, and the reader is required to possess (or soon learn) the cultural and historical background to which the images allude.

The primary focus of the article is the difference between Pushkin's version of Don Juan and those of others, especially the versions of Molière and Mozart–La Ponti. Akhmatova discovers that the poem is autobiographical—once again it is a form of *tainopis* (secret writing), which allows Pushkin to explore aspects of his own personal and public life through literary expression—a device to which Akhmatova turned frequently, culminating in her *Poem Without a Hero.* Juan is transformed by Pushkin from a clever rogue squandering his wealth to a poet with dignity and pride. In Pushkin's version, Don Juan is deeply in love for the first time, but instead of salvation, love brings death. The Commendatore is the symbol of retribution. However, Juan is not afraid of death; what creates his state of despair is the loss of long-sought-for happiness. With great insight, Akhmatova perceives the similarity between the play and Pushkin's short story *The Shot,* in which Silvio, the hero, refuses to shoot his opponent in a duel because the man is young and carefree—life means little to him. He waits several years, until the man is happily married, when his life has become more meaningful and he has much to lose; then the hero comes back to take his shot.

Akhmatova points out that the autobiographical aspects of the work refer to not one, but two of the characters. First is the Commendatore (who in Pushkin's version is not Donna Anna's father, but her husband), because Pushkin was about to marry, and worried about leaving his future wife, Natalya Goncharova, a "merry widow" who would soon remarry. Second, he also identifies with Don Juan, because Pushkin was at an important moral turning point in his life, questioning the nature of his behavior in his youth. Akhmatova too was feeling guilty at this time for the sins of her youth, fearing to confront her former self, the "gay sinner of Tsarskoye Selo," as she said in one of the poems in *Requiem*. Like Pushkin, she began writing an increasing number of works based on the themes of guilt, retribution, and atonement; there is a good reason why *Poem Without a Hero* begins with an epigraph from *Don Giovanni* and is permeated with leitmotifs relating to this theme.

Thus, both Pushkin and Akhmatova make use of the Don Juan motif not as simple reworkings of a world-famous legend, but as profoundly personal expressions of their own experience and attitude toward life.

Although Akhmatova found solace in her research, the regime soon increased the pressure on her "inner peace." On February 28, 1948, Yakovleva-Shaporina was able to record in her diary that Akhmatova looked better. The Moscow Literary Fund had given her 3,000 rubles for her to go to a sanatorium. Akhmatova told her with typical irony the story of how a microphone had been put in her ceiling. She was to recite at the House of Scholars, and it was suggested that her son go with her, but for some reason Lev stayed behind. Suddenly he heard a knocking above the ceiling, the sound of a drill. From two spots in the ceiling pieces of plaster fell right in the middle of the room, onto Akhmatova's pillow.[51]

Akhmatova and her friend then began discussing how out of all the various intellectuals attacked, Akhmatova was the only one who had not publicly repented, had not begged for forgiveness. Akhmatova answered that no one had accused her of anything, so there was no need to reply. However, Akhmatova would soon be forced to "repent" and bow in submission to the powers that be—not for herself but for someone she loved dearly, her son. They arrested Punin first.

"The political clouds continued to thicken," says Olga Freidenberg, describing the atmosphere in academic circles at this time.

The lives of scientists and scholars were poisoned. . . . A meeting of the Philology Department was called to "discuss" persecution. A similar meeting had been held at the Academy of Sciences and the Institute of Literature. All the professors were put to shame. Some, like Zhirmunsky, endured it elegantly and with flair . . . but Professor Tomashevsky . . . a man of cool temperament and not yet old, not even elderly . . . a caustic wit, very calm and lacking in sentiment, walked out into the corridor of the Academy of Sciences after his oral execution and fainted. Professor Azadovsky, a folklorist, already weakened by heart disease, lost consciousness during the meeting and had to be carried out. Any reference to works by foreign scholars was dubbed "cosmopolitanism," a term fraught with dire political consequences.[52]

In 1949, Freidenberg noted in her diary that the best professors had been dismissed, and that any who had managed to survive last year's attacks were dying of strokes or heart attacks. Eikhenbaum had become a complete invalid, and then his wife died. Another great folklorist, Vladimir Propp, had recently fainted in the middle of a lecture and was taken directly to the hospital.[53]

In September 1949, Akhmatova told Yakovleva-Shaporina that Punin had known he probably would be taken away soon. They had already arrested eighteen of his colleagues at the university. He kept hoping that his daughter and granddaughter would be able to return from their vacation before anything happened, but he was arrested shortly before they came back. They did not tell little Anya about the arrest, simply that he had gone away. "I have the most terrible of feelings—pity—I am dying of pity for Irochka and Anya," said Akhmatova. Irina's husband had been killed during the war, and it was difficult to make the little girl learn her lessons. Punin had spent a lot of time with her, and she loved him very much, calling him affectionately "Papa." Now she was sad and cried continually; she kept asking where "Papa" had gone and when he would be back. Gumilyov had been shot on August 25: Punin was arrested on August 26. "In spite of superstition," said Akhmatova, "it still makes you think!" Irina Punina noted that Akhmatova dated her poem "Lullaby" to the day of her father's arrest: "August 26, 1949 (Afternoon)" (the words *bai-bai* or *bayushki-bayu* are typical of Russian lullabies).

> Over this cradle
> I am bending like a black fir.
> Bai, bai, bai, bai,
> Ai, ai, ai, ai . . .
>
> I don't spy a falcon
> Neither far nor near.
> Bai, bai, bai, bai!
> Ai, ai, ai, ai.

On September 19, Yakovleva-Shaporina went to see Akhmatova. It was a Sunday, her day off. At 1:00 P.M. Akhmatova was still in bed. She had not been feeling well the whole summer. Although she did a minimal amount of housekeeping, it still tired her. They went for a walk in the Summer Garden, and that was when Akhmatova told her that Punin had been arrested.[54]

Little Anya's "Papa" was never to return. Punin was sent to Abez, a camp in Siberia, and he died there in August 1953. Anatoly Vaneyev, who had been arrested for writing poetry considered suspect, described meeting Punin in the camp. One day after dinner when everyone was resting, Vaneyev's attention was drawn to a man walking around the wards. He was tall, quiet, and the ordinary patient garb looked on him like the clothes of an elegant dandy. Vaneyev noticed he suffered from a nervous tic, and as he slowly passed along the ward without looking at anyone, he sang in a baritone to himself the Latin "*et in saecula saeculorum.*" Vaneyev learned the man was Nikolay Punin, the art historian who had been accused of being a Formalist and a cosmopolitan the year before. Punin never ate in the dining hall, but got supplies from home. He also had a separate bed on which there were three mattresses, three pillows, and three blankets; he called this contraption "Cleopatra's couch." He had gotten it because, not knowing the proper procedures, he had inadvertently paid twice as much in fees to the people in charge. In return, they had set up the special bed for him.

Punin was convinced he had been arrested not because of his adherence to Formalism, but because of his carelessness. At one of his lectures at Leningrad University, he had said, "We lived through the Tatar attacks and we'll live through this." He enjoyed the fact that in the camp it did not matter at all what anyone said.

Punin spoke only when he was in the mood, which was rarely. Vaneyev described what he was like then: "When speaking, Punin sat in a grand manner, holding his hands on his walking stick, looking with an unseeing glance past his conversation partner. But if inspired, he created a vivid picture of what he was talking about." And Punin talked about many things, from passages in the Bible to analyses of poetry and art. One day he entertained Vaneyev with a story of how Innokenty Annensky recited his poetry to an enraptured audience in his study. He read from sheets that had been pasted together to form a long scroll. Annensky stood in front of his audience, holding the scroll in one hand while gesturing theatrically with the other. When he finished, he rolled up the scroll on the red rug of his study.[55]

When Punin died, he was buried in a cemetery with many nameless mounds. Around the cemetery lay the flat, monotonous tundra, an endless landscape enveloped by blue sky and transparent clouds. It was another unmarked grave for a man Akhmatova had once loved.

Lev was arrested on November 6, 1949, when he came home on a lunch break. Akhmatova was so ill from the shock that she lay unconscious. Irina was in their communal apartment when the arrest took place, and she helped him gather his things.[56] He was put in Lefortovo Prison in Moscow. He says that at the interrogation they shouted: " 'You're guilty! In what form would you like to confess this?' They did not beat me very much, but I remember it well. So they sentenced me to ten years in a camp and sent me to Karaganda. From Karaganda they transferred me to Mezhdurechensk, where Dostoyevsky had once served his time. From there they sent me to Omsk."[57]

Once again Akhmatova burned her papers—manuscripts of poems, notes, letters. She went to Moscow every month to give Lev the allotted sum; as long as it was accepted, it meant he was alive. Nina Olshevskaya says that once Lev was arrested, a totally different epoch in Akhmatova's life began—it became a "tale of two cities." Akhmatova herself was ill and in need of care. Olshevskaya did whatever was necessary calmly, very capably, and with great love. They began to speak about Akhmatova moving permanently to Moscow, but she would not forsake Leningrad. Perhaps this beautiful city in all its transformations—Petersburg to Petrograd to Leningrad—was too much a part of her for her ever to consider leaving it permanently. However, many of her good friends were now in Moscow, and she spent an increasing amount of time there.

Emma Gershtein found out about Lev's arrest from a friend in Leningrad, who had seen Akhmatova in the waiting room of the city prosecutor's office. From behind the office door, crude masculine shouts were heard, then a tall woman came out with her head tossed back proudly, her entire figure expressing intense suffering. "Who is that?" Gershtein's friend asked, and someone in line whispered, "That's Akhmatova. She's come because of her son."[58]

Yakovleva-Shaporina noted in her diary a visit from Akhmatova on December 20, 1949. The doctor had ordered her to stay in bed for ten days, but she had to shop and do other errands. Akhmatova sat silent, looking with half-open eyes out of the window, a tormented, grief-stricken expression on her face. Shaporina asked her why Lev had been arrested, whether it was connected somehow with Punin. "Does there have to be a reason?" Akhmatova replied wearily. A doctor had come to see her from the Maximilian Clinic. "He was like some bandit or provocateur. The first thing he said was, 'I thought I would find something more magnificent,' meaning the state of her apartment, and then, listening to her heart, he asked whether the August Regulation had affected her heart, to which Akhmatova, with her typical understated irony, replied, 'I don't think so.' "[59]

While Lev was still in a Moscow prison, Akhmatova gave him 100 rubles once a month, handing it in at a little window at the prison and receiving a receipt. She told Gershtein the money was from Maria Petrovykh, a close friend whom she had known since 1933; when Akhmatova made a long visit to Moscow, if she was not staying with the Ardovs, she would stay with Petrovykh, with whom she discussed her poems, her Pushkin articles, and her translations. Although little known in the West, Petrovykh is considered one of the best Russian poets and translators of the century. Akhmatova, Mandelstam, and Pasternak all valued her work very highly.[60]

In September, Lev's verdict was handed down: ten years in camp, hard labor, in the Karaganda region; correspondence to be limited. Yakovleva-Shaporina recorded that Akhmatova came to see her on February 1, 1950. She had just spent three weeks in Moscow taking care of various details of her son's transfer to Siberia. "Yes, he is with us—as you have heard," she said, pressing her arms to her chest.[61]

Akhmatova's whole life now revolved around her attempts to care for—and see—her son. Every month Akhmatova sent Lev a parcel. A woman who had worked with Lev at the Ethnographic Museum sent the packages from a post office outside the city, where it was easier to post such mail. In the spring of 1951 Akhmatova spent a long time in Moscow, living with the Ardovs. In May, Gershtein asked her about the packages for Lev. It turned out Akhmatova had no money left for this in Leningrad; she was hoping to get money somehow while in Moscow and send them from there, but had not been able to do so. On May 28, she had a serious heart attack and was taken to the hospital. When she recovered, Gershtein organized raising money. The woman in Leningrad continued to send parcels to Lev while Akhmatova was living there, and when she came to Moscow, Gershtein took care of it for her. Akhmatova was now beginning to earn enough to pay for all this, since she was getting work translating.[62]

Gershtein often went with Akhmatova to the Central Post Office where "the epistolary muse hovered in the air," as Akhmatova put it. Akhmatova would find a free spot at the long table, and while Gershtein stood in line in the huge hall to the sound of banging doors and shuffling feet, the staccato din of the mail being rubber-stamped and the names of cities shouted out, Akhmatova wrote letters to her son in the camp.[63]

In 1950, Akhmatova finally decided to "repent" and make her compromise with the Stalinist regime. She used the only weapon she had to attempt to set her son free—her poetry. She wrote verses for a cycle entitled *In Praise of Peace,* simple poems with a clear message: Five years had passed since the war and the country was now growing strong.

> Where the tank roared—there is a peaceful tractor now,
> Where conflagrations flared—a fragrant garden blooms,
> And along the once demolished highway,
> Light autos fly.
>
> (II, p. 839)

Nadezhda Mandelstam recalled how her husband Osip Mandelstam had also done what was necessary to survive:

> To be sure, M. also, at the very last moment, did what was required of him and wrote a hymn of praise to Stalin, but the "Ode" did not achieve its purpose of saving his life. It is possible, though, that without it I should not have survived either. . . . By surviving I was able to save his poetry. . . . When we left Voronezh, M. asked Natasha to destroy the "Ode." Many people now advise me not to speak of it at all, as though it had never existed. But I cannot agree to this, because the truth would then be incomplete: leading a double life was an absolute fact of our age, and nobody was exempt. The only difference was that while others wrote their odes in their apartments and country villas and were rewarded for them, M. wrote his with a rope around his neck. Akhmatova did the same, as they drew the noose tighter around the neck of her son. Who can blame either her or M.[64]

Akhmatova took her drafts of the poems to the Tomashevskys. When Boris Tomashevsky, the great Pushkin scholar, looked at them, he did not say a word but sat down at the typewriter and retyped the poems to be sent to Moscow. Without asking Akhmatova, he corrected her crude language and stylistic errors. Lydia Ginzburg, who describes this incident in her notes, says, "When poets do not say what they think—they do not speak in their own language."[65]

Akhmatova sent the poems to Nina Olshevskaya, who made contact with Fadeyev, now secretary of the Writers' Union, and Surkov, the editor of the magazine *Ogonyok*. In spite of their disavowal of Akhmatova right after the 1946 Regulation—an action typical of those members of the intelligentsia who did what the Party required in order to survive—both men respected Akhmatova, knew very well the greatness of her poetry, and did what they could to help her publish these poems. They are dated from May to July 1950 and appeared in *Ogonyok* that year.[66]

Some of her friends were not sure how to react to the work. A year before, in 1949, Makogonenko was preparing a volume of the works of Alexander Radishchev, an eighteenth-century writer who exposed the ills of serfdom under Catherine the Great and was sent to Siberia as a result. Makogonenko asked Akhmatova to translate letters Radishchev had written in French from his Siberian exile. When she had finished, Makogonenko read the first letter, in which Radishchev talks about how his tormented heart suddenly felt some joy when his sister brought his two little children to see him. Akhmatova commented: "It's interesting, isn't it, that someone condemned to slow death in a remote jail in Siberia says that he can still be happy." And she thanked Makogonenko for the work. Although she received an honorarium, the translations were published without her name.

Now in 1952 Makogonenko was preparing an anniversary edition of Radishchev, marking 150 years since the poet's death, and he went to see Akhmatova to ask if she wished to revise her translation in any way. He had not seen her for a while and noticed that her face had become sterner, the wrinkles around her eyes more prominent. When Makogonenko came in and greeted her, she stared at him as if waiting for something. "How did you like my Derzhavin imitation?" she finally asked. "Excuse me, I don't understand," replied Makogonenko. "Haven't you seen *Ogonyok* with my verses?" Then Makogonenko understood what she was talking about—her Socialist Realist poems praising the Soviet State. He did not know how to respond, whether to tell her what he really thought of them or to empathize—either would be tactless. After a long pause, he muttered, "I read them . . ." She then compared herself to the famous eighteenth-century poet Derzhavin, who found himself in similar circumstances, forced to employ his art in the service of the state in order that he or someone dear to him be allowed to survive. "Good," she replied. "You, of course, remember when Derzhavin was under attack and wrote his ode 'Felitsa.' Well, now, it's me. . . . Let's

talk about our Radishchev." Her translations of the letters were published in the
new volume, but this time her name was allowed to appear. When Akhmatova
heard about this, she said: "Is it possible after all that has happened, I can now
say like Radishchev that I can be happy?"[67]

At the beginning of the 1950s, the Arctic Institute laid claim to the quarters
in which Akhmatova and Irina's family were living. They wanted Irina and her
family to move to Teatralnaya Square and have Akhmatova live somewhere else,
but Irina refused. Finally, after many complicated negotiations, in March 1952
they all received a place in a communal apartment on the second floor of a building
near the Smolny Cathedral. Krasnaya Konnitsa Street had formerly been called
Kavalergardskaya, and Akhmatova had been at this address, No. 20, many times
in 1910–20 to visit acquaintances. She lived there until 1961. The building had
once served as a hostel for coachmen. A pub was on one floor and rooms for the
coachmen as well as for permanent residents above. Akhmatova's room looked
out onto a military hospital where Mussorgsky had died. However, she would
miss the House on the Fontanka, where she had spent so much of her life. Upon
leaving, she wrote wistfully:

> I don't have special claims
> On this illustrious house,
> But it happens that almost my whole life
> I have lived under the celebrated roof
> Of the Palace on the Fontanka . . . As a pauper
> I arrived and as a pauper I will leave . . .
>
> (II, p. 634)

Akhmatova's neighbor in the communal apartment, Anna Anaksagorova, a
teacher, said the apartment had belonged to Sergey Krylov, a professor of international law, before the war. It had five rooms, and Anaksagorova was there
looking after N. A. Essen, the daughter-in-law of Admiral N. O. Essen. Alexey
Batalov, the movie actor, star of *The Cranes Are Flying,* who is the son of Nina
Olshevskaya by her first marriage, stayed in the apartment with Akhmatova when
he was acting in his first film in the 1950s.[68]

The apartment consisted of a long dark corridor with rooms. There was very
little furniture, but still not enough room for all of Akhmatova's books, which
were lying everywhere. The surroundings reflected the life of a person totally
devoted to art and literature. Batalov said there were shades of great artists,
writers, actors in this room—their presence could be felt everywhere. At times
they almost seemed alive, materializing out of phrases uttered by Akhmatova, or
from the pages of old photos and engravings and books. For Batalov, Akhmatova
was not only a sibyl who prophesied the future but one of the few links with the
past, with Imperial Russia.[69]

Batalov tells how when he was a child, Akhmatova used to take him and other children to Tsarskoye Selo on excursions. The last time he went with her was after World War II. Nothing in particular happened, but just being there with Akhmatova made it exceptional. It was ten years after the war, and Batalov, who knew that Akhmatova seemed to have parted forever with the places associated with her youth, was surprised at her desire to go to Tsarskoye Selo that particular day. There were few people around. The grounds were still in ruins—the restoration had only just begun. They wandered for a long time along neglected *allées* and overgrown paths. In the autumn air he listened to the calm, even voice of Akhmatova. He remembers how her head was covered that day by a large black scarf. The quiet, dim day, so typical of Russian autumn, the half-ruined railing of the bridge with its smashed ornamental bases, the still, black water and the overgrown shore, the empty, rickety marble pedestals seemingly abandoned by their sculptures, and the dark figure of an older woman in a scarf—"All this composed a world of some kind of Russian picture from an old book of prints, especially striking since it was alive and permeated by the damp air, the piercing cries of birds, the unhurried murmuring of the water flowing across the dams."

As usual, Akhmatova was restrained in expressing what she was feeling at that moment. She did not stop and recall what had happened in the various places they passed. "She walked like someone who found himself on the ashes of a house that had burned down, where amid the fragments distorted by fire one could make out with some difficulty the remains of objects one had known since childhood." " 'On hot days he [i.e., Pushkin] loved to hide here,' " Akhmatova said, with a barely caught nuance of some slender, curved tree trunks, the rusted skeleton of an iron bench that had been there in the times of the Lyceum when Pushkin was a pupil studying in Tsarskoye Selo. Batalov suddenly felt the presence of Pushkin and his time and was overwhelmed by the courage and spiritual strength of this great woman. Memory and dignity were all that she could oppose to a monstrous reality.

Batalov describes what a typical day was like at the Ardovs' apartment on Ordynka Street, where Akhmatova often stayed in Batalov's former room when she was in Moscow:

One must say that under the guidance of Ardov, breakfast in our house became an endless feast, often turning into lunch. Everyone who came during the first half of the day—whether it was the children's school friends, students from my course, actors coming to see Ardov on business, or Nina Olshevskaya's acting pupils or guests of Akhmatova—was immediately invited to sit down at the table and after drinking tea or coffee . . . inevitably ended up in the circle of news and totally unexpected conversation. And the cups and simple food which would keep changing were no more than a pretext for getting together. . . . In this rotation the only constant figures were Akhmatova and Ardov—he with his back to the window, she next to him, in the corner on the couch.

Once when "eating breakfast" turned into noon, a shy young admirer of Akhmatova suddenly appeared. Overwhelmed by the familiarity and confusion in the presence of her idol, after a long silence she humbly asked Akhmatova to inscribe the book she was holding in her hand like some holy object. The sincerity and excitement in her voice made everyone at the table feel abashed. They pulled themselves together as if suddenly recalling the significance of Akhmatova and took on the role one ought to play in the presence of a great poet. Akhmatova excused herself and invited the guest into her little room. While she was gone, the conversation quickly resumed, but in muted tones. After a while Akhmatova returned with the admirer and offered her a cup of tea, taking her place at the table. The girl silently swallowed the tea, but even Akhmatova's soothing words could not ease the tension. Finally, to everyone's relief, she swallowed the last drop, silently bowed, and left; but no one at the table could begin the conversation again. There was a long pause, and Akhmatova, without looking at anyone, took up her cup. Then, in a lofty tone that was pure Akhmatova, she raised her eyebrows and slowly and dramatically declaimed the lines from her early youth that had made her so famous, but which by this time had been repeated by so many generations they had become almost a cliché:

She wrung her hands under the dark veil . . .
"Why are you so pale today?"

She raised her slyly laughing eyes to her friends. The tension broke, and from that day on, says Batalov, any time an admirer of Akhmatova's visited, they all carried out this same ritual.[70]

In 1952, an important person reappeared in Akhmatova's life: Lydia Chukovskaya. She had not been allowed to return to her native city after the war, but was told to move to Moscow, where she had to begin a new life.[71] She had not seen Akhmatova since their estrangement in Tashkent at the beginning of the war. Chukovskaya cried when she read about Akhmatova's expulsion from the Union of Soviet Writers. She had also heard of Lev's arrest in 1949, and that in 1951 Akhmatova had suffered a bad heart attack. In the summer of 1952 she learned that Akhmatova was spending a month near Moscow in the sanatorium in Bolshevo, and that she was now at the Ardovs'. It made no sense to Chukovskaya any more not to see Akhmatova, no matter what had happened in Tashkent. She wrote a letter asking to see her again and had it dropped in the mailbox by the Ardovs' door. In two hours she received a telegram from Akhmatova, asking Chukovskaya to phone her. When she called, Akhmatova said, "Please come as soon as possible. I will be waiting for you; I hope to see you in twenty minutes." And with these words Chukovskaya's new diary on Akhmatova began.

When they met on June 14, 1952, they had not seen each other for ten years, and Chukovskaya was nervous. Akhmatova opened the door herself. Chukovskaya was struck by the change—her old friend was now entirely gray and quite heavy. Akhmatova led Chukovskaya into her little room, looking out onto the courtyard. A couch and bed took up the entire space, along with a desk and chair. Akhmatova's face had lost its angularity, but her voice and the way she looked at you remained the same. And the silence. Akhmatova read her some lines from Lev's last letter. They spoke about Tolstoy, Gogol, Dostoyevsky. Not only was what Akhmatova had to say important but the fact that the channel of communication between her and her companion, her diarist, had been opened once again. As a result, her public could learn about the last years of Akhmatova's life through the perceptions of an intelligent, sensitive, and loving friend.

The Thaw: 1953–1958

Not with the lyre of someone in love
Do I try to captivate people—
A leper's rattle
Sings in my hand.
        —AKHMATOVA
        (II, p. 643)

On March 5, 1953, an event occurred that changed the life of Akhmatova and millions of others in the Soviet Union: Joseph Stalin died.

The final months of Stalin's regime were marked by increased fear that another period of purges was on its way. Riasanovsky describes the volatile atmosphere that prevailed at this time:

It could be that the madness that kept peering through the method during his entire rule asserted itself with new vigor. In any case, the events which then transpired will have to be elucidated by future historians. With international tension high, dark clouds gathered at home. In January 1953, nine doctors were accused of having assassinated a number of Soviet leaders, including Zhdanov. Beriya's police were charged with insufficient vigilance. The press whipped up a campaign against traitors. Everything pointed to another great purge.[1]

After Stalin's death there was a period of struggle for succession, and the Soviet Union was ruled by collective leadership, including Malenkov, Beriya, Molotov, Bulganin, Mikoyan, and Khrushchev. On January 13, 1953, *Pravda* had published an article about the indictment of the Jewish doctors who had allegedly caused the death of key Soviet figures. In April, after Stalin's death, the "doctors' plot" was declared invalid, and it was revealed that the doctors' confessions had been obtained by torture. Beriya, head of the secret police, was arrested, and in December 1953 he was shot. Nikita Khrushchev became First Secretary of the Communist Party in September 1953, and within two years he was the Soviet leader, ushering in the Khrushchev era and "the Thaw," when the severe oppression of the Stalinist years was finally eased. Certain famous Communist leaders who had suffered under the Terror were rehabilitated. However, one must be careful not to oversimplify this very complicated period, which was characterized by subtle and often overt swings in mood and atmosphere, from great freedom of expression to severe repression, as in the case of Pasternak and eventually Solzhenitsyn, who initially was symbolic in this period of the new easing of restraints on artistic creativity by the state. While Khrushchev may have denounced certain aspects of Stalin's reign, he was a confirmed Communist and continued to stand for total control of all facets of life by the Party.

One of the most important events of this period was Khrushchev's speech in February 1956 to a closed session of the Twentieth Party Congress, at which he addressed a carefully selected audience of high Party functionaries. Khrushchev denounced Stalin as a cruel, bloodthirsty tyrant. The speech was directed against the "cult of personality," at how this "cult" deviated from the precepts of Leninism.

However, the fact that the Thaw did not mean giving up on communism as an ideal form of government became clear on January 17, 1954, when Khrushchev spoke at the Chinese Embassy and modified his statements about Stalin. He described Stalin's actions as deviations that had harmed the cause. "But even when he committed mistakes and allowed the law to be broken, he did so with the full conviction that he was defending the gains of the Revolution, the cause of socialism. That was Stalin's tragedy." In defense of the cause of socialism, Khrushchev emphasized that he wished everyone would fight as Stalin had. This attitude remained in force until October 1961, when, at the Twenty-Second Congress of the Communist Party, Stalin was finally labeled a murderer who had seriously violated Lenin's principles. Stalin's body was then removed from Lenin's tomb and buried along the Kremlin wall.[2]

It was not clear how far reforms would be allowed to go in the intellectual and artistic world, and these years saw artists and thinkers "testing their limits." The great swings in attitude by Khrushchev and the regime can be seen in the developments from 1954 to the end of the decade. Initially, Party bureaucrats and adherents to the system put up fierce opposition to the criticism of Soviet society that was beginning to appear in literature and the other arts. In 1954, the poet Alexander Tvardovsky, the relatively liberal editor of *Novy mir* (*New World*), the most important literary journal in the Soviet Union, was replaced by Konstantin Simonov, who adhered more closely to the Party line. The strongest critics of Socialist Realism were dismissed from their jobs and were not allowed to attend the Second All-Union Congress of Soviet Writers in Moscow in December 1954, which was held to discuss the developments that had taken place since the new liberal atmosphere had been introduced. The Congress reasserted that Socialist Realism was the only creative trend in the literature of a Socialist society, and that Soviet literature must continue to serve as the Party's agent in educating the masses about Communist society. Although works criticizing the policy of previous years continued to appear, in 1957 Khrushchev summoned leading Soviet authors to a meeting and warned them against any more rebellion against the Party. However, unpredictably, at the Third All-Union Congress of Soviet Writers in May 1959, Khrushchev addressed the group in milder tones and guaranteed that there would be no return to Stalinism. Alexey Surkov, who had been appointed secretary of the Union of Soviet Writers, was replaced by Konstantin Fedin, and Tvardovsky was reinstated as editor of *Novy mir*.[3]

Two of Akhmatova's letters to Lev during this period have been recently published. He was still in prison camp.

July 1 [1953]

My dear son Lyovushka, again I have not written to you for a long time and I do not even have the usual excuse—work.

I'm resting now after the sanatorium, where it was very nice and cool, with a separate room and a generally pleasant atmosphere.

But I went wild. It is difficult for me to be among so many people. . . . Like you, it's difficult for me to imagine my life in Leningrad since my life in the House on the Fontanka is over. However, the Neva flows on, the Hermitage is standing in place, the white nights wander the street and peep into the windows. So at least it seems to me from Moscow, which is also beautiful in its own way: ten fountains are running, the linden fragrance penetrates even the buses, poppies are blooming, and above it all is the tender middle-Russian sky.

On June 29th I was at A. A. Osmyorkin's funeral. He died working with a brush in his hand, like a real artist. I'm writing from the post office—it seems it's the only place where the epistolary muse visits me.

I'll write you a real letter from Leningrad, my dear Lyovushka. I won't be there for long, because I was invited to a dacha near Kolomna where I rested last year. Take care of yourself—don't drink too much strong tea. Well, I think the rain is coming to an end and the letter is coming to an end as well. I can go home now. In July I will send you 200 rubles by mail and, of course, a package.

I warmly embrace you.

Mama

In the second letter, Akhmatova talks of her son's interest in Asian studies— an interest she had shared for a long time, but which developed as she continued to translate Oriental poetry. She would be sending him a package for his birthday, October 1.

September 20, 1954

. . . Only today, my dear Lyovushka, I sent you two packages. . . . The day is bright and the sky is like summer. The celebration package for you is still not ready but all the provisions have already been bought.

In the Chinese anthology which I'm continuing to read there is again a reference to the Huns. Now it is the first era of our century. Two Chinese (Generals S and W) and Li Ling were taken prisoner by the Huns, where they spent nineteen years. Then one of them (Sa Wu) returns to his homeland, and the other sings a song which has been translated into English without rhyme. [She provides a Russian translation.] Did I write you that I saw the Peking edition of Tzu Wan 1954 in English? A Chinese writer translated it.

I kiss you. Mama.

P.S. Did you get my excerpts from the anthology and the gloss? Perhaps you find them interesting?[4]

Regardless of what Akhmatova endured during these years, she never wavered in her allegiance to her native land. She was always upset when foreigners attempted to use her name and situation to condemn the Russian people. There is a fine line between rightly calling attention to the abuses in Soviet society and arousing hostile feelings in the West against the Russian people and Russian culture in general. Moreover, at this time, in the early 1950s, she found herself in a particularly delicate situation, where anything she said or did could have an impact on her son's situation. This explains her behavior in May 1954, when a group of twenty British students visited Leningrad. They did not ask to see Akhmatova or Zoshchenko, according to Max Hayward, but the Leningrad branch of the Union of Soviet Writers had the idea of having the two authors appear before the students—perhaps as examples of repentant members of the intelligentsia who had been punished. Akhmatova mistakenly thought they were from Oxford. Her neighbor in the communal apartment, Anna Anaksagorova, reported that one morning she overheard Akhmatova saying in an irritated voice, "Leave me in peace." When Anaksagorova asked her what was wrong, Akhmatova replied that some students from Oxford's Department of Literature had arrived and had demanded a meeting with her. Members of the Union of Soviet Writers were also present at the meeting. Both Akhmatova and Zoshchenko were asked what they thought of the Central Committee's Resolution. As Haight says, "The poet [i.e., Akhmatova] felt very strongly that it was not the business of those who had come from abroad to ask such questions." Zoshchenko replied that at first he was astonished and then realized it was correct. Akhmatova simply said she agreed with the Union's Regulation and subsequent events.[5]

Akhmatova was directly affected by the Khrushchev reforms when amnesty decrees were issued by the Presidium of the Supreme Soviet. The historian Dmytryshyn explains what the amnesty meant: "Under the 1953 and 1957 amnesty decrees, all persons serving short-term sentences (up to five years) for lesser offenses were freed, as were all pregnant women, women with small children, juveniles, men over sixty, women over fifty-five, and all those who were incurably ill. The 1955 and 1956 amnesty decrees freed all those who had been sentenced in person or in absentia to ten-year imprisonment for collaboration with the enemy during World War II or for surrender to the enemy."[6]

On March 1, 1956, the eve of the third anniversary of Stalin's death, Akhmatova asked Chukovskaya to celebrate with her. Akhmatova talked a lot that night about the past.

What we lived through, yes, yes, all of us, because the torture chamber threatened all of us!—not a single piece of literature was printed. Shakespeare's dramas—all these effective villainies, passions, duels—are trifles, child's play, in comparison with what we had to live through. I won't even dare speak about what those punished or sent to the camps endured. This cannot be expressed in words. But each of our wonderful lives is a Shakespearean drama raised to the thousandth degree. Mute separations, mute black, bloody events in every family. Invisible mourning worn by mothers and wives. Now the arrested are returning, and two Russias stare each other in the eyes: the ones that put them in prison and the ones who were put in prison. A new epoch has begun. You and I will wait for it together.

Chukovskaya said that many people, especially the young, were confused by the exposure of Stalin. How could such a thing happen? They were told he was a genius, one of the leading lights of science, and he turned out to be a master executioner.

"That's stupid," Akhmatova replied calmly. " 'The narcotic has worn off,' as the doctors say. But I don't believe that no one understood anything before.

Except for babes at their mother's breast." Chukovskaya did not agree with her. She said she had met people who were sincere and had been deceived. Akhmatova responded passionately:

> That's not true! Stones shout, reeds find speech, but according to you, a human being does not see and does not hear? That's a lie. They were pretending. It was useful for them to pretend to others and to themselves. You understood everything completely even then—don't deceive yourself now. Well, of course, like you and I, they did not have the possibility to learn by heart the immortal decrees in the original, but in terms of "enemies of the people," everything was a lie, slander, bloody filth—everyone understood this. They did not want to understand—that's another matter.[7]

On March 20, 1956, Chukovskaya recorded a similar conversation. She asked Akhmatova why they felt such heaviness in their souls when they should all be happy now that so many were returning. Everyone should have been rejoicing, yet somehow the joy had been poisoned by something. Perhaps it was shame before those whose fate Chukovskaya had escaped? Shame for the silence when others had been tormented? Akhmatova answered:

> Why? Because unconsciously, without knowing it yourself, you wish those years had never happened, but they did. It is impossible to erase them. Time does not stand still; it moves on. It is possible to return the people who were arrested from the camps. But it is impossible for you or them to return to that day when you were separated. That day was terrible both for you and for them, but it was one day in your life, and you wish not only that the people would come back, but that this day would return as well, and the life which had been forcefully interrupted, that it would begin happily again from where it had been broken off. That it could be glued together where it had been chopped apart by an ax. But it hasn't turned out that way. There is no such glue. The category of time in general is much more complicated than the category of space.[8]

Lev Gumilyov was freed on May 14, 1956, and officially exonerated by the Supreme Soviet on June 2, 1956. Akhmatova and Emma Gershtein had made numerous attempts to free him. After Stalin's death, all Akhmatova's thoughts had turned to freeing her son. However, in every school and every institution, children continued to read the Regulation of the Communist Party against her, and she knew that it was going to be difficult.[9]

In June 1953, when Akhmatova went to the artist Osmyorkin's funeral, Lev Rudnev, an architect, spoke to her. At that time he was involved in the project to plan new buildings for Moscow University on Lenin Hills. He told her he often met with Kliment Voroshilov, the military marshal and faithful Stalinist who had become Chairman of the Presidium of the Supreme Soviet after Stalin's death. Rudnev suggested he might talk to him about Lev. Akhmatova waited a while, and then in February 1954 she decided to take Rudnev up on his offer. Akhmatova, Gershtein, and Chukovskaya drafted a letter, and Gershtein took it to Rudnev, who immediately phoned Voroshilov's personal assistant. The assistant agreed to give Voroshilov the letter. The next day Gershtein went with Akhmatova to the guardhouse at the Trinity Gate of the Kremlin, where Akhmatova handed over the envelope containing her letter and a letter Rudnev had written supporting it.

They waited for half a year without any news. Finally in the summer a letter came for Akhmatova, not from the Supreme Soviet, but from the Prosecutor of the USSR, informing "Citizenness Akhmatova" that there were no grounds for reexamining the case of Lev Gumilyov. After receiving this, Akhmatova was sick for a week. She had thought that now there was a new regime, she had a chance, yet she had received a refusal: it meant the case was hopeless. Twice they went to the Military Prosecutor's Office, but with no result. Soon several academics wrote letters in Lev's support. The scholar Vasily Struve wrote a petition describing Lev as a talented scholar of Central Asian studies, leaving out the name of the addressee so Akhmatova could give the letter to whoever seemed necessary.

There were certain indications that the regime was beginning to allow Akhmatova some recognition at last. At the end of December 1954, she was chosen as a delegate to the Second All-Union Congress of Soviet Writers. At that time Emma Gershtein received a telegram from Lev somewhere near Omsk saying, "Remind Mama that she should take care of me." After the final session in the Kremlin there was a reception. Lev imagined she would shout, "Save my innocent son!" But as Gershtein points out, a single false step would have ruined everything. Instead, she consulted with Ilya Ehrenburg, and he wrote to Khruschev himself about Akhmatova, adding the letter from Struve in support of Lev. He sent the materials directly to Khrushchev, again with no results. In spring 1955, Gershtein went to the Military Prosecutor to ask whether Ehrenburg's letter had been sent there from the Secretariat of Khrushchev, but she was told to come back in a month. When she returned, she was told it had arrived and was under consideration. She kept coming back month after month; in July she was told the affair of Lev Gumilyov was now being considered by the Chief Military Prosecutor of the Soviet Union. Akhmatova decided now to turn to Mikhail Sholokhov, who was a favorite writer with the regime and had promised to help. She spoke with him, but according to Gershtein he did nothing. However, on September 27, Chukovskaya reports that hopes were raised. Akhmatova had a new expression in her eyes—an anxiety, something like August 1939, when Lev had been arrested, although that was on the eve of their separation, and now perhaps they were on the eve of seeing one another again. They kept saying the same things over and over. Akhmatova sat on her bed, and with both hands pulling her shawl around her, said, "Just like in Tatyana's dream. Remember?" And she quoted the strange dream of Tatyana in Pushkin's *Eugene Onegin:*

Now the mill is dancing a Russian dance . . .
Now the witch with the bearded goat,
Here the skeleton prim and proud . . .

Here a dwarf with a tail and now
A half-crane and half-cat . . .

Barking, laughter, singing, whistling, and banging . . .

"This all happened to us, but not in a dream," said Akhmatova. "In real life we also heard and saw barking and singing and the mill doing a Russian dance. . . ."[10]

In December, Gershtein went to see M. I. Artamonov, director of the Hermitage in Leningrad. He had known Lev since he was a young man and had taken him on archeological expeditions. Artamonov gave Gershtein a very strong letter of recommendation for Lev. Letters from various scholars were sent to the Prosecutor's Office. And Lev himself wrote Gershtein a letter in which he explained what he had been accused of: "17-58-8,10. contents of the affair: twice brought to trial: in 1935 with *corpus delicti*—conversations at home—and in 1938, without *corpus delicti,* but being condemned, he considered his arrest in no way justified." Lev had been condemned again in 1950 as a "repeater," that is, a person whom they decided to continue to punish without any cause on his part. Gershtein showed Surkov the letter, and he phoned a deputy of the Military Prosecution, Terekhov. Surkov spoke about Akhmatova's poems in *Ogonyok*; he stressed that she had been a delegate at the All-Union Congress of Soviet Writers and that Lev was a good scholar; and he related the positive things said about Lev in the letters of recommendation that Gershtein had given him. Still there was no response.

After the Twentieth Congress of the Communist Party in February 1956, Gershtein went again to the Prosecutor's Office. Everything had changed, and they greeted her almost joyfully. They told her the General Prosecutor himself would make an official protest. Gershtein wrote to tell Lev about this, and he replied, "I received your postcard today from March 1st. I'm absolutely overjoyed, even sick from it. It's like the Resurrection." Akhmatova wrote a letter to Fadeyev, who although no longer secretary of the Writers' Union, still had a lot of power. He was then in the hospital, and he called Akhmatova and asked her to come to see him. On March 2, Fadeyev sent the General Prosecutor a letter about Lev Gumilyov. He wrote that although he himself did not know Lev, he believed that prominent members of the scholarly and literary community thought he had been treated unjustly. He then dealt directly with the topic of Akhmatova:

After the well-known decree of the Communist Party concerning the magazines *Zvezda* and *Leningrad,* his mother, A. A. Akhmatova, had shown herself to be a true Soviet patriot; she has decisively rebuked all attempts of the Western press to make use of her name and has printed patriotic Soviet poems in our journals. At present she has shown herself to be a translator of the highest caliber in the West or the East. The patriotic and courageous behavior of this fine, elderly poet after such a stern decree has called forth deep respect in writers' circles and Anna Akhmatova was a delegate to the Second All-Union Conference [Congress] of Soviet Writers.

In considering the case of L. N. Gumilyov, it must be taken into consideration that, despite the fact that he was only nine years old when his father died, he, Lev Gumilyov, as the son of N. Gumilyov and A. Akhmatova, may have been "used" by careerists and inimical elements in making what accusations they chose against him. I think that it is perfectly possible for this matter to be considered objectively.[11]

On May 9, Akhmatova was told by the Prosecutor's Office that the General Prosecutor, Rudenko, had made a protest that had gone to the Military Collegium of the Supreme Court of the USSR; they would take it under consideration in about two weeks. She quickly wrote Lev but received an air-mail postcard back with the words, "The addressee left May 14." The Mikoyan Commission had decided to hasten the return home of those imprisoned who were awaiting rehabilitation. On May 15, Lev was already in Moscow, and he soon left for Leningrad. A session of the Supreme Court, which took Lev's case under consideration, convened three weeks later and he was officially pardoned.

Akhmatova arrived in Moscow on the 14th. Not having heard from her, Chukovskaya went to the Ardovs' on the 15th. It was wonderful to see Akhmatova looking younger, with a new voice. They went into her small room. It was filled with smoke. "Lyovka smokes!" Akhmatova said in a maternal voice, waving away the smoke with her hand. It made Chukovskaya very happy to see Akhmatova like this.[12]

On May 15, Chukovskaya noted in her diary:

Lyova [Lev] returned.
Fadeyev committed suicide.
This is the "beginning of the end," the culmination of an epoch: one begins a new life, the other finishes his in expiation for the old life.[13]

Akhmatova herself told Chukovskaya, "I have no right to judge Fadeyev. He tried to help me free Lyova." Chukovskaya notes that he helped not only Lev but many others during the war. One day, perhaps fifty years from now, she added, someone would write *The Tragedy of Alexander Fadeyev.*[14]

Lev Shilov, an archivist at the Literary Museum in Moscow, said Fadeyev had not been kind to Akhmatova right after the Regulation; but, like Surkov, he fell into the category of those people in the Soviet Union who "did things if they needed to be done." But after Stalin died, both Fadeyev and Surkov helped Akhmatova. On April 13, she inscribed her book of translations: "To a great writer and a good person" for all Fadeyev had done to help liberate Lev.[15]

Guy De Mallac, one of Pasternak's biographers, has attempted to explain Fadeyev's suicide:

An almost logical consequence of the Thaw was Fadeyev's suicide in May, 1956. Fadeyev was perhaps one of the most tragic victims of the Stalin years. Initially talented and sincere, he had become a moral and emotional cripple long before he physically perished. In 1955–56 he was acidly attacked for his many nefarious actions during the Stalin regime. . . . Since Khrushchev was also denouncing Stalinism, Fadeyev may well have felt that there was no longer a place for prominent Stalinists in Russia. His alcoholism and the personal attacks upon him enforced his sense of helplessness and led the former Secretary of the Writers' Union to his tragic end.[16]

Pasternak's reaction was one of both condemnation for Fadeyev's former actions and deep sympathy for his final act: "It [his suicide] absolves him of any of the wrongs he did, willingly or unwillingly."[17]

On July 30, 1956, a statement was issued by the Chief Military Prosecutor, addressed to Citizenness Emma Gershtein, for Citizenness A. A. Akhmatova.

30 July 1956
12. No. 500443-49
Moscow, Center 41, Kirov St.

I wish to inform you that the case whereby GUMILYOV, Lev Nikolayevich, was condemned in 1950 has been examined.

It has been established that Gumilyov, L. N. was condemned without good reason.

On the protest of the General Prosecutor of the USSR by the determination of the Military Collegium of the Supreme Court of the USSR from June 2, 1956, the Regulation of the Special Communication at MGB USSR of September 13, 1950, in respect to GUMILYOV Lev Nikolayevich has been removed and because of lack of evidence of any crime, the case has been curtailed.

Military Prosecutor of Section GVP
Lieutenant Colonel of Justice
L/C Kuraskua[18]

An unpleasant incident occurred in February 1957, after Lev had already been released. Akhmatova told Chukovskaya that she was eating dinner quietly one night when the telephone rang. "Comrade Akhmatova. This is the Military Prosecutor. Will you come to see us?" "What floor is it on?" she asked. "The fifth," he replied. "It will be difficult for me without an elevator." "You can walk slowly." She went at the appointed hour. At each step she thought, "What do they want to talk to me about?" It turned out to be connected with the Livshits affair. The poet Benedikt Livshits had been shot back in 1938. Under persecution and nervous shock, he lost his reason, and when the prosecutor interrogated him, he accused dozens of innocent people. Akhmatova said she closed the Livshits affair: "They showed me seventy-nine names. I knew thirty-five of them. I immediately warned them that I could not say anything about a single one except something good."[19]

However, in the midst of the increasing fear and paranoia that began to permeate the Khrushchev period, there were also many moments of great joy, when Akhmatova was surrounded by good friends. Korney Chukovsky, the critic and father of Lydia Chukovskaya, had not seen Akhmatova from the time she was expelled from the Union of Soviet Writers until 1954, when he was visiting the home of one of Russia's most gifted scholars, Vyacheslav V. Ivanov. Chukovsky describes Akhmatova then:

> She was gray-haired, calm, corpulent, straightforward, not at all resembling that stylish, shy, and at the same time arrogant slender poet to whom Gumilyov had introduced me in 1912. She spoke about her catastrophe calmly and with humor: "I was famous, then I was very infamous, and I am convinced that essentially it's one and the same thing." I again felt that excitement in her presence that I had when I was young. I felt the grandeur, nobility, the enormity of her talent and of her fate.[20]

In 1956, something unexpected happened: the man who was to become the "Guest from the Future" in her great work *Poem Without a Hero*—Isaiah Berlin— suddenly returned to Russia. This was the famous "meeting that never took place." In her poem, "A Dream" (August 14, 1956), Akhmatova writes:

> This dream was prophetic or not prophetic . . .
> Mars shone among the heavenly stars,
> Becoming crimson, sparkling, sinister—
> And that same night I dreamed of your arrival.
>
> It was in everything . . . in the Bach Chaconne,
> And in the roses, which bloomed in vain,
> And in the ringing of the village bells
> Over the blackness of ploughed fields.

And in the autumn, which came close
And suddenly, reconsidering, concealed itself.
Oh my August, how could you give me such news
As a terrible anniversary?

(II, p. 247)

Another poem, "In a Broken Mirror" (1956), has the poet compare Petersburg to Troy at the moment when Berlin came before, because the gift of companionship that he brought her turned out to poison her subsequent fate:

The gift you gave me
Was not brought from afar.
It seemed to you idle diversion
On that fiery night.
And it became slow poison
In my enigmatic fate.
And it was the forerunner of all my misfortunes—
Let's not remember it! . . .
Still sobbing around the corner is
The meeting that never took place.

(II, p. 251)

On August 23, 1956, Chukovskaya recorded what Akhmatova told her about this "meeting that never took place." After they had talked of various topics, suddenly Akhmatova became silent. Then she began to speak in a confidential tone, lowering her voice:

A certain gentleman—you can guess of course, who I'm talking about, you and two or three friends know what this is all about—called me and was surprised when I refused to meet with him. Although I think he could have guessed that *after everything* I did not dare risk anything again. . . . He gave me some interesting news: he married only just last year. Just think, what politeness toward me: *only!* I found congratulations too sweet for the given occasion. I said: "Well, how nice!" to which he replied . . . well, I won't tell you what he replied.[21]

Chukovskaya says that although Akhmatova was smiling, she spoke in a slow, deep, passionless voice, and Chukovskaya understood that Akhmatova had called her to come over so she could tell her of this "non-meeting" with Isaiah Berlin. Akhmatova had refused to see the man who had meant so much to her in these years of hardship—the man for whom she had composed one of the most beautiful cycles of love poems ever written, *Cinque*— because she would not jeopardize her son and was afraid of the repercussions such a meeting might have. By this point Akhmatova understood, like so many others, that these were precarious times, and the liberal atmosphere of the so-called Thaw at any moment could swing back to repression; she was not going to take any chances.

Berlin gives his own account in his memoirs:

> I did not see her on my next visit to the Soviet Union, in 1956. Pasternak told me that though Anna Andreyevna wished to see me, her son, who had been rearrested some time after I had met him, had been released from his prison camp only a short while before, and she therefore felt nervous of seeing foreigners, particularly as she attributed the furious onslaught upon her by the Party at least in part to my visit in 1945 . . . but she wished me to telephone her.

Pasternak told Akhmatova that he had met Berlin, and his new wife, who he thought was delightful, and was sorry that she could not meet her. Perhaps Pasternak had not understood the meaning behind Akhmatova's love poems written to Berlin, but it was yet another of the hurtful remarks these two dear friends made to each other that would be long remembered. Berlin reports his conversation with Akhmatova:

> Later that day I spoke to her over the telephone. "Yes, Pasternak told me that you were in Moscow with your wife. I cannot see you, for reasons which you will understand only too well. We can speak like this because then they know. How long have you been married?" "Not long," I said. "Exactly when were you married?" "In February of this year." "Is she English, or perhaps American?" "No, she is half French, half Russian." "I see." There followed a long silence. "I am sorry you cannot see me, Pasternak says your wife is charming." Another long silence.[22]

Her grief and disappointment, as in the past, were transformed into poetry, into a cycle entitled *Sweetbriar in Blossom*. In one poem she compares herself with Dido, who was abandoned by Aeneas when he left her to fulfill his destiny in founding Rome.

But Akhmatova also made valuable new friends at this period, among them Natalya Ilyina, a writer. In her memoirs, Ilyina says she had known the name of Akhmatova and her poetry since childhood. When she was a little girl, through the door of their room she and her sister overheard their parents reading Akhmatova's poetry. To Ilyina, Akhmatova was a figure out of legend, and it was difficult to imagine her as a real human being. The two women met when Ilyina was spending the summer of 1954 in the small town of Golitsyno near Moscow, where she had a room and took her meals at the House of Writers. One day she saw Serafima Ivanovna, the director, looking very excited, and learned that Anna Akhmatova was coming to spend some time. Akhmatova appeared with Nina

Olshevskaya, and Ilyina had the same feeling she had experienced when she saw Falconet's statue of Peter the Great for the first time: "Am I really looking at this very monument?"²³ Akhmatova came out onto the veranda where they were eating, and all the chattering voices suddenly became very still. It was not just a matter of their knowing who she was and having read her poetry. She had the same effect on people who knew nothing about her. Her silence, her bearing, her expression, her calmness, all inspired respect, even shyness.

Akhmatova and Olshevskaya liked to sit in the garden on beautiful sunny days. Ilyina made their acquaintance very unexpectedly. She happened to have some English detective novels with her, a genre that Akhmatova adored, and Olshevskaya asked her if she would lend some to Akhmatova. Ilyina brought along some books and then a few days later learned that Akhmatova was alone, that Olshevskaya had left. They began to go on walks together, but Ilyina did most of the talking. Akhmatova remained silent and inscrutable, until one day she asked Ilyina to come and see her in her room. Akhmatova then became the gracious hostess and asked Ilyina to talk about her life, to tell her something about herself. Ilyina explained that she had just finished at the Literary Institute, and as the conversation continued, she felt more at ease with Akhmatova. They began to take walks every day together, but spoke only on general topics. Akhmatova never talked of herself or her own life, and Ilyina never asked.

Akhmatova left in September, but Ilyina saw her again in Moscow when the poet came to attend the Second All-Union Congress of Soviet Writers in December. At the Ardovs', Akhmatova was different, laughing at Ardov's jokes, and affectionate with Olshevskaya and the children. Ilyina also visited Akhmatova at the Ardovs' in the summer of 1955, when Akhmatova was staying with them. That was when one day Akhmatova invited her into her room and read her passages from *Poem Without a Hero*. That autumn Ilyina accompanied Akhmatova for two weeks to Golitsyno. At meals Akhmatova was still severe and grand, distant and reserved; Ilyina now realized this was a form of armor which the poet donned in the presence of strangers. But Akhmatova was starting to share her private thoughts with Ilyina. She was upset by the publication of the memoirs of Lyubov Mendeleyeva, the wife of the Symbolist poet Alexander Blok. Mendeleyeva had revealed vulgar aspects of her affairs with other men. With the typical ironic, understated wit that Akhmatova used in her conversations with friends, she said: "In order for the Beautiful Lady to remain, one thing is required of her: to keep still!" For it was Mendeleyeva who had been raised to the heights of the allegorical figure Sophia, Holy Wisdom, by both Blok and Andrey Bely at the turn of the century.

Ilyina noticed that Akhmatova loved jewelry—necklaces, brooches, rings—but it was not important to her if she did not have any. If she had a new dress, fine; if not, she could do without it. For years she went around in an old fur coat with a frayed collar. But this elderly lady with her grand bearing lent beauty to anything she wore, including the old fur. She could also transform the most banal of topics into something poetic and wonderful. One day Ilyina was complaining about the nasty weather. "What's wrong with you!" Akhmatova chided. "It's fantastic. Such a tragic autumn. The wind is tearing off the last leaves, the sun comes out to take a look at this, wrings its hands, and then vanishes in despair."

In November Akhmatova was in Leningrad, but at the end of the month she returned to Moscow, where she stayed for a while, since she was involved in negotiations on her translation of Korean poetry, which she accomplished with the aid of a gloss. Ilyina recalls how one evening a friend, A. A. Reformatsky, came over when Akhmatova was visiting and said he had just heard a line of her verse that was new to him: "Gold rusts and steel decays." "Who did you hear this from?" she asked excitedly. Reformatsky stopped smiling, suddenly realizing this was serious. He explained that he was smoking in the corridor by the window when Vinogradov walked by and, commenting on Reformatsky's reddish beard turning gold in the sun shining through the window, said: "Do you remember in Akhmatova? 'Gold rusts and steel decays.' " "And that's all? Nothing more?" Akhmatova demanded. "Nothing," Reformatsky replied. Akhmatova said they must phone Vinogradov as soon as possible: perhaps he would remember the rest of the poem or perhaps he had written it down. They were lines from her burned notebook, which she had long since forgotten. She phoned Vinogradov, and he recited the entire poem to her. Vinogradov, the great linguist and critic, was one of the first to write significant studies of her work.

That winter Akhmatova led her "nomad life," moving from friend to friend in Moscow. An older relative was staying with the Ardovs, so Akhmatova went to various friends—Ilyina, Maria Petrovykh, the actress Faina Ranevskaya, among others. In December 1955 she had an appendicitis attack, but the doctors decided not to operate (the operation finally took place a few years later). Akhmatova stayed on in Moscow through March 1956, and would often visit Ilyina, who drafted her own prose on the typewriter while Akhmatova sat quietly reading. Then in the evening after supper Ilyina would accompany Akhmatova to wherever she was staying at the time. In May 1956, Akhmatova returned to Leningrad, and then came back to Moscow. In June, when she was again in Leningrad, Ilyina went to see Akhmatova in her apartment on Krasnaya Konnitsa Street. Shortly before this the State Literary Fund (*Litfond*) had allowed Akhmatova to have a small dacha at Komarovo near Finland. Akhmatova christened it *Budka* (The Guard's Stall), comparing it to the stalls by city gates in which city guards used to sit in the olden days.

When Akhmatova was in Moscow, she also visited her friend Emma Gershtein, who had done so much to help her free Lev from the prison camp. Gershtein lived on Serpukhovka Street, on the grounds of a hospital garden. Akhmatova usually came to see her after lunch, when the patients were in their wards, and they could go into the huge empty garden and sit on a bench and talk. Gershtein recalls that a year after Akhmatova's first heart attack, in May 1951, she went with her to Kolomenskoye, the beautiful town near Moscow. It had been a favorite retreat of the tsars, featuring a famous wooden palace built by Tsar Alexey, father of Peter the Great, in 1667, which was torn down by Catherine the Great, although she had a model made of it that can be seen in the museum there today. The most memorable building at Kolomenskoye is the Church of the Ascension, built by Vasily III in 1532 to celebrate the birth of his son, who would later become known as Ivan the Terrible. It is the first church in Russia known to break with the Byzantine tradition of domes, built instead in the form of a cone-shaped tower or "tent" soaring into the heavens. The church was open when Akhmatova and Gershtein visited. Akhmatova looked silently at the narrowing vault sweeping upward, at the "tsar's place" where Ivan the Terrible used to sit.[24]

At the end of 1958, Ilyina bought a car, and Akhmatova loved to make small excursions with her around the city and to the surrounding areas. Once they went to the great Trinity Sergey Monastery a few hours away, in Zagorsk. The monastery had been founded in the fourteenth century by St. Sergey, and was one of the few active monasteries in the Soviet Union. It was October 1959 and the weather was warm, with a drizzling rain. Ilyina says Akhmatova also loved the birch grove near the Uspensky Highway. There were only birches, all approximately the same height, with almost no underbrush and not a single other species, giving the impression of gleaming whiteness. They first went there in the autumn, and when they returned in winter, Akhmatova said, "Can it really be? Does it really exist? I think somehow it is a dream."[25] In her autobiographical notes, the poet recorded her impressions:

> First of all, no one has ever seen birches like this. I am scared to recall them. A hallucination. Something threatening, tragic, like the "Pergamon Altar," magnificent and inimitable. And I think there must be ravens there. And there's nothing in the world more wonderful than these birches, enormous, powerful, as ancient as the Druids and even older. Three months have passed, and I cannot come back to my senses. It was like yesterday, but I still do not wish it to be a dream. I need them now, in the present.[26]

When Akhmatova was in Leningrad, she visited her childhood friend Valeriya Sreznevskaya, who had suffered from mental problems before the war. When Akhmatova returned after the war, Sreznevskaya often came to see her. Then, at the beginning of 1946, Valeriya's daughter Lyulya came over one day to tell Akhmatova her mother had been arrested. Apparently she had had another nervous attack the evening before when, worn out and hungry, she had stood in line and began arguing with someone, and they took her away. No testimony about her poor health helped, and she was given seven years in the camps. Akhmatova sent her money and packages. Lyulya continued to visit Akhmatova. In 1953, Sreznevskaya returned to Leningrad, and after much trouble Lyulya was able to obtain a pension for her. She could only get a widow's pension, and at that time one needed dozens of letters of reference even for that. Akhmatova obtained these letters in both Leningrad and Moscow, stressing at great length how much the Sreznevskayas were deserving of support. (Sreznevskaya's husband had been a leading psychiatrist in Leningrad for many years.)[27]

Another important but rarely mentioned person came into Akhmatova's life at this time, Nika Glen. She was working on Bulgarian literature at the publisher Khudozhestvennaya Literatura. She became acquainted with Akhmatova in 1956, and from 1958 to 1963 became Akhmatova's personal assistant, helping her with manuscripts and correspondence. (After 1963, Anatoly Nayman took over in this capacity.) From the end of 1962 to the beginning of 1963 Akhmatova stayed with Nika Glen in Moscow, and in the summer and autumn of 1962, Glen stayed with Akhmatova in her little cabin in Komarovo.[28]

In a short memoir, Glen tells how she met Akhmatova. She says that in her mind Akhmatova lived somewhere in time past, in the epoch of Alexander Blok, and the fact that now someone could just pick up the phone and call her seemed absolutely unbelievable. When Glen began to prepare a book by the Bulgarian poet Elisaveta Bagryana, she turned to Akhmatova for advice, and then slowly she began to help Akhmatova in various ways, soon becoming her assistant. The feeling of wonder every time Akhmatova read her a poem never left her until the end of Akhmatova's life.

Another of Akhmatova's friends, Margarita Aliger, was responsible for getting Akhmatova published again.[29] She came to visit in 1953 on a trip from Moscow to Leningrad. Aliger was amazed by the poet's memory, by the kinds of details about the city that she recalled. For example, Akhmatova told her that on the corner of Suvorovsky Street there was a drugstore called *Slonovaya* (Elephant) that got its name from the fact that once medicine used to be prepared there for an elephant that had been brought to Petersburg by some foreign circus. Many times Akhmatova would take Aliger for a walk and show her some new aspect of the city she loved so much.

Aliger says that Akhmatova was known not only for her vast scholarly erudition but for her grasp of current events and even new scientific discoveries. If the conversation turned to politics, Akhmatova would discuss some political figure as if he were a close acquaintance. The same was true of historical figures. She read in several languages, often several books at once, and when she had finished, she remembered almost everything she had read. Once, for example, Aliger had a copy of James Frazer's *The Golden Bough* with her—the mammoth four-volume compendium of beliefs and rituals of peoples all over the world. Akhmatova was able to recite whole pages of it by heart.

At the end of 1955 Aliger, who had become a member of the editorial board of a new Moscow journal, *Literaturnaya Moskva* (*Literary Moscow*), asked Akhmatova for some poetry.[30] They published several of her poems and an extract from *Poem Without a Hero*. As a result, Aliger and her journal got into trouble. It was becoming increasingly clear that the "Thaw" was now over. In March 1957, at a special meeting of the Moscow section of the Union of Soviet Writers, Aliger was forced to defend the journal, saying it was not directed against the Soviet system but against the "varnished reality" or idealization typical of Socialist Realism, which the Twentieth Congress had also criticized. However, the attacks increased. Khrushchev himself appeared at the May 19 meeting at which the journal was discussed and said that he found the ideas in *Literaturnaya Moskva* alien and the editors apparently disrespectful to friendly criticism. He also shouted vulgarly at Aliger. The editors finally decided there was no way out except "repentance," but the Party determined this was not enough. Then, at one of the meetings of the Union of Soviet Writers that October, Aliger said, "I've made some mistakes; I've thought it over, I've been passive." This was reported in *Literaturnaya gazeta* on October 8.

Although Akhmatova's appearance in print was still rare, when her poems were published, they still aroused attacks. Chukovskaya noted in her diary for April 6, 1957, that Akhmatova was extremely upset by an article by Ognev, which appeared in the journal *Oktyabr* (October) reviewing the collection *Den poezii* (*Day of Poetry*) (Moscow, 1956). In it Akhmatova's famous poem from the Northern Elegies, "There are three ages . . .", appeared. In criticizing this great work about the stages in one's life, Ognev said, "There is so much weakness of soul, coldness, devastating lack of belief in life." Akhmatova was not the only target of Ognev's attack. She said the critic was obviously hard of hearing. He was clever enough to condemn Pasternak, Akhmatova, and Petrovykh, all in one paragraph. "A bouquet of masterpieces. One must have an ear like Ognev's to practice literary criticism," she said acidly.[31]

In 1958, the first collection of Akhmatova's poems to appear since the Stalinist period was published. It was called simply *Poems*—a small book in a red binding. She had been working for several years on it with Alexey Surkov. Lev Ozerov, the respected scholar who had written articles on many Russian writers, was one of the first who dared to write a positive review of Akhmatova's works during these precarious times. Sensitive to the possible accusation that her verses did not reflect the contemporary age, he said, "The poet has made every effort to find a way to her new reader. This path leads in the direction of the present day and not away from it."[32] In his Introduction, Surkov, also aware of the difficulty of getting her poems accepted, emphasized Akhmatova's patriotism, pointing out that during the war she looked at the world around her with new eyes. In the first year after the war her works had reflected a despondent mood, he continued, and in 1946 this received a strong reprimand; but then she wrote *In Praise of Peace*, which was more in keeping with what was expected of a Soviet writer.

In spite of the fact that a collection of her works had finally been published after so many years, Akhmatova was disappointed in the book. Of the 127 pages, one quarter was translations, and many of the poems were from her early period. Chukovskaya says Akhmatova told her the book was nonsense and would only confuse readers, meaning that they would get a distorted view of her entire corpus since she was now writing more philosophical poems, as well as poems that reflected the history of her country. But Chukovskaya herself nevertheless thought it was to the great credit of Surkov that the book had been published at all, even though what was most important was missing: the tragic path of the great poet, her most significant poems. And yet, says Chukovskaya, what was included was Akhmatova's "Prehistory." "The tragedy remained beyond the covers of the book, but the voice to which it had been given to heal the soul rang out."[33]

When Akhmatova gave Aliger a copy, the poet said bitterly, "It will be necessary to justify my reputation. Just imagine someone who did not grow up reading my poems taking this into his hands. 'So much experience, so much grief, so many upheavals, and she says nothing about herself except her love affairs.' That's what I would think."[34]

Soon after Lev had returned, he moved out of the apartment, perhaps because he was not getting along with Akhmatova.[35] He took a room on Srednyaya Rogatka Street, on the sixth floor without an elevator. Akhmatova did everything she could to help him get his book published. Lev had completed *The Huns* in the camps; he says that his teacher Nikolai Kyuner helped by sending him valuable material he needed. Lev was allowed to receive scholarly books. The camp doctor declared him an invalid, and that way he was able to work in the accounting office or the library, or simply sit in the barracks. This gave him enough time to write.

Although he had moved, Lev continued to see his mother. On March 8, 1958, Chukovskaya noted that she was working with Akhmatova for several days on some poems. Suddenly the door opened and in walked a man with a wrinkled forehead and strong features:

"Do you know each other?" Anna Andreyevna asked me.
"No."
"This is my son."
Lyova!
I didn't recognize him because it was so unexpected, although I knew he was in Moscow.
It was a feeling of hugeness and smallness at the same time. It's like that in love. Fortunetelling by poems; strange coincidences in dates; one's heart torn to pieces with every telephone call and knock on the door from the mailman; only a human being: neither more nor less . . . the greatest and most ordinary trifles: a human being. And now he was standing in front of me. . . . Not mine—but all *her* sleepless nights, non-meetings and meetings, little windows [at the prison] . . . poems in the fire. . . . Two decades of her life. And it turns out this is simply a human being—and he is here, in this very room. It is possible to touch him by the hand or call him by name. "Mama." "Little son." "My boy."
The walls of this room were permeated by thoughts about him, poems

to him. And snow, and trees, and the dawn outside the window. And scars from heart attacks.[36]

The last time Chukovskaya had seen Lev was in 1932, when he was quite young and was visiting her family. He was awkward, shy, not handsome, strongly resembling his father; he wore a quilted jacket, which was strange even for that time. Even earlier, when she was a child, he was known as Lyovushka-Gumilyovushka—a little boy with golden curly hair, brought by his father to visit, and they played Cowboys and Indians, jumping from the windowsill to the couch. Now the resemblance to his father had vanished, and in some way which Chukovskya could not fathom, he resembled Akhmatova. He spoke with a stutter. He was dressed like everybody else, but something made him very different. Chukovskaya says Lev saw less and less of his mother as the years went on.[37]

In April 1958, Akhmatova told Chukovskaya that Zoshchenko had been to visit her. "Poor Mishenka," Akhmatova said. He was suffering from persecution mania and megalomania at the same time. Akhmatova said it was impossible to talk to him because he would not listen—he would not reply to questions, but would answer with something totally unrelated. "Let me show you what a typical conversation with him is like. 'Are you going to leave the city this summer?' I ask. Then Akhmatova intoned slowly and solemnly, 'Gorky said that I'm a great writer.' "[38] Zoshchenko died later that year, with no comment from the Soviet press. That same year a censored edition of his stories was published and sold out; it was reissued in 1959. These were the only editions of his works in twelve years.[39] He taught people how to laugh at the absurd conditions under which they were living, and in this way helped them to survive. On the ground floor of the House of Writers on the Griboyedov Canal, where he used to live, there is now a museum in his honor.[40]

Akhmatova lost another link with the past when her friend Mikhail Lozinsky, one of Russia's best translators of Dante and Shakespeare, died in 1955. She wrote in her autobiographical notes:

In some mysterious way this tore the thread of my memories. I am no longer able to recall something that he can verify (about the Guild, Acmeism, etc.). Because of his illness we rarely met in recent years, and I was not able to read him my poems of the thirties (that is, *Requiem*). Because of this he thought I was the way he knew me in Tsarskoye. I found this out in 1940, when we were looking at proofs together for the collection *From Six Books*.[41]

Pasternak: The Nobel Prize and Death, 1958–1960

He who compared himself to the eye of a horse,
He glances sideways, looks, sees, recognizes,
And instantly puddles shine
As melted diamonds, ice pines.
>   —AKHMATOVA, 1936
>   (II, p. 85)

On May 30, 1960, Akhmatova lost another friend and Russia lost a great poet: Boris Pasternak. In 1929 he had written a poem to Akhmatova, which begins:

> I think I'm choosing words
> Resembling your primordial being
> And if I am mistaken, it's all the same to me,
> I will still not part from my mistakes.

He noted how important the city of Petersburg was in her life and work. The poem ends:

That's how I see your image and glance.
It inspires me not with that pillar of salt
By which five years ago
You set in rhymes your fear of looking back

But as it springs in all your early work,
Where crumbs of unremitting prose grew strong,
In all poems like wires conducting sparks.
Your work throbs high with our real past.[1]

Theirs was a difficult relationship. Part of the reason was that they were inspired by two different cities and grew up in two different milieux. Akhmatova and Mandelstam developed as young poets together: they met at Ivanov's Tower, went to the same soirées, and were part of the flow and ebb of Acmeism. They also spent difficult times together after the Revolution, and Akhmatova shared his suffering and pain when Mandelstam was arrested and exiled. A member of an earlier poetic generation, Alexander Blok figured strongly in the life of the young Akhmatova—almost as a mythical figure for her when she began her poetic career. His work served as a point of departure for her own, and he became the prototype of the Symbolist poet, the poet of the decadence and decline of Imperialist Russia. Akhmatova was never as close to Pasternak as a person or as a poet, although in times of need Pasternak was always there to support her, both emotionally and financially, which he also did for Mandelstam.

Vitaly Vilenkin recalls that in the last years of her life Akhmatova would often say nasty things about Pasternak—not malicious but nasty. Yet Vilenkin points out it was the kind of nastiness we express toward people we really love, people who are very dear to us. After a flourish of unjust accusations, Akhmatova would usually calm down, not rejecting what she had just said, but instead reciting one of her verses devoted to Pasternak, such as the lines written in 1958:

Here everything belongs to you by right
The drowsing drizzle stands like a wall
Give up the toy of the world—glory—to others,
Go home and don't expect anything.[2]

Apparently some of her remarks reached Pasternak, and in his last years the relationship grew strained. But she would still recall with gratitude how he had worried about her, had come to see her in Leningrad, had helped her with money in the difficult days, how he had even been in love with her.

When she spoke to Isaiah Berlin about Pasternak at Oxford in 1965, she described Pasternak as a "magical poet," one of the greatest in Russian history.

Every sentence he wrote, in verse and prose, spoke with his authentic voice, unlike any other she had ever heard. Blok and Pasternak were divine poets; no Frenchman, no Englishman, not Valéry, not Eliot, could compare with them—Baudelaire, Shelley, Leopardi, that was the company to which they belonged . . . he did not really read contemporary authors he was prepared to praise—not Bagritsky or Aseyev, or Maria Petrovykh, not even Mandelstam (for whom he had little feeling as a man or a poet, though of course he did what he could for him when he was in trouble), nor her own work—he wrote her wonderful letters about her poetry, but the letters were about himself, not her—she knew that they were sublime fantasies which had little to do with her poems. "Perhaps all great poets are like this." He was a generous giver, but not truly interested in the work of others; interested, of course, in Shakespeare, Goethe, the French symbolists, Rilke, perhaps Proust, but "not in any of us."

Berlin says Akhmatova ended her discussion of Pasternak by saying that she missed Pasternak's existence every day of her life.[3]

Pasternak's childhood was just as privileged as Akhmatova's, but in a different way. His parents were Jews, members of the middle-class intelligentsia. His father, Leonid, was a recognized artist, and his mother, Rosalie, was a fine pianist, both highly respected by Moscow's cultural elite. They were from Odessa, the birthplace of some of the most gifted Jewish artists, musicians, and writers in the Russian Empire, including Yasha Heifetz and Isaak Babel.

Leonid Pasternak was on the faculty of one of the most important art institutions in Russia, the Moscow School of Painting, Sculpture, and Architecture. His paintings, influenced by the Impressionists, were very popular. Rosalie née Kaufman Pasternak was a child prodigy who gave up a very promising career to devote herself to her family. However, she did not give up performing, and such famous musicians as Scriabin, Chaliapin, Heifetz, and Koussevitsky would often appear at music evenings at the Pasternak household. The family lived on the premises of the Moscow School of Painting, Sculpture, and Architecture.

Pasternak was born on February 10, 1890 (January 29, Old Style). He recalls in his memoirs not only renowned musicians but famous literary figures who came to visit. As a child he woke once in the middle of the night to the sound of music, which aroused in him a sweet, tormenting feeling. In response to his sobbing, his mother brought him in to see the guests, including Tolstoy, whose work, *Resurrection*, was being illustrated by Leonid Pasternak.[4] Akhmatova has her own version of this event, which she told to Chukovskaya on that first day she saw her again, on July 13, 1952:

Did he ever tell you about the first time he saw Tolstoy? No? Borenka [Pasternak] was three years old. He was sleeping. And suddenly he woke up in his bed, aroused by divine music. He listened, listened, and began to cry. He climbed out of bed and peeped into the next room: his mother at the piano, and sitting next to her, an old man listening to the music and crying. This was Tolstoy. The brilliant Borya knew when to wake up, didn't he?[5]

At first inspired by Scriabin, from 1903 to 1909 Pasternak devoted himself to music; then he turned to philosophy, and after several years of study at Moscow University, went to Marburg in Germany, one of the most important centers of Neo-Kantian philosophy as taught by Hermann Cohen. It is a beautiful university town, full of medieval timbered houses and colorful Jugendstil mansions; swans float on the River Lahn. Luther lived there, and the Brothers Grimm came to study law and left to collect fairy tales. Pasternak spent only a short—but significant—time in Marburg, for it was here that he realized his temperament was not suited to the restraints of academic discipline, that professors do not "collapse in bouts of creativity," as he put it. Knowledge and understanding of the world were to be gained not by the logical syllogisms of the scholar, but by the creative intuition of the poet.[6] He wanted to transform his inspiration and revelations into great works of poetry rather than tomes of dry academic prose. Like Akhmatova, his poems span a range from superb love lyrics to poems about the wonders of nature to philosophical meditations.

When Pasternak returned to Moscow, he continued to study philosophy, but his main focus was poetry. The year 1913 was an important one for Pasternak: not only did he graduate from Moscow University with a degree in philosophy, but his first collection of poems, *Twin in the Stormclouds,* was published. The next year he joined the Moscow group Centrifuge, poets who were seeking new styles and themes. In 1920 the artist Yury Annenkov characterized Pasternak: "Large eyes, puffy lips, a proud and dreamy look, tall stature, a harmonious gait, and a beautiful and resonant voice. On the street passersby—particularly women—not knowing who he was, would instinctively stare at him."[7] In May 1914, the Futurists, led by Mayakovsky, quarreled with Centrifuge, and they came together for a historic confrontation at the Café Grek on Tverskaya Street, which many of the Moscow bohemians frequented. Sergey Bobrov, a poet and one of the key members of Centrifuge, describes the incident. Pasternak was sitting opposite Mayakovsky.

"What do you intend to speak about?" Pasternak asked Mayakovsky. "If it's about poetry, then I agree; it's a worthy theme, and I believe it is not unknown to you." Mayakovsky looked at him ironically and incredulously. "Why do you think that?" Mayakovsky asked Pasternak. Borya shrugged his shoulders and cited Lermontov, and then said: "Well, must I really explain what originality is in art? I don't know how you'll answer me, but I think for you, simply as a talented person, it is the simplest thing."

I still recall the phrase of Mayak [Mayakovsky]: "Are you really a philosopher?"

"Every poet has something like this in his soul," answered Borya. "Would you really like to argue with this?"

And finally:

"But there are limits where a literary quarrel ends and just shouting and pounding of fists begins . . . indeed isn't this what you call art?"

Borya's face expressed fatigue and anxiety, and Mayak's face gradually softened, and then relaxed completely . . . he began to listen to Borya attentively, fascinated.[8]

Like Akhmatova, when Pasternak looked back at 1914, the year in which the war began, he saw it as a turning point in the history of all their lives. His own description of his fateful meeting with Mayakovsky makes this clear: "This was May 1914. The turning point of history was so near. But who thought about it? The tasteless city burned like enamel and tinsel, as in the opera *The Golden Cockerel.* The lacquered green of the poplars glistened. . . . I was obsessed with Mayakovsky and already missed him."[9] Pasternak was overwhelmed by Mayakovsky; indeed, he feared Mayakovsky's influence on his own poetry, and consciously adopted a style in direct contrast to Mayakovsky's.

Pasternak was not drafted, because of an injury he had suffered as a child when thrown by a horse. He spent part of the war at a factory in the Urals, arranging for deferrals of military service for local peasants and workers involved in important civilian tasks.[10] In 1917 he published the collection that made him famous, *My Sister-Life,* written mainly in the summer between the February and October revolutions.

One relatively neglected aspect of Pasternak's poetry is the influence of Akhmatova's work. In his first volume on Pasternak's life, Christopher Barnes suggests that Pasternak recalled reading Akhmatova for the first time in 1915, and envied her ability to "capture particles of reality by such simple means." This quote appeared in Pasternak's autobiography, *People and Attitudes,* in 1956. Barnes seems to see no relationship between the poetry of the two, saying that Pasternak's "own modernist tastes . . . were far removed from her restrained classicism and their aesthetic views and biographies began converging only in the 1920s."[11]

In the passage quoted by Barnes, Pasternak said he thought the collection he was reading was *Plantain.* But he clearly was mistaken, since *Plantain* was not published until 1921. However, Pasternak does not say this is the first time he ever read or heard any of Akhmatova's works. And even if he first read Akhmatova in print only in 1915, he belonged to many literary groups, which meant he had frequent opportunities to have heard her work, especially from Mayakovsky, who quoted Akhmatova profusely every time he was in love (which was often), and he had already had direct contact with her many evenings at the Stray Dog.[12]

In comparison with Akhmatova, Pasternak's early poems are rhapsodic, as one image tumbles over another in a burst of emotion. However, in comparison with Mayakovsky, for example, they are the epitome of restraint. We need only look at a passage from Mayakovsky's "Cloud in Trousers":

> You would not be able to recognize me now:
> a sinuous huge creature
> groans
> writhes.
> What can such a clod want
> Though a clod, he wants a lot.[113]

and compare it to Pasternak's lines. Pasternak too can express strong emotions, but he is more controlled, as when he relates his grief on being rejected by Ida Vysotskaya in his poem "Marburg":

> I shuddered. I flared up and then died down.
> I shook. I suddenly made a proposal,
> But too late. I was scared, and then—she refused me.
> How sad her tears! I'm more blessed than a saint.[14]

As various critics have pointed out, it is difficult to call Pasternak a Futurist, although many contemporaries saw the young Pasternak as part of this movement. His poetry differs both from Mayakovsky's urban worship of technology and Khlebnikov's primitivistic verse. He had no passion for the achievements of the industrial age, no nostalgia for a distant, primitive past. Although Pasternak created new and fresh images in his works, he was never interested in transrational language (*zaum*) for its own sake.[15] What Pasternak does have in common with Mayakovsky and Akhmatova, however, is a technique typical of modernist poetry: the juxtaposition of images and metaphors without apparent logical connection or smooth transitions, a collage of fragments of reality, a montage that reflects inner speech, the way we think. It is a free association of images that are linked through private meanings in the mind of the poet, through his own internal logic.

Pasternak is also similar to Akhmatova in his use of metonymy to express human feelings, a psychological event. When the poet puts the left-hand glove on her right hand, it is Akhmatova's way of conveying the character's disturbed state of mind through a simple gesture:

> Then helplessly my breast grew cold,
> But my steps were light,
> I pulled the glove for my left hand
> Onto my right.

(I, p. 225)

Roman Jakobson has pointed out that metaphor is certainly an important component of Pasternak's work, establishing a network of correspondences amidst the diverse aspects of the universe; but Jakobson then continues: "However rich and refined Pasternak's metaphors may be, they are not what determines and guides his lyric theme. It is the metonymical, not the metaphorical, passages that lend his work an 'expression far from common.' " In comparison with Maya-kovsky's poetry, says Jakobson, the lyrical hero in Pasternak is absent or thrust into the background because so much of the poetry is devoted to objects, scenes, nature. But this relegation of the hero is only apparent, because here too the hero is in fact present:

It is merely a case of being metonymically presented. . . . In Pasternak's poetry, images of the surrounding world function as contiguous reflec-tions, or metonymical expressions, of the poet's self. . . . Instead of the hero, it is, as often as not, the surrounding objects that are thrown into turmoil; the movable outlines of roofs grow inquisitive, a door swings shut with a silent reproach . . . when the poet is turned away by the girl he loves, he finds that "the mountain had grown taller and thinner, the town has become lean and black" . . . the hero is as if concealed in a picture-puzzle, he is broken down into a series of constituent and sub-sidiary parts, he is replaced by a chain of concretized situations and surrounding objects, both animate and inanimate.

Jakobson then turns to the poem "Marburg" to illustrate his point:

The paving stones glowed white hot, and the street's brow
Was swarthy, and from under their lids the cobblestones
Looked up at the sky, and the wind, like a boatman, was rowing
Through the lindens. And each was a likeness.

But, be that as it may, I avoided
Their glances. I did not notice their greeting.
I did not want to know of their riches.
I burst out of there so as not to start howling.[16]

Clearly, objects associated with the poet's surroundings reflect his spiritual state of mind: "The theme of the poem is the poet's rejected proposal of marriage, but the principal characters in the action are flagstone, paving stone, wind, 'innate instinct,' 'new sun,' chicks, cricket and dragonfly, tile, midday, Marburger, sand, impending storm, sky, etc."[17] Like Akhmatova, Pasternak's vision perceives the whole by means of an individual detail, which is why both poets can seem de-ceptively simple—often requiring great sensitivity and intuition in order to com-prehend the real meaning of a poem. The reader "has to exercise creative association in order to follow the poet . . . to reconstruct the whole by one detail."

Another feature inherent in Akhmatova's verse as well as Pasternak's, as Olga Hughes points out, is that while remaining within the limits of the familiar and the everyday, the poet succeeds in demonstrating the accessibility of the spiritual experience.[18] An example of this technique is Pasternak's poem "Out of Superstition" (1917), where the poet tells a woman what she means to him through a simple image from everyday life:

> Is it a sin—you're not a vestal virgin
> You came with a chair,
> As if from a shelf, you took my life down
> And blew the dust away.[19]

In 1926, Abram Lezhnyov published an essay examining Pasternak's technique, in which he discussed Pasternak's works in terms of presenting everyday reality—ordinary objects, nature, people, events—from a unique perspective, and thereby forcing the perceiver to look at the everyday world in a new way. The Russian Formalist critics called this technique *ostraneniye*, or "defamiliarization"—and it has since become a well-known technique used in literary criticism in the West. This was Akhmatova and Pasternak's contribution to Russian poetry at the beginning of the twentieth century. Lezhnyov also pointed out that it was not the object itself but the emotional coloring the poet invests in that object that is important. Like Akhmatova, Pasternak omits associative links, which often makes it difficult to understand his poems, but this is a deliberate aesthetic choice. "Things, splintered into sensations and created anew by the combination of these sensations, turned out to be different things, never seen before."

And there is another aspect of Pasternak's technique that Akhmatova shares: "The displacing of levels and the omission of associative links leads to a rupture of meaning, to difficulty in understanding," as Lezhnyov noted. "Something which otherwise would have sounded workaday or banal acquires novelty and significance when you are obliged to guess at it, when what is supposed to be shown is only partly visible, only an edge of it to be seen."[20] This method is termed *zatrudneniye*, literally "making it difficult," because the reader is forced to participate in the work by supplying the associative links in order to decode the message, idea, or feeling behind the poem.

Akhmatova often juxtaposed seemingly disconnected images, which are in fact linked by associations in the poet's mind. In "My heart beats calmly . . . ," the speaker recalls moments in the past—when she and her lover were together under the Galernaya Arch or in the Summer Garden. Now the affair is over, and the poet says she is calm; but the last lines belie this statement:

> You are free, I am free,
> Tomorrow will be better than yesterday—

Over the Neva's dark waters,
Under the cold smile
Of Emperor Peter.

(I, p. 357)

The dark waters of the Neva, the cold smile of Falconet's statue of Peter the Great, evoke the same feeling of despair that torments the heroine.

"When you're drunk . . . ," written in 1911, when Akhmatova was close to Modigliani, again typifies the juxtaposition of images that convey how the everyday world was transformed in the mind of the poet through her guilty love (Akhmatova was married to Gumilyov at the time):

When you're drunk it's so much fun—
Your stories don't make sense.
And early fall has stung
The elms with yellow flags.

We've strayed into the land of deceit
And we're repenting bitterly,
Why then are we smiling these
Strange and frozen smiles?

We wanted piercing anguish
Instead of placid happiness
I won't abandon my comrade,
So dissolute and mild.

(I, p. 237)

The poem shifts suddenly from the speaker talking to her lover to the metaphor of yellow autumn leaves resembling flags fluttering in the wind—then abruptly returns to the speaker's feelings of guilt and joy. Through the metaphor, the vision of the yellow leaves is heightened and transformed.

Although nature as a vehicle for expressing the poet's spiritual state has been more closely identified as a technique in Pasternak's poetry than in Akhmatova's, it is still an important device in her works as well. "The heart's memory . . ." was written in January 1911. Here the dying of nature in autumn and the sudden freeze are juxtaposed to reflect the heroine's emotions when love has gone out of her life:

The heart's memory of the sun grows faint.
The grass is yellower.
A few early snowflakes blow in the wind,
Barely, barely.

The narrow canals have stopped flowing—
The water is chilling

Nothing will ever happen here—
Oh, never!

The willow spreads its transparent fan
Against the empty sky.
Perhaps I should not have become
Your wife.

The heart's memory of the sun grows faint
What's this? Darkness?
It could be! . . . One night brings winter's first
Hard freeze.

(I, p. 221)

At first the poem seems to be describing the transformation of autumn into winter. The pace is slow and calm, reflecting the slow extinguishing of the sun and the freezing of nature. Only in the third stanza, abruptly, without any transition, does the poet juxtapose the human condition to what is occurring in nature, when she says, "Perhaps I should not have become/Your wife." Repeating the first line, the poem returns just as abruptly to nature slowly fading, then dying all at once, in one night—implying the slow, dull ache one feels over time when a love relationship slowly turns sour and suddenly becomes too much, turns into intense pain, and is over. Several years after Akhmatova wrote this poem, such events actually occurred when she finally told Gumilyov she wanted a divorce in 1918; or again, at the end of the 1930s when she made the decision to cut off her relationship with Punin, although she continued to live in the same communal apartment with him.

Similarly, Pasternak's poem "February" (1912) uses images from everyday life, but the comparisons are so unusual they are almost shocking:

February. Get your ink and weep!

Write about February in sobs.
While the thundering slush
Burns like black spring.

Get a hired cab. For six miles,
Through church bells ringing, through the clank of wheels
You will go where the showers
Are louder still than ink and tears.

Where, like charred pears,
From the branches thousands of rooks
Break away into the puddles and bring down
Dry sadness to the bottom of your eyes.

Beneath it thawed patches are black,
And the wind tore through with shouts,
And the more randomly, the surer
Are poems forming in sobs.[21]

It is the time of year before the real beauty of spring, yet winter is already over, as
the white sparkling snow of December and January turns to dirty slush, and spring
is still black in its "thawed patches" of earth, like the black rooks which resemble
charred pears, like the blackness of the ink with which the poet composes his verse—
the color of sorrow and pensive melancholy, the color associated with grief.

Pasternak himself admitted his debt to Akhmatova in the letter he wrote to
her in 1940, upon the appearance of her book *From Six Books,* when he said that
her name "has its previous power to recall the time when I would not have dared
believe that I would ever know you, or have the honor and good fortune to write
you a letter. . . . It is likely that I, Severyanin, and Mayakovsky are infinitely
more indebted to you than one normally assumes, and this indebtedness goes far
deeper than any of us recognizes, because it is unconscious. How much all this imprinted itself on our imagination has been shown by how often it has been echoed
and imitated! What examples of refined painting in words and precise accuracy!"[22]

In the final analysis, both Akhmatova and Pasternak reach back to the poet
Annensky. The reason lies in Annensky's style. The critic Khardzhiyev noted that
"What is typical of Annensky is syntactical tension in the line, the unexpected
train of impressionistic metaphors and comparison dislocating the usual relations
to objects, the interruptions of lofty poetical diction by prosaisms. . . . All these
elements of construction have had development in Pasternak's poetry."[23]

When the Revolution broke out in February 1917, Pasternak was still in the
Urals and did not return until March 1918. Like many of the intelligentsia, he
was enthusiastic about the Revolution, the feeling of freedom. He was optimistic
that somehow all the many factions would work together to create a new and
better society. Although upset by initial acts of terrorism, he did not resist the
Bolsheviks in October 1917. Perhaps Pasternak thought the Bolsheviks could be
effective where the Provisional Government had failed; in fact, the government
seemed totally paralyzed in the weeks preceding the Revolution.

Initially, however, Pasternak's poems reflected little reaction to the momentous events that were taking place. In one, "About These Poems" (1917), he even
seems to imply that he intends to shut himself off from recent events:

In a muffler, supported by my palms,
Through the casement window I'll shout to the children:
Dear children, which century
Is it in the courtyard?

Who beat a trail to my door,
To the hole strewn with sleet,

> While I smoked with Byron,
> While I drank with Edgar Poe?[24]

The sentiments expressed here are similar to those in Akhmatova's "We're all drunkards here," in which the poet and her friends are in the cellar cabaret carousing, firmly shutting out the demonstrations and oppression outside:

> Forever are the windows boarded up.
> What's out there—frost or thunder?[25]

Pasternak did not recite his poetry in the "café period" during the Civil War (1918–21), when it was difficult to get material printed and poets chose to recite at cafés and cabarets. However, this did not mean he did not attend. Pasternak was often seen at cafés socializing with his colleagues.

During the early years of the Soviet State, Pasternak's works were much more enthusiastically received than Akhmatova's. In 1922, *My Sister-Life* appeared. Like Akhmatova, he received some negative reviews at this time. Valeryan Pravdu-khin claimed that Pasternak's sole response to the age was a shudder, and that he was a "hothouse aristocrat of our society's private residences," even though Pasternak came from the middle class.[26] What is interesting, however, are the number of critics who excused Pasternak's complex metaphors, his strange syntax, and difficult imagery, as inaccessible to the average Soviet reader. His poetry also exhibited a lack of revolutionary themes, and yet for the most part Pasternak was not castigated for this at a time when Akhmatova was being branded as an outcast for writing on personal themes. One critic, Nikolay Aseyev, warned readers not to be put off by the complexity of Pasternak's verse because "He is your contemporary, who sings on your behalf." Bryusov noted that in spite of Pasternak's intellectual anemia and philosophizing, there was still hope for the poet: "Pasternak has no separate poems about the revolution, but his verses, maybe without the poet's own knowledge, are saturated with the spirit of modernity." He believed that Pasternak's views could only have been formed under contemporary conditions, and therefore his poetry was a reflection of his age.[27]

Pasternak himself wondered at the special treatment that his clearly non-revolutionary works were being accorded: "It is simply laughable what fortune *Sister* has had. An apolitical book, to say the least . . . this book ought to have attracted the most routine and ordinary attacks, and yet—one can forgive the terminology—it is recognized as being 'most revolutionary.' "[28] Pasternak wrote Yury Yurkun to say that he had sent a copy of *My Sister-Life* to Akhmatova, who was "a person who has unjustly suffered from friendly criticism, which prematurely proclaims someone a master, canonizes them according to the measure of its moderate demands, and then requires nothing more from them."[29] Pasternak also wrote to Akhmatova himself, expressing his sympathy in the inscription dated June 6, 1922, on a copy of *My Sister-Life* that he sent her:

> To Anna Akhmatova, poet and comrade in misfortune. To a modest, youthful and less than half-exploited sensitivity, and therefore a special and exclusive victim of criticism that is incapable of feeling and tries to be sympathetic, the victim of unsolicited and ever inopportune summings-up and schemes.[30]

However, Pasternak's earlier remarks about Acmeists such as Mandelstam and Gumilyov show that he was not initially enchanted with members of this group. As late as 1920, Pasternak had expressed contempt for what he thought were the "trivial thematic concerns" of these two poets: "They only harness toy horses up to the cab." He clearly had not paid attention to some of their most important works. Four years later he reread Mandelstam and ruefully admitted his mistake.[31] Soon after the Revolution he began to feel close to Akhmatova as a fellow member of his own generation—poets who were still relatively young, but who were already considered antiquated and were threatened by a new, alien world which they were forced either to become a part of or to leave. As Pasternak wrote to Yury Yurkun on June 14, 1922:

> I consider close to me those people whose sensitivity and expressive abilities blossomed at the start of the war. A maxim has been established about them, referring to some "pre-revolutionary quality," to their having been "heard out to the end" by their readers, to the fact that they have "said their last word leaving no remnant of artistry," to their "Symbolism, Acmeism, bourgeois quality" and so on. And as you well know, in the now-established view—a mere hour ago on our clocks—this means they have well nigh prehistoric origins. Yet would these 1917s and 1918s and so on be at all worthwhile—let alone the years of a great revolution— if these years had not been my own or your thirtieth, or somebody's fortieth or fiftieth? or their sixtieth?[32]

In 1922 Pasternak decided to leave Russia. Before setting off for Berlin, he was called in by Trotsky for a talk about literature. Trotsky asked Pasternak why he had avoided social themes. Pasternak noted that "My answers and explanations were reduced to a defense of true individualism, as one social cell of a new social organism."[33] By coincidence, Pasternak sailed from Petrograd on August 17 on the same ship as Arthur Lourie, the composer and recent Soviet Commissar of Music, with whom Akhmatova was living at the time. Yevgenia Pasternak, the young and beautiful artist whom Pasternak had recently married, always recalled how amazing it was to see Akhmatova's distinctive profile as she waved goodbye from the pier.

Pasternak was not happy in Berlin. The enormous Russian émigré community seethed with constant squabbles among the various factions, from monarchists to left-wing liberals, visiting Communists, and those, like Alexey Tolstoy and Ilya Ehrenburg, who had not made up their minds exactly where they stood. The situation was exacerbated by the severe financial problems in Weimar Germany, which was quickly heading for a crisis. Pasternak soon returned to Moscow for other reasons as well. Like Akhmatova, as a poet he felt it was important to write in his native tongue and to be within a milieu that understood the culture he loved so much.

However, his return did not mean an enthusiastic acceptance of the new Soviet State. One of the first indications of Pasternak's developing ambivalent attitude toward the Revolution was *Lofty Malady* (1923–28), a verse epic about the Civil War years, in which Pasternak presents positive aspects of the Revolution but also points to the problematic relationship of the intelligentsia after the new Soviet State was established.[34] The work was first published in *LEF* in 1924, the journal edited by Mayakovsky that featured works by some of the finest members of the avant-garde, such as Eisenstein, Mayakovsky, Brik, and Rodchenko. In 1928, Pasternak addded lines praising Lenin's speech at the Ninth Congress of Soviets in 1921. The addendum about Lenin may be less an indication of adoration of the leader than an assessment that foreshadows a statement in *Doctor Zhivago,* that "wars and revolutions, tsars and Robespierres are history's organic agents, its fermenting yeast. Revolutions are produced by men of action, one-sided fanatics, narrowminded geniuses."[35] Pasternak's later autobiography in the mid-1950s presents a positive estimation of Lenin that he was forced to include:

Lenin was the soul and conscience of such a rare splendor, he was the fact and the voice of the great Russian storm, unique and exceptional. With the fervor of genius and unhesitatingly, he took upon himself responsibility for bloodshed and breakage such as the world had never seen. He did not fear to cry out to the people to summon them to realize their most secret cherished hopes. He allowed the ocean to rage, and the hurricane passed over with his blessing.[36]

One feature that differentiates Pasternak from Akhmatova is that he turned to prose early in his career (Akhmatova waited until much later in life before she felt secure with this medium). Pasternak's novella *Lyuvers' Childhood,* which appeared in 1922, is based on the same technique of juxtaposing images and associations as in his poetry. The work focuses on the developing consciousness of a child, and it is a masterpiece of poetic prose.

Pasternak and Akhmatova saw each other sporadically in the 1920s. Lev Gornung, the Moscow poet who was collecting materials on Gumilyov, very much wanted an opportunity to speak to Akhmatova. He noted in his memoirs that on March 8, 1926, Pasternak called him to say that Akhmatova was in Moscow and he had seen her. She was staying in Shileiko's apartment. Pasternak arranged for Gornung to meet her in the former Morozov mansion on Prechistenka, where the Museum of Modern Western Art was then located. Akhmatova arrived a week after there had been a benefit to raise much-needed funds for the poet Maximilian Voloshin. Pasternak suggested that an event be planned to raise funds for her as well, but she was too proud and would not accept charity.[37] In a letter on March 9 Pasternak wrote to a friend:

> Anna Andreyevna came here for three days. I have not seen her for two years. I think she is feeling much better. She seems younger and not as sad. I was afraid to ask her how she was doing financially, because it's been a year since the rumor was going around about her illness and difficult situation, and I, Aseyev, and Mayakovsky thought of doing something about it. . . . But indirectly I learned (not from A. A. and not from her friends) that she would find this insulting.[38]

At a time when Akhmatova wrote little poetry and was leading a relatively secluded life, Pasternak turned again to the *poema,* the long narrative poem, focusing on public and historical themes. In 1927, the tenth anniversary of the Revolution, he published "1905" and "Lieutenant Schmidt." The first work, "1905," is a set of vignettes reflecting revolutionary activity during the tumultuous year 1905, including the mutiny on the *Potyomkin* which became famous in Sergey Eisenstein's film. "Lieutenant Schmidt" is about a military leader, a politically ambiguous figure who carries out a mutiny in Sebastopol in 1905. Pasternak also published an autobiography, *Safe Conduct* (1929)—a genre to which Akhmatova turned very late in her life, and which exists now only as a set of fascinating fragments.

In 1929, Pasternak's attitude toward his poetry and the unique style that had become identified with his works began to change radically. He published a revised version of his collection of poems *Above the Barriers,* attempting to simplify the style; but as several critics have shown, the poems still often remained elusive and difficult to understand. However, what was important was that he was shifting to a style that he was determined would be more transparent and comprehensible to the ordinary reader, and eventually he succeeded. His later poems are much simpler, the metaphors and other images easier to grasp, and *Doctor Zhivago* is written in relatively straightforward narrative prose. As Akhmatova was to point out later, their literary careers moved in opposite directions: her works became more complex, with radical shifts in time and space, and often erudite allusions to world culture, even as Pasternak's poetry and prose avoided these techniques in order to achieve immediacy of comprehension.

Around 1937 Pasternak wrote a series of poems to various members of the intelligentsia, including Meyerhold, Tsvetayeva, and Akhmatova. He sent Akhmatova one poem in a letter dated March 6, 1929, asking her permission to publish it and sharing his fear that his creative powers were waning. It appeared in 1929 in the journal *Krasnaya nov* (*Red Virgin Soil*). "The last remnant of lyric feeling is alive," he wrote her, "and it is still only burning out in me in the form of a living (and, of course, unpayable) debt to a few important people and friends. I have written something to you, to the Meyerholds, and Mayakovsky."[39]

He also wrote a poem to Pilnyak in 1931, after Pilnyak and Zamyatin had been subjected to humiliation and criticism in 1929. The poem was published in *Novyi mir* (1931), with the title "To a Friend" (the manuscript version says "To Boris Pilnyak"). This important poem would be cited constantly by enemies to question Pasternak's loyalty to the Communist state.

> As if I do not know that groping in the dark,
> Ignorance would never find light,
> Or am I a monster, and the happiness of the hundreds of thousands,
> Is not dearer to me than the empty happiness of a hundred?
>
> Don't I use the Five-Year Plan as a standard,
> Don't I fall and rise with it?
> But what am I to do with my rib cage,
> And with that which is more inert than inertia itself?
>
> It is unfortunate that at the time of great decisions,
> When preference is given to a higher passion,
> The post of poet is retained;
> It is dangerous, if not vacant.[40]

The poet has attempted to accept Socialist reality, the Five-Year Plan. Yet, as one critic interprets it, "Pasternak regrets retaining the post of poet at a time when social and political concerns have, presumably, an indisputed priority."[41] The work can also have a more sinister meaning: that it was dangerous at this time for anyone to be a poet, especially considering the date of the poem, soon after Mayakovsky's suicide and the Party's attack on Pilnyak for publishing his book abroad.

Although Pasternak's former works were reissued in the 1930s, which was not the case with Akhmatova, like her, he began to write less and less poetry and turned to translations instead. His relations with Stalin at this time were complex. In November 1932, Stalin's wife committed suicide. Pasternak wrote an addendum to a condolence letter sent by various writers to Stalin. The letter included the signatures of Boris Pilnyak, Yury Olesha, and Alexander Fadeyev. Pasternak had made several trips to Georgia, Stalin's birthplace, and he fell in love with its culture. His translations of Georgian poetry have made it possible for Russians to read great poetry from this rich but largely unknown culture in the West. Perhaps this influenced Stalin's behavior toward Pasternak. Critics have said Pasternak genuinely admired Stalin, which in the 1930s was not unique among intellectuals, who thought that the worst oppression was over. The standard of living was getting better, illiteracy was being overcome, and until 1932, when Socialist Realism was declared the official doctrine in the arts, there was a feeling that one could still write as one wished within the parameters of the Communist state. However, Yevgeny Pasternak says the critics are wrong. Moreover, Pasternak was soon sent on two trips to the Urals as part of an effort to use writers to gather material on new developments in the Soviet State. His impressions of collectivization were distressing, and it was at this time that his "period of silence" began, when little original work was created.

As the state became more oppressive, as friends and colleagues began to be arrested, and especially after Kirov's assassination in 1934 when the purges began, Pasternak's inner peace began to be destroyed. As Akhmatova said about Zoshchenko's semi-madness after he was expelled from the Writers' Union, women are better at surviving situations that seem to be too much for the human mind to bear. Soon Pasternak began to suffer from nervous trauma.

At the First All-Union Congress of Soviet Writers in 1934, in the keynote speech, Bukharin praised Boris Pasternak as one of the greatest poets of Soviet literature. But Pasternak was also attacked when Surkov claimed there was little Bolshevik sentiment in his works. In his own speech at the Congress, Pasternak dared to warn poets against becoming dignitaries of the state and writing what they thought was required only to achieve a certain status.[42]

In 1935 Pasternak was sent—much against his will—to the International Writers' Congress in Defense of Culture, organized in Paris by André Malraux, André Gide, and Ilya Ehrenburg to show a united front against the rise of Fascism. Pasternak was under extreme nervous tension at this time, and exhausted physically, in no condition to go abroad and represent the Communist regime at an event that would attract publicity. However, he had little choice. Malraux and Gide insisted on having both Isaak Babel and Pasternak attend, and Pasternak received a call from Stalin's personal secretary ordering him to go. He traveled through Germany, but although his parents were in Munich, he said he did not go to see them because he did not want them to see him in such a pathetic condition, though his sister saw him in Berlin. The Congress greeted him enthusiastically. Malraux said: "Before you is one of the greatest poets of our time." He saw the Russian poets Vladislav Khodasevich and Marina Tsvetayeva; the latter told him she hoped to return to Russia. He tried to dissuade her, but to no avail. Pasternak returned in a state of total depression. He came back via Leningrad and spent some time visiting with Akhmatova. They took walks around the city together.[43]

At a meeting of the executive board of the Union of Soviet Writers in 1936 in Minsk, Pasternak vigorously attacked Socialist Realism, its commands from above on how to write, saying, "Art is unthinkable without risk and spiritual self-sacrifice; freedom and boldness of imagination have to be gained in practice. . . . Don't expect a directive on this score."[44]

Although Pasternak helped Mandelstam when he got in trouble, he had warned him of the consequences of writing satires and serious poems against Stalin: "This is not a literary fact, but an act of suicide, of which I do not approve and in which I have no desire to take part."[45] However, when Mandelstam was arrested, Pasternak stood by the couple loyally, helping in every way he could, and was one of the few to visit Nadezhda Mandelstam immediately after she found out about her husband's death.

During these difficult times, Akhmatova was inspired to write several poems, and one of them, "The Poet," written in January 1936, was devoted to Pasternak. She picks up many motifs typical of Pasternak's own work: immersion in nature; the Daryal area in Georgia, where he had spent many happy hours; the reference to Laocoon from his long poem "1905":[46]

He who compared himself to the eye of a horse,
He glances sideways, looks, sees, recognizes,
And instantly puddles shine
As melted diamonds, ice pines.

In lilac haze repose backyards,
Station platforms, logs, leaves, clouds.
The whistle of a steam engine, the crunch of watermelon rind,
In a fragrant kid glove, a timid hand.

He rings out, thunders, grates, he beats like the surf
And suddenly grows quiet—it means that he
Is cautiously advancing through the pines,
So as not to disturb the light sleep of space.

And it means that he is counting the grains
From the stripped stalks, it means that he
Has come back to a Daryal gravestone, cursed and black,
After some kind of funeral.

And once more, Moscow weariness burns the throat,
Far off, a deadly little bell is ringing . . .
Who lost his way two steps from the house,
Up to the waist in snow and no way out?

Because he compared smoke to the Laocoon,
And celebrated cemetery thistles,
Because he filled the world with the new sound
Of his verse reverberating in new space—

He was rewarded with a kind of eternal childhood,
His generosity and keen-sightedness shone,
The whole earth was his inheritance,
And he shared it with everyone.

(II, p. 85)

The path Pasternak had to follow in the 1930s because of his public persona was very different from that of Akhmatova, who had essentially retired from the literary scene and was mainly worried about the survival of her son and Punin. She was never put in the position of being asked to sign petitions supporting death sentences for Party leaders or fellow intellectuals. Pasternak was—not only because he was a prominent poet, but because he was a leading figure in the public intellectual apparatus, serving on boards of writers' groups and so on. In 1936 there was talk of a new, more liberal constitution and a parliament, and again Pasternak and other intellectuals hoped for an easing of restrictions. As a result, Pasternak wrote two poems in praise of Stalin at Bukharin's request. The situation at the time was extremely complex, as Lazar Fleishman points out; there was also the increasing threat of Fascism in Italy and Germany, and the poems reflected Pasternak's hope for the establishment in his country of "socialism with a human face."[47]

Pasternak was subjected to very difficult choices during these years. As a member of the board of the Union of Soviet Writers he was told to sign a note demanding the death penalty for Zinovyev and Kamenev, Stalin's enemies, and his name appears among the writers listed on the note. Yevgeny Pasternak says Pasternak actually refused to sign the note and his name appeared without his permission. However, he refused to support the campaign in Russia against Gide's book, which revealed the French author's disillusionment with Stalinism after his visit to the Soviet Union. Nor would Pasternak sign a petition in 1937 by a group of writers that supported the death penalty for key Soviet generals, even though his second wife, Zinaida, was pregnant and feared for their lives.[48] People dear to him became victims of the Terror. In August 1937 he heard about the suicide of his dear friend, the great Georgian poet Paolo Yashvili. Soon another Georgian poet and friend, Titsian Tabidze, was arrested. Later, in *People and Attitudes,* Pasternak wrote: "Why were these two people sent to me? How can one describe our relationship? Both became an essential part of my personal world. I did not prefer one to the other, they are so inseparable, so much supplement each other. The fact of both together along with the fate of Tsvetayeva had to become my greatest grief."[49]

When Akhmatova's collection *From Six Books* appeared briefly in the summer of 1940 and was then banned, Pasternak wrote a very moving letter to her on July 28.

It is the rival significance of your new writings in *Willow* and the latest insertions, your present style of writing which is still too much a law unto itself and too authoritative to seem like a continuation or modification of the early style. One might talk of the appearance of a new artist, unexpectedly emerging next to the former you, as a result of the prevalence of total realism over the impressionist element, veering toward impressionability, and also the complete independence of the ideas from any rhythmic influence.[50]

What Pasternak means by "the impressionist element" is a series of images from everyday reality juxtaposed not in simple, linear, chronological fashion but as personal or historical associations rendered in the poet's stream-of-consciousness style. By 1940, the images of both Pasternak and Akhmatova are easier to decipher, and the connections among such images are much more straightforward, although cultural and biographical information is still often required. For Akhmatova, *The Way of All Earth,* the verse sections of her play, *Prologue,* and especially *Poem Without a Hero* are the chief places where she returns to her earlier style and then carries it way beyond her early work.

Pasternak praises Akhmatova for the power of her first books (reprinted in *From Six Books*) to evoke their own time, which he believes upon rereading is stronger than ever. He finds especially "beautiful clusters" of poems in *Rosary* and admits how the style in these works influenced his own works and those of Mayakovsky: "It is precisely as one such cluster that one could classify the whole future world in *Above the Barriers,* the atmosphere in which it came into being, i.e., all that which I had touched up in passing in reference to our indebtedness, about the magic impact of your pictorial power."[51]

His second letter to her, written on November 1 of the same year, reflects his attempt to soothe Akhmatova because of the harsh criticism her book received. It also reflects the tense atmosphere of the months before the impending fury of war. Akhmatova had been to see him that August, and he tells her it was then "You reminded me how unequivocally dear you are to me." His parents had moved from Germany to Oxford because of the threat to their lives as Jews, but there was now a threat to England as well: "the British are holding out, but Akhmatova is being attacked. If only between those two items of news which affect me equally closely there could be some kind of osmosis, so that the sweetness of one could soften the pain of the other!"[52]

The Terror was beginning to have a closer impact on Pasternak's own life. In January 1939, the great theater director Meyerhold planned to produce *Hamlet* at the Pushkin Theater in Leningrad, where he had been invited to work, and he commissioned Pasternak to do the translation. But before he was able to produce the work, Meyerhold was arrested—in June 1939—and swiftly executed. Pasternak finished his translation at the end of that year, although it was not staged until much later. (He did recite the translation in public in the spring of 1940.) The translation removed much of the complex metaphorical passages typical of Shakespeare, and instead produced a style that is clear and transparent, like the later poems of Pasternak himself. It differs radically from the most famous translation of *Hamlet* in Russian until that time, by Akhmatova's good friend Mikhail Lozinsky. Lozinsky's version is much more faithful to the original, retaining the richness and complexity of Elizabethan English and Shakespeare's own style.

Akhmatova knew Shakespeare well and had read him in the original. She knew many of his plays by heart, and she had a keen sensitivity to the music of his verse, to the form which could not be divorced from the meaning. She herself had been working on translations of passages from *Macbeth* in the early 1930s. Although Akhmatova later criticized Pasternak's translations of Shakespeare for being unfaithful to the original, at this time she praised his work to Chukovskaya, commenting that Pasternak's version was much better for the contemporary stage:

I love it. I'm so happy for Boris Leonidovich: everyone praises him, everyone likes it, and Boris Leonidovich is satisfied. The translation is really excellent; a powerful wave of verse. And no matter how strange it seems, there is nothing of Pasternak. Marshak told me he thinks in Pasternak's translation *Hamlet* is too much of a schoolboy, simplified, but I don't agree. I'm only sorry that Pasternak's translation now will be praised at the expense of Lozinsky's. It's also very good, but different. Lozinsky's translation is better to read, like a book, but Pasternak's is better to hear on the stage. There's really no reason to neglect one at the expense of the other. One must simply be glad for such a holiday in Russian culture.[53]

By 1957, however, Akhmatova had changed her mind. She told the literary critic Abram Gozenpud then that for her, Lozinsky's was the ideal translation:

I have often heard that actors prefer Pasternak's translation as more lively, more natural than Lozinsky's. It's true that when spoken by Hamlet himself, the verses of Boris Leonidovich are easier to pronounce. Lozinsky, who achieved a miracle of freedom and lightness in his translation of the Spaniards, is solemn and grand in *Hamlet,* which is more faithful and corresponds better to the spirit of Shakespeare. . . . In attempting to free the text from rhetoric and bombast, Boris Leonidovich purposely simplifies and brings the vocabulary down to earth. Actors, directors, and yes, even spectators who haven't glanced at the original think that this makes Shakespeare come closer to our time, makes him a realist. But is the text of *Hamlet* not characterized by a hypertrophy of metaphors, ornamentation, even mannerism—is it not this that one can call the gift of the baroque? . . . Is it right for us to sacrifice the particular features of a poetic style in the name of notorious lightness and accessibility? I think the solemn grandeur of Lozinsky's style better answers the spirit of tragedy. . . . And what richness of registers of poetic speech—each character has his own voice, his own intonation.

She also changed her mind about Pasternak's ability to capture the original at the expense of imposing the power of his own creative personality on the work he was translating: "Just as Pasternak is on a much higher plane than Lozinsky as a poet, to the same extent he must yield to him as a translator. In the realm of poetry Boris Leonidovich is an autocratic sovereign, the center of the Solar

System. Lozinsky is rather a satellite of that planet into whose orbit he is drawn, be it Dante or Shakespeare. But he conveys to us the clear light of its rays."[54] Akhmatova admitted that Pasternak had made many discoveries and clarified passages that often had been obscure; but there were also unjustified simplifications of poetic thought that she felt should not be allowed, or the full implication of the meaning could be lost.

In 1941 Pasternak was evacuated to Chistopol, leaving on the same train from Moscow with Akhmatova, although after arriving in Chistopol she went on to Tashkent. He arrived too late to save Tsvetayeva and would never forgive the writers like Trenev and Aseyev, who were in authority, for not helping her. In 1943 he wrote a poem about his guilt over her death, and how much he knew Russia had lost when she committed suicide:

Akh, Marina, the time is long gone,
And it is not so much toil
To bring from Yelabuga
Your forsaken dust in a requiem.

. . .

What can I do for you?
Please let me know somehow.
In the silence of your departure
There is a reproach left unexpressed.[55]

Although he spent part of the war years with his family in Chistopol, Pasternak lived during the winters in Peredelkino, the writers' colony outside Moscow where he had been given a dacha in 1936. He spent increasingly more time there, surrounded by nature, though he also had an apartment in a House of Writers in Moscow. In August 1943 he visited the front, along with other prominent Soviet authors.

In 1946 Pasternak met Olga Ivinskaya, who was working at the journal *Novyi mir*. Blond and voluptuous, she was much younger than Pasternak (she was born in 1912) and, as in many such relationships, perhaps she made him feel young again. She became his mistress and companion for the rest of his life. But his family remained important to him, and no matter how difficult relations became between him and his second wife, he never got a divorce, dividing his time between two households. Many of his later poems were written to Ivinskaya, and she was the inspiration for Lara in *Doctor Zhivago*. Ivinskaya had a decisive influence on Pasternak's activities during the *Zhivago* affair, when Pasternak finally suffered the attacks that Akhmatova and Mandelstam had endured for so long.

Pasternak had hoped that the war would introduce a new atmosphere, encouraging optimism and freedom in the USSR, but the August 1946 Resolution against Akhmatova and Zoshchenko and their subsequent expulsion from the Writers' Unon quickly disillusioned him. He refused to attend any meetings of the board related to this affair, for which he was dismissed. Pasternak appeared with Akhmatova in Moscow in 1946 during the series of successful poetry evenings devoted to works by Moscow and Leningrad poets. Pasternak arranged for Akhmatova to receive money for translations, and also a loan.

The generally oppressive atmosphere after the war and the attacks against major members of the art world now led to attacks against Pasternak as well. He was criticized at literary gatherings, and Alexander Fadeyev, secretary of the Writers' Union from 1946 to 1953, said at this time: "He represents the spirit of individuality which is so profoundly alien to our society." He was condemned in the press; and at the end of 1948, the director of a major publishing house, Sovetskii pisatel, was denounced for attempting to republish Pasternak's works. Alexey Surkov wrote a scathing article against Pasternak that appeared in 1947 in *Kultura i zhizn* (*Culture and Life*). From 1946 until 1954, no original work by Pasternak was published, only his translations.[56]

But he was now working on completing the novel he had been writing since autumn 1945. In September 1948, a manuscript version of the first chapters of *Doctor Zhivago* circulated in Moscow. This amazing hero must surely have created a stir:

> This scion of the Russian intelligentsia is, successively, a doctor, a poet, a citizen in sympathy with the outbreak of revolution, a family man struggling to survive the material hardships of the early Soviet years, an involuntary member of the Red partisan army during the long civil war, a disgraced member of the former bourgeoisie, an internal refugee obliged by political dangers to part from the woman he loves, the extralegal husband of the daughter of a former family servant—through all this—a man whose external life goes to seed while in his writings he keeps alive a full measure of spiritual and creative integrity.[57]

In the same year that Lev Gumilyov was arrested after the war, 1949, Pasternak's mistress Ivinskaya was taken away by the secret police. She was sent to the camps for five years, charged with anti-Soviet political activities. Apparently her arrest and exile had not so much to do with her relationship with Pasternak as her association with someone who had been accused of embezzlement.[58] Her arrest and detention, instead of dampening Pasternak's enthusiasm, spurred him to work on the novel with renewed energy. He wrote his cousin Olga Freidenberg on August 7, 1949:

> For some reason my heart is heavy. No longer does my life matter to me. It is a role that is set and fixed; I must play it out with dignity. With God's help, if I live, I will finish the novel. I will finish everything. It is important, and I must see that those near and dear to me are happy. . . .
> Again things are plentiful, beautiful and marvelous here at the dacha.[59]

Olga wrote back on November 27 in reply to his complaints about becoming old: "History is a chronicle not of the past but of the eternal present. Time will never make an old man of you because the spirit that your name stands for does not age. . . . You will go on writing splendidly, your spirit will remain alive."[60]

After Stalin's death, Pasternak began to read to small circles of friends, and his poems were published, as well as a short story. At the Second Congress of the Writers' Union, his name was rarely mentioned. The novel was completed in 1956 and submitted to *Znamya* and *Novyi mir*. In 1956 an agreement for publication was concluded by Goslitizdat (the State Literary Publishing House).

Ivinskaya was released in the autumn of 1953. In the camps she had become acquainted with the writer Nadezhda Adolf-Nadezhdina, a friend of Lydia Chukovskaya's. After Ivinskaya's return, Chukovskaya, who had come to know Ivinskaya when they worked together in 1946–47 at *Novyi mir,* gave her money for packages for Nadezhdina, and sometimes food, clothes, and books that had been donated by various friends. It turned out Nadezhdina did not receive a single package. This went on for two and a half years. Chukovskaya suspected something, since Nadezhdina never mentioned having received anything in her letters to her mother and aunt. Finally, when Adolf-Nadezhdina returned in April 1956, she confirmed Chukovskaya's suspicions that she had not received a single package.[61]

When Chukovskaya discussed this with Akhmatova at the beginning of June 1956, Akhmatova's initial reaction was silence. She did not say anything, just lowered her eyes. Ivinskaya had never been a favorite with Akhmatova: although she herself had a difficult relationship with Pasternak's second wife, Zinaida, she still respected her and admitted she was a devoted wife and mother. Akhmatova had nothing but contempt for Ivinskaya. Now, calmly and slowly, she said that Ivinskaya had always been a thief, but to have been freed and living on the generosity of Pasternak's income and then to rob a friend who was imprisoned and dying of hunger was too much. "I've never heard of such a thing even among gangsters—among themselves. I hope you have explained to Boris Leonidovich who this is he is singing about, for whom he is strumming his resounding lyre?" Chukovskaya said she would never tell Pasternak—it would bring him too much pain, and moreover he would never believe her. He adored Ivinskaya.[62]

After Ivinskaya was released, she helped Pasternak with his literary affairs. In 1954, ten of the poems from *Dr. Zhivago* were published in *Znamya*. He had given a copy of the manuscript to Sergio D'Angelo, a member of the Italian Communist Party who worked for Italian radio in Moscow and who had been introduced to Pasternak by the Soviet ambassador. D'Angelo immediately passed it on to a Milan publisher, Giangiacomo Feltrinelli, who decided to publish the novel in an Italian translation. Pasternak told Feltrinelli that he would be happy if it were published, but warned him: "If the publication here, which has been reported by many journals, is held up and you do it first, the situation will be very difficult for me." Pasternak made no attempt to conceal the Italian publication from the Soviet literary bureaucracy.

Soon there began to be problems with the publication of the novel in the

Soviet Union. Other novels criticizing aspects of the Soviet State, such as Ehren-burg's *The Thaw,* were apparently less problematic. But *Doctor Zhivago*

> posed a more fundamental challenge. It called into question the theo-retical basis for the existence of a socialist state—the doctrines of Marx-ism—and advanced an alternative set of values. . . . The novel was devoted to the Revolution and civil war—but as the first readers noticed, the author showed in telescopic form that the main features of Stalin's time flowed inevitably from the very nature of the Bolshevik Party and Soviet power. This conclusion was especially heretical and subversive: Stalin's indictment at the Twentieth Party Congress had been accom-panied by protestations that the cult of personality was an alien phenom-enon, having nothing in common with the essence of the Soviet order and socialism in general. It was an accidental historical abberation that could never happen again.[63]

Ehrenburg's novel was one of the first to be published after Khrushchev took over, when writers were still testing their limits under the new reforms. By 1956, the Party was getting nervous about how far liberalization should go, especially after the uprisings in Hungary and Poland in October and November 1956. *Novyi mir* rejected Pasternak's novel in September 1956. This led Pasternak to believe that the work would not appear in his own country, even in abridged form, although Goslitizdat had indicated a willingness to publish it, but in a heavily edited form. The book was to be released in Italy in September 1957, but Soviet officials demanded that Pasternak request a release. Pasternak complied only when it was clear it was too late to stop the production. He also sent Feltrinelli a confidential letter at the same time saying he should go ahead and publish.[64] The protests of the Soviet government only increased interest in the novel in the West; when *Doctor Zhivago* finally appeared, numerous articles were written about it in the European and American press. No work of Russian literature had received such publicity since the time of the Revolution.[65] But publication of the book at Goslitizdat remained frozen.

At the beginning of 1958 there was talk in the Western press that Pasternak would be nominated for a Nobel Prize. On October 23, 1958, Pasternak received a cable informing him he had indeed won the prize. He soon received a visit from an old friend, Konstantin Fedin, now head of the Moscow section of the Union of Writers, who urged him to refuse the prize. On October 24, notice of the award appeared in the world press, and the attacks against Pasternak in the Soviet media followed shortly thereafter. He was expelled unanimously from the Union of Writers, which meant loss of any opportunity to earn a living.

On October 29, Pasternak sent a cable to the Swedish Academy saying that in view of the interpretation his winning the prize had been given in his country, he had to refuse it. One of the main reasons for Pasternak's action may have been that he feared another series of purges such as had accompanied the events associated with Zamyatin and Pilnyak in 1929 and with Akhmatova and Zo-shchenko in 1946, when it became clear these famous figures were only symbolic of numerous others who would suffer as well. Fleishman also points out that Pasternak had never actively sought publicity or personal fame. "No matter how flattering the fact that he was the first Slavic poet to receive the highest literary distinction, he was glad to receive it primarily as a sign of his victory in a long and unequal fight with the state for the right to free expression and not as an honorary title of personal merit." Pasternak's refusal of the Nobel Prize was less a manifestation of momentary weakness than a carefully thought-out reaction to what had happened and what might occur, according to Fleishman. The Writers' Union voted to exile Pasternak, which led to his letter at the end of October to Khrushchev in which he stated: "I am tied to Russia by birth, by life, and by work. I cannot imagine my fate separated from and outside Russia."[66] Pasternak was finally allowed to remain in the Soviet Union and had the right to do translations. But his intense bitterness is expressed in a poem entitled "The Nobel Prize":

What vile thing have I done?
Am I a murderer and scoundrel?
I have made the whole world weep
Over the beauty of my land.[67]

It is difficult to trace Akhmatova's relationship with Pasternak after the war, since no letters are available from this period, and Chukovskaya did not see her again until 1952, when she resumed noting down their conversations. Although there are some notes in the archives indicating that Akhmatova intended to write her memoirs of Pasternak, she never set down more than a few lines. However, Pasternak's son and daughter-in-law, Yevgeny and Yelena Pasternak, have indicated that Pasternak and Akhmatova were close and that Pasternak was always there for her—and Mandelstam as well—when they needed him most.[68] An example occurred in 1948. Lev Gornung wrote in his diary on June 27, 1948, that he had seen Pasternak, who told him that he could get 3,000 rubles for Akhmatova from the *Litfond* (State Literary Fund), but she would have to make an application, which she refused to do. Pasternak then phoned the Communist Party Central Committee and the Union of Writers, and it was decided to aid her without an application. It was also recommended that Moscow publishers give her translating work.[69]

Lev Ozerov, who has written many important articles on Akhmatova, recently published his notes of his meetings with her. He describes one time when he could tell she was speaking on the phone to Pasternak. The conversation was clearly related to Ivinskaya. "You, Boris Leonidovich, with pleasure. I will receive you any time. Especially since there are many good reasons for conversation. But [a visit] from your companion, please . . ." She then put down the receiver and said to Ozerov: "Can you guess who we're speaking about? . . . She will be the end of him. Adventuress! Everyone understands this except Boris."[70]

Nina Olshevskaya says that whenever Pasternak was feeling bad or had quarreled with his wife, he went to Leningrad and stayed with Akhmatova. He would lay his coat on the floor and spend the night there, and Akhmatova would not disturb him. In fact, in a startling revelation, Akhmatova told Chukovskaya that Pasternak had even proposed to her many times, indicating an important aspect of Akhmatova's life—Pasternak's romantic attachment to her—that may remain a mystery because there is so little evidence available.[71]

Akhmatova told Chukovskaya,

> Boris never understood women. . . . He has no luck with them. The first, Yevgenia, was sweet and intelligent, but, but, but . . . she imagined she was a great artist, and because of this, Boris had to cook soup for the entire family; Zina is a dragon on eight paws, crude, vulgar, the embodiment of anti-art; when he got together with her, Boris stopped writing poetry, but at least she raised his son and is generally a decent woman. But a thief like Olga. . . . He proposed to me three times. . . . But I didn't want him at all. No, not here, but in Leningrad; with particular insistence when he had returned from abroad after the anti-Fascist meeting. I was married then to Punin, but this did not bother Boris at all. And he had an affair with Marina [Tsvetayeva] abroad.[72]

In 1956 Akhmatova told Chukovskaya that she believed Pasternak had read few of her poems before 1940, when he sent her his letter praising *From Six Books*. In his autobiography *Safe Conduct* (1931), Pasternak notes how in 1915 he was struck by a collection of Akhmatova's works, which he thinks is *Plantain*, although it had to be either *Evening* or *Rosary*, since *Plantain* had not yet been published. He praises Akhmatova's simplicity and sense of reality, but makes no comment whatsoever on the influence she had on his work, which he had noted in his letter to her in 1940. He devotes an enormous amount of space, however, to Marina Tsvetayeva, saying that for a long time he did not appreciate her properly, and continuing, "I underestimated many others in a variety of ways: Bagritsky, Khlebnikov, Mandelstam, Gumilyov." Yet he does not mention Akhmatova in this list, nor does he mention any of her later works or their friendship.[73] Chukovskaya understood it was not so much the confusion of *Plantain* and an earlier collection that upset Akhmatova, "though that was typical." But "*In Lieu of a Preface* as a whole is perceived as a history of the poetry of the twentieth century, and in the history Akhmatova hardly exists for the author. Only one confused paragraph is devoted to her, while whole pages, for example, are given over to Marina Tsvetayeva."[74]

Although she sometimes got upset with Pasternak because of episodes like this, Akhmatova's admiration for him was revealed to Chukovskaya in a conversation recorded on December 31, 1952. Akhmatova commented on how handsome Pasternak had become: "Pale, handsome, the head of a nobleman." Although she had complained about his Shakespeare translations elsewhere, she told Chukovskaya that his translation of the history plays was remarkable and his version of *Macbeth* quite precise. But she was unhappy with Pasternak's famous translation of Goethe's *Faust:*

> It varies. The beginning where the angels are singing is better than in Goethe! But sometimes Margarita is more vulgar than necessary. In Goethe she is a young girl. Looking at the jewels, she says: "Ah, how much they are worth. And we are so poor." In Pasternak this passage is not as naive; it sounds much more adult. But further on it is more precise, and again he succeeds in conveying Margarita-the-maid.[75]

Pasternak's love and respect for Akhmatova at this time is reflected in the inscription on the two-volume translation of Shakespeare which he gave her. "To Anna Andreyevna Akhmatova, the acme of refinement and polish, to one who has always encouraged me and given me joy, to one who is close and kindred to me and one who is higher and greater than me. B. Pasternak. May 10, 1952."[76]

A few years later, on January 20, 1954, Chukovskaya asked Akhmatova about Pasternak, whom she had not seen for a long time. Akhmatova said she adored him. The following passage shows just how much affection Akhmatova had for her friend of so many years—years that had been so difficult for both of them:

> Well, he's unbearable. He rushed in yesterday to explain to me that he's a nonentity. And what did that mean? I said to him, "Dear friend, calm down, even if you have not written anything for the past ten years, you are still one of the greatest poets in the twentieth century in Europe." What did he look like? He's an old man, but a handsome old man. Thick gray hair, intelligent eyes full of life. A lovely old age. I don't like these youngish old men: you don't know whether they're thirty-five or eighty-five. . . . I've been told to dye my hair. I don't want to. Now they give me a seat in the bus because of my gray hair, and if I would dye it they'd say, "Hey, stand up, lady!"[77]

On May 8, Chukovskaya recorded the overwhelming feeling she had when she was in the presence of both of these remarkable poets for the first time. Pasternak no longer appeared to be the "youthful older man" Akhmatova had described a few months before:

> In the presence of both of them I looked at the world as if I were on a new planet. The room: a little table covered with a torn tablecloth, a trunk on a chair, an ottoman which was not really a proper ottoman, but

a pillow with a gray blanket on it, a student's lamp on the little table, outside the window, bare branches. And the two of them. And the flow of time could be felt keenly, as if it had settled down there today, in this little room. And I was also there—and should have left, but it was difficult to leave. The room was too small for his voice, stormy and rumbling. The same voice as before, but he was no longer the same as before. I had not seen him for a long time. While before he had been enthusiastic, there was now an air of suffering about him.[78]

She cites lines from his poem "August":

Then my former voice prophetically
Rang out, untouched by disintegration . . .

The voice was as before, untouched, but he had been touched—perhaps by sickness, by grief. And his new look touched Chukovskaya's heart. What she saw was not the strength of old age, but an exhausted old man, whose movements until recently had seemed so youthful and were now somehow inappropriate. And his tormented eyes were horrible. He was upset by an evening he had gone to devoted to Hungarian poetry that had been arranged somewhere difficult to reach, on purpose, so no one would go. He spoke of an evening of *Faust* at the Union of Writers, where he had begun to cry while he read a scene between Faust and Margarita. And he spoke of many other things that Chukovskaya did not remember, because she was so overwhelmed by the exhaustion and suffering reflected in Pasternak's eyes.

However, by 1956 the relationship between Akhmatova and Pasternak was beginning to show signs of stress. On August 23, Akhmatova told Chukovskaya that she had just been to see Pasternak, which made Chukovskaya happy, since she knew Akhmatova had not seen him for a while.

No, no, don't be so happy, Lydia Korneyevna! The friendship will not last! Someone sent him to see me on business. . . . He's dazzling: a dark blue peacoat, white pants, thick gray hair, slender face, no swelling, and a well-made jaw. . . . He wrote fifteen new poems. Did he read them? Of course not. The time has passed when he would rush to me with every new four-liner. . . . This is how he told me about his new poems: "I told them at Goslit [the publishers] that I need more money." You can guess, of course, what the problem is? Olga demands as much as Zina. They suggested he write some new poems so the volume does not end with the ones from *Zhivago*. . . . Well, so he wrote them: fifteen new poems. I got so angry I shouted with the shrill voice of an old peasant: "What a great fortune for Russian culture, Boris Leonidovich, that you need extra money!"

Akhmatova's tirade hurt Chukovskaya, because she wanted them to love each other. Akhmatova then showed why she was upset. "I sent him my little book with the inscription, 'To the first poet of Russia.' I gave him a copy of *Poem* [*Without a Hero*] . . . he told me: 'I lost it somewhere. . . . Someone must have taken it. . . .' That was his response. You understand, of course, who stole it?" (She meant Olga Ivinskaya.)[79]

Pasternak told Akhmatova in 1957 that his novel would be published in the Soviet Union by Goslit. On January 3, 1957, Chukovskaya went to see her. Akhmatova had eaten lunch at Pasternak's, and he had told her the news. A contract had been signed, and Pasternak told Akhmatova he was happy. But as Chukovskaya put it, again there was a "black cat" between them. It was something petty, something he had said offhandedly, "I think you have such a book—*Evening?*" (meaning the key work in her career). This only reconfirmed in Akhmatova's eyes that for Pasternak, she had never grown beyond her first early book. She asked Chukovskaya what would have happened if she had asked him, "I think you have such a book—*Above the Barriers?* He would pretend not to know me, would stop saying hello to me on the street, I assure you. . . . He writes that *Plantain* was lying on his table on the eve of the war. But *Plantain* came out in 1921." Pasternak had also asked her to receive Olga Ivinskaya. "Can you believe it? And it's not the first time. I kept quiet and pretended I was deaf."[80]

On December 4, 1957, Akhmatova told Chukovskaya she had read *Zhivago* through to the end. There were pages which she found totally unprofessional and she even suggested they had been written by Ivinskaya. "Don't laugh. I'm speaking seriously. As you know, Lydia Korneyevna, I've never had any editor's experience, but here I feel like grabbing a pencil and crossing out page after page. But in this novel there are landscapes. . . . I sincerely assure you there's nothing in Russian literature equal to them. Not in Turgenev or in Tolstoy or in anyone else. They're brilliant."[81]

When Akhmatova's friend Nadezhda Rykova asked her if she had read the novel, Akhmatova replied that Pasternak had sent her a copy of the manuscript when she lay in the hospital with a heart attack in Moscow. It was not a question of whether she liked it or not. She found many pages that were remarkable, pure poetry, especially the descriptions of emotions and of nature. The problem was that Pasternak did not think this was very important. Instead, in this book he wanted to be some kind of "teacher of life," a prophet, an apostle, and in Akhmatova's opinion, he did not succeed. And there was a good reason why the best thing in the novel was the addendum—the poems of Zhivago. Here, Akhmatova believed, Pasternak had achieved poetic perfection:

I consider it a misfortune for Russian literature that some of its most famous figures in old age begin to imagine themselves as teachers of the truth, called upon to preach the truth and show the way. When Gumilyov was young and we were man and wife, he once said to me: "You know, if I live to old age and suddenly decide I've been summoned to lead the people to a bright future, you must quietly poison me." Unfortunately he did not live to old age.[82]

On April 22, 1958, Chukovskaya interrupts her diary on Akhmatova, and beginning with this date, until November 26, 1958, her entries concentrate on Pasternak, although they include conversations with Akhmatova. She provides an invaluable account of Pasternak's ordeal at this time, calling the week in October 1958 Pasternak's "Passion Week." Chukovskaya went to see Pasternak on October 28 to tell him the news—he had been expelled from the Union of Writers of the USSR on October 27. He said, as she walked in, "Expelled?" She nodded. He had not yet received any mail or newspaper. He told her he could not understand why people made such a fuss over his poetry. The only thing he had done that was really important, he said, was this novel. After she returned home, Chukovskaya received a call from Akhmatova, who was staying with the Ardovs. The next day Chukovskaya took a taxi to see Akhmatova. The taxi driver said to her: "Have you read, comrade? Some writer—Paster I think is his name—sold out to foreign enemies and wrote a book that shows how much he hates the Soviet people. He got a million dollars for it. He eats our bread and then plays dirty tricks on us. Here, in the newspaper." And he handed Chukovskaya a copy of *Pravda*.[83]

Akhmatova had summoned Chukovskaya to find out how he was, thinking she might have heard something while she was in Peredelkino, but she never imagined that Chukovskaya had actually seen him. Chukovskaya conveyed Pasternak's every word, every gesture, to Akhmatova. Akhmatova then spoke again about why she thought the novel was a failure. "Boris lost himself in it. That's why the novel is bad, except for the landscapes. Speaking frankly, this is a Gogolian failure—the second volume of *Dead Souls* [where Gogol begins to preach]. . . . Because of this he has put the people very close to him, as well as his friends, in such a horribly difficult position."[84]

Chukovskaya had not attended the meeting on October 31, 1958, of the Moscow Union of Writers when they decided to expel Pasternak from the Soviet Union. She told Akhmatova on November 8 she felt she was a traitor and would feel so until she died, although she had gone to the meeting because she was afraid for her father's health: Korney Chukovsky was old and sick, and he was extremely upset about what was happening to Pasternak. Chukovskaya wished she had gone and had the courage to shout something at the meeting. Akhmatova comforted her, replying that this would only have made her father worse. Then she went on, "You did a great deed. Yes, I'm not joking. You went to see Boris Leonidovich and were with him on a day when, I'm sure, not a single other person went to see him, when everyone was running away from him like the plague." At this point Chukovskaya began to cry; it was all too much for her.[85]

However, Olga Ivinskaya's desire to see Akhmatova continued to be a source of dissension between her and Pasternak. On November 26, Akhmatova told Chukovskaya that Pasternak had called her. She was bitter. She had been happy to hear from him, but then he said: "In Leningrad this summer a woman very close to me and her daughter came to visit. But she was not allowed to see you without a letter from me!" Akhmatova said angrily, "Of course, he was speaking of Olga. He called me on her instigation. But I maintained the border to the castle. I do not wish to meet with this bandit." However, she said she intended to go with Nina Olshevskaya to see him at his dacha. "This will be a visit of condolence, but without any expression of condolence. I'll have the taxi wait and will stay for half an hour. No longer. Not a word about his problem—you can talk about the weather, nature, whatever you wish. If he is not at home, I will leave him a note, like you, and that's it." Chukovskaya felt sad that Akhmatova should be angry with him. This was not the time for anger.[86]

On December 7, 1958, Chukovskaya recorded another conversation about Pasternak. One must remember what Akhmatova went through when she was expelled from the Union of Writers in 1946. She did not write any letter of apology, and her ration card was taken away. It was only because of the compassion of friends, including Pasternak, and unknown admirers, that she had enough to eat, although she was allowed to retain her small room in the communal apartment with the Punins. Later she was forced to move. She points out that in comparison to what she went through, the situation with Pasternak was a "battle of butterflies":

> The kind old woman Moscow made it appear as if the Swedish king had sent our government a telegram with a request not to take the "lodging at Peredelkino" away from Pasternak. Of course, this is nonsense. But if it were, he is not a king but a fool: where was he when they evicted me from the Sheremetev Palace? He didn't say a single word! And really, in comparison with what they did with me and Zoshchenko, the story of Boris is—a battle of butterflies![87]

This upset Chukovskaya, who thought to herself, "And in comparison with what they did to Mandelstam . . . the story of Akhmatova and Zoshchenko is—a battle of butterflies." However, Chukovskaya admitted that in comparison to Pasternak, Akhmatova's torment was incomparable because Lev had been sent to a camp, while Boris's sons, thank God, were at home. And Akhmatova was a pauper, while Pasternak was rich. But she felt the comparison was absolutely unnecessary. What purpose was there, Chukovskaya said, in calculating who suffered the most?

Another incident occurred at the thirtieth-birthday party of Vyacheslav Ivanov, the brilliant young scholar whose father was the writer Vsevolod Ivanov, and who lived next door to the Pasternaks in Peredelkino. On September 12, 1959, Chukovskaya saw Akhmatova, who told her about the party and Pasternak:

He no longer knows how to behave. I was at Koma's [Vyacheslav Ivanov] party. There was Boris and his wife. On a piece of paper it was written he was to sit next to me. No, he sat in another place. It was absolutely indecent. It was Koma's party, and Boris spoke the whole time only about himself, about the letters he was receiving. Well, was this right? . . . Then for a long time, in a totally boring way, he played the coquette when they asked him to read. After I read, he asked me, shouting across the whole table: "What do you do with your poetry? Pass it around to your friends?" Shostakovich visited me at Komarovo. I looked at him and thought: he carries his fame like a hunchback, used to it from birth. But Boris—like a crown which just fell down over his eyes, and he shoves it back in place with his elbow.[88]

On May 22, 1960, Akhmatova was taken to a hospital in an ambulance, then transferred to the Botkin Hospital four days later, where she was under the supervision of the famous cardiologist, Boris Votchal. At this time Pasternak was dying of cancer. Akhmatova's recovery was slow. But when Chukovskaya came to see her, she wanted to know about Pasternak, and Chukovskaya told her the truth.

Pasternak died on May 30. When Chukovskaya learned of Pasternak's death, she first had to break the news to her father, who had known him for so long and had been a good friend. His hands began to tremble and he broke out in a dry sobbing without tears. He wanted to be alone. The Union of Writers told Pasternak's wife they would take care of the funeral, but she refused. When Chukovskaya went to his home on June 1, Pasternak was lying in a coffin surrounded by flowers on a table. His face was peaceful, as if he had relaxed from great torment.

The day after Pasternak's death, Vitaly Vilenkin went to the hospital to see Akhmatova and prepare her for the blow. Maria Petrovykh, the poet and close friend of Akhmatova, took on the burden of actually telling her.

Shortly before Pasternak's death, Vilenkin had suddenly heard the phone ringing at one in the morning. When he picked up the receiver, he heard Akhmatova's voice: "I wanted to tell you in particular. I was at Peredelkino." She had gone to see Pasternak, and told Vilenkin she had the feeling there had been a reconciliation between the two of them. She had not been allowed into the room to see him, but he was told she was nearby. "I'm happy I went to see him. It was awful. He was so tormented. Our poor Borisik . . ." She used that pet name only rarely when she spoke of him.

For a long time it was difficult for Akhmatova to shed the tears that were often welling up inside her. She envied those who could cry easily. But when she was told about Pasternak's death, her eyes were full of tears, and Maria Petrovykh told Vilenkin she would never forget this.[89]

Chukovskaya describes the funeral: the grief, exhaustion, intense heat, the plainclothes detectives and police. While the coffin was still on the table, Maria Yudina played from morning on, and Svyatoslav Richter came shortly before the

coffin was taken out and played Bach. The coffin was carried in silence to the cemetery. Bareheaded men and women in scarves stood along the fences as they passed.

Chukovskaya said that at first Akhmatova was full of grief. There was no
room for any other feeling. But when Chukovskaya went to see her on June 20,
the initial shock was over, and Akhmatova again spoke about Pasternak with both
love and irritation, as in the past.

> For days I've been arguing with one of my friends about Pasternak. Just
> imagine, he said Boris Leonidovich was a martyr, persecuted, etc. What
> nonsense! Boris Leonidovich was an unusually happy man. First of all,
> by nature happy from birth: he loved nature so passionately, he found
> so much joy in it! Secondly, how was he persecuted? When? What per-
> secution? Everything was always published, if not here—then abroad. If
> something was not printed here or there—he gave his poems to two or
> three admirers and immediately they were distributed by hand. Where is
> the persecution? There was always money. His sons, thank God, are fine.
> (She crossed herself.) If you compare his with other fates: Mandel-
> stam's . . . Tsvetayeva's—whomever you take, Pasternak's fate was happy.[90]

Chukovskaya did not agree. Born in comfortable circumstances, happy by nature,
Pasternak learned to feel another's pain. Here was a man created for happiness.
Yet this is what he wrote at the end:

> Soul of mine, lamenter,
> For all in my circle,
> You became a burial vault
> Of those tormented by life.[91]

His sons were not imprisoned in camps, said Chukovskaya, but he helped those
who did have sons in camps and generously shared his money with Akhmatova
when she was in trouble. Pasternak's suffering was great enough that he died of
it. Everyone has a different power of endurance. Pasternak was meant to live for
a hundred years, but he died when he was seventy. And he did not die, but was
driven into his grave. At sixty he was active, capable of work, as amorous as a
young man, and within ten years he died of cancer.

Chukovskaya said all this to Akhmatova, who did not say a word. Then,
suddenly, Akhmatova handed her a piece of paper, saying a friend had brought
her a poem she had written to Pasternak in 1949 (although it is dated in her
collections as 1947), when the newspapers began to criticize him.[92]

> And once more the autumn blasts like Tamerlane
> There is silence in the streets of Arbat.

Beyond the little station or beyond the haze
The impassable road is dark.

So here it is, the latest one! And the rage
Subsides. It's as if the world had gone deaf . . .
A mighty, evangelical old age
And that most bitter Gethsemane sigh.

(II, p. 307)

Chukovskaya thought to herself, "But the Gethsemane sigh—this is the sigh before Golgotha. Why is she arguing with me? It means she understood his torment, and more than understood it—she predicted it."

Vilenkin commented that in spite of all Akhmatova's reproaches and the often unjust things she said about Pasternak, no other poet accompanied someone on his last journey with such bitter sighs when he died.[93]

I

Yesterday the inimitable voice fell silent,
And he who conversed with the groves abandoned us.
He became a life-giving ear of grain
Or the first rain of which he sang.
And all the flowers in the world
Bloomed to greet this death.
But suddenly it became quiet on the planet
Bearing the humble name of . . . Earth.

(II, p. 308)

II

Like the little daughter of blind Oedipus,
The Muse led the prophet toward death.
And a single frenzied linden tree
Blossomed in this funereal May—
Opposite the window, where once
He revealed to me that before him
Wound a path, winged and golden,
Where he would be protected by the will of the Most High.

June 11, 1960
Botkin Hospital,
Moscow
(II, p. 309)

The Gay Little Sinner Repents:
Poem Without a Hero

I dedicate this poem to the memory of its first audience—my friends and fellow citizens who perished in Leningrad during the siege.
     —Akhmatova (II, p. 399)

At the Twenty-Second Congress of the Communist Party in October 1961, Khrushchev finally denounced Stalin as a murderer who had violated Lenin's principles. Stalin's remains were then removed from Lenin's mausoleum and relegated to the Kremlin wall, and the city of Stalingrad was renamed. This opened the way for a new thaw in Soviet cultural affairs. There was a feeling of euphoria when Alexander Solzhenitsyn's work *One Day in the Life of Ivan Denisovich* was published in the 1962 issue of *Novyi mir,* but this was soon followed by regulations warning the intelligentsia not to go too far in their criticism of the regime. The fear and suspicion in the government about the possible results of loosening restrictions on its citizens was evident. In 1963, a series of conferences between Party leaders and intellectuals took place. One occurred in March, when Khrushchev addressed a group of writers, reminding them that they were to continue to remain loyal to communism and to depict it as a superior way of life. Many of the writers at the meeting were chastised. Ilya Ehrenburg, who had written *The Thaw* at the beginning of the Khrushchev era (1954), daring to complain that it was impossible for real art to flourish under Soviet conditions, was reprimanded for his memoirs, *Men, Years, Life,* which was criticized for representing life in gloomy colors. Khrushchev's policy toward the intellectuals did not remain in force long, for on October 15, 1964, he stepped down from power. On that day there was an official announcement that at a meeting of the Central Committee of the Communist Party, Khrushchev had requested to be relieved of his duties because of ill health, and Leonid Brezhnev became the new head of state. The Brezhnev era, which lasted from 1964 until 1982, was characterized by similar swings of policy between reform and repression to those that had marked the Khrushchev era. In foreign policy it was the time of the suppression of the "Prague Spring" in 1968, when Czechoslovakia attempted to become more independent of the Soviet regime, and of the crushing of protests in Poland in 1970 and 1980. In the intellectual world, dissent became stronger and punishment soon followed. These were the years of the trials and later expulsion of Joseph Brodsky, Andrey Sinyavsky, and Yuli Daniel (the second two publishing abroad under pseudonyms: Abram Tertz and Nikolay Arzhak, respectively), the expulsion in 1973 of Solzhenitsyn after he had published more works clearly antagonistic to the Soviet regime; and the exile of Andrey Sakharov, the outspoken internationally renowned physicist, to the city of Gorky.[1]

These were also the last years of Akhmatova's life, and while she sympathized and as always felt deeply the suffering of others, for her they were years of recognition as a great poet by her own nation and abroad. New friends appeared who played an important role in her life—among them Lev Kopelev and his wife Raisa Orlova. Kopelev is a specialist in German studies, who spent time in a Russian prison camp after the war. He was released in 1956 and returned to Moscow, where he taught at the university. His wife Raisa was a literary scholar, who was active in the Union of Writers.[2]

In their touching and beautifully written memoirs on Akhmatova, Kopelev and Orlova each describe how they came to know her. Kopelev had read the works of Akhmatova when he was fifteen, and imagined her as a stylishly dressed lady in a large hat, with a terrifying beauty. Many years later, during World War II, he read her poem "Courage." Kopelev was in a Russian prison camp after the war when he learned of the 1946 Regulation against Akhmatova and Zoshchenko and their expulsion from the Union of Writers. He could not understand why this had happened, after Russia's victory.[3]

Orlova first heard of Akhmatova's poetry in 1935 from a friend, but only actually looked at her books fifteen years later; like so many others she concentrated on Akhmatova's love poetry, and assumed that Akhmatova could never surpass Alexander Blok in this genre. Then in the mid-1950s the full range of Akhmatova's poetry and her fate began slowly but inevitably to fill Orlova's life.

Kopelev first met Akhmatova in May 1962, when Nadezhda Mandelstam brought him to the Ardovs'. Akhmatova was in a lilac dress, looking quite magnificent. Normally very expansive and not a shy man, Kopelev was absolutely mute. Akhmatova began reciting her *Requiem*. As she read, he could not take his eyes off her, and gradually lost his shyness. Although Akhmatova was used to this reaction to her poem, Kopelev said she was still very pleased by it and needed every new listener. Her voice was calm, tragically peaceful. Kopelev was soon overcome by emotion. Because she would not allow him to write the poems down, he was grateful that she recited them again so he could try to memorize them. Suddenly she became transformed in his eyes into a queen. What captivated him was her unpretentious simplicity, her lack of any attempt to assert herself in any way. When she asked if he liked the poems, he replied that if she had written nothing but these works, she would be the greatest poet of their time. She did not even smile at this, and he understood that for her any praise would be redundant.

Kopelev memorized fragments of *Requiem* and recited them to Raisa when he returned home, who promptly memorized them as well. They were friends of Lydia Chukovskaya, and once when they were all sitting in the little garden of their courtyard, Raisa began to recite *Requiem*. Chukovskaya seems to have resented their having been let in on this secret, the poem she had kept in her head for so many years. She said, "We—I think there were ten of us—have kept quiet about this for more than twenty years." Raisa said she thought she even caught a note of displeasure that a stranger had been let into the secret of the "chosen."

On May 20, 1962, Chukovskaya introduced Raisa to Akhmatova, because Akhmatova hoped Raisa could help in the attack on her friend Emma Gershtein. At that time Raisa was secretary of the Criticism section of the Union of Writers. Gershtein had been attacked in the journal *Oktyabr* for an article about Pushkin's death, which was always a problematic subject to the regime in power, since Pushkin had become symbolic of the poet's struggle for freedom against the state. Raisa promised to do what she could to defend Gershtein. Chukovskaya told Akhmatova that Raisa's husband had recently met and had fallen in love with Akhmatova, and Raisa had begun to look on her as a rival. Without the shadow of a smile, Akhmatova said grandly, "I understand. We women are always like that."

Akhmatova spoke about *Poem Without a Hero*: Alexander Tvardovsky was considering publishing fragments from it in *Novyi mir*. Akhmatova told Raisa that it was extremely important for her to find someone who did not know the work so that it could be read with new eyes. She had not found any such person in Moscow or Leningrad. Later Akhmatova gave Raisa a manuscript version and Raisa became that person "with new eyes."

Kopelev tells how, in the summer of 1962, Solzhenitsyn came to their dacha in Zhukov and asked about Akhmatova. When he found out they had a copy of *Poem Without a Hero,* he began to copy it down. He soon met Akhmatova herself. At the end of October, Chukovskaya records in her diary that Akhmatova was very excited about meeting this new author. Chukovskaya had come to visit Akhmatova, who was staying with Maria Petrovykh, and was met by her in the hall.

Akhmatova immediately began to talk about Solzhenitsyn. Kopelev had introduced him to her. "A bearer of light!" she said solemnly. "And very special—fresh, cheerful, young, happy. We've forgotten that such people exist. Eyes like precious stones. Serious, listens to what he's saying." Chukovskaya says that when Akhmatova said of someone that he was careful in expressing his thoughts, this was a great compliment. Akhmatova had been quite overwhelmed by Solzhenitsyn and made it clear how much she valued his prose; but she also was honest about her misgivings over his poetry, which caused problems between her and this oversensitive young author. Chukovskaya quotes the conversation:

> I read to him. . . . He said: "I thought so, that you are not silent, that you are writing something that is impossible to print." He knows the *Poem Without a Hero* by heart. This is what he said about it: "At first everything was incomprehensible, but then the incomprehensible became comprehensible." . . . He read me his poems. I still can't make them out. He reads very strangely. . . . They are weak. . . . I told him: "You know that in a month you will be the most famous person on earth?" "I know. But this will not be for long." "Can you endure fame?" "I have very strong nerves. I endured the Stalin camps." "Pasternak could not endure fame. It is very difficult to endure fame, especially late fame." Oh, Lydia Korneyevna, you should have seen this person. He is unimaginable. You have to see him for yourself, not just read *One Day*. . . ."[4]

Akhmatova also spoke to Kopelev: "A Viking came in. And totally unexpectedly, and young and kind. Amazing eyes. I said to him: 'I want two hundred million people to read your story.' I think he agreed." Soon after he had seen her, Solzhenitsyn came to see Kopelev and Orlova. He asked Kopelev who he considered the greatest contemporary Russian poet. Kopelev mentioned Akhmatova, Tsvetayeva, Pasternak, and from a later generation, Tvardovsky and Samoilov. Solzhenitsyn replied, "But for me there is only Akhmatova. She is unique—magnificent. Pasternak has some good poems—from the last evangelical ones. . . . But generally he is too artificial. . . . I am convinced she [Akhmatova] is the greatest." Akhmatova also told Kopelev of her reservations about Solzhenitsyn's poetry. They were sentimental love poems, she said, that resembled the works of the nineteenth-century Russian poet Semyon Nadson. Perhaps in reaction to Akhmatova's remarks, Solzhenitsyn criticized the poems in *Requiem*. He spoke to Kopelev about this:

> I listened to the whole thing. Very attentively. Some poems she read again. Of course, the poems are good. Beautiful. Resonant. But really, the nation suffered, tens of millions, and here are poems about one single case, about one single mother and son. . . . I told her that it is the duty of a Russian poet to write about the suffering of Russia, to rise above

personal grief and tell about the suffering of the nation. . . . She thought
it over. Perhaps she didn't like this—she is used to praise, to flattery.
But she is a great poet. And the theme is very imposing.[5]

When she reported Solzhenitsyn's comment to Chukovskaya, Akhmatova pointed
out that Ivan Denisovich was also only one individual case, but he stood for the
suffering of millions. Kopelev tried to argue with Solzhenitsyn, but it was hopeless.
Solzhenitsyn never saw Akhmatova again, and Kopelev and Orlova never spoke
about him to her.

Kopelev was amazed at how interested Akhmatova was in everything that
was going on in Moscow—how Yevgeny Yevtushenko and Andrey Voznesensky
were behaving, what kind of work the modern sculptor Ernst Neizvestny was
showing, and why they were attacking Kopelev for "abstract humanism." Akhmatova found the rhetorical, dramatically exaggerated readings of Yevtushenko
and Voznesensky to a stadium of thousands of admirers very alien. She continually
contrasted them with Brodsky, who, she believed, wrote a deeper, more philosophical kind of poetry, without the theatrical effects that, she believed, were
typical of these other poets.[6]

In the last years of her life, Akhmatova received visits from foreigners—poets
and admirers of Russian poetry. Robert Frost traveled to Russia in September
1963 and came to Komarovo to see Akhmatova. He was accompanied by the
noted scholar and translator of Russian literature F. D. Reeve and Mikhail Alekseyev, a Soviet literary scholar and specialist in Pushkin. Alekseyev toasted Frost
and Akhmatova, and said he considered this meeting one of the greatest literary
events of the time: each was a leading poet of their country, of an entire national
literary culture and tradition. They ate a seven-course dinner, and the conversation
turned first to American and English writers, then to the Greek and Roman
classics. Asked to recite a poem, Akhmatova chose "The Last Rose," which she
said referred to "four powerful, passionate women from world history who directed their passion to serve the integrity of the nation in which they had trans-
cendent faith":[7]

The Last Rose

> *You will write about us on a slant.*
> —Joseph Brodsky

I have to bow with Morozova,
Dance with Herod's stepdaughter,
Fly up with the smoke of Dido's fire,
Only to return to Joan of Arc's pyre.

Lord! You see I am tired
Of living, and dying and resurrection.

> Take everything, but grant that I may feel
> The freshness of this crimson rose again.
>
> (II, p. 317)[8]

The noblewoman Morozova was persecuted for her resistance to religious reforms in the seventeenth century. In reading these lines, Russians recall the famous painting by V. I. Surikov (1887) of Morozova being dragged off on a sled to exile. Morozova symbolizes the resistance not only of women, but of a great historical figure who resisted the pressure of the state. Joan of Arc similarly is a martyr who fought against political authority and died for her religion and her people. The other two women endured *Liebestod*—death caused by love. Dido, the proud queen of Carthage, was abandoned by her lover Aeneas, who left her to fulfill his destiny, the founding of Rome. In despair, Dido committed suicide and was burned on a pyre. Salome loved John the Baptist, who was destined to serve Christ and not participate in the joys or suffering of earthly love. In revenge, Salome performed her dance of the seven veils and was rewarded by Herod with the head of the man she wanted as her lover, who instead became a saint. "The whole group was so caught by the immediacy of the poem and by the life and understanding which it represented," Reeve says, "that for a few seconds we were silent, still. . . . Frost remembered this and he remembered Akhmatova's expression, for he commented later how grand she was but how sad she seemed to be."[9]

Akhmatova's version of this event, which she related to Orlova and Kopelev, is marked by her inimitable irony. The authorities would not allow her to receive Frost in her little cabin; instead, she was taken to the academician Mikhail Alekseyev's large dacha, which served, as Akhmatova put it, as a "Potyomkin village." (When Catherine the Great came to visit her lover Potyomkin's conquered lands in the Crimea, to impress the empress, whole villages were painted on flats that were seen from a distance as her coach rushed by. Ever since, such "false facades" have been known as "Potyomkin villages.")

> I still don't know where they got such a tablecloth and crystal. They combed my hair elegantly and dressed me up, since everything I had was old. Then the handsome Reeve, a young American Slavicist, came for me. . . . Everyone was already there, talking excitedly. And then the old man arrived. An American grandfather . . . red-faced, gray-haired, cheerful. We sat next to each other in wicker chairs. All kinds of food [was] served and wine was poured. We talked without rushing. And I kept thinking: "Here are you, my dear, a national poet. Every year your books are published. . . . They praise you in all the newspapers and journals, they teach you in the schools, the President receives you as an honored guest. And all they've done is slander me! Into what dirt they've trampled me! I've had everything—poverty, prison lines, fear, poems remembered only by heart, and burned poems. And humiliation and

grief. And you don't know anything about this and wouldn't be able to understand if I told you. . . . But now let's sit together, two old people, in wicker chairs. A single end awaits us. And perhaps the real difference is not actually so great?"[10]

Orlova was one of those who did know of Akhmatova's suffering and drew strength from it. In August 1963, Orlova had just experienced a difficult operation and was recovering in the hospital. She had become totally apathetic and refused to read or see anyone. Then Kopelev brought her a small volume of Akhmatova's poems, which became for Orlova a bridge back to the world. Later she wrote Akhmatova, telling her what those poems meant to her at this very difficult period in her life:

I have often thought about you, about your fate, an example of unusual, rare courage, but it is only now that I understand what is most impor-tant—you *know* that man is mortal. You know about human tragedy. You know both in the abstract-philosophical and most concrete earthly sense—you teach people how to live without covering their eyes (as I have lived). Before your poems seemed lovely but cold, lovely but marble, and only now—perhaps because I'm also suffering—I felt the red-hot lava that the artist captured. In Tsvetayeva's poetry, suffering pours over the edge, seizes the reader with pain and trembling. . . . But here suf-fering is overcome . . . and this is the reason for the great victory of the artist, a moral and aesthetic victory. This overcoming, this modest suf-fering, seems a very Russian feature, connected with nature, with birch trees, with the small, quiet rivers. One may object that an explosion of suffering in Dostoyevsky is also a special feature of Russians. But what you possess is not reconciliation, but the ability to endure. It is remaining oneself and not allowing anyone to crush you, not going to pieces in suffering but rising up again. Please forgive me for these disconnected thoughts—Again, thank you. I bow low before you for the fact that you exist, for everything that you have written and are writing now, lovely young poems. I see your portrait before me—not the one in the book, but my favorite, all in white, where the grand, usually happy woman is portrayed, the great poet—Olympian at the peak of glory, crowned by all imaginable laurels of the fatherland and from abroad, collections of works, etc. . . . The most important laurels, however, are in the readers' hearts—they really exist and are not illusions. Thank you, with the hope of seeing you soon—if you will allow it—we will come in November to Komarovo.

In reply, Orlova received a telegram: "Your letter brought comfort and aid in a difficult hour. I thank you. Yours, Akhmatova."[11]

Akhmatova and Irina Punina and her family were forced to move once again in June 1961 because of renovations on the building on Krasnaya Konnitsa Street. They were given rooms in a communal apartment at 34, Lenin Street (Apt. 23). Akhmatova thought the move temporary, but it turned out to be permanent. Her clothes and books in the new apartment got soaked because of flooding, and for a while she lived with her friends, the literary scholars Vladimir Admoni and his wife Tamara Silman. Akhmatova had become acquainted with Admoni at a meeting of the Commission on Alexander Blok at the end of the 1930s. They soon became friends and took walks together. At first Admoni would recite his own poetry to her, but soon she began to recite her new poems to him, including those in *Requiem*. He was overwhelmed by the power of these new verses, in which the poetic voice of the earlier Akhmatova—the poems that had excited him in his childhood—still resounded. She still possessed the proud and strange beauty of her youth, but also a beauty reflecting someone exhausted by suffering. They discussed Akhmatova's strong feelings about Tolstoy's *Anna Karenina*. Akhmatova protested vehemently against the attempt by Tolstoy to forbid freedom of feelings to his heroine, the right to determine one's own life. Admoni and Akhmatova continued to meet in Tashkent, and she read him *Poem Without a Hero*. She also became acquainted with his wife Tamara. At this time Admoni came to know those qualities often identified with her—an external calm, firmness in words and actions, but a feeling of inner anxiety and fear which she would reveal only to someone really close to her. But then, says Admoni, somewhere in the very depths of her soul, in spite of the fear, there was courage, a strength that overcame her insecurity. After they all returned to Leningrad they continued to be friends, and the Admonis went on seeing Akhmatova after she was expelled from the Union of Writers. When she had to move to her new apartment on Lenin Street and wait until her new room was no longer flooded, she went to stay with them. The Admonis were living in rooms in the former apartment of the composer Glazounov on Plekhanov Street. While she was there, she loved to hear Tamara read her translations of Rilke.[12]

Akhmatova's most important creative work during this period was on *Poem Without a Hero*. She was continually changing it and modifying it, adding and removing verses and images, writing a ballet version and then returning to the literary one. On June 30, 1955, Akhmatova went to Peredelkino to see Lydia Chukovskaya's father, Korney. Lydia soon understood that Akhmatova had come not because of the fresh air but exclusively for her poem: "Evidently in her tragic, tormented life, the Poem is the only ray of hope, the only illusion of happiness. She came to speak about the Poem, to hear praise about the Poem, to live for a time by her Poem. . . . She divided the world into two unequal parts . . . those who understood her poem and those who did not."[13]

Akhmatova had begun the work in 1940, the year so many of her poems turned toward the past. She continued to work on it during the war in Tashkent, but only finished it much later, in the 1960s. Akhmatova herself commented that Tashkent was a magical cradle for the poem; then toward the end of the war back in Leningrad, living in the House on the Fontanka amid the ruins of her city, she wrote the Epilogue, and continued refining and polishing "amid the little pines of Komarovo."[14]

Akhmatova attributes the origins of the work to the evening of February 25, 1917, when she was standing with her companion Boris Anrep on Nevsky Avenue after the dress rehearsal of Meyerhold's famous production of Lermontov's *Masquerade,* a work about Fate punishing pleasure seekers for their sins. However, the actual stimulus in 1940 for the torrent of memories associated with the year 1913 was various objects left behind by Olga Sudeikina for Akhmatova when Olga left for Paris in 1924, such as her portrait, porcelain candlesticks, and icons: "The Poem is a peculiar revolt of things. Olga's things, among which I had lived for a long time, suddenly assumed their place under the poetic sun. They came to life for a moment, as it were, but the sound that was left continued to vibrate over many long years."[15]

In one of her "Letters to N.N." (N.N. is the equivalent of "X" in English, and the reference is to letters chronicling her ideas, addressed to no one in particular, and stored in her trunk, along with all her other important manuscripts) she relates in more detail how the poem came into being:

In the autumn of 1940, while sorting out my old papers (which later perished during the siege), I came across some poems and letters which I had had for a long time but had not yet read. (The Devil made me rummage in the packing case.) They concerned the tragic events of 1913 that are related in *Poem Without a Hero.* I then wrote the verse fragment "To Russia you came out of nowhere." . . . During that sleepless night of December 26–27, this fragment unexpectedly started to grow and turn into the first sketch of *Poem Without a Hero.*[16]

At the opening of the work, entitled "In Place of a Foreword," she discusses the poetic process. The poem is not something she willed into being—it came crashing down upon her against her own volition. "I did not summon it. I was not even expecting it on that dark, cold day of my last winter in Leningrad." She goes on: "That night I wrote down two sections of Part One ('1913' and 'Dedication'). In the beginning of January, almost to my own surprise, I wrote "The Other Side of the Coin' and in Tashkent (in two tries) 'Epilogue,' which became the third part of the poem. I also made several substantial insertions into the first two parts."[17] In her "Prose About the Poem," written in March 1959, Akhmatova relates how the poem took on layers of meaning as she continued to insert passages reflecting thoughts at different periods of her life: "The rhythm born from these shock waves, abating at times, then rising again, accompanied me during periods of my life that were completely unlike. The Poem proved to be more capacious than I first thought. It imperceptibly assumed events and feelings from different layers of time, and now that I have finally rid myself of it, I see it as a complete and single entity."[18] Akhmatova, however, never really rid herself of this work. For several years she would continue to touch and retouch it, like a painter who is never satisfied with his greatest picture.

Arthur Lourie read the poem in America, where he had moved from Paris during the war, and was very excited by it. He realized that the various masquerade figures—Faust, Don Juan, Hamlet, the Iron Mask—were puppets that Olga had made and kept in special boxes that she took out when friends came over. He probably read it in the version that appeared in 1960 and 1961 in the émigré journal *Vozdushnye puti* (*Air Paths*), where he later published some measures of music for the poem.[19]

Poem Without a Hero must be examined in the context of other works written or begun in 1940 in order to appreciate its true significance. In his excellent study on Akhmatova's works of this period, Kees Verheul points out that

> The year 1940 forms an unequalled high point in the creative biography of the poet Akhmatova. Neither in an earlier nor in a later period do we find a moment at which her artistic powers reached such an intensity of concentration, surveying the private, historical, and literary past and creating almost all the forms that the poet will spend the rest of her years refining into the perfect embodiment of the basic themes of her artistic maturity.[20]

The return through memory to the past would be merely a personal reminiscence if any poem from this period were viewed in isolation, says Verheul. But seen in relation to the other works written at this time, these poems reveal a vision of a lost world of which the heroine has once been a part and to which she now looks back with a sense of shame. In her memoirs, Akhmatova talks about memory and the year 1940:

> My memory has become unbelievably sharp. The past has engulfed me and demands something. What? Dear genies of the remote past seem to speak with me. Perhaps this is their last chance, when bliss, which people call oblivion, may pass them by. Where do the words spoken half a century ago, and which I haven't recalled for over fifty years, come from?[21]

One poem from this period is "The Cellar of Memory" (January 18, 1940). Verheul interprets the original purpose of the speaker's return to the past, the descent, as a desire to recover a lost idyll of her youth. There is, however, another slightly different but related interpretation.

The Cellar of Memory

But it is pure nonsense, that I live grieving
And that reminiscence gnaws at me.

I don't often visit memory
And it always surprises me.
When I descend with a lamp to the cellar,
It seems to me—a landslide
Rumbles again on the narrow stairs.
The lamp smokes, I can't turn back,
And I know that I am going toward the enemy.
And I beg, as if for charity . . . But there
It is dark and quiet. Finished, my holiday!
It is already thirty years since they bid the ladies good-bye,
And that mischievous wag died of old age . . .
I am too late. What a misfortune!
I am forbidden to appear anywhere.
But I am touching the paintings on the walls,
And warming myself by the fireplace. How marvelous!
Through this mold, these fumes and slime,
Flashed two green emeralds,
And the cat mewed. Well, let's go home!

But where is my home and where is my reason?

(II, p. 125)

From the very beginning, memory is distinguished from "recall," as in stanza 14 of *Poem Without a Hero,* which reads:

> Between "remember" and "recall," friends,
>   The distance is like that between Luga
>   And the land of satin dominoes.

(II, p. 453)

Luga is near Petersburg, and "the land of satin dominoes" is Venice—the distance between them is great. To remember is an involuntary act: memories rush in, not just idyllic moments but many we would like to forget and hope never to have to confront. But to recall is a moral act, an act of will, because it forces us to face our former self, a self whose acts we may find it necessary to judge and condemn. Memory thereby becomes the agent of one's conscience.

In the first lines of "The Cellar of Memory," the poet confesses that she rarely visits memory, that is, rarely consciously attempts to recall the past. Moreover, reminiscence (i.e., her conscience) does not often "gnaw" at her. But when memories do return, the process is involuntary, it "surprises" her, and her subconscious then becomes transformed into the image of a cellar, which is also a telling sign—the memories are not in some high, bright place but somewhere dark below the surface, where we hide things we wish to forget, and the descent is not gradual but sudden, as memories surge through her brain. The visit is not to friends—it is a visit to hostile forces, to one's former self, to shades of the past who might once have been friends, as Kuzmin had been in Akhmatova's own past, but who are now alien figures threatening the heroine. "Thirty years since" would be 1910, the time of Tsarskoye Selo, the era of the frivolous upper classes and bohemian artists who displayed indifference to the sufferings of their con-temporaries—and the year of the "gay little sinner of Tsarskoye Selo," as Akh-matova calls herself in one of the poems in *Requiem.* She says, "I am forbidden to appear anywhere"—for many years Akhmatova had not recited nor had her poems been published. Any comfort this cellar may bring, such as the warmth of the fire, is soon dispelled by mold, the fumes and slime. The poet now wishes to go home, to forget again; but she has no refuge, no real home of her own, and metaphorically no place where her guilty memories can be laid to rest. In a typical line, the poet juxtaposes two seemingly unrelated images—her home and her reason—but within the context of the poem, home represents perhaps the more rational aspect of the mind as opposed to the irrational subconscious that has suddenly taken possession of her.

In *The Way of All Earth,* written in 1940, the heroine again attempts to "go home" to a more peaceful past, but a sly voice says that no matter how many attempts the poet makes she can never return: "And again you will strike/Against unyielding diamond," and advises her to go to the "paternal garden," that is, to give up and die, to go "the way of all earth." But the problem of the heroine facing her past is much more complex in *Poem Without a Hero,* and the ending more ambiguous. As in so many of her works, including the early lyrics, grief, suffering, and despair are resolved not by death but by overcoming and trans-forming what the poet herself has endured into poetry, thus giving others the voice they required to articulate what they too felt and experienced.

The recollection in *Poem Without a Hero* is of the year 1913, the culmination of the Silver Age, when many turned to a worship of beauty and pleasure for their own sake, or a form of religion that was a mixture of Nietzscheanism and strong sensuality that often seemed more like worship of the Devil than of God.

Nadezhda Mandelstam discusses the theme of memory in Akhmatova's works, and turns back to the poem "Lot's Wife," written in 1924. She says *Poem Without a Hero* is a last, backward glance at the "red tower" of the poet's "native Sodom"—a temptation hard to resist, even knowing the price she would pay. Mandelstam also posits the idea of memory in moral terms. For Akhmatova, at the time she wrote *Poem Without a Hero,* to forget was to commit a mortal sin: one remembers one's misdeeds, atones, and achieves redemption. As Mandelstam says: "We answer for everything, but there are many ways of trying not to. First is by deliberately not recalling something (as opposed to passively 'remembering it'). The first way of evading responsibility is not to recollect at all, the second is to embellish it, deceive oneself. . . . The operation can be performed on an individual life history or on the past of a whole nation."[22]

At the end of her life, Akhmatova told Anatoly Nayman: "The human memory is so organized that it works like a searchlight, illuminating certain objects but leaving impenetrable darkness all around them. Even someone with a magnificent memory can and should forget some things."[23] The human psyche cannot endure too much pain; it is too fragile. But in certain cases it is necessary to remember, for private memory is transformed into collective memory, forcing not just the individual but the whole nation to confront those dark parts of its past that it must never repeat again. Akhmatova contributes to that collective memory in what is considered by many to be her greatest work.

The Russian philosopher Berdyaev discussed the difference between remembering and recollecting when writing his autobiography. He says memory of the past is a creative, transforming memory, which does not merely reproduce passively, but selects. "In remembering the past, I consciously achieve the creative act of rethinking, giving meaning and comprehending, and transformation." And he mentions the consequences of believing in Nietzsche, whose ideas dominate many of the symbolic figures in the *Poem* who represent intellectuals from the turn of the century. Nietzsche "passionately, tormentedly, with unusual talent expressed the theme: how is an exalted state, heroism, ecstasy, possible if there is no God, if God is dead? But not only is God dead, it turns out man is dead as well, and the horrible image of the Superman arose."[24]

Poem Without a Hero is Akhmatova's rethinking of the past—her own individual past and the past of her generation, one of the most creative and complex epochs in Russian history. She attempts to give this period meaning and to comprehend her role in its context. Berdyaev says: "Time is the greatest metaphysical secret. . . . That is why it is so difficult to write about the past." But Akhmatova did write about the past and succeeded in creating one of the greatest works of the twentieth century.

In the poem, the author acts as a master of ceremonies, introducing the protagonists and commenting on the action. As Zhirmunsky observed, "The poet is both hero and author of the poem, contemporary and guilty along with the people of her generation but at the same time a judge pronouncing a verdict over them."[25]

Part One, entitled "The Year 1913: Petersburg Tale," opens with the poet sitting in the House on the Fontanka on New Year's Eve, 1940. After lighting ritual candles, and before the clock begins to strike midnight, shades from the year 1913, dressed in costume, including Don Juan and Faust, arrive uninvited. Suddenly lights flash, sirens howl, and the walls expand, transforming the poet's little room on the grounds of the Sheremetev Palace into the mirrored ballroom of the palace. In the Intermezzo, a scrap of conversation is overheard about going to the Stray Dog cabaret.

The second half takes place in the cabaret. A handsome young poet-soldier is in love with a beautiful actress from the Stray Dog, but she proves unfaithful. Later that evening she returns home with another lover. When the young officer— waiting across the street for her arrival—witnesses her infidelity, he commits suicide. The poem ends in 1942, when the poet addresses her beloved city of Leningrad, now in ruins, saying that she is inseparable from it: her shadow is on its walls, her reflection in its canals, the sound of her footsteps in the halls of the Hermitage.

In Part Two, entitled "The Other Side of the Coin," the author is reproached by her editor for making the work so obscure. There are also many references to the Silver Age and the period around 1940. Part Three is the Epilogue, which takes place in August 1942, after Leningrad has been bombed and the city is in ruins. She has a vision of the prisoners behind barbed wire in Siberia, including her "double"—her son Lev, or perhaps Mandelstam, or both. The poet then soars off in an airplane as she is evacuated to Central Asia, to the East. (Akhmatova herself actually left Leningrad at the end of September 1941 for Moscow, and then Central Asia.)

The plot is loosely based on reality. A young poet, Vsevolod Knyazev, once the lover of the poet Kuzmin, fell in love with Olga Sudeikina and wrote many passionate verses to her; but after being coldly rejected, he shot himself on April 5, 1913 (New Style), and died on April 7.[26] John Malmstad has traced the beginning and eventual disintegration of the homosexual relationship between Kuzmin and Knyazev. Knyazev was handsome, slender, with warm brown eyes and blond hair. His father was a professor, but he chose to go into the dragoons. Kuzmin devoted a cycle of poems, "Autumn May," to Knyazev in 1910. Their enforced separation due to Knyazev's military duty in Riga put a strain on their relationship. As Malmstad says, Kuzmin was "not a model of constancy," and dedicated cycles of verse to other men while his affair was going on with Knyazev. Knyazev was also a poet, albeit a mediocre one, and he composed poems to Kuzmin. In one of them he refers to Kuzmin as Antinous, the handsome lover of the Roman emperor Hadrian:

> And every moment, obedient, quiet,
>   I bow before the straight arrow like a slave;
> He will come, Antinous, so handsome, he will come,
>   But I am too weary, too mute to meet him . . .[27]

They wrote a mutual collection of poems in 1912 with the suggestive title *The Arrow's Prick*. Kuzmin made several trips to Riga to see Knyazev, but by autumn, the relationship had cooled. Kuzmin had moved out of Vyacheslav Ivanov's apartment and moved in with the Sudeikins, and a homosexual affair began between Kuzmin and Sudeikin. Olga found out by reading Kuzmin's diary and promptly threw Kuzmin out.[28]

Johannes Guenther mentions that it became clear that Olga was having an affair with Knyazev when she came to Riga to spend a few days with him. But Olga's husband was not upset by this, since he had a whole harem of schoolgirls. Eventually Olga divorced Sudeikin, who married Vera Bousset (later the wife of Igor Stravinsky).

Early in 1912, Knyazev began to write poems on his unrequited love for a woman who resembled the beautiful romantic nineteenth-century Russian portraits of Bryullov. She is the Columbine to his Pierrot. It soon becomes clear the poems are to Olga Sudeikina:

> You—are sweet, tender Columbine,
> All rosy in powder blue.
> A portrait beside an antique clavesin
> Of a white maid with a yellow flower!
> They kissed tenderly, after they closed the door
> And on her hat a yellow feather . . .
> And isn't it painful, painful for the heart
> To know that I'm only Pierrot, Pierrot? . . .[29]

But Olga soon tired of Knyazev, and her attitude turned from coolness to total indifference. In despair, Knyazev shot himself in Riga and died shortly afterward of his wounds. He was buried at the Smolensk Cemetery in Petersburg. Akhmatova recalled that after Blok's burial in 1921, she and Sudeikina looked for Knyazev's grave by the wall in the cemetery, but could not find it.[30]

Suicide was popular at the time. Zhirmunsky notes that the Symbolist poet Sologub had published an article entitled "Russian Decadents and Suicide" in *Den* [*The Day*], and Wedekind's play, *Spring Awakening,* also about suicide, was being performed at the Komissarzhevskaya Theater. "In those years," Chukovsky comments, "there were an enormous number of suicides, especially among young people. It became an epidemic, and even the fashion. . . . This prompted Akhmatova to make one of the personages of her story about that period a suicide. On the eve of war not only the officer Pierrot but everyone lived under the sign of death. . . . Akhmatova's entire narration from the first to the last line is permeated by this apocalyptic 'feeling of the end.' "[31]

There are very few references to Knyazev's suicide in Kuzmin's poetry published that year, and Akhmatova later accused him of not responding to this loss. Soon after Knyazev's death, Kuzmin went to Kiev, where he fell in love with Yury Yurkun, a Lithuanian by birth, who was eighteen and playing in a band in Kiev. He too wrote poetry, and he became Kuzmin's life companion after moving to Petersburg. Kuzmin did write one very moving poem which Malmstad believes refers to Knyazev, and which was published in 1914. The poet tells his friend not to be upset by the halting of their horses, and not to destroy their friendship by awkward explanations: everything happens because it is predestined to happen.

Perhaps this reflects Kuzmin's stoicism in the face of loss and death. "Kuzmin did not weep for the dead, not because he had no conscience but rather because death and the sadness of loss were accepted as inevitable attributes of life."[32]

Some critics conjecture that the more obvious allusions to Knyazev and Sudeikina in *Poem Without a Hero* are really a cover for a relationship Akhmatova herself had with some young man who committed suicide after she rejected him. In "Prose About the Poem," Akhmatova says, "The first impulse, which I concealed from myself for decades, was, of course, a note by Pushkin: 'Only the first lover leaves an impression on a woman, like the first casualty in a war.' Vsevolod was not the first casualty and never was my lover, but his suicide was so similar to another catastrophe that for me they have merged forever."[33]

Vilenkin reports a conversation he had with Akhmatova after reading excerpts from the poem. She told him that Knyazev was not the hero, but someone else, "an analogy."[34] Timenchik says that what she calls the "other catastrophe" was the suicide of Mikhail Lindeberg, a member of the Vladikavkaz artillery brigade and son of the director of the Petersburg cadet corps. The event was described in a Vladikavkaz newspaper in December 1911, which reported that the suicide was committed for romantic reasons.[35]

Whether the poem's plot is based on reminiscences of a boy soldier who wrote mediocre verse or an affair in which Akhmatova was personally involved, the guilt for his senseless death is elevated to a universal and philosophical level. It becomes the guilt of those who refused to assume responsibility for the suffering of their fellow beings, who turned away from the apocalyptic rumbling in the air warning of retribution for their indifference, a sound which was heard by Alexander Blok and expressed in his poetry before the war and the Revolution. They retreated from the impending chaos and made merry at their *Feast During the Time of the Plague,* resembling the characters in Pushkin's play who feast to the accompanying moans of the sick and dying.[36] The descent into the cellar of the Stray Dog is a metaphorical descent into Hell, an encounter with death: salvation is possible only through one's conscience, by returning in memory to the time of one's guilt in order to expiate and atone for one's actions—and in the Russian Orthodox tradition (in which Akhmatova firmly believed) to imitate Christ, not only atoning for one's own sins but also taking on those of others so that future generations may live in a better world. In *Poem Without a Hero,* the poet curses the beauty of an art associated with death and guilt.[37]

Timenchik claims Akhmatova's poem is in part a polemic against Kuzmin's works, especially his long poem, *The Trout Breaks the Ice,* which Akhmatova was reading when she started *Poem Without a Hero.*[38] The work appeared in 1929 and Lydia Ginzburg gave a copy of it to Akhmatova in 1930. Akhmatova's use of rhythm is similar to part of Kuzmin's work; the poem is also related to Kuzmin's novel *Travelers by Land and by Sea* (1916), in which several of the same figures that Akhmatova portrays appear at "The Owl," a cabaret based on the Stray Dog. The heroine Yelena resembles Olga Sudeikina. In Kuzmin's "The Trout,"

uninvited guests come for tea, and the dead interact with the living. The poet
meets a young man, the first incarnation of the lyrical hero, and they swear eternal
love, but the young man leaves. Later the poet receives a letter from him posted
from a Scottish town, where the young man has fallen in love with a woman,
Ellinor. Numerous episodes allude to the history, philosophy, and personal associations of Kuzmin's own life.[39] The work is based on complex shifts of time.
It may have influenced not only specific themes and motifs, but also the formal
structure of Akhmatova's poem, which also relies on constant shifts in time, and
on associative rather than sequential relationships.

Akhmatova's early work is predominantly concerned with intimate relationships rather than public events, and there are few allusions to erudite cultural
material or key artistic figures of her epoch, unless, as in the poems to Blok and
Mandelstam, they were an important part of her personal or creative life. However,
Akhmatova's early poetry already treated public themes, especially when she was
confronted by war and revolution, with the choice of leaving one's homeland or
suffering with it. Moreover, when she turned to public themes, it was not done
abstractly but by showing how it affected the poet's life in particular. In this way
she continues the tradition in Russian literature typified by Tolstoy's *War and
Peace,* where historical events and major figures are viewed through the prism of
how they affect the lives of ordinary people.

Akhmatova's early works, as we have seen, also feature the juxtaposition of
images linked not by logic but by personal associations that the reader decodes
through an awareness of the poet's cultural and personal context. Therefore, she
did not have to turn to Kuzmin to learn this technique. *Poem Without a Hero* is
thus not a deviation from Akhmatova's "simple style." Her style was always
difficult. Although she uses simple, ordinary language, her poems mirror interior
monologue, the way we speak to ourselves, a mode of thinking through phrases,
sudden and abrupt shifts in images and thought patterns that resonate within one's
own personal experience. Interior speech has been characterized by the great
Russian psychologist Lev Vygotsky, who spent many years examining this phe-
nomenon:

> Inner speech is condensed, abbreviated speech. Written speech is de-
> ployed to its fullest extent, more complete than oral speech. Inner speech
> is almost entirely predicative because the situation, the subject of thought,
> is always known to the thinker. Written speech, on the contrary, must
> explain the situation fully in order to be intelligible. The change from
> maximally compact inner speech to maximally detailed written speech
> requires what might be called deliberate semantics—deliberate structur-
> ing of the web of meaning.[40]

What is different in this new work is the complexity of Akhmatova's allusions—not only metaphors and other figures of speech, but the lines and phrases

from other people's works in the form of *tainopis,* "secret writing." However, since the 1930s her poems, both published and unpublished during her lifetime, had become increasingly full of oblique references that had to be decoded by the reader; the poem is thus a culmination of a development that had been gradually intensifying.

In distinguishing between logical, straightforward narrative and poetic prose based on the association of images, which is clearly the way Akhmatova's own poetic style functions, Wolf Schmidt points out that memory in literature is always reductionist: it selects and discards. His discussion of modern poetic prose is relevant to modern poetry as well. Poetic prose mirrors the way memory works. A story is based on analogy and association rather than on temporal or cause-effect relationships. There is a simultaneity and bringing into juxtaposition of key related moments of the past in order to give them new meaning within the new context, and these fragments become equivalent in relevance. Networks of relationships are established among the images presented by the artist, and at each node in the net numerous relations cross. In realistic literature, connections are linear, but in this mode of writing, the network of images reaches out in all directions at the same time. This also requires a different form of perception on the part of the reader: "Modern poetry asks the reader to suspend the process of individual references temporarily until the entire pattern of internal references can be apprehended as a unity. . . . Joyce cannot be read. . . . He can only be reread."[41]

Osip Mandelstam remarked that Acmeism is the passion for world culture: it retrieves from the collective memory of culture fragments from the arts, history, politics, and the personal biographies of great masters. And through ellipsis—leaving out information—the reader understands by means of critical commentary or a common cultural heritage how to interpret the work and supply the necessary connections. The reader thus becomes an active participant in the poetic act. These ideas, summarized by Yuri Lotman, resemble the theories of Vsevolod Meyerhold, the great Russian theater director, who also wrote about the perceiver (in the case of a theatrical performance, the audience) as a major component in communicating the message and understanding a work of art. The author, actors, and director can only convey an artistic code, which must be interpreted by the audience; only then does a text become a complete work of art.

Lotman shows how aspects of another work of art may undergo important transformations when they appear in a new context. Certain texts have been forgotten in our culture, he points out, but they are potentially latent. When recalled by an author and cited in some way—by allusion or actual citation of lines and phrases—they are transformed. If cultural texts of the past are retrieved by memory, they are not then preserved in a passive way, but the process is generative—they create new texts and new meanings. "Memory is not only a passive preserver of culture but a component part of its text-forming mechanism."[42]

Kees Verheul's study of time in Akhmatova's *Poem Without a Hero* is the classic work on this subject. Instead of the traditional narrative development, Akhmatova provides the result of the enfolding action at the very beginning: Leningrad is going to be attacked in an impending catastrophic war. The poem is based on a concentric cyclical structure: "The story moves . . . not by a temporal progression from beginning to end, but rather by what may be called a concentric development, in which the principal elements of a cyclic recurrence of suspense and a connected catastrophic denouement are carried through a series of variations and expansions."[43]

Verheul suggests that the second and third parts of the poem differ in method from the first. Part Two, "The Other Side of the Coin," contains a set of numbered stanzas, many of which contain references to particular cultural and biographical motifs—an allusion to Byron's *Manfred,* to the difficulty of the editor understanding the poem, or to a Russian Orthodox hymn. The thematic movement is improvisatory, "as the thoughts of the speaker seem to turn associatively from one subject to the next," whereas the thematic movement of Part Three, the Epilogue, reflects a more recognizable linear character, beginning with an evocation of besieged Leningrad, interrupted by a digression about the camps in Siberia, and subsequently, a description of the successive stages of the poet's journey and other places of evacuation.[44] However, the "improvisatory" nature of motives linked by association is exactly the same principle of "inner speech" as that on which the first part is based; and the last section of the poem proves also to be based on this structure, as we will see.

The feeling conveyed in the three parts is different. The first part tells the story of the love triangle, conjuring up the drama of characters who lived in the Silver Age of elegant decadence. The second part is not dramatic in the sense of reflecting dialogue or action. It is, rather, the musings of a poet about the nature of poetry, the difficulties of style in modern verse, and the problem of borrowing from other works. It also covertly refers to the problem of the relationship between the artist and the state. The third part is reflective: the poet, now in the East, where she has been evacuated, contemplates separation from her beloved city and what this means to her, and her thoughts about those in Siberia (also in the East).[45]

Although the metrical scheme is the same throughout, the difference in layout of the verses on the page in each part influences the way one perceives the poetry. The poem is written in the *dolnik* form, with a predictable number of accents but no predictable number of syllables per line. However, there is a predominance of anapest lines—three syllables with the accent on the third syllable—which lends the poem a driving, "winged," rhythmic movement, soaring ahead, "forward, with arms thrown wide," as Pasternak wrote Akhmatova. Chukovsky calls this passionate, stirring rhythm the "Akhmatova rhythm."[46]

In each section, however, the layout is different. The first part contains three-

line units that are set out on the page in "ladder fashion," as in the Third
Dedication:

> Long enough I have frozen in fear,
>> Better to summon a Bach Chaconne,
>>> And behind it will enter a man,
> He will not be a beloved husband to me
> But what we accomplished he and I,
>>> Will disturb the Twentieth Century.
>>>> (II, p. 407)

The rhyme scheme is complicated. The rhymed units cover two stanzas: *aabcbc;*
the first two lines are a rhymed couplet, then the next four lines form a crossed-
rhyme scheme. In Russian, it appears as follows:

> *Polno mne ledenet ot strakha,*
>> *luchshe kliknu Chakonu Bakha,*
>>> *a za nei voidyot chelovek,*
> *on ne stanet mne milym muzhem,*
>> *no my s nim takoye zasluzhim,*
>>> *chto smutitsya Dvadtsatyi vek.*

Within this six-line pattern there is still room for some experimentation, with
different combinations and fragmentation, as in lines 38–54:

> I'm not afraid of publicity . . .
>> What to me are Hamlet's garters!
>>> What to me the whirlwind of Salome's dance,
>>>> What to me the tread of the Man in the Iron Mask!
>>>> I am more iron than they . . .
> And whose turn is it to be frightened,
>> To flinch, to step back, to give in
>>> And ask forgiveness for an old sin?
> It's all clear:
>>> If not I, who then?
>> This supper wasn't prepared for them,
>>> And they won't walk this path with me.
> Under his tails he has hidden his tail . . .
>> He is so lame and elegant! . . .
>>>>>> However . . .
>>> I hope you have not dared
>>>> To bring the Prince of Darkness here?
>>>>> (III, pp. 413 & 415)

Many studies have been written on the possible prototypes for Akhmatova's characters, as well as for the citations from other works, which in Russian literary criticism is referred to as *chuzhoye slovo,* or "alien word."[47] In "The Other Side of the Coin," the poet predicts that she will be accused of plagiarism. T. S. Eliot addressed this concern in his essay on "Tradition and the Individual Talent," cautioning not to judge a poet only on those aspects of his work that least resemble others'. Indeed, the best of a poet's work may be the parts in which "the dead poets, his ancestors, assert their immortality most vigorously."[48] Akhmatova's thoughts on this subject were recorded by Luknitsky on June 7, 1927:

A genius is a usurper. He collects, snatches words, similes, images from everywhere—the simplest and even those often not noticed by anyone— but the best. He takes them, and until he does, they are not worth anything. They are in free circulation everywhere. Anyone can utter them. But when the genius takes them, he pronounces them in such a way that they become unrepeatable. He puts his own stamp on them. They become his property, and it is forbidden. For the stamp of genius is upon them.[49]

But what is most important is the way Akhmatova followed her own analysis of how such borrowings should be employed.[50] The manner in which she employs these allusions is breathtaking: within the context of other images and phrases in the work, they become transformed. They become constituent elements in a rich fabric, and she imparts to them her own private symbols and meanings. The poem is not merely a patchwork quilt of allusion and direct citations of others' works, but a complex whole, where phrases and words take on new meanings by their masterful placing into juxtaposition with each other. The phrases and motifs are based on an underlying theme, to which all the parts are organically related. Numerous studies have been written on the individual parts of *Poem Without a Hero.* Now it is time to look at the work as a whole.

The key lies in the epigraph to "The Other Side of the Coin"—"My future is in my past." This epigraph reflects lines in several different poems by T. S. Eliot. In 1947, Vyacheslav Ivanov wished to give Pasternak a gift—a volume of Eliot. But at this stage of his life Pasternak found the style too complex, too removed from his present simpler technique. He told Ivanov to give it instead to Akhmatova, saying, "And you can be sure, she'll understand everything."[51] Perhaps this was when she first became more interested in Eliot's works.

The most obvious reference is to the opening line of "East Coker" in *Four Quartets:* "In my beginning is my end." However, other parts of the *Quartets* discuss the role of the past in determining one's future. Toporov points to the lines from "Burnt Norton":

> Time present and time past
> Are both perhaps present in time future
> And time future contained in time past . . .
> What might have been and what has been
> Point to one end, which is always present.

These lines may refer to an individual as well as to a more universal level of history. Eliot's third quartet, "The Dry Salvages," contains lines that are more similar to those in *Poem Without a Hero*. Here not only the individual but a whole nation confronts its past in order to account for or attempt to understand what is occurring in the present and to predict what may happen in the future:

> . . . I have said before
> That the past experience revived in the meaning
> Is not the experience of one life only
> But of many generations—not forgetting
> Something that is probably quite ineffable:
> The backward look behind the assurance
> Of recorded history, the backward half-look
> Over the shoulder, towards the primitive terror.[52]

While God determines the destiny of the world, the human individual chooses between good and evil, between a metaphysical truth and the illusion of well-being and worldly power that passes for truth in the present. The future Eden will feature retribution for those who have sinned and vindication for those who have upheld the faith.[53] A similar apocalyptic pattern is described by M. H. Abrams in his discussion of the English and German Romantics before the French Revolution and the Russian Symbolists before the Bolshevik Revolution:

> [Their works] are written in the persons of the visionary poet-prophet, "the Bard," who present, past, and future sees; they incorporate the great political events of their age in suitable grandiose literary forms, they present a panoramic view of history in a cosmic setting, in which the agents are in part historical and in part allegorical or mythological and the overall design is apocalyptic; they envision a dark past, a violent present, and an immediately impending future which will justify the history of suffering man by its culmination in an absolute good; and they represent the French Revolution (or else a coming revolution which will improve on the French model) as the critical event which signals the emergence of a regenerated man who will inhabit a new world uniting features of a restored paradise and a recovered Golden Age.[54]

Akhmatova's work fits into this pattern, with one important difference: the lack of a future Eden, the reward for upholding the faith. *Poem Without a Hero* has no paradise as a reward for suffering and atonement, no explicit New Jerusalem. The poem seems to end in despair, as the pattern of crisis and judgment lacks its third component, its resolution—vindication. There is no direct intimation that the world will be redeemed either here or in an afterlife. However, as we will soon discover, there are subtle hints and allusions to the possible salvation of the Russian land and its people.

The title itself is a puzzle. It has been suggested that it derives from lines in Byron's narrative poem *Don Juan:*

I want a hero: an uncommon want,
    When every year and month sends forth a new one
Till, after cloying the gazettes with cant,
    The age discovers he is not the true one:
Of such as these I should not care to vaunt,
    Therefore take our ancient friend Don Juan—

Another suggestion is that the title comes from Mandelstam's prose piece, *The Egyptian Mark:* "Our life . . . is a story without a poet and hero, made out of trifles and glass, out of passionate murmuring of some depression, from Petersburg influenza raving."[55] Commentators often refuse to accept the title's literal meaning and continue to search for the poem's "real hero." Perhaps, like Byron, Akhmatova could not find anyone in the epoch who was worthy of being called a hero—certainly not the Soldier-Poet, who instead of stoically overcoming his disappointment or facing his rival commits suicide at the threshold of a momentous historical event—World War I, when he might have died a true hero's death. Nor would Akhmatova be apt to choose as her hero the Demon Poet, the villain, the sinner who symbolizes the reason for retribution. Perhaps instead, as in Mandelstam's story, the epoch is peopled with anti-heroes, heirs to Dostoyevsky's protagonist in *Notes from the Underground,* who are drowning in self-reflection and inaction as they passively contemplate their doom.

The subtitle "Triptych" immediately endows the work with religious connotations, bringing to mind the great altarpieces in three parts that depict scenes representing the life of Christ or a saint.[56] The epigraph on the title page of *Poem Without a Hero* features the words spoken by the Commendatore's statue in *Don Giovanni:* "You will stop laughing before the dawn" (*Di rider finirai/Pria dell'aurora*). Retribution will come at last, and Don Giovanni will pay for his sins. Thus at the very outset the poet sounds the theme: Retribution. This epigraph is also an allusion to Alexander Blok's "The Steps of the Commendatore," which plays a key role in Akhmatova's work. Blok's poem follows:

A heavy, thick curtain at the entrance,
    Behind the night's window—fog,

What is your tedious freedom now worth,
    Don Juan, now that you know fear?

It is cold and empty in the sumptuous bedroom,
    The servants sleep, and the night is mute.
From some land blessed and unknown, far away
    The crowing of the cock is heard.

What can sounds of bliss mean to a traitor?
    Life's moments are numbered.
Donna Anna sleeps, hands crossed on her heart.
    Donna Anna dreams . . .

Whose cruel features froze,
    Reflected in the mirrors?
Anna, Anna, is it sweet to sleep in the grave?
    Is it sweet to envision unearthly dreams?

Life is empty, mad and fathomless!
    Go to battle, ancient fate!
And in reply—triumphant and in love—
    A horn sounds in the snowy mist. . . .

Like fires in the night, flashing by in the night
    A motor car, black, quiet, like an owl flies by.
With quiet, heavy steps
    The Commendatore enters the house . . .

The door flings open. From the immense cold
    Comes a sound like a clock striking hoarsely in the night—
The striking of the clock: "You asked me to supper.
    I've come. Are you ready?" . . .

To the cruel question there is no reply,
    No reply—only silence.
In the sumptuous bedroom is fear at the hour of dawn,
    The servants are asleep, and the night is pale.

At the hour of dawn it is cold and strange,
    At the hour of dawn—and the light is dim.
Maiden of Light! Where are you, Donna Anna?
    Anna! Anna!—Silence.

Only in the threatening morning mist
    The clock strikes for the last time:
Donna Anna will rise at the fatal hour.
    Anna will rise at the fatal hour.[57]

Akhmatova introduced *Requiem* with "In Place of a Preface," in which the poet explains how the poem came to be written. There she uses "In Place of a Foreword" as a structural component of the work itself.

The epigraph to this prose introduction, *"Deus conservat omnis"* (God preserves everything), was the motto on the coat of arms of the Sheremetev Palace. It is more than just a metonymic reference to where Akhmatova lived—it is the sole mention of God within the entire work. Any retribution for people's sins implies either a God to carry it out or a more abstract agent of retribution such as Providence, Fate, or history. The motto may function in the same way as the epigraph does in *Anna Karenina,* where the biblical citation, "Vengeance is mine, I will repay," clearly refers to God punishing those who sin. Dostoyevsky interprets this to mean that God alone should judge another man's sin, and also that God forgives. Sin is not inevitable; sinning is the result of man's free choice, and if he atones, he will be expiated by mercy and love. But Anna Karenina accepted a superficial, hypocritical society's condemnation of her, and perished by committing suicide. In *Poem Without a Hero,* the end seems to fail to confirm the promise of redemption made at the beginning, for the country itself is perishing. And yet for a Russian Orthodox believer, there is still hope, since the poem becomes a means of expiation. As Dostoyevsky suggests in his most profound works, in the Russian Orthodox Church the individual frequently not only atones for his own sins but takes on the sins of others as well. Here the poet imitates Christ: the poem itself becomes a ritual of expiation. The country and its people have the possibility of being purged of their sins, and then the divine force will preserve and protect them from harm. But redemption can come only after expiation.

In the introduction, datelined April 8, 1943, Tashkent, Akhmatova discusses how poetry is created: she does not consciously call forth her creative work, but the sounds, the rhythms, the words crashed in upon her on the night of December 27, 1940. "I did not summon it. I was not even expecting it on that dark, cold day of my last winter in Leningrad." The poem is immediately associated with present events—the Siege of Leningrad—and from the very beginning the reader is meant to search for relationships between the catastrophic events occurring in the poet's city in the present and what took place in 1913 when it had another name, St. Petersburg: "I dedicate this poem to the memory of its first audience—my friends and fellow citizens who perished in Leningrad during the siege. I hear their voices and remember them when I read the poem aloud, and for me this invisible chorus is an everlasting justification of the work" (II, p. 399).

Akhmatova added another prose passage in November 1944, after her return to Leningrad, saying she would not take the advice of others and make the poem more comprehensible. Her decision is couched in biblical terms, citing Church Slavonic, the sacred language of the Orthodox Slavs into which the Bible and the Divine Liturgy have been translated: *"Yezhe pisakh—pisakh"* (What I have written—I have written), the words of Pontius Pilate. This adds another religious dimension to the work. However, Akhmatova expresses her clear intention to write a "difficult" poem, one that will be understood only by those who actively participate in decoding her allusions; she will not write an "easy" work, typical of Socialist Realism, in which the author reduces art to a simplistic level in order to make it comprehensible to the masses.

Three characters are introduced through dedications. The first is the Soldier-Poet:

In memory of Vs.K.

. . . .

Isn't it the sea?
        No, it is only pine needles
on a grave, and, in boiling foam,
closer, ever closer . . .
            Marche Funèbre . . .
                    Chopin . . .
                    (II, p. 403)

This First Dedication was part of the original concept, dated December 27, 1940, and written the first night she began the work. The most obvious reference is to Knyazev, as the epigraph indicates. However, scholars have also noted Osip Mandelstam's role in the poem and the possible allusion to him. Nadezhda Mandelstam provides evidence that Akhmatova had her husband in mind, blurring his image with that of Knyazev, since both were victims of the age. Akhmatova originally dated the dedication December 28, but when Nadezhda showed her the slip of paper from the Registrar's Office declaring Mandelstam's death on December 27, Akhmatova used that date instead. The "dark lashes of Antinous" may also refer to Mandelstam, since his friends frequently alluded to his long lashes.[58]

More probably the reference to Antinous refers to Kuzmin and Knyazev. In 1906, Kuzmin and two of his friends founded a society called *Haifizschenke* in honor of the poet Hafiz. Each member had a nickname—Kuzmin's was Antinous. In 1919 Kuzmin began a novel, *Roman Miracles,* set in the Rome of the emperor Hadrian, and in the second chapter young Roman aristocrats discuss Hadrian's favorite lover, Antinous.[59]

What is important is how all this helps us in understanding the way the Soldier-Poet is characterized in the poem. The clear reference to Knyazev in the epigraph indicates he is the main model for the character—which means he is young, bisexual, a poet, and a soldier. These aspects of Knyazev are confirmed by the reference to "writing on the first draft" of a work by this character (we assume it is the first draft of a poem, and the allusion to Antinous indicates he is homosexual). The "greenish haze" alludes to similar phrases in Kuzmin's "The Trout," whose hero is similar to Knyazev. The fact that the epigraph reads "In memory of Vs.K.," and that Chopin's *Marche Funèbre* (Funeral March) is coming ever closer tells the reader the hero is soon to die, probably by taking his own life over unrequited love, as Knyazev did. As the plot develops, it becomes clear that the Soldier-Poet has far more to do with Knyazev than Mandelstam, but all three have in common the role of innocent victim, although—depending on the author's attitude toward homosexuality—Knyazev may not be entirely innocent. If homosexuality is deemed a sin, then Knyazev is yet another representative of the decadence of the age. He also showed his weakness by committing suicide rather than attempting to overcome his suffering. Knyazev's action cannot be compared with Mandelstam's attempted suicide—the latter was already on the verge of madness, driven insane by a cruel and oppressive regime.[60]

The Second Dedication is to Olga Sudeikina and is dated the year of her death, May 25, 1945:

O.A. G.-S.

Is it you, Confusion-Psyche,
    Fluttering your black-white fan,
        Bending over me?
You want to tell me secretly
    That you are beyond the River Lethe
        And breathing in another springtime.
Don't dictate to me, I can hear it myself:
    A warm shower presses on the roof,
        I hear the ivy whispering.
Someone small has decided to live,
    Has turned green, has fluffed out, and will try,
        Tomorrow, to shine in his new cloak.
I sleep—
    She alone hovers over me—
The one people call spring,
    I call loneliness.
I sleep—
    I dream of our youth,
    The cup that passed *him* by:
        Waking, I'll give it to you,
If you want, as a souvenir,
    Like a pure flame in a dish of clay
        Or a snowdrop in an open grave.

                    (II, p. 405)

Sudeikina and Akhmatova lost touch after Sudeikina left Russia, but Akhmatova always kept a portrait of her. Sudeikina died in January 1945 in Paris, but the poet did not learn of her death until 1946, after she had already written the dedication. Confusion-Psyche is a combination of two roles played by Sudeikina in 1910 and 1912–1913, in plays by Yury Belyaev produced at the Suvorin Theater. *Confusion, or the Year 1940* was produced at the Maly Theater in Petersburg, with Olga in the starring role, from January 2 to April 24, 1910. In 1912–13, she played in Belyaev's *Psyche*.[61] The Lethe is mentioned in Akhmatova's poem for the first time—the river in Hades where dead souls drink in order to forget their past lives. Soon the Neva River is paired with it as Neva-Lethe, and thereby also becomes a "river of forgetfulness." "Someone small" who has decided to live refers to the Soldier-Poet, who will appear in his new cloak. The cup that passes to him may be the cup of life or of the youth that Knyazev never had, since he died so young.

The Third Dedication was written much later and dated January 5, 1956, the year when Akhmatova refused to see Isaiah Berlin for fear of what might happen to her and her son.

> *Once on Epiphany Eve . . .*
> —Zhukovsky

Long enough I have frozen in fear,
　　Better to summon a Bach Chaconne,
　　　　And behind it will enter a man,
He will not be a beloved husband to me
　　But what we accomplish, he and I,
　　　　Will disturb the Twentieth Century.
I took him by mistake
　　For someone mysteriously bestowed,
　　　　The most bitter of fates.
He will come to me in the Fountain Palace
　　To drink New Year's wine
　　　　And he will be late this foggy night.
And he will remember Epiphany Eve,
　　The maple at the window, the wedding candles
　　　　And the poem's mortal flight . . .
But it's to the first branch of lilac,
　　Not a ring, not the sweetness of prayers—
　　　　It is death that he bears.

January 5, 1956 (Le jour des rois)

(II, p. 407)

The epigraph cites a line from a poem by the early nineteenth-century Romantic poet, Vasily Zhukovsky, "Once on Epiphany Eve." Anyone familiar with Russian folklore knows that Yuletide (*Svyatki*), which lasts from Christmas Eve through Epiphany (Twelfth Night), has many rituals, including fortunetelling. In one, two small mirrors are placed opposite each other in the bathhouse; holding up one of the mirrors, young, unmarried girls look without blinking into the other, which is lit by two candles. The setting for the ritual includes a table set for two. It begins with the girl saying, "Intended groom, come to me to supper!" She continues to look into the mirror until a vision appears, hopefully the face of her intended bridegroom. In Akhmatova's poem "High in the Sky," which appeared in her first collection, *Evening,* there is a similar reference to this ritual: "On Epiphany Eve I cast fortunes about him/In January I was his friend" (I, p. 223). The custom was made famous by Pushkin in *Eugene Onegin,* V.4: "Epiphany they observed very solemnly/When all the serf-maids told fortunes/For the young ladies of the manor."[62] The line in the Dedication is quoted from Zhukovsky's ballad *Svetlana.* The heroine, trying to divine the future, sits before her mirror with a candle at midnight and sees a messenger. He takes her to her fiancé, who is dead—then she wakes up and next day finds out that her beloved is alive.

The Bach Chaconne is mentioned in "A Dream" (August 1956), in the cycle including poems about Isaiah Berlin. The poet says she dreamed of his arrival:

It was in everything . . . in the Bach Chaconne,
And in the roses, which bloomed in vain,
And in the ringing of the village bells
Over the blackness of ploughed fields.

(II, p. 247)

In the Dedication here, the poet says the two of them will "disturb the Twentieth Century," as indeed they did when Akhmatova was expelled from the Union of Writers in 1946, very probably because of Berlin's visit. Certainly Akhmatova's expulsion exacerbated the hostility between the Soviet Union and the West. The maple at the window outside the poet's apartment will become a leitmotif in the poem, appearing at various key points in the tale. In the last lines, the poet notes that the Guest brings not what a woman would expect from a potential bridegroom on this Epiphany Eve—flowers, a ring, a prayer—but death. It is interesting that Akhmatova puts *Le jour des rois* (Day of the Kings) next to the date, especially since for the Russian Orthodox, Epiphany is devoted chiefly to the celebration of Christ's baptism in the Jordan rather than the coming of the Magi. Perhaps she is attempting to add a European flavor to the poem, which is about a city that merged European and Russian culture. Or perhaps she wishes to play up the theme of "bearing gifts," for the Three Kings brought salubrious gifts to the Christ Child, while the Guest from the Future bears death—that is his gift.

The Introduction was added on August 25, 1941. August had always been a bad month for Akhmatova—the month Alexander Blok died and Nikolay Gumilyov was arrested and shot. War had been declared between Germany and Russia, guns, grenades, and Molotov cocktails were piled on streetcar platforms, guns were mounted on trucks, and observation posts established in the rotunda of St. Isaac's Cathedral, on the roof of the Lenin flour mill, at the Troitsky

Cathedral, and in the Red Banner factory. Harrison Salisbury says that Leningrad in August 1941 was a "city . . . sown with dragon's teeth—great cement blocks to bar the passage of German tanks. Railroad iron was crisscrossed into jungles along the outskirts of the city where the Nazis might break through." He then cites a passage from Pavel Luknitsky's diary, describing his visit to Akhmatova on August 25:

> Anna Akhmatova was sick in bed, but she greeted Luknitsky with her usual politeness. She was in good spirits, despite her illness, despite the danger to her beloved Leningrad. She had been invited, she told Luknitsky, to speak on the radio. "She is a patriot," Luknitsky wrote in his diary, "and the consciousness that her spirit is shared by all fills her with courage." . . . Thus Leningrad, a city of three million people, a city of cowards and of patriots, of sleazy sharpers and men and women of endless dedication, of plundering military men and feuding Party leaders, moved toward the time of trial.[63]

In the Introduction, the poet looks back at her past as if from a tower:

FROM THE YEAR NINETEEN FORTY
    AS IF FROM A TOWER, I SURVEY EVERYTHING:
        AS IF BIDDING FAREWELL AGAIN
            TO WHAT I PARTED FROM LONG AGO;
                AS IF CROSSING MYSELF
                    AND THEN DESCENDING TO DARK VAULTS.

(II, p. 409)

Chukovskaya says Akhmatova's friend Tamara Gabbe was the source of the tower image. After reading an early version of the poem, Gabbe told Akhmatova: "One has the impression that you climbed up on a high tower and that from there, from the height of another era, you looked down, you examined the past."[64] However, the passage also recalls Akhmatova's "The Cellar of Memory," written the year before, on January 18, 1940, with its metaphor for the memory of her past and all that is contained within.

The date in the title of Part One—"The Year 1913: Petersburg Tale"— represents the year Knyazev actually committed suicide; but 1913 was also the year *before* the war, before what Akhmatova would soon call the "real twentieth century," just as the tale really begins on New Year's Eve 1940, ushering in the year (for the USSR) of World War II, 1941.

New Year's Eve is not solely a time of amusement in Russia. The night is full of ritual and folklore, with fortunetellers prophesying what the future year will bring; as during Carnival week before Lent, people dress up in costumes and attend masked balls. It is a night full of hope and expectations, as the old year is bidden farewell and the new year brings promise of better things to come. But this New Year's Eve would usher in the last year before the war, which many in Russia saw as the beginning of an apocalypse.

In the first scene the poet is alone in her small, narrow room on the grounds of the Sheremetev Palace. To initiate the New Year's ritual, she lights *sacred* candles. This setting is reminiscent of the tales of Hoffmann, who wrote the wonderful *Kunstmärchen* (art fairy tales), philosophical fantasies conveying profound ideas about life and death told through the guise of a fairy tale. There is a specific allusion to one of the Hoffmann tales, "New Year's Eve Adventure," in the line "The flame sinks in the crystal." This tale also takes place on New Year's Eve. Strange visions appear in mirrors, and as the hero takes a glass of wine, "little flickering blue flames licked around the goblet."[65] In fact, this is the very story in which the demonic Dr. Dapertutto appears, the name taken by the director Meyerhold when he published his journal *Love for Three Oranges,* and the name by which he is referred to in *Poem Without a Hero.*

The Hoffmannesque quality is a key feature of the work, which reveals the very different styles and attitudes toward poetry of Akhmatova and Pasternak at this point in their lives. As Pasternak strove for simplicity, Akhmatova's works became infinitely more complex, culminating in *Poem Without a Hero.* Pasternak commented on this complexity and its relation to the tales of Hoffmann:

> I have never liked nor even understood the fantastic or romantic elements themselves (nor have I believed in their existence) as an independent domain. I have never liked nor understood the strangeness of E. T. A. Hoffmann or Carlo Gozzi, for example. For me art is a possession, and the artist is a man attached, stricken, possessed by reality, by an everyday existence which becomes even more fairy-like to a lively and expanded sensitivity precisely because of the unretouched, prosaic element.[66]

For Akhmatova, however, the idea of a philosophical fairy tale was the perfect vehicle for her musings about confrontation with one's past, and the themes of retribution and expiation. It was the perfect form for a work that slips from everyday reality into the fantastic and the grotesque and, without warning, back again, as in the Petersburg Tales by Gogol, who also came under the spell of this great German writer.

As the poem begins, the clock is about to strike the hour of midnight. Suddenly the bell rings—but the poet is not expecting any guests, and the unbidden masqueraders frighten her. She tells them to go away:

You are mistaken: The Venice of the Doges—
    Is next door . . . But your masks

> And cloaks and staffs and crowns,
> You'll have to leave them in the entrance hall today.
>   (II, p. 413)

Akhmatova has carefully chosen the masks that appear: each character is associated with a famous figure from literature or history who has attempted to destroy an innocent victim—such as Don Juan and Faust—or represents the victim himself—such as Jokanaan (St. John the Baptist). Some of these figures do not appear again, but others, such as Don Juan, will return at different points in the work, taking on further meaning each time they reappear. The goat-legged nymph who is introduced here will appear later as the Actress, and corresponds to Olga in her famous performance in this role at the Stray Dog:

> I'm not afraid of publicity . . .
>   What to me are Hamlet's garters!
>   What to me the whirlwind of Salome's dance,
>   What to me the tread of the Man in the Iron Mask!
>   (II, p. 413)

Akhmatova is referring to the moment in *Hamlet* when the prince is most vulnerable, feigning madness but close to actually going mad, as Ophelia describes: "His doublet all unbraced/No hat upon his head, his stockings foul'd/Ungartered, and down-gyved to his ankle" (Act II, sc. i). The Man in the Iron Mask was the alleged twin brother of Louis XIV, the hero-victim of Dumas's novel who spent most of his life in prison. The poet says that unlike some of these figures, who have suffered and lost, she has overcome her suffering and endured.

Suddenly the walls part, lights flash, sirens howl, and her room turns into the White Hall of Mirrors in the Sheremetev Palace, where the masquerade ball unfolds before us.[67] And as it begins, the poet poses a question, which becomes the main theme of the work:

> And whose turn is it to be frightened,
>   To flinch, to step back, to give in
>   And ask forgiveness for an old sin?
> It's all clear:
>   If not I, who then?
>   This supper wasn't prepared for them,
>   And they won't walk this path with me.
>   (II, p. 415)

At the end of the poem she will answer the question, acknowledging that it is her turn, and the turn of her people, to atone for the sins of the past so that Russia may be purged of its evil and forgiven, and a new life of hope and grace can begin. The shades of the past will not "walk this path" with her—they are dead, but she has been left alive to undergo the ritual of expiation for the sins she shares with them.

Suddenly the Prince of Darkness himself appears—and perhaps this refers to Kuzmin. When she began writing *Poem Without a Hero,* we know that Akhmatova was thinking about him and portrayed him as the embodiment of evil to Chukovskaya:

> We took everything seriously, but in Kuzmin's hands everything turned into a toy. . . . Kuzmin was very nasty and malicious. He loved saying awful things about everyone. He could not bear Blok because he envied him. . . . His salon had a bad influence on young people—they thought it was the culmination of thought and art but it was actually corruption where everything was taken as a game, everything was mocked. . . . He could not endure me.[68]

In 1913, however, when the poem takes place, Kuzmin and Akhmatova were friends. He wrote the Preface to *Evening,* and had the insight to prophesy her greatness. In fact, Akhmatova was still friendly with Kuzmin after the Revolution. In 1920, Kuzmin published his collection of erotic poems, *Forbidden Garden,* illustrated with provocative drawings by Milashevsky. The poems are about both heterosexual and homosexual love. In 1921 Akhmatova and Sudeikina attended a gathering at which these poems were read. Perhaps what turned Akhmatova against Kuzmin was an article by him which appeared in 1923, in which Kuzmin warned Akhmatova as a friend not to fall into the trap of repeating a successful formula and turn out poems with the same themes and style as before the Revolution, but rather to seek new paths of creativity as an artist. Perhaps this scolding—at a time when other critics were attacking her work more vociferously—made Akhmatova particularly sensitive to his words. Kuzmin had also attacked Gumilyov's work earlier, which was not appreciated by Akhmatova.

However, by the time Akhmatova began writing *Poem Without a Hero,* she was far removed from the "gay little sinner of Tsarskoye Selo," in a period of profound reevaluation. Malmstad says that in interviewing Akhmatova's friends in Leningrad in 1969, he found out that Akhmatova often spoke sarcastically, even cruelly, about Kuzmin to others. "They could explain her attitude only as a kind of moralizing, almost prudish view of Kuzmin's homosexuality and the 'sins' of her own youth. This was compounded in the last decades of her life by an egocentricity which caused her to belittle almost all her contemporaries, even Mandelstam at times."[69] This is certainly an unfair evaluation of Akhmatova in her later years. In the last decades of her life she wrote her touching and appreciative memoir about Mandelstam as a beloved friend; and whatever disagreements she might have had with Pasternak, especially over his relationship with Ivinskaya and Akhmatova's evaluation of his novel, she felt his death as a great loss, and wrote a poem to him on his death that is a moving and powerful tribute not only to a great poet but a dear friend. But her feelings for Kuzmin are not the result of petty egotism. Nor does Akhmatova condemn Kuzmin alone, but herself and her whole generation as well. According to the Judeo-Christian tradition, homosexuality and adultery are sins,[70] yet such behavior was flaunted by Akhmatova's generation. It is for this attitude, as well as their indifference to the suffering around them, that they are condemned.

Some may view this as prudishness on Akhmatova's part, when she confronts her past and judges it by standards and beliefs different from those she held as a young poet who was part of a gay, bohemian crowd. But rather than see this as a result of egotism or age, it is possible to see it as a return to the beliefs and traditions of the religion in which she was raised, beliefs that Dostoyevsky also held and on which his great works are based—those of the Russian Orthodox Church. The underlying theme of *Poem Without a Hero* is the same as that of such great works as *Crime and Punishment* and *The Brothers Karamazov* by Dostoyevsky, who, along with Dante, the Bible, and Shakespeare, was one of the most important influences on Akhmatova's life. And when Akhmatova writes the following lines about the Prince of Darkness (who very well may be Kuzmin), it is not petty egotism but a profound moral belief:

> Minion and mocker of us all—
>> Before him the most putrid sinner—
>>> Is blessedness personified. . . .

In "Prose About the Poem," Akhmatova noted:

> Most of all I will be asked who the "Prince of Darkness" is. . . . He is, very simply, the Devil. He is also in "The Other Side of the Coin": "That most elegant Satan." I don't really want to speak about it, but for those who knew the entire history of 1913, it is no secret. I will say only that he was probably born under a lucky star: he is one of those for whom everything is possible. I won't begin now to list everything that was possible for him; if I were to do so the hairs of today's reader would stand on end.[71]

After the passage on the Prince of Darkness, the poet asks, "How did it come to pass/That I alone of all of them am still alive?" (lines 62–63). It is a question she restated in a brief, but powerful, two-line poem allegedly written in 1958:

> All the unburied ones—I buried them,
>> I mourned for them all, but who will mourn for me?
>>> (II, p. 653)

Here the speaker identifies with the ancient heroine Antigone, who ensured that her dead brother was buried with respect. Akhmatova's *Poem Without a Hero* is also a way of mourning for the dead, a funeral lament, what Isaiah Berlin called a Requiem for Europe. In this work the poet does not ask, "Who will mourn for me?" but instead realizes that not only must she mourn for the dead, but she must take on the burden of their sins:

> Tomorrow morning they'll wake me,
> > And nobody will sentence me,
> > > And the blue beyond the windowpane
> > > > Will laugh in my face.
> But I am afraid: I myself will enter,
> > And not removing my lace shawl,
> > > I will smile at them all and fall silent.
> I don't want to meet again
> > The woman I was then,
> > > Wearing a necklace of black agate
> > > > Until the Valley of Jehosaphat. . . .
> > > > > > (II, p. 415)

Nobody will sentence her because she is the only one left alive who knows what her past and the past of her own generation was like, and if they are all to be judged, it will only be by her own conscience. She will retrieve the past from her own memory and make it immortal, part of collective memory, through her art, through this poem. Although the sky is blue and the sun is shining and "everything is all right with the world"—it is only seemingly so. This vision of New Year's Eve gaiety is but a momentary reprieve from what has gone before and the necessary atonement that must follow. That is why the poet is afraid—afraid to confront the woman she was then, the woman wearing "a necklace of black agate." She hopes to put off this confrontation until the Day of Judgment, which according to the Bible will take place in the Valley of Jehosaphat.

Akhmatova follows up this passage with lines about how the future is already present in the past:

> As the future ripens in the past
> > So the past rots in the future—
> > > A terrible festival of dead leaves.
> > > > > (II, p. 417)

They recall Eliot's "Burnt Norton" and "The Dry Salvages." Akhmatova's lines go further, however, than Wordsworth's notion that "the child is father of the man." The metaphor of the past rotting like dead leaves is a powerful negative image—the past is associated here with decadence and decay for which we in the future will now pay. What is conveyed in these lines is not only that our present is the product of our past, but much more than that—for what happened in our past could have resulted in a joyous present. Instead, what happened in Russia's past led to death and sterility, a culture that bore dead fruit.

The next passage about the Guest from the Future was added later:

T	*The sound of steps, those that don't exist,*
H	*Across the shining parquetry,*
E	*And bluish cigar smoke.*
W	*And reflected in all the mirrors*
H	*Is the man who didn't appear,*
I	*Who could not get into the hall,*
T	*He is no better than the others and no worse,*
E	*But he doesn't waft on Lethe's chill,*
H	*And his hand is warm,*
A	*The guest from the future—Is it true*
L	*That he really will come to me,*
L	*Turning left at the bridge?*

(II, p. 417)

The "bluish cigar smoke" is a metonymic motif that associates this figure with Isaiah Berlin, as does the mirror.[72] Both appear in the poem "In Reality"—in the cycle *Sweetbriar in Blossom*—which was written on June 13, 1946 (Akhmatova had last seen Berlin in January 1946):

Away with time and away with space,
I described everything through the white night:
The narcissus in crystal on your table,
And the blue smoke of a cigar,
And that mirror, where, as in pure water,
You might be reflected right now.
Away with time and away with space . . .
But even you can't come to my aid.

(II, p. 243)

In *Poem Without a Hero*, the Guest from the Future has difficulty making an appearance. He cannot pass through the mirrors, but is reflected in them all. He is not dead like the others—"he doesn't waft on Lethe's chill," that is, he does not come from Hades, and his hand is warm, the hand of someone alive. But the poet anticipates that he will eventually appear, as he turns left at the bridge en route to the Sheremetev Palace.

Finally the last important guest arrives, and at this point there is some confusion:

> . . . Since childhood I have feared maskers;
>> It always seemed to me
>>> That some superfluous shadow
> With "*neither face nor name*"
>> Slipped in among them . . .

After the pause indicated by ellipses at the end of the line, the poet announces the beginning of the celebration of New Year's:

>> Let's open the proceedings
>> On this joyous New Year's Day!
> I won't tell the whole world
>> About the midnight Hoffmannia
>>> And I would ask the others . . .
>>>>> Wait,
> You don't seem to be on the list
>> Of Cagliostros, magi, Lyciscas—
>>> Dressed as a striped milestone,
> Painted lewdly and gaudily—
>> You . . .
>>> Contemporary of the Mamre oak,
>>> Ancient interlocutor of the moon.
>>>> (II, p. 419)

Is the poet speaking about the same person in both passages? In December 1959, Akhmatova wrote that "The Demon was always Blok, the Milepost—the Poet in general . . . (something like Mayakovsky)."[73] Therefore, two different characters are represented in these passages: first, the Demon Poet, with "neither face nor name"; and second, the Milestone, the Poet in General.

Scholars have shown that the character with "neither face nor name" alludes to works by Blok, hence this figure is the Demon Poet. The person dressed as one of those brightly painted striped poles in Russia that marked the miles along highways may instead stand for the Poet in General. Some identify him with Nedobrovo, since he hands down laws, and Nedobrovo was known for teaching poets of his generation about the laws of poetry. However, this could also refer to Gumilyov, since he too taught poetry to groups of followers after the Revolution, and discussed the nature of poetry in his column in *Apollon* as well as in the various artistic groups of which he was a key member. Several scholars identify the Milestone with Mayakovsky, as Akhmatova did in her "Prose About the Poem."

It is important, however, while not disregarding what the author herself said,

to examine how this character functions within the poem. If it is indeed Mayakovsky, he adds a new element to the tone and changes the relationship of the
themes and other characters to this figure. Although Akhmatova certainly recognized the genius of Mayakovsky—especially his works before the Revolution,
and his innovations in form and language—his poems were antithetical to her
own. Her early works reflected everyday reality, and in that they marked a strong
contrast to the ornate style of the Symbolists. However, the "everyday reality"
conveyed in Akhmatova's works was a reality of the upper-class intelligentsia,
restrained and refined. Mayakovsky, in contrast, deliberately attempted to reflect
the reality of "the streets." In his great poem written before the Revolution,
"Cloud in Trousers," he shouts emphatically:

> I spit on the fact that nowhere
> in the Homers and Ovids of this world
> are there people like us,
> pock-marked with soot.

He identified himself with John the Baptist, prophesying not the coming of
Christ—peace on earth and goodwill toward men—but Revolution:

> I, mocked, by my contemporaries
> like a prolonged
> dirty joke
> I perceive whom no one sees,
> crossing the mountains of time.

> I,
> laughed at by today's tribe like a long
> scabby joke,
> I see coming across the mountains of time
> Someone no one else sees.

> Where men's eyes stop short,
> at the head of starving hordes,
> in the thorny crown of revolution
> the sixteenth year approaches.[74]

Mayakovsky was off by one year: the Revolution came in 1917, and he became
its poet laureate—at least for a while, until he began to criticize what he viewed
as a betrayal of its goal and ended up putting a bullet through his head.

Although the Futurists were creating their works during the Silver Age, this
era is associated not with them, but with the Russian version of Jugendstil, Fa-
bergé, the Symbolists and Acmeists, elegant salons, decadence, cabarets featuring
the *chansons* of Alexander Vertinsky. This was also the period of avant-garde

art—the primitivism of Goncharova and Larionov, the wild experimentation of Malevich and Kandinsky, the disharmonies of Stravinsky and Prokofiev—and even though the members of these various groups met and clashed with their more refined counterparts, the sensibility of the Silver Age differed from that of the avant-garde.

If, indeed, the Milestone is related to Mayakovsky, then it is a marker for the introduction of the new age of the Futurist Utopia, of harsh and discordant sounds and colors, of an energy that is missing from the languor and ennui of the Silver Age. But it also changes the whole tone of *Poem Without a Hero*, which otherwise is marked by a sensibility of elegance and refinement, the carnival atmosphere of Alexander Benois's beautiful designs for the ballet *Petrouchka*, an *aestheticized* version of folk fairs rather than the more primitive versions of the Russian folk portrayed in *The Rite of Spring* or Goncharova's paintings.

It seems more probable that the Milestone represents the "Poet in General," but one who shares many of the attitudes and beliefs of the Silver Age. As depicted in the poem, the poet is ancient—he is a contemporary of the Mamre oak, as old as the oak in Genesis, the setting for the three angels telling Sarah she will bear a child. He writes "iron laws" like the great lawgivers of antiquity, laws concerning the writing of verse. He is not modest:

> He doesn't wait for gout and fame
>> To bundle him hastily
>>> Into a splendid jubilee armchair,
>>>> But across blooming heather,
>>>>> Over wastelands he carries his triumph.
>>>>>> (II, p. 419)

The next lines are also difficult to interpret:

> And he is not guilty of anything: either of this,
>> Nor of that, nor of the third . . .
>>> Sins
>> Are generally not suitable to poets.
> Either dance before the Ark of the Covenant
>> Or disappear! . . .[75]

The German translation of the third and fourth lines by Heinz Czechowski interprets them as follows:

> *Die Dichter, sie leben*
> *Jenseits von Gut und von Böse.*[76]
>> Poets, they live
> Beyond good and evil.

This associates the lines with Nietzsche, who borrowed his ideas from the negative aspect of Dostoyevskian characters like Raskolnikov in *Crime and Punishment.* If God is dead (and Nietzsche assumes he is, a fantasy made up by weak-minded men), then all is permitted. Without God there is no absolute morality, no absolute good or evil. Each person generates his own arbitrary moral system. The lines in the poem do not mean that Akhmatova agrees with the idea that "all is permitted," for critics have always emphasized that what differentiated her work from typical Symbolist poetry (for example, Bryusov and Gumilyov's early work) was that it did *not* convey the idea that the artist must know all of life's experiences in order to be able to transform such experiences into art. Instead, the poem presents a character (the Poet in General) who does believe this, someone who typifies the Silver Age in Russia, whereas the Poet-Narrator herself shares Dostoyevsky's view—that there is a God whose moral laws are absolute and must not be transgressed, and that transgression inevitably brings retribution for one's sins.

However, the line that sins "Are not appropriate to poets" may also mean that art is moral, that poets must not sin at all, it is not appropriate for them to do so, and then the following lines become meaningful: "Either dance before the Ark of the Covenant/Or disappear!" This refers to a passage in II Samuel 6:15, when King David rejoices in the Lord, makes a sacrifice, and dances before the ark: "So David and all the house of Israel brought up the ark of the Lord with shouting, and with the sound of the trumpet." Thus not only must the poet not sin, but like his great predecessor, King David, he must rejoice in the Lord—or disappear.

The crowing of the cock that follows serves as a warning on two levels. It may refer to the passage in Matthew 26:75: "And Peter remembered the word of Jesus, which said unto him, 'before the cock crows, thou shalt deny me thrice.' And he went out, and wept bitterly." In Akhmatova's poem, the poet says, "To us the cock's crow is just a dream"—she and her generation refused to heed the warning. The image of the cock providing a warning also appears in Blok's famous poem about Don Juan, "The Steps of the Commendatore." At dead of night the bedroom is cold and empty: "From some blessed, unknown, far-away land comes the sound of the cock crowing." It is a sign of dawn, a sign that the Commendatore will arrive as the agent of retribution, taking vengeance for Don Juan's sins. When the Commendatore says to the sinner: "You asked me to supper. I have come. Are you ready?" there is no reply—only silence. However, there is yet a third allusion—to the cock in *The Golden Cockerel,* the Pushkin tale which served as the subject of Akhmatova's first published article on Pushkin. This too is a tale of sin and retribution: when the lazy, egotistical tsar fails to keep his promise to the forces that aided him, he is pecked to death by the cock. In all these examples the allusion has a similar meaning, associated with betrayal and retribution.

This interpretation is corroborated by the lines that follow, as the masqueraders continue to pursue their pleasure, totally oblivious to impending disaster:

Death is somewhere near, evidently,
But thoughtless, shameless, nonchalant,
The masqueraders babble on . . .
(II, p. 419)

Suddenly the masqueraders run off, and the ballroom is like an empty stage. The protagonist, the Soldier-Poet, is called to center stage. Set off in italics is a warning of what is to come. It is a "rehearsal" of the ultimate suicide, the pseudo-hero's solution to his problems. Akhmatova uses words from Knyazev's own poetry to Olga:

I hear a whisper: "Farewell! It's time!
I will leave you alive,
But you will be my *widow,*
You—Dove, sun, sister!"

And then we have an anticipation of the actual suicide scene, ending in the words that Mandelstam spoke to Akhmatova during the 1930s as his mental state became increasingly distraught: "I am ready to die."

On the landing two shadows merged . . .
Then . . . the flat steps of the staircase,
A scream: "You didn't have to!" and from afar
A clear voice:
"I am ready to die."
(II, p. 421)

The vision is over, the torches go out, the ceiling descends, and the white-mirrored ballroom becomes once again the author's bedroom. Her thoughts are externalized in the form of "words from the darkness." Another vision appears to her, but now in the smallness of her narrow room, someone standing between the cupboard and the stove—like Kirilov in Dostoyevsky's *Devils*. If the allusion is a conscious one, then it appropriately develops the theme of the inevitable consequences when a person thinks he is above or beyond God's law, or, what is even worse in Dostoyevsky's eyes, that God does not exist. Kirilov believes the act of suicide will prove he has control over his own destiny. But his act is futile. The Soldier-Poet, however, does not kill himself for an idea, but because he cannot bear rejection by the Actress. His choosing to die in this way instead of the possible fate awaiting him—death in battle for his people—corroborates his role as an anti-hero.

The next section is the "Interlude." It takes place on the landing of a stair-case, presumably still in the palace, for the figures are reflected in mirrors.

Snatches of conversation are overheard. Again masqueraders appear in the guise of famous figures from world culture—mainly those associated with sin and retribution—Casanova, Lot, Aphrodite, and Helen of Troy. But masqueraders disguised as Don Quixote also appear, those kind, naive, idealistic souls who believe that good will ultimately triumph over evil. A woman, the "best dressed and tallest of all," relates to Salomea Andronikova, a Petersburg beauty and one of Akhmatova's best friends, who left Russia for England after the Revolution. Here she appears in conjunction with Mme. de Lamballe, Duchess Maria Teresa de Lamballe (1749–1792), a favorite of Marie-Antoinette, who is connected in the people's minds with the frivolous indifference of their queen to the people's suffering ("Let them eat cake. . . ."). Mme. de Lamballe was torn to pieces by the crowd in September 1792, and her head was raised on a pike to the windows of the prison where the queen was incarcerated and could contemplate the fate that was in store for her.

From the Palace Grotto, a goat-legged nymph is led out—the Actress finally appears. The nymph is an allusion to Olga's role in Ilya Satz's ballet *The Goat-Legged Nymph,* at the Miniature Theater in Petersburg. The work was related to Nijinsky's *Afternoon of a Faun* and was said to border on the pornographic. The stage directions give several possible backdrops for the nymph—a hall, on stage, in Hell, or on the peak of Goethe's Brocken, one of the mountains in the Harz which in Goethe's *Faust* is the setting for the witches' sabbath that occurs every April on *Walpurgisnacht.* A few lines from Goethe describing the gathering of witches and devils illustrate the atmosphere that Akhmatova is also attempting to convey:

They throng and push, they rush and clatter.
They hiss and whirl, they pull and chatter.
It glistens, sparks, and stinks and flares;
Those are indeed the witches' airs.[77]

Watching the nymph dance is the Soldier-Poet, now compared to "Ivanushka of the old fairy tale." In Russian fairy tales, there are two typical types of hero: Ivan the Prince, who is handsome and brave but usually requires the aid of a helper (i.e., a wolf, or some magic object such as a flying carpet), and Ivan the Fool, who is usually from the lower classes, the youngest of three brothers. He is only seemingly a fool, because he is naive rather than crafty and cynical. Ultimately he always wins the hand of the princess through his courage and kindness. In the poem, the Soldier-Poet is identified with this archetypical hero in contrast to his opposite—the Demon Poet.

The "Second Chapter" takes place in the bedroom of the Actress. The epigraph relates to a poem by Akhmatova from the year 1913, "The Voice of Memory":

Or do you see him at your knee,
The one who broke your spell for white death?

The sequence is devoted to Sudeikina, and wonders at her indifference to being
the cause of Knyazev's death.

Over the bed are three portraits. One is the goat-legged nymph, the role in
which the Actress has already appeared. Another is Confusion-Psyche, the role
with which she was associated in the Second Dedication. The third, say the stage
directions, may be Columbine or Donna Anna from Blok's "The Steps of the
Commendatore." Meyerhold's pantomime adaptation of Schnitzler's *Columbine's
Scarf* reflects the general Silver Age interest in the Commedia dell'Arte.[78] The
Italian tradition had by then become an integral part of Russian popular culture,
and performances featuring this tradition appeared regularly at folk fairs during
Carnival week and after Easter. One of the reasons the tradition was popular in
Russia among artists and in the theater at the turn of the century was the avant-
garde generation's wish to break away from realistic illusion as practiced in the
Moscow Art Theater and by the so-called Wanderers in painting. The Commedia
consciously broke such illusions, working with blatantly stylized conventions and
archetypical symbolic characters. Meyerhold endowed the tradition with a slightly
grotesque feeling in his production of the Schnitzler play, and the atmosphere
reflects the Hoffmannesque quality that appears later in *Poem Without a Hero*.
Rudnitsky describes this scene in his book on Meyerhold:

> Especially interesting was the ball scene where "during the old-fashioned
> quadrille here, there, in windows and doors, Pierrot's white sleeve ap-
> pears; the dances, first faster, then slower, take on the terrible quality of
> a nightmare, more so than in life—strange Hoffmann-like creatures gri-
> macing under the direction of a large-headed orchestra leader, who from
> a chair conducts four improbable musicians. . . . All the fantasy and
> unreal terror of these short scenes," wrote Zosko-Borovsky, "was trans-
> mitted with agonizing passion and intensity, and the duality between
> truth and the intentional was presented with great force, knocking the
> audience off balance."[79]

The portrait of Donna Anna has several interpretations. In Akhmatova's own
discussion of Donna Anna as she appears in Pushkin's *The Stone Guest* (as Wendy
Rosslyn points out), Donna Anna represents the divine nature within Don Juan
which he can express and discover through love. However, in a later version of
her article, Akhmatova believes Donna Anna bears a relationship to Pushkin's
own wife—coquettish and curious; and Pushkin is afraid his own wife will soon
forget him as apparently Donna Anna has her own husband (in Pushkin's version—the Commendatore) should he meet an untimely death. The Donna Anna
portrait in *Poem Without a Hero* is explicitly associated with the Blok poem,

where she is already dead. Life has become empty and meaningless for Don Juan without her, but it is unclear whether she is saint or sinner, and the latter is not excluded.[80] In this case she fits well among the other portraits characterizing the Actress.

It is New Year's Eve at midnight. As at the beginning of the poem, a candle is burning. The portrait of the Actress comes to life and steps out of its frame. (Art turning into life, and vice versa, was a favorite theme of the Silver Age.) In Blok's play, *The Fairground Booth,* when the Clown is wounded, cranberry juice instead of real blood pours out of his wound, and characters appear as dolls transformed into real human beings. In Meyerhold's production of this, the mystics were painted onto a flat at a long table, with holes for the actor's heads and hands. Meyerhold himself described this famous scene:

> The long table at which the mystics were sitting was covered with black cloth which reached the floor so the audience saw just the lower part of their figures. Frightened by some reply, the mystics lowered their heads in such a way that they became headless and armless. It turns out that these are cardboard cutouts of figures, with the suits and cuffs drawn in charcoal and chalk. The actors' hands had been pushed through the round holes cut in the cardboard busts and their heads had been leaning against cardboard collars.[81]

In Stravinsky's ballet *Petrouchka,* the puppets at the carnival fair come to life; in Nikolay Tcherepnin's ballet *Pavillon d'Armide,* a tapestry comes to life; and at The Bat, a famous Moscow cabaret, numerous numbers were based on figures painted on flats with holes for heads and arms of actors, and toys and porcelain figures also came to life.

The scene begins with the poet warning the Actress that "the day of reckoning is at hand." What follows is a stream-of-consciousness flow of images conjuring up the atmosphere of Petersburg in 1913—both everyday reality such as lines of grain carts, daubed tea-rose paintings, and the constellation of great Russian figures in the world of art which made the Silver Age one of the greatest epochs in world history: Anna Pavlova as the "Dying Swan," Fyodor Chaliapin, the great Russian bass, Stravinsky's ballet *Petrouchka* (which relates to *Poem Without a Hero* not only because of art-turning-into-life but because it is also based on the archetypal Harlequin triangle), and "blackamoors," who are seen throwing snowballs outside the Actress's window. The last is a reference to the figures dressed as eighteenth-century blacks in Meyerhold's production of Molière's *Don Juan.* They were another means used by Meyerhold to break the realistic illusion, and they functioned as stage hands, moving props around in front of the audience. Alexander Golovin, the stage designer for this production, describes the effect: "The stage was served by the so-called 'liveried little blackamoors' who, bustling like kittens, lit the lights, rang the silver bell before the start, burned perfume, carried out 'Intermission,' reported events like Il Commendatore's appearance, brought chairs and stools, and greatly contributed to the general liveliness with their running about."[82] They also function in the poem as yet another allusion to the Don Juan theme.

We soon find that this enumeration of images provides not only a feeling for the period but the background for a tragedy, and we are about to witness the traditional last fifth act:

> Everyone who's needed is in place:
>   From the Summer Garden the fifth act
>   Wafts . . .

But there is more—the "phantom of Tsushima's hell," a reference to the destruction of the Russian fleet in Tsushima in 1905, in the Russo-Japanese War, which produced such a strong impression on the young Akhmatova. It was the first time a historical event affected Akhmatova's consciousness; the blow to national pride was a shock that was felt throughout the Russian land.

> Then suddenly the Demon Poet appears, alone:
> His sharp profile against the wall.
>   My beauty, is your paladin
>   Mephistopheles or Gabriel?
> The demon himself with Tamara's smile,
>   But such sorcery is hidden
>   In this terrible, smoky face
> . . .
> Was he the one in that crowded hall
>   Who sent the black rose in the goblet
>   Or was all that a dream?
> And wasn't it he who stole—with dead eyes,
>   With a dead soul—into the accursed house
>   Where he met the Commendatore?
>   (II, p. 429)

The character in the last stanza clearly refers to Alexander Blok. At the end of her life, Akhmatova wrote: "I consider Blok not only the greatest poet of the first quarter of the twentieth century, but the man of the epoch, that is, the most characteristic representative of his age." Here he combines features of romantic demonism and tragic doom. The poet is not a Gabriel but a Mephistopheles— he does not save but destroys. He is the "demon himself with Tamara's smile"— an allusion to the mid-nineteenth-century narrative poem by Lermontov, who hopes his love for a mortal, the Georgian princess, Tamara, will save him. His kiss destroys her, but her soul is taken to heaven by an angel. The reference to the black rose in the goblet refers to another famous poem by Blok, "In the Restaurant," in which the hero sends a black rose to a strange woman—or perhaps only dreams that he sent it to her.

The Poet says that these two figures—the Demon Poet and the Actress—appear together at the mouth of the Lethe-Neva. The river on which Petersburg was built now becomes identified with the Lethe in Hades, whose waters make the dead forget their past. But the underlying theme of the poem is that to forget is a mortal sin, and thus the "river of forgetfulness" associated with Hell is another motif in this fabric of sin and retribution. The poet overcomes the power of forgetfulness, and by remembering her past, atones for it.

Suddenly the Demon Poet disappears, and the Actress is left alone to dance without a partner. The author herself will be the fatal chorus, not only providing commentary but, like the Greek chorus, condemning or praising the actions of the principal figures.

The poet now provides a long and loving passage about the Actress, the "Columbine of the 1910–20s," the star of the artistic cabaret, the Stray Dog. She is the poet's double, a Doppelgänger from a Hoffmann tale, where there are two very different aspects of a character-within-a-character. Here the Actress reflects the "gay little sinner" aspect of the author, who now condemns the Actress, and therefore herself as well. And yet in her description of the Actress, she shows there was something very wonderful and attractive about this beautiful creature, who devoted her life to aesthetic and sensual pleasure.

The music that appears is the whistling of the wild wind of Leningrad. The author has a vision of court skeletons, recalling the grotesque ball of Pushkin's story "The Gravedigger." There is an allusion to a wedding, but rather than bringing joy, it reeks once again of death, for the candles are going out and the church hymn sung in an Orthodox wedding ceremony, "Come, O Innocent One!", is sung here to Olga, the seducer of men.

Many features of the Actress's apartment resemble those of Olga's own home, and some of the objects that surrounded her were given to Akhmatova when Olga left Russia in 1924:

> Your house was gaudier than a circus wagon,
>> Decrepit cupids guarded
>>> The altar of Venus.
> You didn't cage your songbirds,
>> You decked out your bedroom like an arbor
>>> (II, p. 433)

Songbirds flying freely around the room characterized Olga's apartment in Paris, where she lived under the roof in a seven-story house. She lived the "high life of a poor artist," says Arthur Lourie, and earned her bread by selling embroidery. Olga was often invited to Lourie's studio before he moved to America, and gave sensitive renderings of Blok's poems, especially the cycle *Snow Mask*. But she also read the French Symbolists—Verlaine, Rimbaud, Baudelaire, Mallarmé. At this time she had a passion for birds. It started when a friend, Meller-Zakomelsky, left her a beautiful birdcage. First there was a canary, then parakeets, sparrows, and turtle doves. She knew each one and allowed them to fly freely around the room, and they never stopped chirping. Before he left Paris, Lourie convinced her to take his apartment, but she could not bring her birds with her. During the bombardment of Paris, a shell fell on Olga's mansard apartment. Olga was returning home, so neighbors dragged her to the basement, but the birds were killed. Olga never recovered from the shock—she soon fell ill and died.[83]

The next lines are puzzling unless one realizes their relationship to Olga:

> The jolly *skobar* wouldn't recognize
> His neighbor, the village wench.

Skobar is a derogatory term for someone from Pskov. Although Olga herself was born in Petersburg, her ancestors were from Pskov. Holy icons only play the role of decoration in the apartment of this Petersburg Venus:

> Spiral staircases hidden in the walls,
> And saints hung on the azure walls—
> And these goods are semi-stolen . . .
> (II, p. 433)

The hidden spiral staircase recalls Pushkin's *Queen of Spades,* another tale of love and deceit set in Petersburg at the beginning of the nineteenth century, which was popular in its operatic version by Tchaikovsky and was staged in a famous production by Meyerhold in the 1930s.

The setting moves to the Actress's bedroom, where she receives her friends, among them the Soldier-Poet, now identified as "Pierrot." Through a famous biblical reference, the author now warns the Actress that she will not be saved:

> I don't mark houses with crosses,—
> Come out courageously to meet me—
> *Your horoscope was cast long ago. . . .*

This refers to the story of the plagues sent against the Pharoah in Exodus, when God sends the worst plague of all, the killing of the firstborn. The Lord told Moses that in order to save their children, he should order the Jews to smear their doorposts with blood from the Passover lamb: "For the Lord will pass through to smite the Egyptians; and when he seeth the blood upon the lintel, and on the two side posts, the Lord will pass over the door, and will not suffer the destroyer to come in unto your houses to smite you" (Exodus 12:23).

The "Third Chapter" is essentially a lyrical digression. One of the epigraphs, lines taken from a poem by Mandelstam (November 1920), is particularly sinister:

> In Petersburg we'll meet again,
> As if it were there we buried the sun.

The poem was written when the Bolsheviks were establishing power, and the Petersburg that Mandelstam and Akhmatova knew and loved was being transformed into Soviet Leningrad. The sun, the former life, has been extinguished, and in the "black velvet of the Soviet night . . . the capital arches its back like a wild cat."[84]

In this chapter, it is not the poet but the wind that speaks, in a digression conjuring up the Petersburg of 1913 through an accumulation of familiar images. (Carriages sliding off bridges appear in one of Gogol's Petersburg tales, "Nevsky Avenue," which is also a Hoffmannesque tale hovering between the real and the fantastic.)

> Bonfires warmed the Christmas holidays,
>> And carriages slid off the bridges,
>>> And the whole mournful city floated
> Toward some mysterious goal
>> With the Neva's current or against it—
>>> Only away from its graves.
> The Galernaya Arch darkened,
>> In the Summer Garden the weathervane squealed,
>>> And the silver crescent moon brightly chilled
>>>> Over the Silver Age.
>
> (II, p. 435)

It is a city doomed from the very beginning, when Tsarina Avdotya Lopukhina, the first wife of Peter the Great, who was abandoned by him, hurled her curse at the new capital: "May this place be empty." The city is "Dostoyevskian and possessed."

> And ever-present in the freezing, prewar,
>> Lecherous, terrible, stifling air,
>>> Lurked an incomprehensible rumble.
>> (II, p. 437)

This incomprehensible rumble recalls the many references by Blok before the Revolution to a rumbling sound hovering in the air, symbolizing the apocalyptic events that were to come. And now the "real" twentieth century appears:

Just as in the mirror of a horrific night
>   A man is possessed and does not want
>   To recognize himself,
Along the legendary embankment
>   The real—not the calendar—
>   Twentieth Century draws near.

(II, p. 439)

In her autobiographical notes, Akhmatova pointed out that

> The twentieth century began with the war in the fall of 1914, just as the
> nineteenth century began with the Congress of Vienna. Dates of the
> calendar have absolutely no meaning. Our revolt against Symbolism was
> entirely legitimate because we thought of ourselves as people of the
> twentieth century and did not wish to remain in the previous century.[85]

Now the poem suddenly switches from the cold, wet mists and wild winds of
Petersburg to a calmer, gentler winter scene in Tsarskoye Selo, as the poet attempts
to find her way home—in her mind, in her memory—as she passes the lovely
Cameron Gallery with statues of the muses near the Catherine Palace. Perhaps
the addressee of this section is Nikolay Nedobrovo, the elegant connoisseur of
poetry who was intimate with Akhmatova for several years before the Revolution,
and wrote an article on her poetry in 1915 that Akhmatova always considered
one of the best assessments of her work, differentiating her strong, restrained
style from the more typically sweet and sentimental poetry written by most women
poets. In this digression, Tsarskoye Selo represents a brief reprieve in memory—
an idyllic spot where the aristocracy ignored the warning signs of imminent war
and revolution until it was too late.[86]

The "Fourth Chapter" of the Petersburg Tale takes place in front of the
Actress's house, facing the Field of Mars, which was used for military maneuvers
and promenades. The name derives from the military parades that were held here
in the early nineteenth century: it is one of the famous landmarks of Petersburg.
The bells of the Church of the Saviour of the Blood are heard—the church built
on the spot where Alexander II was assassinated in 1881—another cursed spot.
A mirage of a palace ball appears through the snowstorm on the Field of Mars.

The chapter begins with an epigraph from a poem by Knyazev.

Love abated and the mortal features
became close and clear.

(II, p. 439)

And now the drama reaches its tragic denouement. The scene is set, as the Soldier-
Poet takes the stage:

Who stands frozen at the darkening window,
   Next to his heart "the pale yellow curl,"
      Darkness before his eyes?
          (II, p. 439)

The phrase, "the pale yellow curl," is from another poem by Knyazev, "How many times . . ."(1911): "How many times I saw the pale yellow curls,/When the wind played with them tenderly . . ."

Now we hear "invisible hooves"—perhaps the hooves of the famous statue of Peter the Great which comes alive in Pushkin's narrative poem *The Bronze Horseman* (1828), when at night after the terrible flood of 1824, the young clerk Yevgeny has a vision of the statue chasing him around the square. This is one of Pushkin's greatest works about the relation between the crushing might of the state and the "little man," the meek subject who is oppressed.

And now the last act begins. She describes the Soldier-Poet:

Who has only a little life left,
   Who asks God only for death
      And who will be eternally forgotten.
          (II, p. 439)

Perhaps these lines allude to another anti-hero, Lensky in Pushkin's *Eugene Onegin*. He too is a poet, a gentle, weak creature whose talent never reaches fruition because he perishes in a duel over love. He also has an Olga in his life, but she is a silly, provincial girl who becomes the Muse in Lensky's overromanticized view of the world. After he dies, he is soon forgotten by his beloved Muse—who marries and leads the very unromantic life of a provincial matron. And Knyazev is also swiftly forgotten by his Muse—Olga Sudeikina.

Soon the Actress returns from a performance of *The Road from Damascus,* a stylized miracle play which was performed at the Stray Dog. However, the words also have more erotic overtones, since they recall lines from one of Knyazev's poems to Olga written in January 1913:

I kissed the "gates of Damascus,"
Gates with a shield, twined in moss,
Let the mask now be put
On me, the happiest of all![87]

The Actress is not alone—she is accompanied by her lover, "with neither face nor name." He is the Demon Poet, and now the words that served as an omen at the start are repeated, as the prophecy is realized:

> "You, Dove, sun, sister!
> I will leave you alive,
>   But you will be *my* widow."[88]

The Soldier-Poet commits suicide, and the author as chorus comments that his death could have been far more noble had he died in the coming war, in the "accursed Mazur swamps" or "on the azure Carpathian heights."

> *Of all the ways for a poet to die,*
> *Foolish boy: He chose this one—*
> *He could not bear the first insult,*
> *He did not know on what threshold*
> *He stood and what road*
> *Spread its view before him . . .*
>   (II, p. 441)

In the short Epilogue, the poet imitates Pushkin's metapoetic digressions, where in the midst of a poem he suddenly discusses the poetic process—what rhymes to use, what techniques to employ at a certain point, the very process of poetic creation. The poet has laid the poem aside—or so she thinks, but it comes crashing down again upon her. This is what actually happened to Akhmatova, who was possessed by the work for at least twenty years. Setting the Epilogue in capital letters conveys the effects of reciting at the top of one's voice:[89]

> ALL IS IN ORDER: THERE LIES THE POEM
> AND, AS USUAL, IT HAS FALLEN SILENT:
> BUT WHAT IF SUDDENLY A THEME BURSTS FORTH;
> KNOCKS ON THE WINDOW WITH ITS FIST—
> AND FROM AFAR, RESPONDING TO THIS APPEAL,
> COME THE TERRIBLE SOUNDS—
> OF GURGLING; GROANS AND SCREAMS
> AND A VISION OF CROSSED ARMS . . .
>   (II, p. 443)

Part Two, "The Other Side of the Coin," was originally devoted to Vladimir Garshin, the doctor Akhmatova hoped to marry after she returned from Tashkent—his name was removed after she learned her hopes were an illusion. But he was a collector of rare coins, and the first section here is named "Tails"—if this "other side of the coin" appears when the player tosses the coin, he loses. It is subtitled "Intermezzo"—like the comic plays performed between acts in early plays. It is an interesting diversion before the full tragic Epilogue.

The first epigraph, "My future is in my past," echoes the earlier lines in its motif: the past determines our future. These words are attributed to Mary Queen of Scots, but clearly relate to various phrases cited earlier by T. S. Eliot. The motif of Lethe reappears in the second epigraph, in the form of a quote from Pushkin's comic poem "House in Kolomna":

> I drink of the waters of Lethe,
> My doctor forbade despondency.

The epigraph is ironic, for the theme of Akhmatova's poem is exactly the opposite of Pushkin's playful parody on the *Rape of Lucretia*. In Pushkin's work, licentiousness and deceit are lauded, and the ability to forget is a way to avoid feeling guilty for one's sins.

The setting is time present, but an interval has passed since the poem began on December 27, 1940. The war is coming closer: it is now January 5, 1941. The motif of the maple appears again—covered now with snow and looking like a specter. What is left of the vision in Part One, of the New Year's Eve drama, is only the debris "common to any holiday or funeral procession"—the smoke of torches, flowers trampled underfoot, sacred souvenirs lost forever.

The poet says the stanzas that follow come from the wind howling in the stovepipe; one can also divine snatches of *Requiem* in the wind.[90] The allusion to *Requiem* is ambiguous. It may be Mozart's *Requiem*, and in this way would be associated with Isaiah Berlin, who said later that *Poem Without a Hero* was a Requiem for all of Europe. However, *Requiem* is also the name of Akhmatova's great cycle of poems about a mother watching her son and her people suffering. She can only stand aside and allow their destiny to be fulfilled: her role is to act as mourner, as lamenter for those who suffer, to reach God through prayer, to bring comfort to these suffering souls.

The text is prefaced by an epigraph from a poem by Klyuev to Akhmatova, "The Revilers of Art." It is a superb tribute to Akhmatova and the horror of her silence, when she writes so little, and what she writes is not allowed to be published. He is angry that for ten years Akhmatova did not give a handful of oats to the horse of poetry, with its diamond-studded bridle, its golden-shod hooves. The poem ends with the comparison of Akhmatova to a jasmine bush:

> Akhmatova is a jasmine bush
> hemmed in by gray tarmac.
> Did she lose her way to the cave
> where Dante walked and the air was thick
> and a nymph spins crystal flax?
> Among Russian women, distant Anna
> shines through like a white little cloud
> seen in the evening through the gray willows.[91]

It was for this poem that Klyuev was sentenced to exile in the camps.

The stanzas in Part Two are numbered, and yet they are often interconnected, and sometimes the end line of one stanza is completed in the next. The section begins with a quarrel between the poet and her editor, who finds the poem too difficult to decipher. It calls to mind a Pushkin poem, "The Poet and the Crowd" (1828), in which the masses cannot understand what the poet is attempting to communicate. There the crowd, in disbelief, also asks the poet what use his poetry can be to anyone.[92] Thus this section not only relates to problems during the Soviet period but is raised to a more universal level: the role of poetry in society in general.

The poet mentions works where the world of dream and vision seems more real than real life—the world conjured up in Keats's sonnet "To Sleep," which begins, "O soft embalmer of the still midnight"; the fantasy world of Maurice Maeterlinck's play *The Blue Bird,* in which two children search for the blue bird of happiness in the kingdom of dreams; or the parapets of Elsinore, where the ghost of Hamlet's father appeared to him—another work on sin and retribution.

The poet discusses the poetic process: she does not wish to write this work but it obsesses her, and she is powerless to rid herself of the haunting, grotesque images, including the figure of Cagliostro-Satan, which is a clear reference to Kuzmin (who, according to many, did not mourn the death of his former lover Knyazev):

I can't get clear of this motley trash;
   Here's old Cagliostro acting the fool—
     Elegant Satan himself,
Who won't weep for the dead with me,
   Who doesn't know what conscience means,
     And why conscience exists.
               (II, p. 449)

Kuzmin wrote a life of Alessandro di Cagliostro, published in 1919. Count Cagliostro (Giuseppe Balsamo, 1743–1795) was a Sicilian alchemist and charlatan famous at the time of the French Revolution for his fake miracles and false prophecies.

A reference to the "Hymn of the Cherubim" (as Amert points out) is a covert allusion to the suppression of religion after the Revolution, the destruction and desecration of churches and their conversion into warehouses and museums:

This does not smell like a midnight
   Roman carnival. The Hymn of Cherubs
   Trembles at the closed churches.
               (II, p. 449)

The hymn is an important part of the Russian Orthodox liturgy, sung when the central doors of the iconostasis, the screen of icons leading to the altar, are

opened, which symbolizes the beginning of the high point of the service, communion.[93]

An allusion to the suppression of her works is conveyed by the poet when
she mentions her "half dead and mute" *Seventh,* that is, her last book of poems.

> And with me is my Seventh,
>   Half dead and mute,
>   Its mouth is numb and open,
> Like the mouth of a tragic mask,
>   But it is daubed with black paint
>   and stuffed with dry earth.
>   (II, p. 449)

Akhmatova'a last collection, *From Six Books,* was published in 1940 and
withdrawn a few months later on Stalin's orders. Only in 1965, a year before her
death, was her seventh book published—*The Flight of Time* (*Beg vremeni*), which
included poems from 1936 to 1964. The Seventh would also refer to her uncom-
pleted Seventh Elegy, on which she was working in 1958–64, whose theme is her
deadly silence:

> And I have been silent, silent for thirty years.
> The silence of arctic ice
> Stands through innumerable nights,
> Closing in to snuff out my candle.
> The dead are silent like this, but that's understandable
> And not as horrible.................
>   (II, p. 721)

What follows are a series of stanzas filled mainly by lines of ellipses. In her
footnotes to the poem, Akhmatova says: "Missing stanzas—imitation of Pushkin.
See 'About *Eugene Onegin:* "It is humbly acknowledged that in *Don Juan* there
are two stanzas left out," wrote Pushkin.' " (II, p. 470). These lines allude to
the metapoetic game Pushkin played in his own works, where he purposely left
some stanzas out, which fits in with the rest of "The Other Side of the Coin."
But another explanation for these "empty stanzas" is that Akhmatova wanted to
call attention to the fact that there were certain themes not allowed by the censor
to be discussed overtly, which had to be removed from her work. V. A. Chernykh,
in his edition of Akhmatova's poems, *Ya—golos vash* (1989), says that because
Akhmatova could not publish certain stanzas relating to the purges and the camps,
she substituted lines of ellipses, thus making an ironic statement. Struve includes
three lines of the possible expurgated stanzas:

And the decades file by,
>   Tortures, exiles and deaths . . . I can't sing
>   In the midst of this horror.

(II, p. 451)

Another editor, Kralin, does not include any of the empty stanzas in his edition of the poem, but replaces them with those that appear in Chukovskaya's diaries:

The enemy tortured: "Come on, tell!"
>   But not a word, nor a groan, nor a cry
>   Did the enemy hear.
And the decades file by,
>   Tortures, exiles and deaths . . . I can't sing
>   In the midst of this horror.

As my contemporaries—
>   Convicts, hundred-and-fivers, prisoners—
>   And we will tell you
How we lived in unconscious fear,
>   How we raised children for the executioner,
>   For prison and for the torture chamber.

Sealing our bluish lips,
>   Mad Hecubas
>   and Cassandras from Chukhloma,
We roar in silent chorus
>   (We, crowned with disgrace):
>   "We are already on the other side of hell." . . .

(II, p. 473)

Her contemporaries, the "hundred-and-fivers," were like the Mandelstams at the end before Osip's arrest—persons who were refused permission to live closer than 105 kilometers to any major city. In the last stanza, Akhmatova identified with modern-day Hecubas and Cassandras: "Sealing our bluish lips . . . We roar in silent chorus." This recalls the woman with bluish lips who stood with Akhmatova in the prison lines and asked her, "Can you describe this?" Hecuba is another famous figure with whom Akhmatova identifies—the wife of Priam, King of Troy, who laments at the end of the *Iliad* as Troy burns and her son, the great hero Hektor, dies. Akhmatova had been identifying with the Trojan princess Cassandra since her early youth—Hecuba's daughter was forced to become the mistress of Agamemnon, leader of the Greek forces. She rejected Apollo, and he cursed her with a gift of prophecy, but no one would heed her warnings. These are great archetypal females, who symbolize the deep suffering women must endure as mere observers of a tragedy played out by men, and who survive them as prophets of doom and lamenters of the dead.

The lines following the empty stanza continue the theme of the poet and the state. The author refuses to "melt away in an official hymn," that is, to write civic verses in praise of the state. This is not entirely true in life, for Akhmatova did finally write the cycle *In Praise of Peace* in the Socialist Realist mode, in order to help get her son out of the camps.

The poet then contrasts Sophocles to Shakespeare, saying that she is more like the ancient Greek dramatist than Shakespeare. Perhaps this is because Shakespeare's plays are more psychological than those of Sophocles—in the latter, the outcome is determined by Fate, which dictates the sudden reversals in characters' lives.[94] However, one might also interpret the last line to mean that destiny did not totally determine the poet's life, but created a life with possibilities that were not foreseen by her. A similar theme is expressed in the third of the "Northern Elegies." Moreover, Shakespeare's plays are not just psychological but concerned with destiny. The individual does have freedom of choice within the confines of the situation in which he or she has been placed by destiny. Hamlet has been told about his father's murder; he knows it is his duty as a son and as Prince of Denmark to avenge it, but he hesitates, and therein lies his tragedy. In *Macbeth,* destiny in the form of the three witches prophesies Macbeth's fate, that he will rule Scotland but his heirs will not. The witches never tell him to sin in order to achieve his end; he makes a conscious choice along with his wife to commit murder in order to attain the throne, and is punished for his sin.

Sophocles' plays also traced the evolution of a character's consciousness when confronted by a dilemma in which destiny had placed him. This is a basic difference between Sophocles and Aeschylus. The theme of Aeschylus' tragedies is moral law outraged, whereas in Sophocles the hero's will is important. In *Oedipus Rex,* the drama focuses on the decisions of Oedipus. "The gods only predict," says the critic H. D. F. Kitto, "they do not compel."[95] Oedipus committed murder in a fit of rashness. The deed was greater than he knew, for his own father was his victim. However, the focus of the play is not on this action, but on how Oedipus behaves when he and his people begin to suffer—for a plague is visited upon his state as punishment for his deed. Oedipus is not a passive victim of Fate, for what is important is how he behaves once he has gained knowledge of what he has done, what choices he makes through his own free will. It is Oedipus himself who sets the forces in motion to discover the cause of the plague, continuing to seek the truth even at the risk that the knowledge may harm him. When he learns what he has done, he blinds himself, thereby replacing physical sight with insight. Perhaps Akhmatova means that Sophoclean drama is more concentrated than that of Shakespeare—it does not mix comedy with tragedy, and *Poem Without a Hero* has that same intense concentration on the tragic without comic relief.

The poet addresses another issue associated with poetry—the fine line be-

tween alluding to others' works and pure plagiarism. She also discusses the issue
of the obscurity of so much of her poem:

> This much is sure; if they accuse me of plagiarism . . .
>> Am I more guilty than others?
>>> Anyway, it's all the same to me.
> I admit to failure
> And I'm not concealing my confusion . . .
>> The box has a triple bottom.
>
> But I confess that I used
> Invisible ink . . .
>> I write in mirror writing,
> There's no other road open to me—
>> I stumbled on this one miraculously
>>> And I am reluctant to put it by.
>>>> (II, p. 453)

Akhmatova insists that her work is different from the classic *poema*, or long
narrative poem, which had become a popular genre in Russian literature in the
nineteenth century, when Pushkin borrowed it from the English Romantic poets.
It had taken numerous forms, from Nekrasov's description of a vision that appears
to peasant women in "Grandfather Frost" to Mayakovsky's anticipation of the
Revolution in "Cloud in Trousers" and Blok's brutal portrayal of the period after
the Revolution in "The Twelve." The *poema* appears in the form of a "hundred-
year-old charmer," but the poet insists that she will have nothing to do with
tradition—her work is different.

> But the hundred-year-old charmer
>> Suddenly wakes up and wants
>>> To play. It has nothing to do with me.
> She drops her lacy handkerchief,
>> Narrows her eyes languidly and, from behind the lines,
>>> Lures with a Bryullovian shoulder.
>>>> (II, p. 455)

It is tempting just to follow the readymade pattern set for her by Russian literary
tradition. The "charmer" lures her with those wonderful, sensual shoulders depicted in the paintings of Bryullov in the mid-nineteenth century. But Akhmatova
goes way beyond the traditional *poema* handed down to her. While Blok's "The
Twelve" may move rapidly from the basic plot to other motifs, it never reaches
the extremes of Akhmatova in terms of abrupt shifts in time; it never becomes a

fabric that at first seems woven of threads of totally disconnected images, but which, as the reader soon learns, is tightly interconnected through an enormous web of cultural and personal associations.

Akhmatova refers to two great English poets who were masters of the long narrative poem, Byron and Shelley:

> To the darkness under Manfred's fir tree,
>   And to the shore where lifeless Shelley,
>   Staring straight up at the heavens, lies—
> And all the world's skylarks
>   Burst the abyss of the ether,
>   And George holds the torch.
>   (II, p. 457)

There are several important links between *Manfred* and *Poem Without a Hero*. Byron's poem also begins at midnight; spirits appear, although not against the hero's will—he consciously conjures them up through charms and invocations. Memory also becomes a moral imperative in this work. Manfred has previous sins on his conscience and wishes to be rid of them, imploring the spirits for the gift of forgetfulness of the past. But they refuse:

> We are immortal, and do not forget!
> We are eternal; and to us the past
> Is, as the future, present.[96]

Akhmatova's stanza about Manfred also relates to Shelley, who was drowned in 1822. George Gordon Byron and other poets burned Shelley's body on the shore—the tragic loss of another poet.

The speaker then tells the author that she is not that "English lady," that is, she is not just a continuation of the English Romantic *poema,* nor is she Clara Gazoul (the fictitious Spanish author of romantic works written by the French writer Prosper Mérimée). Nor, however, does the poem wish to serve Akhmatova's "dubious reputation which has lain twenty years in the ditch"—a reference to the many years Akhmatova has been slandered, attacked, and left unpublished. She will reward the poet's midnight malice with a royal kiss.

Part Three is the Epilogue, and we now return to the time frame of the poet looking back. However, it is no longer the same "present" as when the reader first met the poet. It is June 1942. The war has ravaged the city of the poet, and it now lies in ruins.

The Epilogue begins with three epigraphs, all relating to Petersburg, and they have been ordered very carefully—there is a progression from Pushkin's adulation of Petersburg in *The Bronze Horseman* to the curse of Avdotya, Peter the Great's first wife, and finally to Annensky's nightmarish vision of Petersburg as a city of mute squares and executions.[97] Akhmatova once told Chukovskaya that the city was made for catastrophe: "This cold river, over which there are always heavy clouds, these threatening sunsets, this horrible operatic moon. . . . The black water with yellow flecks of light . . . It is all horrible. I cannot imagine how catastrophes and misfortunes would look in Moscow: there is none of this there."[98]

Although the poet does not mention it, the date on which the scene takes place is Akhmatova's birthday, June 24.[99] It is just over a year since the Soviet Union was invaded and Leningrad was bombed. The maple tree outside the poet's window, a symbol perhaps of the city itself, has been mutilated, but reaches out toward the poet:

> A witness to everything in the world,
>   From dusk to dawn,
>   The old maple looks into the room.
> And, foreseeing our separation,
>   Stretches out to me, as if to help,
>   Its desiccated black hand.
>   (II, p. 461)

The Epilogue is narrated by the author 7,000 kilometers away—she has been evacuated to the East (Akhmatova was sent to Tashkent in Central Asia). Lines 19–30 relate to Garshin. They differ greatly from the original version, when Akhmatova was still very much in love with him, written on August 18, 1942, in Tashkent. The earlier version reads:

> You are my formidable one and my last,
> Bright listener of dark ravings,
> Hope, forgiveness, honor.
> You burn before me like a flame,
> You stand over me like a banner,
> And you kiss me like flattery.
> Put your hand on the top of my head . . .
> Now let time stand still
> On the watch you gave me.
> Misfortune will not pass us by,
> And the cuckoo does not cuckoo
> In our burned woods.[100]

The lines that replace these in the final version are quite different. They were written after Garshin and she had separated forever and Akhmatova had returned to Leningrad.

> You, neither the first nor the last
>   Dark listener to bright babbling,

What revenge are you planning for me?
You are not drinking, only sipping
    This grief from the very depths—
        The news of our parting.
Don't place your hand on my head—
    Let time stop forever
        On the watch you gave me.
Misfortune will not pass us by,
    And the cuckoo does not cuckoo
        In our burned woods. . . .

(II, p. 461)

The next stanzas introduce another "double." In the earlier "Petersburg Tale" of 1913, the Actress was the poet's double. Now the author turns to Siberia, and her double is her son. He returns from an interrogation with emissaries from the "Noseless Slut"—death.

And from behind barbed wire,
In the very heart of the taiga—
I don't know which year—
Having become a heap of "camp dust,"
Having become a terrifying fairy tale,
My double goes to the interrogation,
And then he returns from the interrogation
With the two emissaries from the Noseless Slut.

The next lines are some of the most famous in the poem, when the poet returns her gaze to Leningrad. Although physically separated, she and her beloved city are inseparable, for her shadow is on its walls, her reflection is in its canals, the sound of her footsteps is in the halls of the Hermitage where her friend walked with her—an allusion to the times she shared with Garshin visiting this great museum before the evacuation.

The poet takes up the theme of exile, of never being able "to go home again." She talks of her own evacuation as a form of exile, but also recalls those who left after the Revolution for other lands:

And that happy phrase—at home—
    Is known to no one now,
        Everyone gazes from some foreign window.
Some from New York, some from Tashkent,
    And bitter is the air of banishment—
        Like poisoned wine.

(II, p. 463)

The one gazing from the window in New York is Arthur Lourie, the first Soviet Commissar of Music, with whom Akhmatova was living before he left Russia for good in 1922. "Bitter is the air of banishment" relates to her earlier poem in 1922: "I am not with those who abandoned their land . . .":

> Dark is your road, wanderer,
> The bread of strangers smells like wormwood.

The end of the poem has several possible interpretations. Before the poet lies the road to Siberia, the road her son had trod.

> Seized by mortal fear
>   Of what had turned to dust
>   And recognizing the hour of vengeance,
> Lowering her dry eyes
>   And wringing her hands, Russia
>   Fled before me to the east.
>   (II, p. 465)

This could mean that the "hour of vengeance" was punishment in Siberia. However, one must recall that Akhmatova was a descendant of the Tatar ruler Ghenghis Khan and had royal Tatar blood flowing in her veins. She was always fascinated by the East, and translated poetry from Korea and other Oriental countries. When she came to Tashkent, she identified strongly with her ancestors, who conquered the Russian land in the mid-thirteenth century:

> I haven't been here for seven hundred years
> But nothing has changed . . .
> In the same way the grace of God still pours
> From unassailable heights
>   (II, p. 201)

The last lines could be interpreted to mean that Russia finally turned away from the West and looked instead to the East for salvation. Akhmatova's son was very much an advocate of the Eurasian theory, which had been popular at the beginning of the twentieth century in Russia. The Eurasian theorists did not object to the Western technological innovations introduced into Russia by Peter the Great and his followers, but to the secularization of Russian culture, which they felt was the influence of the West—a turning away from religion and mysticism shared with the East, to a total reliance on logic and science as the final solution to humanity's problems. The sentiments contained in Eurasianism were expressed in a different way by the artist Natalya Goncharova, one of the leading members of the avant-garde at the beginning of the twentieth century:

I shake the dust from my feet and leave the West . . . my path is toward the source of all arts, the East. The art of my country is incomparably more profound and important than anything that I know in the West. . . . We have not learned the most important thing: not to make stupid imitations and not to seek our individuality, but to create, in the main, works of art and to realize the source on which the West draws is the East and us. . . . I express my deep gratitude to Western painters for all they have taught me. After carefully modifying everything that could be done along these lines and after earning the honor of being placed alongside contemporary Western artists—in the West itself—I now prefer to investigate a new path.

Goncharova goes on to say that she now intends "to draw my artistic inspiration from my country and from the East, close to us."[101] While Akhmatova certainly loved and admired Western European culture, she was never tempted to leave Russia, which she considered unique, and whose beauty and profundity is partly explained by its Eastern legacy.

Some critics have interpreted *Poem Without a Hero* as wholly pessimistic. But this is to limit the poem to the context of Akhmatova's other works and her own beliefs. It is very different from works written after the war by Western Existentialists like Camus and Sartre, who viewed the world as godless and absurd. In their interpretation, the greatness of mankind lay in its ability to endure in a basically senseless world, where destiny played dirty tricks on humanity. Instead, implicit in the *Poem Without a Hero* is Akhmatova's belief that good will ultimately triumph in a world ruled by a just God. When Akhmatova looked back at her life and that of her generation before the Revolution, she judged their behavior as wrong and deserving of punishment. But she also believed that through atonement, retribution could be avoided—sins could be expiated, because a just God is also a forgiving God, and she believed Russia and its people could be regenerated. The poem then becomes a ritual of atonement.

Akhmatova also wrote a version of this poem as an (unfinished) ballet libretto, dated December 1959. It lacks the framework—the setting before and during World War II. Instead, it begins in the past with a woman named "X" in a shawl (Akhmatova's attribute) sitting at a table with two place settings. At some point there were to be scenes characterizing Petrograd in 1920, and the last part was to be set in 1941: "The first bombing has begun. Everyone has died long ago."

But there are many similarities to the original poem. It is just before midnight, the bell rings, and masqueraders arrive—not only the same ones as in the poem but others as well. The focus of the ballet is the scene in the Actress's bedroom, when the Soldier arrives and eats breakfast. Mozart's *Requiem* is heard. An extensive list of ballet numbers follows: the Actress receives guests and forgets the Soldier, Klyuev and Yesenin perform a wild Russian peasant dance, Ivanov's artistic salon—"the Tower"—and the altar of Pergamon come to life, Oedipus and Antigone appear. There is even a vision of pagan Russia, recalling Stravinsky's *Rite of Spring,* and a character referred to as the "Superfluous Shade."

In another version, the Superfluous Shade signifies Fate, continually appearing and disappearing, presaging misfortune. There is a scene at the Stray Dog—in particular, the evening with the ballerina Tamara Karsavina. In a later version numerous representatives from the pre-Revolutionary epoch are present at the masquerade, including Marina Tsvetayeva, Mikhail Vroubel (the artist who painted many versions of Lermontov's Demon), Stravinsky, Meyerhold as Dr. Dapertutto, Blok, Khlebnikov, Ivanov, Rasputin, Mayakovsky, and Nijinsky. Here Fate appears in the form of a one-legged old organ grinder, who is also a fortuneteller able to reveal the future.[102]

The focus of the ballet is the love story. It is not really a confrontation with the past, nor are there abrupt transitions in level. Instead, the form reduces the roles to character dances. The complex interweaving of themes and motifs in the literary version is totally missing here.

Finally, we should note that the problem of the accessibility of the literary text is related to reception theory, a theory that is popular today among literary critics. Many of Akhmatova's images and allusions were perfectly clear to the intelligentsia of her era, just as most of the allusions in Dante's *Divine Comedy* were clear to his contemporaries, even a part of their everyday lives. Similarly Robert Wilson, John Cage, and Merce Cunningham, who are currently "household names" among the American intelligentsia, may be quite obscure in fifty years' time to those who did not share our cultural experience. Akhmatova did not write *Poem Without a Hero* in order to be obscure, but to provide a work rich in cultural allusions to some of the most important artistic figures and historical events in Russian history. It is surely one of the great works of the twentieth century.

Joseph Brodsky: Arrest and Exile, 1963–1965

You will write about us on a slant.
—JOSEPH BRODSKY

One of those who became close to Akhmatova at the end of her life, and who was made to suffer and stood his trial with dignity, was the poet Joseph Brodsky. When Akhmatova first met him, he was young, rash, and brilliant—famous by the time he wa twenty, his poems recited and put to music later by many of the 1960s generation. It is important to view the Brodsky trial in the context of other events of Soviet society at the time, as part of an overall pattern. Brodsky was brought to trial in 1964, a time when everyone still remembered what happened to Pasternak and soon became wary of the "Thaw." A month after the publication in 1962 of Solzhenitsyn's *One Day in the Life of Ivan Denisovich*, Khrushchev visited an art exhibition in the Manezh hall, in the former riding arena, where military exercises had been held during the times of the tsars, and which had become a major venue for art exhibitions under the Soviets. The exhibition featured abstract art, which triggered off a campaign against modernism. On December 12, 1962, at a session of the Supreme Soviet, Khrushchev declared that the Party had criticized Stalin's excesses but had not denied his merits and contributions to communism. A few days later, on December 17, at a meeting of the

Party and government leaders which included people in the arts, there was a denunciation of Formalism, allegedly an imitation of the worst in the art of the bourgeois West. A Secretary of the Central Committee of the Communist Party, Leonid Ilyichov, gave a speech distinguishing between criticizing the cult of personality—Stalin—and criticizing Communist society and culture in general. Solzhenitsyn was present at this meeting. In his *Essays on Literary Life,* he writes:

> At that first Kremlin meeting they still praised me, applauded me—but *Ivan Denisovich* was like the last breath of the explosion of the Twenty-Second Congress. A general counterattack of Stalinists began which the nearsighted Khrushchev supported wildly. We heard from him that literature was a long-range weapon and had to be verified by the Party, that he was not an advocate of the rule "live and let live"; that ideological co-existence is morally filthy and that the struggle did not allow for compromise.[1]

A conversation Chukovskaya had with Akhmatova on December 21 reflected these events. Akhmatova had hoped, with the coming of the Thaw, that there might be a chance for her *Requiem* to be published, but she quickly realized the potential danger to art that the Manezh affair symbolized. Chukovskaya said, "The gap is closing. The mighty Solzhenitsyn crack is beginning to be riveted shut." "Yes," replied Akhmatova, "and the Manezh. . . . My *Requiem* will not have any success if the Manezh affair also affects literature." Chukovskaya discussed the main topic going around Moscow—Ilyichov's speech and the words of Khrushchev, that not all of Stalin's acts should be condemned. Chukovskaya points out that it was possible to live under Stalin—they *had* lived under him—and possible to listen and read words of praise for Stalin—they had done so for thirty years. But now after everything (meaning the Thaw and the condemnation of Stalin), to have to listen to any praise of Stalin was unthinkable.

"It is impossible to endure a 'repetition,' " Akhmatova went on. "When you remember that in 1948–49 they began taking people away again who had returned after 1937—I know that among those who were waiting for yet another arrest there were many suicides. Waiting for the second arrest was too much for them. Can we really endure praise of Stalin—again?"[2] During the first few months of 1963 there were more meetings with Khrushchev, at which he warned intellectuals to be careful about how far they went in their criticism of the state, and that their art must be accessible and comprehensible to the masses.

This was the atmosphere in which Joseph Brodsky's trial took place. Brodsky was born in Leningrad in 1940; his father was a newspaper reporter and photographer. The family lived in a room and a half in a communal apartment, which by coincidence had been occupied by the Symbolist poets so popular at the turn of the century, Dmitry Merezhkovsky and Zinaida Gippius, who advocated a synthesis of sensual paganism and spiritual Christianity in their poetry. Brodsky says in his autobiographical sketch that it was from his family's apartment that Gippius, the elegant red-haired aristocrat, shouted abuse to the revolutionary sailors—the pair left for Paris soon after the Revolution.

After high school, instead of going on to the university, Brodsky began taking odd jobs, working in a factory, as a stoker in a boilerroom, as janitor in a morgue, and he also went on a geological expedition. But all the time he continued to write poetry. He taught himself English and Polish and began doing translations.[3] His poetry is not wildly experimental, but it is brilliant and profound. He was awarded the Nobel Prize in 1987 for the "unusual intensity of the spiritual and intellectual life of his poems, his broad cultural horizons and artistic form."[4] One of his most popular early poems is "Pilgrims":

By the coliseums, the robbers' dens,
by temples and bars,
by chic cemeteries
by large bazaars
by peace and grief,
by Mecca and Rome,
burnt by the blue sun
along the earth go
the pilgrims.

They are maimed, hunchbacked.
Hungry, half dressed.
Their eyes are full of the sunset,
Their hearts are full of the dawn.
Behind them sing the deserts,
lightning flashes,
stars tremble above them,
and birds shriek hoarsely at them,
that the world will remain the same.

Yes. Will remain the same.
Blinding as snow.
And doubtfully tender.
The world will remain deceitful.
The world will remain eternal.
Perhaps, accessible,
but nevertheless endless.

And this means there will be no sense
in a belief in yourself or in God.
And it means, the only thing left
was Illusion and a Road.

And there will be sunsets over the earth.
And there will be dawns over the earth.

It will be fertilized by soldiers.
It will be approved by poets.[5]

There is nothing political in this poem—as Efim Etkind points out in his book
on Brodsky's trial. It is about people today wandering around without aim or
meaning, believing that nothing will ever change, and that any idea of earthly
paradise is only an illusion.[6] But from the Socialist Realist point of view, "Pilgrims"
is a political poem: it implicitly suggests the failure of the Communist state by
what it does *not* do. The poem does not promote the idea that communism will
eventually produce a paradise on earth; rather, it projects a cynical view of a
world without hope.

According to Yakov Gordin, who was one of Brodsky's closest friends and a
student at the university with him, the attitude of the authorities toward Brodsky
was based on two factors: his own individual personality and the political climate
of the time. Brodsky was a free spirit, who hated any kind of conformity. He
often behaved wildly and did not follow the rules of the game, which even under
the Thaw were still quite rigid and confining. It was his public behavior, even
more than his poetry, that provoked the authorities. In 1958, he began reciting
his poetry at student halls and experienced an enormous success. They especially
loved the way he chanted the lines, making them come alive. In 1960, he read in
a poets' competition held at Leningrad's Gorky Palace of Culture.[7] "The Jewish
Cemetery" in particular created a sensation:

The Jewish cemetery near Leningrad.
A crooked fence of rotten wood.
Behind the crooked fence lay all in a row
Lawyers, merchants, musicians, revolutionaries.

They sang for themselves.
They saved up for themselves.
They died for others.
But at first they paid taxes,
                              respected the police,
and in this world, absolutely materialistic,
they interpreted the Talmud,
                              remaining idealists.

Perhaps they saw more.
Perhaps they believed blindly.
But they taught the children to be patient
and to become persistent.

And not sow bread.

                        Never to sow bread.

Simply to lie down
in the cold earth, like grain.
And fall asleep forever.
And then earth would be sprinkled on them,
and candles lit,
and on memorial day
hungry old men with high voices
choking from the cold, shouted about keeping calm.

And they found it.

                    In the form of the decay of matter.
Not remembering anything.
Not forgetting anything.
Behind the crooked fence of rotten wood,
    kilometers from the end station of the trams.[8]

Samizdat, the term given to underground publications of forbidden material, was only just beginning, and Brodsky's poems were passed around on sheets of paper. He became close friends with three fellow poets, Dmitry Bobyshev, Anatoly Nayman, and Yevgeny Rein. Bobyshev said they were "Akhmatova's orphans." All three were students at the Leningrad Technical Institute in the early 1950s, and were soon joined by Brodsky in their poetic endeavors. They read their works to each other and received invitations to recite in people's homes at literary associations and evenings devoted to poetry. Nayman said they had no doubts about their talent—they believed in their stars.

Nayman met Akhmatova first. A few weeks later, Bobyshev and Rein went on their own to her apartment to introduce themselves. Akhmatova was packing to move, and piles of books were lying all over the floor. Having accepted their offer to help her, she led them to the next room and commanded: "Read!" She approved of their verse, saying they "would do," but advised them to write more concisely. "And how happy we were," wrote Bobyshev in his memoir of these years. "My God! Our poems were approved by Akhmatova herself, when they were rejected by every almanac, magazine, and publisher in Moscow and Leningrad. This gave us great confidence."[9]

Brodsky met Akhmatova when Yevgeny Rein brought him to her dacha in Komarovo. He was twenty-two years old. He recited some of his poems and she liked them. Then he came with Rein and Nayman several more times. He says he still did not quite grasp the full significance of who she was—until one day, returning from Akhmatova's by train to Leningrad, he suddenly understood. From then on he went as often as possible to visit her, and even rented a cabin in Komarovo one winter just to be able to see her every day. At that point he had only read her early works: "The Gray-Eyed King," and the poem about putting the glove on the wrong hand. He said as a "normal Soviet" it was difficult for him to respond to such poems. In fact, except for Mandelstam, he did not like the poets of the Silver Age, and found Blok impossibly melodramatic. It was only when he read Akhmatova's later work that her poems became meaningful to him.[10]

The four young poets waited for a "dedication"—a touch of the magic wand, a tap of the sword on the shoulder, some symbolic "handing down of the lyre." They all devoted verses to Akhmatova with the undisguised hint that she write poems back to them. In 1962, she wrote a poem to Brodsky:

> I don't weep for myself now,
> But let me not be on earth to witness
> The golden stamp of failure
> On this yet untroubled brow.
>
> (II, p. 223)

With her usual gift for prophecy and insight, she predicted destiny would soon test Brodsky's ability to endure adversity.

One time, in 1962, Bobyshev brought Akhmatova a poem he had written for her, along with a bouquet of five beautiful roses. It was her birthday, and she was staying at Komarovo. Akhmatova mentioned the roses on his next visit, saying, "Four of them soon faded, but the fifth bloomed extraordinarily well and created a miracle, almost flying around the room." Soon the young poets found out what this "miracle" was—Akhmatova had written poems to them. "The Last Rose" was devoted to Brodsky, "The Fifth Rose" to Bobyshev, and "Non-existence" to Nayman. The poem to Brodsky was the one she recited to Robert Frost when he came to see her. In it she asks God to let her live a simple life and not share the terrible fate of famous women in history like Joan of Arc and Dido. She opens with an epigraph containing a line from Brodsky: "You will write about us on a slant," which appeared when Akhmatova's poem was first published, but disappeared after Brodsky's trial.

Brodsky had written his poem to her earlier that year:

> . . . I did not see, will not see your tears,
> I will not hear the rustling of wheels,
> carrying you to the bay, to the trees,
> along the fatherland without a memorial to you.
>
> In a warm room, as I recall, without books,
> without admirers, but there you are for them,
> resting your brow on your palm,
> you will write about us on a slant.

You will mutter then: "O, my Lord!
This air is only thickening the flesh
of thoughts which left their own recognition,
and not your new creation!"[11]

Brodsky's life quickly became more complicated. As a result of Khrushchev's meetings with intellectuals in 1963, Leningrad decided to "clean the city." Brodsky's trial was the first, but certainly not the last attempt to punish artists for their individualism. Gordin says the court condemned Brodsky as a real opponent because he was a free spirit. Although he did not plot to overthrow the regime, his very existence was a threat to the status quo. They felt this instinctively, and therefore in their eyes they were not condemning a totally innocent victim.

The campaign against Brodsky began with a nasty article that appeared in *Vechernii Leningrad* in November 1963. The person who had organized the major attack against Brodsky was Yakov Lerner. In 1956 he had been director of the Technological Institute, where a newspaper, *Kultura* (*Culture*), had been put out by the students. As self-appointed guardian of the purity of Communist ideology, Lerner attacked several articles in this paper—those on film by Nayman and on Paul Cézanne by Rein. Lerner became head of one of the vigilante groups that took the law into their own hands and carried out unwarranted searches. Later Lerner himself would be charged with black marketeering and sentenced to prison. But on November 29, his article, "Subliterary Drone," appeared in *Vechernii Leningrad*. Its basis was a relatively new Regulation against people who allegedly were not working and were sponging off Communist society. The article was signed by Lerner, A. Ionin, and M. Medvedev.[12]

The only aspect of Lerner's article that was correct was the spelling of Brodsky's name. It claimed that some years ago a young man calling himself a poet appeared in velvet pants carrying a briefcase stuffed with papers. Friends called him simply "Osya," but elsewhere he was known as Joseph Brodsky. He was a loner who had not joined any literary circles. His poetry was full of pessimism, a mixture of decadence, modernism, and simple gibberish. Brodsky, it was asserted, had not even finished high school. The authors quoted poems that were not written by Brodsky, and then criticized them. They accused Brodsky of not working, mentioned people identified as friends, among them a mystic and a criminal. They charged that Brodsky met an American in Samarkand to whom he wanted to give a forbidden manuscript, then lost his nerve. He allegedly planned to leave the country with his friend O. Shakhmatova, who was with him in Samarkand—they were going to steal a plane and fly it abroad.

Lerner enlisted the support of Alexander Prokofiev, head of the Leningrad Writers' Union. Vladimir Admoni says that Prokofiev was a real poet and did not have the features of an executioner. He was good-natured, sympathetic; a short man, with a round peasant's face, who had a genuine lyric gift. He actually tried to promote young poets rather than help destroy them. Yet he was against the public readings of Yevtushenko and Voznesensky in Moscow, and seemed jealous of the popularity achieved by Brodsky, Andrey Bitov, and others. Without his sanction, Brodsky could not be arrested. Lerner showed him a falsified epigram, saying it had been written by Brodsky against Prokofiev, who believed it. After Lerner's article appeared, Brodsky wrote a reply, but no newspaper would accept it.

At that point Efim Etkind, a distinguished scholar at the Herzen Pedagogical Institute who had been deeply impressed by Brodsky's works and the poet Gleb Semyonov asked Gordin to go to Moscow to deliver a letter to Etkind's friend Frieda Vigdorova, explaining what had happened. The literary scholar Vladimir Admoni knew Vigdorova from Tashkent during the war. Vigdorova wrote children's books and was a journalist whose columns appeared in such important newspapers as *Literaturnaya gazeta* and *Pravda,* chiefly essays on material from letters sent to the editors, begging for help and talking about injustices encountered in everyday life. A strong person, she was also restrained and quiet, and often managed to overcome tremendous difficulties in order to help people. She became a member of the District Soviet Council, where she listened to endless pleas; although they exhausted her, she continued to help people in any way she could. In the late autumn of 1963 Vigdorova came to visit Leningrad, and Admoni showed her an article attacking young Leningrad writers, in particular Brodsky. Vigdorova decided to devote herself to helping Brodsky during this period of his arrest and trial. But she developed terminal cancer, and in August 1965 she died at just over fifty years old.[13]

There are various interpretations as to why Brodsky became the victim of the regime's attack at this particular moment in Russian history. For his trial was not just an individual affair, but a turning point in the history of the relationship between the poet and the state. In the second half of the 1950s, a large number of talented young writers and poets had appeared in Leningrad. In first place, according to Admoni, was Joseph Brodsky, because of the power of the poetry that poured from his soul. Most of the work of the Leningrad writers was nonpolitical; there was no one comparable to Yevtushenko in Moscow. Yet the works of the Muscovites were often published—admittedly sometimes meeting with opposition from the regime—whereas the works of the Leningrad writers were not.

A series of attacks appeared during the 1960s, and the rumor was that Brodsky would be only the first victim—others would follow. Therefore, many people rallied to Brodsky's cause not only because he was a remarkable poet but because they wanted to protect all poets from the arbitrary will of the state, which had been punishing artists and intellectuals for so long. This time there was hope that things would be different, and some very brave intellectuals like Admoni and Etkind dared to make a public protest. As Gordin says: "The soul, the conscience, the mind rose up against the shameless, cold cynicism of state figures who punished, who had the unlimited right to pulverize innocent people on their grindstone. It was only a handful of people who protested, but they were members of the Union of Writers."[14] The Brodsky trial became a symbol of the active dissent in the sixties, and its suppression in Soviet society. There would soon be other such events—the trial of Daniel and Sinyavsky, the support for Solzhenitsyn and Sakharov—but Brodsky's case was the first.

Akhmatova was in Moscow in December 1963, and she invited Shostakovich to come see her at the Ardovs'. He was then the deputy to the Supreme Soviet for the area of Leningrad where Brodsky lived. Shostakovich told Akhmatova that nothing could be done for Brodsky, because he had been meeting with foreigners. However, Shostakovich did speak with Tolstikov, head of the Leningrad City Council.

It was clear when the articles appeared that Brodsky had to leave Leningrad. He lived for a while near Moscow in the Kaluga district, but then he found out that the woman he loved was having an affair with another poet, someone he considered a good friend, and Brodsky returned immediately to Leningrad.[15] On February 13, 1964, Brodsky was arrested on the street. At 9:30 P.M. three men approached him, and without any documents proving their legal right to do so, they put him in a car and took him to the police station, where he was placed in solitary confinement. Subsequently he was put in the same prison as Lev Gumilyov had been, Kresty [Crosses], made famous in Akhmatova's *Requiem* cycle.

On February 18, the trial began in the Dzerzhinsky District Court. Vigdorova did all she could beforehand to help. She turned to several important writers, found a lawyer and witnesses. Three formal legal witnesses appeared for the defense: Admoni, Etkind, and Natalya Grudinina, the head of a seminar of young poets in which Brodsky had once taken part. Admoni appeared not because he had had any strong ties earlier with Brodsky, but on principle—he could not remain silent. It was the first time, said Admoni, that someone had appeared at such a trial chiefly as a matter of conscience. Admoni and his wife both thought the result of his appearance at best would mean he would lose his job and be expelled from the Union of Writers, and at worst that he would be arrested and sent to a camp. And yet his wife, the scholar Tamara Silman, did not attempt to dissuade him. "For many long decades we had preserved the inner strength of our souls, and refused to turn to the executioners," Admoni wrote. "And now, for the first time, a chance appeared to reveal this strength—a chance to prevent the executioners from carrying out their intentions. And it seemed that our secret inner spiritual freedom meant nothing if it were not transformed into action at the appropriate moment—even if it was doomed to failure."[16]

Admoni added that something like this would have been absolutely unheard of during the Stalinist period. Now a different time had come—with the death of Stalin, the curtailment of the horrible trial against the Jewish doctors, the execution of Beriya, the condemnation of Stalin at the Twentieth Congress. But then Khrushchev began to return to the old ways. The basis of the system had not changed. However, something inside people's souls *had* changed and the former mute silence became impossible. There was a feeling that protest might at last be effective. Once the decision had been made, it was necessary to go all the way, even if it meant sacrifice. As someone who had spent his life at an institute teaching young people to love literature, Admoni said to himself, "Who if not me?"

It was not so easy to rally writers of the older generation in Leningrad behind Brodsky. Brodsky had insulted many of them, treating their works with mocking irony and sometimes even with contempt. He was often arrogant, but Admoni felt it was a kind of naive arrogance, the pride of someone who was aware how great his own talent was, but not wise enough to hide his pride. But they knew how much he respected Akhmatova and was close to her, and this made a difference in their minds. Akhmatova had shown Admoni poems by Brodsky, and Admoni realized immediately the great gift of this poet. Admoni thought Brodsky and Akhmatova understood each other because they shared many important things in common: a disregard for external circumstances that might otherwise have crushed them; an unpretentiousness; their ability never to lose their great dignity in spite of persecution and poverty. She along with Chukovsky, Marshak (the noted author of children's books), and many others sent letters and telegrams to the KGB and the court.

The court was on Vosstaniya Street: a crowd gathered outside the entrance, and also stood in the corridors and filled the hall on the second floor. They were mainly young people who came to show their moral support. Gordin, an influential figure among the students, asked them not to get out of control, and they behaved well, knowing any scandalous action would only work to the detriment of the accused. Brodsky's parents sat with their eyes glued to the door, waiting for their son to appear. Judge Savelyeva arrived—a vulgar, ignorant woman, who knew just how much power she held in her hands. There was no barrier behind which the accused normally stood. Brodsky just stood alone, isolated, near his parents on the bench. His face reflected that inner peace which Akhmatova radiated her entire life, no matter how bad her situation. Savelyeva could not really insult him, reach his inner core, and he was never frightened by her shouting. Gordin says Brodsky's calm was more than just a form of courage. His simple, biblical features expressed confusion at the authorities' inability to comprehend him, and he in turn could not understand this strange woman, her unmotivated maliciousness.

Vigdorova wrote to Chukovskaya on February 22, 1964: "Perhaps one day he will become a great poet, but I will never forget how he looked—helpless, with an expression of astonishment, irony, and challenge all at the same time." Sitting in court and taking meticulous notes, Vigdorova wrote down the essence of what occurred, and then made this information available both in the USSR and abroad. Her reporting made people aware of what was really going on. Vigdorova was on her own: for the first time in her life she could not obtain an assignment from a newspaper or get a press pass. She and Chukovskaya both wrote the KGB and Union of Writers but got no reply. Any contacts Vigdorova may have had either could not or did not wish to help. Even the popular Voznesensky, Yevtushenko, and Akhmadulina, to whom the regime often listened, could not get a response in this particular case.

The judge began by asking Brodsky what he did. He replied, "I write poetry. I translate." The judge asked if he had any regular work, and Brodsky said, "I thought that was regular work." He told her he had contracts with publishers. The judge asked who had recognized him as a poet, and Brodsky replied, "No one. Who was it who decided I was a member of the human race?" The judge wanted to know where Brodsky had studied to be a poet. Brodsky replied, "I didn't think you learned that . . . I think this is . . . from God." Brodsky's lawyer was experienced and proved that the allegations in the newspaper articles had been false, that Brodsky earned money from translations, lived at home, and had few expenses. After the trial, Judge Savelyeva was amazed to discover so many people standing in the corridor. Israel Metter told her, "It's not every day they judge a poet."[17] Actually, Metter adds, that was not quite accurate. Poets were judged every day in the Soviet Union, but the regime did not usually take such an active interest.

The next three weeks were the hardest for Brodsky. He was sent to a psychiatric clinic to be tested to see if he was fit to be sent into exile, and had to submit to all sorts of ill treatment during the tests. On March 13, Brodsky's second trial began. It took place at the Club of Building Renovators on 22, Fontanka, next to the Leningrad City Court, which had once been the headquarters of the tsar's secret police. By this time Brodsky had many prestigious people writing letters and telegrams and collecting money for him. A number of these supporters, including Admoni and Etkind, testified on his behalf at the trial; but witnesses for the prosecution, ordinary workers and pensioners who had never met Brodsky before or read his poetry, nevertheless condemned him as harmful to society.

This time Brodsky was asked by the judge how he had participated in building communism. Brodsky replied, "Building communism is not just standing at a lathe or behind a plough. It is also the work of the intelligentsia." Admoni and Etkind both gave brilliant speeches in Brodsky's defense.

Admoni says that in the pause before the verdict, everyone somehow quite senselessly hoped that he would be pardoned. All the accusations and the witnessing against him was such clear nonsense, and after his own testimony and that of other scholars, and the lawyer's speech and Brodsky's own concluding words, plus telegrams from Akhmatova and Shostakovich, it seemed somehow impossible that the verdict would go against the poet. However, it had been decided beforehand: five years' exile to the village of Norinskaya near Konosha in the district of Archangel region. And they then understood just how naive and childish their hopes had been. They could not win against the impenetrable political machine. On this level, nothing had changed. The verdict was read at one o'clock in the morning. Brodsky was led out by the police. As Admoni, Vigdorova, and some others walked slowly along the Fontanka, through the cold, wet darkness of the March night, they were silent.

Etkind relates how this trial pitted two traditional foes against each other, the bureaucracy and the intelligentsia. Brodsky represented Russian poetry.

The lot had fallen on him by chance. There were many other talented poets at the time who might have been in his place. But once the lot fell upon him, he understood the responsibility of his position—he was no longer a private person but had become a symbol, the way Akhmatova had been in 1946, when she was picked out of hundreds of possible poets to be punished, and became a national symbol of the Russian poet, as Brodsky had become that day. It was hard for Brodsky—he had bad nerves, a bad heart. But he played his role in the trial impeccably, with great dignity, without challenge, and with fervor, calmly, understanding that by the way he answered he evoked deep respect not only from his friends but from those who once had been indifferent to him or even hostile.[18]

The second trial lasted five hours and exhausted everyone. Etkind says Vigdorova was never the same. It was as if something had disrupted the calm balance in her soul—something had broken the harmony of her inner world. Vigdorova and Chukovskaya worked incessantly—obtaining signatures, making phone calls, filing petitions—and the "Brodsky affair" took over their lives.

Everyone thought that things had changed after the Twentieth Congress, and in some ways they had: millions had returned from the camps, forbidden books were finally printed. That was why Brodsky's trial was so shattering. Everyone was afraid the repression of the Stalin era was returning. Reading Vigdorova's notes on the trial, many felt the need to protest. Scholars, writers, journalists, and students sent letters to the Communist Party, the Supreme Court, the Secretary of the Leningrad Council, and the Chairman of the Presidium of the Supreme Soviet, as well as to the Writers' Union, all to no avail.

Vigdorova wrote to Konstantin Fedin, secretary of the Writers' Union, that she was weak and exhausted and therefore was now going to shift the responsibility for the fate of the talented young poet to him. But plans were afoot to expel her from the Union of Writers. Then, on October 15, 1964, Khrushchev was removed, and Prokofiev was soon removed from the Union of Writers as well. Grudinina, Admoni, and Etkind—the main witnesses for the defense at the Brodsky trial—were voted in as members of the Secretariat of the Union of Writers. Vigdorova was not expelled, but in November came the shattering news that she had terminal cancer. She felt she was a failure because she had not succeeded in getting Brodsky freed. While she was ill, she asked Chukovskaya, "Well, how is our red-haired boy?" Chukovskaya told her that Yevtushenko had just returned from Italy and had sent in his report to the KGB. He had met with representatives of the intelligentsia and it was clear that the "Brodsky affair" was damaging the prestige of the Soviet Union. Yevtushenko urged Brodsky's release as soon as possible.[19]

Nayman describes the conditions under which Brodsky was living in exile. He was actually settled in the village of Norinskaya, where he was renting a house. People treated him kindly. In the evening, Brodsky could get the BBC and Voice of America on the radio. "There was enough to eat, enough firewood, and enough time for poetry, too. Letters came, books were sent. It was sometimes possible to telephone Leningrad from the post office in the neighboring village of Danilovo."[20]

Nayman compares the association in people's minds at that time between Brodsky and Akhmatova:

It goes without saying that when compared with " '37," "the Brodsky case" was "a battle of butterflies," as Akhmatova liked to say. It meant suffering, poetry, and fame for him, and Akhmatova, while doing what could be done to help him, spoke approvingly of the biography they were "making for our Ginger." *Requiem* began to circulate clandestinely at approximately the same time, in the same circles and in the same number of copies as Vigdorova's transcript of Brodsky's trial. Public opinion unconsciously made a link between these two things, though not one which could be named openly: the poet defends the right to be a poet and not to have any other occupation so that he or she should be able when necessary to speak on everyone's behalf. The transcript of the poet's trial sounded like poetry on the most profound themes of public concern; and *Requiem*, poetry on the most profound themes of public concern, sounded like a transcript of the repressions, a kind of martyrology, a record of acts of self-sacrifice and martyrdom.[21]

With the removal of Khrushchev, there was hope that Brodsky might be freed. Admoni wrote a petition to the Supreme Court, and many others tried to help as well. In September 1965 the Supreme Court reviewed the case; although the verdict was not repealed, Brodsky was finally freed. On September 11, Nayman received a telegram from Komarovo: "REJOICING STOP ANNA SARRA EMMA STOP." Sarra Arens was helping take care of Akhmatova and Emma Gershtein was staying with her. Brodsky had been released and Akhmatova was celebrating.

When he was freed, Brodsky went to see Chukovskaya, and together they called up Akhmatova and his parents. Then Chukovskaya called Vigdorova's daughter and told her, "Sashenka, Joseph has returned." There was silence at both ends. They were both too filled with emotion to speak. Chukovskaya thought to herself, "Go to the grave. Whisper these words to the earth. 'Fridochka, Joseph has returned.' "[22]

Admoni relates that he saw a photocopy of a page from one of Akhmatova's notebooks, a note made that September: "Joseph has been freed by the decision of the Supreme Court. This is a great joy. I saw him a few hours before this news. He was horrible—he seemed to be on the verge of suicide. He (at least I think so) was saved by Admoni, who met him at the train, when this madman was returning from seeing me." Apparently Admoni and his wife were at the Komarovo train station, waiting for the train to go to the city, when they suddenly saw Brodsky running by. Admoni called him over and asked him what was going on. Brodsky muttered something. Admoni invited him to come with them to Leningrad. Brodsky asked Admoni about the Van Gogh Museum in Amsterdam, which the couple had just visited. When they got to Leningrad, they found Brodsky a taxi and accompanied him home. The next day they learned about the review of the case.[23]

Etkind's book on the trial ends with a letter written by Brodsky on June 4, 1972, when he left the Soviet Union, addressed to Leonid Brezhnev. In it he said that he was not leaving Russia of his own free will, and hoped that he would remain a part of Russian literature:

> I belong to Russian culture, I recognize myself as part of it and do not want to leave. . . . The measure of a writer's patriotism is how he writes in the language of the people among whom he lives and not the oaths from a podium. I am bitter to have to leave Russia. I was born here, grew up here, lived here and everything I have in my soul I owe to it. . . . Once I stop being a citizen of the USSR I will not stop being a Russian poet. I believe I will return; poets always return—in the flesh or on paper . . . the only righteousness is goodness. No one ever wins with evil, anger or hatred, even when it is justified. . . . I hope you will understand what I am asking for. I ask you to give me the possibility to continue to exist in Russian literature, in the Russian land. I do not think I am guilty before my Homeland of anything. . . . I don't know what your reply will be or whether there will ever be one. It's a pity I did not write you sooner, and now there is no longer any time. But I will tell you that in any case, even if my people do not need my body, my soul will still be important for them.[24]

In 1987, Joseph Brodsky won the Nobel Prize for Literature. His prophecy has now come true: his poems are being read and admired in his native land. He recently married and has a daughter named Anna, after Akhmatova.

The Last Years: The 1960s

And the voice of eternity beckons
With unearthly irresistibility,
And over the blossoming cherry trees
The crescent moon pours radiance.
    —AKHMATOVA, 1958 (II, p. 279)

In 1965, a great collection of Akhmatova's poetry was published at last: *The Flight of Time*. The volume was over 400 pages long and featured poems from 1909 to 1965, including *The White Flock, Plantain, Anno Domini MCMXXI*, plus two unpublished collections, *Reed* and *Seventh Book*. It was divided into three basic sections: prewar poems; war poems of the Tashkent cycle; and poems written after Akhmatova's return to Leningrad. Some of the poems are arranged in cycles, such as *Secrets of the Craft*.

The ballerina Tatyana Vecheslova once asked Akhmatova how she wrote poetry. They were sitting at a table with a number of people. Vecheslova says, "She answered quietly in my ear, 'It's a mystery.' "[1] *Secrets of the Craft* is devoted to an examination of this mystery. In the first poem of the cycle, "Creation" (1936), Akhmatova perceives creation as relatively passive, a form of possession, inspiration as described by Plato in the *Ion*. The poet first hears sounds in the air—sounds of everyday reality such as a clock striking, the peal of thunder—

but then follows the process of selection, as one triumphant sound overrides the rest. This sound is then transformed into words and rhymes. The lines are "dictated" rather than being called forth by the poet at will:

But now words are beginning to be heard
And the signaling chimes of light rhymes—
Then I begin to comprehend,
And the simply dictated lines
Lie down in place on the snow-white page.
(II, p. 155)

Pasternak had a similar view of poetry, convinced that it was "a direct product and consequence of life. The artist does not think up his images, he gathers them from the street, helping nature in her work of creation, but never supplanting her by his own interference."[2] The poet is spectator, but more receptive to sensation than others. One of Pasternak's most famous expressions of this idea occurs in his poem "Poetry":

Poetry! Be like a Greek sponge with suckers
And amongst this sticky verdure
I would have put you upon the wet board
Of a green garden bench.
Grow yourself sumptuous frills and farthingales,
Soak up clouds and ravines,
But at night, poetry, I will squeeze you out
To the health of the thirsty paper.[3]

Mandelstam had a similar image of how poetry is born from the chaos of disconnected images and sounds, expressed in "I have forgotten the word . . ." (1920):

No birds are heard. The mortelle does not bloom.
The night herd's manes are transparent.
In the dry river an empty boat is drifting.
Among the grasshoppers the word is unconscious.

And it rises slowly, like a tent or a temple,
Then suddenly rushes headlong like crazed Antigone,
Then like a dead swallow it flings itself at her feet
With Stygian tenderness and a green branch.[4]

Akhmatova described the passive nature of the poet in the creative process to Punin, and he noted it down in his diary on February 21, 1946. When he said to her, "Poets are not professional," she agreed. "Yes, we know that. It's like a camera. Like a nonexistent camera. They sit and fish; perhaps once a century they will catch something. They mainly fish for only an intonation; everything else is there. Painters, actors, singers . . . these are all professionals; poets—are catchers of intonations. If a poet wrote a poem today he has no idea whether he will write one tomorrow or really ever again."[5]

In 1959, in pages from her own diary, Akhmatova wrote about how a poet does not have full control over his or her inability to conjure up poems at will. She talks about those times when none came to her: "I confess that at times the air around me lost its moisture and its ability to conduct sound, that the bucket being lowered into the well brought forth a dry thump on stone rather than a joyful splash, and that, in general, I was unable to breathe for several years." And she goes on, "X asked me whether it was difficult or easy to write poetry. I answered that when somebody dictates it to you, it's quite easy, but that when there is nobody dictating—it's simply impossible."[6] In her last years, Anatoly Nayman, who acted as Akhmatova's literary secretary, watched her at work and corroborated her own description of how she wrote:

> It would not be correct to say of Akhmatova that "she wrote poetry":
> in fact, she wrote poetry down. She would open a notebook and write
> down the lines which had already formed in her head. She often replaced
> a non-existent line, one which had not yet come, with dots and then
> carried on, filling in the omitted lines afterwards, sometimes several days
> later. . . . [W]hen she was "composing poetry" the process never let up
> for a moment: suddenly, while someone was speaking to her, or she was
> reading a book, or writing a letter, or eating, she would half-sing, half-
> mutter, "hum" the almost unrecognizable vowels and consonants of the
> incipient lines, which had already found their rhythm. This humming was
> her outward expression of the constant vibration of poetry which the
> ordinary ear cannot detect. Or, it was the transformation of chaos into
> poetic cosmos.[7]

One of Akhmatova's most famous poems, "I don't need martial hosts" (January 21, 1940), appears next in *Secrets of the Craft*. It is essentially Akhmatova's credo, setting her apart from the Symbolists who preceded her: her poetry does not require lofty themes or ornamental discourse; it is derived from the simple things of life—the fresh smell of tar, or mold on a wall.

If only you knew from what rubbish
Poetry grows, knowing no shame,
Like a yellow dandelion by the fence,
Like burdock and goosefoot.

An angry cry, fresh smell of tar,
Mysterious mold on the wall . . .

and suddenly a line rings out, lively, tender,
To my delight and yours.

(II, p. 157)

Timenchik points out that "mold on the wall" alludes to Leonardo da Vinci's famous reference to how one can discern figures and features of landscape from a mold on a wall—his way of describing the artist's unique ability to see patterns in what appear as amorphous forms to the more ordinary sensibility. Arthur Lourie says when Akhmatova lived with him and Sudeikina, looking out through the window onto the courtyard wall one could see a "Leonardo" mold of a figure in cape and tall hat. Olga said it was the poet Gérard de Nerval running around Paris.[8]

In his brilliant interpretation of the Akhmatova cycle, Jerzy Faryno points out that the third poem, "The Muse," again related to the previous one. Here Akhmatova presents two opposing concepts of the Muse: One is the stereotype, shown through clichés such as "the divine babble"; the other is the actual, concrete experience of the poet herself. In the first, more popular and idyllic version, the poet is a partner of the Muse. But the speaker's actual experience of the Muse is quite different: the Muse attacks her victim "more savagely than fever," and then is silent for a whole year, not inspiring any sound at all.[9]

In the next poem, "The Poet" (1959), the speaker feels slightly guilty about the ease with which she can write poems, once inspired. Again poetic creation is typified as a form of eavesdropping, which is then transformed into words:

I take from the left and from the right,
And even, without feeling guilt,
A little bit from cunning life,
And everything—from the silence of the night.

(II, p. 158)

"To the Reader" (1959) is a tribute to her readers. The poem is touching, especially since the amount of praise the poet received for her poems was limited for many years, restricted by the slander of critics who wished to see her as an outdated relic of the past. But Akhmatova does not lose her faith in her readers' ultimate ability to appreciate her work. While the poet "flings everything wide," that is, reveals what is within, and the lights shine upon the poet as they do upon an actor on the stage, each reader is like a mystery, difficult to fathom. But the poet appreciates the reader's faith:

Our time on earth is fleeting
The appointed round constricting,
But he—the poet's unknown friend—
Is devoted and everlasting.

(II, p. 161)

"Latest Poem" (1959) is a beautiful rendition of the various moods that envelop the poet while writing—inspiration can strike like a thunderbolt or quietly steal up, then slip through her hands. But then comes that dread moment, which may last for many months or years, as in the case of certain periods in the lives of Akhmatova, Pasternak, and Mandelstam, when inspiration vanishes and the poet confesses that "without it . . . I will die."

The satirical seventh poem, "Epigram" (1958), was written about Akhmatova's imitators.

> Could Biti, like Dante, create,
> Could Laura glorify love's heat?
> I taught women to speak . . .
> But Lord, how to make them cease!
> (II, p. 163)

It reflects a humorous side that the poet rarely reveals in her works. Chukovsky notes that Akhmatova revealed a similar humor when the poem about the glove appeared in *Evening*. She said, laughingly, "With . . . [and she named one of the silliest women poets of the time] tomorrow she will write in her poems: 'I will put my right galosh on my left foot.' " Akhmatova was referring of course to her own "Song of the Last Meeting," when the speaker, in total confusion after her lover leaves her, puts the left-hand glove on her right hand. Chukovsky says Akhmatova was correct. "Right after *Evening* and *Rosary* appeared, along came female doggerel—mannered, tasteless, hysterical, vulgar, with none of that feeling . . . that is one of the achievements of the Russian lyric."[10]

One of Akhmatova's shabby imitators was Natalya Poplavskaya, who mimicked Akhmatova's famous poem, "Under her dark veil" (1911). Poplavskaya's attempt reads:

> Today we had a terrible quarrel,
> Is it possible he won't come?
> I ran down the stairs from the tower,
> I ran after him to the gate.
> I said: "My friend, it was a joke,
> I love you eternally and I'll wait."
> He answered directly and terribly:
> "I won't come see you today."[11]

The ninth poem in the cycle is dedicated to Mandelstam, and was originally part of another unrealized cycle, *Wreath to the Dead,* which featured poems to people important in Akhmatova's life who had died. The speaker muses about

poems that she calls the "black, tender news of our bloodstained youth." She
then refers to certain motifs that appear in Mandelstam's poems, such as Eurydice
and the myth of Europa and the bull. These motifs also were current in the Silver
Age, when Mandelstam was writing. Eurydice became popular as an image once
people had attended Meyerhold's production of Gluck's opera *Orpheus* in 1911
at the Mariinsky, and *The Rape of Europa* was painted in 1910 by Valentine Serov.

Not included in *Secrets of the Craft* but related to the same theme is the poem
"Our holy trade," written in 1944 after Akhmatova's return to Leningrad. In it
she points to the great role of the poet throughout history. But that role is still
limited, for the poet is only mortal; no matter how true his gifts of prophecy and
insight, the mysteries of the universe remain known only to divine beings:

> Our holy trade
> Has existed for a thousand years . . .
> With it even a world without light would be bright.
> But not one poet has ever yet said
> That there is no wisdom and no old age,
> And that possibly there is no death.
>
> (II, p. 171)

World War II is the focus of several poems in another cycle, published in *The
Flight of Time,* entitled *In the Fortieth Year.* Although war had not yet been
declared in the Soviet Union, it was already raging in Europe and Stalin had
invaded Finland. And two cycles, *The Wind of War* and *Victory,* contain poems
directly reflecting the war—and its impact—in the Soviet Union.

In "Grandly they said good-bye . . ." (1943), Akhmatova presents an enormous range of emotions about war in just a few, concise lines. It is one of the
most impressive anti-war poems ever written. The poet begins with the romantic
idea that war is a glorious game, a form of amusement, and the players are dressed
in pretty uniforms. But in the second stanza the mood grows grim: all the soldiers,
no matter which rank, face a common end, for death is the great leveler.

> Grandly they said good-bye to the girls,
> On the way kissed Mother,
> All dressed in brand-new clothes
> As if they were going to play soldier.
>
> No bad, no good, no in-between . . .
> They all took their place,
> Where there is neither first, nor last . . .
> They all lay down to sleep.
>
> (II, p. 181)

The Wind of War also includes Akhmatova's famous poem "Courage," read throughout the Soviet Union during the war, and "Knock with your little fist . . ." (April 23, 1942) about the grief Akhmatova felt when she heard that the child Valya Smirnov, whom she had taken care of in the communal apartment, had perished during a bombing raid.

> Knock with your little fist—I will open.
> I always opened the door to you.
> I am beyond the high mountain now,
> Beyond the desert, beyond the wind and the heat,
> But I will never abandon you . . .
>
>   (II, p. 187)

Another poem in this cycle, "Nox" (May 30, 1942), reflects the amazing feat of the Soviet Union in protecting its art treasures during the war—either by burying them or evacuating them to remote areas such as Central Asia. The Latin *Nox* is a reference to the statue of *Night* in the Summer Garden in St. Petersburg.

> Little night!
> Draped in stars,
> In funereal poppies, with a sleepless owl.
> Little daughter!
> We hid you under
> The garden's fresh dirt.
> Empty now are the cups of Dionysus,
> The gazes of love are stained with tears . . .
> Passing over our city are
> Your terrible sisters.
>
>   (II, p. 189)

Five cycles are associated with Akhmatova's period in Tashkent, where she was evacuated during the war. In one, *The Moon at Zenith* (1942–44), the poet says that here in Tashkent, she recalls with pride her Tatar identity and her ancestors, and she is struck by the beauty of this Central Asian city. Some of the poems recall those of Pushkin when he was in the Ukraine, Moldavia, and the Crimea, surrounded by warm, lush scenery that contrasted strongly with the cold mists of Petersburg.

Akhmatova suffered from typhus in Tashkent, and faced the ultimate experience—death. In a two-poem cycle called *Death*, she writes about this experience. The second poem contains the powerful image of death as a ship leaving one's native land. She wrote it in 1942 in Dyurmen, near Tashkent, where she was recovering:

And I am standing on the threshold of something
That befalls everyone, but at different cost . . .
On this ship there is a cabin for me
And wind in the sails—and the terrible moment
Of taking leave of my native land.

(II, p. 207)

There are several poems in the Tashkent cycle *Housewarming* that refer to acquaintances of Akhmatova. "The Hostess" (August 5, 1943) is dedicated to Yelena Bulgakova, whose room Akhmatova lived in after Bulgakova left. Akhmatova refers to Mikhail Bulgakov's amazing novel, *The Master and Margarita*. She read the novel in manuscript form—it was not published in Russia until 1966. In another poem from this cycle, "Guests" (1943), two branches swaying in the wind make the poet think of Don Juan and Faust, two figures from *Poem Without a Hero*, on which she continued to work in Tashkent. The last two poems relate to two men, one in Tashkent and the other somewhere else—perhaps one is the composer Kozlovsky, who lived in Tashkent for many years and was close to Akhmatova while she was there, and the other Garshin, whom Akhmatova hoped to marry upon her return to Leningrad. Perhaps Akhmatova did have an intimate relationship with Kozlovsky and was feeling guilty, because this meant a betrayal of Garshin:

Betrayal

Not because the mirror cracked,
Not because of the wind to the chimney,
Not because something foreign
Was already filtering into my thoughts of you—
Not because, not at all because
On the threshold I met him.

(II, p. 215)

In *The Flight of Time*, the Tashkent cycles are followed by a cycle of four-line poems entitled *A Group of Quatrains*, from 1910 until 1963. The title of the entire book comes from a phrase in one of them, written in 1962 when Akhmatova was in her seventies and knew she did not have much longer to live—to experience the joys and sorrows of life.

What is war, what is plague?—Their end is near,
Their sentence is about to be proclaimed.
But who will defend us from the horror
That once was named the flight of time?

(II, p. 217)

On June 3, 1940, Chukovskaya came to visit Akhmatova, who said she wanted to recite some poems for her. They were about Gumilyov and Tsarskoye Selo, and Akhmatova told Chukovskaya that she had never read them to anyone before.[12] They were all written in 1921, probably right after Gumilyov's death, although no month is given. The year 1940 was the year that the shades of the past appeared in *Poem Without a Hero,* and in Verses such as "Teacher," in which Akhmatova remembered Annensky; it was also the year she began the cycle called *A Wreath to the Dead,* recalling dead figures in her past, when memories of Gumilyov overwhelmed her. She wrote in an autobiographical sketch:

And who would have believed that I was fated to live so long, and why didn't I know it? My memory has become unbelievably sensitive. I'm surrounded by the past and it is demanding something from me. But what? The dear shades of the distant past are particularly talking to me. Perhaps for them it's the last chance for bliss, which people call oblivion, to pass by. Words spoken a half century ago, which I have not recalled once in these fifty years, are surfacing from somewhere. It would be strange to explain away all of this as merely my summer solitude and the nearness to nature, which, for a long time now, has reminded me only of death.[13]

While Akhmatova was recalling other shadows of the past, she experienced an overwhelming longing for Gumilyov. She had not made her peace with him in life. They apparently remained friends after their divorce, yet strong feelings of resentment and hostility persisted. Akhmatova and Gumilyov had grown up together, two sensitive poets, both of whom hid their feelings behind a mask of restraint, but who shared each other's profound love of European culture, passionate attachment to their native land, and a strong attraction to the wisdom of the East.

Over the years their mutual hurt and pain might have been reconciled, but fate did not allow them that chance. Gumilyov's early death was a shock, and the true significance of her husband in Akhmatova's life became clear only over the years. She spent a long time with Pavel Luknitsky in the 1920s, who had come to her as a young student to learn more about Gumilyov so he could write about him. (Though we have learned recently that he was also working for the Cheka, the secret police, and informing on Akhmatova's life and relationships.)[14] She provided Luknitsky with material and personal connections so that he could write a biography of Gumilyov, preserving the memory of his life and work. But Luknitsky himself was not able to write that book. It was finally completed by Luknitsky's wife, with the help of her son, using material that could be published only after Gorbachev and the reforms in the Soviet Union.[15] In the last years of her life, Akhmatova summoned Luknitsky once again to help rehabilitate Gumilyov's memory. Perhaps this effort brought her some peace, for she always felt guilty about Gumilyov's distraught state of mind after she left him.

One of the poems about Gumilyov that Akhmatova read to Chukovskaya that day in June 1940 was the "Sixth Elegy" (1921), dated the year Gumilyov died. In it the poet pleads with someone, now dead, to help her account for her feeling of dread while she and Gumilyov lived together in the house in Tsarskoye Selo:

It was dreadful to live in that house,
And not the patriarchal glow of the hearth,
Not the cradle of my child,
Not the fact that we were both young
And full of ideas,
[. . . and that good fortune
Didn't dare take a step from the door
For seven years]
Nothing diminished that feeling of fear.
    . . .
Now that you're there, where everything is known—tell me:
What else lived in that house besides us?

(II, p. 357)

Two other poems relating to Gumilyov are in the part of *Flight of Time* entitled "Seventh Book." In one, also dated 1921, "All the souls of my loved ones . . ." (II, p. 227), she writes that there is now "no one left to lose." The air of Tsarskoye Selo, she says, was created for the "echoing of songs." Indeed, Tsarskoye was strongly associated with Pushkin, Annensky, and Gumilyov. The speaker now believes there is room for her lyre as well. A silver willow is mentioned, which Toporov associates with the mythological tree of life.[16] Here it is associated with beauty and art, and becomes a symbol, like the cherry trees in Chekhov's *The Cherry Orchard,* of the irretrievable past. The poem shows that as early as 1921 Akhmatova already felt abandoned and left alone to mourn the dead. "How good it is that here is no one left to lose/And one can weep," she says ironically. But it was not good, and she turned once again to this poem in 1940 when she was feeling more than ever the absence of those she loved so much.

In the second poem related to Gumilyov, "Like the fifth act of a drama" (1921), Tsarskoye Selo represents a past to which the speaker is clinging, pretending that her beloved friends have not died. But she knows sooner or later she must face reality:

With a frail hand it's possible to hold
A heavily laden boat to the pier

(II, p. 229)

Eventually the boat will leave, and she must say farewell. The fifth act of a drama is always the last—there is no more.

Akhmatova turned to Tsarskoye Selo again in later poems, which appear in the section of *The Flight of Time* entitled "Odd Number." In "Seaside Sonnet" (1958), the poet senses the impending end of her life. Everything in Komarovo—from the decrepit starling houses to the sea breeze—will outlive her. In the second stanza she turns toward eternity, which beckons her to new horizons. But she also turns back to the peaceful landscape of her youth:

> . . .
> Here everything will outlive me.
> Everything, even the decrepit starling houses,
> And this breeze, a vernal breeze,
> Finishing its flight from across the sea.
>
> And the voice of eternity beckons
> With unearthly irresistibility,
> And over the blossoming
> The Crescent moon pours radiance.
>
> And it seems so clear,
> Growing white in the emerald underbrush,
> The road to—I won't say where . . .
>
> There among the tree trunks it's brighter still,
> And everything resembles the allée
> Along the pond at Tsarskoye Selo.
>   (II, p. 279)

Tsarskoye Selo figures in two other poems in this section, in a cycle devoted to the *City of Pushkin*. In "Oh, woe is me . . ." (November 8, 1945), it again symbolizes her peaceful past, but in deadly contrast to what greeted the poet when she visited Tsarskoye Selo after the war. The Nazis have burned it to the ground. What she sees are only remembrances of things past—the spot where the fountain was, where she walked down the lovely *allée*. The poem evokes two major themes of Akhmatova's work: the inability to return to the past, and that of Tsarskoye Selo as a "toy town," a place not quite real, to which people escaped or where they lived a womblike existence before the Revolution, away from the chaos and suffering they would have encountered in Petersburg. These themes become more obvious in the version first published in *Zvezda* (no. 1) in 1945:

> They burned my little toy town,
> And there's no loophole back to the past.
> There was a fountain there, green benches
> The tsar's huge park in the distance.[17]

However, in the final version, Tsarskoye symbolizing the frivolity of Akhmatova's youth gives way to a new vision of the town's beauty—with its fountains and walkways, and the precious moments of one's youth, like one's first kiss, which took place here. It is a sacred place, representing art and beauty in Russian culture, which the Nazis destroyed. The contrast between Tsarskoye as it once was and as Akhmatova saw it in November 1945 is especially poignant. The epigraph is a line from Pushkin's poem "To Chaadayev," written by the poet when he was in exile, recalling the carefree days of his early youth in Tsarskoye Selo. But for Akhmatova there was "no loophole back to the past."

The second poem of the cycle, "The leaves of this willow," again deals with the theme of inability to return. It was written in October 1957, when Akhmatova felt close to death. The beauty of Tsarskoye Selo and the leaves of the willow had already been immortalized by Pushkin in his "Hymns from the Lyceum." The speaker says that while she cannot physically return to the Tsarskoye Selo of the past, its memory will be taken by her to the grave and beyond—even Lethe will not erase this image:

And I can't return! But even beyond Lethe I will take with me
The living outlines of my gardens at Tsarskoye Selo.
                                        (II, p. 289)

In her autobiographical notes, Akhmatova discusses this theme more explicitly:

My generation is not threatened with a melancholy return, because there is nowhere for us to return to. . . . Sometimes (when it's so deserted and fragrant in the parks) it seems to me that you could get in a car and drive to the days of the opening of the Pavlovsk Station, to those places where a shadow inconsolably searches for me, but then I begin to realize that this is not possible, that one shouldn't bury oneself (never mind in a gasoline tin can) in memory's mansions, that I would not see anything and that I would only blot out what I see so clearly now.[18]

One of the last poems to mention Tsarskoye Selo, "Tsarskoye Selo Ode: The 1900s" (August 3, 1961), is very different from her earlier ones. Here there are no philosophical motifs and no sense of regret. The "toy town" and its fantastic world—ephemeral and lovely, with snowdrifts, carriages from the court—is juxtaposed with the world of the commonplace. Along with these aesthetic aspects of Tsarskoye are "a very decent pub," the railway, a gypsy telling fortunes, soldiers swapping dirty jokes, smoking cheap tobacco, singing and swearing. The poet contrasts Tsarskoye with Temnik (Temnikov), the location of a Stalinist camp. She will do for Tsarskoye what Chagall did in his painting for his own town of Vitebsk:

she will immortalize it. The poem ends with an allusion to Alexander III, portrayed as a cavalryman—the "giant cuirassier."

> A crow croaked the praises
> Of this phantasmagorical world . . .
> And the wide sledge was steered
> By a giant cuirassier.
>
> (II, p. 313)

This recalls an early poem by Mandelstam, "Tsarskoye Selo," written in 1911, in which Mandelstam uses the same mixture of images from the court and the more mundane soldiers' barracks and brawling:

> Let's go to Tsarskoye Selo!
> Free, frivolous and drunk,
> There the uhlans smile,
> After galloping on their strong saddles . . .
> Let's go to Tsarskoye Selo!
>
> Barracks, parks and palaces,
> And in the trees—clumps of cotton,
> And thundering "hellos" rang out
> A shout—"Hello, brave men!"
> Barracks, parks and palaces . . .[19]

From 1925 to 1940, Akhmatova composed fragments of what was intended to be a long poem devoted to Tsarskoye Selo, "The Russian Trianon." The title evokes comparison between Tsarskoye Selo and Marie-Antoinette's palace in France, thereby suggesting an impending revolution and, in particular, the collapse of the tsarist regime. The fragments contrast the speaker's childhood—when the granddaughters of Pushkin's beauties strolled with their lapdogs—with the historic events now changing the face of Russia. Those immersed in the sounds of the choir singing hymns and the moon reflected on the diamond snow remain unaware of events—until history intrudes in the form of a machine gun placed on the White Tower. Pushkin is now only a memory, and Tsarskoye Selo has become a whole way of life—a place where people attempt to hide in the gentle, languid atmosphere, refusing to face the brutality of contemporary times.

The cycle of five poems written between November 26, 1945, and January 11, 1946, *Cinque* (the number "Five" in Italian) is about Akhmatova's first meeting with Isaiah Berlin. Scholars have attempted to explain the strong emotion that Berlin evoked in her. Most attribute her feelings to the fact that he was the first person to visit her who was born and brought up in the Russian Empire, but who had spent much of his life in the West and could relate to her his experiences and tell her about her friends now living in the West. But Isaiah Berlin was more than that in Akhmatova's life, much more. Berlin has a penetrating mind and a keen perception of life, an encyclopedic knowledge of world culture that Akhmatova shared; he would have immediately understood and added his own insights to any cultural allusions she made. She also had just been bitterly disappointed by Vladimir Garshin, whom she had hoped to marry, and Berlin had the same powerful attraction for her. Berlin was certainly well aware of the pain and suffering the Terror had wrought, and strongly condemned the Stalinist regime, yet he shared Akhmatova's love of Russian culture and the Russian people. And he was a kindred spirit, a man with great sensitivity, respect, and understanding for Akhmatova's ideas and the people who meant most in her life. Akhmatova uses the image of a door slamming shut to convey that at this point in her life, she hid and suppressed her feelings as a defense against ever getting hurt again; but Berlin half opened it once more. The cycle opens with the poem "As if on the rim of a cloud" (November 26, 1945), and the epigraph contains lines from a poem by Baudelaire, lines that appear to be more hopeful than probable, considering her experiences of the past:

> *"Just as you are faithful to him, he will be faithful to you*
> *And constant, until death."*

As if on the rim of a cloud,
I remember your words,

And because of my words to you,
Night became brighter than day.

Thus, torn from the earth,
We rose up, like stars.

There was neither despair nor shame,
Not now, not afterward, not at the time.

But in real life, right now,
You hear how I am calling you.

And that door that you half opened,
I don't have the strength to slam.

(II, p. 235)

The next cycle in *Flight of Time, Sweetbriar in Blossom,* is also about her relationship with Berlin; it includes poems written soon after Berlin left Russia in 1946, and the theme here is the difficulty of separation. The poet mentions the "blue smoke of a cigar," a motif she uses in describing the Guest from the Future in *Poem Without a Hero.* Some of the other poems in the cycle were written in

1956, when Berlin returned to the Soviet Union and spoke with Akhmatova on the phone; she was afraid to see him for fear it might jeopardize her son, who had only just been released. Other poems in the cycle were written in 1961–64, when she again recalled their relationship. These poems are not just pessimistic, treating their inability to meet and the grief Akhmatova felt when she learned that Berlin was now married; they are even sinister, and she raises their first meeting to the level of a mythical event. In "A Dream," the poet says she had a prophetic vision that Berlin would come: it was augured in everything, including the Bach Chaconne, another motif associated with the Guest from the Future. The poem that best conveys the general tenor of these works is "You invented me. . . . " (August 18, 1956):

> You invented me. There is no such earthly being.
> Such an earthly being there could never be.
> A doctor cannot cure, a poet cannot comfort—
> A shadowy apparition haunts you night and day.
> We met in an unbelievable year,
> When the world's strength was at an ebb,
> Everything was in mourning, everything withered by adversity,
> And only the graves were fresh.
> Without streetlights, the Neva's waves were black as pitch,
> Thick night enclosed me like a wall . . .
> That's when my voice called out to you!
> Why it did—I still don't understand.
> And you came to me, as if guided by a star
> That tragic autumn, stepping
> Into that irrevocably ruined house,
> From whence had flown a flock of burnt verse.
>
> (II, p. 251)

Four of the seven verses in the cycle *Midnight Verses* also may refer to Berlin. They were written in 1963, and again reflect a sinister attitude toward the relationship. In "And the Last" (July 1963) the poet talks about love, which she compares in the last stanza to a swallow:

> By day she circled before us as a swallow,
> Bloomed as a smile on our lips.
> But at night, with an icy hand, she strangled
> Both of us at once. In different cities.
>
> (II, p. 277)

Leonid Zykov, husband of Punin's granddaughter Anna Kaminskaya, suggests that several of the poems in *Midnight Verses* refer to Punin. He cites in particular

"Through the Looking Glass," saying that the woman in the poem who is associated with Venus is Marfa Golubeva, the young woman who was Punin's assistant
at the Hermitage and with whom he began to have an affair in the mid-thirties,
and who, unlike Punin and Akhmatova, was born in the twentieth century:[20]

Through the Looking Glass

> *O quae beatam, Diva, tenes*
> *Cyprum et Memphis. . . .*
> [O Goddess, who keeps blessed
> Cyprus and Memphis. . . .]
> —Horace

She's very young, this beauty,
But not from our century,
We're never alone together—she, the third,
Won't leave us, ever.
You move an armchair for her,
I generously share my flowers with her . . .
What we are doing—we ourselves don't know,
But every moment is more frightful.
Like convicts released from prison,
We know something about each other,
Something horrible. We are in an infernal circle.
But perhaps, this is not us at all.

(II, p. 271)

Akhmatova wrote two poems under the title "A Small Page from Antiquity,"
about the relationship of the poet to the state. In 1957, she told Chukovskaya
that she had begun reading Sophocles again after fifty years.[21] In "The Death of
Sophocles" (1961), the poet is considered so sacred that the god Dionysus appears
to a conquering monarch in a dream, warning him to suspend his siege until
Sophocles' funeral has been celebrated. Chukovskaya notes that Akhmatova was
angry at her for finding the poem cold. " 'Cold,' Akhmatova answered in a rage.
'Red hot! You have no ear for antiquity. . . . The childhood of Dionysus and the
legend of the death of Sophocles—for you are empty sounds. But it must be
within, right here,' and she pointed to her chest. 'You must live with it . . . and
my poem about the death of Sophocles is absolutely essential for an understanding
of the relationship between art and power.' "[22] In the second poem, "Alexander
at Thebes" (October 1961), the warrior-king, Alexander the Great, recalls the
lessons of his teacher Aristotle: when he orders the city attacked, he spares the
house of the poet (Pindar).

Another poem in which an allusion is made to a figure from antiquity is "All
the unburied ones . . . " (suggested date 1958), which was unpublished during

Akhmatova's lifetime. Akhmatova indirectly alludes to Antigone, who ensured that her dead brother was buried with respect. In this two-line poem, the speaker mentions how she has mourned for the unburied ones and wonders if anyone will mourn for her in return.

In 1964, Akhmatova's lifelong friend, Valeriya Sreznevskaya, died. She was probably privy to more of Akhmatova's real thoughts and secret feelings than anyone else, but she kept those secrets discreetly to herself. Sreznevskaya's children, Olga and Andrey, recall that Akhmatova and Sreznevskaya had a secret language they shared. When Akhmatova spoke to their mother, a few words were enough for each to understand, but the children found it impossible to follow. Their mother was refined and well educated, had known all the famous intellectuals of the Silver Age, and like many who remained after the Revolution, she found it difficult to adjust to the new reality. Akhmatova had lived with the Sreznevskys from January 1917 to the autumn of 1918. Sreznevskaya recalls:

> She lived in a small . . . but warm and nice room with a window looking out onto our small quiet garden at the clinic. The door to my room was almost always open, so that we spoke without having to leave our rooms. I had a good ear, and sometimes at night I shouted to Anya: "Why aren't you sleeping?" "And how do you know that?" "By the rhythm of your breathing." And then she often came into my room, and sitting on my bed, told me the reason for her insomnia. She often mumbled verses at night, trying to hear how they sounded.[23]

"To the Memory of V. S. Sreznevskaya" was written on September 9, 1964, when Akhmatova felt her own death very near. She ends with these lines:

> But your ringing voice calls out to me from there,
> And asks me not to grieve, but to wait for death as for a miracle.
> All right! I'll try.

(II, p. 319)

A cycle entitled *Shards,* written at the end of the 1940s but not included in *The Flight of Time,* describes more explicitly than *Requiem* does the ordeal Akhmatova endured when her son was held prisoner. Given the subject matter and its treatment, it clearly had no chance of being published in the Soviet Union while Akhmatova was alive. One of the poems deals with another related theme— her poetic silence. Akhmatova railed for many years against the belief by foreigners such as Gleb Struve that she no longer was writing poetry. In fact, Struve and B. A. Filipoff did an extraordinary job of compiling and publishing Akhmatova's poems in the West, when it was forbidden to publish them in the Soviet Union. Yet Akhmatova complained bitterly when Struve wrote that she was no longer composing poetry, that her "incomparable gift had died out." This is

Griboyedov Canal near apartment of the Tomashevskys, where Akhmatova stayed before she was evacuated in 1941. (courtesy Roberta Reeder)

Boris Tomashevsky (1939), leading Pushkin scholar and friend of Akhmatova. (courtesy Zoya Tomashevskaya collection)

Boris Pasternak (1942). By this time Pasternak and Akhmatova had become friends and showed a mutual respect for each other's work. (courtesy Pasternak family archive)

ABOVE: Akhmatova. (drawing by A. G. Tyshler, courtesy Moscow collection)

LEFT: Akhmatova with Smirnov children in the communal apartment in the wing of the Sheremetev Palace. One of the boys died in the Siege of Leningrad. (courtesy Akhmatova Museum)

ABOVE: Alexander Kozlovsky, a Russian composer in Tashkent with whom Akhmatova became close during the war years. (courtesy Moscow collection)

RIGHT: Faina Ranevskaya, famous actress and close friend of Akhmatova. (courtesy Akhmatova Museum)

BELOW: Tashkent Bazaar (1940s). (courtesy Akhmatova Museum)

Akhmatova and Anna Kaminskaya,
daughter of Irina Punina and
granddaughter of Nikolay Punin.
(courtesy Akhmatova Museum)

Letter from Akhmatova to Irina
Tomashevskaya, April 14, 1943. She
asks Irina to send *Poem Without a
Hero* to Garshin. (courtesy Zoya
Tomashevskaya)

RIGHT: Irina Punina, Nikolay Punin and Anna Kaminskaya. (courtesy Akhmatova Museum)

BELOW LEFT: Nina Olshevskaya, actress and close friend to Akhmatova, who often stayed with her on her extended visits to Moscow. (courtesy Moscow collection)

BELOW RIGHT: Vladimir Admoni, poet and scholar. He became a good friend of Akhmatova's in Tashkent during World War II and remained close to her until her death. (courtesy Moscow collection)

ABOVE: Tatyana
Vecheslova, ballerina who
became part of
Akhmatova's circle of
friends in her later years.
(courtesy Akhmatova
Museum)

LEFT: Boris Pasternak
(May 1946). (courtesy
Pasternak family archive).

RIGHT: Akhmatova (1946).
(courtesy Moscow collec-
tion)

Sir Isaiah Berlin, whose visit to Akhmatova right after World War II was one of the reasons for her expulsion from the Union of Writers. (courtesy Akhmatova Museum)

Akhmatova (1950s). (courtesy Akhmatova Museum)

Korean Classical Poetry, translated by Akhmatova. The dedication is to Irina and Boris Tomashevskaya, "who were my friends in need." May 4, 1956. (courtesy Akhmatova Museum)

ABOVE: Lev Gumilyov (1956), the year he returns from exile in the camps. (courtesy Moscow collection)

LEFT: One of the porcelain figures by Olga Sudeikina, the prototype for the heroine in *Poem Without a Hero*. (courtesy Moscow collection)

BELOW: Anichkov Bridge on Nevsky Boulevard, which is featured in *Poem Without a Hero*. (courtesy Moscow collection)

LEFT: Joseph Brodsky (mid-1950s).
(courtesy Moscow collection)

RIGHT: Joseph Brodsky in exile in the
village of Norensky, Archangel Province.
(courtesy Moscow collection)

BELOW: Akhmatova and Viktor Ardov,
writer and husband of the actress Nina
Olshevskaya. Akhmatova often stayed
with them in Moscow when she visited.
(courtesy Akhmatova Museum)

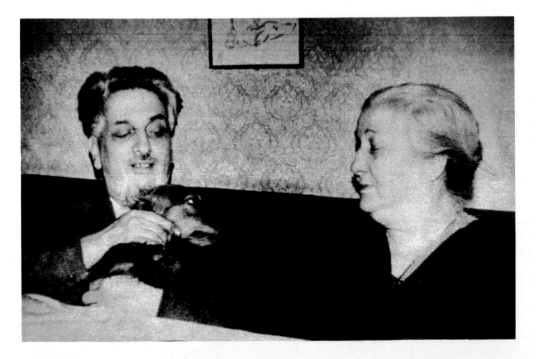

TOP: Akhmatova and the poet Olga Berggolts on her right. (courtesy Akhmatova Museum)

ABOVE: Membership card in Society of Writers of the Community of Europe. (courtesy Akhmatova Museum)

RIGHT: Akhmatova (1958). (courtesy Moscow collection)

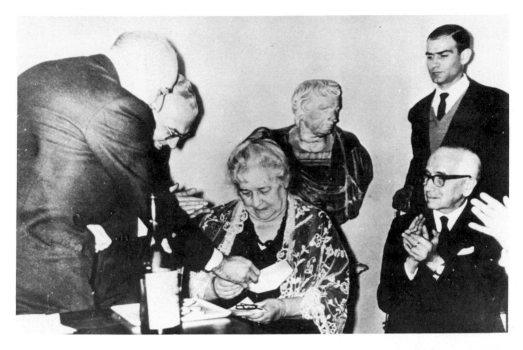

ABOVE: Akhmatova in Italy (1964) to receive the Taormina prize, bust of Marcus Aurelius in background. (courtesy Moscow collection)

RIGHT: Lenin Street, 51, Leningrad. The last apartment in which Akhmatova lived. (courtesy Zoya Tomashevskaya)

BELOW: Nadezhda Mandelstam. (courtesy Akhmatova Museum)

LEFT: Lev Gumilyov and his wife. (courtesy Akhmatova Museum)

BELOW: Mikhail Meilakh, literary scholar and Akhmatova's friend at the end of her life. (courtesy Roberta Reeder)

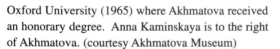

Oxford University (1965) where Akhmatova received an honorary degree. Anna Kaminskaya is to the right of Akhmatova. (courtesy Akhmatova Museum)

ABOVE: Mosaic by Boris Anrep. Floor of
National Gallery, London (1952). Akhmatova
as model for "Consolation." Background is the
Siege of Leningrad. (courtesy Moscow collection)

RIGHT: Boris Anrep (Paris, 1965), friend from
her youth whom Akhmatova saw in Paris on
her way back from England. (courtesy Moscow
collection)

BELOW: Akhmatova and Anatoly Nayman
(1960s) at the writers' colony in Komarovo.
(courtesy Moscow collection)

ABOVE: St. Nicholas Cathedral, where Akhmatova's funeral took place. (courtesy Roberta Reeder)

BELOW: Funeral of Akhmatova, March 1966. Left—Anatoly Nayman and Lev Gumilyov. (courtesy Akhmatova Museum)

LEFT: Cross on Akhmatova's grave, Komarovo. (courtesy Roberta Reeder)

BELOW: Plaque on wall at Akhmatova's grave, Komarovo. (courtesy Roberta Reeder)

LEFT: Marker: "The estate of Slepnyovo was here. At the beginning of the twentieth century the poet Nikolay Gumilyov and his wife, the poetess Anna Akhmatova lived and worked here." (courtesy Akhmatova Museum)

Akhmatova in Komarovo (1960s).
(courtesy Moscow collection)

LEFT: Lev Kopelev and Raisa Orlova, members of the intelligentsia and close friends of Akhmatova in her later years. Kopelev won the Prize for Peace in Germany in 1981. (courtesy Lev Kopelev)

expressed in one of the works in *Shards*. (It is clear that, without mentioning his name, the poem is addressed to Stalin.)

> You raised me up, like a slain beast
> On a bloody hook
> So that sniggering, and not believing,
> Foreigners wandered in
> And wrote in their respectable papers
> That my incomparable gift had died out,
> That I had been a poet among poets,
> But my thirteenth hour had struck.
>   (II, p. 635)

The "Northern Elegies" are long poems written at various points in Akhmatova's life. She says that soon after the end of World War II, she wrote two long poems in blank verse, apparently the "Third" and "Fourth Elegies," and she then added two other poems, the "First Elegy" (1940–42), about the Dostoyevsky years; and the "Sixth Elegy" (1921), relating to Gumilyov. The "Seventh" was never finished.

The "First Elegy" is subtitled "Prehistory" and conjures up the years of Dostoyevsky's Russia, the years when Akhmatova's mother was a young girl. The poem contains a tribute to her mother:

> And a woman with translucent eyes
> (Of such deep blue, that to gaze into them
> And not think of the sea was impossible).
> With the rarest of names and white hands,
> And a kindness that as an inheritance
> I have from her, it seems—
> useless gift for my harsh life . . .
>   (II, p. 343)

The era is beautifully conveyed through representative images of the time: wives of bankers and railroad magnates, wild bars, plush armchairs of the bourgeoisie, dancing classes, money changers' signs. Akhmatova mentions places associated with Dostoyevsky—Staraya Rusa, where *The Brothers Karamazov* takes place; Optina, the famous monastery of pilgrimage; and Baden-Baden in Germany, where Dostoyevsky lost at roulette. But she ends the elegy with a reference to Dostoyevsky as a writer who suffered for his beliefs—he is "the convict from Omsk," where he lived from 1850 to 1854, after his release from prison. She also alludes to Semyonov Square, where he was sent to be executed because of his association with Socialist circles, but was pardoned at the last minute and sent into exile instead.

The country shivers, and the convict from Omsk
Understood everything and made the sign of the cross over it all.
Now he shuffles everything around
And, over this primordial chaos,
Like some kind of spirit, he rises. Midnight sounds.
His pen squeaks, and page after page
Stinks of Semyonov Square.

(II, p. 343)

And this is the time when Akhmatova and her generation "decided to be born." Chukovsky has called Akhmatova a master of historical landscape: people, objects, and events are almost always presented against a historical background. The "First Elegy," says Chukovsky, shows for the first time this mastery, which he believes is the essence of her later works, in full. The poem is a distant prehistory of those enormous events that took place in the early period of Akhmatova's life, and their inevitability is confirmed.[24]

The "Second Elegy" was written in March 1942 in Tashkent, when Akhmatova was still feeling bitter about the disintegration of her relationship with Punin. By this time she had already left Leningrad, but she writes as if she is in the city under bombardment—the sky has become a flaming abyss and the sounds she hears are as if from another world. She talks of the many years spent with Punin, and ends with bitter irony: Guests are summoned to celebrate the silver anniversary of the day they met—a day that should be marked by rejoicing. But she greets it only with regret:

. . .
Fifteen years ago, with what rejoicing
You greeted this day, you begged the heavens
And the choirs of stars and the choirs of oceans
To salute the glorious meeting
With the one you left today . . .

So this is your silver anniversary:
Summon the guests, stand in splendor, celebrate!

(II, p. 347)

Punin kept an important record of the months in Leningrad during the bombing before he left in September 1942 for Samarkand. Akhmatova had already gone to live with Boris and Irina Tomashevsky and their family. Just before she left Leningrad for Central Asia, Punin made a diary entry on September 25, 1941. It indicates that they were still friends:

Today Garshin came over and said that An. [Akhmatova] would fly the day after tomorrow out of Leningrad. (She left here a long time ago and has recently been living at the Tomashevskys' at the House of Writers, where there is a bomb shelter. She is very afraid of air raids.) After he said this, Garshin patted me on the shoulder, began to cry, and said: "Well, now, N.N. [Nikolay Nikolayevich], so ends another period of our life." He was depressed. Through him I sent An. a note: "Greetings, Anya, whether we will see each other again or not. Farewell; just stay calm." I find it strange that Anya is so frightened. I'm so used to hearing her talk about death, about her desire to die. And now, when it is so easy and simple to die. Well, let her fly. Only let her reach her destination.[25]

The "Third Elegy" (1945) is perhaps Akhmatova's most famous and most quoted poem.[26] It is a philosophical meditation on her life and what it might have been. It is dedicated to Nina Olshevskaya, with whom Akhmatova often stayed, as well as to Nina's husband, Viktor Ardov. The Elegy originally began with an epigraph from Tyutchev's poem "Cicero":

Blessed is he who visited this world
In its fatal moments.

Akhmatova depicts her life as a river that somehow got rechanneled and adopted a different course. The "life I might have led" was already a theme of an early poem written in 1915, in which Akhmatova compared what she might have been to what she in fact became:

Somewhere there is a simple life and a world,
Transparent, warm and joyful . . .
There at evening a neighbor talks with a girl
Across the fence, and only the bees can hear
This most tender murmuring of all.

(I, p. 411)

In fact, the poet lives a life of suffering, lives with difficulty, and although she might have enjoyed a more pleasant life in other cities, she chose Petersburg— the "granite city of fame and calamity." However, after exploring the "life that never was," she says that had she lived such a life, she would have envied the life she actually chose:

But had I observed from there
The life I am living today,
I would finally discover envy . . .

The theme of the "Fourth Elegy" (February 1945) is a familiar one in many poems of Akhmatova's later period—that of memory. There are three ages to memory: The first features tears, but laughter as well, and a kiss. It is remembered as unique, but this stage is brief. The second age is remembrance of a house now desolate—"People walk to this house as if to their grave." It is probably the Gumilyov house where Akhmatova lived after she was married, a place marked by bitter memories. But the third age is the most devastating of all. "Names of cities change." In this last age there are no remaining witnesses to events, "no one to weep with, no one to remember with." And once again Akhmatova recognizes that "you can't go home again," you cannot ever return again to the past:

> . . .
>
> And waking one morning we realize that we have forgotten
> Even the path to that solitary house,
> And, choking with anger and shame,
> We run there, but (as it happens in dreams)
> Everything has changed: the people, the objects, the walls,
> And nobody knows us—we are strangers.
> We don't find ourselves there . . . My God!
>
> (II, p. 351)

The poet and her generation must face the truth: Time is sequential and moves in a linear progression. Everything changes—nothing is ever the same again. The poet understands that the life of her youth no longer makes any sense from the perspective of the person she has become today. She can no longer live the way she lived then:

> And then it is that bitterness wells up:
> We realize that we couldn't have fit
> That past into the boundaries of our life.
> And that it is almost as foreign to us
> As to our next-door neighbor.
>
> (II, p. 353)

Akhmatova ends the Elegy with a thought from Voltaire's *Candide:* "Everything turned out for the best . . . " However, there is a great difference between the two works. Voltaire's is an amusing satire, an attack on Lessing's belief in a universe that, in spite of all its cruelty and suffering, contains some divine plan that accounts for catastrophes. In Akhmatova's Elegy, there is no satirical irony intended. Life may seem absurd, suffering and pain inexplicable, but in the end the poet realizes it was through the trials she experienced and her ability to overcome them that she became capable of creating works far beyond those of the "gay little sinner of Tsarskoye Selo." When Akhmatova says "everything turned out for the best," she is alluding to the last words of the "Third Elegy."

The next Elegy, the "Fifth," was not written until 1955. In it the poet again returns to her childhood and her years as a young poet. Hers was not a normal childhood, no "freckles and toy bears and curls,/ And doting aunts and scary uncles, or even/ Friends among the river pebbles." There is an implicit comparison to Russian saints' lives, where the blessed person who will achieve something special in life is already marked out in childhood as different from others. Her childhood seems more like "someone's dream or delirium." Without a transition, the speaker slips into her years as a young poet, when unexpectedly she achieved sudden fame, which terrified her, because she felt that in some way she would eventually pay for it.

. . .

The more people admired me,
The more frightful it was to live in the world,
And the more I yearned to awaken,
For I knew that I would pay dearly
In prison, in the grave, in the madhouse,
Wherever someone like me must awaken—
But the torture dragged on as good fortune.
                    (II, p. 355)

The "Sixth Elegy" was written long before, in 1921, and is devoted to Gumilyov. Of all the poems Akhmatova read to Chukovskaya about Gumilyov, the most frightening was "Terror, fingering things in the dark," dated August 27–28, 1921, which is when many believed the poet was executed.

Terror, fingering things in the dark,
Leads the moonbeam to an ax.
Behind the wall there's an ominous knock—
What's there, a ghost, a thief, rats?
                    (I, p. 585)

Chukovskaya says that Akhmatova had intended to incorporate this poem into the "Sixth Elegy." She wrote other lines instead, but the feeling of fear, of being watched, of being in danger even in one's own home, works equally well in this Elegy. The poet asks the addressee, now dead, to tell her finally what it was they feared:

Now that you're there, where everything is known—tell me:
What else lived in that house besides us?
                    (II, p. 357)

The reply might very well be that Akhmatova, with her gift of prophecy, felt the atmosphere of doom hovering over the land and her house, although when she lived in this house she did not yet know what shape or form the Terror would take.

The "Seventh Elegy" was never finished. Its theme is silence—the silence Akhmatova was forced to keep for thirty years.

> And I have been silent, silent for thirty years.
> The silence of arctic ice
> Stands through innumerable nights.
>
> (II, p. 721)

She did not cease writing poetry, but as she was no longer able to publish, she had lost her role as "the voice of the people." She worked on this elegy from 1958 to 1964, although by then the political atmosphere had changed and her work was once again being published. The "Seventh Elegy" ends on a pessimistic note:

> It is deforming my fate,
> It almost devoured my soul,
> But I will break it some day
> To summon death to the whipping post.

It—the silence—is oppressive, makes it difficult to breathe, she says. But Akhmatova did not die in silence, and *The Flight of Time* crowned the very last years of her life.

Akhmatova, who produced some of the most renowned translations in the Russian language, was always ambivalent about her work as a translator. For many years she earned her living translating works by major authors from places as distant and remote as Armenia, Korea, Serbia, and India. She frequently complained that it was ruining her creativity and taking time away from her own work. Nadezhda Mandelstam notes that Akhmatova often gave the translations to other people and shared the fees. "She managed it very shrewdly and saved needy people by getting them paid handsomely for their drudgery."[27] However, it is doubtful that Akhmatova would let anything appear under her name that was less than the highest quality, whether it was her own poetry, an article on Pushkin, or a translation of another poet's work. Perhaps others produced a basic version, and like an artist with apprentices, the real poet did the final job of polishing the text and transforming it into a work of art. In her biographical sketch, *Briefly About Myself*, Akhmatova wrote: "I have been interested in the problems of literary translation for a long time. I translated a great deal in the postwar years. And I am translating now."[28]

The poet Semyon Lipkin believes Akhmatova's love and real empathy for the works of other cultures enabled her to produce these great translations. He notes that previous Russan translators made the Bengali poet Rabindranath Tagore's work sound stilted and cold, whereas in Akhmatova's version, he speaks clearly, simply, and musically, without any superfluity.

> She is present in every line of the translation, just as an original author is present in every phrase of his hero. But a translator must not stifle the author or we lose the feeling of the original. Akhmatova does not impose anything on the author; she helps him state his relationship to the world in another language, helps him express his thoughts, his feelings. . . . If letters, diaries, biographical notes of a poem can help us enter his world and understand more profoundly this world, then the translation by a real poet will serve us as an invaluable guide to this world. Reading her translations, we again return to Akhmatova's original poems and see what we had not noticed before.[29]

Another poet, Arseny Tarkovsky, comments that her edition of Tagore should sit next to Akhmatova's own poetry on the reader's shelf. He assumes Akhmatova selected the poets she translated, although others do not agree and say she was simply assigned authors. If she did indeed choose whom she wished to translate, then Tarkovsky is correct when he says that that choice reveals something about her:

> Like any other art, a poetic translation begins with selection. A painter chooses the single part of the world that best answers his ideas. The poet-translator finds in the literature of another language what at any given moment of historical, social, and personal life signifies for him something important and expressive, and under the hand of our contemporary, something that recently seemed strange, perhaps written long ago, is reborn and answers the needs of our time, our national milieu.[30]

Akhmatova's interest in Georgian poetry led to her translations of works from that nation. Akhmatova had met the famous Georgian poets Paolo Yashvili and Titsian Tabidze through Boris Pasternak at the beginning of the 1930s. She said, "Once Pasternak brought Titsian and Paolo to see me at 34, Fontanka, where I was living. At my request, they read me poems in Georgian. I wanted to penetrate further into the music of Georgian verse."[31]

Abram Gozenpud, the literary scholar and translator, came to know Akhmatova because he wanted her to do some translations for him. He first met her in 1956, and was impressed that she never attempted to dominate any conversation, but preferred instead to remain a listener, while always raising the person to whom she was speaking to her level. Like many others, Gozenpud at first felt shy in her presence, but sensing this, Akhmatova helped subtly. He told her she resembled Catherine the Great. "You're not the first to say that," she replied. "I hope you're mistaken. I can't bear her. In general, I don't like famous women. There is something reeking of bad theater in them. And what's more, they were invented by men."[32]

In 1957, Gozenpud was compiling an edition of the great Ukrainian poet Ivan Franko. The works had to be translated into Russian, many for the first time. One of Franko's best-known works, *Fading Leaves,* had never been translated very well. It is a lyric drama about unrequited love, and each poem serves as a link in the chain. If even one is poorly translated, it ruins the effect of the whole. Ten different people had translated twenty-nine of the sixty-one poems for the 1941 edition; as a result, there was no stylistic unity. What was needed was a single translation by a real poet, someone who was close to the theme and images. Gozenpud turned to Anna Akhmatova, and she willingly agreed. "This is my theme," she said. And yet, in spite of a certain commonality, one cannot imagine two more different poets. Gozenpud suggests that perhaps it was this essential difference that attracted Akhmatova most. She once compared the poet-translator to the actor: a truly talented actor never wants to be confined by roles that are most congenial to him. He seeks to take on new and challenging ones to avoid sterility and even self-parody. Akhmatova noted the close connection in Franko's work between the development of action and the change of meter and rhythm, the transition from an expression of feeling to a lyrical coloring of the landscape. "*Fading Leaves* was not an imitation but an echo," says Gozenpud of her translation.[33]

The care that Akhmatova took to make sure her translations were close in feeling and rhythm to the original is exemplified by how she went about translating from Korean. Before she began work, she invited students from Korea to visit her. They sang and played on their musical instruments. Akhmatova listened carefully, keeping time and learning the rhythm and meter; subsequently, she wrote translations of poems that conformed well to the meaning and mood of the original.[34]

When Lev Ozerov was preparing an anthology of nineteenth-century Lithuanian poets, he invited Akhmatova to contribute. She agreed, outlining her philosophy of translation: "You don't have to look for material that is congenial to me, like what I write. Sometimes what is more remote is more comprehensible and closer to me. Is that strange? You have to penetrate the original in something that is different from you, live with the original, illuminate it while you yourself remain in the shadow. If you do not wish to reproduce someone else's poetry, but just inspire it with your own, then you might as well just write your own poetry."[35]

While Akhmatova was in Tashkent, she had begun working on her prose and verse play, *Enuma Elish (When above . . .*). She burned it after the war. Much later, at the beginning of the 1960s, Akhmatova said, "It thought of returning to me." She attempted to restore, or more precisely, to re-create the lost text. Shortly before her death, she collected what was finished in an envelope with the inscription: "A. A. Akhmatova. Prologue (Dream within Dream). 1965." Fragments appear in other notebooks. After Akhmatova's death, scholars attempted to order the fragments and produce a more or less complete work, but because of the experimental nature of the play and the use of stream-of-consciousness techniques in the imagery, it is difficult to hypothesize what the whole might have been like.[36] Many of the new passages written after the war relate to her relationship with Isaiah Berlin as the "Guest from the Future." In the fourth poem of the cycle *Cinque,* again connected with the Guest from the Future, there is a reference to the "dedication of the burnt drama from which no ashes are left."

In *Hope Abandoned,* Nadezhda Mandelstam talks about the difficulties Akhmatova had in working on her play after the war:

Akhmatova was not able to reconstruct Prologue. She started trying as soon as Lev came back from the camp [1956], but there was no one who could help her. . . . In vain she begged them to jog her memory by recalling some little part of it. Although nothing came of this, she could not let it rest there and decided to write something similar in its place. But by this time she had entered her final phase of resigned old age. . . . [T]he second prologue . . . was written . . . when, in recollecting the past, [Akhmatova] began to add up all the things she had missed or been deprived of during her life because the "cruel age" had deflected it.[37]

Enuma Elish is the title of an ancient Babylonian poem about the creation of the world and the generation of the gods. It includes the passages on *Gilgamesh.* The prose framework is a satire set during World War II, dramatizing the trial of a poet before a writer's tribunal—a parody of the typical inquisitions against intellectuals during the Stalinist period. The "Dream Within a Dream" is a drama in verse, performed before an audience onstage. A mysterious dream appears to the sleeping heroine, in which two lovers, "He" and "She," or the Guest and X, engage in a sado-masochistic discourse. The third part of the play returns to prose. It portrays the trial of the author-heroine after the failure of her play, and ends with her tragic death. The characters are reduced to a few anonymous figures such as "She," "He," and the "Blind Man." The male and female protagonists each bring great joy and great pain to the other's life. There are clear references to Akhmatova's own life. In one fragment the heroine says no one has been more homeless than she has. The male has appeared to her in a dream and condemns her. As in her earlier poetry, Akhmatova employs a natural setting to evoke a dark atmosphere:

So curse once again the creak of the well,
The rustle of pines, the black cry of crows,
The earth on which I walked,

The yellow star in my window,
What I was and what I became.

(II, p. 385)

"She" identifies with a forbidden book, a falconer—and "He" is her favorite
bird, that is, her favorite victim. But there is constant role reversal:

How many times we changed roles,
And death did not save us.
Now you penned me in a dungeon,
Now I was carrying your head,
Because you were my Orpheus,
My Holofernes, my Johannes,
These cruel dreams of mine became our tenderness,
And our own beauty we didn't recognize.

(II, p. 387)

A few lines later, "She" identifies with Phaedra, and "He" becomes her stepson
Ippolyte, her innocent victim.

The verses in which "He" speaks are equally sadistic, and his goal is to inflict
pain upon the heroine. "He" will use his favorite weapon—not a sword but his
poetry—to achieve his goal:

Though you are three times more beautiful than angels,
Though you are the sister of the river willows,
I will kill you with my singing,
Without spilling your blood on the ground.

(II, p. 387)

Both are caught in an inextricable web; no matter how much pain they bring each
other, they cannot bear to be apart. He tells her:

Better for me to look for you among the graves
Than for you not to have existed at all.
. . .

Sinful, criminal, holy—
But our bond—that must be.
. . .

You alone were my fate,
I would have done anything for you.

(II, p. 388)

In fact, they seem to have lived throughout history, playing the same sado-masochistic roles. He says:

> I was your murderer, it seems,
> Or were you? I don't remember anything.
> As a Roman, as a Scythian, a Byzantine,
> I was a witness to your shame.

There is a final end ahead when both will be judged and either be saved or receive divine retribution. The First Voice says:

> We tasted the forbidden knowledge,
> And in the bottomless abyss of conscience,
> The more transparent the buildings, the more frightening,
> And the final hour was already visible . . .

The Second Voice echoes her despair:

> Already the distant thunder rumbles . . .
> And that which we call music
> Because we have no better name,
>   Can it save us?
>   (II, p. 393)

There are fragments of this play (published in Kralin's edition) that show more direct allusions to Akhmatova's meeting with Isaiah Berlin. In one scene, "She" tells "Someone" (He) that it will be three years until their next meeting. "She" prophesies that he will come to her out of mere curiosity, and when he comes, he will understand that everything has gone wrong. "He" replies:

Someone: Alas! I already remember how the tragic autumn will reek, when I will come see you in order to destroy you, without touching your hands, without looking into your eyes.

She: And you will depart, leaving the door open to misfortunes which you cannot even imagine.

Someone: And you?

She: For a long time and in a strange way I will be faithful to you and with cold eyes will look on all misfortune until the Last One comes.

Someone: And who is she?

She: The one behind the gates. They did not show her to me when in my typhus delirium I had a vision of everything that would happen to me. Everything . . . up to the gate.[38]

It becomes clear that the "Last One" is the Last Misfortune. "Someone" asks her if she knows what awaits her and she replies that she does: Zhdanov (who expelled Akhmatova from the Writers' Union).

In another version, "She" tells "He" that it is August 28, 1963, and only a year until they will have their last meeting. This was more prophetic than Akhmatova knew, for she would see Isaiah Berlin again in 1965, when she went to Oxford to receive an honorary degree. "She" warns that if they meet again, it will mean they will never see each other again. This will be the last, "eternal farewell." There is another version in which the Guest from the Future has a dialogue with Ix, the heroine, in a cave.

In one fragment there is an "Intermezzo," to be performed between acts. She then discusses in prose what happened to various characters in the play and others associated with it. One seems to be a reference to Arthur Lourie, who actually did write some music for *Poem Without a Hero*. The fragment says he met an apocalyptic fate: society divided him into two equal parts. The first put his name among the most brilliant luminaries, the second said nothing would come of him, and some asked, "Are you sure there really is such a composer?" Perhaps she wrote this after she received a very moving letter from Lourie telling her how difficult it had been for him to find a reception for his music in America.[39]

It is difficult to interpret a work which even in its original completed version was hard to comprehend. Like Bulgakov's novel, *The Master and Margarita*, the play *Enuma Elish* combined radically different styles. For example, Bulgukov's novel uses biting satire and irony to expose the vices of Moscow in the 1920s, then adopts a lovely lyrical tone in the Master's story about Pontius Pilate. It appears, from Nadezhda Mandelstam's description, that the trial at the end would be written in a grotesque farcical style, reflecting the ironic humor. However, in the fragments we have devoted to the "Dream Within a Dream" verse portion of the play, another style is employed, recalling that of Leonid Andreyev's *Life of Man* from the beginning of the century. The characters include nameless allegorical figures like "Man" and "Someone in Gray." It is a Symbolist play, staged by both Stanislavsky and Meyerhold in experimental productions. In Stanislavsky's version, the characters were placed against a background of black velvet; the scenery was made out of white ropes against a black velvet background, like lines in a drawing marking the contours of a room, windows, doors, tables and chairs, as if white lines had been drawn on black paper. The actors were dressed in black velvet, with white outlines defining their bodies, and against the black background they seemed to be "moving drawings." People sounded the way voices do on early phonograph records. It was a strange and haunting production, very popular at the time. Although Akhmatova was in the Ukraine and Crimea in 1907 when Stanislavsky staged his version of the work, she may still have been aware of it.[40]

In the fragments of Akhmatova's play we can piece together a very complex allegory reflecting two major themes—man's inhumanity to man and the complex love-hate relationship between the sexes.

In February 1966, when Akhmatova was very sick, she was reading Alain Robbe-Grillet's book *Last Year at Marienbad,* which experiments with shifts in time and space and has other coincidental similarities to her work. She was afraid people would accuse her of getting her ideas for her play from him, even though she was just now reading his work for the first time: *"L'année dernière à Marienbad* will be the death of my Prologue. This is both bad and good. I'm reading it with a pain in my heart. My God! There is also a theater there. Who will believe that I wrote 'Dream Within a Dream' without knowing this book?" But in a diary entry written shortly before she died, she noted: "On the other hand, the Frenchman [Alain Robbe-Grillet] does not portray the era—it could have happened at any time at all," and goes on to point out important differences between his work and her own.[41]

Vilenkin connected *Enuma Elish* with Kafka's *The Trial,* which fascinated Akhmatova. Once at a gathering at Vilenkin's home, Akhmatova entered the room in the middle of a conversation about Kafka, who at this time was not very well known in Russia. She sat down in an armchair and, without a pause, joined in the conversation, soon dominating it. They were astounded when she began to retell Kafka's tale in her own words, and had the impression that they were listening to the author himself. There was not a single superfluous word in the flow of detail. This went on for over an hour, but she was not at all tired and her eyes glittered. Vilenkin realized that *Enuma Elish* had something in common with *The Trial.* In her play, the accused was interrogated by lowly officials, helped by "witnesses to the prosecution" who held parcels from which fish heads and tails protruded. This was written before Akhmatova returned to Leningrad, yet the detail anticipated the story of Akhmatova's own discovery that she had been accused of disloyalty in August 1946, when after returning home from shopping, she opened the newspaper she had been carrying fish in and read the headlines. The horror in the play is that the accused can never understand what she has been accused of. When she attempts to speak in verse, she is interrupted by shouts: "That's not allowed. How dare you!" Vilenkin cites lines from one of Akhmatova's poems dating from the mid-1950s, where Kafka is mentioned:[42]

Others go off with their loved ones—
I don't look after them with envy.
I've been sitting alone in the prisoners' dock
For almost half a century,
Surrounded by quarrels and crowds
And the cloying smell of ink.
It's like something invented by Kafka
And played by Chaplin.
And in these momentous arguments,
As in the tenacious embrace of sleep,

Three generations of juries
Decided: "She is guilty."

(II, p. 641)

Gozenpud relates how in response to her request that he get Akhmatova a French translation of Kafka's *Metamorphosis,* she commented that the significance of this story was not that a person had been crushed after having been transformed into a repulsive insect. She cited instead Kafka's depiction of the agony, the torment without any enlightenment, any relevation before death—in contrast to Tolstoy's *Death of Ivan Ilyich.* She thought it a cruel and tormented tale, and felt a bond with Kafka: "How alone he was, and probably his life was an agony extended for many years."[43]

During the fifties and sixties Akhmatova continued to work on articles on Pushkin that resembled biographical studies rather than analyses of his work. Nadezhda Mandelstam comments on Akhmatova's ability to make figures from the past such as Pushkin come alive, to the point where Akhmatova is even jealous of the women in his life:

Akhmatova, in resurrecting figures from the past, was always interested in the way they lived and their relations with others. I remember how she made Shelley come alive for me—this was, as it were, her first experiment of this kind. Next began her period of communion with Pushkin. With the thoroughness of a detective or a jealous woman, she ferreted out everything about the people around him, probing their psychological motives and turning every woman he had ever so much as smiled at inside out like a glove.[44]

Two articles, "Pushkin and Mickiewicz," about Pushkin's relationship to his famous Polish contemporary, and "Pushkin and Dostoyevsky," which Akhmatova considered her best study, both perished in the blockade. However, other articles written after the war were published after Akhmatova's death.[45]

Akhmatova became interested in Pushkin's death, and sifted through an enormous amount of material, both published and in the archives, focusing on details neglected by other scholars. Pushkin died in a duel with the French officer Georges d'Anthès, who had been adopted by Baron Lis de Heeckeren, the Dutch ambassador to Russia. There were rumors of an affair between Pushkin's wife Natalya and d'Anthès. To avert suspicion, d'Anthès married Natalya's sister, Catherine. However, the rumors continued unabated. Pushkin sent an insulting letter to Heeckeren, which led d'Anthès to challenge him to a fatal duel in 1837.

Akhmatova concentrates on Natalya's responsibility for the death of her famous husband. Akhmatova says Natalya was under the illusion that d'Anthès was in love with her, but Akhmatova—like many of Pushkin's contemporaries—was convinced d'Anthès was only using Natalya to hurt Pushkin. There was presumably a homosexual involvement between Heeckeren and d'Anthes, and Heeckeren hoped that once Pushkin learned of the alleged affair between his wife and d'Anthès, he would remove Natalya from the capital. (Akhmatova alludes to the affair between Heeckeren and d'Anthès, which most other scholars do not.) However, Heeckeren accepted that d'Anthès could marry Catherine, since he assumed there was no love between them. Akhmatova clearly sees Natalya as Heeckeren's accomplice, saying, "Without her help, Heeckeren would have been helpless." She characterizes Natalya as willful, depriving her husband of peace of mind, bringing her sisters into the household (which created further financial problems), renting expensive dachas, and in general making the life of the famous poet not easier, but impossible. In reading the actual correspondence between Pushkin and his wife, one becomes convinced that Akhmatova is correct. Natalya *was* frivolous and egotistical, with little understanding of the brilliant man she had married—the man considered by many to be Russia's greatest poet.

In an article entitled "Alexandrina," Akhmatova argues effectively against the rumor of a romance between Pushkin and his sister-in-law Alexandra, Natalya's sister. Akhmatova's research, using letters and diaries from the period, revealed no evidence for this rumor. Akhmatova also dispels A. P. Arapova's characterization of Pushkin. Arapova (*née* Lanskaya) was the daughter of Natalya Goncharova and her second husband. She described Pushkin as a failure who squandered his inheritance, an uncouth bore and vulgar libertine, the wicked husband of a long-suffering, tormented victim. "It never occurred to Arapova," Akhmatova points out, "to take a look at the tender, caring, and most beautiful letters that Pushkin wrote to his wife." And Akhmatova reveals the good relationship Arapova had with the man who had killed Pushkin, Baron d'Anthès, and his wife Catherine, Natalya's other sister.

Akhmatova's work on Pushkin gives us an insight into her own life. "Pushkin and the Banks of the Neva" includes a discussion of Pushkin's story "The Solitary Hut on Vasilevsky Island" (1828), which features a description of Golodai Island. Akhmatova incorporates other works such as Pushkin's narrative poem *The Bronze Horseman,* and then focuses on the unknown graves of five rebels executed after the Decembrist uprising in 1825, including the poet Ryleyev and others close to Pushkin. At the end, Akhmatova notes: "Pushkin fully shared the lofty belief of antiquity (see Sophocles, *Oedipus at Colonus*) that the grave of a just man is a national treasure and a blessing from the gods."

Nikolay Gumilyov was buried in an unmarked grave believed to be located on Golodai Island, which Akhmatova visited with the Mandelstams. And Irina Punina also recalls having been taken as a child by Akhmatova to the place where Gumilyov was shot and presumably buried. There are also possible allusions in the article to Mandelstam, since he too was buried in an unmarked grave.[46]

In "A Word About Pushkin" (1961), one of Akhmatova's last pieces on Pushkin and also one of her most powerful, she observes how at the end the house of Pushkin became sacred to his homeland:

> Little by little, the entire era . . . came to be called the Pushkin era. All the beauties, ladies-in-waiting, mistresses of the salons, Dames of the Order of St. Catherine, members of the Imperial Court, ministers, aides-de-camp and non-aides-de-camp, gradually came to be called Pushkin's contemporaries, and were later simply laid to rest in card catalogues and name indices . . . to Pushkin's works. He conquered both time and space . . . In the palace halls where they danced and gossiped about the poet, his portraits now hang and his books are on view, while their pale shadows have been banished from there forever.[47]

Akhmatova says what is most terrifying is what they could have heard from Pushkin himself:

> You will not be answerable for me,
> You can sleep peacefully.
> Strength is power, but your children
> Will curse you for me.

She refers to another famous poem by Pushkin, "I build a monument to myself . . ." (1836). The poet's monument will be "made without human hands"—his poetry will outlive any monuments to tsars and political leaders. By implication, Akhmatova's works will long outlive any bronze monuments erected by the Communist regime to the heroes of socialism.

Although Akhmatova's works were finally being published and she was achieving renown, her life in the early 1960s was still not easy. Natalya Ilyina says that in many ways Akhmatova became more dependent on those around her. However, she was discreet and considerate in her demands on other people. Her memory remained exceedingly keen. Ilyina had to be careful not to offend Akhmatova's pride: Akhmatova hated anyone to feel sorry for her. Sometimes Ilyina took her friend for rides around Moscow; she would say to Akhmatova, "I'll take you," and Akhmatova would severely reprimand her: "You mean, we are going together?"[48] Ilyina recalls one beautiful spring day in 1961 when Akhmatova's new collection of poems had just been published. That day they drove to Peredelkino. Akhmatova wanted to bring her book as a gift to Chukovsky. The evening was quiet, warm, with a rosy glow in the sky:

> How lovely they were together—Akhmatova and Chukovsky! She, heavy, gray, magnificent in a simple silk dress, and he in a white coat with a white lock on his dark forehead, lean, tall, slightly and reverently leaning

toward her. . . . I left the two of them on the bench, admiring them from afar, strolling down the road, and it was strange for me that these two people whose names I had known my whole life, were here right next to me, and I thanked fate for giving me the chance to meet them and that they were so kind to me.[49]

Through a simple outburst in one conversation, Ilyina grasped Akhmatova's theory of poetic creativity—it is not a matter of will, of following simple rules set out by poets of the past, but a combination of craftsmanship and true inspiration that cannot be willed. Once Ilyina asked Maria Petrovykh about a certain young female poet. "She is capable," replied Petrovykh, to which Akhmatova replied angrily, "There are no capable poets! Either someone's a poet or not! It's not the kind of work where you get up early in the morning, wash, and sit down at the table: Well, let's see, I'll immerse myself. Poetry is a catastrophe. Only in this way can it be written. If not this way—the reader will immediately understand this and feel it!"[50]

Ilyina describes a visit to Akhmatova at her little cabin in the writers' colony in Komarovo, in 1964. She captures the wonderful noisy atmosphere when people came to visit. There was always someone to look after Akhmatova. Often, as in 1963, it was Lev Arens, the brother of Punin's first wife, and his wife Sarra. They had known Akhmatova for years, when they visited the Punins and possibly even before Akhmatova lived with them. Sarra was a little old lady of nearly seventy who wore an apron from morning to night and always had a smile on her small, wrinkled face, though her eyes were sad.

> Quiet, affectionate, obliging and selfless, she was afraid of Akhmatova, but could not restrain her ineradicable desire to report on expenses; she would find a moment to mutter something about the rising price of curd cheese, to which Akhmatova would immediately respond with fury: "Sarra, I've forbidden you to talk to me about curd cheese!" Lev was also short with an expressive face, lively, laughing eyes, and a long white beard that blew in the wind when he rode his bicycle. He was a botanist. Lev had once been the victim of one of the repressions and when asked by an interrogator, "How is it that an enlightened man like you believes in God?" he replied, "It is because I am an enlightened man that I believe."[51]

Silvia Gitovich, wife of the poet and translator A. I. Gitovich, lived with her husband in a dacha in Komarovo near Akhmatova. Often at night a bonfire was lit in front of Akhmatova's house, and she would drag out an armchair with a high back and sit for a long time, watching the fire burn. After sunset she liked to sit on a little narrow bench under the windows of the veranda and rest. The Gitoviches moved next door to her. Little by little Akhmatova's cabin was furnished: old chairs with curved legs and torn upholstery, a narrow table fashioned from some attic door, and a mattress resting on eight bricks. Akhmatova said, "I've gotten quite used to my bricks. After all, Pushkin's bed stood on birch logs, and mine is on bricks."[52] She worked at a long, narrow desk, a strange hybrid of a high bench with a narrow commode on which stood her marvelous light blue porcelain candlesticks and a porcelain inkstand with a bronze top. She had a radio and phonograph as well as a wardrobe for her clothes. There were flowers everywhere—in vases, pitchers, jars. Usually toward evening she went for a walk with guests up to a little bench opposite the pale blue two-story house of the writer Plotkin. Once, on arriving there, Akhmatova pointed to the house and said, "Oh, this foundation is standing on my drops of blood." (Plotkin had taken an active part in the persecution of Akhmatova after the August 1946 Regulation.)[53]

However, there were not always guests. Silvia says often Akhmatova was left alone and grew bored. Frequently after taking a walk she would stop in at the Gitoviches' and drink tea with them, sitting and chatting for a long time.

In 1959, on a hot summer day, Silvia celebrated Akhmatova's seventieth birthday with her. There were no guests—just the two of them. They took a walk, drank tea. In the evening a telegram arrived from Moscow—from Akhmatova's dear friend, the actress Faina Ranevskaya. Silvia did not want to leave Akhmatova alone that day, since it would have been depressing for her to spend her birthday alone. Silvia stayed the night with her, sleeping in the little room called "the Gray Room" in Akhmatova's cabin.

Often the artist Tonya Lyubimova would visit; she was always making drawings of Akhmatova and would do errands for her. In 1960, Silvia Gitovich took care of Akhmatova, since Irina Punina said she could find no one that summer to do so. It was not easy—Silvia's husband woke up early at seven and Akhmatova at eleven, and Silvia was afraid to leave her alone at night, since Akhmatova had recently had a heart attack. Akhmatova would often go for walks gathering mushrooms, and she had a little companion, Alik, the son of the nursemaid who worked in the day-care center next door; he picked the mushrooms for her, since it was difficult for her to bend. He would come back with her and chat and keep her company. By her porch he arranged pine cones in a pattern, saying, "This is for the writer who lives all alone and thinks up everything out of her head."[54] Finally Irina arranged for a maid to take care of Akhmatova.

However, in the next few years things changed. Young poets such as Brodsky and Nayman started to call, and many other young people arrived—those who wrote poetry and those who wrote nothing at all, those who knew her well and those who knew her not at all—to pay their respects to Akhmatova's poetry or simply to look at her just so they could say, "I spent an evening at Akhmatova's. It was absolutely marvelous."[55]

Israel Metter says people who did not know Akhmatova thought of her as a national monument, and many also treated her as one. This evoked contradictory feelings in her. Deprived so long of public recognition, Akhmatova appreciated the respect and even adulation, but the idea of herself as an icon tired and annoyed her as well. Metter mentions how amazed he was at Akhmatova's conversation, the words she used, how contemporary they were—not street slang, but expressions that had not yet become standard. He could not fathom where she had picked them up, since she did not stand in long lines at stores or use public transportation. Akhmatova was not like many people her age who were just enveloped in memories of the distant past.[56]

Alexey Batalov, the actor who had known Akhmatova since he was a child when she stayed with his mother, Nina Olshevskaya, said Akhmatova possessed a secret strength as well as a clear vision of her very special place in the world. She was always genuinely interested in what others were trying to achieve. This was why his generation found it so easy to show her their poems or drawings, to argue with her about art, or simply tell her funny anecdotes. The older, more conservative visitors who came to see Akhmatova in her cabin, who did not have a sense of humor, expected to find the quiet abode of a famous poet tucked behind an old fence. Instead, it was open house day and night. During her last years there were bicycles, motorcycles, young people dressed informally always in attendance. Depending on who the frightened guest was and how serious his purpose, everyone would quiet down and appear respectful. Akhmatova would lead him very calmly to her room and speak to him, give him a cup of tea or coffee, and if necessary, invite him out on the veranda, where the rest of her visitors congregated. The guest would sit in polite silence, slightly confused, and then finally leave.[57]

One of the people who became a close companion in her last years was Anatoly Nayman, who could slip as gracefully as Akhmatova from subject to subject, who had a broad cultural background but was young and knew the contemporary scene from his own personal experience. Nika Glen, who served as Akhmatova's literary secretary from 1957, says in her memoirs that she often felt Akhmatova told her things especially so she would note them down for posterity, but writing was not her gift. In 1962, Nayman began serving in this capacity, helping Akhmatova with her manuscripts and running errands for her.

Zoya Tomashevskaya describes how she introduced Nayman to the poet. Zoya knew Nayman's wife, who worked as an art historian in the Hermitage. Through her she came to know Nayman, who constantly begged her to introduce him to Akhmatova. One summer day, when Zoya was going to bring some fruit and flowers to Akhmatova, she finally gave in and brought Nayman with her. As they were walking down the path to Akhmatova's cabin, Nayman ran ahead, and when Zoya approached, Nayman was already sitting and chatting with Akhmatova.[58] Many say he reminded Akhmatova of Modigliani—the same handsome, dark features—and that was one of the reasons she found him so attractive. Nayman soon left his wife and spent much of his time with Akhmatova. They worked on a translation of the Italian poet Leopardi together. Some believe a few of the poems in her cycle *Midnight Verses* are to him. In one, written on March 10,

1963, in Komarovo, she is possibly thanking Nayman for being her companion.
Yet it might also be Punin, who died but remained always in her memory:

Elegy Before the Coming of Spring

> . . . *toi qui m'as consolée.*
> —Gérard de Nerval

The snowstorm hushed among the pines.
But, intoxicated without wine,
There, like Ophelia, silence itself
Sang to us all through the night.
And the one who appeared only to me
Was betrothed to that quietness,
Having said farewell, he generously remained,
He remained with me until death.

(II, p. 269)

In his memoirs, Nayman describes the enormous amount of activity around
Akhmatova whenever she traveled:

> In her last years . . . moving from place to place became increasingly
> difficult, mainly because of her heart trouble. An hour before she had
> to leave the house she would get symptoms of *Reisefieber,* travel fever,
> and sometimes her heart would play up. She would only travel with a
> female companion—some close acquaintance or a relative. They would
> arrive at the station long before the train came into the station. . . . One
> of the young people would be put in charge of Akhmatova's luggage and
> someone was always at her side with nitroglycerine for her heart condition
> to hand—another bottle of nitroglycerine was always kept in her handbag.
> She would walk slowly to the carriage, leaning on someone's arm, and
> stopping to rest from time to time.[59]

Often in the evenings Akhmatova listened to music on the radio—Mozart,
Vivaldi, Stravinsky. Nayman records how particular pieces would captivate her at
different times. In 1963, it was Beethoven sonatas, then in the autumn Vivaldi;
in the summer of 1964, Shostakovich's eighth quartet, in the spring of 1965 Per-
golesi's *Stabat Mater,* and that summer and autumn Monteverdi's *L'Incoronazione
di Poppea* and Purcell's *Dido and Aeneas* in the performance with Elizabeth
Schwarzkopf.

On the morning of June 24, 1964, Silvia cut a special bouquet of lilacs from
her garden. It was Akhmatova's seventy-fifth birthday, and her cabin was full of
flowers. The postman brought packets of congratulatory telegrams—from Moscow, from the Writers' Union, from different publishers, from friends and

strangers. The chauffeur Vasya from the Writers' Union came on June 25 with all the telegrams received at the Leningrad Writers' Union. No special guests had been invited, but her friends were there. Then after dinner Alexander Prokofiev, secretary of the Leningrad section of the Union of Soviet Writers, arrived with a delegation. They celebrated with champagne and flowers.[60]

In the summer of 1964 Natalya Ilyina arrived with her sister Olga, who had married a Frenchman and was visiting Russia with her young daughter Katya. Katya was not happy at the prospect of visiting a famous poet. "Will there be any children there?" she asked, and was annoyed when told there would be none. Ilyina informed her that one day she would be very proud she had visited this elderly lady—that she was a great Russian poet. But nothing impressed little Katya. They assumed they had come too late to be served a meal, since in France everything is served on a strict schedule. But they arrived to find the cabin full of people. Someone was cooking in the kitchen, and on a table out on the veranda Nina Olshevskaya was cleaning mushrooms she had just picked. Several young people were visiting, and one of them went to get some vodka and took Katya along, which made her happy. A Leningrad artist was drawing Akhmatova in her room. Akhmatova was dressed in a simple lilac dress and sat at the table, looking magnificent. Finally the sitting was over. Ilyina thought the drawing looked more like the Statue of Liberty than Akhmatova. The artist disappeared, and Akhmatova came out on the veranda, where they all had supper. Boris Ardov, Nina's son, appeared with some young poets and actors. Yevgeni Chukovsky, nephew of Lydia Chukovskaya, was there with his wife, Galina Shostakovich, and they had brought along a tape recorder and a tape of her father's new work. Faina Ranevskaya was living nearby, and someone went to invite her to join them. The meal went on for a long time, and it was an event young Katya would long remember.[61]

Mikhail Meilakh, a noted literary scholar and editor of Akhmatova's poems, came to know her in her last years. His father was also a literary scholar, and Mikhail grew up in a family where Akhmatova was more like a myth than a real person. It was difficult for him to believe she actually lived in the same city of Leningrad. When he was fifteen years old, he took her collection *From Six Books* off the shelf, then cut some branches of lilac in his Komarovo garden and presented them to Akhmatova. She inscribed the book to him. Several years had passed when he met her at the Ardovs' on Ordynka. Meilakh had just returned with Nayman from visiting Brodsky in exile. She asked in detail about Brodsky. After this he visited her more frequently. At first he was excruciatingly shy, but he kept bringing her flowers, records, and books, and soon began to help her when she traveled, as well as running errands for her. He recalls how amazing her memory was: she not only retained events from long ago but remembered everything that was going on in the present.[62]

Ignaty Ivanovsky, a translator, recalls her wit. Shortly before her death, Akhmatova had to have her appendix removed. After this a representative of the Union of Soviet Writers appeared in the hospital ward, bearing flowers and suggesting that she be moved to a nicer hospital. Akhmatova answered coldly, "Thank you. I've already been cut in two."[63]

Many noticed Akhmatova's eagerness to hear how her poems were being received by the intelligentsia and the general public. She was also aware of the increased interest in her work in the West. The last years of her life were filled with people's admiration, and she thrived on this. Ilyina described how one would arrive for a visit and sit down, and then Akhmatova, with a mysterious look, would take out of her black purse a piece of paper and smooth it out. The paper would be either a letter from a reader who had only just discovered Akhmatova and was amazed by her poems, or a note from some institute where someone was doing research on her works and asking for information. Sometimes she would read a newspaper clipping or a page from a magazine, hoping her listener would praise the reviewer's sensitivity, or say of the institute, "Well, it's about time!" One had to express approval of such missives or she would be upset. Ilyina found this rather trying.[64]

As she grew older, Akhmatova became more accessible, and people who met her for the first time found it less difficult to converse with her. Although in some respects this may have been to the good, it also meant total strangers would often overwhelm her with bad poetry and small talk. Silvia Gitovich recalls how one morning some young man appeared at Akhmatova's cabin with a guitar tucked under his arm. Staring insolently at Akhmatova drinking tea on the veranda, he informed her he had to recite his poems to her alone. "Have you been writing for a long time?" she asked. "For two months already," he replied. It was absolutely impossible to get rid of him; he would not move until he had recited two whole notebooks' worth of verses.[65]

Sometimes Ilyina would overhear someone saying, "Well, Akhmatova believes this . . . ", "Akhmatova thinks that . . . " Ilyina knew that the person was barely acquainted with Akhmatova and would think to herself, "Lord, why did she allow this person to come see her? And why does she need this madding crowd?" Although less severe, especially with strangers, Akhmatova's basic personality remained the same—her mysterious gift of song, her penetrating mind, the magnificent irony, her ability to characterize concisely a person or event. But she was neither a saint nor a statue, just a very human being. In a letter, Leo Tolstoy once wrote while working on *Anna Karenina:* "You write and write (something quite unique!), and there finally comes a time when it is absolutely necessary that you are praised. And a genius needs this as well."[66]

Vilenkin also noted that Akhmatova did not want to be forgotten. To many this seemed like vanity, the way she would eagerly grab at any testimony to the popularity of her poetry. She once told him with great satisfaction how when she was in the hospital recovering from her appendicitis attack, an orderly who was combing her hair suddenly told her, "They say you write good poetry," and in reply to Akhmatova's question as to how she knew this, the orderly said, "Dasha, who works in the cafeteria, told me." Vilenkin experienced the same confusion that Ilyina did when Akhmatova would ask him whether he had heard whether her book had "created a scandal" when it appeared in Moscow and Leningrad, that it had sold out within a half hour, that huge lines of people were waiting for it, and so on. She wanted all this fuss and fame. Yet there was no egocentrism in her behavior, and she never treated people with condescension. Vilenkin was always struck by how easily and naturally Akhmatova became the focus of any gathering—theatrical or literary, of the old or young—without the least intention of taking center stage. It simply happened naturally by right of her talent, her vast knowledge, and her keen insights.[67]

An extraordinary range of people wrote to Akhmatova, total strangers from all walks of life. One, K. G. Starokadomsky, told her about his prison camp experiences:

November 4, 1960, Karaganda

Unjustly convicted, I lived for twelve years in the extreme North under difficult conditions, with no books or art. I'll never forget and probably will never be able to convey to you what poetry meant in our lives—the only form of art available to us. Of course, we did not have any printed collections, only handwritten sheets of paper with poems that were passed from hand to hand—yours, your husband's, Alexander Blok's are in the first and most honored place. This was the single thread connecting us in the polar night (in both the literal and figurative sense) with the world of great art. Don't worry about the number of your editions (for example, it is impossible to get last year's edition here); lovers of poetry preserve your pearls in their memory and give them to each other for their birthdays. I think for a poet—this is much more important.[68]

Akhmatova told Dmitry Khrenkov about perhaps the most touching tribute to her. She showed him a newspaper from Bashkir with a photograph of an unusual book. On it was an inscription, "Edition of this book—one copy," printed not on paper but on birch bark: seven pages bound with a simple string, filled with the poems of Anna Akhmatova. The article explained that it was difficult to write, since there was no ink or paper.

Akhmatova sometimes heard unexpectedly from shades of the past. One was the composer Arthur Lourie. After he left Russia in 1922, he settled in Berlin, then Paris, and married his second wife, Tamara Peritz. He went to the United States after the outbreak of World War II, and stayed there. Lourie had been an outstanding figure in the Paris music world of the 1920s and 1930s, although his own style became more conservative. In 1940 he married a Russian countess Elizaveta Belevskaya-Zhukovskaya, related to the tsar and to the Russian poet Vasily Zhukovsky.

A converted Catholic, Lourie was of Jewish origin, and it would have been dangerous for him to remain in Europe. He was able to emigrate to the United

States because of an invitation from Serge Koussevitsky, the conductor of the
Boston Symphony, whom Lourie had known in Russia in 1910–20. After Koussevitsky died, it was difficult for Lourie to find an audience for his music. In 1946
he became acquainted with a writer, Irina Graham, in New York, where he was
living on East 54th Street in a tiny apartment. With a grant from the Koussevitsky
Foundation, he began writing an opera, *The Moor of Peter the Great,* based on
the story by Pushkin about his ancestor, the black Ethiopian prince adopted by
Peter the Great. Irina Graham worked on the libretto. For the rest of his life
Graham helped support him. After spending time with Graham in San Francisco
and returning to New York, at the end of his life, in 1961, Lourie and his wife
Elizaveta moved to Princeton, where he lived in a villa left to him by Raissa
Maritain, wife of the philosopher Jacques Maritain, with whom Lourie had been
close in Paris.

Clarence Brown, a professor of comparative literature at Princeton, often
spoke with Lourie and said, "He was always cordial, though I understand he could
be difficult and suspicious. He did not seem to have much respect for the other
musicians in Princeton. He was, I think, homesick for Russia. He missed Europe,
too."[69] A recent article on Lourie describes him as a genuinely Russian composer
with a specific national sensibility that developed by way of Greece, Byzantium,
and the East, as well as the influence of the music of the peoples who made up
the Russian Empire.

On November 9, 1958, Lourie wrote to Salomea Andronikova Halpern, one
of Akhmatova's friends before the Revolution, who was now living in England.
Salomea had barely known him in Petersburg and rarely saw him when she was in
Paris. He sent her Akhmatova's poem "Willow," which he had set to music. In
1961 she wrote to Lourie at Akhmatova's request, and they corresponded for four
years. In one letter to Salomea dated March 5, 1962, Lourie wrote that he was not
happy in Princeton. There were cultured people but few Russians. "In general,
Princeton is the American elite. Life stopped here a hundred years ago and since
then nothing has changed. There is a certain charm in this, but also a certain
monotony. A closed circle where everything is repeated."[70] His opinion of San
Francisco was not much better. He found the climate beautiful but the people
boring. Lourie was included on Akhmatova's list of names to receive copies of her
last collection, *The Flight of Time.* He also wrote some music to *Poem Without a
Hero,* which appeared in the émigré journal *Vozdushnye puti* in New York in 1963.

Irina Graham says that the inner bond between Lourie and Akhmatova never
was broken. For his entire life, Lourie was spiritually faithful to Akhmatova, and
sought her image in every other woman with whom he was involved. On March
25, 1963, Lourie wrote to Akhmatova:

> My dear Annushka, recently I read somewhere that when d'Annunzio
> and Duse [the poet-playwright and actress] met after twenty years' sep-
> aration, they both went down on their knees to each other and cried.

What can I say to you? My "fame" has also been lying in a ditch for twenty years, that is, since I came to this country. At first there were moments of brilliant success, but the musicians here took every measure to make sure I did not succeed. I wrote an enormous opera, *The Moor of Peter the Great,* and devoted it to the memory of altars and hearths. This is a memorial to Russian culture, to the Russian people and Russian history. Now it's been two years since I unsuccessfully attempted to put it on the stage. Here no one needs anything and the path for a foreigner is closed. You foresaw everything forty years ago: "foreign bread tastes of wormwood." *The Moor* is my second large work on a Pushkin theme; in Paris I wrote *The Feast During the Plague,* an opera-ballet, which had been accepted by the Opera before the war, but was never performed on stage, only in fragments. In general I'm living a totally empty life, like a shadow. All your photographs look at me the entire day! I embrace and kiss you tenderly. Take care of yourself. I await news from you.[71]

All the women in Lourie's life seemed to be pale imitations of Akhmatova; and by coincidence—or perhaps fate—he died only a few months after she did.

Akhmatova always tried to help her friends. On November 16, 1962, she told Chukovskaya she had just spoken with Surkov about getting an apartment for Nadezhda Mandelstam. He had come to see her, arriving with a bouquet of flowers and declaring, "If only I had known you were in Moscow, I would have brought you flowers from Rome." In response to her request for help for Nadezhda, Surkov said Nadezhda was the wife of a great poet, that she had suffered enough and it was time to change the situation. Surkov, an official first and a lover of poetry second—according to Chukovskaya, who did not trust him—did eventually make good on his promise. Nadezhda was given a place to stay in Moscow and a pension.[72]

For a long time relations between Akhmatova and her son had not been good. Lev felt he had stayed in the camp for so long due to his mother's indifference. Chukovskaya comments on how sad this all was. She herself had witnessed for so many years Akhmatova's constant worrying, her efforts to release Lev. She had tried everything—letters, petitions, connections with influential people. For many years she subordinated her whole life to her efforts to get him released. On many occasions she quietly humiliated herself, by writing poems that would please Stalin, for example, and by saying what would please the authorities when the English students asked her how she felt she was being treated by the regime. She translated hundreds of lines in order to earn enough to send Lev packages, work that took up time she otherwise would have devoted to her poetry.

Chukovskaya attempts to explain Lev's attitude toward his mother. She said not only had the camps affected him, but his difficult childhood. He was raised by his grandmother instead of his own parents, felt abandoned by both his parents, and sensed the disharmony between them. He was a worshipped grandchild as well as a beloved only son, but both Akhmatova and Gumilyov were always more interested in their own internal warfare than in him, says Chukovskaya. His mother was tormented by "fame, love, life, and slander." His father had been killed, and for many years Lev lived in the home of Punin, who in his role of stepfather did not make the boy feel welcome.

On January 1, 1962, Lydia congratulated Akhmatova on Lev's defense of his dissertation, and said Professor Konrad considered him a great scholar. "This great scholar did not come to see me in the hospital a single time in three months," Akhmatova answered gloomily. "God be with him, with Lyova. He is a sick person. They destroyed his soul there [in the camps]. They suggested to him—your mother is so famous. She just has to say the word and you will be home. And he won't admit I'm sick. 'You were always sick even when you were young. It's all pretending.' "[73]

On September 28, 1962, Chukovskaya noted it was Lev's birthday. Akhmatova seemed sad that day, immersed in herself. She and Nika Glen were deliberating whether Lev would be angry if she sent him a telegram congratulating him, which she decided to go ahead and do anyway. Nika gave her some paper and she wrote something, read it over, crossed it out, and wrote something else. Her hands were shaking. Chukovskaya left. The pathetic scene was too much for her.[74]

Chukovskaya also noted that by the end of December 1962, the relationship between Akhmatova and Viktor Ardov, the husband of her dear friend Nina Olshevskaya, had deteriorated. Akhmatova had wanted to stay with Nina at that time, but when she learned that Ardov was returning from his vacation early, she made sure she left the apartment before he returned.[75]

In general, however, the last years of Akhmatova's life were happy ones. Khrenkov, editor-in-chief at Lenizdat, interviewed her at the beginning of 1965 and found her in good spirits. A small volume of her poems had just been published in Poland, the last version of *Poem Without a Hero* was finished, 800 lines of her translation of poems by Tagore had been completed, and cycles of her new poems had appeared in *Novyi mir* and *Znamya*. "There is no old age for anyone used to hard work," she said. She frequently wrote about death, said Khrenkov, but thought only about life.[76]

Chukovsky paid tribute to her at the end of her life:

For the entire half a century that we were acquainted I do not remember on her face a single pleading . . . or pathetic smile . . . even when waiting in line for kerosene and bread, even in the trams in Tashkent, anyone who did not know her felt her "calm importance" and treated her with a certain respect, although she behaved in a simple and friendly manner.[77]

He also noted how she was always giving away things to make her friends happy—books, old candlesticks, Oriental fabrics, engravings. Anything that appeared in her modest surroundings tended to disappear in a few weeks. The single thing that always remained with her was her trunk of manuscripts.

In her last years, Akhmatova loved noise and commotion. Emma Gershtein recalls: "The most horrible thing in the cosmos is absolute quiet, she would say. She loved the noise coming from the courtyard: one person beating rugs, another calling the children home, car doors banging, dogs barking. . . . She laughed at those writers who tried to isolate themselves from the sounds of life going on beside them."[78]

Akhmatova always retained her spiritual side. According to Israel Metter, her belief was quite pure, and in no way obtrusive to anyone else. When she rose up out of her armchair and accompanied guests to the hallway, on the threshold she would say, "Christ be with you," and would quickly cross herself as she said goodbye.[79]

Although Akhmatova and Shostakovich were never close, she always enjoyed his music. In 1958, she had written a poem to him:

Music

D.D.S.

Something miraculous burns in her,
Edges are faceted before her eyes.
She alone speaks to me
When the rest are afraid to come near.
When the last friend averted his gaze,
She was with me in my grave,
As if the first thunderstorm were singing,
Or as if all the flowers broke into words.

(II, p. 281)

In November 1961, Akhmatova wrote in her diary that a waltz she had heard in a ballet suite by Shostakovich recalled the iridescent beauty of a dragonfly. "It is a miracle. I think it is elegance itself dancing. Perhaps one can do with the word what he does with sound?"[80] When she gave him a copy of her poems, Akhmatova wrote: "To Dmitry Shostakovich, in whose epoch I live on earth." He was ecstatic. He loved her poetry, especially *Requiem,* but when he was once asked why he had never written music for a single one of Akhmatova's poems, he replied, "I am not worthy of her talent."[81] In his discussions with Solomon Volkov, Shostakovich says he met Akhmatova around 1918 at the home of the surgeon Grekov, who had a literary salon where Shostakovich was asked to perform. Shostakovich says Akhmatova did not exhibit any great interest in music at that time. She was beautiful then, very beautiful, and enveloped in an aura of majesty. He said in later years she attended premieres of his works.[82] Akhmatova particularly loved Shostakovich's Seventh Symphony, and alludes to it at the end of the first variant of *Poem Without a Hero*.

> And after me, sparking with a mystery
>> And having named herself the seventh
>>> She rushed to an unprecedented feast . . .
> Pretending to be a musical score,
>> The famous Leningrader
>>> Returned to her native ether.

(II, p. 465)

The honors accorded her were public as well as more private. On May 30, 1964, a special ceremony took place at the Mayakovsky Museum to celebrate the fiftieth anniversary of the first appearance of *Rosary*. Zhirmunsky gave a very moving speech:

> The end of March marked fifty years since *Rosary* appeared, the book that established Akhmatova's fame in Russian poetry. Fifty years is a long time, the same amount of time from when Pushkin died to Russian Modernism. However, as you see, these poems did not grow old. We have gathered here to listen to the poems of a great Russian poet, to poems that are already classical but still contemporary, which have been translated into every language in the world.[83]

Fifty years earlier, Zhirmunsky had reviewed this collection; now he read the poems he had known and loved as a young man.

Lev Kopelev describes the visit of the famous German writer Heinrich Böll when he came to Leningrad in August 1965. He was working on a scenario for a film on Dostoyevsky and Petersburg. Admoni and his wife, Tamara Silman, took Böll to see Akhmatova in Komarovo. He told her he had read her work in English and German, as Kopelev interpreted. Akhmatova gave him useful information about places connected with Dostoyevsky. She discussed the eternal significance of Dostoyevsky's work, his meaning for Russia. The two got along very well. When he finally said goodbye, Böll kissed her hand, which was the first time Kopelev had ever seen him do that. Böll said solemnly, "I am very happy, very proud that I have seen the leader of Russian literature." Akhmatova described him as probably the most wonderful foreigner she had ever met. "They are almost all wild beasts. But he is a wonderfully sweet person."[84]

At the end of 1963, Akhmatova met Amanda Haight, an American who had just completed courses in Russian at the School of Slavonic and Eastern European Studies at the University of London, and was now beginning to do research on her dissertation on Akhmatova. In order to finance her stay in Russia, she was working as a governess for an English family working at the embassy, and had obtained a reader's card to the Lenin Library. She began reading everything available on Akhmatova. Akhmatova saw in Haight someone who could help dispel the distorted image of her and those close to her, such as Gumilyov, which was being projected by Russian émigrés abroad. Haight for her part felt privileged to be able to be useful to others in some way, to help correct the errors and false impressions of Akhmatova's life by writing a biography. It was first published in 1976 and has recently been translated into Russian. Although it contains some factual errors, it is sensitively written and stands as the first real biography of Akhmatova.[85] In his tribute to Haight at the beginning of the Russian version, Nayman relates that when she arrived in Moscow in 1989 for the centennial of Akhmatova's birth, she told him she had only a few months to live. She revealed this calmly and with great courage. They reminisced about the times they had shared with Akhmatova many years before. Even at the end of her life (she died in 1989), Haight showed her generosity and love for Akhmatova by continuing her work of making Akhmatova's life and poetry known at home and abroad.[86]

Akhmatova devoted a great deal of time to trying to restore the reputation of Nikolay Gumilyov. In 1962, she was reading Western memoirs of Petersburg's cultural life in the first post-Revolutionary years and was upset by the portrayal of Gumilyov and his relationship with her. She invited Pavel Luknitsky, who by that time had moved to Moscow, to come see her. At Akhmatova's request, Luknitsky went to the prosecutor Malyarov and acquainted himself with the archives on the Gumilyov case. He subsequently did everything possible to remove the ban against Gumilyov and allow his poetry to be published again. Valentin Golosev, one of the editors of the newspaper *Izvestiya*, gave a lot of support to Akhmatova in this venture as well.

Luknitsky was visiting Akhmatova in Komarovo for a week in January 1962. He wrote her a letter in response to her desire for something in writing from people she knew about their views of *Poem Without a Hero*. In it he first discusses the ostensible difficulty of understanding the poem, which he believes is not true in this case. He suggests one reason others may find it so difficult is that the poem requires the reader's active participation and perception—one must study its allusions carefully. The poem is dressed in a kind of armor, which defends it from any foolish ignorance in approaching it. One must have a heritage of learning and culture, the legacy of many centuries, nations, and peoples. *Rosary,* he says, is two-dimensional. The third dimension, which is present in *Poem Without a Hero,* derives from life experience, an accumulation of the poet's wisdom. The poem's words are actually simple, but they construct for us a world visible only at night, when the fathomless universe opens up, strewn with stars. Luknitsky calls *Rosary* and *White Flock* the "daytime" Akhmatova, although they contain prophetic, nightlike visions of the third dimension. But the "nighttime" Akhmatova transformed all her ravings, all her years of torment into a gigantic, miraculous, transparent prism. Three dimensions—a clear and pure view of the world, seen through a huge, transparent crystal cube. The world viewed through this cube is weightless, purified of any earthly dust, so it is transparent. Gazing through, one can grasp the entire world, the entire twentieth century, with all its spiritual and emotional life. The first level of this universal picture is personal—the love of the author for her city—Petersburg, Petrograd, Leningrad—uttered by the wind of the fifty-year-old Akhmatova's lyrical breath, in which black nights alternate with white ones.

Luknitsky says he was delighted to have spent a week with Akhmatova after such a long time. He had gotten out of the habit of immersing himself in the world of poetry of the beginning of the century and the 1920s. He had been preoccupied, and thought she would never understand the new world of which he had become part, that she would never overcome the pain and abuse she had suffered because of this new world. But this was not the case. Indeed, her strength was truly amazing.

You found in yourself the will, and most important—in a form at times wild and terrible—a life-giving spirit capable of magnificent flights. It took enormous nobility, a deed of selflessness for you to do this, and the even greater deed, after having understood what was so important, of passing into another epoch greeting you like a hurricane, an opposing wind—to pass over without losing yourself, without betraying either yourself or a single principle of Humanity or your native Russia, a land which at all times and epochs of past, present and future is indivisible in the greatness of its people. Not with a penitent look . . . but with head proudly raised (because there is nothing for you to repent—one must repent *before you*), daring and self-confident—like an Islamic righteous person walking along the hair of the prophet over the pit to heaven . . . you walked into the new epoch.

Even the Sphinx of our times, immersing his claws in the sand of lifeless deserts singed by his steady and enigmatic gaze—even this Sphinx, mysterious and cruel, but imprinted by history for thousands of years— you were able to regard without preconception, were able calmly to look straight in the eye, with unwavering pride. And the Sphinx lowered his eyes. This is easy for many to do now, when his stony eyes are covered forever, and everyone knows that his lids will never be raised. I think it was then that you were able to perceive everything with understanding— both the terrible and the magnificent. It is from the impartial, proud, wise penetration into the essence of the horrible and magnificent, characterizing our striking epoch, promising so much, that *Poem Without a Hero* was born, and you assuredly know very well that there is a hero in this poem nevertheless, and this hero is—Russia. Blok would have been happy about your poem. It would have been close to his spirit. And in another way, his own special way, that conjuror of words, Osip Mandelstam, would have been happy. The transparent violet cube through which you viewed the twentieth century of your homeland suits your poem, with its endless unassailable crystal purity. It is also a witness of our age, just as a trilobite or fossil was the witness of geological epochs when man was not yet on our planet. It is amazingly simple and clear. I repeat, there are in it complex and difficult ideas, but their verbal expression is distinguished by extreme clarity. That is why the *poema* is comprehensible and in the future will be accessible . . . close to everyone, just as in their time the works of Pushkin were accessible and close to everyone.[87]

Foreign honors for Akhmatova also poured in. In 1964, she received an Italian literary prize from the Communita Europea degli Scrittori (European Community of Writers). Jean-Paul Sartre and Simone de Beauvoir congratulated her by telegram. In a letter to Juan Carlo Vigorelli, Akhmatova wrote:

Your letter informing me that I am to receive the Taormina Prize has brought me great joy. I do not wish to shine with wit on this occasion, to hide behind false modesty, but this news, coming to me from a country which I have loved tenderly all my life, has shed a ray of sunshine on my work. I beg of you, dear Juan Carlo, to convey my thanks to the friends who have chosen me.[88]

Nayman says that her trips at the end of her life were the opposite of the travels of her youth. When Akhmatova was young, she went where she pleased; now she was taken. At that time she gazed at the world; now it gaped at her. One trip was to Italy, to receive the Taormina Poetry Prize. It took several months for her documents to be processed, and her train ticket was issued on the day she was to leave. "What do they think—that I won't come back?" she asked. "That I stayed here when everyone was leaving, that I've lived my whole life in this country—and what a life!—in order to change everything now!" She growled, "Before, you'd only have to call the house supervisor, give him a few rubles, and he'd bring a foreign-travel passport from the police station at the end of the day."[89]

Akhmatova was supposed to be accompanied by Nina Olshevskaya, but Nina had a sudden stroke in Minsk, where she was performing, so Irina Punina went instead. They traveled first to Rome and then to Sicily, where they stayed in Taormina in a hotel that was a converted monastery, San Dominico; Akhmatova was awarded the prize in the castle of Urbino in Catania. From Rome she sent a postcard of the Piazza di Spagna to Nayman, dated December 7, 1964, describing a dazzling pink and scarlet autumn. Another card followed, two days later, of the Trevi Fountain, saying, "Today was a very special day—we drove down the via Appia—the Romans' most ancient cemetery. A hot rusty summer and graves and more graves all around us." They also visited Raphael's tomb in the Pantheon. In Taormina, when they arrived, everything was "flowering, shining, and smelling sweet." She wrote Nayman that she would read the Prologue from the *Novyi mir* text. She had just been to see the ancient Graeco-Roman theater at the top of the hill.[90]

Nayman points out that Vigorelli's association was pro-Soviet, and Surkov, as head of the Union of Soviet Writers, was trying to establish friendly relations with the West. Akhmatova was the perfect person to receive the award—she had written *Requiem,* had been persecuted, and yet wrote patriotic poems. "Her prestige, authority, and reputation suited everyone."[91] Zoya Tomashevskaya says that her brother, an eminent translator of Italian literature into Russian, was the one who suggested to Vigorelli that the prize be awarded to Akhmatova as the greatest living Russian poet.[92] One might also add that Surkov supported the award not only for the cynical reasons Nayman suggests, but because he genuinely admired Akhmatova, had helped her print the poems to Stalin that she hoped would get Lev released, and after many years had published the first collection of her poems to appear since the 1946 Resolution. He and a delegation of other representatives of the Soviet Union were also present at the awarding of the prize. Arseny Tarkovsky, the poet and critic, whose first poetry collection was printed in 1962, was there, as was Alexander Tvardovsky, the editor of *Novyi mir*. The delegation arrived before Akhmatova did, and the Italian director Paolo Pasolini invited them to see his new film, *The Gospel of St. Matthew.*

Irina Punina describes the wild ride they had when she and Akhmatova were driven on December 12 from Taormina to Catania, where the award ceremony was to take place. It was a winding road along the Ionian Sea and the driver wanted to show them the Cyclops formation. He would point to the cliffs with one hand and to his forehead with the other (illustrating the one-eyed Cyclops from Greek mythology), with both hands off the steering wheel, at a speed of 100 kilometers an hour, on a road with hairpin turns and a steep drop to the sea. Akhmatova was frightened out of her mind and upset by this mad Sicilian who would not listen to their pleas and warnings. She tried speaking in French, but he kept talking loudly in his own dialect. Irina informed him that they understood very well what "Cyclops" meant and knew what he was trying to say, which made him very happy, but he still refused to keep his hands on the wheel. Later Akhmatova created a whole scenario about how Vigorelli had abandoned them, how the chauffeur had driven them over a precipice while talking with his hands and forgetting to steer the car. It would become one of Akhmatova's favorite stories to tell visitors when they asked about the trip.

They finally reached the Hotel Exselsior, a skyscraper, very different from the Dominican monastery in Taormina. It was packed with reporters, photographers, American sailors, and curious onlookers. Akhmatova walked in, leaning on Irina's arm. They had been assigned a small room with one bed in the middle. Irina told the manager this was impossible and they soon got a different room with two beds and a telephone.

Surkov was with Georgy Breitburd, the secretary of the Soviet section of the European Community of Writers. The two of them had promised to come by at 4:00 P.M. However, by five o'clock no one had arrived. Irina called Surkov, but no one answered. Akhmatova was afraid to stay alone and would not let Irina go downstairs to find out what was wrong. Finally Irina went out onto the balcony. Opposite was a huge administrative building. When she looked down, she saw Konstantin Simonov and some other people that she knew, and attempted to call them, waving her arms, but no one heard her from the eighth floor; the square was full of buses and people, and it was too noisy. Irina then went out into the hall, and there were Breitburd and Simonov knocking madly on the door of the first room they had been assigned. Surkov was absolutely terrified—they had been knocking for half an hour on the wrong door. Akhmatova created a whole other scenario from this, saying everyone thought she and Irina had run off somewhere.

They all went downstairs into waiting cars to go to the Palazzo Urbino, a medieval castle, the seat of the first parliament in Sicily, which began in 1402. However, to reach it one had to climb an enormous stone staircase. In her narration of the trip, Irina said when she found out there was no other entrance, she nearly died. She knew how difficult it was going to be for Akhmatova. But Akhmatova leaned on Irina's arm and began to climb. Later the poet confessed to Yeventov that "the solemnity and grandeur of the occasion demanded that even if I hesitated for a moment, they would have quickly put me in a chair and carried me up. I would not allow such a disgrace. I bravely forged ahead. And so I climbed to the peak of fame—choking and groaning."[93]

An important leftist German author and journalist, Hans Werner Richter, wrote a description of the event. He first saw Akhmatova in the garden of the Dominican cloister in Catania, now a hotel. She was sitting on a white-lacquered garden chair, accompanied by her "lady-in-waiting," Irina, in the distance. Here at last was the grand duchess of poetry holding court.

And before her stood poets from all countries of Europe . . . young and old, conservatives and liberals, communists and socialists, standing in line to kiss the hand of Anna Akhmatova, and I, too, joined them. She held out her hand as each one walked in front of her, bowed, and received a kind nod . . . each performed this ceremony in the manner of his country: the Italian with charm, the Spaniard with grandness, the Bulgarian with devotion, the English with restraint. Only the Russians knew the style Akhmatova expected. They stood before their tsarina, knelt down, and kissed the ground. No, they did not do this, but it seemed as if they did. It was as if when they were kissing Akhmatova's hand, they were actually kissing the Russian soil, the tradition of its poetry and the magnificence of its literature.[94]

Richter describes the poetry recital she gave, at which two hundred guests gathered in formal attire in one of the cloister halls. Akhmatova wore a long gown of brown silk and recited in Russian in a voice that recalled a distant tempest. Each of the other poets in turn read poems to Akhmatova:

It was like the New Year's reception at the court of an empress. The tsarina of poetry accepted the homage of the diplomatic corps of world literature. . . . Finally she grew weary and walked out, a grand woman, above all the poets, a statuesque figure, and as I watched her leave, I suddenly understood why Russia could be ruled by a female tsarina. I saw her once more . . . when she received the Taormina Prize. She thanked the Minister of Culture with a few words, and in this speech there was not a single superfluous word or phrase. It was the thanks of a tsarina to her subject.[95]

Mikola Bazhan, a Ukrainian member of the Soviet delegation, described the award ceremony: "Daughter of the Ukraine, in her features she retained the pensive beauty of the black-haired southern women. In addition, having lived almost all her life in the north, in the severe magnificent Leningrad, she seemed to carry in her figure the imprint of this severity and grandness."[96]

In his remarks, Tvardovsky said that Akhmatova's "so-called 'chamber poetry' responded to the great and tragic moments in the life of the country." He read some of her poems, and Akhmatova, touched, rose from her chair and embraced him. Pasolini read a poem devoted to the famous guest. Other writers and poets came up and paid their respects. Finally, Akhmatova herself rose and began her speech, pronouncing each word slowly and clearly. Although she spoke in Russian, she cited Dante and Leopardi in Italian. She read her poem "Dream" and her verses about Dante. She alluded to the book of Leopardi translations that she was working on with Nayman, and her love of Italian culture.

After the ceremony, the poet invited the members of the Soviet delegation back to her room at the hotel. As they left, it was already dark, and preparations were being made for Christmas. In store windows and on balconies were nativity scenes, all tastefully lit with little candles. That Saturday the city was particularly lovely. The ringing bells reminded Akhmatova of her childhood, when the evening service ended. She felt as if Catania was greeting Akhmatova with bells. Many people came to congratulate her that evening. From her trunk Akhmatova solemnly drew out jars of caviar, jam, all kinds of sweets. "On the table," she said, "there will only be ours [our kind of food]. I brought everything, even black bread, and even this"—and she solemnly held up a bottle of Stolichnaya vodka. The celebration lasted late into the night. At one point Akhmatova turned to Mikola Bazhan and said, "You know, I have Ukrainian blood. My father was of Cossack origin. I was born in Odessa and finished school in Kiev." She then said that was where she learned Ukrainian, though not well enough to translate by herself, and that she needed help when she was working on *Fading Leaves,* Ivan Franko's beautiful cycle of poetry.[97]

Akhmatova was struck by the difference in the meaning poetry had for Western Europe and her own country, which she described to Kopelev upon her return. She used to condemn Yevtushenko and Voznesensky for "playing to the crowds," calling them "variety show types." However, she now felt this was not so bad. After all, having thousands of admirers come and listen to poetry was quite wonderful. In Italy, she said, poets were isolated, sitting alone in different cities with no audience to read them or listen to them, nor did they read to each other.

Kopelev calls the event a triumph. Dozens of poets from different countries gathered to pay her tribute, confirming her international renown. Akhmatova, characteristically wry, showed Kopelev a photograph of an ancient bust. "I think this is Marcus Aurelius . . . See how mean he looks. He's probably saying, 'Who's this? A poetess? I know Sappho—but Akhmatova—it's the first time I've ever heard of her.' " Akhmatova also told him that some Italian journalist had come to see her who wrote absolute nonsense. "She hoped I would stay, that I would choose the free world. And did she lie! And the whole time it was, 'Akh, Pasternak! Akh, Mandelstam!' . . . I've lived through everything."[98]

The following year, 1965, Akhmatova went to Oxford to receive an honorary doctorate. Once again she was required to climb a high staircase when they awarded her the degree. But the English broke a long-standing tradition, and it was not Akhmatova who ascended the staircase, but the rector of the university who descended to her.[99] This time she was accompanied by Anna Kaminskaya, Punin's granddaughter, and Amanda Haight.

Elaine Bickert, who attended the ceremony, wrote: "In silence, a heavy woman dressed in black beneath the traditional crimson robes, advanced slowly on the arm of a young companion. Thick gray hair crowned the face of an Oriental empress."[100] Later Bickert was introduced to her by the Russian émigré artist Yury Annenkov in a small hotel room. Annenkov had come from Paris for the occasion. They spoke about Sudeikina, on whom Bickert was writing a dissertation. Bickert saw Akhmatova again in Paris shortly thereafter, and the poet appeared to be more relaxed, full of humor and wit. Four years after Akhmatova's death, Bickert visited Leningrad and wrote that just as Akhmatova had predicted in *Poem Without a Hero,* she was indeed present in "every stone, every reflection on the Neva, every leaf of a willow."[101]

In Oxford, Akhmatova again met the "Guest from the Future," Sir Isaiah Berlin. He wrote that she told him of her life during the many years since they had last seen each other. She told him with pride of the numerous gifted young poets Russia now had; "the best among them was Joseph Brodsky, whom she had, she said, brought up by hand—a noble poet in deep disfavor, with all that this implied." Berlin says she mentioned others, marvelously gifted, whose verses could not be published, "and whose very existence was testimony to the unexhausted life of the imagination in Russia." Akhmatova said,

They will eclipse us all, believe me, Pasternak and I and Mandelstam and Tsvetaeva, all of us are at the end of a long period of elaboration which began in the nineteenth century. My friends and I thought we spoke with the voice of the twentieth century. But these new poets constitute a new beginning—behind bars now, but they will escape and astonish the world.[102]

Akhmatova also went to Stratford to visit Shakespeare's birthplace. Vladimir Retsepter, an actor and poet, recalls Akhmatova's theories about the authorship of plays allegedly written by Shakespeare. "Do you really think the actor Shakespeare wrote all those plays?" She claimed all the signatures on the manuscripts were different. She was sure the author of the thirty-seven plays was well educated, had knowledge of many areas, while facts revealed about the actor Shakespeare showed him to be a barely literate, commercially oriented drinker who had not left a single book. According to Akhmatova, the author of the plays was a real aristocrat, someone close to the court who had to conceal his true identity and used the actor Shakespeare as a mask. She thought *Macbeth* was really about Mary Stuart and suspected that the author hiding behind Shakespeare had a right himself to the throne. Akhmatova also thought that different plays ascribed to Shakespeare were by different authors. Retsepter said that in 1957 she had outlined a book on various aspects of Shakespeare's work, which she never completed.

Akhmatova received her honorary degree on June 4. Afterward she spent two days in Stratford. She visited the house where Shakespeare was born. They went to Trinity Church, where there is a gravestone and a famous bust of Shakespeare. Akhmatova did not think the face looked like someone with the great spirit of the person who wrote the plays.[103]

During her trip to Europe, Akhmatova renewed her acquaintance with many old friends. She saw Salomea Andronikova Halpern, who had been one of the beauties of Petersburg circles in the Silver Age. Georgy Adamovich, living in Paris, recalled how one night he received a call from London. There were some words in English, and then he heard, "Akhmatova speaking. I will be in Paris tomorrow. We will see each other, yes?" He was overjoyed. But when he looked at the clock, he thought, "Mother Russia has remained as she always was. A telephone call at 2:00 A.M.? In the West we had gotten unused to that." The next day he came to see her at the Hôtel Napoléon. Adamovich describes the initial shock many friends had on first seeing Akhmatova after so many years. She was no longer the slender, fashionable young Petersburg lady they had remembered, but a dignified, older, portly woman. But he soon realized that her brilliance and refined nature had not changed.

Tolstoy once said that the first moment you see someone after a long separation you notice all the changes. However, a moment later the changes become less clear, and it seems as if the person had always been the same. That's what happened with me. In the armchair sat a portly old woman, beautiful and grand, smiling pleasantly, but it was only by this smile that I was able to recognize Akhmatova. Yet it was exactly as Tolstoy had said, in a moment or two before me was Akhmatova, only more talkative, more sure of herself. . . . What did we talk about? Mainly about poetry. We strolled around Paris, and she recalled Modigliani.[104]

Yury Annenkov had made two portraits of Akhmatova in 1921, one in pen and ink, the other a colored portrait in gouache. He had gone to Oxford to witness the ceremony and soon afterward received a call from Akhmatova asking him to come see her. He returned to Paris, and on June 17 she arrived for a few days. The Hôtel Napoléon was managed by Ivan Makovsky, the son of Sergey Makovsky, editor of the journal *Apollon,* where she had published her early verses. He invited her to come to lunch with her companions. On the walls of his study and library were portraits of famous Russians—Pilnyak, Babel, Eisenstein, Pudovkin, Malevich—and the gouache portrait of Akhmatova. "I think I have returned to my youth," Akhmatova said. Annenkov replied, "I have, too, because you are here."[105]

Adamovich took her around Paris on one of those early, fresh, clear summer days when the city is at its best. They went to the rue Bonaparte where she had once stayed. Then to the Bois de Boulogne, where they sat on the terrace of a café, and to Montparnasse, where they ate at a restaurant where bohemians, poets, and writers had met every night before the war.

Akhmatova had very much wanted to see Boris Anrep while she was in England, but he was apprehensive about such a meeting. In his letter to Gleb Struve describing the ring Akhmatova had given him, and their friendship, Anrep says that after he left Russia in 1917, he sent Akhmatova two packages of food and received a brief note with a ring, in reply: "Dear Boris, thank you for feeding me. Anna Akhmatova." He wanted to write but was afraid that might get her into trouble.

Anrep wore the ring on a chain, but once when he was undressing, the chain broke, so he put it in a box where he kept other objects of sentimental value. The years passed, but he never forgot the ring. At the beginning of World War II when the Nazis invaded Paris, he was about to leave for London. But before he could leave, his studio was bombed, and when he came by the next morning, the box with the ring was gone. He met Gleb Struve in London during the war, and Struve gave him many of Akhmatova's works that had been published in Russia and abroad. Anrep was moved by her poems and felt even guiltier. When he heard Akhmatova was coming to Oxford, he did not want to stand in line with her admirers. He asked Struve, who had come for the ceremony, to relay his greetings.[106] Anna Kaminskaya said that Akhmatova desperately wanted to see him, and when he did not appear, it hurt her very deeply.[107]

Anrep left for Paris, where he was working on a commission for a mosaic. He wanted to preserve the memory of the beautiful, fresh, young girl he had left in 1917. But the phone rang and it was Akhmatova. She invited him to come see her the next evening. He was a nervous wreck the entire day, wondering what to do if she asked about the ring. When he came in, he kissed her hand, and they both assumed stern expressions. They talked about Nedobrovo, and then she asked if he had read *Requiem*. "Yes," he replied. "It is a great tragic work, written in your blood. It is painful to read." Akhmatova then opened a small notebook and began reading. He realized he had not heard anything like this for so long. Later, he kissed her hand and said goodbye, then rushed out of the hotel room in a trance, wandered along the Champs-Elysées, and sat in a café until midnight.

Nikita Struve, nephew of Gleb Struve and publisher of the YMCA Press in Paris, also met Akhmatova in Paris. Like many others, he was struck by the strange, haunting quality of her presence, especially when she read her poems aloud. "She recited for me. To describe in words the magic of her recitation is impossible. The kind, mocking smile, which never abandoned her during conversation, disappeared. Her face became more concentrated, more serious. The poems seemed to come from within."[108]

Adamovich describes her last moments before she left Paris forever.

At our last meeting she finally spoke about herself. "Fate did not leave anything out for me. Everything anyone could possibly experience fell to my lot." People came with flowers, candy. It was time to get ready. There was less than an hour before the train left. She stood helpless in the middle of the room, trying to smile. "Well, goodbye, don't forget me. Not farewell, but 'see you again'! God willing, I'll come to Paris again next year. If God wills it, I will come again to Paris. Thank you." We shook hands and I asked her why she had thanked me. "Well, for everything. Not for the past, but for the future. We all owe something to each other. Especially now." As I was leaving, I turned around at the door. Akhmatova made the sign of the cross and said, "Christ be with you, *au revoir*." But there was no more meeting again—and would never be.[109]

Annenkov went to the station to see her off. She left from the Gare du Nord on June 21. As the train began to move, Akhmatova and Kaminskaya stood at the open window and waved a tender goodbye until they disappeared from his view.[110]

After her trip to Europe, Akhmatova continued to write sketches for her autobiography. In 1957, she had called the autobiography "A book which I will never write, but which nevertheless exists."

In the beginning I wanted to write all of it, but now I've decided to insert several segments from it into the narrative of my life and the fate of my generation. . . . I started to write my autobiography several times, but, as they say, with mixed results. I was eleven years old the first time I set out to write my autobiography in my mother's red, ruled notebook, which had been used to record the household expenses (for the year 1900).[111]

Her sharp memory went back to when she was two years old. She wrote the sketch "Sukhardina's House" (where she grew up in Tsarskoye Selo) in a delirium, while she was sick with typhus in Tashkent. She also wrote a sketch about Leningrad after the blockade, about a poetry reading at the front in Terioki, and another, "Three Lilacs," again about Tsarskoye. She was unsure of these attempts at prose, noting:

> Prose always seemed to be both a secret and a temptation. From the very beginning I knew everything about poetry—I never knew anything about prose. Everybody praised my first attempt very highly, but, of course, I did not believe them. I invited Zoshchenko over. He suggested that some things should be cut and said that he agreed with the rest. I was happy.[112]

Akhmatova felt that she ought to write about her life, a "cousin" to *Safe Conduct* (Pasternak's autobiography) and *The Noise of Time* (Mandelstam's). But she feared that in comparison to its elegant cousins, her book would seem like a simpleton, a Cinderella. She pointed out that both Pasternak and Mandelstam wrote their memoirs when they were still fairly young, when everything they were recalling was not a fairy tale away. "But to see the 1890s from the altitude of the middle of the twentieth century without becoming dizzy is almost impossible."[113]

She characterizes the process of memory the way one would characterize her own poems—a stream of consciousness in which one image evokes another through personal associations rather than a linear succession of events in chronological order. "Every attempt at a continuous narration in memoirs is a falsification. Not a single human memory is so constructed that it remembers everything in order. Letters and diaries often turn out to be poor aids." She warns the reader that at least 20 percent of anyone's memoirs are counterfeit in one way or another. Either an event or a person is remembered dimly, or wrongly, or completely forgotten: "The human memory is constructed so that it works like a projector that throws light on individual moments, while leaving the rest in impenetrable darkness. One can and should forget something, even with a splendid memory."[114]

What she has left us—fragments and autobiographical sketches—is very beautiful and revealing. The material has been put into more or less chronological order and published in Russian and in English. Although this is the best that could be done by editors under the circumstances, the reader should be aware that it is not what the final form of the work would be like. Sergey Eisenstein's *Que Viva Mexico,* which he never edited in his lifetime, has appeared in several versions ordered in a simple way—totally untypical of the genius of Eisenstein, his gift for montage, for ordering images by association and not simple logic. Given Akhmatova's propensity for "thinking in images" and stream of consciousness, one must assume that the work would probably have been as experimental as *Poem Without a Hero* or Alain Robbe-Grillet's *Last Year at Marienbad*, which she was reading before she died.

In the last years of her life, Akhmatova was very conscious of her own impending death. Nayman says she would initiate conversations with him about this, which upset him. She wrote a quatrain at this time:

It's dawn—this is the Judgment Day,
And meeting is more pain than parting.
And deathly fame will come to take
Me—from your hands and from the living.[115]

Instead of answering him directly when he protested her allusions to death, she handed him a letter dated March 31, 1964, in which she said, "I am now finally convinced that all conversations on this subject are destructive and I promise never to begin one again. We shall simply live like Lear and Cordelia in a cage, translate Leopardi and Tagore, and trust each other. Anna."[116]

In November 1965, Akhmatova was in Moscow when she suffered another heart attack and was taken to the Botkin Hospital. She remained there until February 1966, when she moved to the Ardovs'. Excerpts from her diary in February show how much she hated being in the hospital. By February 10 she had been there for three months: "Today makes three months that I've been in the hospital. Now I can definitely write down the following: There exists a law whereby after a lengthy stay every hospital slowly turns into a prison, and after six days they declare a quarantine to make the picture complete: 'parcels' are delivered in pillow cases, the entrance is locked (like in a madhouse), the doctors, nurses, and orderlies wear masks, and there is unrelenting boredom."[117] In her last diary entries, she mentions music several times, especially Prokofiev:

Last evening I listened to Prokofiev's "Possession." Richter performed.
It was marvelous, I still haven't come to my senses. No words (of any
kind) can even remotely convey what it was like. It is almost impossible
that such a thing occurred. A gigantic symphony orchestra, directed by
an otherworldly force (moreover, with Satan himself as the first violinist),
enveloped the entire space as it streamed towards the blue, frosty
window.[118]

Margarita Aliger says that Akhmatova's friends set up a strict schedule for visitors, and anyone wishing to see her had to make an appointment in advance. This was to prevent her from getting overtired by the constant stream of guests. However, it also affected her son Lev. After the long separation from her, he came to Moscow to see his mother, but when he arrived at the hospital, he was not allowed to see her, only to send her a note. The woman with whom Akhmatova shared a room said how upset Akhmatova was by the note and what had occurred. "How come my friends don't understand that this is my only son, the person closest to me, my only heir?"[119]

Aliger saw her when Akhmatova finally moved to the Ardovs'. On February 18, she left the hospital. Aliger says she was calm, felt all right, was getting ready to go to a sanatorium, and was making plans for the future. It was the last time Aliger would ever see Akhmatova.

At the beginning of March, Akhmatova went with Nina Olshevskaya to the sanatorium in Domodedovo, near Moscow. Although at first she described it as "a big, empty house," on March 4 she wrote in her diary, "It is simply so nice and so enchantingly quiet here." She was excited by the discovery of the Dead Sea Scrolls at Qumran and the information they contained. The next day, March 5, 1966, she died peacefully.

That evening on the radio they announced the death of Anna Akhmatova. Strange coincidences were occurring even after her death. Once again she was under the roof of the Sheremetevs, for her body was brought to the morgue of the Skilfosovsky Institute in Moscow, formerly the Sheremetev Almshouse, with the same coat of arms that adorned the gates of the Sheremetev Palace in Leningrad, where she had lived for so long. Natalya Ilyina only heard the news the morning of March 6, and on March 8 she received a telegram: "Farewell on the 9th from ten to eleven A.M. in the Skilfosovsky morgue. Funeral Leningrad the 10th."[120] On March 7, the pianist Maria Yudina arranged a memorial ceremony in a church in Moscow. Forty people gathered to honor Akhmatova's memory. In the evening there was a funeral meal for her friends, and they listened to a tape of her reciting her poetry.

Lev Kopelev and Raisa Orlova have provided the best description of what it was like on the days immediately following Akhmatova's death.[121] From March 6 to March 8, Kopelev received phone calls continuously. The Union of Writers asked Tarkovsky, Ozerov, and Viktor Ardov to accompany the coffin to Leningrad. And what about the Moscow Union of Writers? According to Kopelev, they were afraid of a demonstration. The Moscow Union of Writers wanted everything to take place as quickly as possible.

Akhmatova's friends in Moscow wanted to pay homage to her, but there was little time left. March 8 was Women's Day in the Soviet Union, a day set aside to honor women, when they do not have to work. This further complicated matters, since the workers in the baggage section of the airport that would be dispatching the coffin to Leningrad were women. Anna Kaminskaya called and said the coffin was to fly on March 9 at 3:15 P.M. and had to be at the airport by midday. This would make it difficult for Akhmatova's friends in Moscow to have the memorial gathering. Tarkovsky's voice was shaky. "I don't know what to do. Everyone says it's too late. Tomorrow is the eighth. There is no one to ask. At the airport all the workers in the baggage section are women, and they have a holiday!" Ardov also gave up.

Kopelev decided to act in the name of the "Commission of the Union of Writers for Akhmatova's Funeral." He knew there was one hope—instead of appealing to the big bosses, he would talk to the workers themselves. He called the freight section of the airport, and in a velvet voice congratulated the women on the approaching holiday, explaining that Anna Akhmatova was a great woman, and it was very sad that she had died on the eve of Women's Day. He finally persuaded them and received permission to bring the coffin three hours later than planned. That allowed time for a memorial service at the morgue before the coffin was removed.

On March 8 Efim Etkind and Mikhail Dudin, poet and secretary of the Leningrad branch of the Union of Soviet Writers, arrived at dawn. Kopelev called the airport to confirm the plans. By ten o'clock he was at the morgue. There was a cool rain. In a small gray room on a pedestal stood the coffin, and beside it were Nina Olshevskaya, Anna Kaminskaya, Nadezhda Mandelstam, Nika Glen, and Yulya Zhukova, all standing silently. Ilyina met Semyon Lipkin on the way and found many familiar faces among those gathered. It was warm, and there was a strong fragrance from the flowers covering the coffin. Everyone who entered came up, kissed Akhmatova's hand and forehead, and then gave way to the next person. Ilyina recalled Akhmatova's "Seaside Sonnet" (June 1958):

And the voice of eternity beckons
With unearthly irresistibility,
And over the blossoming cherry trees
The crescent moon pours radiance.

(II. p. 279)

Lev Ozerov spoke: "Akhmatova! The name conjures up an entire epoch. These words burst from the lips of Marina Tsvetayeva fifty years ago. And we repeat them today. And we will repeat them forever, because for a great artist there is no death, only the day of birth. . . . The great life of Anna Akhmatova has ended. And now immortality begins, has already begun."

Efim Etkind followed: "In an article on Pushkin, Akhmatova wrote that Nicholas I and Benkendorf [head of the secret police] are now known only as the persecutors of Pushkin, as his insignificant contemporaries. . . . We live in the epoch of Akhmatova. And our descendants will refer to the persecutors of Akhmatova as we today refer to the persecutors of Pushkin."[122]

That evening there was a meeting in the Moscow Union of Writers. Someone from the Presidium declared: "Anna Akhmatova has died. Let us honor her memory by standing." Tamara Ivanova (Vyacheslav Ivanov's mother, wife of the Soviet writer Vsevolod Ivanov) said angrily, "I was terribly ashamed today for our organization when I was in the courtyard of the morgue. There was enough time. There could have been a gathering." Mikhalkov said he wanted to make a correction. People were asking why the Moscow writers had not paid a formal farewell to Akhmatova. He said she died in a sanatorium, and it was correct for her then to be sent to the morgue. It was the eve of Women's Day, and it was impossible to do anything. At the request of relatives, there had been a requiem according to the Russian Orthodox ritual, and there would be a funeral in Leningrad.

At midnight, March 9, Kopelev left for Leningrad with Ivan Rozansky and Vyacheslav Ivanov. There was a crowd at the station. Mikhail Ardov and his friends arrived with Akhmatova's trunk containing her manuscripts and notebooks, from which she was never parted, even when she traveled.

The next morning the funeral took place at St. Nicholas Cathedral, a beautiful Baroque church, blue with white trim, built by the Russian architect S. I. Chevakinsky in the mid-eighteenth century with five gilded domes. Akhmatova lay in an open coffin, in the black brocade dress she loved to wear, her head covered by black lace that had been given to her by Salomea Halpern when Akhmatova met her at Oxford. The church was dark. At each side of the coffin stood a small church candelabrum.

The mass began in the middle of the nave. The coffin stood in the middle of the church opposite the altar, surrounded by wreaths. Lev Gumilyov and Anna Kaminskaya were on the right. By noon the church was filled, and it was impossible to move. Students formed a human chain around the coffin, trying to keep a narrow passageway free. The Requiem began. The bright chandeliers were lit. There were photographers and film cameras everywhere. Lev shouted at them to show some respect, that they were in a cathedral. A small choir sang, five in all. The service ended, and then the Orthodox ritual of saying farewell began, which lasted two hours.

Kopelev says that Joseph Brodsky stood, pale and disheveled, next to Anatoly Nayman. One after another people walked past the coffin—old ladies from Petersburg with little caps, well-dressed young women, young men, the intelligentsia, workers. They kissed her forehead; some cried quietly, others lamented loudly. Akhmatova's face was calm and noble as it had been in life. Kopelev was one of those who helped carry the coffin to the hearse. On the church porch he could hear beggars chatting loudly: "She was pious, serious. . . . She always gave us something, and a whole ruble when it was a holiday. She was a good woman, may the kingdom of heaven be hers. . . ."[123]

There was a crowd at the House of Writers and a line for several blocks. On the second floor, a civil funeral for Akhmatova took place; only members of the Writers' Union who had tickets could attend. In the middle of the room was a pedestal, and along the walls were wreaths from scholarly institutions like Pushkinsky Dom, from composers and writers. Shostakovich had sent a wreath of white hyacinths. The coffin was brought in, and Boris Tichenko played the music he had composed for Akhmatova's *Requiem* on the piano. There was also a trio from the Conservatory. First Mikhail Dudin spoke, then Olga Berggolts. Mikhail Alekseyev said, "A famous poet has departed, a poet of unprecedented strength, who glorified Russian verse far beyond the borders not only of her native city but of her entire land, because sunny Sicily and misty Oxford were also able to value the strength of this poetic voice."[124]

Then a procession left for Komarovo in buses and cars. They were welcomed by a crowd waiting at the cemetery. First Mikhalkov read, then Tarkovsky, who held back his tears with difficulty, and the last to speak was Makogonenko. It was already getting dark. After the last kiss, the priests scattered some earth over the body and the coffin was closed. Lev and her closest friends went back to the cabin, where there was one last service.

"Akhmatova's orphans"—Brodsky, Nayman, Rein, and Bobyshev—had by this time parted, but Akhmatova's death brought them together again for one last time. Bobyshev wrote a poem for the occasion, "All Four," one of his "Mourning Octaves":

Having closed my eyes, I first drained
The poison to the bottom.
And, nailed to the cemetery cross
My soul regained its sight: in the line of the bereaved
Come Osya, Tolya, Zhenya, Dima
Akhmatova's orphans all in a row.
Only looking straight ahead not at each other
The four poetmakers—sworn brothers.
Their friendship, as life, is irretrievable.[125]

Kopelev gave a speech at the first evening in memory of Akhmatova, which was arranged by students of the mathematics faculty of Moscow University on March 31.

The poetry of Akhmatova, her fate, her image is beautiful and magnificent—it embodies Russia in its most difficult tragic years of its one-thousand-year history. . . . "Anna of all Rus"—this is what Marina Tsvetayeva called her. Anna of all Rus! This is pride, unbending both in humiliation and in mortal anxiety. This is humility—humility not meekness—and mocking sobriety even in moments of greatest triumph. . . . The powerful elegant thought of the scholar, the clairvoyance of the stern prophetess in genuine naive amazement when faced with beauty, with the mysteries of life, that wise self-control when a sorceress is herself bewitched by love, by the breathing of the earth, by the magical harmonies of the magic word. . . . Anna of all Rus double-crowned—the crown of thorns and the starry crown of poetry. . . . She is as immortal as the Russian word.

Others close to Akhmatova also participated—Tarkovsky, Aliger, Lipkin, Ozerov, and Vyacheslav Ivanov. Then they listened to Akhmatova's voice, followed by a moment of silence. Kopelev said her inimitable voice rang out that evening in a totally different way than he had always heard it—a new way that was at once sad and solemn.[126]

And everyone followed after me, my readers,
I took you with me on that unrepeatable road.
    —AKHMATOVA, 1958[1]

Akhmatova died as she had lived, with calm dignity. Sometimes her outward
serenity masked an inner turmoil which she revealed only to those close to her;
however, most of the time she maintained a quiet inner peace in the face of the
great trials she suffered along with her country. Her friend Nadezhda Chulkova
says:

> I saw Akhmatova in the bloom of fame and in the misfortune that befell
> her. She lived through everything with dignity and bore courageously
> the burden and bitterness of life's adversities. . . . Several times in her
> life she shared her thoughts with a person she loved, but this bond, which
> sometimes lasted a long time, would be torn—and again there was lone-
> liness and again poems full of bitterness and courage. I asked her, "Are
> you all right?" She answered, "I'm like Eugene in Pushkin, remember?
> He was deafened by the noise of inner anxiety." . . . I saw her in thin,
> old shoes and threadbare dresses and in luxurious clothes, with a precious
> shawl on her shoulders; but no matter what she wore, no matter what
> grief was tearing her apart, she always walked with a calm step and refused
> to give in to the attempts to humiliate her.[2]

Akhmatova remained firm in her conviction to the very end that she had
made the right choice by not leaving her homeland. As late as 1961 she wrote
the memorable lines that were finally set as the beginning of the cycle *Requiem:*

No, not under the vault of alien skies,
And not under the shelter of alien wings—

I was with my people then,
There, where my people, unfortunately, were.
                    (II, p. 95)

Had Akhmatova made the choice to follow her friends in emigration, she might have faced the same indifference to her work as many other contemporaries found when they went abroad. The lack of knowledge of Russian would have been a barrier to understanding her work; but perhaps even more important is the frequent lack of awareness in the West of the culture from which Akhmatova derived her inspiration and many of her themes. And as Akhmatova herself found out when she went abroad at the end of her life, the Russian passion for poetry is unique to her people. David Bethea cites the fate of a fellow poet who did choose to leave, Vladislav Khodasevich:

One reason we can speak of Khodasevich's fate as tragic even against the background of Mandelstam in a Stalinist camp or Tsvetayeva's Yelabuga is that Khodasevich had the especially agonizing experience of living through his own eclipse as an artist. It is arguable that no other modern Russian poet of comparable status has suffered more from literary politics, from the legacy of his own silence, and from what Simon Karlinsky calls "Western self-censorship"—"the conviction, inherited from the thirties, that a Russian writer who resides outside the Soviet Union cannot be of any interest for a Western reader."[3]

At the end Akhmatova understood—perhaps better than anyone else still alive from her generation—all the cruelty and suffering her country had experienced. But she was always proud of the other side of the Russian people, a side that the West often fails to admit or purposely overlooks: their compassion and kindness, their creativity, and their ability to endure.

Akhmatova believed in the future of Russia. She believed that its tradition of great culture would be carried on by new generations, by poets and prose writers who would ensure that the Russian word stayed alive and strong:

If poetry is fated to blossom in the twentieth century in my Homeland, I dare say, I am always a happy and reliable witness. . . . And I am sure that even now we do not entirely know the magic chorus of poets we possess, that the Russian language is young and flexible, that we only just recently began writing verse: we love it and believe in it.[4]

Russia is different from many other Slavic countries. A large part of its territory lies in Asia, and for several hundred years it was ruled by the Tatars. Many, like Akhmatova herself, have Tatar blood in their veins—and they are proud of it. Akhmatova inherited the wisdom of her ancestors, their ability to preserve calm in the midst of chaos. She inherited their resignation in confronting pain and suffering, which to Western eyes may look like a passive acceptance of injustice. In fact, the ability to overcome pain transforms it into something profoundly spiritual. Through both her Eastern and her Russian Orthodox heritage, Akhmatova inherited the idea that although there is evil and sin in the world, it is balanced by the good. These traditions also share the idea of a delicate balance between the free individual and the caring community. To live in harmony with one's fellow beings does not necessarily imply the suppression of one's own individuality. Chinese painting teaches us that "Harmony does not mean sameness. . . . Harmony is creative, sameness is sterile."[5]

Many of the mysteries of her life and work will only be revealed in the future. However, the material that is available now, especially what has been released in the last few years, confirms what Nikita Struve said of Akhmatova—that she was "not only a great poet but a remarkable, unusual, great human being."[6] Akhmatova was gifted by God to perceive the beauty in everyday life, and to transform the anguish and suffering of her people in this century into one of the greatest collections of poems ever written. The transforming power of her art is expressed in a poem to the singer Galina Vishnevskaya, written in 1961 when Akhmatova was overcome by the beauty of her voice:

> A woman's voice is rushing like the wind,
> Black, it seems, damp, and of the night.
> And whatever it touches in its flight—
> Becomes instantly transformed,
> With a diamond shining it pours,
> Somewhere, something silvers for a moment
> And an intriguing garment
> Of fabulous silks rustles.
> And such a compelling power draws the bewitched voice on,
> As if ahead there were no grave,
> But the flight of a flight of mysterious stairs.

(II, p. 683)

The following abbreviations are used throughout the Notes and Bibliography:

AA: *Anna Akhmatova: 1889–1989,* ed. Sonia I. Ketchian. Modern Russian Literature and Culture. Berkeley: Berkeley Slavic Specialties, 1993.

AS: *Akhmatovskii sbornik,* ed. Serge Deduline and Gabriel Superfin. Bibliothèque Russe de l'Institut d'Etudes slaves, vol. LXXXV. Paris: Institut d'Etudes slaves, 1989.

BP: *Boris Pasternak 1890–1960: Colloque de Cerisy-la-Salle 11–14 September 1975.* Paris: Institut d'Etudes slaves, 1979.

CCPL: Osip Mandelstam. *The Complete Critical Prose and Letters,* ed. Jane Gary Harris, trans. Jane Gary Harris and Constance Link. London: Collins Harvill, 1991.

CPP: *Contemporary Poetry and Poetics,* XXXIX (Fall 1988).

DG: *Anna Akhmatova: Desyatye gody,* ed. R. D. Timenchik and K. M. Polivanov. Moscow: MPI, 1989.

HAH: Nadezhda Mandelstam. *Hope Against Hope,* trans. Max Hayward. New York: Atheneum, 1970.

H-M: Amanda Haight. *Anna Akhmatova: poeticheskoye stranstviye: dnevniki, vospominaniya, pisma,* trans. M. Timenchik, ed. S. Dubovik, commentary V. Chernykh, et al. Moscow: Raduga, 1991.

H-N: Amanda Haight. *Anna Akhmatova: A Poetic Pilgrimage.* Oxford: Oxford University Press, 1990.

LO: *Literaturnoye obozreniye.*

Mandrykina: Anna Akhmatova. "Avtobiograficheskaya proza," ed. A. A. Mandrykina and Anna Akhmatova, *Sochineniya,* II. Moscow: Khudozhestvennaya literatura, 1986.

MHC: Anna Akhmatova, *My Half Century: Selected Prose,* ed. Ronald Meyer. Ann Arbor: Ardis, 1992.

NG: Nikolay Gumilyov. Vera Luknitskaya, *Nikolay Gumilyov: zhizn poety po materialam domashnego arkhiva syemi Luknitskikh.* Leningrad: Lenizdat, 1990.

NGVS: *Nikolay Gumilyov: Vo vospominaniyakh sovremennikov,* ed. Vadim Kreid. Paris and New York: C.A.S.E.–Third Wave; Düsseldorf: Blue Rider, 1989.

OAA: *Ob Anne Akhmatovoi,* ed. M. M. Kralin and I. I. Slobozhan. Leningrad: Lenizdat, 1990.

Pasternak-Davie: *Pasternak: Modern Judgements,* ed. Donald Davie and Angela Livingstone. London: Macmillan, 1969.

PBG: *Poema bez geroya,* ed. R. D. Timenchik with V. Ya. Morderer. Moscow: MPI, 1989.

PV: *Posle vsego,* ed. R. D. Timenchik and K. M. Polivanov. Moscow: MPI, 1989.

Requiem, ed. R. D. Timenchik and K. M. Polivanov. Moscow: MPI, 1989.

RLT: *Russian Literature Triquarterly.*

S-F: Anna Akhmatova, *Sochineniya,* ed. G. P. Struve and B. A. Filipoff, Vol. 1. 2nd ed. Munich: Inter-Language Literary Associates, 1967. Vol. 2. Munich: Inter-Language Literary Associates, 1968. Vol. 3. Paris: YMCA Press, 1983.

S-L: *Soviet Literature.*

SMV: *Svoyu mezh vas yeshchyo ostaviv ten . . . ,* Akhmatovskiye chteniya, ed. N. V. Korolyova and S. A. Kovalenko. Moscow: Naslediye, 1992.

SP: *A Sense of Place: Tsarskoe Selo and Its Poets: Papers from the 1989 Dartmouth Conference Dedicated to the Centennial of Anna Akhmatova,* ed. Lev Loseff and Barry Scherr. Columbus, OH: Slavica Publishers, 1994.

SUE: *The Speech of Unknown Eyes: Akhmatova's Readers on Her Poetry,* ed. Wendy Rosslyn. 2 vols. Nottingham: Astra Press, 1990.

TR: *Tainy remesla.* Akhmatovskiye chteniya, ed. N. V. Korolyova and S. A. Kovalenko. Moscow: Naslediye, 1992.

TRAS: *Transactions of the Russian-American Scholars of USA* (New York).

TsS: *Tsarstvennoye slovo.* Akhmatovskiye chteniya, ed. N. V. Korolyova and S. A. Kovalenko. Moscow: Naslediye, 1992.

VAA: P. N. Luknitsky. *Vstrechi s Annoi Akhmatovoi.* Vol. I: 1924–25 gg. Paris: YMCA Press, 1991.

VOAA: *Vospominaniya ob Anne Akhmatovoi,* ed. V. Y. Vilenkin and V. A. Chernykh. Commentary A. V. Kurt and K. M. Polivanov. Moscow: Sovetskii pisatel, 1991.

ZAA: Lydia Chukovskaya. *Zapiski ob Anne Akhmatovoi.* Vol. I (1938–1941). Paris: YMCA Press, 1976. Vol. II (1952–1962). Paris: YMCA Press, 1980.

PROLOGUE

1. See Akhmatova's poem, "We met for the last time" (January 1914) in *Rosary.*

CHAPTER 1: The Wild Child Becomes a Poet: 1889–1909

1. See Richard Charques, *The Twilight of Imperial Russia* (London: Oxford University Press, 1958).
2. Anna Akhmatova, "Korotko o sebe," in Amanda Haight, *Anna Akhmatova: Poeticheskoye stranstviye: dnevniki, vospominaniya, pisma* (Moscow: Raduga, 1991, cited henceforth as H-M), p. 212.
3. Anna Akhmatova, "Budka," in H-M, p. 215. See also Anna Akhmatova, "Pages from a Diary," *My Half Century* (Ann Arbor: Ardis, 1992, cited henceforth as MHC), p. 1. See Yevgeny Glebov, "Akhmatovskii memoriyal," *Vechernyaya Odessa,* June 24, 1989, p. 4, on the plaque. In the nineteenth century the Russian calendar was twelve days behind the Western calendar, and in the twentieth century it was thirteen days behind. After the Revolution the Soviets adopted the Western calendar. When dates are referred to according to the older pre-Revolutionary calendrical system, they will be termed "Old Style."
4. For a description of the rituals and songs sung on this night, see *Russian Folk Lyrics,* trans. and ed. Roberta Reeder (Bloomington: Indiana University Press, 1992).
5. See Joseph Brodsky, "Sretene," *Posvyashchaetsya Akhmatovoi,* ed. Pamela Davidson and Isia Tlati, for his poem dedicated to Akhmatova commemorating the story of St. Anna (Tenafly, NJ: Hermitage), p. 133. See Luke 2:22. The infant Jesus was brought by his parents to the temple for the Jewish purification ceremony, and the prophetess

Anna, who lived in the temple, gave thanks to God when she witnessed the event and "spoke of him to all who were looking for the redemption of Jerusalem." See the *Pravoslavnyi tserkovsnyi kalendar* (Moscow: Moskovskaya Patriarkhiya) for listing of the day of St. Anna. The baptismal certificate shows that Akhmatova was baptized December 17, 1889, in the Transfiguration Cathedral in Odessa. See "Svidetelstvo No. 4379," *Anna Akhmatova: Desyatye gody,* ed. R. M. Timenchik and K. M. Polivanov (Moscow: MPI, 1989, cited henceforth as DG), p. 6.

6. The "Bestuzhev courses" were founded in 1878 in St. Petersburg and named after the historian Constantine Bestuzhev-Ryumin. See Richard Stikes, *The Women's Liberation Movement in Russia 1860–1930* (Princeton: Princeton University Press, 1978).

7. The note on p. 12 of DG says, "In the reference section of *Deyateli revolyutsionnogo dvizheniya v Rossii* (1934, Vol. II, issue 2, p. 904) Anna Gorenko is mentioned as a participant of the People's Will circle." Yevgenia Gorenko, another of Andrey's sisters, was occupied with conspiratorial activity.

8. M. I. Budyko, "Rasskazy Akhmatovoi," *Ob Anne Akhmatovoi,* ed. Mikhail Kralin and I. I. Slobozhan (Leningrad: Lenizdat, 1990, cited henceforth as OAA), p. 471. See also Roman Shuvalov, "Otets poeta. K 100-letiyu so dnya rozhdeniya Anny Akhmatovoi," *Vechernyaya Odessa,* June 14, 1989, p. 3.

9. From *Deyateli revolutsionnogo dvizheniya . . . ,* cited in DG, p. 10.

10. See the obituary of Andrey Gorenko which appeared in *Odesskii listok,* September 7, 1915, cited in DG, p. 10.

11. See Victor Gorenko, "Interview," *RLT,* no. 9 (Spring 1974), p. 501.

12. Anna Akhmatova, "Northern Elegies," *The Complete Poems of Anna Akhmatova,* trans. Judith Hemschemeyer, ed. Roberta Reeder (Somerville, MA: Zephyr Press, 1990), Vol. II, p. 343. Henceforth all translations of Akhmatova's poems are from this edition unless otherwise noted.

13. Lydia Chukovskaya, *Zapiski ob Anne Akhmatovoi,* Vol. I: 1938–1941 (Paris: YMCA Press, 1976), p. 170. This and Vol. II: 1952–1962 (Paris: YMCA Press, 1980), cited henceforth as ZAA.

14. Ibid, p. 8.

15. Hannah Gorenko, "Iz ocherka 'Mat Akhmatovoi,' " DG, p. 8. From memoirs given to Timenchik.

16. Victor Gorenko, "Interview," p. 499.

17. Ariadna Tyrkova-Williams, "Teni minuvshego," DG, p. 31.

18. Cited in Chukovskaya, ZAA, I, p. 170.

19. Budyko, "Rasskazy Akhmatovoi," p. 470. See Charles J. Halperin, *Russia and the Golden Horde* (Bloomington: Indiana University Press, 1987) for a discussion of the Tatar invasion and the episode concerning Akhmat.

20. Shuvalov, "Otets poeta," p. 3.

21. Anna Akhmatova, "Avtobiograficheskaya proza," H-M, p. 216.

22. Ibid.

23. Akhmatova, "Korotko o sebe," H-M, p. 212. See also MHC, p. 25.

24. Valentin Krivich, "Iz vospominanii," in DG, p. 36. Valentin Krivich is the pseudonym of V. I. Annensky (1880–1936), son of Innokenty Annensky, the poet.

25. Chukovskaya, ZAA, I, p. 113.

26. Dmitry Klenovsky, "Poety tsarskoselskoi gimnazii," *Nikolay Gumilyov: Vo vospominaniyakh sovremennikov.* Ed. Vadim Kreid (Paris and New York: C.A.S.E.–Third Wave, Düsseldorf: Blue Rider, 1989; cited henceforth as NGVS), p. 25.

27. "Dom Shukhardinoi," H-M, p. 217. See also MHC, p. 2.

28. Akhmatova, "Korotko o sebe," H-M, p. 212. See also MHC, p. 25. Timenchik cites A. Tinyakov's discussion of the influence of Nekrasov on Akhmatova in *Zhurnal*

zhurnalov, no. 6 (1915). See R. D. Timenchik, "Khram premudrosti boga . . . ," pp. 297–317. See also Milivoe Jovanovich, "Krazboru 'Chuzhikh golosov' v *Rekvieme* Akhmatovoi," *Russian Literature*, XV (1984), p. 170.

29. Valeriya Sreznevskaya, "Dafnis i Khloya," OAA, p. 17.
30. Anatoly Nayman, *Remembering Anna Akhmatova*, trans. Wendy Rosslyn (New York: Henry Holt & Co., 1991, cited henceforth as Nayman-Rosslyn). See also P. N. Luknitsky, *Vstrechi s Annoi Akhmatovoi*, Vol. I (Paris: YMCA Press, 1991, cited henceforth as VAA), p. 56.
31. Alexander Pushkin, "Bronze Horseman," *The Heritage of Russian Verse,* ed. Dimitri Obolensky (Bloomington: Indiana University Press, 1964), p. 113.
32. Akhmatova, "Gorod," DG, p. 25.
33. Carnival *(Maslenitsa)* is a holiday that goes back to the pagan period and celebrates the return of the sun. Pancakes in the shape of the sun are the ritual food eaten during this time of year. It takes place the week before Lent and is celebrated by welcoming a straw effigy representing Carnival. At the beginning of the week the "god" appears, and at the end it is buried in the earth so that its energy will help plants grow in the spring. See Reeder, *Russian Folk Lyrics*. During this week there were great fairs in Petersburg and Moscow. Stravinsky's ballet *Petrouchka* is based on this holiday.
34. Akhmatova, "Dalshe o gorode," DG, p. 26.
35. Akhmatova, "Zapakhi Pavlovskogo vokzala," DG, p. 22.
36. Chukovskaya, ZAA, II, p. 30.
37. Valeriya Sreznevskaya, "Iz vospominanii," DG, p. 37.
38. Anna Akhmatova, "Kogda . . . ," DG, p. 34.
39. Chukovskaya, ZAA, I, p. 148. Akhmatova does not say to which gymnasium she is referring, the one she attended in Tsarskoye Selo or the one in Kiev.
40. Chrysostum is a reference to the early Christian saint, John Chrysostum (the goldenmouthed). The Tsvetayeva poem in which the phrase appears is "zlato ustoi Annevseya Rusi," June 27, 1916. Akhmatova mentions becoming "friends with the sea" in "Korotko o sebe," H-M, p. 212.
41. Korney Chukovsky, "Chukovsky ob Akhmatovoi: Po arkhivnym materialam," *Novyi mir* (March 1987), p. 223.
42. Chukovskaya, ZAA, I, p. 187.
43. Ibid.
44. Sreznevskaya, "Iz vospominanii," DG, p. 15.
45. Luknitskaya, Vera. *Nikolay Gumilyov. Zhizn poeta po materialam domashnego arkhiva semi Lukniskikh* (Leningrad: Lenizdat, 1990, cited henceforth as *Nikolay Gumilyov*), pp. 15–16.
46. Ibid, p. 62. See also Edith W. Clowes, "Vulgarization of the Superman," *Nietzsche in Russia*, ed. Bernice Glatzer Rosenthal (Princeton: Princeton University Press, 1986), p. 318. The articles in this book are excellent for an overview of the influence of Nietzsche in Russia at the turn of the century.
47. Nikolay Punin cited in Luknitskaya, *Nikolay Gumilyov*, p. 30.
48. Ibid., p. 25.
49. V. V. Ivanov, "Zvezdnaya vspyshka," Nikolay Gumilyov, *Stikhotvoreniya i poemy*. Biblioteka poeta, bolshaya seriya. 3rd ed. (Leningrad: Sovetskii pisatel, 1988), p. 14.
50. Sergey Makovsky, "Nikolay Gumilyov (1886–1921)," NGVS, p. 58.
51. Based on the version in *Heritage of Russian Verse*, p. 253.
52. Luknitskaya, *Nikolay Gumilyov*, p. 34.
53. H-M, p. 251. For good discussions of this period, see Michael T. Florinsky, *The End of the Russian Empire* (New York: Collier Books, 1961), pp. 11–31; Basil Dmytryshan, *USSR: A Concise History* (New York: Charles Scribner's Sons, 1984), pp. 14–36;

Nicholas Riasanovsky, *A History of Russia* (London: Oxford University Press, 1969), pp. 448–464; Charques, *The Twilight of Imperial Russia;* Roberta Thompson Manning, *The Crisis of the Old Order in Russia* (Princeton: Princeton University Press, 1982); and Sheila Fitzpatrick, *The Russian Revolution 1917–1932* (Oxford: Oxford University Press, 1982), pp. 10–33.

54. Trans. Roberta Reeder. Valery Bryusov, "Na novyi, 1905 god," *Sobranie sochinenii,* Vol. I (Moscow: Khudozhestvennaya literatura, 1973), p. 44.

55. Alexander Blok, *Sobranie sochinenii,* ed. V. N. Orlov, Aa. A. Surkov and K. I. Churkovsky, Vol. III (Moscow and Leningrad: Khudozhestvennaya literatura, 1960), p. 331. Trans. Roberta Reeder. See also Sam Driver, "Akhmatova's 'Poema bez geroja' and Blok's 'Vozmezdie' " in *Aleksandr Blok Centennial Conference,* ed. W. Vickery and B. Sagatov (Columbus, OH, 1984), pp. 89–99.

56. Vladimir Orlov, *Hamayun. The Life of Alexander Blok* (Moscow: Progress Publishers, 1980), p. 46.

57. N. Skatov, "Rossiya u Aleksandra Bloka i poeticheskaya traditsiya Nekrasova v mire Bloka," *Sbornik statei* (Moscow: Sovetskii pisatel, 1980), p. 89.

58. Georgy Chulkov, "Anna Akhmatova," in Chulkov, *Nashi sputniki 1912–1922* (Moscow: N. V. Vasilev, 1922), p. 87.

59. Arnold Haskell, *Diaghileff: His Artistic and Private Life* (New York: Da Capo Press, 1935), p. 137.

60. Cited in Margarita Aliger, *Tropinka vo rzhi* (Moscow: Sovetskii pisatel, 1980), p. 354.

61. Luknitskaya, *Nikolay Gumilyov,* p. 35.

62. Amanda Haight, *Anna Akhmatova: A Poetic Pilgrimage* (Oxford: Oxford University Press, 1990; cited hereafter as H-N), p. 12.

63. N. I. Petrovskaya cited in Luknitskaya, *Nikolay Gumilyov,* p. 46.

64. Akhmatova, "Iz perepiski A. Akhmatovoi," H-M, p. 325.

65. Vera Beer, "Listki iz dalyokikh vospominanii," DG, p. 39.

66. Ibid., pp. 40–41.

67. Her certificate lists good grades for all her subjects, which included Russian literature, religion, German, French, math, history, geography, natural sciences, physics, and drawing. See "Attestat," DG, pp. 42–43.

68. See Nikolay Berdyaev, *Samopoznaniye* (Moscow: Mysl, 1991), p. 127.

69. Cited in Gabriel Superfin and Roman Timenchik, "A Propos de deux lettres de A. A. Akhmatova à V. Brjusov," *Cahiers du monde russe et soviétique,* XV (1974), p. 190.

70. Andrey Bely, "Na ekrane, Gumilyov," NGVS, pp. 33–35.

71. Yury Aikhenvald, *Poety i poetessa* (Moscow: Severnye dni, 1922), p. 42.

72. There are disagreements as to how many trips Gumilyov made to Africa. His sister-in-law, Anna Gumilyov, says in her memoirs that he first realized his dream of going to Africa in 1907 and talks about this in letters sent by friends to his parents. She does not mention the specific countries he visited. Moreover, she did not marry Dmitry Gumilyov until 1909, and her account of Gumilyov's life until that point is based on what her husband told her. See Anna Gumilyova, "Nikolay Stepanovich Gumilyov," NGVS, p. 116. Akhmatova says Gumilyov's first trip to Africa was in 1908.

73. Vadim Bronguleyev, "Afrikanskii dnevnik N. Gumilyova," *Nashe naslediye,* no. 1 (1988), p. 80.

74. Ibid.

75. Luknitskaya, *Nikolay Gumilyov,* p. 48.

76. Trans. Roberta Reeder. For original see Nikolay Gumilyov, *Stikhotvoreniya i poemy,* ed. M. D. Elzon, Biblioteka poeta, Bolshaya seriya, 3rd ed. Leningrad: Sovetskii pisatel (1988), p. 89.

77. Alexey Tolstoy, "N. Gumilyov," NGVS, pp. 38–39.
78. Anna Akhmatova, "Iz perepiski A. A. Akhmatovoi," H-M, p. 317. See also "To Sergei von Shein," MHC, pp. 271–282. Akhmatova was living at Meringovskaya Street, house no. 7, apt. 4, in Kiev. According to the commentary in H-M, p. 376, Akhmatova lived with her cousin Mariya Zmunchilla, and her family in 1906–07 while studying in the eighth class of the Fundukleyevskaya Gymnasium in Kiev. (Mariya later married Akhmatova's brother Andrey.) She spent her holidays with her aunt, Anna Vakar (née Stogova), the older sister of Akhmatova's mother, and her uncle Victor Vakar.
79. Akhmatova, "Iz perepiski . . . ," p. 318.
80. Ibid., p. 321.
81. Ibid., p. 322.
82. Ibid., p. 323.
83. Luknitskaya, *Nikolay Gumilyov,* pp. 61–62.
84. Bronguleyev, "Afrikanski dnevnik," p. 80.
85. See Tyrkova-Williams, "Teni minuvshego," DG, pp. 28–29, and John Malmstad, "Mikhail Kuzmin: A Chronicle of His Life and Times," in M. A. Kuzmin, *Sobraniye stikhov,* Vol. III (Munich: Wilhelm Fink Verlag, 1977), p. 119.
86. Berdyaev, *Samopoznaniye,* p. 137.
87. Chukovskaya, ZAA, I, p. 147.
88. Berdyaev, *Samopoznaniye,* p. 131.
89. Chukovskaya, ZAA, II, p. 451.
90. For the relationship between Akhmatova and Bryusov, see Superfin and Timenchik.
91. Berdyaev, *Samopoznaniye,* p. 139.
92. Wladimir Weidle, "Iz stati 'Tri Rossii,' " *Poema bez geroya,* ed. R. D. Timenchik with V. Ya. Morderer. Moscow: MPI, 1989, p. 90. (Cited hereafter as PBG).
93. Orlov, *Hamayun,* p. 238.
94. Luknitskaya, *Nikolay Gumilyov,* p. 71.
95. Ibid., p. 75, and Makovsky, NGVS, pp. 77–78.
96. Alexey Tolstoy, "N. Gumilyov," NGVS, p. 40.
97. Johannes von Günther, "Pod vostochnym vetrom," NGVS, pp. 135–138.
98. Luknitskaya, *Nikolay Gumilyov,* p. 99.
99. Maksimilian Voloshin, "Vospominaniya o Cherubine de Gabriak," NGVS, p. 146.
100. Luknitskaya, *Nikolay Gumilyov,* pp. 93 and 96, and Alexey Tolstoy, "N. Gumilyov," pp. 40–43.
101. Trans. Roberta Reeder. See Nikolay Gumilyov, "Potomki Kaina," *Stikhotvoreniya i poemy,* p. 116.
102. Luknitskaya, *Nikolay Gumilyov,* p. 103.

CHAPTER 2: Petersburg, Poetry, and the Cabaret: 1910–1914

1. Roman Timenchik, "Khram premudrosti boga . . . ," *Slavica Hierosolymitana,* 5–6 (1981), p. 309.
2. Yuri Molok, "Kak v zerkalo, glyadela ya trevozhno . . . ," *Akhmatovskii sbornik,* ed. Serge Deduline and Gabriel Superfin. Bibliothèque Russe de l'Institut d'Etudes slaves, vol. LXXXV (Paris: Institut d'Etudes slaves, 1989, cited henceforth as AS), p. 44.
3. Luknitskaya, *Nikolay Gumilyov,* pp. 104–105.
4. Ibid., p. 107.
5. H-N, p. 24. Russian version, Sreznevskaya, "Vospominaniya," DG, p. 16.
6. Akhmatova, "Amedeo Modilyani," H-M, p. 296, and "Korotko o sebe," H-M, p.

213. See also "Amedeo Modigliani," MHC, p. 81, and Akhmatova, "Briefly About Myself," MHC, p. 26.

7. See Akhmatova, "Pages from a Diary," MHC.

8. Luknitskaya, *Nikolay Gumilyov,* p. 109. See also Makovsky, "Nikolay Gumilyov (1886–1921)," NGVS, p. 59.

9. Akhmatova, "Avtobiograficheskaya proza," H-M, p. 213.

10. Sreznevskaya, archival material cited by Valentin Valenkin, *V sto pervom zerkale* (Moscow: Sovetskii pisatel, 1987), p. 184.

11. Sreznevskaya, DG, p. 16.

12. On June 10, 1910, Kuzmin noted in his diary that he had just met Akhmatova and that "she was nothing special but was very sweet." Elsewhere he wrote he had met her in Pavlovsk in June "reading her own poems in a shy voice to her husband's friends, who had not yet become her friends." Mikhail Kuzmin, cited by Superfin and Timenchik, p. 191. First cited by E. A. Znosko-Borovsky, "O Bloke," *Zapiski nablyudatelya,* I (Prague, 1924), p. 125.

13. Chukovskaya, ZAA, I, p. 61. See also Akhmatova, "V desyatom godu," H-M, p. 324.

14. Luknitsky, VAA, p. 141.

15. Marc Slonim, *From Chekhov to the Revolution* (New York: Oxford University Press, 1962), p. 83.

16. Vyacheslav Ivanov, "Zavety simvolizma," *Borozdy i mezhi* (Moscow: Musaget, 1916), pp. 118–144. Originally printed in *Apollon* (May-June 1910) with Blok's lecture. Aleksandr Blok, "O sovremennom sostoyanii russkogo simvolizma," *Sobraniye sochinenii,* V, p. 431.

17. Valery Bryusov, "O sovremennom sostoyanii russkogo simvolizma (Po povodu doklada V. I. Ivanova)," April 2, 1910, *Sobraniye sochinenii,* pp. 147–158.

18. Mikhail Kuzmin, "O prekrasnoi yasnosti (otkryvki)," *Russkaya literatura XX veka,* compiled by N. A. Trifonov (Moscow: Gosudarstvennoye uchebno-pedagogicheskoe izdatelstvo, 1962), pp. 433–434. See also John Malmstad,"Mikhail Kuzmin," in *Sobraniye stikhov,* III, pp. 135–139.

19. Vladimir Pyast, DG, p. 46. From his book *Vstrechi.* Pyast is the pseudonym of Vladimir Postovsky (1886–1940).

20. Luknitskaya, *Nikolay Gumilyov,* p. 112.

21. Akhmatova, "Avtobiograficheskaya proza," H-M, p. 213.

22. Georgy Chulkov cited by Roman Timenchik and A. V. Lavrov, "Materialy A. A. Akhmatovoi v rukopisnom otdela pushkinskogo doma," *Yezhegodnik rukopisnogo otdele pushkinskogo doma na 1974* (Leningrad: Nauka, 1976), p. 67.

23. Akhmatova, "Avtobiograficheskaya proza," H-M, p. 228.

24. See Sergey Makovsky, "Nikolay Gumilyov," NGVS, p. 64.

25. Ibid., p. 223.

26. See N. Khardzhiyev, "O risunke A. Modilyani," H-M, pp. 302–304, where he suggests the influence of Michelangelo's *Night* on Pope Julian's sarcophagus. Passage translated by Roberta Reeder from Anna Akhmatova, "Amadeo Modilyani," H-M, p. 296. See English version of Akhmatova's memoir of Modigliani, Anna Akhmatova, "Amadeo Modigliani," MHC, pp. 76–83.

27. Cited by Timenchik and Lavrov, "Materialy . . . ," p. 67.

28. Akhmatova, "Korotko o sebe," p. 213. "Briefly About Myself," MHC, p. 27.

29. In the 1930s the former Gumilyov home was moved from Slepnyovo to the neighboring village of Gradnitsa and became a school. In the middle of the 1980s a plaque appeared, "In this house from 1911–1917 lived the Russian poets Anna Akhmatova and Nikolay Gumilyov." See T. Arkhangelskaya and V. Radzishevskii, " ' . . . K sebe domoi' ":

Pervyi Akhmatovskii prazdnik poezii," *Literaturnaya gazeta,* June 22, 1987, p. 7, for a celebration of the two poets with the participation of leading scholars, and D. Kuznetsov and V. Potapov, "Pered vesnoi," *Sovetskaya kultura,* March 4, 1989, pp. 9–10.

30. Akhmatova, "Slepnyovo," H-M, p. 227. See "Slepnyovo," MHC, p. 9.

31. H-M, p. 226, and MHC, p. 8.

32. Sergey Deduline, "Iz besedy s Dmitriyem Bushenom," DG, p. 89. Published originally in the Literary Supplement no. 3/4 to *Russkaya mysl* (Paris, June 5, 1987).

33. Vera Nevedomskaya, "Vospominaniya o Gumilyove," NGVS, pp. 151–160.

34. Luknitskaya, *Nikolay Gumilyov,* p. 119. For a description of the house, see ibid., pp. 120–121. Akhmatova took Pavel Luknitsky to see the house in April 1925.

35. Makovsky, "Nikolay Gumilyov po lichnym vospominaniyam," NGVS, p. 91.

36. Anna Gumilyova, "Nikolay Stepanovich Gumilyov," NGVS, p. 119.

37. Chukovskaya, ZAA, I, p. 80.

38. B. Kats and R. Timenchik, *Akhmatova i muzyka: Issledovatelskiye ocherki* (Leningrad: Sovetskii kompozitor, 1989), p. 52.

39. Cited by Yury Annenkov, "Anna Akhmatova," *Dnevnik moikh vstrech: Tsikl tragedii,* Vol. I (Munich: Inter-Language Literary Associates, 1966), p. 116.

40. Korney Chukovsky, "Chukovsky ob Akhmatovoi. Po arkhivnym materialiam," *Novyi mir* (March 1987), p. 232.

41. Cited in Gabriel Superfin, and Roman Timenchik. "A Propos de deux lettres de A. A. Akhmatova à V. Brjussov," *Cahiers du Monde russe et soviétique,* nos. 1–2, XV (January–June 1974), p. 192.

42. Boris Pasternak, "A Safe-Conduct," *Selected Writings and Letters,* trans. Catherine Judelson (Moscow: Progress Publishers, 1989).

43. For an excellent work discussing these concepts, see V. Delson, *Skryabin* (Moscow: Muzyka, 1971).

44. Anna Akhmatova, "Iz vospominanii o Mandelstame," H-M, p. 282. See also "Osip Mandelstam," MHC, p. 85.

45. See Nadezhda (Buchinskaya) Teffi, "Iz 'Vospominanii,' " PBG, p. 94. The memoirs were written at the end of her life. From a copy of her memoirs in a private collection.

46. Nikolay Punin, "Iz 'vospominanii," PBG, p. 337.

47. Trans. Roberta Reeder. For the original Russian, see Osip Mandelstam, *Sobraniye sochinenii,* ed. G. P. Struve and B. A. Filipoff, Vol. I (Washington, DC: Inter-Language Literary Associates, 1964), p. 119. The Struve-Filipoff edition dates the poem to 1910, although Akhmatova says she was not introduced to Mandelstam until 1911.

48. Arthur Lourie. From "Cheshuya v nevode," PBG, p. 295. Originally in *Vozdushnye puti,* no. 2 (1963).

49. Osip Mandelstam, "On the Nature of the Word," in Mandelstam, *The Complete Critical Prose and Letters,* ed. Jane Gary Harris, trans. Jane Gary Harris and Constance Link (Ann Arbor: Ardis, 1979, cited henceforth as CCPL), p. 128.

50. Adamovich, "Moi vstrechi," OAA, p. 95.

51. Nikolai Gumilev, "Symbolism's Legacy and Acmeism," trans. Robert T. Whittaker, Jr., RLT, no. 1 (Fall 1971), p. 140. Originally "Naslediye simvolizma i akmeizma," *Apollon,* I (1913), pp. 42–45.

52. Sergey Gorodetsky, "Nekotorye techeniya v sovremennoi russkoi poezii," *Apollon,* I (1913), pp. 46–50.

53. Cited by Luknitsky in P. N. Luknitsky, *Vstrechy s Annoi Akhmatovoi,* Vol. I (Paris: YMCA Press, 1991, cited hereafter as VAA), p. 204. See also Luknitskaya, *Nikolay Gumilyov,* pp. 156–157, for Akhmatova's version of the relationship between Gumilyov and Gorodetsky.

54. Vasily Gippius, "Tsekh Poetov," DG, p. 84.
55. Bryusov, cited in Superfin, p. 186.
56. See in particular the perceptive analysis by Elaine Rusinko, "Russian Acmeism and Anglo-American Imagism," *Ulbandus* (1978), pp. 37–49.
57. Adamovich, "Moi vstrechi," OAA, p. 95.
58. Luknitskaya, *Nikolay Gumilyov,* p. 124. See also Kreid, note to Makovsky, NGVS, p. 87. Masha died in Italy in Ospidaletti at twenty-two and was buried in Bezhetsk.
59. See Akhmatova, "Gumilyov," MHC, for Akhmatova's view of his development.
60. V. Zhirmunsky, "Preodolevshiye simvolizm," *Voprosy teorii literatury* (The Hague: Mouton, 1962), p. 284.
61. See Lydia Ginzburg, *O lyrike* (Moscow and Leningrad: Sovetskii pisatel, 1964), p. 300. See also Vsevolod Setchkarev, *Studies in the Life and Works of Innokentij Annenskij* (The Hague: Mouton, 1963), and Janet G. Tucker, *Innokentij Annenskij and the Acmeist Doctrine* (Columbus, OH: Slavica Publishers, 1986). For an English translation of Annensky's poems, see Innokenty Annensky, *The Cypress Chest,* trans. R. H. Morrison, bilingual edition (Ann Arbor: Ardis, 1982).
62. See Andrey Fyodorov, "Poeticheskoye tvorchestvo Innokentiya Annenskogo," in Innokenty Annensky, *Stikhotvoreniya i tragedii,* ed. A. V. Fyodorov. Biblioteka poeta, Bolshaya seriya, 2nd ed. (Leningrad: Sovetskii pisatel, 1959), pp. 46–55, for a detailed discussion of Annensky's poetic style.
63. Mikhail Kuzmin, "Predisloviye M. A. Kuzmina k pervoi knige stikhov Anny Akhmatovoi," in Akhmatova, Struve-Filipoff ed., III, pp. 471–473. See also DG, pp. 530–532.
64. Mandrykina, "Nenapisannaya Knigu," p. 74.
65. Chukovsky, *Lyudi i knigi,* Vol. V, p. 754.
66. Mandelstam, "Storm and Stress," CCPL, p. 177.
67. Chulkov, *Nashi sputniki . . . ,* p. 71.
68. See Yuri K. Shcheglov, "Cherty poetichskogo mira Akhmatovoi," *Wiener Slawistischer Almanach,* III (1979), pp. 27–56.
69. See Kees Verheul, *The Theme of Time in the Poetry of Anna Akhmatova* (The Hague: Mouton, 1971), p. 6.
70. Mandelstam, "A Letter About Russian Poetry" (1922), CCPL, p. 157.
71. A. S. Pushkin, *Sobraniye sochinenii,* ed. D. D. Blagoi, et al., Vol. I (Moscow: Khudozhestvennaya literatura, 1959), p. 108. Trans. Roberta Reeder.
72. For a discussion of Akhmatova's style, see V. V. Vinogradov, *Anna Akhmatova* (Munich: Wilhelm Fink Verlag, 1970), which is a reprint of *O poezii Anny Akhmatovoi* (Leningrad, 1925), and "O simvolike A. A. Akhmatovoi," *Literaturnaya mysl,* I (1922). Vinogradov discusses what he calls "nests": Akhmatova's technique of forming groups of objects with shared associations which are then often juxtaposed with other "nests," resulting in even further sets of associations. The image "song," for example, is related to "voice," which may be the voice of the wind, an organ, a bird. The bird, in turn, is a symbol of the poet's childhood: a white bird recalls sweet memories of a happy past, the dove symbolizes love, betrayed love is a crow, and swans are associated with Tsarskoye Selo. See also T. V. Tsivian, "Materialy k poetike Anny Akhmatovoi," *Trudy po znakovym sistemam* III (Tartu: Tartu State University, 1967), pp. 180–208.
73. Wendy Rosslyn, *The Prince, the Fool and the Nunnery* (Amersham, Bucks: Avebury Publishing Co., 1984), p. 24.
74. Anthony Hartmann, "The Versification of the Poetry of Anna Akhmatova," Ph.D. dissertation (University of Wisconsin, 1978), p. 24. In the *dolniki,* there can be one or two syllables between accents. See also M. L. Gasparov, "Stikh Akhmatovoi: chetyre Yego etapa," *Literaturnoye obozreniye,* no. 5 (1989) cited henceforth as LO,

pp. 26–28, and "The Evolution of Akhmatova's Verse," *Anna Akhmatova 1889–1989,* ed. Sonia I. Ketchian (Berkeley: Berkeley Slavic Specialties, 1993), cited henceforth as AA, pp. 168–174.

75. For many excellent examples of Russian folk poems employing parallelism, see the section on vocal songs on love, *Narodnye liricheskiye pesni,* ed. V. Ya. Propp (Leningrad: Sovestskii pisateli (1961), pp. 113–181. See also *Russian Folk Lyrics,* trans. and ed. Roberta Reeder (Bloomington: University of Indiana Press, 1992), pp. 109–114.

76. See Sam Driver, *Anna Akhmatova* (New York: Twayne Publishers, 1972), p. 100.

77. See Howard Goldman, "Anna Akhmatova's *Hamlet:* The Immortality of Personality and the Discontinuity of Time," *Slavic East European Journal,* vol. XX, no. 4 (1980), p. 485.

78. Critics have suggested the influence of Annensky's "The Bronze Poet" on this poem. However, except for the fact the poet is not named, and the poem refers to Pushkin and Tsarskoye Selo, there is little in common with Akhmatova's poem. Annensky's verses refer to the bronze statue of Pushkin sitting on a bench, which had been recently set up in Tsarskoye Selo. The poet imagines the statue coming down from his pedestal.

79. The "dark-skinned youth" refers to Pushkin's African heritage. His great-grandfather, Avram Hannibal, godson of Peter the Great, was the son of royalty in an Ethiopian tribe in Abyssinia. He was brought to Constantinople as a hostage and bought by a Russian envoy, who then took him to Petersburg. He became a court favorite and was sent by Peter the Great to France to become an engineer. See Pushkin's story, "The Moor of Peter the Great" for his tale about his ancestor. Arthur Lourie has composed an opera on this subject.

80. "Reminiscences in Tsarskoye Selo" (1814) in Pushkin, Vol. I, p. 8, trans. Roberta Reeder. See also p. 662, where Pushkin's friend V. P. Gorchakov discusses what Tsarskoye Selo meant to the poet: "Pushkin seemed really to be transported to that society where his first poetic life blossomed with all its specters and charms. At those moments Pushkin sometimes grieved; and in the midst of this grief, reason gave way to the impressions of his young heart." This citation is from M. A. Tsyavlovsky, *Kniga vospominanii o Pushkine* (Moscow, 1931), p. 170. Roman Timenchik points to a Kuzmin poem on Pushkin that was written at approximately the same time as the Akhmatova poem and published in 1912. It is not clear which was created first:

With what strange force
Do words reign over us . . .
But one word "three cornered hat"
Reigns over me now,
For over the course of thirty years
And more: Pushkin, the lyceum,
But I've had enough of fashion.

Timenchik, "Akhmatova i Pushkin," *Pushkinskii sbornik, uchyonye zapiski,* Vol. 106 (Riga: Latvia University, 1989), p. 130.

81. Vasily Gippius, "Anna Akhmatova 'Vecher,' " in DG, p. 80. Originally published in the journal *Novaya zhizn,* no. 3 (1912).

82. Timenchik, "Poslesloviye," DG, p. 276.

83. Cited by Timenchik, ibid.

84. Cited by Timenchik, ibid., p. 277.

85. Bryusov, cited in Superfin, p. 186.

86. Valerian Chudovsky, "Po povodu stikhov Anny Akhmatovoi," PBG, p. 111.
87. Cited by Wiktor Woroszylski, *The Life of Mayakovsky,* trans. Beleslaw Taborski (New York: Orson Press, 1970), p. 26.
88. Trans. Roberta Reeder. For original see Vladimir Mayakovsky, *Polnoye sobraniye sochienii,* Vol. I (Moscow: Khudozhestvennaya literatura (1955), p. 185.
89. See V. Sayanov, "Akmeism," *Ocherki po istorii russkoi XX veka* (Letchworth, Herts: Prideux Press, 1972), pp. 43–86.
90. Cited by Valentin Katayev, *The Grass of Oblivion,* trans. Robert Daglish (New York: McGraw-Hill, 1969), p. 56.
91. Trans. Roberta Reeder. For original, see Gumilyov, *Stikhotvoreniya i poemy,* p. 168.
92. Luknitskaya, *Nikolay Gumilyov,* p. 138.
93. Ibid., p. 135.
94. Ibid., p. 136.
95. Sergei Makovsky, "Nikolay Gumilyov po lichnym vospominaniyam," NGVS, p. 92.
96. Sreznevskaya, DG, p. 18.
97. Superfin. "A propos . . . ," p. 200.
98. Sreznevskaya, DG, p. 19.
99. Vera Luknitskaya, *Pered toboi zemlya* (Leningrad: Lenizdat, 1988), p. 291.
100. Orest Vysotsky wrote in a recent letter that his mother died in January 1966 in Tiraspol. He was on the faculty at Kishinyov University and is now retired. (This information was provided by Prof. Elaine Rusinko, through a personal communication.) See also the Appendix to Jessie Davies's biography, *Anna of All the Russias* (Liverpool: Lincoln Davies & Co., 1988), pp. 134–135, for a translation of an interview with Orest Vysotsky that appeared in *Soviet Weekly,* May 14, 1988, p. 5, in which he says he and his mother became acquainted with Akhmatova and Lev Gumilyov in 1936 in Leningrad, where Orest was studying at the Forest Engineering Academy.
101. Trans. Roberta Reeder. For original, see Gumilyov, *Stikhotvoreniya i poemy,* p. 167.
102. Gumilyov, "Symbolism's Legacy and Acmeism," trans. Robert T. Whittaker, Jr., RLT, no. 1 (Fall 1971), p. 143.
103. Akhmatova, "Iz perepiski," H-M, p. 345.
104. Vadim Bronguleyev, "Afrikanskii dnevnik N. Gumilyova," *Nashe nas_lediye,* no. 1 (1988), p. 89.
105. Luknitsky, VAA, p. 41.
106. Trans. Roberta Reeder. For original, see Gumilyov, *Stikhotvoreniya i poemy,* p. 220.
107. Luknitskaya, *Nikolay Gumilyov,* p. 155.
108. Sreznevskaya in conversation with Luknitsky. See Luknitskaya, *Nikolay Gumilyov,* p. 162.
109. Chukovsky, "Chukovsky ob Akhmatovoi . . . ," *Novyi Mir,* p. 230.
110. Nikolay Punin, "Iz dnevnika," PBG, p. 336.
111. V. M. Zhirmunsky, *Tvorchestvo Anny Akhmatovoi* (Leningrad: Nauka, 1973), p. 38. For further information on images of Akhmatova in art, see Yuri Molok, "Vokrug rannikh portretov," LO, no. 5 (1989), pp. 81–85.
112. Jeanne van der Eng-Liedmeier, "Reception as a Theme in Akhmatova's Early Poetry," *Dutch Contributions to the Eighth International Congress of Slavicists,* ed. Jan M. Meijer (Amsterdam: John Banjains b.V., 1979), p. 211.
113. Orlov, *Hamayun,* p. 323.
114. Woroszylski, *Life of Mayakovsky,* p. 179. See also Dora Kogan, *Sergey Yurevich. Sudeikin* (Moscow: Iskusstva, 1974), p. 80, and Yu. Sazonovaya, "Novogodneye," *Posledniye novosti* (Jan. 1, 1938), cited by R. D. Timenchik, V. N. Toporov, and T.

V. Tsivyan, "Akhmatova i Kuzmin," *Russkaya Literatura*, VI, no. 3 (July 1978), p. 279.

115. Cited in Woroszylski, *Life of Mayakovsky*, p. 137.
116. Luknitskaya, *Nikolay Gumilyov*, p. 150. See also pp. 130 and 159 for allusions to the Stray Dog.
117. Andrey Levinson, "Iz ocherka . . . ," PBG, p. 136.
118. Livshits as cited in Woroszylski, p. 138. For the original, see B. Livshits, *Polutoroglazyi strelets* (Leningrad: Izdatelstvo pisatelei, 1923), p. 261.
119. Adamovich, "Moi strechi . . . ," OAA, p. 90.
120. Trans. Roberta Reeder. For original, see in Mandelstam, *Sobraniye sochinenii*, Vol. I, p. 37.
121. See Tamara Shileiko, "Legendy, mify i stikhi," *Novyi mir*, no. 4 (April 1986), pp. 199–213, for an in-depth analysis of Shileiko's relationship to Akhmatova.
122. Vera Garteveld, from *Vospominaniye*, cited in PBG, p. 321. See I. S. Yeventov, "Ot Fontanki do Sitsilii," OAA, p. 376, on Akhmatova's conversation with him on Shileiko.
123. Chukovsky, "Anna Akhmatova," p. 746.
124. Arthur Lourie, "Olga Afanasevna Glebova-Sudeikina," *Vozdushnye puti*, no. 3 (1963), p. 139. Andrey Bely describes Sudeikina as "a fragile, youthful, charming blond, twittering pleasantly like a bird, reminding one of a Ceylonese butterfly with a swash of silks in a cloud of muslin," cited by Timenchik, et al., "Akhmatova i Kuzmin," note 84.
125. Dora Kogan, *Sergey Yurvich Sudeikin* (Moscow: Iskussto, 1974), p. 88. See also Sergey Sudeikin as cited in Luknitskaya, *Nikolay Gumilyov*, p. 160.
126. V. Krasovskaya, *Russkii baletnyi teatr nachala XX veka*, Vol. I (Leningrad: Iskusstvo, 1971), p. 502.
127. K. M. Azadovsky, "Menya nazval 'kitezhankoi': Anna Akhmatova i Nikolay Klyuev," LO, no. 5 (1989), p. 67.
128. Adamovich, "Moi vstrechi," p. 92.
129. Cited by Woroszylski, p. 137.
130. Adamovich, "Moi vstrechi," p. 93.
131. Ibid., p. 93.
132. E. Dobin, *Poeziya Anny Akhmatovoi* (Leningrad: Sovetskii pisatel, 1968), p. 16.
133. Akhmatova told this to her friend Nina Olshevskaya. See Emma Gershtein, "Besedy ob Akhmatovoi s N. A. Olshevskoi-Ardovoi," LO, no. 5 (1989), p. 92.
134. C. E. Bechofer, "Letters from Russia," *The New Age* (London, January 28, 1915), cited in Kats and Timenchik, *Akhmatova i muzika*, p. 45.
135. "Chukovskaya," ZAA, I, p. 141.
136. Cited by Kats and Timenchik in *Akhmatova i muzika*, p. 39. In E. T. A. Hoffmann's tale "The Sandman," the narrator sees the world through his romantic illusions and is convinced a doll is really a beloved woman. The story was turned into the famous ballet *Coppélia*. See also Anatoly Shaikevich, *Most vzdokhov cherez Nevu* (Paris: Orion, 1947), pp. 136–137.
137. On Gumilyov in the Stray Dog, see Livshits, "Polutoraglazyi strelets," NGVS, p. 161, and Luknitskaya, *Nikolay Gumilyov*, p. 265.
138. For the best book on Arthur Lourie, his life and his music, see Detlef Gojowy, *Arthur Lourie und der russische Futurismus* (Laaber: Laaber Verlag, 1993). See Mikhail Kralin, *Artur i Anna* (Leningrad: Kralin, 1990). This book is based on information from letters between Kralin and Irina Graham, who was Lourie's close friend during the last period of his life when he lived in America and provided him with both

emotional and financial support, and letters between Kralin and Nina Konge, wife of Lourie's brother who remained in the Soviet Union. Ms. Graham has provided me with biographical information based on what she learned from Lourie, and says he was born in Petersburg. Recently Gidon Kremer has been promoting Lourie's music both in the West and in Russia through festivals, concerts, and recordings. Lourie came from a Sephardic Jewish family, and traced his ancestry to Rabbi Isaak Luria, a medieval philosopher and mystic.

139. Kron in PBG, p. 340.
140. See Kats and Timenchik, pp. 38–46, on music in the Stray Dog and Lourie's role in performing his own music and music of the avant-garde during this period.
141. Adamovich, "Moi vstrechi," p. 93.
142. Vasily Gippius, "Tsekh poetov," DG, p. 84.
143. Lutnitsky, VAA, I, p. 164.
144. Anna Akhmatova, "Pisma," in Anna Akhmatova, *Sochineniya v dvukh tomakh,* ed. Mikhail Kralin, II (Moscow: Pravda, 1990), pp. 188 and 189.
145. Gizetti cited by Rosslyn, *The Prince,* p. 6. For the original in Russian, see A. Gizetti, "Tri dushi (Stikhi N. Lvovoi, A. Akhmatovoi, M. Moravskoi)," *Yezhememesyachnyi zhurnal,* 12 (1915), pp. 147–166. Sam Driver and Vinogradov agree that the use of religious imagery is a treatment of the love theme or part of her cultural background, but not an indication of profound religious belief. See Driver, *Anna Akhmatova,* p. 114.
146. Driver, *Anna Akhmatova,* p. 114.
147. See Boris Eikhenbaum, *Anna Akhmatova: opyt analyza* (Paris: Lev, 1980). This is a reprint of the edition published in Petrograd in 1923.
148. Korney Chukovsky, "Akhmatova i Mayakovsky," *Dom isskustv,* I, p. 26. Reprinted in *Voprosy literatury,* no. 1 (1988), pp. 177–205.
149. See Osip Mandelstam, "On Contemporary Poetry," CCPL, p. 107 (first published in Petrograd 1916), and Nadezhda Mandelstam, *Hope Abandoned,* trans. Max Hayward (New York: Atheneum, 1974), p. 227.
150. For a good analysis of Petersburg in Akhmatova's poetry, see Sharon Leiter, *Akhmatova's Petersburg* (Philadelphia: University of Pennsylvania Press, 1983). See also Driver, *Anna Akhmatova,* p. 77.
151. Leonid Grossman, *Sobraniye sochinenii,* Vol. IV (Moscow: Sovremennye problemy, 1928), p. 36.
152. Chukovskaya, ZAA, II, p. 562.
153. Written in 1830, *The Feast During the Time of the Plague* is based on a play by John Wilson. It is one of Pushkin's *Small Tragedies,* a collection of short plays that includes *The Stone Guest* (about Don Juan) and *Mozart and Salieri,* with a theme similar to that of *Amadeus* by Peter Shaffer. Great aesthetic power is achieved in these works through their conciseness and concentration on a climactic moment in the life of the protagonists.
154. Trans. Roberta Reeder.
155. Trans. Roberta Reeder. Originally "Vospominaniya ob Aleksandre Bloke," H-M, p. 277. See also D. Maksimov, "Akhmatova o Bloke," *Zvezda,* no. 12 (December 8, 1967), p. 187.
156. Viktor Zhirmunsky, "Anna Akhmatova i Aleksandr Blok," *Alexander Blok: An Anthology of Essays and Memoirs,* ed. and trans. Lucy Vogel (Ann Arbor: Ardis, 1982), p. 147.
157. Trans. Roberta Reeder.
158. Nikolai Gumilyov, *Nikolai Gumilev on Russian Poetry,* ed. and trans. David Lapeza (Ann Arbor: Ardis, 1977), p. 142.

159. Rosslyn, *The Prince,* p. 4.
160. V. Gippius, "Anna Akhmatova," DG, p. 216. Original appeared in *Kuranty,* no. 2 (1918).
161. Nikolai Gumilev, "Review of Akhmatova's *Beads* (Petersburg, 1914)," trans. Robert T. Whittaker, Jr., RLT, no. 1 (Fall 1971), pp. 144–146.
162. Ilya Brazhnin, "Obayaniye talanta," *Novyi mir,* no. 12 (December 1976), pp. 235–244.

CHAPTER 3: The Twilight of Imperial Russia: 1914–1917

1. Petersburg was founded by Peter the Great as a European city, which not only imitated European architecture but translated "Peter's City" into the Germanic "Petersburg." The name Petersburg was too closely associated with Germanic roots, and instead the old Slavic term for city, *grad,* was used to form the new name of the city, Petrograd.
2. Anna Akhmatova, "Avtobiograficheskaya proza," H-M, p. 233.
3. See Charques, *Twilight of Imperial Russia,* p. 211. For further information, see Nicholas V. Riasanovsky, *A History of Russia,* 2nd ed. (New York: Oxford University Press, 1969), and John E. Rodes, *Germany: A History* (New York: Holt, Rinehart and Winston, 1964).
4. Akhmatova, "Avtobiograficheskaya proza," H-M, p. 235.
5. Friedrich Nietzsche, *Thus Spake Zarathustra,* trans. Thomas Common (New York: The Modern Library, n.d.), p. 48.
6. Akhmatova, "Avtobiograficheskaya proza," H-M, p. 226.
7. Luknitskaya, *Nikolay Gumilyov,* p. 168.
8. Ibid., p. 168.
9. Ibid.
10. Trans. Roberta Reeder. For original, see Mayokovsky, *Polnoye sobraniye sochinenii,* Vol. I, p. 75.
11. Ibid., p. 140.
12. Ibid., p. 141.
13. Ryszard Przybylski, *Essay on the Poetry of Osip Mandelstam,* trans. Madeline G. Levine (Ann Arbor: Ardis, 1987), p. 139. For original Russian version, see Mandelstam, *Sobraniye socheinenii,* Vol. I, p. 61.
14. Ibid.
15. Luknitskaya, *Nikolay Gumilyov,* pp. 168 and 172.
16. Ibid., p. 176.
17. Trans. Roberta Reeder. For original, see Gumilyov, *Stikhotvoreniya i poemy,* p. 260.
18. Cited in V. V. Ivanov, "Zvyozdnaya vspyshka," p. 19.
19. Orlov, *Hamayun,* p. 345.
20. H-N, p. 28.
21. Cited in Annenkov, "Anna Akhmatova," p. 120.
22. Boris Kremnev [G. I. Chulkov], "Pisma so storony," IV, *Golos zhizni,* no. 20 (1915), p. 18. Cited in Superfin, "A propos . . . ," p. 189. See Yugurta [A. Toporkov], *Severnye zapiski,* no. 6 (1916), p. 133.
23. Vl. Valters, *Spolokhi,* Vol. I (1922), p. 40, cited in Superfin, "A propos . . . ," p. 189.
24. Yuliya Sazonova-Slonimskaya, "Nikolay Vladimirovich Nedobrovo: opyt portreta," PBG, p. 232. Original *Russkaya mysl,* nos. VI–VIII (1923).
25. "Pisma, N. V. Nedobrovo k Bloku," ed. M. Kralin, *Literaturnoye nasledstvo: Aleksandr Blok, novye materialiy i issledovanii,* kn. 2 (Moscow: Nauka, 1981), p. 292.

26. Letter of Vera Znamenskaya (1895–1968) cited by Lazar Fleishman, "Iz akhmatov-skikh materialov v arkhive Guverovskogo Instituta," *Akhmatovskii sbornik,* Vol. I, p. 178. She was a good friend of Nedobrovo's and knew Akhmatova for more than half a century, but had never met Anrep. She had old letters from Nedobrovo to Anrep which had been given to her for Akhmatova, who in turn had received them in 1962 from Struve through one of his acquaintances who was in the Soviet Union. Upon Anrep's request, she wrote her reminiscences about Nedobrovo and Akhmatova.

27. "Pisma N. V. Nedobrovo k Bloku," ed. Kralin, p. 292.

28. Lazar Fleishman, "Iz akhmatovskikh materialov v arkhive Guverovskogo instituta," AS, p. 174.

29. She told this to Anatoly Naiman. See Nayman-Rosslyn, p. 77.

30. Gleb Struve, "Akhmatova i Nikolay Nedobrovo," S-F, III, p. 381; Fleishman, "Iz akhmatovskikh," p. 188.

31. Both poems translated by Roberta Reeder. Nedobrovo, cited in Timenchik and Lavrov, "Materialy . . . ," p. 63.

32. Trans. Roberta Reeder. Original appears in *Russkaya Mysl,* 1915.

33. R. D. Timenchik, "Anna Akhmatova 1922–1966," *Posle vsego,* ed. R. D. Timenchik and K. M. Polivanov (Moscow: MPI, 1989, cited henceforth as PV), p. 6.

34. Sheelagh Graham, "Amor Fati: Akhmatova and Gumilev," in *The Speech of Unknown Eyes: Akhmatova's Readers on Her Poetry,* ed. Wendy Rosslyn, Vol. II (Nottingham: Astra Press, 1990, cited henceforth as SUE), p. 77.

35. N. V. Nedobrovo, "Anna Akhmatova," trans. Alan Myers, RLT, no. 9 (Spring 1974), p. 232. See also for original, N. Nedobrovo, "Anna Akhmatova," PBG, p. 250–272.

36. Chulkov in Timenchik and Lavrov, p. 69.

37. Luknitskaya, *Nikolay Gumilyov,* p. 178.

38. Kats and Timenchik, *Akhmatova i muzyka,* p. 52.

39. "Iz perepiski N. S. Gumilyova i A. A. Akhmatovoi," H-M, p. 349.

40. Luknitskaya, *Nikolay Gumilyov,* p. 179.

41. Ibid.

42. Luknitsky, VAA, I, p. 65.

43. Trans. Roberta Reeder.

44. K. M. Azadovsky, "Menya nazval 'kitezhankoi' . . . ," p. 68. See also Chukovskaya, ZAA, I, p. 74.

45. Cited in Orlov, *Hamayun,* p. 348.

46. Ibid., p. 338.

47. Luknitskaya, *Nikolay Gumilyov,* p. 184.

48. Ibid., and A. N. Engelhardt cited in ibid., p. 207.

49. Ibid., p. 185.

50. See Cathy Porter, *Larissa Reisner* (London: Virago Press, 1988).

51. Luknitskaya, *Nikolay Gumilyov,* p. 189.

52. Ibid., p. 190.

53. Ibid., p. 191.

54. Ibid., p. 192.

55. Marina Tsvetayeva, "Iz ocherka 'Nezdeshnii vecher,' " in PBG, pp. 354–357.

56. Trans. by Roberta Reeder.

57. Chukovskaya, ZAA, II, p. 265. Bunin poem translated by Roberta Reeder. For original, see Dmitry Khrenokov, *Anna Akhmatova v Peterburge-Petrograde-Leningrade.* (Leningrad: Lenizdat, 1989).

58. Wendy Rosslyn, "Boris Anrep and the Poems of Anna Akhmatova," *Modern Language Review,* LXXIX (October 1979), p. 885. Neither Luknitsky nor Chukovskaya

notes any mention by Akhmatova of her knowledge of Anrep's affair with Maitland.

59. Wendy Rosslyn, "A propos of Anna Akhmatova: Boris Vasilyevich Anrep (1880–1969)," *New England Slavic Journal,* no. 1 (1980), p. 27.
60. Ibid., p. 29.
61. Cited in Fleishman, "Iz akhmatovskikh . . . ," p. 178.
62. Haight, personal communication.
63. G. Struve, "Akhmatova i Nikolay Nedobrovo," S-F, III, p. 386.
64. Boris Anrep, "O chyornem koltse," in S-F, III, p. 440.
65. Ibid., p. 442. Trans. Roberta Reeder.
66. Ibid., trans. Roberta Reeder.
67. *The Heritage of Russian Verse,* p. 92.
68. "The Lay of Igor's Campaign," in ibid., p. 4.
69. Vasily Gippius, "Anna Akhmatova," DG, p. 216. Originally in *Kuranty,* no. 2 (1918).
70. Sergey Rafalovich, "Anna Akhmatova," DG, p. 220. Originally in the Tbilisi, Georgia, journal *Ars,* no. 1 (1919).

CHAPTER 4: The Revolutionary Years: 1917–1922

1. Anna Akhmatova, "Avtobiograficheskaya proza," H-M, p. 227. See also MHC, p. 9.
2. Luknitskaya, *Nikolay Gumilyov,* p. 195.
3. See Adam Ulam, *Stalin: The Man and His Era* (Boston: Beacon Press, 1973), p. 130. See also von Rauch, *A History of Soviet Russia,* pp. 35–123.
4. Luknitskaya, *Nikolay Gumilyov,* p. 196.
5. Cited in Konstantin Rudnitsky, *Meyerhold the Director,* trans. George Petrov (Ardis: Ann Arbor, 1981), p. 231. Roman Timenchik mentions that in her autobiographical notes Akhmatova said she went to the performance with Anrep. See Boris Anrep, "O chyornom koltse," DG, p. 192.
6. Rudnitsky, *Meyerhold,* p. 235.
7. N. Drizen, "Iz stati 'Teatr vo vremya revolyutsii," PBG, p. 147.
8. Luknitskaya, *Nikolay Gumilyov,* p. 196.
9. Anna Akhmatova, "Iz pisem k Mikhailu Lozinskomu," DG, p. 212.
10. Riasanovsky, *A History of Russia,* p. 512.
11. Chukovskaya, ZAA, II, p. 206.
12. Anrep, "O chyornom koltse," DG, pp. 191–211.
13. Dmitry Segal, "Sumerki svobody: o nekotorykh temakh russkoi ezhednevnoi pechati 1917–1918 gg," *Minuvsheye,* no. 3 (1987), p. 162.
14. See von Rauch, *A History of Russia,* pp. 75–70, and Dmytryshan, pp. 78–79.
15. Mandelstam, trans. Roberta Reeder.
16. Chukovskaya, ZAA, I, p. 19.
17. "Iz besedy s L. S. Ilyashenko," *Requiem,* ed. R. D. Timenchik with K. M. Polivanov (Moscow: MPI, 1989, cited henceforth as *Requiem*), p. 27.
18. See Tatyana Nikolskaya, "Akhmatova v otsenke literaturnogo Tiflisa (1917–1920)," AS, I, pp. 83–88.
19. Chulkov, "Vchera i segodnya," *Narodopravstvo,* no. 12 (Oct. 16, 1917), cited in Malmstad, "Mikhail Kuzmin," p. 225.
20. Arthur Lourie, "Iz ocherka 'Nash marsh,' " PBG, p. 352. Original Lourie, "Nash march," *Novyi zhurnal,* no. 4 (1969), pp. 127–142.
21. See Camilla Gray, *The Russian Experiment in Art 1863–1922,* revised Marina Burleigh-Motley (London: Thames and Hudson 1986), pp. 219–244. Quotation at p. 224.
22. Akhmatova, "Mandelstam," H-M, p. 286. See also MHC, p. 94.

23. See also Lourie's beautiful passage on Mandelstam in "Detskii rai," PBG, p. 348. Original *Vozdushnye puti,* no. 3, 1963.
24. See Przybylski, *An Essay on the Poetry of Osip Mandelstam,* pp. 141–144. For original of poem, see Mandelstam, *Sobraniye sochinenii,* S-F, I, p. 70.
25. Przybylski, *Essay,* p. 142.
26. G. P. Makogonenko, "Iz tretei epokhi vospominanii," OAA, p. 267. Trans. Roberta Reeder.
27. Luknitskaya, *Nikolay Gumilyov,* pp. 146–201.
28. Ibid., p. 188.
29. Elaine Rusinko, "Gumilev in London: An Unknown Interview," RLT, no. 16 (1979), pp. 73–85.
30. Luknitskaya, *Nikolay Gumilyov,* pp. 201–202. For Larionov on Gumilyov's visit, see "Pisma M. F. Larionova o N. S. Gumilyove," Gumilyov, *Sobraniye sochienii,* S-F, I, pp. 403–411.
31. See B. Filippoff, cited in Luknitskaya, *Nikolay Gumilyov,* p. 203. Gumilyov left his papers with Anrep before returning to Russia. They were given to Struve, and are now in the Hoover Institute at Stanford in California.
32. Cited in Luknitskaya, *Nikolay Gumilyov,* p. 204. See Anrep, "O chyornom koltse," Akhmatova, S-F, III, p. 448.
33. Vyacheslav V. Ivanov, "Zvyozdnaya vspyshka (Poeticheksii mir N. S. Gumilyov)" in N. Gumilyov, *Stikhi, pisma o rusksom poezii* (Moscow: Khudozhestvennaya literatura, 1989), p. 18.
34. Luknitskaya, *Nikolay Gumilyov,* p. 204. See also Chukovskaya, ZAA, I, p. 161.
35. Personal communication.
36. Luknitsky, VAA, I, p. 273.
37. Chukovskaya, ZAA, I, p. 69.
38. Luknitsky, VAA, I, p. 44.
39. Sreznevskaya, DG, p. 213.
40. See Tamara Shileiko, "Legendy, mify i stikhi," *Novyi mir,* no. 4 (April 1986), pp. 199–213. Tamara Shileiko has carefully preserved a family archive on Shileiko, which she was kind enough to show me.
41. Ibid., p. 208. Nadezhda Mandelstam said Shileiko took Akhmatova to the house manager's office and registered the marriage there, although the manager was not authorized to approve marriages. She said nobody was quite certain in those days about the procedure for getting married, and Akhmatova thought this was sufficient. "Only when they parted did she understand the difference between the Register's Office [at the official House of Marriage] and the house manager's office," *Hope Against Hope,* p. 448. Nayman reports yet another version—that in those days it was sufficient for a couple wishing to register their marriage to make a declaration to the house management committee, and the marriage was considered legal when the house manager had made an entry in his book. Akhmatova found out when they separated that Shileiko had not done this. Anatoly Nayman, *Remembering Anna Akhmatova,* ed. and trans. Wendy Rosslyn (New York: Henry Holt and Co., 1991), p. 73.
42. Chukovskaya, ZAA, II, p. 34.
43. Luknitsky, *Pered toboi zemlya,* p. 314. He includes a sketch of the apartment.
44. Yeventov, "Ot Fontanki do Sitsilii," OAA, p. 376. Akhmatova told him that she and Shileiko moved immediately into the Marble Palace after they returned from Moscow.
45. Chukovskaya, ZAA, I, p. 71.
46. Yeventov, OAA, "Fontanki," p. 376.
47. Luknitsky, VAA, I, pp. 36 and 44.

48. H-N, p. 56.
49. See Tamara Shileiko. See also Nayman, p. 72.
50. Trans. Roberta Reeder. For original, see Shileiko, "V ozhestochyonnye . . . ," PBG, p. 328.
51. Luknitsky, VAA, I, p. 65.
52. Tamara Shileiko, p. 208. The Shileikos showed me a copy of the divorce certificate dated 1926.
53. Ibid., p. 207.
54. N. P. Kolpakova, "Stranitsy dnevnika," AA, p. 122.
55. George Fedotov, "Iz ocherka 'Tri stolitsy,' " PBG, p. 74. Original in *Versty*, no. 1 (Paris, 1926). Fedotov was a historian and journalist.
56. For an excellent article on the three houses, see Barry Scherr "Notes on Literary Life in Petrograd 1918–1922: A Tale of Three Houses," *Slavic Review*, vol. XXXVI, no. 2 (June 1977), pp. 256–268.
57. Vladislav Khodasevich, "Dom iskusstv," *Literaturnye stati i vospominaniya* (New York: Chekhov, 1954), pp. 399–411.
58. Adamovich, "Moi vstrechi," p. 105.
59. See Barry Sherr, "Notes on Literary Life."
60. Vladislav Khodasevich, "Gumilyov i Blok," NGVS, p. 204.
61. Luknitskaya, *Nikolay Gumilyov,* p. 208.
62. Chukovskaya, ZAA, I, p. 107.
63. Luknitskaya, *Nikolay Gumilyov,* p. 213.
64. Cited in ibid., p. 215.
65. Ida Nappelbaum, cited in ibid., p. 263.
66. Nikolay Otsup, "N. S. Gumilyov," NGVS, p. 176.
67. Ibid.
68. Luknitskaya, *Nikolay Gumilyov,* p. 225.
69. See ibid., p. 220.
70. Cited in ibid.
71. Anna Akhmatova, "Mandelstam," MHC, p. 91.
72. Anrep, "O chyornyom koltse," S-F, III, p. 447.
73. Anna Akhmatova, "Listki iz dnevnika [O Mandelstame]," ed. V. Vilenkin, *Voprosy literatury*, no. 2 (1989), p. 197.
74. Cited in Luknitskaya, *Nikolay Gumilyov,* p. 221.
75. Ibid., p. 190.
76. Chukovskaya, ZAA, I, p. 62.
77. Ibid.
78. Cited in *Requiem*, p. 31.
79. Luknitsky, VAA, I, p. 46.
80. Marina Tsvetayeva, "Iz stati 'Geroi truda,' " *Requiem*, p. 32. See Simon Karlinsky, *Marina Tsvetaeva* (Cambridge: Cambridge University Press, 1986), p. 97.
81. Luknitskaya, *Nikolay Gumilyov,* p. 228.
82. Ibid., p. 236.
83. V. V. Ivanov, "Zvyozdnaya vspyshka," p. 5.
84. Trans. Roberta Reeder. For original, see Gumilyov, *Stikhotvoreniya i poemy*, p. 331.
85. Cited in Luknitskaya, *Nikolay Gumilyov,* p. 230.
86. See Sheila Fitzpatrick, "NEP and the Future of the Revolution," *The Russian Revolution 1917–1932* (Oxford: Oxford University Press, 1982) pp. 85–109.
87. Nayman-Rosslyn, p. 201.
88. Akhmatova, "Amedeo Modigliani," MHC, p. 82.
89. Chukovsky, "Chukovsky . . . ," p. 234.

90. Luknitskaya, *Nikolay Gumilyov,* p. 247.
91. Cited in Luknitskaya, *Nikolay Gumilyov,* p. 248.
92. Ida Nappelbaum, "Fon k protretu Anny Andreyevny Akhmatovoi," OAA, pp. 198 and 200.
93. Timenchik and Lavrov, p. 62. See p. 64 for a copy of the actual handwritten charter. See also Aleksey Remizov, "Gorky. A Memoir," trans. Roberta Reeder, *Yale/Theatre* (1976), p. 99.
94. Vladislav Khodasevich, *Literaturnye stati i vospominaniya* (New York: Chekhov, 1954), p. 399.
95. Vladislav Khodasevich, *Nekropol* (Paris: YMCA Press, 1976), p. 123.
96. Luknitskaya, *Nikolay Gumilyov,* p. 249.
97. Cited in Woroszylski, *Life of Mayakovsky,* p. 202.
98. Ibid., p. 210.
99. Cited in Luknitskaya, *Nikolay Gumilyov,* p. 252.
100. Gleb Struve, "Blok and Gumilyov: A Double Anniversary," *Slavonic and East European Review* (1966), p. 176.
101. Blok, cited in Orlov, *Hamayun,* p. 457.
102. Ibid., p. 460.
103. Cited in ibid., p. 463.
104. Alexander Blok, "Pushkinskomu domu," Blok, Vol. III, pp. 376–377. Trans. Roberta Reeder.
105. Ibid., p. 446.
106. Vilenkin, *Vospominaniya,* p. 443.
107. Korney Chukovsky, "Excerpt from 'A. A. Blok—the Man,'" *Alexander Blok: An Anthology of Essays and Memoirs,* ed. and trans. Lucy Vogel, p. 75.
108. "Iz pisma V. Lyublinskoi," DG, p. 253.
109. E. Ts. Chukovskaya, ed. "Pisma Bloka k K. I. Chukovskomu i otryvki iz dnevnika K. I. Chukovskogo," *Literaturnoye nasledstvo: Aleksandr Blok, novye materialy i issledovaniya,* kn. 2 (Moscow: Nauka, 1981), pp. 256–257.
110. Larisa Reisner, "Iz pisma k A. A. Akhmatovoi," PV, p. 19.
111. Luknitskaya, *Nikolay Gumilyov,* p. 254.
112. For a detailed account of the so-called Tagantsev Affair, see Mikhail Heller and Aleksandr M. Nekrich, *Utopia in Power: The History of the Soviet Union from 1917 to the Present* (New York: Summit Books, 1986), pp. 139–140.
113. Cited in Luknitskaya, *Nikolay Gumilyov,* p. 200.
114. Ibid., p. 234.
115. Khodasevich, cited in Struve, "N. S. Gumilyov: Zhizn i lichnost," p. xxxvii.
116. Riasanovsky, *History of Russia,* p. 541.
117. Whether there had actually been a plot by Tagantsev or whether the whole thing had been fabricated on the orders of the Petrograd secret police will not be known until the KGB files are released. Key documents from the file that Luknitsky's wife and son looked at appear in their biography, *Nikolay Gumilyov,* published in 1990 in Leningrad. See Luknitskaya, *Nikolay Gumilyov,* pp. 265–298, for a detailed account of the files and Pavel Luknitsky's attempts to get Gumilyov rehabilitated. See also G. A. Terekhov, "Vozvrashchayas k delu N. S. Gumilyova," *Novyi mir,* no. 12 (December 1987), pp. 257–258.
118. Luknitskaya, *Nikolay Gumilyov,* p. 294. Davies, *Anna of All the Russias,* translates Orest's article from *Soviet Weekly* (May 14, 1988); it appears at pp. 134–135.
119. Adamovich, "Pamyati Gumilyova," NGVS, pp. 243–244.
120. Otsup, "N. A. Gumilyov," p. 180. See also Nikolay Volkovysky, "Delo N. S. Gu-

milyova," DG, p. 257, published first in Riga, *Segodnya* (February 3, 1923), p. 148, cited in Luknitskaya, *Nikolay Gumilyov,* p. 293.

121. Luknitskaya, *Nikolay Gumilyov,* p. 293. Most accounts say Gumilyov was shot on August 25. The preface to Gumilyov, *Izbrannoye (Selected Works),* says August 24, and Khodasevich says Gumilyov died August 27. The document condemning him to death is dated August 24, 1921 (see Luknitskaya, p. 295). On p. 271, in Paper No. 3, it says "K." initiated the arrest. Yevgeny and Yelena Pasternak, who discussed this material with me, suggest that this might refer to Mikhail Kalinin, Chairman of the Central Executive Committee of the Soviet, who had been sent to Kronstadt to attempt to prevent the rebellion.

122. Viktor Gorenko, "An Interview," p. 505.

123. Luknitskaya, *Nikolay Gumilyov,* p. 242, and Luknitsky, VAA, I, p. 53.

124. Chukovskaya, ZAA, II, p. 432.

125. Marina Tsvetayeva, "Pismo k Anne Akhmatovoi," *Requiem,* p. 34. See also notice advertising "Evening in memory of AA" in *Requiem,* p. 36. Tsvetayeva dates the letter according to the Old Style pre-Soviet calendar—after 1917 the Russian and Western calendars were the same.

126. Timenchik, "Predisloviye," *Requiem,* p. 8.

127. See Roberta Reeder, "Tsarskoe Selo in the Poetry of Anna Akhmatova: The Eternal Return," SUE, II, pp. 285–302, and Vitaly Vilenkin, "Tsarskoselskaya muza," *V sto pervom zerkale* (Moscow: Sovetskii pisatel, 1987), pp. 179–211.

128. Boris Eikhenbaum, "Roman-lirik," DG, p. 247. The review was published in the journal *Vestnik literatury,* nos. 6–7 (1921).

129. Luknitsky, VAA, I, p. 46.

130. Chukovsky, "Chukovsky . . . ," p. 234. Akhmatova's ballet libretto is based on Blok's collection of poems, "Snow Mask" (1908), dedicated to Natalya Volokhova, an actress with whom Blok was infatuated for some time. In her ballet scenario for *Poem Without a Hero,* Akhmatova depicts in the second vignette the actress looking through her window at a vision from "Snow Mask."

131. Annenkov, "Anna Akhmatova," *Dnevik,* I, p. 124.

132. Chukovsky, "Chukovsky . . . ," p. 234.

133. "Pisma Blok K. I. Chukovskomu i otryvki iz dnevnika K. I. Chukovskogo," ed. E. Ts. Chukovskaya, p. 253.

134. Anna Akhmatova, "Avtobiograficheskaya proza," H-M, p. 244.

135. Cited in Timenchik, *Requiem,* p. 9. From *Novyi put,* Riga (Dec. 22, 1921).

136. Mikhail Zenkevich, "U kamina s Annoi Akhmatovoi," PV, pp. 20–23.

137. Ida Nappelbaum, "Fon k portretu," OAA, p. 203.

138. Khodasevich, "Torgovlya," *Requiem,* pp. 43–44. Published in *Ogonyok,* no. 13 (1989).

139. Arthur Lourie, "Detskii rai," PBG, pp. 341–352. It first appeared in *Vozdushnye puti,* no. 3 (New York, 1963).

140. Ibid.

141. Trans. Roberta Reeder. Velimir Khlebnikov, "Odinokii litsedei," *Tvoreniya,* ed. M. Ya. Polyakov (Moscow: Sovetskii pisatel, 1986), p. 166.

142. Trans. Roberta Reeder.

143. See Yevgeny Pasternak, *Boris Pasternak: Materialy dlya biografii* (Moscow: Sovetskii pisatel, 1989), p. 370. See Gojowy, *Arthur Lourie,* p. 69, for a list of poems suggested by Irina Graham as dedicated by Akhmatova to Lourie. By the time Lourie and Akhmatova were living with Olga Sudeikina, her husband Sergey had left her for Vera de Bosset, who later became Igor Stravinsky's wife.

144. Luknitsky, VAA, I, p. 40.

145. See Anna Akhmatova, "Primechaniya," *Stikhotvoreniya i poemy,* ed. V. M. Zhirmunsky, Biblioteka poeta, Bolshaya seriya, 2nd ed. (Leningrad: Sovetskii pisatel, 1979), p. 474.

146. Luknitsky, VAA, I, p. 217.

147. Chukovsky, "Chukovsky . . . ," p. 235.

148. Chukovsky, "Pisma Blok," p. 258.

149. See Anna Akhmatova, "Pyostrye zametki," DG, p. 262, and "Random Notes," MHC, p. 35.

150. Ibid.

151. See Timenchik, "Khram premudrosti . . . " for an excellent analysis of Akhmatova's Kiev poems. He suggests the subtext of "Khram premudrosti . . . " is Nekrasov's work *Grandfather Frost,* about the peasant mother who has just buried her husband and to whom *Grandfather Frost* brings comfort as she dies of cold in the forest.

152. See Tamara Shileiko, p. 208. Trans. Roberta Reeder.

153. See Luknitsky, VAA, pp. 36 and 273, for her relationship with Lourie. Akhmatova tells Luknitsky that Shileiko was often difficult, but a good person (p. 273).

154. Jeanne van der Eng-Liedmeier notes that the turn to a historical or biblical figure by a Russian poet goes back to the Decembrist poets. They obliquely referred to forbidden political masters through quasi-historical descriptions of figures from the Bible or classical antiquity. See *Tale Without a Hero and Twenty-Two Poems* by Anna Akhmatova, trans. and ed. by Jeanne van der Eng-Liedmeier and Kees Verheul, Dutch Studies in Russian Literature, 3 (The Hague: Mouton, 1973), p. 23.

155. Arthur Lourie, "Pismo k Anne Akhmatovoi," PBG, p. 339.

CHAPTER 5: The Great Experiment: 1922–1930

1. See Dmytryshyn, "The Experimental Twenties," in *USSR: A Concise History,* pp. 115–156, and Gray, *The Russian Experiment in Art 1863–1922.*

2. Berdyaev, *Samopoznaniye,* p. 218.

3. Ibid., p. 311.

4. Nadezhda Mandelstam, *Hope Abandoned,* p. 11.

5. Mandelstam, "On the Nature of the Word," CCPL, p. 131.

6. Trans. Roberta Reeder.

7. Nayman-Rosslyn, p. 14.

8. Wladimir Weidle, "Iz ocherka 'Umerla Akhmatova,' " in *Posle vsego,* ed. R. D. Timenchik and K. M. Polivanov (Moscow: MPI, 1989, cited henceforth as PV), p. 71.

9. Chukovsky, "Chukovsky . . . ," p. 235.

10. Boris Eikhenbaum, *Anna Akhmatova: Opyt analiza* (Paris: Lev, 1980, first published 1922), p. 7.

11. Ibid., p. 114.

12. Annenkov, "Anna Akhmatova," *Dnevnik,* I, p. 120.

13. Chukovsky, "Akhmatova i Mayakovsky," *Dom iskusstv,* I (1920), p. 42.

14. Cited by Mikhail Kralin, "Kakaya yest. Zhelayu vam druguyu . . . ," OAA, p. 557.

15. Kuzmin, "Uslovnost," *Stati ob iskusstve* (Petrograd, 1923), p. 166, cited in Zhirmunsky, *Tvorchestvo,* p. 39.

16. Ibid.

17. Vladimir Mayakovsky, "Vystupleniye na pervom vechere 'Chistka sovremennoi poezii,' " in Vladimir Mayakovsky, *Polnoye sobraniye sochinenii,* ed. L. Yu. Brik, XII (Moscow: Khudozhestvennaya literatura, 1959), p. 460.

18. In Chukovskaya, ZAA, I, pp. 84 and 95.
19. Alexandra Kollontay, 'O 'drakone' i 'beloi ptitse,' " *Molodaya gvardiya* no. 2 (9) (1923), pp. 164–175, cited in Zhirmunsky, *Tvorchestvo*, p. 41. See also Kollontay, "Pisma k trudyashchesisya molodyozhi," *Requiem*, pp. 54–58.
20. Nikolay Osinsky (Obolensky), *Pravda*, (July 4, 1922), cited in Zhirmunsky, *Tvorchestvo*, p. 41. See also N. Osinsky, "Pobegi travy," *Requiem*, pp. 49–52.
21. V. Arvatov, "Grazhdanka Akhmatova i tovarishch Kollontay," *Molodaya gvardiya*, IV–V (1923), pp. 147–151, cited in Zhirmunsky, *Tvorchestvo*, p. 40.
22. P. Vinogradskaya, "Voprosy morali, pola, byta i t. Kollontay," *Krasnaya nov*, VI, no. 1 (1923), pp. 204–214, cited in Zhirmunsky, *Tvorchestvo*, p. 40.
23. G. Lelevich, "Anna Akhmatova," *Na postu*, nos. 2–3 (September–October 1923), p. 202, in *Na postu*, Vols. 1–6, 1923–25 (Munich: Wilhelm Fink, 1971). Lelevich is the pseudonym of Labor Kalmsanson (1910–1937), who was arrested at the end of 1934 and later shot. See also G. Lelevich, "Anna Akhmatova," *Requiem*, pp. 64–66.
24. Leon Trotsky, *Literature and Revolution*, trans. Rose Strunky (Ann Arbor: University of Michigan Press, 1971), p. 41.
25. N. N. Punin, "Revolyutsiya bez literatury," *Minuvsheye* (1989), p. 346.
26. Chukovsky, "Chukovsky . . . ," p. 228.
27. Nadezhda Chulkova, "Iz vospominanii," *Requiem*, p. 43.
28. Luknitsky, VAA, I, p. 8.
29. The poem on one level is about the relation of the average man and the state, and on another the relationship of man and nature. The prelude describes the rise of Petersburg from a swamp to grand capital of the Russian Empire. However, the story of the flood of 1824 is depicted in terms of how it affects Eugene, a simple clerk, who is overwhelmed by the power of the state embodied in Falconet's statue of Peter the Great, and who is also a victim of nature's attempt to destroy what man has built to overcome and destroy nature itself.
30. Valentina Shchogoleva, see R. D. Timenchik and A. V. Lavrov, "Materialy A. A. Akhmatovoi v rukopisnom otdele Pushkinskogo Doma," *Ezhegodnik rukopisnogo otdela Pushkinskogo Doma za 1974,* ed. Alekseyev, et. al., pp. 53–83.
31. See Chukovsky, "Iz dnevnika," *Requiem*, p. 70.
32. Luknitsky, VAA, I, p. 8.
33. A Sergeyev, "Iz stati 'Vcherashneye segodnya,' " *Requiem*, ed. Timenchik, p. 71. Original in *Pravda* (April 19, 1924).
34. H-N, p. 80.
35. Chukovskaya, ZAA, II, p. 46.
36. Nikita Struve, "Kolebaniya vdokhnoveniya v poeticheskom tvorchestve Akmatovoi," AS, p. 158.
37. Innokenty Basalayev, "Zapiski dlya sebya (1926–1939)," OAA, p. 172.
38. Matthew Frost, "Nikolai Punin and the 'Science' of Criticism,' " *Transactions of the Association of Russian-American Scholars in the USA,* vol. XIX (1986), pp. 253–269. On Punin, see also Arthur Lourie, "Nash marsh," *Novyi zhurnal*, no. 4, kn. 94 (1969), p. 140.
39. "Arestovannaya literatura," *Gosudarstvennaya bezopastnost i demokratiya*, no. 3 (Moscow, 1992), p. 37. I would like to thank Konstantin Azadovsky for making this source available to me.
40. Luknitsky, VAA, I, p. 88.
41. Ibid.
42. In a letter allegedly dated 1926, Akhmatova informs Shileiko that Manya is no longer working for her. Kralin says this is a reference to Mariya Lyubimova, who was Akhmatova's maid in the early 1920s. This obviously contradicts the information about

the extreme poverty and difficult conditions under which Akhmatova was living. See her letter to Shileiko, Anna Akhmatova, "Pisma," *Sochineniya v dvukh tomakh,* II, p. 194, and notes by Kralin, p. 369. See also Luknitsky, VAA, I, p. 92.

43. Luknitskaya, *Pered toboi zemlya,* p. 319.
44. Luknitsky, VAA, I, pp. 55 and 134.
45. Ibid., p. 44.
46. Akhmatova, "Mandelstam," MHC, p. 96. Akhmatova describes how much Mandelstam disliked Tsarskoye Selo. She said it was not "his element," and he was not at all impressed by its beauty or the fact that famous Russian writers had lived there.
47. Luknitskaya, *Pered toboi zemlya,* p. 334.
48. Luknitsky, VAA, I, p. 160.
49. Akhmatova, "Pisma," *Sochineniya,* ed. Kralin, II, p. 192. Akhmatova's mother was living with her sister, Anna Vakar. See also Luknitsky, VAA, I, p. 300, for her relationship to her mother.
50. Luknitskaya, *Pered toboi zemlya,* p. 300.
51. Ibid., p. 260.
52. See Luknitsky, VAA. Pavel's wife Vera Luknitskaya says her husband began visiting Akhmatova in the Sheremetev Palace (in the Punins' apartment) in 1927. Alexey and Tamara Shileiko kindly showed me the divorce certificate between Shileiko and Akhmatova, dated 1926, as well as photographs of Shileiko's wedding with Alexey's mother, Vera Andreyeva, in 1926.
53. Ibid., p. 217.
54. Trans. Roberta Reeder.
55. Woroszylski, *Life of Mayakovsky,* pp. 386 and 388.
56. Ibid., p. 392.
57. Trans. Roberta Reeder.
58. Trans. Roberta Reeder.
59. Luknitsky, VAA, I, p. 312.
60. Luknitskaya, *Pered toboi zemlya,* p. 319.
61. H-N, p. 80.
62. Luknitsky, VAA, I, p. 262.
63. Ibid., p. 320.
64. Translation based on Jessie Davies, *Anna of All the Russias* (Liverpool: Lincoln Davis & Co., 1988), p. 56. Original cited in Luknitskaya, *Pered toboi zemlya,* p. 297.
65. Tamara Shileiko, p. 209.
66. Luknitskaya, *Pered toboi zemlya,* p. 323.
67. Karlinsky, *Marina Tsvetaeva,* p. 115.
68. Marina Tsvetayeva, "Pismo k Akhmatovoi," *Requiem,* p. 83.
69. Lydia Ginzburg, "Iz starykh zapisei," OAA, p. 183.
70. Ibid., p. 184.
71. Luknitskaya, *Pered toboi zemlya,* p. 314.
72. See "O genii" in ibid., pp. 346–365, on Akhmatova and Pushkin.
73. H-N, p. 83.
74. Nadezhda Mandelstam, *Hope Against Hope,* trans. Max Hayward (New York: Atheneum, 1970, cited hereafter as HAH), pp. 173–174.
75. Akhmatova, "Mandelstam," ed. Vilenkin, p. 200. See also MHC, p. 97.
76. See Davies, *Anna of All the Russias,* p. 55.
77. H-N, p. 82.
78. Akhmatova, "Pisma," *Sochineniya,* II, ed. Kralin, p. 193.
79. Tamara Shileiko, p. 210.

80. Luknitskaya, *Pered toboi zemlya,* p. 380.
81. See the history of the non-publication of these two volumes in Timenchik, "Predis-loviye," *Requiem,* p. 10.
82. Ibid.
83. Luknitsky, "Iz dnevnika," *Requiem,* p. 86.
84. N. Osinsky, cited in Woroszylski, *Life of Mayakovsky,* p. 444.
85. Ibid., p. 509.
86. Ibid., p. 510.
87. Ibid., p. 526.
88. Ibid., p. 530.

CHAPTER 6: The Great Terror: 1930–1939

1. Nadezhda Mandelstam, HAH, p. 96.
2. Ibid., p. 113.
3. D. Usov, "Iz pisma k V. Rozhdestvenskomu," *Requiem,* p. 91.
4. N. Ya. Rykova, "Mesyatsa besformennyi oskolok . . . ," OAA, p. 175.
5. Chukovskaya, ZAA, I, p. 152.
6. Ibid., p. 128.
7. Vsevolod Petrov, "Fontannyi Dom," intro. L. S. Lukyanova and E. V. Tersky, *Nashe naslediye,* IV (1988), pp. 103–108.
8. Zamyatin sent the following letter February 1933: "Dear Zinaida, Just so in all the tumult of Paris I do not forget about Akhmatova—and you don't either, I'm writing you immediately upon my arrival. It would be best for Akhmatova if the package for her is sent to the following address [Agrafena Grozdova]. This is best, because she is sick and cannot go to customs for the package." Yevgeny Zamyatin, "Pismo k Z. Shakovskoi," *Requiem,* p. 104.
9. Yury Olesha, "Iz knigi *Ni dnya bez strochki*," *Requiem,* p. 94.
10. Roman Timenchik, "Predisloviye," *Requiem,* p. 19.
11. Nadezhda Mandelstam, HAH, p. 247. She notes on p. 174: "In two articles in *Russian Art* (Kiev) there were critical remarks about Akhmatova which were also a concession to the times. . . . The logic of the times demanded that M. part company with Akhmatova, his only possible ally. It is no easier for two than for one to swim against the tide, and he made this one attempt to cut himself off from her. But he very soon came to his senses. In 1927, when he was gathering his article together as a book, he threw out one of the pieces that had appeared in *Russian Art* and removed his attack from the other."
12. Clarence Brown, "Introduction," Osip Mandelstam, *Selected Poems,* trans. Clarence Brown and W. S. Merwin (New York: Atheneum, 1983), p. xiii.
13. Akhmatova, "Mandelstam," H-M, p. 289, and MHC, p. 99.
14. Nadezhda Mandelstam, HAH, p. 258.
15. Georgy Klychkov, "Nevyanyi istochnik-Sergei Klychkov, stikhi 30-kh godov," *Nashe naslediye* V, no. 11 (1989), p. 93.
16. Yelena Tager, "Iz vospominanii," *Requiem,* p. 93.
17. Tamara Silman and Vladimir Admoni, *My vospominayem* (St. Petersburg: Kompozitor, 1993), p. 201.
18. Akhmatova, "Mandelstam," H-M, p. 289, and MHC, p. 99.
19. Nadezhda Mandelstam, HAH, p. 314.
20. Akhmatova, "Mandelstam," H-M, p. 289, and MHC, p. 99.

21. Trans. Roberta Reeder. For the original, see Mandelstam, *Sobraniye sochinenii,* I, p. 167.
22. Trans. Roberta Reeder. For original, see Mandelstam, *Sobraniye sochinenii,* Vol. I, p. 195.
23. Akhmatova, "Mandelstam," H-M, p. 290, and MHC, p. 101.
24. Nadezhda Mandelstam, HAH, p. 15.
25. Akhmatova, "Mandelstam," H-M, p. 291, and MHC, p. 102.
26. Ibid., H-M, p. 291, and MHC, p. 103.
27. Nadezhda Mandelstam, HAH, p. 68.
28. Merle Fainsod, *How Russia Is Ruled* (Rev. ed. Cambridge, MA: Harvard University Press, 1963), p. 80.
29. Boris Pasternak and Olga Freidenberg, *The Correspondence of Boris Pasternak and Olga Freidenberg: 1900–1954,* trans. Elliott Moss and Margaret Wettlin (New York: Harcourt, Brace, Jovanovich, 1982), p. 175.
30. L. V. Yakovlev-Shaporina, "Leningrad v marte 1935 goda," ed. V. N. Sazhin, *Requiem,* p. 110. Lyubov Yakovleva-Shaporina (1885–1967) was an artist working with the puppet theater and wife of the composer Yu. A. Shaporin. She became friends with Akhmatova in Detskoye Selo (Tsarskoye Selo) in 1931. See her description of this period in *Requiem,* pp. 105–114.
31. Nadezhda Mandelstam, HAH, p. 91.
32. Ye. S. Bulgakova, "Iz dnevnika," *Requiem,* p. 116. Cited from Yelena Bulgakova, *Chudakova M.: zhizneopisaniye Mikhaila Bulgakova* (Moscow, 1988).
33. Timenchik, "Predisloviye," *Requiem,* p. 18.
34. Lev Gumilyov, " . . . Inache poeta net," *Zvezda,* no. 6 (1989), p. 129.
35. Ye. S. Bulgakova, "Iz dnevnika," *Requiem,* p. 116.
36. Ibid., p. 116, and Nayman-Rosslyn, p. 71. Akhmatova and others refer to Punin as her husband. They were never legally married. See also Chukovskaya, ZAA, II, p. 347.
37. See Ye. Pasternak, *Boris Pasternak,* Ye. Pasternak, personal communication.
38. Nayman-Rosslyn, p. 70.
39. Teren Masenko, "Iz romana *Vita pochtovaya*," *Requiem,* pp. 116–117. This excerpt also appeared in LO, no. 5 (1989), pp. 73–75. Teren Masenko (1903–1970) was a Ukrainian poet.
40. See Marc Slonim, *Soviet Russian Literature: Writers & Problems 1917–1967* (London: Oxford University Press, 1969), p. 66.
41. Trans. Roberta Reeder. Original Russian cited in K. M. Azadovsky, "Menya nazval 'Kitezhankoi,' " LO, no. 5 (1989), p. 65.
42. Ibid., p. 69.
43. See Ye. Pasternak, *Boris Pasternak,* p. 514.
44. Nadezhda Mandelstam, HAH, p. 162.
45. Gershtein, "Besedy ob Akhmatovoi s N. A. Olghevskoi-Ardovoi," LO, no. 5 (1989), p. 90.
46. Aleksey Batalov, "Ryadom s Akhmatovoi," *Neva,* no. 3 (1984), p. 158.
47. See chapter 31 of Nadezhda Mandelstam, HAH, for their life in Voronezh.
48. E. G. Gershtein, *Novoye o Mandelshtame* (Paris: Atheneum, 1986), pp. 272–281. This book is extremely important for clarifying errors in facts and evaluations of people's characters by Nadezhda Mandelstam. The book contains letters between Rudakov and Osip Mandelstam, entries from Rudakov's diaries, letters from Rudakov to his wife, and an analysis by Gershtein. See ibid., pp. 116–130, for a discussion of this episode. Gershtein says she does not know exactly when Akhmatova

gave Rudakov the files, but she received a telegram from Akhmatova, Mandelstam, and Rudakov from Leningrad in 1937 when Mandelstam was visiting Akhmatova.

49. Przybylski, *Essay*, p. 25. Mandelstam said, "Self-compassion is a parasitical emotion corrupting both the soul and the organism," "François Villon," CCPL, p. 56.
50. Lydia Ginzburg, *O lyrike* (Moscow and Leningrad: Sovetskii pisatel, 1964), p. 434.
51. Przybylski, *Essay*. The poem also appears on p. 195.
52. Nadezhda Mandelstam, HAH, p. 217.
53. See Akhmatova, *Sochineniya*, I, ed. Kralin, p. 402. The poem first appeared in *Leningrad*, no. 2 (1940), p. 9, without the last lines.
54. Nadezhda Mandelstam, HAH, p. 293.
55. Ibid., p. 314.
56. Akhmatova, "Mandelstam," H-M, p. 294, and MHC, p. 108.
57. Nadezhda Mandelstam, HAH, p. 369.
58. Akhmatova, H-M, p. 295, and MHC, p. 108.
59. Nadezhda Mandelstam, HAH, p. 377.
60. Akhmatova, H-M, p. 295, and MHC, p. 108.
61. Nadezhda Mandelstam, HAH, p. 369.
62. Ibid.
63. Cited in Yakovleva-Shaporina, "Iz dnevnika," p. 101.
64. Lev Gumilyov, " . . . Inache poeta net," p. 128.
65. Cited in Davies, *Anna of All the Russias*, p. 134, from *Sovietskii nedelnik (Soviet Weekly)*, May 14, 1988, p. 5.
66. Von Rauch, *A History of Soviet Russia*, p. 243.
67. Lydia Zhukova, "Iz knigi *Epilogi*," *Requiem*, p. 155. From *Epilogi* (New York, 1983), Vol. I.
68. Akhmatova, "Pages from a Diary," MHC, p. 13.
69. Nayman-Rosslyn, p. 127.
70. Milivoe Jovanovich, "K razboru . . . ," p. 171.
71. Joseph Brodsky, "The Keening Muse," in Brodsky, *Less Than One: Selected Essays* (New York: Farrar, Straus & Giroux, 1986), p. 51.
72. Amanda Haight, Akhmatova's first biographer, suggests that these lines harken back to the poems written right after the Revolution, such as "To the Many":

I—am your voice, the warmth of your breath,
I—am the reflection of your face,
The futile trembling of futile wings,
I am with you to the end, in any case.

(I, p. 619)

H-N, p. 100.
73. Michael Basker, "Dislocation and Relocation in Akhmatova's *Rekviem*," SUE, I, p. 9.
74. See "The Lay of Igor's Campaign," *The Heritage of Russian Verse*, p. 4.
75. In America the black prison van is known as "the Black Maria." A poem by Langston Hughes incorporates this image in his poem "Must be the Black Maria," in which the poet says he hopes "it ain't coming for me." See Langston Hughes, *Selected Poems of Langston Hughes* (New York: Vintage Books 1974,), p. 118.
76. In Akhmatova, "Mandelstam," MHC, p. 101, Akhmatova says she quoted lines from this poem when she was visiting Mandelstam, and he thanked her for them. However,

she makes it clear she originally wrote it for Punin: "That poem is from *Requiem* and refers to the arrest of Nikolai Punin in 1935."

77. See Efim Etkind, "Die Unsterbichkeit des Gedachtnisses: Anna Achmatova's poem 'Requiem,' " *Die Welt der Slaven,* XXIX (1984), p. 363.
78. Reeder, *Russian Folk Lyrics,* p. 155.
79. Basker, "Dislocation," p. 11.
80. Trans. Roberta Reeder.
81. See Etkind, "Ob Fontanki," p. 373.
82. Zoya Tomashevskaya, "Introduction" to Anna Akhmatova, "Requiem," *Oktyabr,* no. 3 (1987), p. 130.
83. H-N, p. 105.
84. The Requiem service, called *pannykhida,* is held immediately after death, when the reading of the Psalter begins by the dead person's coffin. The body is later taken to a church burial, and a funeral service is held. A manual of the Orthodox Church's Divine Service describes the remembrance days—days set apart by the Church for the commemoration of all deceased Christians, apart from private commemoration of the deceased at the wish of friends and relatives. The services for these general days are called "Universal Requiems" and the days are called "ancestral days." One of the most important is on Monday or Tuesday of St. Thomas week, the week after Easter, when families go to the cemetery and feast at the side of the ancestral graves. D. Sokolof, *A Manual of the Orthodox Church's Divine Services* (Jordanville, NY: Holy Trinity Monastery, 1975), p. 157.
85. Chukovskaya, ZAA, I, p. 8.
86. Ibid.
87. Ibid., p. 10. Chukovskaya recorded this conversation November 10, 1938.
88. Personal communication.
89. Chukovskaya, ZAA, I, p. 245.
90. Ibid., pp. 30–33. The diary entry is August 28, 1939.
91. Ibid., p. 8.
92. Ibid., p. 10.
93. Dmitry Khrenkov, "Ob Anne Akhmatova," in Anna Akhmatova, *Stikhi i prozy* (Leningrad: Lenizdat, 1976), p. 6.
94. Chukovskaya, ZAA, I, p. 49.
95. See Riasanovsky, *A History of Russia,* p. 584, where he cites Zhdanov's speech: "We demand that our comrades, both as leaders in literary affairs and as writers, be guided by the vital force of the Soviet order—its politics. Only thus can our youth be reared, not in a devil-may-care attitude and spirit of ideological indifference, but in a strong and vigorous revolutionary spirit."
96. Cited in Emma Gershtein, "Poslesloviye," Anna Akhmatova, *Anna Akhmatova o Pushkine* (Leningrad: Sovetskii pisatel, 1977), p. 280.
97. Ibid.
98. Chukovskaya, ZAA, I, p. 259.
99. Chukovsky, "Chukovsky . . . ," *Novyi mir,* p. 233.
100. Chukovskaya, ZAA, I, p. 145.
101. Ibid., p. 38.
102. Ibid., p. 50.
103. Ibid., p. 128.
104. Ibid., p. 144.
105. Ibid., p. 183.
106. See letter to Shileiko, suggested date 1926, in Akhmatova, "Pisma," *Sochineniya v*

dvukh tomakh, II, p. 194, where she informs Shileiko, "Manya is no longer working for me," and Kralin's note, p. 369, saying this refers to Mariya Lyubimova, who was Akhmatova's maid at the beginning of the 1920s.

107. Chukovskaya, ZAA, I, p. 133.
108. Ginzburg, "Iz starykh zapisei," OAA, p. 190.
109. Vadim Shefner, "Poeziya silnee, chem sudba," OAA, p. 412–414.
110. M. V. Latmanizov, "Besedy s A. A. Akhmatovoi," OAA, p. 528, and Timenchik, "Predisloviye," *Requiem,* p. 21.
111. V. Pertsov, "Chitaya Akhmatovu," *Requiem,* p. 159.
112. Cited in H-N, p. 111.
113. Chukovskaya, ZAA, I, p. 138. Centrifuge was the group based in Moscow from 1913 to 1917, which included Boris Pasternak, Sergey Bobrov, and Nikolay Aseyev. Although the members considered themselves associated with Futurism, they were much less radical than Futurists such as Mayakovsky and Khlebnikov.
114. Haight omits this passage in her book. Trans. Roberta Reeder. Orig. "Pasternak—Akhmatova," in Boris Pasternak "Iz perepiski s pisatelyami," ed. Ye. B. and Ye. V. Pasternak, *Literaturnoye nasledstvo* (Moscow: Nauka, 1983), p. 661.
115. Boris Pasternak, "It seems I'm choosing . . . ," trans. Roberta Reeder.
116. Chukovskaya, ZAA, I, p. 70.
117. Yeventov, "Ot Fontanki do Sitsilii," OAA, p. 360. See also the excellent article on Mayakovsky and Akhmatova, S. A. Kovalenko, "Akhmatova i Mayakovsky," *Tsarstvennoye slovo,* ed. N. V. Korolyova and S. A. Kovalenko (Moscow: Naslediye, 1992), pp. 166–180.
118. Nayman-Rosslyn, p. 89.
119. Karlinsky, *Marina Tsvetaeva,* p. 222.
120. Viktor Ardov, "Iz *Vospominanii ob Anne Akhmatovoi," Den poezii 1982* (Moscow: Sovetskii pisatel, 1982), p. 79.
121. Cited in Chukovskaya, ZAA, II, p. 534. See also Tsvetayeva, "Iz dnevnika," PBG, p. 367.
122. Cited in Adamovich, "Moi vstrechi," p. 110.
123. H-N, p. 111. See also Nina Olshevskaya's description of the Tsvetayeva-Akhmatova meeting, in Emma Gershtein, "Besedy ob . . . ," LO, no. 5 (1989).
124. Chukovskaya, ZAA, II, p. 374.
125. Ibid., p. 98.
126. The Roman poet Ovid, banished to the Black Sea, represented for Pushkin the archetypal "poet in exile" who longed for his native city. Pushkin identifies with Ovid in his poem "To Ovid" since he had been banished by the tsar to the same area. Pamela Davidson, "Akhmatova's 'Dante,' " in SUE, II, pp. 201–204.
127. Trans. Roberta Reeder.
128. See notes to poem, Zhirmunsky in Akhmatova, *Stikhotvoreniya,* 1979, p. 478.
129. Chukovskaya, ZAA, I, p. 143.
130. See Kralin, "Notes," Akhmatova, *Sochineniya v dvukh tomakh,* I, p. 417.
131. Sonia Ketchian, "The Genre of Podrazheniye and Anna Achmatova," *Russian Literature,* XV (1984), p. 163.
132. Trans. Roberta Reeder.
133. Nadezhda Mandelstam, HAH, p. 3.

CHAPTER 7: The War Years: 1939–1945

1. Harrison E. Salisbury, *The 900 Days: The Siege of Leningrad* (New York: De Capo Press, 1985; first published 1965).
2. Dmytryshn, p. 212. See also von Rauch, *A History of Soviet Russia,* p. 279.
3. Von Rauch, "The Winter Campaign Against Finland," pp. 289–292.
4. Pasternak, *Selected Writings and Letters,* trans. Catherine Judelson, p. 389.
5. H-N, p. 116.
6. See Azadovsky, "Menya nazval 'Kitezhankoi,' " p. 69. Akhmatova says she wrote a draft of *The Way of All Earth* the night of the storming of Vyborg. See "From a Letter to ***," MHC, p. 13.
7. Cited by Zhirmunsky in Akhmatova, *Stikhotvoreniya i poemy,* p. 511. Trans. Roberta Reeder.
8. H-N, p. 116.
9. Dmytryshn, p. 216.
10. Salisbury, *The 900 Days,* p. 66.
11. Ibid., p. 133.
12. Ibid., p. 175.
13. Ibid.
14. Pasternak and Freidenberg, *The Correspondence,* p. 226.
15. Ibid., p. 211.
16. Olga Berggolts, *Bibloteka izbranoi liviki* (n.p.: Molodaya guardiya, 1964), pp. 11–12. Trans. Roberta Reeder.
17. Pasternak and Freidenberg, *The Correspondence,* p. 227.
18. H-N, p. 122.
19. Cited by A. I. Pavlovsky, *Anna Akhmatova* (Leningrad: Lenizdat, 1982), p. 99.
20. G. P. Makogonenko, "Iz tretei epokhi vospominanii," OAA, p. 263.
21. Z. B. Tomashevskaya, "Ya—kak peterburgskaya tumba," OAA, p. 420–426.
22. Cited by Salisbury, *The 900 Days,* p. 364.
23. Nadezhda Chulkova, "Iz vospominanii," *Requiem,* p. 167.
24. Tomashevskaya, "Ya—kak peterburgskaya tumba," OAA, p. 429.
25. Aliger, *Tropinka vo rzhi,* p. 341. See also Ye. Pasternak, *Boris Pasternak,* p. 556.
26. Karlinsky, *Tsvetaeva,* p. 245.
27. Chukovskaya, ZAA, I, p. 191.
28. Ibid., p. 191.
29. Ibid., p. 196.
30. A personal friend of Akhmatova's has suggested that Akhmatova did not like the way Chukovskaya was treating Nadezhda Mandelstam.
31. Cited in Pavlovsky, "Eto pleshchet Neva o stupeni . . . ," p. 197.
32. Chukovskaya, ZAA, II, p. xv.
33. Akhmatova, "Pisma," Kralin, II, p. 201.
34. Tomashevskaya, "Ya—kak peterburgskaya tumba," OAA, p. 572.
35. H-N, p. 128.
36. Svetlana Somova, "Mne dali imya—Anna," *Moskva,* no. 3 (1984), pp. 184 and 187.
37. Ibid., p. 188.
38. Chukovskaya, ZAA, I, p. 15.
39. Joseph Czapski, *The Inhuman Land,* trans. Gerard Hopkins (London: Chatto & Windus, 1951), p. 191.
40. Cited in Rostislav Aleksandrov, "Dobrota svetilas v nei . . . ," *Vechernyaya Odessa,* July 21, 1989, p. 3.
41. Somova, "Mne dali imya," p. 189. See also Svetlana Somova, "Ten na glinyanoi stene:

Anna Akhmatova v Tashkente, pt. 2," *Moskva,* no. 10 (1986), p. 182. For an extensive list of Akhmatova's works set to music, see "Muzykalnye sochineniya na stikhi Anny Akhmatovoi," compiled by B. Rozenfeld in Kats and Timenchik, *Akhmatova i muzyka,* pp. 280–307.

42. Pushkin was exiled to the south of the Russian Empire from 1820 to 1824. It was a very creative period of his life. He wrote poems reflecting the exotic nature in the area and the cosmopolitan atmosphere, where Greeks, Serbs, and Gypsies lived among the Ukrainian and Russian population. Still, Pushkin longed to be back in Petersburg with his friends.

43. Chukovskaya, ZAA, II, p. xix.

44. Somova, "Mne dali imya," p. 183.

45. Trans. Roberta Reeder.

46. Cited in I. Sluzhevskaya, "Tak vot ty kakoi, Vostok!" *Zvezda vostoka,* no. 5 (1982), p. 96.

47. Akhmatova, "Korotko o sebe," H-M, p. 214. See also "Pages from a Diary," MHC, p. 27.

48. Akhmatova, "Vospominaniya," H-M, p. 249.

49. See Somova, "Mne dali imya," p. 186, on Akhmatova's illness in Tashkent.

50. Akhmatova, "Pisma," *Sochineniya,* Kralin, II, p. 219.

51. Pasternak, "Novyi sbornik," *Zvezda,* no. 6 (1989), p. 146.

52. See de Mallac, *Boris Pasternak,* p. 168.

53. Akhmatova, "Pisma," *Sochineniya,* ed. Kralin, II, p. 218.

54. Ibid., p. 371.

55. Babayev, "Na ulitse Zhukovskoi . . . ," LO, no. 7 (1985), pp. 99–104.

56. Akhmatova, "Pisma," *Sochineniya,* ed. Kralin, II, p. 205.

57. Ibid., p. 204.

58. Vilenkin, *Vospominaniya,* p. 145.

59. Kralin, "Notes," in Akhmatova, *Sochineniya,* ed. Kralin, II, p. 370.

60. Somova, "Mne dali imya," pp. 188–190.

61. Nadezhda Mandelstam, *Hope Abandoned,* p. 352.

62. Zhirmunsky in Akhmatova, *Stikhhotvoreniya i poemy,* p. 509.

63. See notes to Zhirmunsky edition, pp. 508–510.

64. Admoni, *My vspominayem,* p. 287.

65. Nadezhda Mandelstam, *Hope Abandoned,* p. 352.

66. Tomashevskaya, "Ya—kak peterburgskaya tumba," pp. 426–430.

67. Budyko, Yu. I., "Istoriya . . . ," p. 236. Aliger writes that Garshin's wife died in the winter of 1941 (*Tropinka,* p. 349).

68. Aliger, *Tropinka vo rzhi,* p. 349.

69. Nadezhda Mandelstam, *Hope Abandoned,* p. 449.

70. Budyko, Yu. I., "Istoriya . . . ," p. 237.

71. Akhmatova, "Pisma," *Sochineniya,* II, ed. Kralin, p. 201.

72. Ibid., p. 203.

73. Gershtein, "Besedy ob . . . ," p. 91.

74. N. D. Kolpakova, "Stranitsy dnevnika," OAA, p. 127.

75. Aliger, *Tropinka vo rzhi,* p. 348.

76. Budyko, Yu. I., "Istoriya . . . ," pp. 237–238.

77. Gershtein, "Besedy ob . . . ," p. 91.

78. Budyko, Yu. I., "Istoriya . . . ," p. 238.

79. Ibid., p. 238.

80. Akhmatova, "Vospominaniya," H-M, p. 214.

81. Yakovleva-Shaporina, "Iz dnevnika," *Requiem,* p. 192.

82. Makogonenko, ". . . Iz tretei epokhi vospominanii," p. 265.
83. Silvia Gitovich, "Ob Anne Andreyevne," OAA, p. 335.

CHAPTER 8: The Cold War Begins: 1946–1952

1. See Dmytryshyn, *USSR,* pp. 240–264.
2. Martin Gilbert, *Winston Churchill,* Vol. VIII (London: Heinemann, 1988), pp. 200–203. See Stalin's Election Speech, February 9, 1946, in Dmytryshyn, *USSR,* pp. 491–500.
3. Brodsky, *Less Than One,* p. 4.
4. Her poems were published in 1945–1946 in the journals *Znamya, Zvezda,* and *Leningrad.*
5. Tatyana Vecheslova, "Yeyo tainstvennyi golos," OAA, pp. 282–289.
6. N. N. Punin, "Iz dnevnka," *Requiem,* p. 194.
7. Ibid., p. 195.
8. I. N. Punina, "Sorok shestoi god . . . ," VOAA, p. 465. See Lev Gumilyov, ". . . Inache poety net," p. 128.
9. H-N, p. 140. Svetlana Kovalenko, "Akhmatova i Mayakovsky," *Tsarstvennoye slovo,* ed. N. V. Korolyova and S. A. Kovalenko (Moscow: Naslediye, 1922), identifies the critic who told Berlin about Akhmatova as Vladimir Orlov, p. 171.
10. Isaiah Berlin, "Anna Akhmatova: A Memoir," in Anna Akhmatova, *The Complete Poems,* II, p. 35.
11. Ibid., p. 27.
12. Punina, "Sorok shestoi god . . . ," p. 466.
13. Chulkova, "Iz vospominanii," *Requiem,* p. 226.
14. A. A. Gozenpud, "Neuvyadshiye listya," OAA, p. 324.
15. Nadezhda Mandelstam, HAH, pp. 18–19.
16. See D. E. Maksimov, "Ob Anna Akhmatovoi, kakoi pomnyu," VOAA, p. 119, on this evening.
17. Chukovskaya, ZAA, II, p. 25.
18. Konstantin Simonov, "Iz knigi *Glazami cheloveka moyego pokoleniya,*" *Requiem,* p. 225.
19. Davies, *Anna of All the Russias,* p. 135.
20. Silvia Gitovich, "Ob Anne Andreyevne," OAA, p. 332.
21. H-N, p. 144. For the full text of the Regulation, see KPSS, "O zhurnalakh *Zvezda* i *Leningrad:* iz postanovleniya TsK VKPb); ot 14-ogo avgusta 1946 g," in *Zvezda,* VII–VIII, 1946, and *KPSS v rezolyutsiyakh i resheniyakh 1925–1953* (Moscow, 1953), pp. 1019–1027. For Zhdanov's speech to the Union, see "Doklad t. Zhdanova o zhurnalakh *Zvezda* i *Leningrad,*" *Znamya,* X (1946), pp. 7–22.
22. Slonim, *Soviet Russian Literature,* p. 161.
23. Ida Nappelbaum, "Fon k portretu Ann Andreyevna Akhmatovoi," *Requiem,* p. 232.
24. Innokenty Basalayev, "Iz ocherka na doklade Zhdanova," *Requiem,* p. 232.
25. De Mallac, *Boris Pasternak,* p. 184.
26. Punina, "Sorok shestoi god . . . ," p. 466.
27. Gershtein, "Nina Antonovna," LO, no. 5 (1989), p. 93.
28. Ilya Ehrenburg, *Post-War Years 1945–1954: Men, Years, Life,* Vol. VI, trans. Tatiana Shebunina in collaboration with Yvonne Kapp (London: McGibbon & Kee, 1966), p. 55.
29. Lazar Fleishman, *Boris Pasternak: The Poet and His Politics* (Cambridge, MA: Har-

vard University Press, 1990), p. 249. See also Detlef Gojowy, *Dimitri Schostakowitsch* (Hamburg: Rowohlt, 1983), p. 59.

30. Cited in L. K. Kozlov, "Ten groznogo i Khudozhnik," *Kinovedcheskii zapiski,* no. 15 (1992), p. 41. See also Yon Barna, *Eisenstein: The Growth of a Cinematic Genius* (Boston: Little, Brown, 1973), p. 265.

31. Chukovskaya, ZAA, II, p. xii.

32. Ibid., p. ix.

33. T. Trifonova, "Iz stati 'Ob oshibkakh leningradskikh kritikov,' " *Requiem,* p. 245.

34. I. V. Sergiyevsky, "Iz stati 'Ob antinarodnoi poezii A Akhmatovoi,' " *Requiem,* p. 240.

35. Vs. Vishnevsky, "Iz vystupleniya Vs. Vishnevskogo," *Requiem,* p. 248.

36. Viktor Sidelnikov, "Iz stati 'Protiv izvrashcheniya i nizkopoklonchestva v sovetskoi folkloristike,' " *Requiem,* p. 265.

37. Yakovleva-Shaporina contradicts this. She says Eikhenbaum was the only writer who refused to act against Akhmatova and that he objected that he was an old man and no one would believe him if he should begin criticizing Akhmatova, whom he had always loved. As a result of his refusal to cooperate with the authorities, says Shaporina, he was removed from all his posts and his wife suffered so much that she became ill and died. See Yakovleva-Shaporina, "Iz dnevnika," *Requiem,* p. 260.

38. A. Fadeyev, "Iz stati 'O traditsiyakh slavyanskoi literatury,' " *Requiem,* p. 258.

39. *Dukhovnaya kultura* in Russian means something intellectual, mental, related to the humanities, religion, philosophy, and sociology in contrast to the natural sciences, whereas in English the phrase "spiritual culture" is associated specifically with religion.

40. N. S. Berdyaev, "O tvorcheskoi svobode i fabrikatsii dush," *Requiem,* pp. 252–258.

41. Punina, "Sorok shestoi god . . . ," p. 470.

42. E. K. Galperina-Osmerkina, "Vstrechi s Akhmatovoi," *Vospominaniya,* p. 244.

43. Gitovich, "Ob Anne Andreyevne," OAA, p. 334.

44. Cited in Lev Shilov, *Anna Akhmatova (100 let so dnya rozhdeniya)* (Moscow: Znaniye, 1989), p. 35.

45. Lev Gumilyov, ". . . Inache poety net," p. 131.

46. Makogonenko, "Iz tretei epokhi vospominanii," OAA, p. 271. Evgeny Shvarts wrote a series of satires in the German *Kunstmärchen* tradition, using fairy tale to convey political satire. One example is his play *The Naked Emperor,* an attack against Hitler told in the form of two tales by Hans Christian Andersen—*The Emperor's New Clothes* and *The Princess and the Pea.* See Roberta Reeder, "The Naked Emperor—A Modern Fairy Tale," *Satire Newsletter,* 1971. Shvarts's most famous play in the West is *The Dragon,* which is specifically related to Stalin, but attacks tyranny in general.

47. Makogonenko, "Iz tretei epokhi vospominanii," OAA, p. 273.

48. Makogonenko, "O sbornike Anny Akhmatovoi 'Nechet,' " *Voprosy literatury,* no. 2 (1986), pp. 170–190.

49. Gershtein, "Nina Antonovna," p. 93.

50. Akhmatova, "Kamennyi gost Pushkina," *O Pushkine,* p. 89. See Susan Amert, *In a Shattered Mirror: The Later Poetry of Anna Akhmatova* (Stanford, CA: Stanford University Press, 1992), for a discussion of the relationship between Akhmatova and Pushkin and their reception by readers.

51. Yakovleva-Shaporina, "Iz dnevnika," *Requiem,* p. 264.

52. Pasternak and Freidenberg, *The Correspondence,* p. 277.

53. Ibid., p. 289.

54. Yakovleva-Shaporina, "Iz dnevnika," *Requiem,* p. 266.

55. A. Vaneyev, "Iz ocherka 'Dva goda v Abezi,' " *Requiem*, pp. 266–277.
56. Punina, "Sorok shestoi god . . . ," p. 471.
57. Lev Gumilyov, ". . . Inache poety net," p. 131.
58. Gershtein, "Besedy s N. A.," p. 94.
59. Yakovleva-Shaporina, "Iz dnevnika," *Requiem*, p. 281.
60. Gershtein, "Besedy s N. A.," p. 94. Maria Petrovykh (1908–1979) first published a book of poems, *Distant Tree*, in 1968 in Yerevan, Armenia. Akhmatova considered her poem "Make an Appointment with Me in This World" one of the greatest poems of the twentieth century. See Chukovskaya, ZAA, II, p. 564.
61. Yakovleva-Shaporina, "Iz dnevnika," *Requiem*, p. 281.
62. E. G. Gershtein, "Memuary i fakty (ob osvobozhdenii Lva Gumilyova)," RLT, no. 13 (1976), p. 646.
63. Gershtein, "V zamoskvoreche," LO, no. 7 (1985), p. 106.
64. Nadezhda Mandelstam, HAH, p. 103.
65. Lydia Ginzburg, "Iz zapisei," *Requiem*, p. 280.
66. Gershtein, "Beseda s N. A.," p. 94.
67. Makogonenko, ". . . Iz tretei epokhi vospominanii," OAA, pp. 279–280.
68. A. K. Anaksagorova, "V kvartire na ulitse Krasnoi Konnitsy," OAA, p. 291.
69. Alexey Batalov, "Ryadom s Akhmatovoi," VOAA, p. 560. See also "Ryadom s Akhmatovoi, *Neva*, no. 3 (1984), pp. 155–164.
70. Ibid., p. 564.
71. Chukovskaya, ZAA, II, p. 1.

CHAPTER 9: The Thaw: 1953–1958

1. Riasanovsky, *A History of Russia*, p. 596.
2. Dmytryshyn, *USSR*, p. 277.
3. Ibid., pp. 291–296.
4. Akhmatova, *Sochineniya* . . . , ed. Kralin, II, p. 225.
5. H-N, p. 162. See note by Max Hayward in N. Mandelstam, *Hope Abandoned*, p. 357. See also Anaksagorova, "V kvartire . . . ," OAA, p. 293.
6. Dmytryshyn, *USSR*, p. 278.
7. Chukovskaya, ZAA, II, p. 137.
8. Ibid., p. 144.
9. For the best description of the various phases of the attempt to free Lev, see Gershtein's "Memuary i fakty," pp. 103–114.
10. Chukovskaya, ZAA, II, p. 110. Trans. Roberta Reeder.
11. Citied in H-N, p. 163.
12. Chukovskaya, ZAA, II, p. 152.
13. Ibid., p. 151.
14. Ibid., p. 156.
15. Shilov, *Anna Akhmatova*, p. 36.
16. De Mallac, *Boris Pasternak*, p. 209.
17. Ibid., p. 209.
18. Published in *Requiem*, p. 286. Originally in Gershtein, "Memuary i fakty," Anna Akhmatova.
19. Chukovskaya, ZAA, II, p. 193.
20. Chukovsky, "Chukovsky . . . ," p. 237.
21. Chukovskaya, ZAA, II, p. 171.
22. Berlin, "Anna Akhmatova," p. 37.

23. Natalya Ilyina, "Anna Akhmatova v posledniye gody yeyo zhizni," *Oktyabr,* no. 2 (February 1977), pp. 107–134.
24. Gershtein, "V zamoskvroreche," LO, no. 7 (1985), p. 547.
25. Ilyina, "Anna Akhmatova . . . ," p. 123.
26. Akhmatova, "Beryozy," H-M, p. 256.
27. Punina, "Ob Anne Akhmatovoi i Valerii Sreznevskoi," VOAA, II, p. 597.
28. Chukovskaya, ZAA, II, p. 597.
29. See Margarita Aliger, "V poslednii raz," VOAA, pp. 349–368, for a description of these events.
30. *Literaturnaya Moskva* came out in one volume (1956). The second volume was prohibited.
31. Chukovskaya, ZAA, II, p. 193.
32. H-N, p. 173. See Lev Ozerov, "Stikhotvoreniya Anny Akhmatovoi," *Literaturnaya gazeta,* June 23, 1959, p. 3.
33. Chukovskaya, ZAA, II, p. 230.
34. Aliger, "V poslednii raz," p. 362.
35. See H-N, p. 175.
36. Chukovskaya, ZAA, II, p. 229.
37. Ibid., p. 193.
38. Ibid., p. 245.
39. See Marc Slonim, "Mikhail Zoshchenko," *Soviet Russian Literature,* pp. 90–96.
40. Zoya Tomashevskaya helped establish this museum.
41. *Requiem,* p. 121.

CHAPTER 10: Pasternak: The Nobel Prize and Death, 1958–1960

1. Boris Pasternak, "Anna Akhmatova," *Poems,* p. 159.
2. Vilenkin, *V sto pervom zerkale,* p. 31. Poem trans. Roberta Reeder. This stanza was originally meant for the poem to Pasternak "And once more the autumn blasts like Tamerlane" (*snova osen valit Tamerlanom*). Vilenkin says it then seemed to have the right to exist as a separate poem. It appears in the Kralin edition of Akhmatova's poems as part of "And once more. . . ." See Akhmatova, *Sochineniye . . . ,* ed. Kralin, I, p. 252.
3. Berlin, "Anna Akhmatova," II, p. 41.
4. Boris Pasternak, "People and Attitudes: An Autobiographical Sketch," *Selected Writings and Letters,* p. 249.
5. Chukovskaya, ZAA, II, p. 5.
6. See "Safe-Conduct," *Selected Writings and Letters,* pp. 117–144. For Pasternak's Marburg period, see Boris Pasternak, *Sommer 1912: Briefe aus Marburg,* ed. and trans. Sergej Dorzweiler (Marburg: Blaue Hörner Verlag, 1990). Dorzweiler and Lazar Fleishman are working on a major project examining the influence of the Marburg School of philosophy on Pasternak's works.
7. Cited in de Mallac, *Boris Pasternak,* p. 74.
8. Ye. Pasternak, *Boris Pasternak,* p. 213. Trans. Roberta Reeder.
9. Ibid., p. 214.
10. Fleishman, *Boris Pasternak: The Poet and His Politics,* p. 69.
11. Christopher Barnes, *Boris Pasternak: A Literary Biography,* Vol. I (Cambridge: Cambridge University Press, 1989), p. 187. See also "People and Attitudes," p. 287.
12. See Lily Brik, "Chuzhiye stikhi," *V. Mayakovsky vo vospominaniyakh sovremennikov* (Moscow: Gosudarstvennoye izdatelstvo khudozhestvennoi literatury, 1963), p. 333.

13. Trans. Roberta Reeder. For original, see Mayakovsky, *Polnoye sobroniye,* Vol. I, p. 176.
14. See Boris Pasternak, *Stikhotvoreniya i poemy,* I, Biblioteka poeta, bolshaya seriya, 3rd ed. (Leningrad: Sovetskii pisatel, 1990), p. 114. Poem trans. Roberta Reeder.
15. See Olga Hughes, *The Poetic World of Boris Pasternak* (Princeton: Princeton University Press, 1974), p. 42, and Efim Etkind, "Pasternak, novator poeticheskoi rechi," *Boris Pasternak: 1890–1960* (Paris: Institut d'Etudes slaves, 1979), pp. 117–142.
16. Trans. Roberta Reeder. See Pasternak, "Marburg," *Stikhotvoreniya,* I, p. 114, for the original.
17. Roman Jakobson, "Marginal Notes on the Prose of the Poet Pasternak (1935)," in *Pasternak,* ed. Davie, p. 147. Originally "Randbemerkungen zur Prose des Dichters Pasternak," in *Slavische Rundschau,* VI (1935).
18. Hughes, *The Poetic World of Boris Pasternak,* p. 26.
19. Pasternak, "Iz suyeverya," *Stikhotvoreniya,* I, p. 125. Trans. Roberta Reeder.
20. A. Lezhnyov, "The Poetry of Boris Pasternak," in *Pasternak,* ed. Davie, pp. 85–108.
21. Pasternak, "Fevral," *Stikhotvoreniya,* p. 75. Trans. Roberta Reeder.
22. Pasternak, "Iz perepiski . . . ," p. 661.
23. Cited by Henry Gifford, *Pasternak: A Critical Study* (Cambridge: Cambridge University Press, 1977), p. 40. See Khardzhiev, "Zametki o Mayakovskom," in *Literaturnoye nasledstvo,* LXV (Moscow, 1958), p. 410.
24. Pasternak, *Stikhotvoreniya,* p. 119. Trans. Roberta Reeder.
25. Trans. Roberta Reeder.
26. Fleishman, *Boris Pasternak,* p. 129. The article by Pravdukhin is "Borba za novoe iskusstvo," *Sibirskiye ogni,* no. 5 (1922).
27. Both critics in Barnes, *Boris Pasternak,* p. 285. See Aseyev, "Pisma o poezii," *Krasnaya nov,* no. 3 (1922), p. 251, and Bryusov, "Vchera, segodnya i zavtra russkoi poezii," *Pechat i revolyutsiya,* no. 7 (1922), p. 57.
28. Barnes, p. 288. Cited from Pasternak's letter to Yury Yurkun, 1922.
29. Ibid.
30. Ibid., p. 293.
31. Ibid.
32. Ibid., p. 304.
33. Yevgeny Pasternak, *Boris Pasternak,* p. 367.
34. Ibid., p. 370, and Barnes, *Boris Pasternak,* p. 326. See Boris Pasternak, *My Sister-Life and A Sublime Malady,* trans. Mark Rudman with Bohdan Boychuk (Ann Arbor: Ardis, 1983). For the original, see Pasternak, *Stikhotvoreniya,* I, "Vysokaya bolezn," p. 238.
35. See Barnes, p. 326.
36. Pasternak, "People and Attitudes . . . ," p. 250. Personal communication, Ye. Pasternak.
37. L. V. Gornung, "Zapiski ob Anne Akhmatovoi," *Vospominaniya,* p. 183. See Luknitskaya, *Pered toboi zemlya,* p. 323.
38. Boris Pasternak, "Iz perepiski s pisatelyami," ed. Ye. B. and Ye. V. Pasternak, *Literaturnoye nasledstvo* (Moscow: Nauk, 1983), p. 649.
39. Barnes, *Boris Pasternak,* p. 412. See "Iz perepiski . . . ," p. 657, for original.
40. Pasternak, *Stikhotvoreniya,* I, p. 202. Trans. Roberta Reeder.
41. Hughes, *The Poetic World of Boris Pasternak,* p. 84.
42. Fleishman, *Boris Pasternak,* p. 87. See "Speech at the First All-Union Congress of Soviet Writers (1934)," in *Pasternak on Art and Creativity,* ed. Angela Livingstone (Cambridge: Cambridge University Press, 1985), p. 171; "Speech at the International Congress of Writers for the Defense of Culture" (1935), p. 73; and "On Modesty and

Daring: Speech at the Third Plenary Meeting of the Board of the Union of Soviet Writers (1936)," p. 173, all in Livingstone.

43. See Fleishman, *Boris Pasternak,* p. 195. See also Ye. Pasternak, *Pasternak,* p. 512–14.

44. See Livingstone, *Pasternak on Art,* p. 173, for the speech. See Fleishman, *Boris Pasternak,* p. 197, for a discussion of the role of Pasternak at the meeting in Minsk.

45. Fleishman, *Boris Pasternak,* p. 176. See also Zoya Maslenikova, *Portret Borisa Pasternaka* (Moscow: Sovetskaya Rossiya, 1990), p. 53, for Pasternak's version of this story.

46. See Kiril Taranovsky, "Zhizni dayushchii golos: zametke o Pasternake i Akhmatovoi," *Vozmi nad radest: To Honour Jeanne von de Eng-Liedmeier,* ed. V. J. Amsenga, et al. (Amsterdam: Slavic Seminar, 1980), pp. 149–156.

47. Fleishman, *Boris Pasternak,* p. 195.

48. Ibid., pp. 204 and 211.

49. Pasternak, "People and Attitudes," p. 250. Personal communication, Ye. Pasternak.

50. Boris Pasternak, "To A. Akhmatova," *Selected Writings,* p. 386. This important passage has been left out of the citation by Haight in H-M, p. 111.

51. Pasternak, "To A. Akhmatova," p. 387.

52. Ibid., p. 389.

53. Chukovskaya, ZAA, I, p. 25. See Efim Etkind, "O Gamlete v perevodakh B. Pasternaka i M. Lozinskogo," *Boris Pasternak 1890–1960,* see p. 474.

54. A. A. Gozenpud, "Neuvyadshiye listya," OAA, p. 318.

55. Original, *Stikhotvoreniya,* I, p. 200. Trans. Roberta Reeder.

56. De Mallac, *Boris Pasternak,* p. 190.

57. Ibid., p. 197.

58. Fleishman, *Boris Pasternak,* p. 255.

59. Pasternak and Freidenberg, *The Correspondence,* p. 290.

60. Ibid., p. 296.

61. See Chukovskaya, ZAA, II, p. 551.

62. Ibid., p. 153.

63. Fleishman, *Boris Pasternak,* p. 271.

64. Ibid., p. 280.

65. Ibid., p. 185.

66. Ibid., pp. 292 and 297.

67. Trans. Roberta Reeder.

68. Personal communication.

69. Gornung, "Zapiski ob Anne Akhmatovoi," VOAA, p. 213.

70. Lev Ozerov, "Razroznennye zapisi," VOAA, p. 598.

71. Gershtein, "Besedy s N. A.," p. 92, and Chukovskaya, ZAA, II, p. 358. Diary entry October 8, 1960.

72. Chukovskaya, ZAA, II, p. 358. Akhmatova and Punin were never legally married, although she and her friends frequently referred to Punin as her husband.

73. Pasternak, "People and Attitudes," p. 302.

74. Chukovskaya, ZAA, II, p. 131, and Akhmatova repeats the accusation in 1959, ZAA, II, p. 286.

75. Ibid., p. 14.

76. Pasternak, "Iz perepiski . . . ," p. 649.

77. Chukovskaya, ZAA, II, p. 43.

78. Ibid., p. 50.

79. Ibid., p. 168.

80. Ibid., p. 178.
81. Ibid., p. 213.
82. N. Ya. Rykova, "Mesyatsa besformennyi oskolok . . . ," OAA, p. 183.
83. Chukovskaya, ZAA, II, pp. 251–279. See p. 253 for information on Pasternak's expulsion.
84. Ibid., p. 259.
85. Ibid., p. 269.
86. Ibid., p. 258.
87. Ibid., p. 275.
88. Ibid., p. 291.
89. Vilenkin, VOAA, p. 414.
90. Chukovskaya, ZAA, II, p. 333.
91. Trans. Roberta Reeder.
92. Chukovskaya, ZAA, II, p. 335.
93. Vilenkin, VOAA, p. 415.

CHAPTER 11: The Gay Little Sinner Repents: *Poem Without a Hero*

1. Dmytryshyn, *USSR,* pp. 265–333.
2. Personal communication.
3. Raisa Orlova and Lev Kopelev, "Anna vseya Rusi," LO, no. 5 (1989), p. 101. This is a chapter from their book *My zhili v Moskve 1956–1980* (Ann Arbor: Ardis, 1988). See also "Vstrechi s Annoi Akhmatovoi," *Grani,* XXXIX, no. 131 (1984), pp. 166–237.
4. Chukovskaya, ZAA, II, p. 480.
5. Orlova and Kopelev, "Anna vseya Rusi," p. 103.
6. Chukovskaya, ZAA, II, p. 392.
7. F. D. Reeve, *Robert Frost in Russia* (Boston: Little, Brown, 1963), pp. 80–85.
8. An epigraph from a poem to her by Joseph Brodsky begins: "You will write about us on a slant." Cited in Orlova, "Anna vseya Rusi," p. 105. Alekseyev is not only a Pushkin scholar who has written numerous books on English and French literature; in 1959 he became president of the Pushkin Commission of the Academy of Arts, of which Akhmatova was also a member. See Chukovskaya, II, p. 607.
9. Reeve, p. 82.
10. Chukovskaya, II, p. 428.
11. Orlova and Kopelev, "Anna vseya Rusi," p. 189.
12. Silman and Admoni, *My vspominayem,* pp. 307–321. See also Chukovskaya, ZAA, II, p. 387.
13. Chukovskaya, ZAA, II, p. 96.
14. Akhmatova, "Prose About the Poem," MHC, p. 128.
15. Ibid., p. 127.
16. Ibid., p. 129.
17. Chukovskaya, ZAA, II, p. 399.
18. MHC, p. 127. See Kralin; *Artur i Anna,* pp. 34–37.
19. See Chukovskaya, ZAA, II, note (389), p. 398.
20. Verheul, *The Theme of Time,* p. 93.
21. Cited in Mandrykina, "Nenapisannaya kniga," p. 62.
22. Nadezhda Mandelstam, *Hope Abandoned,* pp. 429, 152.
23. Nayman-Rosslyn, p. 117.
24. Berdyaev, *Samopoznaniye,* pp. 254, 260.

25. Zhirmunsky, "Anna Akhmatova i Aleksandr Blok," p. 77.
26. Malmstad, "Mikhail Kuzmin," p. 185.
27. Trans. Roberta Reeder.
28. J. Guenther, cited by Timenchik, et al., "Akhmatova i Kuzmin," footnotes #58 and 97.
29. Cited in PBG, p. 205.
30. Timenchik, "Akhmatova i Kuzmin," p. 232. See Malmstad, "Mikhail Kuzmin," p. 185, where he cites the notice in the newspaper *Rech,* which appeared on Sunday, April 7, 1913, in the obituaries under "Knyazev, Vsevolod Gavrilovich."
31. Chukovsky, *Lyudi i knigi,* p. 746.
32. Malmstad, "Mikhail Kuzmin," p. 187.
33. Akhmatova, "Prose About the Poem," MHC, p. 128.
34. Vilenkin, *V sto pervom zerkale,* p. 43.
35. Timenchik, "Rizhskii epizod," p. 121.
36. Written in 1830, *The Feast During the Time of the Plague* is based on a work by John Wilson. It is one of Pushkin's *Small Tragedies,* a set of short plays that includes *The Stone Guest* about Don Juan, and *Mozart and Salieri,* which may have been the impetus for Peter Shaffer's *Amadeus.*
37. See Sam Driver, "Akhmatova's *Poema bez geroja* and Blok's *Vozmezdiye,*" *Aleksandr Blok Centennial Conference,* ed. W. Vickery and B. Sagatov, pp. 88–89.
38. See "Poema bez geroya" in S-F, II, pp. 603–605. This article includes a summary of a talk by R. D. Timenchik published in a limited edition, which I could not obtain. The original is Timenchik, "K analizu *Poemy bez geroya,*" *Materialy XII nauchnoi studencheskoi konferentsii* (Tartu: Tartusskii Gosudarstevennyi Universitet, 1967), pp. 121–123.
39. See John Malmstad and Gennady Shmakov's exegesis of this difficult poem in "Kuzmin's 'The Trout Breaking Through the Ice,' " in *Russian Modernism,* ed. George Gibian and H. W. Tjalsma, pp. 132–165. Shmakov, one of the leading scholars on Kuzmin, emigrated from Russia and died recently in the United States.
40. Lev Vygotsky, *Thought and Language,* trans. Eugenia Hanfmann and Gertrude Vakar (Cambridge, MA: MIT Press, 1962), p. 100.
41. Wolf Schmidt, "Narratives Erinnern und poetisches Gedächtnis in realistischer und ornamentaler Prose," *Wiener Slawistischer Almanach,* no. 16 (1985), p. 107.
42. Yuri M. Lotman, "Pamyat v kulturologicheskom osveshchenii," *Wiener Slawistischer Almanach,* no. 16 (1985), pp. 5–9.
43. Verheul, *The Theme of Time,* p. 194.
44. Chukovsky says, "Each of its three parts has its own musical picture, its rhythm within limits of a single meter and, apparently, a single type of structure of the stanza." See Chukovsky, "Chitaya Akhmatovu . . . ," p. 202. Tsivyan compares the structure of the poem to musical forms—a three-part symphony, sonata, or concerto, where independent parts exist that are self-contained yet form a single whole. Themes are interrupted, repeated, varied. See Tsivyan, "Akhmatova i muzyka," *Russian Literature,* 10/11 (1975), p. 200. For an extensive analysis of the role of music in *Poem Without a Hero,* see Kats and Timenchik, *Akhmatova i muzyka.*
45. See Zhirmunsky, "Anna Akhmatova i Aleksandr Blok," p. 78.
46. Chukovsky, "Chitaya Akhmatovu," p. 202.
47. See, for example, Timenchik, et al., "Akhmatova i Kuzmin," V. N. Toporov, "Akhmatova i Blok," V. M. Zhirmunsky, "Anna Akhmatova i Aleksandr Blok," Sam Driver, "Akhmatova's *Poema bez geroja* and Blok's 'Vozmezdie,' " Susan Amert, "The Poet's Lot in *Poem without a Hero,*" *In a Shattered Mirror,* and V. N. Toporov, "K otzvukam zapadnoyevropeiskoi poezii Akhmatovoi (T. S. Eliot)," *International Journal of Slavic Linguistics and Poetics,* XVI (1973), pp. 157–176.

48. T. S. Eliot, "Tradition and the Individual Talent," in T. S. Eliot, *Selected Essays* (New York: Harcourt, Brace, 1950), p. 4.
49. Cited in Luknitskaya, *Pered toboi zemlya,* p. 346.
50. For an encyclopedic compendium of allusions by Akhmatova to her own poetry which provide possible solutions to key symbols like "wine" and "mirrors" in *Poem Without a Hero,* see Elisabeth von Erdmann-Pandzic, *Poem bez geroya von Anna A. Achmatowa* (Köln-Wien: Böhlau Verlag, 1987). Tsivyan and others refer to this use of images and phrases by other authors as "bricolage," a term borrowed from the anthropologist Lévi-Strauss in his structural analysis of cultural myths. See T.V. Tsivyan, " 'Poema bez geroya' Anny Akhmatovoi," *Anna Akhmatova 1889–1989,* ed. Sonia L. Ketchian, p. 241.
51. Vyach. Vs. Ivanov, "Besedy s Annoi Akhmatovoi," VOAA, p. 474.
52. Toporov, p. 158.
53. See David Bethea, *The Shape of Apocalypse in Modern Russian Fiction* (Princeton: Princeton University Press, 1989).
54. M.H. Abrams, *Natural Supernaturalism* (London: Oxford University Press, 1971), p. 54.
55. See Rory Childers and Anna Lisa Crone, "The Mandelshtam Presence in the Dedications of *Poema bez geroya,*" *Russian Literature,* XV (1984), pp. 52–82.
56. See Mayakovsky, "Cloud in Trousers," where as a form of parody or blasphemy against religious forms, he calls this antireligious poem a "tetryptych" with four parts.
57. Trans. Roberta Reeder.
58. N. Mandelstam, *Hope Abandoned,* p. 435. See pp. 433–443 for her discussion of *Poem Without a Hero.*
59. Malmstad, "Mikhail Kuzmin," p. 97.
60. For the last years of Mandelstam's life, see also Emma Gershtein, "Novoye o Mandelstame," *Nashe naslediye,* no. 9 (1989), pp. 101–124, and Gershtein's book *Novoye o Mandelstame.* She often disagrees with Nadezhda Mandelstam's interpretation of events and figures in Mandelstam's life.
61. Elaine Moch-Bickert, *Kolumbina desyatyikh godov . . .* trans. Vera Rumyantseva, ed. Yu. A. Molok (Paris and St. Petersburg: Grzhebina-AO "Arsis," 1993), p. 49.
62. Pushkin, *Eugene Onegin,* trans. Walter Arndt, p. 116.
63. Salisbury, *The 900 Days,* p. 212.
64. Chukovskaya, ZAA, II, p. 121.
65. E. T. A. Hoffmann, "New Year's Eve Adventure," *The Best Tales of Hoffmann,* ed. E. F. Bleiler (New York: Dover Publications, 1967), p. 108.
66. Cited in de Mallac, *Boris Pasternak,* p. 344.
67. The White Hall was built by the great neoclassical architect Giacomo Quarenghi. The emperor Paul would sometimes hide behind the mirrors and eavesdrop on what guests at the ball were saying about him. See *Poema bez geroya,* ed. Timenchik, p. 69.
68. Chukovskaya, ZAA, I, p. 149.
69. Malmstad, "Mikhail Kuzmin," p. 213.
70. See Leviticus 18: 18–22.
71. Akhmatova, "Prose About the Poem," MHC, p. 133.
72. I thank the great Russian actress Alla Demidova for this suggestion, and that special time we spent in her Moscow apartment, when she recited the poem and we discussed every line and every phrase.
73. Akhmatova, "Prose About the Poem," MHC, p. 128.
74. Trans. Roberta Reeder. For original, see Mayokovsky, *Polnoye Sobraniye,* pp. 184–185.

75. Trans. Roberta Reeder.
76. Anna Achmatowa, "Poem ohne Held," in *Poem ohne Held,* ed. Fritz Mierau (Göttingen: Steidl, 1989), p. 201.
77. Johann von Goethe, *Faust,* trans. Walter Kaufmann (Garden City, NY: Doubleday & Co., 1961), p. 359 for the "Walpurgis Night."
78. For a discussion of the Commedia at the Russian folk fairs and its reincarnation in works like Stravinsky's ballet *Petrouchka,* see Roberta Reeder, "Petrushka, a Russian Rogue," *The Puppetry Journal* (January–February 1981), pp. 41–45; Catriona Kelly, *Petrushka: The Russian Carnival Puppet Theatre* (Cambridge: Cambridge University Press, 1990); and A. F. Nekrylova, *Russkiye narodnye gorodskiye prazdniki, uveseleniya i zrelishcha* (Leningrad, 1984) and A. Ya. Alekseyev-Yakovlev, *Russkie narodnye gulyanya* (Leningrad and Moscow, 1948).
79. Cited in Rudnitsky, *Meyerhold,* p. 147.
80. Wendy Rosslyn, "Don Juan Feminised," *Symbolism and After: Essays on Russian Poetry in Honour of Georgette Doncin,* ed. A. McMillan (Bristol: Bristol Classical Press, 1992), pp. 102–121.
81. Cited in Rudnitsky, *Meyerhold,* p. 153.
82. Ibid., p. 107.
83. Arthur Lourie, "Olga Afanasevna Glebova-Sudeikina," p. 143.
84. Osip Mandelstam, *Sobraniye sochinenii,* I, p. 85. The poem is from the collection *Tristia.*
85. Akhmatova, "The 1910s," MHC, p. 11.
86. See Roberta Reeder, "Tsarskoye Selo in the Poetry of Anna Akhmatova: The Eternal Return," SUE, II, pp. 285–302.
87. Trans. Roberta Reeder. Cited by Zhirmunsky in notes to Akhmatova, *Stikhotvoreniya i poema,* p. 517.
88. Trans. Roberta Reeder.
89. This device was often used in the 1920s in Russian avant-garde films by Eisenstein, where subtitles in a silent film "recited" in a quiet voice are indicated by small letters, but a shout is conveyed by large letters.
90. See Zhirmunsky, "Text Variations," *Complete Poetic Works of Anna Akhmatova,* II, p. 467.
91. Cited and translated by Richard McKane in *Anna Akhmatova: Selected Poems* (Newcastle-on-Tyne: Bloodaxe Books, 1989), p. 335. Akhmatova says in her memoirs of Mandelstam that in 1933, when the Mandelstams were visiting Leningrad, Osip recited parts of Klyuev's poem to her. In the notes to their translation of this memoir, Anna Lisa Crone and Ronald Meyer cite the following passage from MHC, p. 374:

    I saw with my own eyes Klyuev's declaration at Varvara Klyuchkova's (sent from the camps, petitioning for amnesty): "I, sentenced for my poem 'The Blasphemers of Art,' and for some mad lines in my drafts . . ." (I took two lines as an epigraph for my "Tails" ["The Other Side of the Coin"].

92. The relevant lines from Pushkin's poem are:

    Why does he sing so sonorously?
    Striking the ear in vain,
    To what goal does he lead us? About what does he strum?
    What does he teach us?
    Why does he trouble, torment hearts
    Like a capricious wizard?
    Like the wind, his song is free,

But, like the wind, it is fruitless, too:
What use is it to us?

> Trans. Roberta Reeder. See Amert, *In a Shattered Mirror,* p. 95, for a discussion of the relationship of the Pushkin poem to this section of *Poem Without a Hero.*

93. Amert, *In a Shattered Mirror,* p. 109. See also Egon Wellesz, *A History of Byzantine Music and Hymnography* (Oxford: Oxford University Press, 1949), pp. 138–139.
94. Amert, *In a Shattered Mirror,* p. 123.
95. H. D. F. Kitto, *Greek Tragedy* (Garden City, NY: Doubleday & Co., 1952), p. 155.
96. Byron, *Manfred,* scene i, *The Poetical Works of Lord Byron* (New York: Hurst & Co., n.d.), p. 330.
97. Annensky's poem is a pessimistic view of Petersburg:

The yellow steam of the Petersburg winter,
The yellow snow covering the flagstones . . .
I do not know where you are and where we are,
I only know that we are closely merged.

Did a tsarist decree create us?
Did the Swedes forget to drown us?
Instead of a fairy tale in the past we had
Only stones and horror tales.

We got only stones from the magician,
And the Neva of a stormy-yellow color,
And deserts of mute squares
Where they executed people before dawn.

And what we had on earth
Why did our two-headed eagle rise
In the dark monasteries a giant on a cliff—
Tomorrow will become a children's game.

Even though he was threatening and daring,
And his furious horse performed well,
The tsar was not able to crush the snake,
And what was squeezed became our idol.

There are neither fortresses, miracles, holy objects
Mirages, tears, nor smiles . . .
Only stones of frozen deserts
And the consciousness of a cursed mistake.

Even in May, when shadows
Of the white night spread over the waves,
There are no charms of a spring dream,
There is no poison of sterile desire.

> Trans. Roberta Reeder. See Innokenty Annensky, *Stikhotvoreniya i tragedii* (Leningrad: Sovietskii pisatel, 1959), p. 199.

98. Chukovskaya, ZAA, I, p. 47, dated November 27, 1939. See also V. N. Toporov, "Ob istorizme Akhmatovoi," AA, p. 242.
99. She was born June 11 (Old Style) which is June 23 (New Style) in the nineteenth century, but June 24 (New Style) in the twentieth century, since thirteen days, not twelve, are added in this century.

100. Akhmatova, *Stikhotvoreniya i poemy,* ed. Zhirmunsky, p. 441, trans. Roberta Reeder.
101. Natalya Goncharova, "Preface to Catalogue of One-Man Exhibition, 1913," in *Russian Art of the Avant-Garde: Theory and Criticism,* ed. Bowlt, p. 58.
102. See Akhmatova, "The Ballet Libretto for 'A Poem Without a Hero,' " MHC, pp. 139–143. For an excellent study of the ballet version as well as balletic elements in the literary version, see Wendy Rosslyn, "Akhmatova's *Poema bez geroia:* Ballet and Poem," SUE, I, pp. 55–72.

CHAPTER 12: Joseph Brodsky: Arrest and Exile, 1963–1965

1. Chukovskaya, ZAA, II, p. 623.
2. Ibid., p. 483.
3. Joseph Brodsky, "In a Room and a Half," *Less Than One,* p. 452.
4. See Efim Etkind, *Protsess Iosifa Brodskogo* (London: Overseas Publications Interchange, 1988), pp. 5–11. This important book includes information and transcriptions of Brodsky's trial as well as excerpts from the writings of Lydia Chukovskaya and Raisa Orlova and Lev Kopelev.
5. Trans. Roberta Reeder. Original in Etkind, *Protsess,* p. 12.
6. Ibid., p. 13.
7. Ya. Gordin, "Delo Brodskogo," *Neva,* no. 2 (1989), p. 136.
8. Trans. Roberta Reeder.
9. Dmitry Bobyshev, "Akhmatovskiye siroty," *Russkaya mysl,* no. 3507 (March 8, 1984), pp. 8–9.
10. Joseph Brodsky and Solomon Volkov, *Vspominaya Akhmatovu* (Moscow: Nezavisimaya gazeta, 1992), p. 6.
11. Joseph Brodsky, *Ostanovka: stikhotvoreniya i poemy* (New York: Chekhov, 1970), p. 10. Trans. Roberta Reeder.
12. See Etkind, *Protsess,* p. 42.
13. Ibid.
14. Ya. Gordin, "Delo Brodskogo," p. 139.
15. Silman and Admoni, *My vspominayem,* p. 377. Anonymous sources have confirmed that the friend was Bobyshev.
16. Ibid., p. 379.
17. Cited in Gordin "Delo Brodskogo," p. 152.
18. Etkind, *Protsess,* p. 111.
19. Cited in Etkind, *Protsess,* p. 104.
20. Nayman-Rosslyn, p. 132.
21. Ibid., p. 135.
22. Etkind, *Protsess,* p. 105.
23. Silman and Admoni, *My vspominayem,* p. 388.
24. Etkind, *Protsess,* p. 137.

CHAPTER 13: The Last Years: The 1960s

1. Vecheslova, "Yeyo tainstvennyi golos," OAA, p. 283.
2. See Sinyavsky, "Boris Pasternak," pp. 170–172, on Pasternak and the creative process. The quotation is at p. 171.
3. Trans. Roberta Reeder.
4. Trans. Madeline G. Levine in Przbylski, *Essay on Mandelstam,* p. 54.

5. Punin, "Iz dnevnika," PBG, p. 335.
6. Akhmatova, MHC, p. 18.
7. Nayman-Rosslyn, p. 148.
8. Lourie, "Detskii rai," PBG, p. 342. Originally published in *Vozdushnye puti,* no. 3 (1963).
9. See Jerzy Faryno, "Tainy remesla Akhmatovoi," *Wiener Slawisticher Almanach,* V (1980), p. 40.
10. Chukovsky, "Chukovsky . . . ," p. 231.
11. Trans. Roberta Reeder.
12. Chukovskaya, ZAA, I, p. 106. Chukovskaya says they were dedicated to Gumilyov.
13. Akhmatova, MHC, p. 15.
14. See Oleg Kalugin in "Arestovannaya Literatura," *Gosudarstvennaya bezopastnost i demokratiya,* no. 3 (Moscow, 1992), p. 50.
15. Luknitskaya, *Nikolay Gumilyov.*
16. Toporov, "Ob istorizme Akhmatovoi," p. 197.
17. Trans. Roberta Reeder.
18. MHC, p. 5.
19. Trans. Roberta Reeder. I would like to thank Vyacheslav Ivanov for pointing this parallel out to me when I presented my paper on "Akhmatova and Tsarskoye Selo" at the Centennial Akhmatova Conference in Nottingham, England, in the summer of 1989.
20. Personal communication. Golubeva was born in "this century," while Akhmatova and Punin were born in the last. On the basis of an enormous of archival material, the Punin family has written a biography of Nikolay Punin which they intend to publish soon. A great deal of work has been put into attempting to decode Akhmatova's poems based on information from Punin's letters and diary.
21. Chukovskaya, ZAA, II, p. 212.
22. Ibid., p. 391.
23. Personal communication. For the passage cited, see Sreznevskaya, "Dafnis i Khloya," OAA, p. 24.
24. Chukovsky, "Chukovsky . . ." p. 228.
25. Nikolay Punin, "Dnevnik," ed. Irina Punina, *Zvezda,* no. 1 (1994), p. 99.
26. This poem has been renamed the "Fifth Elegy" in the paperback edition of *The Complete Poems of Anna Akhmatova,* trans. Judith Hemschemeyer and ed. Roberta Reeder. This was done without my consultation or permission. In the hardback version I followed the ordering of the elegies as they appeared in the authoritative collection of Akhmatova's works, edited by the noted scholar and friend of Akhmatova, Viktor Zhirmunsky, in the Biblioteka poeta series, approved by Akhmatova herself.
27. N. Mandelstam, *Hope Abandoned,* p. 115.
28. Akhmatova, MHC, p. 28.
29. S. Lipkin, "Vostochniye stroki Anny Akhmatovoi," *Klassicheskaya poeziya vostoka* (Moscow: Khdozhestvennaya literatura, 1969), p. 13.
30. Arseny Tarkovsky, "Predisloviye," in *Golosa poetov: stikhi zarubezhnykh poetov v perevode Anny Akhmatovoi,* trans. Anna Akhmatova (Moscow: Progress Publishers, 1965), p . 5. In spite of Tarkovsky's assertions, it is still uncertain whether Akhmatova was actually able to choose the poets she translated.
31. V. Baluashvili, "U Anny Akhmatovoi," S-F, II, p. 298.
32. A. A. Gozenpud, "Nevyadshiye listya," OAA, p. 311.
33. Ibid., p. 313.
34. Ibid., p. 298.
35. Lev Ozerov, "Razroznennye zapisi," VOAA, p. 607.

36. The most extensive publication of the fragments appears in Kralin's 1990 edition of Akhmatova's works, "Enuma Elish," II, pp. 259–312.
37. N. Mandelstam, *Hope Abandoned,* pp. 361.
38. Kralin, II, pp. 278–279.
39. Arthur Lourie, "Pismo k Anne Akhmatovoi," PBG, p. 339.
40. Constantine Stanislavsky, *My Life in Art,* trans. J. J. Robins (Cleveland: World Publishing Company, 1956; first published 1924), p. 532.
41. See Kralin edition, II, p. 312.
42. Vilenkin, *V sto pervom zerkale,* p. 173.
43. Gozenpud, "Nevyadshiye listya," p. 325.
44. N. Mandelstam, HAH, p. 229.
45. Emma Gershtein edited Akhmatova's articles on Pushkin under the title *Anna Akhmatova o Pushkine* (Leningrad: Sovetskii pisatel, 1977). They have been made available in English in MHC.
46. See Susan Amert in "Akhmatova's 'Pushkin i nevskoe vzmore,' " *Transactions of the Association of Russian-American Scholars in the USA,* XXIII (1990), p. 199.
47. Akhmatova, "A Word About Pushkin," MHC, p. 147.
48. Ilyina, "Ann Akhmatova v poslodniye gody," p. 124.
49. Ibid., p. 128.
50. Ibid.
51. Nayman-Rosslyn, p. 141.
52. Gitovich, "Ob Anne Andreyevne," OAA, p. 340.
53. Ibid., p. 345.
54. Ibid., p. 349.
55. Ibid.
56. I. Metter, "Sedoi venets dostalsya ei nedarom," OAA, pp. 380–390.
57. Batalov, "Ryadom s Akhmatovoi," p. 156.
58. Personal communication.
59. Nayman-Rosslyn, p. 181.
60. Gitovich, "Ob Anne Andreyevne," p. 349.
61. Ilyina, "Anna Akhmatova v posledniye gody," p. 129.
62. Mikhail Meilakh, ". . . Svoyu mezh vas eshche ostaviv ten," LO, no. 5 (1989), pp. 95–100.
63. Ignufy Ivanovsky, "Anna Akhmatova," VOAA, p. 619.
64. Ilyina, "Anna Akhmatova v posledniye gody," p. 130.
65. Gitovich, "Ob Anne Andreyevne," p. 349.
66. Ilyina, "Anna Akhmatova v posledniye gody," p. 130.
67. Vilenkin, *V sto pervom zerkale,* pp. 79, 71.
68. "Pisma k. A. A. Akhmatovoi," OAA, p. 541.
69. See Felix Roziner, "The Slender Lyre: Arthur Lourie and His Music," *Bostonian* (Fall 1992), pp. 34–41, 86–87. The best work on Lourie's life and work is Detlef Gojowy, *Arthur Lourie und der russische Futurismus.* One should also look at Mikhail Kralin, *Artur i ya* (Leningrad: published by author, 1992), based on letters between Kralin, Graham, and others. But the hostility that developed among the correspondents influences the credibility of their versions of Lourie's story and his relationship with Akhmatova and others.
70. Kralin, *Anna i ya,* p. 108.
71. Lourie, "Pisma k Anne Akhmatovoi," p. 339.
72. Chukovskaya, ZAA, II, p. 463.
73. Ibid., p. 401.
74. Ibid., p. 442.

75. Ibid., p. 478.
76. Khrenkov, *Anna Akhmatova,* p. 8.
77. Chukovsky, *Lyudi i knigi,* p. 726.
78. Gershtein, "V zamoskvoreche," LO, no. 7 (1985), p. 108.
79. Metter, "Sedoi venets . . . ," p. 381.
80. Akhmatova, MHC, p. 21.
81. Khrenkov, *Anna Akhmatova,* p. 177.
82. Solomon Volkow, *Die Memoiren des Dmitrij Schostakowitsch,* trans. Heddy Pross-Weerth (Hamburg: Albrecht Knaus, 1979), p. 291. The English version is entitled *Testimony.*
83. Cited in Orlova and Kopelev, "Anna vseya Rusi," LO, p. 104.
84. Ibid., p. 106.
85. In the Russian version, either the errors have been corrected or notes are added by the editors informing readers of the facts.
86. Amanda Haight kindly read the manuscript of the biographical introduction that appears at the beginning of *The Complete Poems of Anna Akhmatova.* She also shared valuable information with me about Akhmatova. Professor Peter Brown, her mentor for her dissertation on Akhmatova, told me in a private interview (February 1992) how proud he was of what Haight had accomplished. Brown was Akhmatova's interpreter on her trip to Oxford in 1965.
87. Luknitsky, *Pered toboi zemlya,* p. 382.
88. Akhmatova, "Pismo k Dzhankarlo Vigorelli," S-F, II, p. 307.
89. Nayman-Rosslyn, p. 180.
90. Ibid., p. 175.
91. Ibid., p. 178.
92. Personal communication.
93. I. N. Punina, "Anna Akhmatova na Sitsilii," VOAA, pp. 662–670.
94. Hans Werner Richter, *Euterpe von den Ufern der Neva oder die Ehrung Anna Achmatowa in Taormina* (Berlin: Friedenauer Presse, 1965), p. 8.
95. Ibid., p. 9.
96. Mikola Bazhan, "Etna-Taormina," trans. from Ukrainian by Elena Umanskaya, *Druzhba narodov,* no. 8 (1979), pp. 261–268.
97. Ibid., p. 263.
98. Orlova and Kopelev, LO, p. 106.
99. Yeventov, "Ot Fontanki do Sitsilii," OAA, p. 378.
100. Elaine Bickert, *Anna Akhmatova: Silence à plusieurs voix* (Paris: Editions Resma, 1970), p. 107. See also Elaine Moch-Bikert, Kolombina. . . .
101. Bickert, *Anna Akhmatova,* p. 107.
102. Berlin, "Anna Akhmatova: A Memoir," *Complete Poems,* p. 40.
103. Vladimir Retsepter, "Eto dlya tebya na vsyu zhizn . . . (A. Akhmatova i 'Shekspirovskii vopros')," VOAA, p. 659.
104. Adamovich, "Moi vstrechi," p. 114.
105. See Yury Annenkov, "Anna Akhmatova," in *Dnevnik moikh vstrech,* pp. 114–136.
106. Anrep, "O chyornom koltse," pp. 451–453.
107. Personal communication.
108. Nikita Struve, "Vosem chasov s Annoi Akhmatovoi," S-F, II, p. 346.
109. Adamovich, "Moi vstrechi," p. 114.
110. Annenkov, "Anna Akhmatova," p. 136.
111. Akhmatova, "Pages from a Diary," MHC, p. 14.
112. Akhmatova, "Briefly About Myself," MHC, p. 28.
113. Akhmatova, "Pages from a Diary," MHC, p. 16.

114. Ibid., pp. 15, 17.
115. Nayman-Rosslyn, p. 150.
116. Ibid., p. 151.
117. Akhmatova, "Pages from a Diary," MHC, p. 63.
118. Ibid., p. 62. In MHC the piece is translated "Hallucination."
119. Aliger, "V poslednii raz," VOAA, p. 367.
120. Ilyina, "Anna Akhmatova," p. 133.
121. See Orlova and Kopelev, "Anna vseya Rusi," LO, pp. 107–109.
122. Orlova and Kopelev, "Vstrechi," *Granii,* pp. 215–216. Ozerov showed me a copy of this speech when I interviewed him in Moscow.
123. Ibid., p. 220.
124. Ibid.
125. Dmitry Bobyshev, "Akhmatovskiye siroty," p. 9. Poem translated by Roberta Reeder. Osya is the nickname for Joseph, Tolya for Anatoly, Zhenya for Yevgeny, and Dima for Dmitry. "Sworn brothers" refers to the Slavic custom of men making a pact to become a *probratim* or "brother for life" with another man. All eight octaves have been published in LO, no. 5 (1989), p. 111. For a comprehensive collection of poems devoted to Akhmatova, see *Posvyashchayetsya Akhmatovoi: Stikhi raznykh poetov posvyashchyone Akhmatovoi,* compiled by Pamela Davidson and Isia Tlusty (Tenafly, NJ: Heritage, 1990).
126. Orlova and Kopelev, "Anna vseya Rusi," LO, p. 109.

EPILOGUE

1. Trans. Roberta Reeder. Original in Kralin, II, p. 106.
2. Chulkova, "Ob Anne Akhmatovoi," p. 38.
3. David Bethea, *Khodasevich: His Life and Art* (Princeton: Princeton University Press, 1983), p. 255.
4. Akhmatova, "Pages from a Diary," MHC, p. 24.
5. Mai-mai Sze, *The Way of Chinese Painting* (New York: Vintage Books, 1959), p. 164.
6. N. Struve, "Vosem chasov . . . ," S-F, II, p. 346.

"A. A. Gorenko (Nekrolog)," DG, pp. 10–11. Orig. *Odesskii listok,* September 7, 1915, signed V.L.

Ablitsov, V. "Kyivski adresy Anny Akmatovoi," *Govoryt i pokazuye Ukraina,* no. 25 (June 15), 1989.

Abrams. M. H. *Natural Supernaturalism.* London: Oxford University Press, 1971.

Achmatowa, Anna. *Briefe, Aufsätze, Fotos,* trans. Irmgard Wille, Johanne Peters, Rosemarie Düring, and Kay Borowsky, ed. Siegfried Heinrichs. Berling: Oberbaum, 1991.

———. *Poem ohne Held,* ed. Fritz Mierau. Göttingen: Steidl, 1989.

———. *Requiem,* trans. Rosemarie Düring. Berlin: Oberbaum Verlag, 1987.

Adamovich, G. "Iz stati 'Literaturnaya nedelya,' " PBG, p. 366. Orig. *Illyustrirovannaya Rossiya,* no. 24. Paris, 1929.

———. "Moi vstrechi s Annoi Akhmatovoi," *Vozdushnye puti* (1967), pp. 99–114.

———. "Moi vstrechi s Annoi Akhmatovoi," OAA, pp. 87–108, and VOAA, pp. 65–77.

———. "Pamyati Gumilyova," NGVS, pp. 243–244.

———. "U samogo morya," DG, pp. 189–191. Orig. *Golos zhizni,* no. 19 (1915).

———. "Znakomstvo i druzhba," VOAA, pp. 332–346.

[Adamovich] G.A. "Vecher u Annenskago," *Chisla,* no. 4 (1930–31), pp. 214–217. (No positive identification of G.A. as Adamovich).

Admoni, V. G. "The Laconicism of Akhmatova's Lyric Poetry," SUE, I, pp. 139–150.

———. "Lakonichnost liriki Akhmatovoi," TsS, pp. 29–40.

———. "Na rubezhe shestidesyatykh: Iz vospominanii ob Anne Akmatovoi," *Zvezda,* no. 6 (1989), pp. 65–66.

———. "Znakomstvo i druzhba," VOAA, pp. 332–346.

Aikhenvald, Yuri. *Poety i poetessy.* Moscow: Severnye dni, 1922.

Aiza Pessina Longo. " 'Ya' liricheskoye i 'ya' biograficheskoye v poeme Akhmatovoi 'U samogo morya,' " TsS, pp. 111–118.

Akhmatova, Anna. "A inogda po etoi samoi Shirokoi . . . ," Mandrykina, p. 241.

———. "An Address Broadcast on the Program 'This Is Radio Leningrad,' " MHC, p. 259.

———. "Alexander Blok," MHC, pp. 69–72.

———. "Alexandrina," MHC, pp. 232–243.

———. "Amedeo Modigliani" (English), MHC, pp. 76–83.

———. "Amedeo Modigliani," H-M, pp. 296–301.

———. "Anina komnata . . . ," Mandrykina, p. 244.

———. *Anna Akhmatova o Pushkine: stati i zametki,* ed. E. G. Gershtein. Leningrad: Sovetskii pisatel, 1977.

———. "Avtobiograficheskaya proza," H-M, pp. 212–258.

———. "Avtobiograficheskoye soobshcheniye," *Nashe naslediye*, III, no. 9 (1989), pp. 83–88.

———. "Avtobiografiya i dva pisma," in *Pamyati Anny Akhmatovoi*, 1974, pp. 31–43.

———. "The Ballet Libretto," MHC, pp. 129–146.

———. "Benjamin Constant's *Adolphe* in Pushkin's Work," MHC, pp. 179–199.

———. "Beryozy," Mandrykina, p. 257.

———. "Biograficheskaya kanva Nikolaya Gumilyova (do 1912 goda)," *Nashe naslediye*, III, no. 9 (1989), p. 82.

———. "Biografiyu ya prinimalas pisat . . . ," Mandrykina, p. 252.

———. "Boris Pasternak," MHC, p. 120.

———. "Boyus, chto vsyo, chto ya pishu zdes . . . ," Mandrykina, p. 253.

———. "Briefly About Myself," MHC, pp. 25–28.

———. "Budka," Mandrykina, p. 239.

———. "Chto zhe kasayetsya memuarov . . . ," Mandrykina, p. 254.

———. *The Complete Poems of Anna Akhmatova*, trans. Judith Hemschemeyer and ed. Roberta Reeder. 2 vols. Somerville, MA: Zephyr Press, 1990.

———. "Dalshe o gorode," Mandrykina, p. 249.

———. "Desyat pisem Anny Akhmatovoi (Publikatsiya i vstupitelnaya statya E. Gershtein)," in *Stikhi, perepiska, vospominaniya, ikonografiya*.

———. "Dikaya devochka," Mandrykina, p. 243.

———. "Dom Shukhardina," Mandrykina, p. 240.

———. "Dopolneniya k Listkam iz dnevnika," *Requiem*, pp. 146–148.

———. "XX vek nachalsya osenyu 1914 goda . . . ," Mandrykina, p. 248.

———. *Dykhanie pesni i kniga perevodov*. Moscow: Sovetskaya Rossiya, 1988.

———. "Eti bednye stikhi. . . . ," Mandrykina, p. 245.

———. "Excerpts from the Last Diary Entries," MHC, pp. 61–68.

———. *Golosa poetov: Stikhi zarubezhnykh poetov v perevode Anny Akhmatovoi*. Moscow: Progress Publishers, 1965.

———. "Gorod," *Ya—golos vash* . . . , p. 340.

———. "I dva okna v Mikhailovskom zamke . . . ," Mandrykina, p. 250.

———. "I kto by poveril . . . ," Mandrykina, p. 252.

———. "I yesli poezii suzhdeno tsvesti. . . . ," Mandrykina, p. 258.

———. "Innokenty Annensky," (English) MHC, pp. 109–111.

———. "Innokenty Annensky," H-M, pp. 305–306.

———. "Iskra parovoza," *Ya—golos vash* . . . , p. 341.

———. *Iz armyanskoi poezii*. Trans. Anna Akhmatova. Yerevan: Sovetskan grokh, 1976.

———. "Iz dnevnika," Mandrykina, p. 256.

———. "Iz nenapisannoi knigi (otryvki vospominanii)," S-F, III, pp. 133–138.

———. "Iz perepiski A. A. Akhmatovoi," H-M, pp. 317–343.

———. "Iz perepiski N. S. Gumilyova i A. A. Akhmatovoi," H-M, pp. 344–353.

———. "Iz pisma k N.," SP, II, pp. 97–98.

———. "Iz pisma k (vmesto predisloviya)," Mandrykina, p. 251.

———. "Iz poslednikh dnevnikovykh zapisei," H-M, pp. 259–263.

———. "Iz vospominanii o Mandelshtame (Listki iz dnevnika)," H-M, pp. 281–295.

———. "Izbrannye pisma," *Ya—golos vash* . . . , pp. 343–348.

———. "K pyatidesyatiletiyu lit[eraturnoi] deyatelnosti," LO, no. 5 (1989).

———. "Kak vsyo uzhe bylo davno . . . ," Mandrykina, p. 252.

———. *Klassicheskaya poeziya vostoka. Anna Akhmatova. Perevody*. Moscow: Khudozhestvennaya literatura, 1969.

————. *Koreiskaya klassicheskaya poeziya,* trans. A. A. Akhmatovoi. Moscow: Goslitizdat, 1956 (2nd ed., 1958).

————. "Korotko o sebe," Mandrykina, p. 236.

————. "Kotoryi-to den vozhus s biograficheskoi knigoi . . . ," Mandrykina, p. 253.

————. Leopardi, Dzhakomo. *Lirika. Perevod s italyanskogo Anny Akhmatovoi i Anatoliya Naimana.* Moscow: Khudozhestvennaya literatura, 1967.

————. "Letters," MHC, pp. 284–329.

————. *Lirika drevnego Egipta. Perevod Anny Akhmatovoi i Very Potapovoi.* Moscow: Khudozhestvennaya literatura, 1965.

————. "Listki iz dnevnika [O. Mandelshtame]," ed. and commentary V. Vilenkin, *Voprosy literatury,* no. 2 (1989), pp. 178–217.

————. "Listki iz dnevnika," *Requiem,* pp. 121–145.

————. "Lyudyam moego pokoleniya . . . ," Mandrykina, p. 242.

————. "Mandelstam," trans. Kristin A. De Kuiper, RLT, no. 9 (Spring 1975), pp. 239–254.

————. "Mandelstam," S-F, II, pp. 166–188.

————. "Marina Tsvetayeva," MHC, pp. 121–122.

————. "Mikhail Lozinsky," (English) MHC, pp. 73–75.

————. "Mikhail Lozinsky," H-M, pp. 279–280.

————. "Mne bylo 10 let . . . ," Mandrykina, p. 242.

————. "Mnimaya biografiya," Mandrykina, p. 243.

————. "Modigliani," trans. Kristin A. De Kuiper, RLT, no. 9 (Spring 1974), pp. 255–261.

————. "Moya biografiya," S-F, III, pp. 123–126.

————. "Moyo detstvo tak zhe unikalno . . . ," Mandrykina, p. 243.

————. *My Half Century: Selected Prose,* ed. Ronald Meyer. Ann Arbor: Ardis, 1992.

————. "Na sever ya vernulas . . . ," Mandrykina, p. 245.

————. "Nachinayet sovershenno vsyo ravno . . . ," Mandrykina, p. 254.

————. "Neizdannye stranitsy iz *Vospominanii o Mandelshtame,*" S-F, III, pp. 128–133.

————. "Neizdannye zametki Anny Akhmatovoi o Pushkine," *Voprosy literatury,* no. 1 (January 1970), pp. 158–206.

————. "Nepremenno, 9 Yanvarya . . . ," Mandrykina, p. 253.

————. "Nikolai Gumilyov," MHC, pp. 112–119.

————. "Nikolai Gumilyov and Acmeism," MHC, pp. 42–43.

————. "Notes in the Margin," MHC, pp. 261–264.

————. "O knige, kotoruyu ya nikogda ne napishu . . . ," Mandrykina, p. 252.

————. *O Pushkine,* ed. E. G. Gershtein. Leningrad: Sovetskii pisatel, 1977.

————. "O sebe," S-F, II, pp. 291–292.

————. "O stikhakh N. Lvovoi," PBG, pp. 142–143. Orig. *Russkaya mysl* (1914), no. 1.

————. "Obshcheizvestno, chto kazhdoye uyekhavshii iz Rossii . . . ," Mandrykina, p. 257.

————. ". . . Odnako knizhka—dvoyurodnaya sestra . . . ," Mandrykina, p. 253.

————. "On the History of Acmeism," MHC, pp. 36–41.

————. "On Nadezhda Lvova's Poetry," MHC, pp. 255–256.

————. "Osip Mandelstam," (English) MHC, pp. 84–109.

————. "Otryvki iz vospominanii," S-F, III, pp. 145–156.

————. "Pages from a Diary," MHC, pp. 1–24.

————. "Pasternak," H-M, p. 307.

————. "Pasternak," MHC, p. 120.

————. "Perevody," *Sochineniya,* ed. Chernykh, II, pp. 260–366.

————. "Pervoye stikhotvoreniye ya napisala . . . ," Mandrykina, p. 245.

————. "Pisma," S-F, III, pp. 319–369.

————. "Pismo k Dzhankarlo Vigorelli," S-F, II, p. 307.

————. "Pismo v redaktsiyu zhurnala *Literaturnye zapiski,*" *Requiem,* p. 46. Orig. 1922.

————. *Poems of Akhmatova,* trans. Stanley Kunitz with Max Hayward. Boston: Little, Brown, 1967.

————. *Poezii.* Kiev: Dnipro, 1989 (in Ukrainian and Russian).

————. " 'Pro domo mea.' . . . ," Mandrykina, p. 254.

————. "Prose About the Poem," MHC, pp. 127–138.

————. "Proza ('Iz deyatelei 14 avgusta . . .')," *Requiem,* p. 236.

————. "Proza o Poeme," H-M, pp. 264–275.

————. "Pushkin and the Banks of the Neva," MHC, pp. 244–254.

————. "Pushkin and Children," MHC, pp. 264–266.

————. "Pushkin i deti," *Sochineniya* . . . , ed. Kralin, II, p. 110.

————. "Pushkin's Last Tale," MHC, pp. 149–170.

————. "Pushkin's *Stone Guest,*" MHC, pp. 200–214.

————. "Reminiscences of A. Blok," *Alexander Blok: An Anthology of Essays and Memoirs,* pp. 96–103.

————. *Rekviem.* Munich: Tvorchestvo zarubezhnykh pisatelei, 1963.

————. *Requiem and Poem Without a Hero,* trans. D. M. Thomas. London: Paul Elek, 1976.

————. "Requiem," ed. Zoya Tomashevskaya. *Oktyabr,* no. 3 (1987), pp. 130–135.

————. " 'Samyi neprochitannyi poet.' Zametki o Nikolaye Gumilyove," H-M, pp. 310–316.

————. "Seichas s izumleniyem prochla . . . ," Mandrykina, p. 249.

————. *Selected Poems,* trans. Richard McKane. London: Oxford University Press, 1969.

————. *Selected Poems,* ed. and trans. Walter Arndt. *Requiem,* trans. Robin Kimball. *Poem Without a Hero,* trans. and annot. Carl Proffer. Ann Arbor: Ardis, 1976.

————. *Selected Poems,* trans. Richard McKane. Newcastle-upon-Tyne: Bloodaxe Books, 1989.

————. *Severnye elegii.* Moscow: Kniga, 1989.

————. "Slepnyovo," Mandrykina, p. 246.

————. "Slepnyovo dlya menya . . . ," Mandrykina, p. 247.

————. "Slushala strekoznnyi vals . . . ," Mandrykina, p. 258.

————. *Sochineniya,* ed. G. P. Struve and B. A. Filipoff. Vol. I. 2nd ed. Munich: Inter-Language Literary Associates, 1967.

————. *Sochineniya,* ed. G. P. Struve and B. A. Filipoff. Vol. II. Munich: Inter-Langauge Literary Associates, 1968.

————. *Sochineniya,* ed. G. P. Struve, N. A. Struve, and B. A. Filipoff. Vol. III. Paris: YMCA Press, 1983.

————. *Sochineniya.* 2 vols. Vol. I, ed. V. A. Chernykh with an introduction by Mikhail Dudin, Vol. II, ed. E. G. Gershtein, L. A. Mandry Kina, V. A. Chernykh, and N. N. Gleno. Moscow: Khudozhestvennaya literatura, 1986.

————. Sochineniya v dvukh tomov, ed. N. N. Skatov and M. M. Kralin. Moscow: Pravda, 1990.

————. "Spravka ob avtore," *Requiem,* p. 227. From Anna Akhmatova, *Izbrannye stikhi* (1910–40), ed. A. Surkov, Moscow: Pravda, 1946.

————. ". . . Sredi etikh priyomov . . . ," Mandrykina, p. 257.

————. *Stikhi i proza.* Leningrad: Lenizdat, 1976.

————. *Stikhi, perepiska, vospominaniya, ikonografiya,* comp. E. Proffer. Ann Arbor: Ardis, 1977.

————. *Stikhotvoreniya.* Moscow: Raduga, 1988.

————. *Stikhotvoreniya i poemy,* ed. V. M. Zhirmunsky. Biblioteka poeta. Bolshaya seriya, 2nd ed. Leningrad: Sovetskii pisatel, 1976 and 1979.

————. *Stikhotvoreniya i poemy,* ed. N. A. Zhirmunskaya. Biblioteka poeta. Malaya seriya, 3rd ed. Leningrad: Sovetskii pisatel, 1984.

————. *Stikhotvoreniya i poemy,* ed. I. I. Slobozhan. Introduction and ed. A. I. Pavlovsky, annot. M. M. Kralin. Leningrad: Lenizdat, 1989.

————. *Tale Without a Hero and Twenty-two Poems by Anna Akhmatova,* trans. and ed. Jeanne van der Eng-Liedmeier and Kees Verheul. Dutch Studies in Russian Literature, 3. The Hague: Mouton, 1973.

————. "Ten letters of Anna Akhmatova," trans. Edith Stevens. Introductory article and notes by E. G. Gershtein. RLT (1976), pp. 627–644.

————. "1910-e gody," Mandrykina, p. 247.

————. "Titsian Tabidze and Paolo Yashvili," MHC, pp. 123–126.

————. "Tsarskoe v 20-kh godakh . . . ," Mandrykina, p. 250.

————. "Tsvetayeva," H-M, pp. 308–309.

————. *Twenty Poems,* trans. Jane Kenyon with Vera Sandomirsky Dunham. St. Paul, MN: Eighties Press, 1985.

————. "U poeta sushchestvuyut tainye otnosheniya . . . ," Mandrykina, p. 255.

————. "Uspet zapisat odnu sotuyu . . . ," Mandrykina, p. 253.

————. "V pervyi raz ya stala pisat . . . ," Mandrykina, p. 242.

————. "V seme nikto, skolko glaz vidit krugom . . . ," Mandrykina, p. 240.

————. "V sushchnosti, nikto ne znayet . . . ," Mandrykina, p. 247.

————. "V Tashkente ot 'evakuatsionnoi toski' . . . ," Mandrykina, p. 251.

————. "V Tsarskom Sele ona delala vsyo . . . ," Mandrykina, p. 244.

————. "V 1936-m ya snova nachinaya pisat . . . ," Mandrykina, p. 251.

————. "Vospominaniya ob Aleksandre Bloke," H-M, pp. 276–278.

————. "Vospominaniya ob Al. Bloke," S-F, II, pp. 191–194.

————. "Vsyo bylo podvalstno yemu," *Sochineniya.* . . . , ed. Kralin, II, pp. 133–134.

————. "Vystuplenie A. A. Akhmatovoi v radioperedache 'Govorit Leningrad,' " S-F, II, pp. 289–290.

————. *Way of All the Earth,* trans. D. M. Thomas. London: Secker & Warburg, 1979.

————. *Ya—golos vash . . . ,* ed. V. A. Chernykh. Moscow: Knizhnaya palata, 1989.

————. "Zametki k *Poeme bez geroya,*" S-F, III, pp. 154–166.

————. "Zapakhi Pavlovskogo vokzala . . . ," Mandrykina, p. 242.

————, Vs. Ivanov, S. Bondi, and S. Marshak. "V redaktsiyu *Novogo mira,*" *Voprosy literatury,* no. 3 (1987), p. 286.

Akhmatovskii sbornik, ed. Sergei Deduline and Gabriel Superfin. Bibliothèque Russe de l'Institut d'Etudes slaves, vol. LXXXV. Paris: Institut d'Etudes slaves, 1989.

Akmeyev, B. "Anna Akhmatova *Anno Domini,*" PV, pp. 63–65.

Alexander Blok: An Anthology of Essays and Memoirs, ed. and trans. Lucy Vogel. Ann Arbor: Ardis, 1982.

Aleksandrov, Rostislav. "Dobrota svetilyas v nei," *Vechernyaya Odessa,* June 21, 1989, p. 3.

Alfonosov, V. N. "Poeziya Borisa Pasternaka," *Boris Pasternak: Stikhotvoreniya i poemy.* 2 vols. Leningrad: Sovetskii pisatel. Biblioteka poeta, 3rd ed., 1990, pp. 6–72.

Aliger, Margarita. *Tropinka vo rzhi.* Moscow: Sovetskii pisatel, 1980.

————. "V poslednii raz," VOAA, pp. 349–368.

Almi, I. L. "O liricheskikh syuzhetakh Pushkina v stikhotvoreniyakh Anny Akhmatovoi," TR, pp. 5–19.

Amert, Susan. *Akhmatova's Later Lyrics: The Poetics of Mediation.* Ph.D. Dissertation, Yale University, 1983.

———. "Akhmatova's 'Pushkin i nevskoe vzmore,' " TARA, XXII (1990), pp. 193–211.

———. "Akhmatova's 'Song of the Motherland': Rereading the Opening Texts of *Requiem,*" *Slavic Review,* no. 3, XLIX (Fall 1990), pp. 374–389.

———. " 'Bolshim Mayakovskim putem': Akhmatova and the *kazennyi gimn,*" SUE, II, pp. 257–266.

———. *In a Shattered Mirror: The Later Poetry of Anna Akhmatova.* Palo Alto, CA: Stanford University Press, 1992.

———. " 'Predystoriya': Akhmatova's Aetiological Myth," AA, pp. 13–28.

Amfiteatrov, Aleksandr. "N. S. Gumilyov," NGVS, pp. 239–242.

Anaksagorova, A. K. "V kvartire na ulitse Krasnoi konnitsy," OAA, pp. 290–294.

Anichikov, E. *Novaya russkaya poeziya.* Berlin: I. P. Ladyzhnikov, 1923.

Anikin, A. E. "Chudo smerti i chudo muzyki (O vozmozhnykh istokakh i parallelyakh nekotorykh motivov poezii Akhmatovoi)," *Russian Literature,* XXX (1991), pp. 285–302.

———. " 'Classical' and 'Tsarskoe Selo' in the Works of Annensky: Some Observations in Regard to Acmeism," SP, pp. 191–214.

———. "O literaturnykh istokakh 'detskikh' motivov v poezii Anny Akhmatovoi," *Russkaya rech,* no. 1 (January–February 1991), pp. 23–28.

Anna Akhmatova: 1889–1989, ed. Sonia I. Ketchian. Modern Russian Literature and Culture, vol. 28. Berkeley: Berkeley Slavic Specialties, 1993.

Anna Akhmatova: Portrety. Rukopisi. Illyustratsii. Ocherk tvorchestva, comp. L. Shilov. Moscow: Gosudarstvennyi literaturnyi muzei, n.d.

Anna Akhmatova ta Ukraina: Bibliografichnyi pokazhhchik, comp. and ed. Oleksandr Moskalets and Evdokiya Olshanskaya. Kiev: Derzhavna biblioteka Ukrainy, 1993.

Anna Akhmatova: tri knigi (B. Eichenbaum. Anna Akhmatova. V. V. Vinogradov. O Poezii Anny Akhmatovoi. V. M. Zhirmunsky. Tvorchestvo Anny Akhmatovoi). Ann Arbor: Ardis, 1990.

Annenkov, Yury. "Anna Akhmatova," *Dnevnik moikh vstrech. Tsikl tragedii,* I, pp. 114–146.

———. *Dnevnik moikh vstrech. Tsikl tragedii,* I. New York: Inter-Language Literary Associates, 1966.

———. "Iz knigi *Dnevnik* moikh vstrech," VOAA, pp. 78–82.

———. "Nikolay Gumilyov," *Dnevnik moikh vstrech,* I, pp. 97–112.

———. "Poslednyaya vstrecha," *Neva,* no. 6 (1989), pp. 196–198.

Annensky, Innokenty. *The Cypress Chest,* trans. R. H. Morrison (bilingual edition). Ann Arbor: Ardis, 1982.

———. *Knigi otrazhenii.* Moscow: Nauka, 1979.

———. "O sovremennom liritsisme," *Knigi otrazhenii,* ed. N. T. Ashibayev, et al. Moscow: Nauka, 1979, pp. 238–382.

———. "Pushkin i Tsarskoe Selo," *Knigi otrazhenii,* ed. Ashibayev, et al., pp. 304–321.

———. *Stikhotvoreniya i tragedii,* ed. A. V. Fyodorov. Biblioteka poeta, Bolshaya seriya, 2nd ed. Leningrad: Sovetskii pisatel, 1959.

Anrep, Boris. "O chyornom koltse," S-F, III, pp. 439–465. See also LO, no. 5 (1989), pp. 57–63; DG, pp. 191–211, and VOAA, pp. 83–90.

Antologiya peterburgskoi poezii epokhi akmeizma, ed. George Ivask and H. W. Tjalsma. Centrifuga: Russian Reprintings and Printings, vol. 16. Munich: Wilhelm Fink Verlag, 1973.

Antsiferov, Nikolay. *Dusha Peterburga.* Petrograd: Brokgauz-Efron, 1923.

———. "Iz knigi *Dusha Peterburga,*" PBG, p. 82.

Arbatov, B. I. "Grazh. Akhmatova i tov. Kollontai," *Requiem,* p. 54. Orig. *Molodaya gvardiya* (1923), no. 4/5, p. 151.

Ardov, O. Mikhail. "Legendarnaya Ordynka," *Russkaya mysl,* no. 3982 (June 4–10, 1993, p. 8; June 11–17, p. 10).

———. "Ne 'poetessa.' Poet! Iz besed s Annoi Akhmatovoi," *Literaturnaya gazeta,* January 4, 1989, p. 5.

———. "Post Scriptum," SMV, pp. 174–179.

Ardov, Viktor. "Anna Akhmatova," SL, no. 6 (1989), pp. 94–99.

———. "Iz 'Vospominanii ob Anne Akhmatovoi," *Den poezii.* Moscow: Sovetskii pisatel, 1982, pp. 77–81.

———. "Vstrecha Anny Akhmatovoi s Marinoi Tsvetayevoi," *Grani,* no. 76, XXV (1970), pp. 110–114.

"Arestovannaya literatura," *Gosudarstvennaya bezopastnost i demokratiya,* no. 3 (Moscow, 1992), pp. 35–52.

Ariev, Andrei. " 'The Splendid Darkness of a Strange Garden': Tsarskoe Selo in the Russian Poetic Tradition and Akhmatova's 'Ode to Tsarskoe Selo,' " SP, pp. 51–87.

Arkhangelskaya, T., and V. Radzishevsky. " 'K sebe domoi': Pervyi akhmatovskii prazdnik poezii," *Literaturnaya gazeta,* July 22, 1987, p. 7.

Arkhangelsky, Aleksandr. "Chas muzhestva," LO, I (1988), pp. 48–51.

Artyukhovskaya, M. I. "O traditsiyakh russkoi psikhologicheskoi prozy v rannem tvorchestve Anny Akhmatovoi," *Vestnik Moskovskogo Universiteta,* Seriya 9, Filologiya, II (March–April), pp. 14–21.

Aseev, Nikolai. "Melody or Intonation," *Pasternak*-Davie, pp. 73–84.

Askoldov, S. A. "Iz pisma k A. A. Zolotaryovu," *Requiem,* p. 154. Orig. LO (1989), no. 5.

Astapov, Vasily. "Seansy v Komarove," OAA, pp. 398–410.

Atlas, Dorothy. *Staraya Odessa, yeyo druzya i nedrugi.* Odessa: Lasmi, 1992 (first printed 1911).

"Attestat," DG, p. 42.

Azadovsky, Konstantin. "Akhmatova i Yesenin (K istorii znakomstva)," AS, pp. 77–82.

———. "Menya nazval 'kitezhankoi': Anna Akhmatova i Nikolay Klyuev," LO, no. 5 (1989), pp. 66–70.

———. " 'Proportsiya 'mraka' i 'sveta' v stikakh D. E. Maksimova," LO, no. 4 (1988), pp. 108–112.

———, and R. D. Timenchik. "K biografii N. S. Gumilyova (vokrug dnevnikov i albomov F. F. Fidlera)," *Russkaya literatura,* no. 2 (1988), pp. 171–186.

———, and Boris Yegorov, "O nizkopoklonstve i kosmopolitizme; 1948–1949," *Zvezda,* no. 6 (1989), pp. 157–176.

Azarov, Vsevolod. "Anna Akhmatova na Ukraine," *Vechernyaya Odessa,* June 12, 1989, p. 3.

———. " 'Mezhdu sosen,' " OAA, pp. 357–359.

Babayev, E. G. "A. A. Akhmatova v pismakh k N. I. Khardzhiyevu (1930–1960-e gg.), TR, pp. 198–228. (Also in *Voprosy literatury* [June 1989], pp. 214–247.)

———. "Na ulitse Zhukovskoi . . . ," LO, no. 7 (1985), pp. 99–104, and VOAA, pp. 404–419.

———. "Nadpis na knige. Neizvestnaya epigramma Anny Akhmatovoi," SMV, pp. 12–17.

———. "Pushkinskiye stranitsy Anny Akhmatovoi," *Novyi mir,* no. 1 (January 1987), pp. 153–166.

———. " 'Sokrovennaya rech': Ob odnom stikhotvorenii Anny Akhmatovoi," *Russkaya rech,* no. 3 (May–June 1989), pp. 28–32.

Baer, Joachim T. "Three Variations on the Theme 'Moi Pushkin': Briusov, Akhmatova, Tsvetaeva," TARA, XX (1987), pp. 163–183.

Bakhterev, Igor. "Tot mesyats v Tashkente," OAA, pp. 216–223.

Balashova, T. V. "Slovo frantsuzskoi kritiki v sporakh o tvorchestve Akhmatovoi," TR, pp. 124–131.

Balatov, Alexei, trans. Raissa Bobrova. "In Akhmatova's Presence," SL, pp. 100–107.

Baluashvili, Valentina. "Shtrikhi k portretam: Anna Akhmatova," *Dom pod Chinarami.* Tbilisi: Merani, 1981, pp. 41–48.

———. "U Anny Akhmatovoi," S-F, II, pp. 296–330.

Bannikov, V. V. "Vysokii dar," in Anna Akhmatova, *Izbrannye stikhotvoreniya,* 1952, pp. 535–558.

Baran, Henrik. "Paskha 1917 goda: Akhmatova i drugiye v russkikh gazetakh," AS, pp. 53–76.

———. "Pisma A. A. Akhmatovoi k N. I. Khardzhiyevu," *Russian Literature,* 7/8 (1974), pp. 5–17.

Baranov, Vadim. "The Inevitability of Purification," SL, no. 2 (1989), pp. 133–137.

Barili, Gabriel. "Stati o Pushkine Akhmatovoi i 'Razgovor o Dante' Mandelshtama. Iz nablyudenii," TR, pp. 39–47.

Barnes, Christopher. *Boris Pasternak: A Literary Biography.* Vol. I. Cambridge: Cambridge University Press, 1989.

Barskaya, G. " 'I tam podruzhilas s morem . . .': O prebyvanii poetessy v Krymu," *Sovetskii Krym* (June 23, 1989).

Basalayev, Innokenty. "Iz ocherka 'Na doklade Zhdanova,' " *Requiem,* pp. 232–233. Orig. *Pamyat,* kn. 2 (Paris, 1979).

———. "Zapiski dlya sebya (1926–1939)," OAA, pp. 170–172.

Basker, Michael. "Dislocation and Relocation in Akhmatova's *Requiem,*" SUE, I, pp. 5–26.

———. "Gumilev, Annensky and Tsarskoe Selo: Gumilev's 'Tsarskoselskii krug idei,' " SP, pp. 215–230.

Batalov, Aleksei. "In Akhmatova's presence," SL, no. 6 (1989), pp. 100–107.

———. "Ryadom s Akhmatovoi," *Neva,* no. 3 (1984), pp. 155–164.

Bazhan, Mikola. "Etna-Taormina," trans. from Ukrainian by Yelena Umbaskaya. *Druzhba narodov,* no. 8 (1979), pp. 261–268.

———. "The Etna-Taormina Prize," trans. June Goss. SL, no. 6 (1989), pp. 140–145.

Bazhenov, M. N. "Chetyre moskovskikh inskripta Akhmatovoi," SMV, pp. 180–184.

———. " 'I my sokhranim tebya, russkaya rech' " *Russkaya rech,* I (January–February 1982), pp. 41–42.

———. "I vot uzhe Kryma temneyet gryada . . . : O krym. periode zhizni i tvorchestva A. Akhmatovoi," *Sovetskii Krym* (October 9, 1983).

———. "Moscow and Muscovites in the Life of Anna Akhmatova," trans. Ben Vladyko. SL, no. 6 (1989), pp. 182–189.

Beer, V. A. "Listki iz dalyokikh vospominanii," VOAA, pp. 28–32.

Belinkov, Arkady. "Anna Akhmatova i istoriya i otryvki iz neokonchennoi knigi *Sudba (Pobeda)* Anny Akhmatovoi," *Grani,* L (1985), pp. 120–137.

Beloded, I. K. "Simvolika kontrasta v poeticheskom yazyke Anny Akhmatovoi," *Poetika i stilistika russkoi literatury,* pp. 269–279.

Beloshevskaya, Lyubov. "Ob odnom stilisticheskom aspekte perevoda liriki A. Akhmatovoi na cheshkii yazyk," *Československa Rusistika,* no. 5, XXXV (1990), pp. 265–268.

Bely, Andrey. "Bashennyi zhitel," NGVS, pp. 148–150.

———. "Na ekrane Gumilyov," NGVS, pp. 33–35.

Berdyaev, Nikolay. "Iz knigi *Samopoznaniye,*" PBG, pp. 97–102.

————. "O tvorcheskoi svobode i fabrikatsii dush," *Requiem,* pp. 252–258 Orig. *Russkie novosti,* Paris (October 4, 1946).

————. *Samopoznaniye.* Moscow: Mysl, 1991.

————. "Samopoznaniye: fragmenty knigi," *Nashe naslediye,* VI (1988), pp. 39–55.

Berggolts, Olga. *Biblioteka izbranoi liviki.* n.p.: Molodaya gvardiya, 1964.

————. "Iz knigi Govorit Leningrad," VOAA, pp. 347–348.

————. "Iz pisma k A. K. Tarasenkovu," *Requiem,* pp. 226–227.

Berlin, Isaiah. "Anna Akhmatova: A Memoir," in *The Complete Poems of Anna Akhmatova,* II, pp. 24–45.

————. Iz ocherka "Vstrechi s russkimi pisatelyami," *Requiem,* pp. 197–224. Orig. *Slavica Hierosolymitana,* trans. from English D. Segan, E. Tolstaya-Segal, and M. O. Ronan with aid of Berlin, V–VI (1981).

————. "Iz vospominanii 'Vstrechi s russkimi pisatelyami,' " VOAA, pp. 436–459.

————. "Meetings with Russian Writers in 1945 and 1956," *Personal Impressions.* New York: Viking Press, 1981, pp. 156–210.

Bernadsky, S. " 'Zdes vstretilas s Muzoi . . .': A. Akhmatova v Krymu," *Krymskie kanikuly.* Simferopol, 1981, pp. 279–286.

Bernshtein, I. A. "Skrytye poeticheskiye tsikly v tvorchestve Anny Akhmatovoi," *Izvestiya Akademii nauk SSSR: Seriya literatury i yazyka,* no. 5, XLVIII (September–October 1989), pp. 418–423.

Bethea, David. *Khodasevich: His Life and Art.* Princeton: Princeton University Press, 1983.

————. *The Shape of Apocalypse in Modern Russian Fiction.* Princeton: Princeton University Press, 1989.

Bickert, Elaine. *Anna Akhmatova: Silence à plusieurs voix.* Paris: Editions Resma, 1970.

Billington, James H. *The Icon and the Axe. An Interpretive History of Russian Culture.* New York: Vintage Books, 1970.

Bilokin, S. "Kyivska rodyna Akhmatovoyi," *Molodaya gvardiya,* July 17, 1984.

————, and M. Sulima. "Na pochatku shlyakhu: Z Kyiv. periodu zhittya i tvorchosti Anny Akhmatovoyi," *Molodaya gvardiya,* February 2, 1980.

————. "Z yunykh rokiv Anny Akhmatovoi," *Prapor zmagannya,* December 23, 1981.

Birnbaum, Henrik. "Face to Face with Death. On a Recurrent Theme in the Poetry of Anna Achmatova," *Scandoslavica,* XXVIII (1982), pp. 5–17.

————. "Gedichtroman und Romangedicht im russischen Postsymbolismus," *Text. Symbol. Weltmodell,* pp. 19–36.

————. "Text, Context, Subtext: Notes on Anna Achmatova's 'A Poem Without a Hero,' " in *Text and Context: Essays to Honor Nils Ake Nilsson,* ed. Peter Alberg Jensen, et al. Stockholm: Almqvist & Wiksell, 1987, pp. 139–145.

Bisk, Aleksandr. "Russkii Parizh 1906–1908 gg.," NGVS, pp. 36–37.

Blok, Aleksandr. "Iz dnevnikov, zapisnykh, knizhek i pisem," VOAA, pp. 41–43.

————. "Narod i intelligentsiya," *Sobraniye sochinenii,* V, pp. 318–328.

————. "O sovremennom sostoyanii russkogo simvolizma," *Sobraniye sochinenii,* Vol. II, pp. 147–158.

————. *Sobraniye sochinenii,* ed. V. N. Orlov, A. A. Surkov, and K. I. Chukovsky. Vols. I–IX. Moscow and Leningrad: Khudozhestvennaya literatura, 1950–55.

Blot, Jean. "Anna Akhmatova," *Preuves,* no. 133 (March 1962), pp 3–6.

Bobovich, B. "Iz stati 'Literaturnye vechera: Vecher *Russkogo sovremennika,*' " *Requiem,* pp. 70–71. Orig. *Vechernyaya Moskva* (April 18, 1924).

Bobyshev, Dmitry. "Akhmatovskiye siroty," *Russkaya mysl,* no. 3507 (March 8, 1984), pp. 8–9.

————. "O tak nazyvayemykh 'anti-emigrantskikh' stikakh Anny Akhmatovoi," TARA, XXIII (1990), pp. 163–173.

Bogomolov, N. A. "N. S. Gumilyov (Kratkaya biografiya)," in N. Gumilyov, *Stikhi. Pisma o russkoi poezii*, pp. 431–436.

————. "Takim ya vizhu oblik vash i vzglyad," LO, no. 5 (1989), pp. 37–43.

————. "Vokrug 'Foreli,' " *Mikhail Kuzmin i russkaya kultura XX veka*, pp. 206–211.

Boldyrev, A. N. "Zapiski iz dnevnika," OAA, pp. 301–310.

Bordeaux, Jean-Mark. "Vstrechi s Akhmatovoi, ili kak ya nachal perevodit stikhi," AS, pp. 225–232.

Boris Pasternak and His Time: Collected Papers from Second International Symposium on Pasternak, ed. Lazar Fleishman. Berkeley: Berkeley Specialties, 1989.

Boris Pasternak 1890–1960: Colloque de Cerisy-la-salle 11–14 September 1975. Paris: Institut d'Etudes slaves, 1979.

Boris Pasternak und Deutschland, ed. Sergej Dorzweiler, Bernhard Lauer, and Katharina Linka. Kassel: Brüder Grimm-Museum, 1992.

Böss, O. *Die Lehre der Eurasier. Ein Beitrag zur russischen Ideengeschichte des 20. Jahrhunderts*. Wiesbaden, 1961.

Botsford, Keith. "A Note on the Music of Artur Lourié," *Bostonia* (Fall 1992), pp. 39–41.

Bowlt, John E. "From Practice to Theory: Vladimir Tatlin and Nikolai Punin," *Literature, Culture, and Society in the Modern Age: In Honor of Joseph Frank*. Pt. II. Stanford Slavic Studies, no. 2, IV, Stanford: Stanford University Press, 1992, pp. 50–66.

————, ed. and trans. *Russian Art of the Avant-Garde: Theory and Criticism 1902–1934*. New York: Thames and Hudson, 1976.

Brazhnin, Ilya. "Obayaniye talanta," *Novyi mir*, no. 12 (December 1976), pp. 235–244.

Brik, L. Yu. "Chuzhiye stikhi," *V. Mayakovsky v vospominaniyakh sovremennikov*. Moscow: Gosudarstvennoye izdatelstvo khudozhestvennoi literatury, 1963, pp. 328–354.

Brodsky, Joseph. "The Keening Muse," *Less Than One: Selected Essays*. New York: Farrar, Straus, & Giroux, 1986, pp. 34–53.

————. "Nobel Lecture, 1987," *Brodsky's Poetics*, pp. 1–11.

————. *Ostanovka: stikhotvoreniya i poemy*. New York: Chekhov, 1970.

Brodsky's Poetics and Aesthetics, ed. Lev Loseff and Valentina Polukhina. London: Macmillan, 1990.

Bronguleyev, Vadim. "Afrikanskii dnevnik N. Gumilyova," *Nashe naslediye*, no. 1 (1988), pp. 79–91.

————. "Novoye ob afrikanskikh puteshestviyakh N. Gumilyova," *Nashe naslediye*, no. 8, (1989), p. 27.

Brown, Clarence. "Introduction," in Osip Mandelstam, *Selected Poems*, trans. Clarence Brown and W. S. Merwin, pp. v–xviii.

Bryusov, Valery. *Sobraniye sochinenii*, I. Moscow: Khudozhestvennaya literatura, 1973.

Buchinskaya, Nadezhda (Teffi). "Iz *Vospominanii*," DG, p. 94.

Budyko, M. I. "Rasskazy Akhmatovoi," OAA, pp. 461–506.

Budyko, Yu. I. "Istoriya odnogo posvyashcheniya," *Russkaya literatura*, no. 1 (1984), pp. 235–238.

————. " 'Ya poslal tebe chyornuyu rozu v bokale . . . ,' " *Russkaya literatura*, no. 4 (1984), pp. 217–221.

Bukhshtab, Boris. "The Poetry of Mandelstam," trans. Clarence Brown. RLT, no. 1 (1971), pp. 262–282. Orig. 1919.

Bulgakova, E. S. "Iz dnevnika," *Requiem*, p. 116.

Butyrin, K. M. "Problema poeticheskogo simvola v russkom literaturovedenii (XIX–XX vv.)," *Isslevodaniya po poetike i stilistike*. Leningrad: Nauka, 1972, pp. 248–260.

Byron, Lord George. *The Poetical Works of Lord Byron,* New York: Hurst & Co., n.d.

Camajani, Giovanni. "Arthur Vincent Lourie," *The New Grove Dictionary of Music and Musicians,* ed. Stanley Sadie. Vol. XI. London: Macmillan, 1980, p. 257.

Carlisle, Olga. "Poems by Anna Akhmatova," trans. Robert Lowell. *The Atlantic* (October 1964), pp. 60–61.

———. "A Woman in Touch with Her Feelings," *Vogue* (August 1973), pp. 19–23.

Charques, Richard. *The Twilight of Imperial Russia.* London: Oxford University Press, 1958.

Chechelnitskaya, Inna. "Akhmatova and Pushkin: *Apologia Pro Vita Sua,*" AA, pp. 29–43.

———. "Anna Axmatova: *Poem Without a Hero.*" Ph.D. Dissertation, Brown University, 1982. (This dissertation is locked in a safe at Brown University and cannot be read without the author's permission.)

———. "Number as Cypher in Akhmatova's *Poema bez geroya,*" SUE, I, pp. 73–86.

———. "Skrytoe prisutstviye Gumilyova v *Poeme bez geroya* Akhmatovoi," *Nikolaj Gumilev 1886–1986,* ed. Sheelagh Duffin Graham. Berkeley: Berkeley Slavic Specialties, 1987, pp. 77–101.

Chepik, Irina. "Inspired by St. Petersburg," SL, no. 6 (1989), pp. 191–192.

Chernova, E. B. "Slepnyovo," VOAA, pp. 44–46.

Chernyak, Ya. Z. "Iz tashkentskogo dnevnika," VOAA, pp. 375–377.

Chernykh, V. A. "Anna Akhmatova o Nikolaye Gumilyove,"*Literaturnaya gazeta,* June 13, 1990, p. 7.

———. "Perepiska Bloka s A. A. Akhmatovoi," *Literaturnoye nasledstvo: Aleksandr Blok: novye materialy i issledovaniya,* vol. 92, bk. 4, pp. 571–577.

———. "Rannye avtografy Akhmatovoi i listki iz zapisnykh tetradei: 1910–1911 g.g.," *Izvestiya AN SSSR,* Seriya literatury i yazyka, no. 4, XLIII (July–August 1984), pp. 348–354.

———. "Rukopisnoye naslediye Anny Akhmatovoi i problemy ego publikatsii," TS, pp. 207–216.

———, ed. "Avtobiograficheskaya proza," LO, no. 5 (1989), pp. 3–17.

Chervinskaya, O. V. "Mifotvorchestvo Anny Akhmatovoi," *Voprosy russkoi literatury,* vyp. 2 (54). Lvov: Lvov University, 1989, pp. 3–19.

Chicherov, V. L. *Zimnii period russkogo zemledelcheskogo kalendarya XVI–XIX vekov.* Moscow: 1957.

Childers, Rory, and Anna Lisa Crone. "The Mandelshtam Presence in the Dedications of *Poema bez geroya,*" *Russian Literature,* XV (1984), pp. 51–82.

Chubinsky, P. P. *Kalendar narodnykh obychayev i obryadov.* Kiev: Muzychna Ukraina, 1993.

Chukovskaya, Lydia. *The Akhmatova Journals, 1938–41,* trans. Milena Michalski and Sylva Rubashova with poetry trans. by Peter Norman. New York: Farrar Straus Giroux, 1993.

———. "Polumyortvaya i nemaya," *Kontinent,* no. 7 (1976), pp. 430–436.

———. *Zapiski ob Anne Akhmatovoi,* I (1938–1941). Paris: YMCA Press, 1976.

———. *Zapiski ob Anne Akhmatovoi,* II (1952–1962). Paris: YMCA Press, 1980.

Chukovsky, Kornei. "Akhmatova i Mayakovsky," *Dom iskusstv,* I (1920), pp. 23–42. Reprinted in *Voprosy literatury,* no. 1 (1988), pp. 177–205. (Translated by John Pearson in *Major Soviet Writers: Essays in Criticism,* ed. Edward J. Brown. London: Oxford University Press, 1973, pp. 33–53.)

———. "Anna Akhmatova," *Sobraniye sochinenii v shesti tomakh,* V, pp. 725–755. Moscow: Khudozhestvennaya literatura, 1967.

———. "Anne Akhmatovoi: prisetstvennoye slovo Korneya Chukovskogo," *Oxford Slavonic Papers,* XII. Oxford: Clarendon Press, 1965, pp. 141–145.

——. "Chitaya Akhmatovu," *Moskva,* no. 5 (1964), pp. 200–203.

——. "Chukovsky ob Akhmatovoi. Po arkhivnym materialam," *Novyi mir* (March 1987), pp. 227–239. Also in DG, pp. 249–250, and *Requiem,* pp. 42–43, 67, 70.

——. "Excerpt from 'A. A. Blok: The Man,' in *Alexander Blok: An Anthology of Essays and Memoirs,* pp. 64–89.

——. "Iz vospominanii. Iz dnevnika," VOAA, pp. 48–64.

——. *Lyudi i knigi,* V. Moscow: Khudozhestvennaya literatura, 1960.

Chukovsky, Valeryan. "Po povodu stikhov Anny Akhmatovoi," PBG, pp. 110–119. Orig. *Apollon,* no. 5 (1912).

Chulkov, Georgy. "Anna Akhmatova," *Nashi sputniki 1912–1922.* Moscow: N. V. Vasilev, 1922, pp. 71–125.

——. "Iz knigi *Gody stranstvii,*" VOAA, p. 35, and DG, pp. 48–49.

——. "Iz ocherka 'Samoubiitsy,' " PBG, p. 141. Orig. *Vchera i segodnya. Ocherki.* Moscow, 1916.

——. "Iz pisma k N. G. Chulkovoi," *Requiem,* p. 31. Orig. archives TsGALI.

——. *Nashi sputniki.* Moscow: N. V. Vasilev, 1922.

Chulkova, Nadezhda. "Iz vospominanii," *Requiem,* pp. 43, 167–168, 226.

Chuzhak, N. "Iz knigi *Literatura. Khudozhestvennaya politika RKP. Vserossiiskii Proletkult,*" *Requiem,* pp. 57–58.

Cioran, Samuel D. "Vladimir Solovyov and the Divine Feminine," RLT, no. 4 (Fall 1972), pp. 219–240.

Clark, Katerina. *The Soviet Novel: History as Ritual.* Chicago: University of Chicago Press, 1981.

Clowes, Edith W. "The Integration of Nietzsche's Ideas of History, Time and 'Higher Nature' in the Early Historical Novels of Dmitry Merezhkovsky," *Germano-Slavica,* no. 6, III (Fall 1981), pp. 401–416.

Conquest, Robert. "Iz knigi *Bolshoi terror,*" trans. L. Vladimirov, *Requiem,* pp. 233–234.

Crone, Anna L. "Akhmatova and the Passing of the Swans: Horatian Tradition and Tsarskoe Selo," SP, pp. 88–112.

——. "Anna Akhmatova and the Imitation of Annenskij," *Wiener Slawistischen Almanach,* VII (1981), pp. 81–93.

——. "Antimetabole in *Rekviem:* The Structural Disposition of Themes and Motifs," SUE, I, pp. 27–44.

——. "Blok as Don Juan in Akhmatova's 'Poema bez geroja,' " *Russian Language Journal,* no. 121–122, XXXV (1981), pp. 145–162.

——. "Genre Allusions in *Poema bez geroia:* Masking Tragedy and Satyric Drama," AA, pp. 43–59.

——. "Three Sources for Akhmatova's 'Ne strashchaj menya groznoi sudboi,' " *Russian Language Journal,* no. 109, XXXI (1977), pp. 147–155.

Czapski, Joseph. *The Inhuman Land,* trans. Gerard Hopkins. London: Chatto & Windus, 1951.

——. "Iz knigi *Na zhestokoi zemle,*" trans. M. K. Polivanov, *Requiem,* p. 174.

Davidson, Pamela. "Akhmatova's 'Dante,' " SUE, II, pp. 201–224.

Davies, Jessie. *Anna of All the Russias.* Liverpool: Lincoln Davies & Co., 1988.

Deduline, Serge. "Iz besedy s Dmitriyem Bushenom," DG, pp. 89–93. Original in the literary supplement to the newspaper *Russkaya mysl* (Paris, July 5, 1987).

Delson, V. *Skryabin: ocherki zhizni i tvorchestva.* Moscow: Muzyka, 1971.

Deppermann, Maria. "Russland um 1900: Reichten und Krise einer Epoche in Umbrich," *Musik-Konzepte. Aleksandr Skrjabin und die Skrjayabinisten* 37/38, pp. 61–106.

Des Pres, Terrence. "Poetry and Politics," *TriQuarterly,* LXV (Winter 1986), pp. 17–79.

Deutscher, Isaac. "Pasternak and the Calendar of the Revolution," *Pasternak*-Davie, pp. 240–258.

Dictionary of Russian Women Writers, ed. Marina Ledkovsky, Charlotte Rosenthal, and Mary Zirin. Westport, CT: Greenwood Press, 1994.

Digges, Deborah. "Translation and the Egg," CPP, pp. 27–31.

Dmitriyev, A. L. "Antonimy v poezii A. A. Akhmatovoi," *Russkii yazyk v shkole,* no. 3 (May–June 1987), pp. 73–78.

———. "A. S. Pushkin i yazyk poezii A. Akhmatovoi," *Russkii yazyk v shkole,* no. 3 (May–June 1987), pp. 64–68.

———. " 'Dlya velikoi lyubvi': K 100-letiyu so dnya rozhdeniya A. A. Akhmatovoi," *Russkii yazyk v shkole,* no. 3 (May–June 1987), pp. 80–86.

Dmytryshyn, Basil. *USSR: A Concise History.* New York: Charles Scribner's Sons, 1984.

Dobin, E. "*Poema bez geroya* Anny Akhmatovoi," *Voprosy literatury,* no. 9 (September 1966), pp. 63–79.

———. *Poeziya Anny Akhmatovoi.* Leningrad: Sovetskii pisatel, 1968.

Dolgopolov, L. K. "Dostoyevsky i Blok v *Poeme bez geroya* Anny Akhmatovoi," *V mire Bloka.* Moscow: Sovetskii pisatel, 1989, pp. 454–480.

———. "Po zakonam prityazheniya (O literaturnykh traditsiyakh v *Poeme bez geroya* Anny Akhmatovoi)," *Russkaya literatura,* no. 4 (1979), pp. 38–57.

Dorovatovskaya, V. "Iz stati 'Lyubov i sostradaniye,' " DG, pp. 128–129. Orig. in *Zhizn dlya vsekh,* no. 2 (1917).

Dorzweiler, Sergej. "Boris Pasternak und die deutsche Philosophie," *Boris Pasternak und Deutschland,* pp. 25–37.

Drews, Peter. "Die slawische Avantgarde und der Westen," *Forum Slavicum,* LV. Munich: Wilhelm Fink Verlag, 1983.

Driver, Sam. "Acmeism," *Slavic East European Journal,* no. 2, XXII (1968), pp. 141–156.

———. "Akhmatova: A Selected, Annotated Bibliography," RLT, no. 1 (Fall 1971), pp. 432–34.

———. "Akhmatova's *Poema bez geroja* and Blok's *Vozmezdie,*" *Aleksandr Blok Centennial Conference,* ed. W. Vickery and B. Sagatov. Columbus, Ohio, 1984, pp. 89–99.

———. "Anna Akhmatova: Early Love Poems," RLT, no. 1 (Fall 1971), pp. 297–325.

———. "Anna Akhmatova: Theory and Practice," *Canadian-American Slavic Studies,* nos. 1–4, XXII (1988), pp. 343–351.

———. "Directions in Akhmatova's Poetry Since the Early Period," *Russian Literature* (Spring 1975 supplement), pp. 84–91.

———. "The Supernatural in the Poetry of Anna Akhmatova," in Amy Mandelker and Roberta Reeder, eds., *The Supernatural in Slavic and Baltic Literature: Essays in Honor of Victor Terras.* Columbus, OH: Slavica Publishers, 1988, pp. 217–225.

Drizen, Baron Nikolay. "Iz stati 'Teatr vo vremya revolyutsii,' " PGB, p. 147. Orig. *Slovo* (Riga, November 6, 1927).

Dudin, Mikhail. "Dushi vysokaya svoboda," Anna Akhmatova, *Sochineniya,* ed. Chernykh, I, pp. 5–18.

———. "Nevesyolye priznaniya pri radostnom sobytii," TsS, pp. 6–8.

———. "Okhotnik za pesnami muzhestva," Nikolay Gumilyov, *Stikhotvoreniya i poemy,* 1988.

———. "Slovo ob Akhmatovoi," *Vechernyaya Odessa,* June 1, 1989, pp. 1 and 4.

———, et al. "Pismo v redaktsiyu. My yeshchyo zhivy," *Literaturnaya gazeta,* January 17, 1990, p. 7.

Dutch Contributions to the Eighth International Congress of Slavists, ed. Jan M. Meijer. Amsterdam: John Benjamins, 1979.

Dutli, Ralph. *Ossip Mandelstam "Als riefe man mich bei meinem Namen."* Frankfurt: Fischer Taschenbuch Verlag, 1990.

Dymshchits, A. L. "Poeziya Osipa Mandelshtama," in Osip Mandelstam, *Stikhotvoreniya,* ed. N. I. Khardzhiyev, pp. 5–53.

Ecker, N. "Elemente der Volksdichtung in der Lyrik Anna Achmatowas." Ph.D. Dissertation, University of Vienna, 1973.

Ehrenburg, Ilya. "Anna Andreyevna Akhmatova," *Portrety russkikh poetov.* Berlin, n.d., pp. 7–9.

————. *Eve of War 1933–1944: Men, Years, Life.* Vol. IV. Trans. Tatiana Shebunina with Yvonne Kapp. London: MacGibbon & Kee, 1963.

————. *Post-war Years 1945–1954: Men, Years, Life.* Vol. V. Trans. Tatiana Shebunina with Yvonne Kapp. London: MacGibbon & Kee, 1966.

Eikhenbaum, Boris. *Anna Akhmatova: opyt analiza.* Paris: Lev, 1980 (first published 1922).

————. "Blok's Fate," *Alexander Blok: An Anthology of Essays,* pp. 130–144.

————. "Ob Akhmatovoi" [Lecture, House of Scholars, January 7, 1946, and House of Film, March 17, 1946], PV, pp. 222–226. Orig. *Den poezii,* Leningrad, 1967.

————. "Roman-lirika," DG, pp. 247–249. Orig. in *Vestnik literatury* (1921), nos. 6–7.

Eisenstein, Sergey. *Selected Works.* Vol. I *Eisenstein: Writings 1922–1934,* ed. Richard Taylor. London: BFI Publishing, and Bloomington: Indiana University Press, 1988.

————. *Film Form, Essays in Film Theory.* New York: Harcourt, Brace & Co., 1949.

————. *The Film Sense,* trans. Jay Leyda. New York: Harcourt, Brace & Co., 1942.

————. *Non-indifferent Nature,* trans. Roberta Reeder and Herbert Marshall. Cambridge: Cambridge University Press, 1987.

Eldar. Silva, and Lev Shilov. "Angliiskiye nedeli Anny Akhmatovoi," TR, pp. 132–147.

Eliade, Mircea. *The Myth of the Eternal Return,* trans. Willard R. Trask. Bollingen Series, XLVI. Princeton: Princeton University Press, 1954.

Eliot, T. S. "Tradition and the Individual Talent," *Selected Essays.* New York: Harcourt, Brace and Co., 1950, pp. 3–11.

————. *The Waste Land and Other Poems.* New York: Harcourt, Brace and Co., 1934.

Eng-Liedmeier, Jeanne van der. "Aspects of the Prophetic Theme in Akhmatova's Poetry," SUE, II, pp. 315–334.

————. "Poem Without a Hero," in Anna Akhmatova, *Tale Without a Hero and Twenty-Two Poems by Anna Akhmatova,* pp. 63–114.

————. "Reception as a Theme in Akhmatova's Early Poetry," in *Dutch Contributions to the Eighth International Congress of Slavists,* ed. Jan M. Meijer. Amsterdam: John Benjamins, 1979, pp. 205–231.

————. "Reception as a Theme in Akhmatova's Later Poetry," *Russian Literature,* XV (1984), pp. 83–147.

————. "Some Aspects of Mandelstam's 'Razgovor o Dante' and Axmatova's 'O Puskine,' " *Miscellanea Slavicai: To Honour the Memory of Jan M. Meijer,* ed. B. J. Amserga. Amsterdam: Rodopi, 1983, pp. 235–252.

Erdmann-Pandzic, Elisabeth von. *Poema bez geroya von Anna A. Achmatowa: Variantenedition und Interpretation von Symbolstrukturen.* Bausteine zur Geschichte der Literature bei den Slaven. XXV. Cologne and Vienna: Böhlau Verlag, 1987.

Erge. "Chitaya 'Poemu bez geroya,' " *Vozdushnye puti,* III (New York, 1963), pp. 295–300.

Erlich, Victor. *Russian Formalism.* 3rd ed. The Hague: Mouton, 1969.

Etkind, E. "Die Unsterblichkeit des Gedächtnisses: Anna Achmatovas Poem 'Requiem,' " *Die Welt der Slaven,* XXIX (1984), pp. 360–394.

————. "Pasternak, novator rechi," BP, pp. 117–142.

————. *Protsess Iosifa Brodskogo.* London: Overseas Publications Interchange, 1988.

Fadeyev, Alexander. "Iz stati 'O traditsiyakh slavyanskoi literatury,' " *Requiem*, pp. 258–260. Orig. *Literaturnaya gazeta*, November 16, 1946.

Faryno, Jerzy. "Kod Akhmatovoi," *Russian Literature*, no. 7/8 (1974), pp. 83–102.

——. "Tainy remesla Akhmatovoi," *Wiener Slawistischer Almanach*, V (1980), pp. 19–75.

——. "Whose Messenger Is Akhmatova's *Poema bez geroya*?", SUE, I, pp. 97–112.

——. "Ya pomnyu (chudnoye mgnoveniye . . .)" i "Ya (slovo . . .) pozabyl," *Wiener Slawistischer Almanach*, no. 16 (1985), pp. 29–35.

Fedotov, Georgy. "Iz ocherka 'Tri stolitsy,' " PBG, pp. 74–79. Orig. *Versty*, no. 1. Paris, 1926.

Fedotova, O. A. "Anya Gorenko," OAA, pp. 29–38.

Feinberg, Lawrence E. "Measure and Complimentarity in Achmatova," *Russian Literature*, V, no. 4, pp. 307–314.

Feinstein, Elaine. *Marina Tsvetaeva*. London: Penguin Books, 1989.

Filipoff, Boris. "Chitaya poemu," *Vozdushnye puti*, III (New York, 1962), pp. 295–300.

——. "*Poema bez geroya*," S-F, II, pp. 53–92.

——. "*Poema bez geroya* Anny Akhmatovoi: zametki," *Vozdushnye puti*, II (New York, 1961), pp. 167–183.

——. "Zerkalo-Zazerkale-Zertsalo Klio: Iskonnyi vsesvetnyi motiv v pretvorenii Anny Akhmatovoi," TARA, XXIII (New York, 1990), pp. 139–151.

Finkelberg, Margarita. "O geroye 'Poemy bez geroya,' " *Russkaya literatura*, III (1992), pp. 207–224.

Fitzpatrick, Sheila. *The Russian Revolution 1917–1932*. Oxford: Oxford University Press, 1982.

Fleishman, Lazar. *Boris Pasternak: The Poet and His Politics*. Cambridge, MA: Harvard University Press, 1990.

——. *Boris Pasternak v dvadtsatye gody*. Munich: Wilhelm Fink Verlag, 1981.

——. *Boris Pasternak v tridtsatye gody*. Jerusalem: Magnes Press, 1984.

——. "Iz akhmatovskikh materialov v arkhive Guverovskogo instituta," AS, pp. 165–194.

——. *Poetry and Revolution in Russia 1905–1930: An Exhibition of Books and Manuscripts*. Stanford, CA: Stanford University Press, 1909.

Florinsky, Michael T. *The End of the Russian Empire*. New York: Collier Books, 1961.

Fonyakov, I. "Pomnit Akhmatovu Ukraina," *Literaturnaya gazeta*, September 27, 1989.

France, Peter. *Poets of Modern Russia*. Cambridge Studies in Russian Literature. Cambridge: Cambridge University Press, 1982.

——. "Reading Akhmatova," *Forum for Modern Langauge Studies*, no. 3, XIII (July 1977), pp. 193–203.

Frank, Victor. "Beg vremeni," S-F, II, pp. 39–53.

——. "Beseda s Georgiyem Adamovichem," PV, pp. 227–236. Orig. *Russkaya mysl*, Paris, April 24, 1980.

Friedrich, Hugo. *Die Struktur der modernen Lyrik*. Hamburg: Rowohlts Enzyklopädie, 1985.

Frost, Matthew. "Nikolai Punin and the 'Science' of Criticism," TARA, XIX (1986), pp. 253–269.

Fyodorov, Andrey. "Poeticheskoye tvorchestvo Innokentiya Annenskogo," in Innokenty Annensky, *Stikhotvoreniya i tragedii*, pp. 5–60.

Galperina-Osmerkina, E. K. "Vstrechi s Akhmatovoi," VOAA, pp. 237–244.

Garteveld, Vera. "Iz *Vospominanii*," PBG, p. 321. Orig. archive Columbia University.

Gasparov, M. L. "The Evolution of Akhmatova's Verse," AA, pp. 68–74.

———. "Stikh Akhmatovoi: chetyre yego etapa," LO, no. 5 (1989), pp. 26–28.

Gershtein, Emma. "Akhmatova's Prose," MHC, pp. 335–346.

———. "Besedy ob Akhmatovoi s N. A. Olshevskoi-Ardovoi," LO, no. 5 (1989), pp. 90–95. (Also in VOAA, pp. 258–276.)

———. "Iz vospominanii i pisem Anny Akhmatovoi," *Voprosy literatury* (June 1989), pp. 248–270.

———. "Lishnyaya lyubov: Stseny iz moskovskoi zhizni," *Novyi mir,* no. 11 (1993), pp. 151–185.

———. "Memuary i fakty (ob osvobozhdenii Lva Gumilyova)," RLT, no. 13 (1976), pp. 645–655.

———. "Neizdannye zametki Anny Akhmatovoi o Pushkine," *Voprosy literatury,* I (1970), pp. 158–206.

———. "Novoye o Mandelstame," *Nashe naslediye,* no. 5 (1989), pp. 101–124.

———. *Novoye o Mandelstame.* Paris: Atheneum, 1986.

———. "O Pasternake i ob Akhmatovoi," LO, no. 2 (1990), pp. 96–102.

———. "Poslesloviye," *Anna Akhmatova o Pushkine,* pp. 275–317.

———. "Repliki Akhmatovoi," SMV, pp. 4–11.

———. "Tridtsatye gody," VOAA, pp. 248–257.

———. "V zamoskvoreche," LO, no. 7 (1985), pp. 105–108.

———, and V. E. Vatsuro, "Zametki A. A. Akhmatovoi o Pushkine," *Vremennik Pushkinskoi komissii, 1970.* Leningrad: Akademiya Nauk SSSR, 1972, pp. 30–44.

Gibian, George, and H. W. Tjalsma. *Russian Modernism.* Ithaca, NY: Cornell University Press, 1976.

Gifford, Henry. "Akhmatova i 1940," SUE, II, pp. 45–54.

———. *Pasternak: A Critical Study.* Cambridge: Cambridge University Press, 1977.

Gilbert, Martin. *Winston Churchill.* Vol. VIII. London: Heinemann, 1968.

Ginzburg, Lydia. "Akhmatova: Neskolko stranits vospominanii," *Literatura v poiskakh realnosti.* Leningrad: Sovetskii pisatel, 1987, pp. 124–130. (Also in VOAA, pp. 126–141.)

———. "Iz starykh zapisei," OAA, pp. 186–194.

———. *O lyrike.* Moscow and Leningrad: Sovetskii pisatel, 1964.

———. "Iz zapisei," *Requiem,* p. 280. Orig. *Rodnik,* no. 1 (Riga, 1989).

Gippius, Vasily. "Anna Akhmatova," DG, pp. 215–219. Orig. *Kuranty,* no. 2 (1918).

———. "Anna Akhmatova *Vecher,*" DG, p. 80. Orig. *Novaya zhizn,* no. 3 (1912).

———. "Tsekh poetov," DG, pp. 82–86. Orig. *Zhizn,* no. 5 (1918), Odessa.

Gippius, Zinaida. "Iz stati 'Literaturnaya zapis,' " *Requiem,* p. 77. Orig. *Sovremennye zapiski,* no. 19 (1924), under pseudonym Anton Krainy.

Gitovich, Silvia. "Ob Anne Andreyevne," OAA, pp. 330–356.

———. "V Komarove," VOAA, pp. 205–219.

Glebov, Yevgeny. "Akhmatovskii memorial," *Vechernyaya Odessa,* June 24, 1989, p. 4.

Glen, Nika. "Vokrug starykh zapisei," VOAA, pp. 627–639.

Gojowy, Detlef. *Arthur Lourie und der russische Futurismus.* Laaber: Laaber Verlag, 1993.

———. *Neue sowjetsiche Musik der 20er Jahre.* Laaber: Laaber Verlag, 1980.

Goldman, Howard. "Anna Akhmatova's Hamlet: The Immortality of Personality and the Discontinuity of Time," *Slavic East European Journal,* 4, XX (1980), pp. 484–493.

Gollerbakh, Erik. *Gorod muz.* 2nd ed. Leningrad, 1930. Reprint, Paris: Lev, 1980.

———. "Iz vospominanii o N. S. Gumilyove," NGVS, pp. 15–24.

———. *Obraz Akhmatovoi: Antologiya.* 2nd ed. Leningrad: Leningradskoye obshchestvo bibliofilov, 1925.

Golosa poetov: stikhi zarubezhnykh poetov v perevode Anny Akhmatovoi, trans. Anna Akhmatova. Moscow: Progress Publishers, 1965.

Goltsev, Val. "Dosuzhiye domysly vernogo druga," *Sovetskaya Rossiya* (December 20, 1989), p. 4.

Gorbanevskaya, Natalya. "Yeyo golos," AS, pp. 233–245.

Gorbovsky, Gleb. "Videniye v Komarove," SMV, pp. 142–151.

Gordin, Ya. "Delo Brodskogo," *Neva,* no. 2 (1989), pp. 134–166.

———. "Dialog poetov (Tri pisma Akhmatovoi k Brodskomu)," AS, pp. 221–224.

Gorenko, Kh.V. "Iz ocherka 'Mat Akhmatovoi,' " DG, pp. 8–10.

Gorenko, Victor. "An Interview," *Stikhi. Perepiska. Vospominaniya. A. Akhmatova.* Comp. Allendea Proffer. Ann Arbor: Ardis, 1977. (Also in RLT, no. 9 [Spring 1974], pp. 497–521.)

Gornung, B. V. "Cherty russkoi poezii 1910–kh godov," *Poetika i stilistika russkoi literatury,* pp. 262–269.

Gornung, L. V. "Zapiski ob Anne Akhmatovoi," VOAA, pp. 179–218.

Gozenpud, A. A. "Neudvyadshie listya," VOAA, pp. 311–327.

Graf-Schneider, Marion. " 'Muza' dans l'oeuvre d'Anna Akhmatova," *Colloquium Slavicum Basiliense. Gedankschrift für Hildegard Schroeder,* ed. Heinrich Riggenbach with Felix Keller. Frankfurt: Peter Lang, 1981, pp. 187–201.

Graham, Irina. "Arap Petra Velikogo," *Novoye russkoe slovo,* (1993), p. 3.

Graham, Sheelagh. "*Amor Fati:* Akhmatova and Gumilyev," SUE, II, pp. 247–256.

Gray, Camilla. *The Russian Experiment in Art 1863–1922,* review Marina Burleigh-Motley. Loudon: Thames and Hudson, 1986.

Grigorian, Kamsar N. "Anna Akhmatova's Poetic Translations of Some Poems by Vahan Terian," AA, pp. 75–85.

Grigoryev, K. "Ukraina chtit svoyua zemlyachku," *Literaturnaya gazeta,* June 28, 1989, p. 7.

Grishunin, A. G. "Provody Akhmatovoi v Moskve 9 marta 1966 g.," SMV, pp. 198–200.

Grossman, Leonid. "Anna Akhmatova," *Mastera slova.* Moscow: Sovremennye problemy, 1928.

Gryakalova, N. Yu. "Folklornye traditsii v poezii Anny Akhmatovoi," *Russkaya literatura,* no. 1 (1982), pp. 46–64.

Gryaznevich, Vladimir, and Natalya Orlova. "Zaplanirovannyi zagovor," *Stsena* (August 24, 1991).

Guenther, Johannes von. "Pod vostochnym vetrom," NGVS, pp. 131–141. Orig. *Ein Leben in Ostwind. Zwischen Petersburg und München.*

Gumilyov, Lev " '. . . Inache poety net' (Beseda L. E. Varustina s L. N. Gumilyovym)," *Zvezda,* no. 6 (1989), pp. 127–132.

———. "Korni nashego rodstva," *Sputnik,* no. 5 (1989), pp. 109–112.

———. " 'My absolyutno samobytny . . . ,' " *Nevskoye vremya,* August 12, 1992, p. 3.

———. "O lyudyakh na nas ne pokhozhikh," Interview with Yelena Seslavina. *Sovetskaya kultura,* September 25, 1988, p. 6.

———. " 'Vsem nam zaveshchana Rossiya.' " Interview V. Kazakov. *Krasnaya zvezda,* September 21, 1989, p. 4.

———. "Zametki poslednego Evraziitsa," *Nashe naslediye,* no. 3 (1991), pp. 19–26.

———, and Aleksandr Panchenko. *Chtoby svecha ne pogasla: Dialog.* Leningrad: Sovetskii pisatel, 1990.

Gumilyov, Nikolay. "Afrikanskii dnevnik," *Ogonyok,* no. 15 (April 11–18, 1987), pp. 20–22.

———. "Chitatel," in Nikolay Gumilyov, *Stikhotvoreniya,* ed. V. P. Tetaki. Paris: YMCA Press, 1986, pp. 7–14.

———. "Iz 'Pisma o russkoi poezii,' " DG, pp. 124–127. Orig. in *Apollon,* no. 5 (1914).

———. *Izbrannoye,* ed. N. Otsup. Paris: Librairie des cinq continents, 1959.

——. *Neizdannoye stikhi i pisma*. Paris: YMCA Press, 1980.

——. *Neizdannoye i nesobrannoye*. Paris: YMCA Press, 1986.

——. *Nikolai Gumilev on Russian Poetry*, ed. and trans. David Lapeza. Ann Arbor: Ardis, 1977.

——. "Review of Akhmatova's *Beads*," trans. Robert Whittaker, Jr. RLT, no. 1 (Fall 1971), pp. 144–145.

——. "Review of Mandelstam's *Stone*," trans. Robert T. Whittaker, Jr., RLT, no. 1 (Fall 1971), pp. 146–149.

——. *Sobraniye sochinenii*, ed. G. P. Struve and B. A. Filipoff. 4 vols. Washington, DC.: Victor Kamkin, 1962–68.

——. *Stikhi. Pisma o russkoi poezii*. Moscow: Khudozhestvennaya literatura, 1989.

——. *Stikhotvoreniya i poemy*, ed. M. D. Elzon. Introduction by Vladimir Karpov. Biblioteka poeta, Bolshaya seriya, 3rd ed. Leningrad: Sovetskii pisatel, 1988.

——. *Stikhotvoreniya*, ed. B. P. Betaki. Paris: YMCA Press, 1986.

——. "Symbolism's Legacy and Acmeism," trans. Robert T. Whittaker, Jr., RLT, no. 1 (Fall 1971), pp. 146–149.

Gumilyova, Anna. "Nikolai Stepanovich Gumilyov," NGVS, pp. 111–131.

Gusak, N. "Anna Akhmatova: 'Ya rodilas pod Odessoi . . . ': Iz biogr. poetessy," *Znamya kommunizma*, February 5, 1983.

Haight, Amanda. *Anna Akhmatova: A Poetic Pilgrimage*. New York and London: Oxford University Press, 1976.

——. *Anna Akhmatova: poeticheskoye stranstviye: dnevniki, vospominaniya, pisma*. Haight biography trans. by M. A. Timenchika. Ed. S. Dubovik. Commentary V. Chernykh, E. Babayev and E. Gershtein. Moscow: Raduga, 1991.

——. "Anna Akhmatova's *Poema bez geroya*," *Slavonic and East European Review*, XLV (1967), pp. 474–496.

——. "Chelovek, a ne legenda," VOAA, pp. 670–673. (Also in SMV, pp. 40–42.)

——. "A Letter from Tsvetayeva to Akhmatova," *Slavonic and East European Review*, L, no. 121 (October 1972), pp. 589–594.

——. "Letters from Nikolay Gumilyov to Anna Akhmatova 1912–1915," *Slavonic and East European Review*, L, No. 118 (January 1972), pp. 100–106.

Halperin, Charles J. *Russia and the Golden Horde*. Bloomington: Indiana University Press, 1987.

Hamburger, H. "The Function of the Affective Verb in Some Poems by Anna Achmatova," *Linguistics*, LXII (1970), pp. 20–33.

Hamsun, Knut. *Pan. Schwärmer. Die Nachbarstadt*, trans. S. Angermann and J. Sandmeier, et al. Munich: Deutscher Taschenbuch Verlag, 1991.

——. *Mysterien*, trans. J. Sandmeier and S. Angermann. Munich: Deutscher Taschenbuch Verlag, 1991.

——. *Victoria. Die Geschichte einer Liebe*, trans. J. Sandmeier and S. Angermann. Munich: Deutscher Taschenbuch Verlag, 1991.

Handbook to Russian Literature, ed. Victor Terras. New Haven: Yale University Press, 1985.

Harris, Jane G. "Nikolai Gumilyov," *Handbook to Russian Literature*, pp. 188–189.

Hartman, Anthony. "The Metrical Typology of Anna Axmatova," *Studies in Honor of Xenia Gasiorowska*, ed. L. Leighton. Columbus, OH: Slavica Publishers, 1982, pp. 112–123.

——. *The Versification of the Poetry of Anna Akhmatova*. Ph.D. Dissertation, University of Wisconsin, 1978.

Hayden, Peter. "Tsarskoe Selo: The History of the Ekaterinskii and Aleksandrovskii Parks," SP, pp. 13–34.

Hayward, Max. *Writers in Russia: 1917–1978,* ed. with an introduction by Patricia Blake. New York: Harcourt, Brace, Jovanovich, 1983.

Heller, Mikhail, and Aleksander M. Nekrich. *Utopia in Power: The History of the Soviet Union from 1917 to the Present.* New York: Summit Books, 1986.

Hemschemeyer, Judith. "A Poet and Her Country," CPP, pp. 22–24.

———. "Translating Akhmatova," *Translation Review* (1990), pp. 12–14.

The Heritage of Russian Verse, ed. Dmitri Obolensky. Revised ed. Bloomington: Indiana University Press, 1965.

Hingley, Ronald. *Nightingale Fever: Russian Poets in Revolution.* New York: Alfred A. Knopf, 1981.

Hoffmann, E. T. A. *The Golden Poet and Other Tales,* trans. Ritchie Robinson. New York: Oxford University Press, 1992.

Holthusen, Johannes. "Anna Achmatovas Umgang mit den Dichtern ihrer Epoche in der 'Poema bez geroja,' " *Aspekte der Slavistik: Festschrift für Josef Schrenk,* ed. Wolfgang Girke and Helmut Jachnow. Slavistische Beiträge, CLXXX. Munich: Verlag Otto Sagner, pp. 102–126.

———. "Petersburg als literarischer Mythos," *Russland in Vers und Prosa.* Slawistische Beiträge, LXIX, pp. 9–34. Munich: Verlag Otto Sagner, 1973.

Holmgren, Beth. *Women's Works in Stalin's Time: Lydia Chukovskaia and Nadezhda Mandelstam.* Bloomington: Indiana University Press, 1993.

Hope, A. D. "Safe Conduct: The Poet and the Soviet State," *Helix,* nos. 7–8 (1981), pp. 156–164.

Hopko, Father Thomas. *Worship in the Orthodox Faith.* Vol. II. New York: The Orthodox Church in America, 1972.

Hughes, Langston. *Selected Poems of Langston Hughes.* New York: Vintage Books, 1974.

Hughes, Olga R. *The Poetic World of Boris Pasternak.* Princeton: Princeton University Press, 1974.

———. "Stikhotvoreniye 'Marburg' i tema 'vtorogo rozhdeniya.' Nablyudeniya nad raznymi redaktsiyami stikhotvoreniya 'Marburg,' " BP, pp. 289–302.

Ilyev, S. O. " 'Peterburgskiye povesti' Andreya Belogo i Anny Akhmatovoi *(Peterburg— Poema bez geroya),* " TsS, pp. 150–165.

Ilyina, G. "Krymskiye stranitsy," *Literaturnaya Rossiya,* June 23, 1989, p. 23.

Ilyina, Natalya. "Anna Akhmatova, kakoi ya yeyo videla," VOAA, pp. 569–594.

———. "Anna Akhmatova v posledniye gody yeyo zhizni," *Oktyabr,* no. 2 (February 1977), pp. 107–43.

———. "The Last Days of Her Life," trans. John Crowfoot. SL, no. 6 (1989), pp. 119–137.

———. "Traurige Seiten," *Sinn und Form,* no. 2, XLIII (March–April 1991), pp. 373–395.

Ilyinsky, Oleg. "Osnovnye printsipy poezii Gumilyova: K stoletiyu so dnya rozhdeniya," TRAS/Vol. XXIII (1990), pp. 373–397.

Ilnytska, Margarita. "Vidkryvayuchy neznane," *Muzyka* (March 1991), pp. 26–27.

Ilyashnenko, L. "Iz pisma k A. E. Parnisu," PBG, p. 213.

Ivanov, Georgy. "Iz knigi *Peterburgskiye zimy,*" OAA, pp. 79–86.

Ivanov, Vyacheslav. *Borozdy i Mezhi.* Moscow: Musaget, 1916.

Ivanov, Vyach. Vs. "Akhmatova i Pasternak: osnovnye problemy izucheniya ikh literaturnykh vzaimootnoshenii," *Izvestiya Akademii nauk SSSR: Seriya literatury i yazyka,* XLVIII, no. 5 (September–October 1989), pp. 410–417.

———. "Besedy s Annoi Akhmatovoi," VOAA, pp. 473–502.

———. "K istolkovaniyu stikhotvoreniya Akhmatovoi 'Vsem obeshchaniyam vopreki . . . ,' " AS, pp. 203–204.

———. "*Poema bez geroya*, poetika pozdnei Akhmatovoi i fantasticheskii realizm," AS, pp. 131–136.

———. "Postsimvolizm i Kuzmin," *Mikhail Kuzmin i russkaya kultura XX veka*, pp. 13–16.

———. "Vstrechi s Akhmatovoi," *Znamya* (June 1989), pp. 199–209.

———. "Zvyozdnaya vspyshka (Poeticheskii mir N. S. Gumilyova), " in N. Gumilyov, *Stikhi, pisma o russkoi poezii*, pp. 5–33.

Ivanov-Razumnik, R. V. "Iz knigi *Pisatelskie sudby*," *Requiem*, p. 164. Orig. *Pisatelskie sudby*. New York, 1951.

Ivanovsky, Ign. "Anna Akhmatova," VOAA, pp. 614–626.

———. "Master," OAA, pp. 295–305.

"Iz besedy s L. S. Ilyashenko," *Requiem*, p. 27. Orig. transcribed 1978.

"Iz knigi *Deyateli revolyutsionogo dvizheniya v Rossii*," DG, pp. 11–12. Orig. *Deyateli revolyutsionnogo dvizheniya v Rossii*, III, vyp. 2, p. 904.

Iz lichnoi biblioteki Anny Akhmatovoi: (Sobraniye Ardovykh-Tolstyakova), ed. A. P. Tolstyakov. Moscow: Vneshtorgizdat, 1989.

"Iz obsuzhdeniya postanovleniya TsK VKP (b) o *zhurnalakh* "*Zvezda*" i "*Leningrad*" i *doklada tov. A. A. Zhdanova v Institute literatury (Pushkinskii Dom AN SSSR)*," *Requiem*, pp. 250–251. Orig. *Izvestiya AN SSSR*. Otdelenie literatury i yazyka, V (1946, vyp. 6).

"Iz peredovoi stati *Leningradskoi pravdy* 'Aktivizirovat tvorcheskuyu rabotu pisatelei,' " *Requiem*, p. 164. Orig. in September 27, 1940, issue of *Leningradskaya pravda*.

"Iz perepiski N. S. Gumilyova i A. A. Akhmatovoi," H-M, pp. 344–353.

"Iz pisma neizvestnogo moskvicha," *Requiem*, p. 70. Orig. *Dni*, Paris (May 4, 1924).

"Iz rezolyutsii obshchegorodskogo sobraniya leningradskikh pisatelei po dokladu tov. Zhdanova," *Requiem*, p. 244. Orig. *Kultura i zhizn*, August 30, 1946.

"Iz sokrashchyonnoi i obobshchyonnoi stenogrammy dokladov t. Zhdanova na sobranii partiinogo aktiva i na sobrannii pisatelei v Leningrade," *Requiem*, pp. 236–238.

"Iz vystupleniya A. Surkova," *Requiem*, p. 248. Orig. *Literaturnaya gazeta*, September 7, 1946.

Jakobson, Roman. *Ausgewählte Aufsätze 1921–1971*, ed. Elmar Holenstein and Tarcisius Schelbert. Frankfurt: Suhrkamp, 1993.

———. "The Prose of the Poet Pasternak," *Pasternak*-Davie, pp. 135–151.

———. "Randbemerkungen zur Prosa des Dichters Pasternak," *Slavische Rundschau*, VII (1935), pp. 357–374.

Jones, Lawrence G. "Distinctive Features and Sound Tropes in Russian Verse," in *Russian Poetics*, ed. Thomas Eeknan and Dean S. Worth. Columbus, OH: Slavica Publishers, 1982, pp. 195–208.

Jovanovich, Milivoe. "K razboru 'Chuzhikh golosov' v *Rekvieme* Akhmatovoi," *Russian Literature*, XV (1984), pp. 169–182.

Kalacheva, S. V. "Svoyeobraziye stikha rannei A. Akhmatovoi," *Filologicheskiye nauki*, no. 4 (1986), pp. 73–76.

Kaminskaya, A. G. "Neopublikovannaya statya N. N. Punina ob Akhmatovoi," TR, pp. 262–263.

———. "Pamyat Amandy," SMV, pp. 43–45.

Kanegisser, Leonid. "Anna Akhmatova. Chyotki. Stikhi, 1914," DG, pp. 127–128. Orig. in *Severnye zapiski*, no. 5 (1914).

Kara-Demur, S. "Iz obzora *Leningradskii almanakh*," *Requiem*, pp. 226. Orig. *Vechernii Leningrad*, May 15, 1946.

Karlinsky, Simon. *Marina Tsvetaeva*. Cambridge: Cambridge University Press, 1986.

———, and Alfred Appel, Jr., eds. *The Bitter Air of Exile: Russian Writers in the West 1922–1972.* Berkeley: University of California Press, 1977.

Karp, Poel. "Yedinstvennyi vzglyad. K 100-letiyu so dnya rozhdeniya Anny Akhmatovoi," *Knizhnoye obozreniye,* no. 23 (June 9, 1989), p. 4.

Karpov, V. V. "N. S. Gumilyov: Biograficheskii ocherk," in Nikolay Gumilyov, *Stikhotvoreniya i poemy* (1988), pp. 63–78.

———. "Poet Nikolay Gumilyov," *Ogonyok,* no. 36 (September 1986).

Karsavina, Tamara. *Theatre Street.* New York: E. P. Dutton, 1931.

Katayev, Valentin. *The Grass of Oblivion,* trans. Robert Daglish. New York: McGraw-Hill, 1969.

———. "Iz vystupleniya V. Katayeva," *Requiem,* p. 246. Orig. in *Literaturnaya Gazeta,* September 7, 1946.

Kategoriya opredelyonnosti-neopredelyonnosti v slavyanskikh i balkanskikh yazykakh, ed. T. M. Nikolaeva. Moscow: Nauka, 1979.

Kats, Boris. "Dalnye ekho: Otzvuki tvorchestva Shumana v akhmatovskoi 'Poeme bez geroya,' " LO, no. 5 (1989), pp. 76–81.

———, and R. Timenchik. *Akhmatova i muzyka: Issledovatelskiye ocherki.* Leningrad: Sovetskii kompozitor, 1989.

Katsis, Leonid. "Zametki o stikhotvorenii Anny Akhmatovoi, 'Mayakovsky v 1913 godu,' " *Russian Literature,* XXX (1991), pp. 317–336.

Keats, John. "The Eve of St. Agnes," "To Sleep," and "Isabella; or The Poet of Basil," in John Keats and Percy Bysshe Shelley, *Complete Poetical Works.* New York: The Modern Library, 1975.

Kelly, Catrione. "The Impossibility of Imitation: Anna Akhmatova and Innokentii Anneskii," SUE, II, pp. 231–246.

Ketchian, Sonia. "Akhmatova's 'Uchitel': Lessons Learned from Annenskij," *Slavic East European Journal,* no. 1, XX (1978), pp. 26–29.

———. "Anna Akhmatova," *Handbook to Russian Literature,* ed. Victor Terras, pp. 14–16.

———. "Anna Akhmatova and Armenian Genocide," *Ararat,* no. 1, XXVII (Winter 1986), pp. 25–29.

———. "Anna Akhmatova and Maro Markarian," *Ararat,* no. 2, XXIX (Spring 1988), pp. 2–10.

———. "Anna Akhmatova and W. B. Yeats: Points of Juncture," AA, pp. 86–109.

———. "Axmatova's Civic Poem 'Stansy' and Its Pushkinian Antecedent," *Slavic East European Journal,* no. 2, XXXVII (1993), pp. 194–210.

———. "The Balladic Poems of Anna Akhmatova," TARA, XXIII (1990), pp. 169–175.

———. "The Genre of *Podrazhanie* and Anna Achmatova," *Russian Literature,* XV (1984), pp. 151–168.

———. "Imitation as Poetic Mode in Achmatova's 'Podrazhanie I. F. Annenskomu,' " *Scando-Slavica,* XXV (1979), pp. 57–69.

———. "An Inspiration for Anna Akhmatova's 'Requiem': Hovannes Tumian," *Studies in Russian Literature in Honor of Vsevolod Setschkarev,* ed. S. Ketchian and Julian W. Connolly. Columbus, OH: Slavica Publishers, 1986, pp. 175–188.

———. "Metempsychosis in the Verse of Anna Akhmatova," *Slavic East European Journal,* no. 1, XXV (Spring 1981), pp. 44–60.

———. "Moon Over Akhmatovaland: With a View Toward Pushkin," SUE, II, pp. 303–314.

———. *The Poetry of Anna Akhmatova: A Conquest of Time and Space.* Slavistische Beiträge, Band 196. Munich: Verlag Otto Sagner, 1986.

————. "Returns to Tsarskoe Selo in the Verse of Anna Akhmatova," SP, pp. 120–136.

————. "A Source for Anna Akhmatova's 'A String of Quatrains': Hovannes Tumian's 'Quatrains,' " *Slavic East European Journal*, no. 4, XXXI (Winter 1987), pp. 520–532.

————. "A Unique Device of Akhmatova's Tribute to Mandelstam," *Slavic East European Journal*, no. 4, XX (1976), pp. 400–404.

Khardzhiyev, N. "N. Khardzhiyev o risunke A. Modilyani," H-M, pp. 305–306.

————. "O perevodakh v literaturnom nasledii Anny Akhmatovoi," TR, pp. 229–232.

Khazan, V. I. " 'Takim ya vizhu oblik vash i vzglyad . . . ' (O tvorcheskom sodruzhestve A. Akhmatovoi i B. Pasternaka)," *Izvestiya Akademii nauk: Seriya literatury i yazyka*, no. 5, XLIX (1990), pp. 432–443.

Khellmann, Bena. "O finskom dome Akhmatovoi," AS, pp. 195–198.

Khemalyan, T. E. "Dva perevoda Akhmatovoi iz Charentsa v svete vozdeistviya poezii Mandelshtama." TsS, pp. 194–202.

Khinkulov, L. "Literaturnye progulki po Kievu," *Raduga*, no. 5 (1979), pp. 178–191.

Khlodovsky, R. I. "Anna Akhmatova i Dante," TR, pp. 75–92.

Khodasevich, Vladislav. "Besslavnaya slava," DG, pp. 214–215. Orig. *Voprosy literatury*, no. 2 (1987).

————. *Literaturnye stati i vospominaniya.* New York: Chekhov, 1954.

————. *Nekropol.* Paris: YMCA Press, 1976.

————. "Retsenziya na knigu *Chyotki*," PBG, p. 120. Orig. *Nov*, no. 69 (1914), p. 6.

————. "Torgovlya," *Requiem*, pp. 43–44. Orig. *Ogonyok*, (1989), p. 13.

Kho. [Kersten Holm]. "Lew Gumilyov: Anna Achmatowas Sohn ist gestorben," *Frankfurter Allgemeine*, June 22, 1992.

Khrenkov, Dmitry. *Anna Akhmatova v Peterburge-Petrograde-Leningrade.* Leningrad: Lenizdat, 1989.

————. *Den za dnyom.* Leningrad: Sovetskii pisatel, 1984.

————. "Gumilyov i Blok," NGVS, pp. 203–212.

————. "Ob Anne Akhmatovoi," in Akhmatova, *Stikhi i proza*, pp. 3–8.

————. "Tainy remesla: Beseda s A. A. Akhmatovoi," in S-F, II, 1968, pp. 292–295.

————. "Uroki dobra i mudrosti," *Neva*, no. 10 (1987), pp. 194–202.

Kireyev, Ruslan. "Obreteniye lada," *Znamya*, no. 11 (November 1985), pp. 233–235.

Kitto, H. D. F. *Greek Tragedy.* Garden City, NY: Doubleday & Co., 1952.

Klassicheskaya poeziya vostoka, trans. Anna Akhmatova. Moscow: Khudozhestvennaya literatura, 1969.

Klein, J. "A. Achmatovas 'Kak solominkoi, p'eš' moju dusu . . . ," in Klaus-Dieter Seemann, ed., *Russische Lyrik.* Munich: Fink, 1982, pp. 183–190.

Klenovsky, Dmitry. "Poety tsarskoselskoi gimnazii," NGVS, pp. 25–32.

Kling, D. A. "Svoyeobraziye epicheskogo v lirike A. A. Akhmatovoi," TsS, pp. 59–70.

Klychkov, Georgy. "Nedavnii istochnik: Sergei Klychkov, stikhi 30-kh godov," *Nashe naslediye*, no. 11, V (1989), p. 93.

Knigi. Arkhivy. Avtografy, ed. A. S. Mylnikov, et al. Moscow: Kniga, 1973.

Knyazev, V. "Yesli by . . ." [Poems by Knyazev], PBG, pp. 203–211.

Knyazeva, N. G. "Otryvok iz perevoda *Makbeta*," LO, no. 5 (1989), pp. 18–21.

Kogan, Dora. *Sergey Yurevich Sudeikin.* Moscow: Iskusstvo, 1974.

Kollontay, Alexandra. "Pisma k trudyashcheisya molodyozhi," *Requiem*, pp. 54–56. *Molodaya gvardiya*, no. 2(9) (1923).

Kolobayeva, L. "I muzhestvo i zhenstvennost: o svoyebrazii lirizma Anny Akhmatovoi," *Zvezda*, no. 6 (June 1979), pp. 147–150.

Kolpakova, N. P. "Stranitsy dnevnika," OAA, pp. 119–127.

Kondratovich, A. I. "Tvardovsky i Akhmatova," VOAA, pp. 674–682.

Kondratyev, A. "Iz ocherka 'Blizkie teni,' " PBG, pp. 227–228. Orig. *Volynskoye Slovo.* Rovno, October 22, 1921.

Konshina, Tatyana. "Vospominaniya ob Anne Andreyevne Akhmatovoi," intro. N. Shik, *Zvezda,* no. 6 (June 1979), pp. 166–168.

Korolyova, N. V. "Anna Akhmatova i leningradskaya poeziya 1960–kh godov," SMV, pp. 117–132.

———. " 'Mogla li Biche slovno Dant tvorit . . . ,' Problema zhenskogo obraza v tvorchestve Akhmatovoi," TR, pp. 93–112.

———. "V gostyakh u Anny Akhmatovoi," *Knizhnoye obozreniye,* no. 24 (June 11, 1989), pp. 8–9.

Korona, Aleksandr. "Arthur Lourie (Portret)," PBG, p. 340. Orig. *Fantastichekii kabachok,* Tbilisi, no. 1 (1918).

Korzhavin, N. "Anna Akhmatova i 'serebryanyi vek,' " *Novyi mir,* no. 7 (July 1989), pp. 240–261.

Kosacheva, N. G. "K analizu *Poemy bez geroya* Anny Akhmatovoi," *Russian Language Journal,* no. 109, XXXI (Spring 1977), pp. 135–145.

Kovalenko, S. A. "Akhmatova i Mayakovsky," TsS, pp. 166–180.

Kozlov, L. K. "Ten groznogo i Khudozhnik," *Kinovedcheskii zapiski,* no. 15 (1992), pp. 14–47.

Kozlov, M. V. "Evolutsiya khudozhestvennogo metoda i stilya Anny Akhmatovoi v dorevolyutsionnom tvorchestve," *Voprosy russkogoi literatury,* LVII (1991), pp. 18–26.

Kozlovskaya, G. L. "Moya Shekherezada: O prebyvanii A. Akhmatovoi v Tashkente: Rasskaz prodrugi poetessy [zapisal A. Usmanov]," *Uchitelskaya gazeta* (May 27, 1989), p. 2.

Kraineva, M. I. " 'V etoi zhizni menya uderzhala tolko vera v Vas i Osiyu . . . ': Pisma N. Ya. Mandelstam A. A. Akhmatovoi," LO, no. 1 (1991), pp. 97–105.

Kralin, Mikhail. "Anna Akhmatova i Sergey Yesenina," *Nash sovremennik,* X (1990), pp. 154–156.

———. "Iz zaventnoi tetradi," *Znamya,* no. 12 (December 1990), pp. 133–135.

———. " 'Kakaya yest. Zhelayu vam druguyu . . . ,' " OAA, pp. 555–560.

———. "Khoroshoye nachalo, v knige Akhmatovoi *Belaya staya,*" *Russkaya literatura,* no. 3 (1989), pp. 97–108.

———. "Mladshii brat," *Zvezda,* no. 6 (1989), pp. 148–151.

———. "Nekrasovskaya traditsiya u Anny Akhmatovoi," *Nekrasovskii sbornik,* VIII. Leningrad: Nauka, 1983, pp. 74–86.

———. "Pobedivsheye smert slovo," *Neva,* no. 7 (1988), pp. 198–200.

———. " 'Samoye luchsheye pismo,' " *Neva,* no. 4 (1989), pp. 204–205.

———, and I. I. Slobozhan, eds. *Ob Anne Akhmatovoi.* Leningrad: Lenizdat, 1990.

Krasavchenko, T. V. "Akhmatova v zerkalakh zarubezhnoi kritiki," TR, pp. 113–123.

Krasovskaya, Vera. *Ruskii baletnyi teatr nachala XX veka,* I. Leningrad: Iskusstvo, 1971.

Kravtsova, Irina. "Ob odnom adresate stikhotvorenii Anny Akhmatovoi," *Russkaya mysl,* January 10, 1992, pp. 10–11.

———. " 'Severnye elegii': opyt interpretatsii," *Russian Literature,* XXX (1991), pp. 303–315.

———, et al. *Muzei Anny Akhmatovoi.* Leningrad: Petropol, 1991.

Kravkhin, S. "Pod krovlei Fontannogo Doma," *Izvestiya,* July 20, 1989.

Kreid, Vadim. "Neizvestnaya retsenziya Gumilyova na knigu Akhmatovoi," TARA, XXIII (1990), pp. 153–161.

Kreps, Michail. *O poezii Iosifa Brodskogo.* Ann Arbor: Ardis, 1984.

Krivich, Valentin. "Iz vospominanii," DG, pp. 35–36. Orig. *Pamyatniki kultury. Novye otkrytiya.* Leningrad, 1983.

Krupene, O. "Akhmatova v Tashkente," *Literaturnaya gazeta,* May 3, 1989, p. 7.

Kruzhkov, Grigory. " 'Ty opozdal na mnogo let . . . ,' " *Novyi mir,* no. 3 (March 1993), pp. 216–224.

Krysl, Marilyn, and Lynn Coffin. "The Leper's Rattle," CPP, pp. 40–44.

Kshondzer, M. K. "Stikhotvoreniye 'Nadpis na knige' v kontekste liriki A. Akhmatovoi. (O gruzinskikh motivakh v poeticheskom mire Akhmatovoi)," TR, pp. 65–68.

Kuk, Zenon M. "Anna Akhmatova's *'Requiem,'* " *Proceedings of the Kentucky Foreign Language Conference,* no. 1 (1983), pp. 65–73.

Kupchenko, V. "Voloshin i Akhmatova," *Pobeda.* Simferopol, August 4, 1981.

Kurako, Yu., and R. Shvalov. "Na dache Sarakini: O prebyvanii poetessy v Odesse," *Znamya kommunizma,* June 16, 1989.

———. "Okolo morya, gde ya rodlus . . . ," *Sovetskaya kultura,* January 26, 1991.

Kurbatov, Vladimir. "Iz stati 'Unichtozheniye petrogradskikh sadov,' " PBG, pp. 71–72. Orig. *Starye gody* (1915), nos. 1–2.

Kurt, Anna. "Akhmatova and Translation," SL, no. 6 (1989), pp. 177–181.

———. "Gost iz budushchego," LO, no. 6 (1989), pp. 77–78.

Kushner, A. S. "Poeticheskoye vospriyatiye mira," *Literaturnaya gazeta,* June 21, 1989, p. 3.

———. "U Akhmatovoi," SMV, pp. 133–141.

Kuzmin, Mikhail. "Iz dnevnika," DG, pp. 251–252.

———. "Iz stati 'Parnasskie zarosli,' " PV, p. 52. Orig. almanach *Zavtra,* Berlin, 1923.

———. "O prekrasnoi yasnosti (otryvki)," *Russkaya literatura XX veka,* comp. N. A. Trifonov. Moscow: Gosudarstvennoye uchebno-pedagogicheskoye izdatelstvo, 1962, pp. 433–434.

———. "Pismo v Pekin," *Uslovnosti.* Petrograd, 1923. Cited in Timenchik, et al., "Akhmatova i Kuzmin," p. 217.

———. "Predisloviye M. A. Kuzmina k pervoi knige stikhov Anny Akhmatovoi," S-F, III, pp. 471–473. See also "Predisloviye k knige *Vecher,*" OAA, pp. 39–44.

———. "Putanitsa," PBG, pp. 223–224. Orig. *Apollon,* no. 4 (1910).

———. *Selected Prose and Poetry,* ed. and trans. Michael Green. Ann Arbor: Ardis, 1972.

———. *Sobraniye stikhov,* ed. John E. Malmstad and Vladimir Markov, *Centrifuga,* no. 12, III. Munich: Wilhelm Fink, 1977.

Kuzmina, Jelena. *Anna Achmatowa: ein Leben im Unbehausten,* trans. Swetlana Geier. Berlin: Rowohlt, 1993.

Kuzmina-Karavaeva, E. Yu. "Vstrechi s Blokom," *Aleksandr Blok v vospominaniyakh sovremennikov,* II. Moscow: Khudozhestvennaya literatura, 1980.

Kuzovleva, Tatyana. "'Ya stala pesnei i sudboi . . . ,' " *Sotsialisticheskaya industriya,* June 20, 1989, pp. 3–4.

Lachmann, Renate. *Gedächtnis und Literatur.* Frankfurt: Suhrkamp Verlag, 1990.

———. "Der unabschliessbare Dialog mit der Kultur: Mandelstam und Achmatowa als Gedächtnisschreiber," *Gedächtnis und Literatur,* pp. 372–393.

———. "Vergangenheit als Aufschub: Die Kulturosophie der Akmeisten," *Gedächtnis und Literatur,* pp. 354–371.

Lane, Ann. "Nietzsche Comes to Russia: Popularization and Protest in the 1890s," *Nietzsche in Russia,* ed. Rosenthal, pp. 51–68.

Latmanizov, M. V. "Besedy s A. A. Akhmatovoi," OAA, pp. 507–530.

———. "K 100-letiyu so dnya rozhdeniya A. A. Akhmatovoi. Razgovory s Akhmatovoi (Predisloviye, ed. A. G. Terekhov)," *Russkaya literatura,* no. 3 (1989), pp. 67–96.

Lavrov, A. V. "V. F. Przhedpelski (Yuri Tumanov). Blok na fronte," *Russkaya Literatura,* no. 4 (1980), pp. 151–159.

―――, and R. D. Timenchik. "Innokenty Annensky v neizdannykh vospominaniyakh," *Pamyatniki kultury. Novye otkrytiya. Ezhegodnik 1981.* Leningrad: Nauka, 1983, pp. 61–146.

Leiter, Sharon. *Akhmatova's Petersburg.* Philadelphia: University of Pennsylvania Press, 1983.

Leites, A. "Iz stati 'Sovetskaya literatura i pisateli zapada,' " *Requiem,* p. 261. Orig. *Literaturnaya gazeta,* March 8, 1947.

Lelevich, G. "Anna Akhmatova," *Na postu,* nos. 2–3 (Moscow, September–October 1923), pp. 178–202, in *Na postu,* I–VI (1923–25). Munich: Wilhelm Fink, 1971.

―――. "Iz stati 'Nesovremennyi *Sovremennik,*" *Requiem,* pp. 75–76.

Levin, F. "Iz stati 'Porochnaya metodologiya," *Requiem,* p. 250. Orig. *Literaturnaya gazeta,* October 19, 1946.

―――. "Iz stati 'Ushei ne spryatat . . . ,' " *Literaturnyi ezhenedelnik,* nos. 20–21 (1923), p. 11.

Levin, Yuri. "O sootnoshenii mezhdu semantikoi poeticheskogo teksta i vnetekstovoi real-nostyu (Zametki o poetiki O. Mandelshtama)," *Russian Literature* 10/11 (1975), pp. 147–172.

―――, D. M. Segal, R. D. Timenchik, and V. N. Toporov. "Russkaya simvolicheskaya poetika kak potentsialnaya kulturnaya paradigma," *Russian Literature* 7/8 (1974), pp. 47–82.

Levinson, Andrey. "Anna Akhmatova—russkaya Marselina," LO, no. 5 (1989), pp. 52–56.

―――. "Anna Akhmatova—Marceline à la russe," *Chicago Review,* no. 4, XXXIV (1985), pp. 74–79.

―――. "Blazhenny mertvye," NGVS, pp. 218–220.

―――. "Gumilyov," NGVS, pp. 213–217.

―――. "Iz ocherka 'Tri podvala,' " PBG, Orig. *Novaya gazeta* (1918) under pseudonym "Alibi."

Lezhnyov, A. "Iz obzora 'Sredi zhurnalov,' " *Requiem,* p. 74. Orig. *Krasnaya nov,* no. 4 (November 1924).

―――. "The Poetry of Boris Pasternak," *Pasternak*-Davie, pp. 85–107.

Liaugminas, Tatiana Suchovy. "Anna Akhmatova: The Intimate Relationship Between the Woman and Her Work," *Proceedings of the Kentucky Foreign Language Conference,* no. 1 (1983), pp. 53–64.

Lidin, Vladimir. "An Evening at Pomerantsev Lane," SL, no. 6 (1989), pp. 138–139.

Likhachyov, D. S. "Akhmatova i Gogol," *Literatura-realnost-literatura.* Leningrad; Sov-etskii pisatel, 1981, pp. 173–179.

Lipkin, S. "Vostochnye stroki Anny Akhmatavoi," in *Klassicheskaya poeziya vostoka,* trans. Anna Akhmatova, pp. 5–13.

Lisnyanskaya, Inna. "Taina muzyki 'Poemy bez geroya,' " *Druzhba narodov,* VII (1991), pp. 235–251.

―――. " 'U shkatulki zh troinoe dno . . .': Zmetki o 'Poeme bez geroya,' " LO, no. 5 (1989), pp. 34–36.

Literaturnoye nasledstvo: Aleksandr Blok, novye materialy i issledovaniya, kn. 2. Moscow: Nauka, 1981.

Livingstone, Angela, ed. *Pasternak on Art and Creativity.* Cambridge: Cambridge University Press, 1985.

Livshits, Benedikt. "Polutoraglazyi strelets," NGVS, pp. 160–164.

―――, and E. K. Livshits. "Pamyatnaya zapiska," OAA, pp. 439–445.

Ljunggren, Anna. "Anna Akhmatova's *Requiem:* A Retrospective of the Love Lyric and Epos," AA, pp. 110–126.

Lochner, Jan Peter. "Ist Boris Pasternak ein Dichter der Avantgarde?", *Colloquium Slavicum Basiliense: Gedenkschrift für Hildegard Schroeder,* ed. Heinrich Riggenbach. Bern: Peter Lang, 1981.

Loseff, Lev. "Geroi *Poemy bez geroya,*" AS, pp. 109–122.

———. " 'Strashnyi peizazh' i marginalii k teme Akhmatova/Dostoyevsky," *Zvezda,* no. 8 (1992), pp. 148–155.

———. "The Toy Town Ruined," SP, pp. 35–50.

———. "Who Is the Hero of the Poem Without One?" *Essays in Poetics,* XI, no. 2 (1986), pp. 91–103.

Lotman, Yuri M. "Pamyat v kulturologicheskom osveshchenii," *Wiener Slawistischer Almanach,* XVI (1985), pp. 5–9.

Lourie, Arthur. "Detskii rai," PBG, pp. 341–250. Orig. *Vozdushnye puti,* no. 3. New York, 1963.

———. "Iz ocherka 'Nash marsh,' " PBG, pp. 351–352 and 336. Orig. *Novyi zhurnal,* no. 4, kn. 94. New York, 1969, pp. 127–142.

———. "Iz stati 'Cheshuya v nevode,' " PBG, pp. 295–296. Orig. *Vozdushnye puti,* no. 2. New York, 1963.

———. "Nash marsh," *Novyi zhurnal,* no. 4, kn. 94. New York, 1969, pp. 127–142.

———. "Olga Afanasevna Glebova-Sudeikina," PBG, pp. 215–218. Orig. *Vozdushnye puti,* no. 5, New York, 1963, pp. 139–145.

———. "Pismo k Anne Ahmatovoi," PGB, p. 339.

———. "Smert Don-Zhuana (Iz 'Variatsii o Motsarte')," PBG, pp. 159–162. Orig. *Chisla,* no. 9, Paris, 1933.

Luknitskaya, Vera. "Iz dvukh tysyach vstrech (Acumiana)," *Pered toboi zemlya.* Leningrad: Lenizdat, 1988, pp. 283–383.

———. *Nikolay Gumilyov: zhizn poeta po materialam domashnego arkhiva syemi Luknitskikh.* Leningrad: Lenizdat, 1990.

———. "O Vaginove," LO, no. 5 (1989), pp. 71–72.

———. "Osennyaya Pushkinym," *Ogonyok,* no. 6 (1987), pp. 10–11.

———, and S. P. Luknitsky. "Sledstvennoye delo N. S. Gumilyova," TR, pp. 233–259.

Luknitsky, Pavel. "Dnevnik," *Nashe naslediye,* no. 9, III (1989), pp. 78–81.

———. "Iz dnevnika," *Requiem,* p. 166. Orig. *Skvoz vsyu blokadu.* Leningrad, 1964, p. 99.

———. "Iz dnevnikov," OAA, pp. 128–169.

———. "Iz dnevnikov i pisem," VOAA, pp. 142–178.

———. "Iz stikhotvorenii, posvyashchennykh A. Akhmatovoi," TR, pp. 262–263.

———. "Ob Anne Akhmatovoi," *Nashe nasledie,* VI (1988), pp. 57–72.

———. "Ob avtore (Biograficheskaya spravka)," in Nikolay Gumilyov, *Stikhotvoreniya,* pp. 15–19.

———. "Pochemu oni eto sdelali?", *Sovetskaya muzyka,* no. 2 (February 1991), pp. 82–83.

———. *Skvoz vsyu blokadu.* Leningrad: Lenizdat, 1964.

———. *Vstrechi s Annoi Akhmatovoi: 1924–1925.* Vol. I. Paris: YMCA Press, 1991.

Luknitsky, Sergey. "Doroga k Gumilyovu," *Moskovskiye novosti,* no. 48 (November 26, 1989).

Lure, Samuil. "Pomilovaniye," AS, pp. 245–250.

———. "Zhizn posle smerti," *Zvezda,* no. 6 (1989), pp. 204–296.

Lushchik, Sergei. "Kryostnaya mat," *Vechernyaya Odessa,* June 19, 1989, p. 3.

———. "Literator A. M. Fyodorov," *Vechernyaya Odessa,* June 15, 1989, p. 3.

Lyamkina, E. I. *Vstrechi s proshlym.* Moscow: Sovetskaya Rossiya, 1978.

Lyubimova, A. A. " 'A nautro vstanesh s novoyu zagadkoi . . . ,' " *Komsomolskaya pravda,* June 24, 1989, p. 4. Intro. and ed. A. Kazakov and S. Umnikov.

———. "Iz dnevnika," VOAA, pp. 420–435.

———. "Zapiski o vstrechakh," OAA, pp. 231–259.

Lyublinskaya, V. S. "Iz pisma V. S. Lyublinskoi," DG, p. 253.

Magomedova, D. M. "Annensky i Akhmatova (K probleme 'romanizatsii' liriki)," TsS, pp. 135–140.

Maimin, E. "Boris Mikhailovich Eikhenbaum," LO, no. 5 (1990), pp. 97–101.

Makogonenko, G. P. "Iz tretei epokhi vospominanii," OAA, pp. 261–281.

———. ". . . Iz tretei epokhi vospominanii," *Druzhba narodov,* 3 (1987), pp. 232–240.

———. "O sbornike Anny Akhmatovoi 'Nechet,' " *Voprosy literatury,* no. 2 (1986), pp. 170–190.

Makovsky, Sergei. "Nikolay Gumilyov (1886–1921)," NGVS, pp. 45–72.

———. "Nikolay Gumilyov po lichnym vospominaniyam," NGVS, pp. 104–110.

Maksimov, D. "Akhmatova o Bloke," *Zvezda,* no. 12 (December 1967), pp. 187–191. Excerpts reprinted in Struve's notes to Akhmatova's "Vospominaniya ob A. Bloke," in S-F, II, pp. 411–417.

———. "Ob Anne Akhmatovoi, kakoi pomnyu," VOAA, pp. 96–125.

Malakov, S. "Iz stati 'Lirika kak orudiye klassovoi borby," *Requiem,* p. 91. Orig. *Zvezda,* no. 9 (1931).

Malkov, M. P. " 'Yeyo poeziya nepovtorima . . .': Ya. Ivaskevich ob A. A. Akhmatovoi," *Vestnik Leningradskogo Universiteta. Seriya istorii, yazyka i literatury,* IV (October 1989), pp. 26–31.

Mallac, Guy de. *Boris Pasternak: His Life and Art.* Norman, OK: University of Oklahoma Press, 1981.

———. "Esteticheskiye vozzreniya Pasternaka," BP, pp. 63–81.

Malmstad, John E. "Mikhail Kuzmin: A Chronicle of His Life and Times," in M. A. Kuzmin, *Sobraniye stikhov,* pp. 7–319.

———, and Gennady Shmakov. "Kuzmin's 'The Trout Breaking Through the Ice,' " in *Russian Modernism,* ed. George Gibian and H.W. Tjalsma, pp. 132–165.

Mandelstam, Nadezhda. *Hope Against Hope,* trans. Max Hayward. New York: Atheneum, 1970.

———. *Hope Abandoned,* trans. Max Hayward. New York: Atheneum, 1974.

———. "Iz Knigi tretyei," *Requiem,* pp. 89, 228.

———. "Iz vospominanii" (first variant), PBG, pp. 298–300.

———. "Iz vospominanii," *Requiem,* pp. 119–120. Orig. *Literaturnaya uchyoba,* no. 3 (1989).

———. "Iz vospominanii," *Requiem,* pp. 177–179. Orig. *Vtoraya kniga,* first variant.

———. "Iz vospominaniya," VOAA, pp. 299–325.

———. *Kniga Tretya.* Paris: YMCA Press, 1987.

Mandelstam, Osip. *The Complete Critical Prose and Letters,* ed. Jane Gary Harris, trans. Jane Gary Harris and Constance Link. London: Collins Harvill, 1991.

———. *Complete Poetry of Osip Emilevich Mandelstam,* trans. Burton Raffel and Alla Burago. Albany: State University of New York Press, 1973.

———. "Conversations About Dante," CCPL, pp. 397–442. (Written 1933, published in Russian 1967).

———. "A Letter About Russian Poetry," CCPL, pp. 156–159.

———. "On Contemporary Poetry," CCPL, pp. 105–108.

———. "On the Nature of the Word," CCPL, pp. 117–132.

————. *Selected Poems,* trans. Clarence Brown and W. S. Merwin. New York: Atheneum, 1983.

————. *Sobraniye sochinenii,* ed. G. P. Struve and B. A. Filipoff. 2 vols. Washington, DC: Inter-Language Literary Associates, 1964.

————. "Storm and Stress," CCPL, pp. 170–180.

————. "The Word and Culture," CCPL, pp. 112–116 (first published 1922).

Mandrykina, L. A., ed. Anna Akhmatova, "Avtobiograficheskaya proza," *Sochineniya.* II. Moscow: Khudozhestvennaya literatura, 1986, pp. 236–259.

————. "Iz rukopisnogo nalediya A. A. Akhmatovoi," *Neva,* no. 6 (1979), pp. 196–199.

————. "Nenapisannaya kniga: Listki iz dnevnika A. A. Akhmatovoi," in *Knigi. Arkhivy. Avtografy,* ed. A. S. Mylnikov, et al. Leningrad: Nauka, 1973, pp. 57–76.

Mankovsky, Arkady. "Zapechatlyonnyi golos Akhmatovoi," *Nashe nasledie,* no. 9, III (1989), p. 67.

Manning, Roberta Thompson. *The Crisis of the Old Order in Russia.* Princeton: Princeton University Press, 1982.

A Manual of the Orthodox Church's Divine Services, comp. Arch-Priest D. Sokolof. Jordanville, NY: Holy Trinity Monastery, 1975.

Manuilov, V. Ya. "Podarok sudby," VOAA, pp. 227–236.

Markarian, Maro. "The Lessons of Anna Akhmatova," AA, pp. 127–135.

Markov, Vladimir. " 'Kogda v toske samoubijstva' by Anna Akhmatova," *Text Symbol Weltmodell. Johannes Holthusen zum 60. Geburtstag.* pp. 409–419.

————. "Mysli o russkom futurizme," *Novyi zhurnal [The New Review],* XXXVIII (1954), pp. 169–181.

————. "Russian Crespuscolari: Minskij, Merezhkovskij, Loxvickaja," in *Russian Literature and History: In Honour of Professor Ilya Serman.* Jerusalem: Soviet Jewry Museum Foundation, 1989, pp. 78–81.

————. "Russkiye tsitatnye poety: zametki o poezii P. A. Vyazemskogo i Georgiya Ivanova," *To Honor Roman Jakobson,* II. The Hague: Mouton, 1967, pp. 1273–1287.

Markova, T. M. "Anna Akhmatova v tvorcheskoi sudbe L. Tatyanichevoi," *Russkaya literatura,* no. 3 (1983), pp. 150–155.

Masenko, Teren. "Iz romana *Vita pochtovaya,*" *Requiem,* pp. 116–117. Orig. LO, no. 5 (1989) ed. E. M. Olshanskaya.

————. "Iz vospominanii," *Requiem,* p. 191.

————. "U Pilnyaka: Neopublikovannye stranitsy avtobiograficheskogo romana *Vita pochtovaya,*" LO, no. 5 (1989), pp. 73–75.

Maslenikova, Zoya. *Portret Borisa Pasternaka.* Moscow: Sovetskaya Rossiya, 1990.

Maslin, N. "Iz stati 'O literaturnom zhurnale *Zvezda,*' " *Requiem,* pp. 228–229. Orig. *Kultura i zhizn,* no. 5, August 10, 1946, p. 4.

Mayakovsky, Vladimir. *The Bedbug and Selected Poetry,* ed. Patricia Blake, trans. Max Hayward and George Reavey. Bloomington: Indiana University Press, 1975.

————. *Polnoye sobraniye sochinenii,* ed. L. Yu. Brik. I. Moscow: Khudozhestvennaya literatura, 1955.

————. "Vystupleniye na pervom vechere 'Chistka sovremennoi poezii,' " in Vladimir Mayakovsky, *Polnoye sobraniye sochinenii,* ed. L. Yu. Brik. XII. Moscow: Khudozhestvennaya literatura, 1959, pp. 458–461.

Mayhem, Lenore. "Images from a Life," CPP, pp. 9–11.

McDuff, David. "Anna Akhmatova," *Parnassus* (Fall–Winter 1983 and Spring–Summer 1984), pp. 51–82.

Meilakh, Mikhail. "Anna Akhmatova's poem 'Zaklinaniye,' " SUE, I, pp. 173–182.

————. "Ob imenakh Akhmatovoi," *Russian Literature,* 10 (1975), pp. 33–57.

————. "Review of Kees Verheul's *The Theme of Time in the Poetry of Anna Akhmatova,*" *Russian Literature,* 7/8 (1974), pp. 203–213.

————. ". . . Svoyu mezh vas yeshchyo ostaviv ten," SMV, pp. 152–173. (Also in LO, no. 5 [1989], pp. 95–100.)

————, and V. N. Toporov, "Akhmatova i Dante," *International Journal of Slavic Linguistics and Poetics,* XV (1972), pp. 29–75.

Merkureva, V. A. "Iz pisma k K. L. Arkhippovoi," *Requiem,* pp. 101–102 and 168.

Metter, Israel. "Sedoi venets dostalsya yei nedarom," OAA, pp. 380–390.

Meyerhold, V. E. *Meyerhold on Theatre,* trans. Edward Braun. New York: Hill and Wang, 1969.

Michalewska, Olga. "*Poema bez geroia:* Real Prototypes and the Coherence of the Text," SUE, I, pp. 87–96.

Mickiewicz, Denis. "The Acmeist Conception of the Poetic Word," *Russian Literature* (Spring 1975 supplement), pp. 59–83.

————. "Apollo and the Modernist Poetics," RLT, no. 1 (Fall 1971), pp. 226–261.

Mierau, Fritz. "Anna Achmatowas 'Majakowski im Jahr 1913,' " *Zwölf Arten die Welt zu beschreiben: Essays zur russischen Literatur.* Leipzig: Verlag Philipp Reclam, 1988, pp. 195–211.

————. *Russen in Berlin 1918–1933: eine kulturelle Begegnung.* Weinheim: Quadriga Verlag, 1988.

————. "Vorabend: 1913 und 1940. Anna Achmatowas *Poem ohne Held,*" *Konzepte: Zur Herausgabe sowjetischer Literatur.* Leipzig: Verlag Philipp Reclam jun., 1979, pp. 143–162.

————. "Die Zeit der Achmatowa: Lyric nach der Oktoberrevolution," *Zwölf Arten die Welt zu beschreiben,* pp. 212–223. (Also in *Frauen Literatur Geschichte,* ed. Hiltrud Gnüg and Renata Möhrmann. Stuttgart: JB. Metzlersche Verlagsbuchhandlung, pp. 281–288.)

Mihajlov, Mihajlo. "The Great Catalyzer: Nietzsche and Russian Neo-idealism," *Nietzsche in Russia,* ed. Rosenthal, pp. 127–148.

Mikhail Kuzmin i russkaya kultura XX veka: tezisy i materialy konferentsii 15–17 maya 1990, ed. G. A. Morev. Leningrad: Sovet po istorii. ANSSSR 1990.

Mikhailov, A. L. "Poeticheskii mir Bloka," *V mire Bloka.* Moscow: Sovetskii pisatel, 1980, pp. 135–163.

Mikhailovich, Vasa, B. "The Critical Reception of Anna Akhmatova," *Papers on Language and Literature,* Winter 1969, pp. 95–112.

Mikhailovsky, S. "N. N. Punin. Portret v suprematicheskom prostranstve," *Neva,* no. 6 (1989), pp. 145–159.

Mikhalkov, S. "Iz vystupleniya," *Requiem,* p. 247. Orig. *Literaturnaya gazeta,* September 7, 1946.

Minsky, Nikolay. "Ognennyi stolp," NGVS, pp. 169–172.

Mitsumasa, Tamura. "O chuzhom golose i rannikh stikhakh Anny Akhmatovoi," TsS, pp. 119–125.

Moch-Bickert, Elaine. *Kolombina desyatykh godov . . . ,* trans. Vera Rumyantseva, ed. Yu. A. Molok. Paris and St. Petersburg: Grzhebina-AO "Arsis," 1993.

————. *Olga Glebova-Soudeikina.* Paris: Service de reproduction des thèses université de Lille, 1972.

Mochulsky, Konstantin. "Anna Akhmatova *Anno Domini,*" PV, pp. 54–61. Orig. *Sovremennye zapiski,* no. 10 (1922).

————. "Poeticheskoye tvorchestvo Anny Akhmatovoi," LO, no. 5 (1989), pp. 44–52.

Mogilyansky, M. M. "Kabare 'Brodyachaya sobaka.' Otryvki iz povesti o dnyakh moyei zhizni." Publikatsiya A. Sergeyeva. *Minuvsheye,* XII. Paris: Atheneum, 1991.

Molok, Yuri. " 'Kak v zerkalo, glyadela ya trevozhno . . .'" (Etyud k pervoi glave ikonografii Akhmatovoi), AS, pp. 43–52.

——. "Vokrug rannikh portretov," LO, no. 5 (1989), pp. 81–85.

Moscow Trefoil: Poems from the Russian of Anna Akhmatova and Osip Mandelstam, ed. David Campbell and Rosemary Dobson, trans. Natalie Staples. Canberra, Australia: Australian University Press, 1975.

Muchnic, Helen. "Three Inner Emigres: Anna Akhmatova, Osip Mandelshtam, Nikolai Zabolotsky," *The Russian Review* (January 1967), pp. 13–26.

Muravyova, I. A. "Anna Akhmatova i dokumentalnoye kino," TR, pp. 148–157.

——. "Poslesloviye k filmu," *Zvezda,* no. 6 (1989), pp. 176–181.

Musatov, V. V. "Akhmatova i Mandelshtam," *Russian Literature,* XXX (1991), pp. 357–372.

——. "K probleme analiza liricheskoi sistemy Anny Akhmatovoi," TsS, pp. 103–110.

"Muzhestvo pravdy i poezii," *Pravda,* June 21, 1989.

"Na zasedanii prezidiumy Soyuza pisatelei," *Requiem,* p. 248. Orig. *Kultura i zhizn,* September 10, 1946.

Nag, Martin. "Über Anna Achmatowas *Deviatsot Trinadtsatyi God,*" *Scando-Slavica,* no. 13 (1967), pp. 77–82.

Nagornyi, S. "Iz stati 'Sleduyuschii nomer,' " *Requiem,* ed. Timenchik, p. 164. Orig. *Literaturnaya gazeta,* September 29, 1940.

Nayman, Anatoly. "Akhmatova and World Culture," trans. Galina Kmetyuk. SL, no. 6 (1989), pp. 189–191.

——. "An Analysis and Interpretation of Anna Akhmatova's 'Tvorchestvo,' " SUE, II, pp. 225–230.

——. "Chetyre stikhotvoreniya," LO, no. 5 (1989), pp. 110–112.

——. "Opyt chteniya neskolkikh pozdnikh stikhotvorenii Akhmatovoi," AS, pp. 137–142.

——. "The Place of Tsarskoe Selo in Akhmatova's Poetry" SP, pp. 114–119.

——. "Prostranstvo Uranii: 50 let Yosifu Brodskomu," *Oktyabr,* no. 12 (December 1990), pp. 193–198.

——. *Rasskazy ob Anne Akhmatovoi.* Moscow: Khudozhestvennaya literatura, 1989. (Also in *Novyi mir* [January, February, March 1989].)

——. *Remembering Anna Akhmatova,* ed. and trans. Wendy Rosslyn. New York: Henry Holt and Co., 1991.

——. "Uroki poeta," *Literaturnaya gazeta,* June 14, 1989, p. 8.

Nappelbaum, Ida. "Fon k portretu Anny Andreyevny Akhmatvoi," OAA, pp. 197–213.

——. "Zvuchashchaya rakovina," *Neva,* no. 12 (1987), pp. 198–200.

——, and Innokenty Basalayev. "Vspominaya Akhmatovu," *Ogonyok,* no. 26 (1984), p. 5.

Nebolsin, S. A. "O zhanre 'Pamyatnika' v nasledii Akhmatovoi," TR, pp. 30–38.

Nedobrovo, N. S. "Anna Akhmatova," OAA, pp. 49–68.

——. "Anna Akhmatova," PBG, pp. 250–273.

——. "Anna Akhmatova," trans. Alan Myers, RLT, no. 9 (Spring 1974), pp. 221–239.

——. "Anna Akhmatova," *Russkaya mysl,* no. 17 (July 1915), pp. 50–68.

——. "Anna Akhmatova," trans. Evgeny Filipoff, SL, no. 6 (1989), pp. 148–154.

——. "Pismo k A. Bloku," PBG, pp. 228–229.

Nekrasov, Nicholas. *Poems by Nicholas Nekrasov,* trans. Juliet M. Soskice. Wilmington, DE: Scholarly Resources, 1974. (Reprint of London: Oxford University Press, 1929).

Nekrasov, Victor, trans. June Goss. "In Memory of Anna Akhmatova," SL, no. 6, (1989), pp. 146–147.

Nekrasova, E. A. "Shedevr grazhdanskoi liriki," *Russkaya rech* (January–February 1982), pp. 43–47.

Nemirovich-Danchenko, Vasily. "Rytsar na chas," NGVS, pp. 228–236.

Nepomnyashchii, I. B. " 'I—stranno!—ya yeyo perezhila' (Ob odnom tyutchevskom motive v lirike A. Akhmatovoi)," TR, pp. 57–64.

———. "Ob odnom tyutchevskom motiv v lirike Akmatovoi," *Izvestiya Ak. Nauk SSSR.* Seriya literatury i yazyka, no. 1, XLIX, pp. 75–79.

Nestev, I. "Iz istorii russkogo muzykalnogo avangarda," *Sovetskaya muzyka,* no. 1 (January 1991), pp. 75–87.

Nevedomskaya, Vera. "Vospominaniya o Gumilyove i Akhmatovoi," NGVS, pp. 151–159.

Nikolaev, A. "Muzei na ulitse Kronshtadtskoi," *Neva,* no. 6 (1989), pp. 201–203.

Nikolayeva, T. M. "Smert vlastelina na okhote ('Okhota' N. Gumilyova i 'Seroglazyi korol' Akhmatovoi)," *Russian Literature,* XXX (1991), pp. 343–355.

Nikolaj Gumilev 1886–1986, ed. Sheelagh Duffin Graham. Berkeley: Berkeley Slavic Specialties, 1987.

Nikolay Gumilyov v vospominaniyakh sovremennikov, ed. Vadim Kreid. Paris and New York: C.A.S.E.–Third Wave; Düsseldorf: Blue Rider, 1989.

Nikolay Gumilyov v vospominaniyakh sovremennikov, ed. Vadim Kreid. Moscow: Vsya Moskva, 1989.

Nikolina, N. A. "Obraz Rodiny v poezii A. Akhmatovoi," *Russkii yazyk v shkole,* no. 2 (March–April 1989), pp. 72–79.

Nikolskaya, Tatyana. "Akhmatova v otsenke literaturnogo Tiflisa (1917–1920)," AS, pp. 83–88.

Niquet, Michelle. "Akhmatova i Klychkov," AS, pp. 89–98.

Niveau, George. "Barochnaya poema," AS, pp. 99–108.

Ob Anne Akmatovoi, comp. M. M. Kralin, ed. I. I. Slobozhan. Leningrad: Lenizdat, 1990.

O'Bell, Leslie. "Akhmatova and Pushkin's Secret Writing," AA, pp. 136–148.

Obukhova, Olga. "Glazami italyanskoi pisatelnitsy," AS, pp. 215–220.

———. "Metamorfozy liricheskogo 'ya' v poezii Anny Akmatovoi," *Russian Literature,* XXX (1991), pp. 391–403.

Oksman, Yu. G. "Iz dnevnika, kotorogo ya ne vedu," VOAA, pp. 640–647.

———. "Iz pisma k A. P. Oksman," *Requiem,* p. 196. Orig. "Iz perepiski Yu. G. Oksmana," *Chetvyortye Tynyanovskie chteniya. Tezis dokladov i materialy dlya obsuzhdeniya.* Riga, 1988, p. 151.

Olesha, Yuri. "Iz knigi *Ni dnya bez strochki,*" *Requiem,* pp. 94–95.

Olshankaya, E. M. "Anna Akhmatova i Arseny Tarkovsky (K istorii vzaimootnoshenii dvukh poetov)," *Russian Literature,* XXX (1991), pp. 373–384.

———. "Anna Akhmatova i poety Ukraini: Do 100–richchya z dnya narodzhennya poetesy," no. 6, *Radyanske literaturoznavstvo,* pp. 58–61.

———. "Anna Akhmatova na karti Kyeva," *Novyny z Ukrainy,* no. 27 (1989).

———. ". . . I dolgovechnei—tsarstvennoye slovo . . .," *Molodaya gvardiya,* I (1990).

———. " '. . . I vovse ne znala, chto eto—schastye . . .': O svyazyakh A. Akhmatovoi s Ukrainoi," *Komsomolskoye znamya,* June 24, 1988.

———. "I vsyo-taki uznayut golos moi," *Komsomolskoye znamya,* June 23, 1989.

———. "Poezii tsaritsa: Posle smerti A. Akhmatovoi minulo 25 let," *Pravda Ukrainy,* March 5, 1991.

———. "Pristalo yei prostoye imya Anna," *Knizhnoye obozreniye,* May 19, 1989.

———. "Rankova godyna," *Vechirnyi Kyiv,* February 15, 1986.

———. "Utrennii chas," *Vechirnyi Kyiv,* February 15, 1986.

———. "V to vremya ya gostila na zemle . . .," *Pravda Ukrainy,* June 23, 1989.

Olshevsky, M. "Anna Akhmatova: otnosheniye k moyei Rodine," DG, p. 44.

Orlov, Vladimir. *Hamayun: The Life of Alexander Blok.* Moscow: Progress Publishers, 1980.

Orlova, Raisa, and Lev Kopelev. "Anna vseya Rusi," LO, no. 5 (1989), pp. 100–109. This article is a chapter from their book *My zhili v Moskve 1956–1980.* Ann Arbor: Ardis, 1988.

———. "Vstrechi s Annoi Akhmatovoi," *Grani,* XXXIX, no. 131 (1984), pp. 166–237.

Osetrov, Evgeny. "Gryadushcheye, sozrevsheye v proshedshem," *Voprosy literatury,* no. 4 (April 1965), pp. 183–189.

———. *Kniga o russkoi poezii.* Moscow: Sovetskaya Rossiya, 1982.

Osinsky, N. "Pobegi travy (Zametki chitatelya)," *Requiem,* pp. 49–52.

Ostroumova, M. N. "Iz vospominanii *Peterburgskiye epizody i vstrechi kontsa XIX-nachala XX* (TsGALI)," DG, p. 45.

Otsup, Nikolay. "N. S. Gumilyov," in Nikolay Gumilyov, *Izbrannoye,* pp. 7–31.

———. "N. S. Gumilyov," NGVS, pp. 173–181.

———. "Nikolay Stepanovich Gumilyov," NGVS, pp. 182–199.

Ozerov, Lev. "Beg vremeni," *Neobkhodimost prekrasnogo: Kniga statei.* Moscow: Sovetskii pisatel, 1983, pp. 234–253.

———. *Rabota poeta.* Moscow: Sovetskii pisatel, 1963.

———. "Razroznennye zapisi," VOAA, pp. 595–613.

———. ". . . S neukrotimoi sovetsyu svoei," *Pravda,* June 23, 1989, p. 4.

———. "Touches to Akhmatova's Portrait," SL, no. 6 (1989), pp. 155–163.

Pakhareva, T. " 'Ya byla togda s moim narodom': K 100-letiya so dnya rozhdenii A. Akhmatovoi," *Raduga,* no. 8 (1989), pp. 108–115.

Panin, Gennady. "Vstrecha s Akhmatovoi," *Requiem,* pp. 60–61. Orig. *Sovremennik.* Toronto, 1977, pp. 35–36.

Parnis, A. E. "Khlebnikov v dnevnike M. A. Kuzmina," *Mikhail Kuzmin i russkaya kultura XX veka,* pp. 156–165.

———, and R. D. Timenchik, "Programmy 'Brodyachei sobaki,' " *Pamyatniki kultury: Novye otkrytiya. Ezhegodnik 1983.* Leningrad: Nauka, 1985, pp. 160–257.

Parnok, Sofya. "Iz stati 'Pasternak i drugie,' " *Requiem,* pp. 73–74. Orig. *Russkoye sovremennik* (1924).

Parton, Anthony. " 'Goncharova i Larionov'—Gumilev's Pantoum to Art," NG, pp. 225–242.

Pasternak, Boris. "Boris Pasternak ob Anne Akhmatovoi," ed. Ye. O. Babayev. *Russkaya rech,* IV (July–August 1989), pp. 11–13.

———. "Dve retsenzii," intro. and ed. Ye. B. Pasternak. *Zvezda,* no. 6 (1989), pp. 145–147.

———. "Iz perepiski s pisatelyami," ed. Ye. B. and Ye. V. Pasternak. *Literaturnoye nasledstvo.* Moscow: Nauka, 1983, pp. 649–664.

———. "Iz pisma A. A. Akhmatovoi [17 April 1926]," PV, pp. 126–129.

———. *My Sister-Life and A Sublime Malady,* trans. Mark Rudman with Bohdan Boychuk. Ann Arbor: Ardis, 1983.

———. "Neskolko polozhenii," *Stikhi 1936–1959,* pp. 152–155.

———. "O postanovlenii TsK RKP(b) o literature," *Stikhi 1936–1959,* pp. 157–159.

———. "O skromnosti i smelosti," *Stikhi 1936–1959,* pp. 218–224.

———. "People and Attitudes: An Autobiographical Sketch," *Selected Writings,* pp. 246–300.

———. "People and Situations," in *Alexander Blok: An Anthology of Essays and Memoirs,* pp. 171–174.

———. "Pismo k A. A. Akhmatovoi" [28 July 1940], PV, pp. 126–129.

———. "Pismo k A. A. Akhmatovoi" [2 November 1940], PV, pp. 126–129.

————. *Poems,* comp. Yevgeny Pasternak. Moscow: Raduga, 1990.

————. "Rech na pervom vsesoyuznom syezde sovetskikh pisatelei, 29 avgusta 1934 goda," *Stikhi 1936–1959,* pp. 216–218.

————. "A Safe-Conduct," *Selected Writings,* pp. 91–197.

————. *Selected Writings and Letters,* trans. Catherine Judelson, comp. Galina Dzubenko. Moscow: Progress Publishers, 1989.

————. *Stikhi 1936–1959. Stikhi dlya detei. Stikhi 1912–1957, ne sobraynnye v knigi avtora. Stati i vystupleniya,* ed. G. P. Struve and B. A. Filippov. Ann Arbor: University of Michigan Press, 1961.

————. *Stikhotvoreniya i poemy.* 2 vols. Biblioteka poeta, Bolshaya seriya, 3rd ed. Leningrad: Sovetskii pisatel, 1990.

————. "Tsentralnyi Komitet Kommunisticheskoi Partii Sovetskogo Soyuza. Nikite Sergeyevichu Khrushchevu," *Stikhi 1936–1959,* p. 227.

————. "V redaktsiyu gazety *Pravda,*" *Stikhi 1936–1959,* pp. 228–229.

————. *Vozdushnye puti.* Moscow: Sovetskii pisatel, 1982.

————, and Olga Freidenberg. *The Correspondence of Boris Pasternak and Olga Freidenberg: 1900–1954,* ed. Elliott Mossman, trans. Elliott Moss and Margaret Wettlin. New York: Harcourt, Brace, Jovanovich, 1982.

Pasternak: Modern Judgements, ed. Donald Davie and Angela Livingstone. London: Macmillan, 1969.

Pasternak, Ye. *Boris Pasternak: materialy dlya biografii.* Moscow: Sovetskii pisatel, 1989.

Pasternak, Ye. B., and Ye. V., ed. and intro. "Iz perepiski s pisatelyami," *Literaturnoye nasledstvo: Iz istorii sovetskoi literatury 1920-kh godov.* Moscow: Nauka, 1983, pp. 649–737.

————. "Koordinaty liricheskogo prostranstva; K istorii otnoshenii Osipa Mandelshtama i Borisa Pasternaka," LO, no. 2 (1990), pp. 44–51.

Pavlenko, G. "Plennik ozera Chad: O sudbe N. Gumilyova i yego synovei," *Sovetskaya Moldaviya,* February 21, 1988.

Pavlovich, Nadezhda. "Iz knigi *Nevod pamyati,*" OAA, pp. 109–114.

Pavlovsky, A. I. *Anna Akhmatova.* Leningrad: Lenizdat, 1982.

————. "Anna Akhmatova (1889–1966)," in Anna Akhmatova, *Stikhotvoreniya i poemy,* ed. I. I. Slobzhan, pp. 3–20.

————. "Bulgakov i Akhmatova," *Russkaya literatura,* no. 4 (1988), pp. 3–17.

————. " 'Eto pleshchet Neva o stupeni . . . ,': K devyanosto letiyu Anny Akhmatovoi," *Neva,* no. 6 (1979), pp. 193–199.

————. "Nikolay Gumilyov," in Nikolay Gumilyov, *Stikhotvoreniya i poemy,* pp. 5–62.

"Perepiska Bloka s A. A. Akhmatovoi," intro. and ed. V. Ya. Chernykh. *Literaturnoye nasledstvo: Aleksandr Blok: novye materialy i issledovaniya,* kn. 4, pp. 571–577.

Pertsov, V. "Chitaya Akhmatovu," *Requiem,* pp. 159–162.

————. "Iz stati 'Po literaturnym vodorazdelam,' " *Requiem,* p. 77. Orig. *Zhizn iskusstva,* no. 43 (1925).

Pervushin, N. V. "Akhmatova i Blok," *Russian Language Journal,* XXV (Winter), no. 90, pp. 3–7.

Petrosov, Konstantin. " 'Potomu chto eto moja sudba . . . ' (AA i Marina Tsvetayeva v Starkakh, pod Kolomnoi)," *Knizhnoye obozreniye,* no. 7 (February 17, 1989), p. 6.

————. " 'Shipovnik Podmoskovya . . . ' (Sled zemli kolomenskoi v zhizni i stikhakh Anny Akmatovoi)," SMV, pp. 185–197.

Petrov, S. "Iz stati 'Blagorodnaya missiya sovetskoi literatury,' " *Requiem,* p. 249. Orig. *Sovetskoye studenchestvo,* nos. 6–7 (1946), p. 5.

Petrov, Vsevolod. "Fontannyi Dom," intro. L. S. Lukyanova and E. V. Tversky. *Nashe naslediye,* IV (1988), pp. 103, 108.

———. "Fontannyi Dom," VOAA, pp. 219–226.

———. "Iz memuarov *Fontannyi Dom,*" PV, pp. 75–78.

Pikach, A. " 'A vot kogda my vzdumali roditsya . . . ,' " *Zvezda,* no. 6 (1989), pp. 182–194.

Piotrowiak, Joanna. "The Symblic Function of Concrete Objects in the Poetry of Anna Achmatova and Maria Pawlikowska-Jasorzewska (1910–1937)," *Russian Literature* (1985), pp. 299–310.

"Pisma Bloka k K. I. Chukovskomu i otryvki iz dnevnika K. I. Chukovskogo," ed. E. Ts. Chukovskaya. *Literaturnoye nasledstvo: Aleksandr Blok,* kn. 2. Moscow: Nauka, 1981, pp. 235–272.

"Pisma k A.A. Akhmatovoi," OAA, pp. 531–554.

"Pisma N. V. Nedoborovo k Bloku," ed. M. M. Kralin, *Literaturnoye nasledstvo: Aleksandr Blok,* kn. 2., pp. 292–296.

Platonov, Andrey. "Anna Akhmatova," *Razmyshleniya chitatelya.* Moscow: Sovremennik, 1980, pp. 134–139.

Platonova-Lozinskaya, I. " 'Letom semnadtsatogo goda . . . ': O druzhbe A. Akhmatovoi i M. Lozinskogo," LO, no. 5 (1989), pp. 48–57.

Poetika i stilistika russkoi literatury: Pamyati Akademika Viktora Vladimirovicha Vinogradova, ed. M. P. Alekseyev, et al. Leningrad: Nauka, 1971.

Polivanov, Konstantin. *Anna Akhmatova and Her Circle,* trans. Patricia Beriozkina. Fayetteville: University of Arkansas Press, 1993.

———. "Prosto provintsialnyi muzei: Pismo V. F. Rumyantsevoi M. N. Ikonnikovoi," LO, no. 5 (1989), pp. 88–89.

Pollack, Nancy. "Annensky's 'Trefoil in the Park' (Witness to Whiteness)," SP, pp. 171–190.

Poltavtseva, N. G. "Akhmatova i kultura 'serebryanogo veka' ('vechnye obrazy' kultury v tvorchestve Akhmatovoi)," TsS, pp. 41–58.

Polukhina, Valentina. "Akhmatova i Brodsky (K probleme prityazhenii i ottalkivanii)," AS, pp. 143–155.

———. "The Grammar, Semantics and Function of Negation in the Poetry of Anna Akhmatova," SUE, I, pp. 151–168.

Popov, T. *Russkaya narodno-bytovaya meditsina.* St. Petersburg, 1903.

Popova, Nina. "Kategoriya prostranstva v ekspozitsionnom reshenii muzeya Anny Akhmatovoi v Fontannom Dome," *Russian Literature,* XXX (1991), pp. 385–390.

Porter, Cathy. *Larissa Reisner.* London: Virago Press, 1988.

Portnov, Vladimir. "K. I. Chukovsky o *Poeme bez geroya,*" *Literaturnyi Azerbaidzhan,* December 12, 1973, pp. 118–122.

Posvyashchaetsya Akhmatovoi: Stikhi raznykh poetov, posvyashchyonnye Akhmatovoi. Comp. and ed. Pamela Davidson and Isia Tlusty. Tenafly, NJ: Hermitage Publishers, 1990.

Pound, Ezra. *Selected Poems of Ezra Pound.* New York: New Directions, 1957.

Pozner, Solomon. "Pamyati N. S. Gumilyova," NGVS, pp. 237–238.

Pratt, Sarah. "The Obverse of Self: Gender Shifts in Poems by Tjutchev and Akhmatova," in *Russian Literature and Psychoanalysis,* ed. Daniel Rancour-Laferrière. Amsterdam: John Benjamins, 1989, pp. 225–244.

Prizhiznennye izdaniya Anny Akhmatovoi (v fondakh odesskikh bibliotek), Comp. N. N. Cherny. Odessa: Mayak, 1989.

Proizvedeniya sovetskikh kompositorov na stikhi Anny Akhmatovoi (for voice and piano). Moscow: Sovetskii Kompozitor, 1989.

Prozorova, N. G. "Opyt sravnitelnogo analiza dvukh stikhotvorenii (Aleksandr Blok, 'Krasota strashna—vam skazhut,' Anna Akhmatova, 'Ya prishla k poetu v gosti,')" *Filologicheskiye nauki,* no. 6 (1989), pp. 141–149.

Przybylski, Ryszard. *An Essay on the Poetry of Osip Mandelstam: God's Grateful Guest,* trans. Madeline G. Levine. Ann Arbor: Ardis, 1987.

"Public Orator's Speech at the Oxford Honorary Degree Ceremony," SUE, II, pp. 335–338.

Punin, N. N. "Cycle of Lectures [Extracts], 1919," in *Russian Art of the Avant-garde: Theory and Criticism 1902–1934,* ed. Bowlt.

———. "Dnevnik," ed. Irina Punina, *Zvezda,* no. 1 (1994), pp. 96–104.

———. "Iz dnevnika [1941–1942]," PV, p. 140.

———. "Iz dnevnika [23 February 1945]," *Requiem,* p. 194.

———. "Iz dnevnika [16 November 1945]," *Requiem,* p. 195.

———. "Iz dnevnika [21 February 1946]," PBG, p. 335.

———. "Iz pisma k A. A. Akhmatovoi [14 April 1942]," PV, pp. 140–143. Orig. *Nashe naslediye,* no. 4 (1988).

———. "Iz vospominanii," PBG, pp. 336–337.

———. "Pamyati grafa Vasiliya Alekseyevicha Komarovskogo," PBG, pp. 308–312. Orig. *Apollon* (1914), nos. 6–7, pp. 86–89.

———. "Pismo N. N. Punina A. A. Akhmatovoi," S-F, III, pp. 466–470.

———. "Revolyutsiya bez literatury," *Minuvsheye,* no. 8 (Paris: Atheneum, 1989), pp. 331–349. See same article, TR, pp. 264–270, with companion article by A. G. Kaminskaya, "Neopublikovannaya statya N. N. Punina ob Akhmatovoi," TR, pp. 262–263.

Punina, I. N. "Anna Akhmatova na Sitsilii," *VOAA,* pp. 662–669.

———. "O Valerii Sreznevskoi," OAA, pp. 26–28. (See same article, VOAA, pp. 20–27.)

———. "Sorok shestoi god," VOAA, pp. 465–472.

Pushkin, A. S. *Sobraniye sochinenii,* ed. D. D. Blagoi, S. M. Bondi, V. V. Vinogradov, and Yu. G. Oksman. Vols. I–II. Moscow: Khudozhestvennaya literatura, 1959.

———. *Eugene Onegin,* trans. Walter Arndt. New York: E. P. Dutton and Company, 1963.

Pyanykh, Mikhail. " 'Menya, kak reku, surovaya epokha povernula,' " *Zvezda,* no. 6 (1989), pp. 195–201.

Pyast, V. A. "Iz knigi *Vstrechi,*" VOAA, pp. 33–34.

———. "Vstrechi," NGVS, pp. 104–110.

Radzishevsky, V. "V prisutsvii Anny Akhmatovoi: Postskriptum k yubileinym chteniyam v Moskve, Leningrade," *Literaturnaya gazeta,* March 7, 1990, p. 3.

Rafalovich, Sergey. "Anna Akhmatova," DG, pp. 220–227. Orig. *Ars,* no. 1 (Tbilisi, 1919).

Rannit, Aleksis. "Anna Akhmatova Considered in a Context of Art Nouveau," S-F, II, pp. 5–39.

"Raport praporshchika N. Gumilyova," ed. Igor Kurlyandsky. *Nashe naslediye,* I (1991), pp. 36–38.

Rauch, Georg von. *A History of Soviet Russia,* ed. and trans. Peter and Annette Jacobsohn, 6th ed. New York: Praeger Publishers, 1972.

Reeder, Roberta. "Eisenstein's *Strike:* Puppets, Propaganda, and Posters," RLT (1988), pp. 255–278.

———. "Folk Song," *Handbook to Russian Literature,* pp. 143–146.

———. "The Greek Anthology and Its Influence on Pushkin's Poetic Style," *Canadian-American Slavic Studies,* X, no. 2 (Summer 1976), pp. 205–228.

———. "The Lament," *Handbook to Russian Literature,* p. 242.

———. "Mir iskusstva (The World of Art)," *Handbook to Russian Literature,* pp. 283–284.

———. "Petrouchka—A Russian Rogue," *Puppetry Journal* (January–February 1981), pp. 41–45.

———. "Tsarskoe Selo in the Poetry of Anna Akhmatova: The Eternal Return," SUE, II, pp. 285–302.

———. "Wedding Ritual Songs," *Handbook to Russian Literature*, p. 516.

———, ed. and trans. *The Russian Folk Lyric.* Bloomington: Indiana University Press, 1992.

Reeve, F. D. "The Inconstant Translation: Life into Art," AA, pp. 149–169.

———. *Robert Frost in Russia.* Boston: Little, Brown, 1963.

Reformatskaya, N. V. "S Akhmatovoi v Muzeye Mayakovskogo," VOAA, pp. 543–544.

Rein, Evgeny. " 'S radostyu vpisyvayu v albom Innokentiya Memnovichu,' " *Voprosy literatury,* no. 6 (1981), pp. 308–314.

———. "Sotoye zerkalo. (Zapozdalye vospominaniya)," SMV, pp. 102–116.

Reisner, Larisa. "Iz pisma k A. A. Akhmatovoi," PV, p. 19.

Remizov, Aleksey. "Gorky: A Memoir," trans. Roberta Reeder, *Yale/Theatre* (1976), pp. 95–106.

Retsepter, V. " 'Eto dlya tebya na vsyu zhizn' (A. Akhmatova i 'Shekspirovskii vopros')," *Voprosy literatury,* no. 3 (1987), pp. 195–210. (Also in VOAA, pp. 648–661.)

Reznikova, E., and E. Gabets. "Zvezda pervoi velichiny," *Russkii yazyk za rubezhom,* no. 4 (1989), pp. 107–116.

Riasanovsky, Nicholas V. "The Emergence of Eurasianism," *California Slavic Studies,* (1967), pp. 207–220.

———. *A History of Russia,* 2nd ed. New York: Oxford University Press, 1969.

Richter, Hans Werner. *Erfahrungen mit Utopien Briefe an einen jungen Sozialisten.* Munich: Deutscher Taschenbuch Verlag, 1981.

———. *Euterpe von den Ufern der Neva oder die Ehrung Anna Achmatowas in Taormina.* Berlin: Friedenauer Presse, 1965.

Rilke, Rainer Maria. *Selected Poems,* trans. Albert Ernest Flemming. New York: Methuen, 1986.

Rodov, S. "Iz stati 'Literaturnoye segodnya,' " *Requiem,* pp. 52–54. Orig. *Molodaya gvardiya,* nos. 6–7 (1922), pp. 308–309.

Ronan, Omry. "A Beam upon the Axe: Some Antecedents of Osip Mandelstam's 'Umyvalsja na dvore . . . ,' " *Slavic Hierosolymitana,* I (1977), pp. 158–176.

Rosenthal, Bernice Glatzer, ed. *Nietzsche in Russia.* Princeton: Princeton University Press, 1986.

———. "Stages of Nietzscheanism: Merezhkovsky's Intellectual Evolution," *Nietzsche in Russia,* pp. 69–94.

Roskina, Nataliya. " 'Kak budto proshchayus snova . . . ,' " VOAA, pp. 520–541.

Rosslyn, Wendy. "A propos of Anna Akhmatova. Boris Vasilevich Anrep (1883–1969)," *New Zealand Slavonic Journal,* no. 1 (1989), pp. 35–34.

———. "Akhmatova's *Poema bez geroia:* Ballet and Poem," SUE I, pp. 55–72.

———. "Boris Anrep and the Poems of Anna Akhmatova," *Modern Language Review,* LXXIX (October 1979), pp. 884–896.

———. "Don Juan Feminised in Symbolism and After," *Essays on Russian Poetry in Honour of Georgette Dochin,* ed. A. McMillan. Bristol: Bristol Classical Press, 1992, pp. 102–121.

———. "The Function of Architectural Imagery in Akhmatova's Poetry," *Irish Slavonic Studies,* VI (1985), pp. 19–34.

———. "Not a Whiff of a Roman Carnival: Akhmatova's *Poema bez geroia,*" *Russian and Yugoslav Culture in the Age of Modernism,* ed. Cynthia Marsh and Wendy Rosslyn. Nottingham: Astra Press, 1991, pp. 69–87.

———. "Painters and Painting in the Poetry of Anna Akhmatova: The Relation Between the Poetry and Painting," AA, pp. 170–185.

————. *The Prince, the Fool and the Nunnery: The Religious Theme in the Early Poetry of Anna Akhmatova.* Amersham, Bucks: Avebury Publishing Company, 1984.

————. "Remodelling the Statues at Tsarskoe Selo: Akhmatova's Approach to the Poetic Tradition," SP, pp. 147–170.

————. "Theatre, Theatricality and Akhmatova's *Poema bez geroya,*" *Essays in Poetics,* no. 1, XIII (1988), pp. 89–108.

————. "The Theme of Light in the Early Poetry of Anna Akhmatova," *Renaissance and Modern Studies,* XXIV (1980), pp. 79–91.

Rostovtsev, Evgeny. "Chi my nasledniki," *Stsena,* August 24, 1991.

Rozanov, I. N. "Iz dnevnika," *Requiem,* p. 34. Orig. cited in Mikhail Bulgakov, *Chudakova M.* Moscow, 1988, pp. 157–158.

Rozenfeld, B. "Muzykalnye sochineniya na stikhi Anny Akmatovoi," in B. Kats and R. Timenchik, *Akhmatova i muzyka,* pp. 279–307.

Rozhdestvenskaya, M. V. "Mikhail Kuzmin v arkhive Vs. Rozhdestvenskogo," *Mikhail Kuzmin i russkaya kultura XX veka,* pp. 212–219.

Rozhdestvensky, Vsevolod. "Gumilyov i Blok," NGVS, pp. 223–227.

Roziner, Felix. "The Slender Lyre: Artur Lourié and His Music," *Bostonia* (Fall 1992), pp. 34–41, 86–87.

Rudakov, S. B. "Voronezh—v gosti k Osipu Mandelshtamu," VOAA, pp. 277–280.

Rude, Jeanne. *Anna Akhmatova. Poètes d'aujourd'hui,* no. 179. Paris: Editions Seghers, 1968.

Rudnitsky, Kontantin. *Meyerhold the Director,* trans. George Petrov. Ardis: Ann Arbor, 1981.

Rumyantseva, V. F. "Iz pisma k M. N. Ikonikovoi," VOAA, pp. 245–247.

Rusinko, Elaine. "Acmeism, Post-Symbolism, and Henri Bergson," *Slavic Review,* no. 3, XLI (Fall 1982), pp. 494–510.

————. "Gumilev in London: An Unknown Interview" [Appendix—C. B. Bechhofer, "Interviews"], RLT, no. 16 (1979), pp. 73–85.

————. "*K sinej zvezda:* Gumilev's Love Poems," *Russian Language Journal,* no. 109, XXXI (1977), pp. 155–167.

————. "Lost in Space and Time. Gumilyev's 'Zabludivŝijsja Tramvaj,' " *Slavic East European Journal,* no. 4, XXVI (1982), pp. 383–402.

————. "Russian Acmeism and Anglo-American Imagism," *Ulbandus* (1978), pp. 37–49.

————. "The Theme of War in the Works of Gumilev," *Slavic East European Journal,* no. 2, XXI (Summer 1977), pp. 204–213.

————. "The 'Two Adams': Gumilev's Creative Personality," *Nikolay Gumilyov 1886–1986,* ed. Graham, pp. 243–267.

Rybakova, O. I. "Grustnaya pravda," OAA, pp. 224–230.

Rykova, N. Ya. "Mesyatsa besformennyi oskolok . . . ," OAA, pp. 173–179.

Ryss, Pyotr. "U Tychkova mosta," NGVS, pp. 221–222.

Saakyants, A. A. "Anna Akhmatova i Marina Tsvetayeva . . . ," TsS, pp. 181–193.

Sakharov, V. I. "A. Akhmatova i M. Bulgakov," TsS, pp. 203–206.

Salisbury, Harrison. *The 900 Days: The Siege of Leningrad.* New York: Harper & Row, 1969.

Salmi, Natalya. "Anna Akhmatova i Innokenty Annensky (k voprosu o smene modelei mira na rubezhe dvukh vekov)," TsS, pp. 126–134.

Samoilov, David. "Vremena Akhmatovoi," in Akhmatova, *Ya—golos vash . . . ,* pp. 5–17.

Sampson, Earl D. "In the Middle of the Journey of Life: Gumilev's *Pillar of Fire,*" RLT, no. 1 (Fall 1971), pp. 382–296.

————. *Nikolay Gumilev.* Boston: Twayne Publishers, 1979.

Sandler, Stephanie. "Reading Loyalty in Chukovskaya's *Zapiski ob Anne Akhmatovoi*," SUE, II, pp. 267–284.

————. "The Stone Ghost: Akhmatova, Pushkin, and Don Juan,"*Literature, Culture, and Society in the Modern Age: In Honor of Joseph Frank*, Pt. II. *Stanford Slavic Studies*, no. 2, IV. Stanford: Stanford University Press, 1992, pp. 35–49.

Satin, Maria R. *Akhmatova's "Shipovnik tsvetyot": A Study of Creative Method*. Ph.D. Dissertation, University of Pennsylvania, 1978.

Saulenko, L. L. "Pushkinskaya traditsiya v *Poeme bez geroya* Anny Akhmatovoi," *Voprosy russkoi literatury*, vyp. 2 (36), Lvov, 1980, pp. 42–50.

Sayanov, V. "Akmeism." *Ocherki po istorii russkoi poezii XX veka*. Leningrad: Krasnaya gazeta, 1929 (reprinted, Letchworth, Herts: Prideux Press, 1972).

Sazonova-Slonimskaya, Yu. L. "Nikolai Vladimirovich Nedobrovo," OAA, pp. 70–74.

Schmid, Wolf. "Narratives Erinnern und poetisches Gedächtnis in realistischer und ornamentaler Prosa," *Wiener Slawistischer Almanach*, XVI (1985), pp. 99–108.

Schreiner, Jana. "Die Kategorie des Gedichtumfangs und die Urerzeiler bei Anna Achmatova," *Die Welt der Slaven*, no. 2, XXXIV (1989), pp. 201–236.

Schroeder, Friedrich-Christian. "Rechtsstreit um den Nachlass von Anna Achmatowa," *Osteuropa*, no. 7, XL (July 1990), pp. 647–650.

Sedakova, D. A. "Shkatulka s zerkalom. Ob odnom glubinnom motive A. A. Akhmatovoi," *Struktura dialoga kak printsip raboty semioticheskogo mekhanizma. Trudy po znakovym sistemam*, vyp. 641. Tartu: Tartu University, 1984, pp. 93–109.

Segal, D. " 'Sumerki svobody': o nekotorykh temakh russkoi ezhednevnoi pechati 1917– 1918 gg.," *Minuvsheye*, no. 3 (Paris: Atheneum, 1987), pp. 131–140.

Segal, Harold B. "Cabaret in Russia: More Bats, Crooked Mirrors, and Stray Dogs," *Turn- of-the-Century Cabaret*. New York: Columbia University Press, 1987.

Serbin, P. K. "Funktsii peizazha v lirike Anny Akhmatovoi," *Voprosy russkoi literatury*, LVII (1991), pp. 24–31.

Serog, Youngjoung. *The Concept of Love in the Poetry of Anna Akhmatova*. Ph.D. Dissertation, Ohio State University, 1987.

Setchkarev, Vsevolod. *Studies in the Life and Work of Innokentij Annenskij*. The Hague: Mouton, 1963.

Shapovalova, G. G., and L. S. Lavrenteva. *Traditsionnye obryady i obryadovyi folklor russkikh Povolzhya*, ed. B. N. Putilov. Leningrad: Nauka, 1985.

Sharlaimova, L. M. "Blokovskaya tema v *Poeme bez geroya* A. Akhmatovoi," *Voprosy russkoi literatury*, vyp. 59. Novosibirskii gosudarstvennyi pedagogicheskii institut, Novosibirsk, 1970, pp. 130–137.

Shcheglov, Yu. K. "Cherty poeticheskogo mira Akhmatovoi," *Wiener Slawistischer Almanach*, XXX (1979), pp. 27–56.

————. "Iz nablyudenii nad poeticheskim mirom Akhmatovoi ('Serdtse byotsya rovno, merno . . .')," *Russian Literature*, XI (1982), pp. 49–90.

————. "Iz nablyudenii nad poeticheskim mirom Akhmatovoi ('Ya s toboi ne stanu pit vino . . .')," *Wiener Slawistischer Almanach*, XI (1983), pp. 325–340.

Shcherbina, O. G. " 'Ne zvukopodrazhaniye, a dushepreobrazheniye . . . ,' " *Russkaya rech*, no. 3 (May–June 1989), pp. 37–40.

Shchuplov, Aleksandr. "Russkaya poeziya nikogda ne molchala" (Interview with Boris Romanov), *Knizhnoye obozreniye*, no. 12 (March 24, 1989), p. 9.

Shefner, Vadim. "Poeziya silneye, chem sudba," OAA, pp. 411–416.

Sherr, Barry. "Notes on Literary Life in Petrograd 1918–1922: A Tale of Three Houses," *Slavic Review*, no. 2, XXXVI (June 1977), pp. 256–267.

Shervinsky, S. V. "Anna Akhmatova v rakurse byta," VOAA, pp. 281–298.

Shileiko, Tamara. "Legendy, mify i stikhi," *Novyi mir*, no. 4 (April 1986), pp. 199–213.

Shileiko, Vladimir. "Muza" [and other poems], PBG, pp. 322–328.

Shilov, Lev. *Anna Akhmatova (100 let so dnya rozhdeniya).* Moscow: Znaniye, 1989.

――――. "Zvuchashchiye teksty Anny Akhmatovoi," TsS, pp. 217–231.

Shindin, S. "Anna Akhmatova i russkaya kultura nachala XX veka. Tezisy konferentsii," *Russian Literature,* XXX (1991), pp. 273–283.

Shklovsky, Viktor. "Anna Akhmatova. *Anno Domini MCMXXI,*" PV, pp. 53–54.

――――. "Gumilyov, 'Kostyor,' " NGVS, pp. 167–168.

――――. *Zhili-byli.* Moscow. Sovetskii pisatel, 1964.

Shkolnik, Boris. "Mandelshtam v Peterburge." *Ya vernulsya v moi gorod . . . : Peterburg Mandelshtama.* Leningrad: Svecha, 1991, pp. 23–47.

Shmakov, G. G. "O nekotorykh chertakh prostranstvenno-vremennykh otnoshenii v poezii XX veka i ob osobennostyakh yeyo vospriyatiya," *Mikhail Kuzmin i russkaya kultura XX veka,* pp. 8–10.

Shuvalov, Roman. "Bratya Romanenko i semya Gorenko," *Vechernyaya Odessa,* June 16, 1989.

――――. "Otets poeta. K 100-letiyu so dnya rozhdeniya Anny Akhmatovoi," *Vechernyaya Odessa,* June 14, 1989, p. 3.

Shvetsova, L. "Nikolai Klyuev i Anna Akhmatova," *Voprosy literatury,* no. 5 (1980), pp. 303–305.

Shwartzband, S. "Anna Akhmatova's Second Book: *Chyokti:* Systematic Arrangement and Structure," SUE, I, pp. 123–138.

Sidorin, Ya. "Vspominaya Akhmatovu," *Neva,* no. 1 (January 1984), pp. 197–199.

Silman, Tamara, and Vladimir Admoni. *My vspominayem.* St. Petersburg: Kompozitor, 1993.

Simchenko, O. "K izucheniyu poetiki Akhmatovoi i Tsvetayevoi," *Sovremennye problemy russkoi filologii,* pp. 53–57.

――――. "Tema pamyati v tvorchestve Anny Akhmatovoi," *Izvestiya Akademii Nauk SSSR: Seriya literatury i yazyka,* no. 6, XLIV (1985), pp. 506–517.

Simonov, Konstantin. "Iz knigi *Glazami cheloveka moyego pokoleniya,*" *Requiem,* pp. 229–231. Orig. *Znamya,* no. 3 (1988), pp. 49–50.

Sinyavsky, Andrei. "Boris Pasternak," *Pasternak-*Davie, pp.154–219.

――――. "Odin den s Pasternakom," BP, pp. 11–17.

――――. "Raskovannyi golos (K 75-letiyu A. Akhmatovoi)," *Novyi mir,* no. 6, XL (June 1964), p. 176.

Skatov, Nikolay. "Rossiya u Aleksandra Bloka i poeticheskaya traditsiya Nekrasova," in *V mire Bloka: sbornik statei.* Moscow: Sovetskii pisatel, 1980, pp. 85–114.

――――. " 'Ya—golos vash,' " *Literaturnaya gazeta,* June 21, 1989, p. 3.

Slinina, E. V. "Pushkinskiye motivy v tsarskoselskikh stikakh Anny Akamtovoi," *Uchyonye zapiski: Pushkinskii sbornik.* Pskov: Gosudarstvennyi pedagogicheskii institut, 1973, pp. 129–139.

Slonim, Marc. *From Chekhov to the Revolution.* New York: Oxford University Press, 1962.

――――. *Soviet Russian Literature: Writers and Problems 1917–1967.* Oxford: Oxford University Press, 1964.

Slonimsky, Mikhail. "Iz 'Literaturnykh zametok,' " OAA, pp. 391–392.

Sluzhevskaya, I. " 'Tak vot ty kakoi, Vostok . . .': Aziya v lirike A. Akhmatovoi: tashkentskoi pory," *Zvezda vostoka,* no. 5 (1982), pp. 96–100.

Smirnov, I. P. "K izucheniyu simvoliki Anny Akhmatovoi," *Poetika i stilistika russkoi literatury: Pamiati akademika V. V. Vinogradova,* ed. M. P. Alekseyev, et al. Leningrad; Nauka, 1971, pp. 279–287.

――――. "O spetsifike khudozhestvennoi (literaturnoi) pamyati," *Wiener Slawistische Almanach,* no. 16 (1985), pp. 11–27.

———. "Poeticheskiye assotsiativnye svyazi *Poemy bez geroya*," *Traditsiya v istorii kultury.* Moscow: Nauka, 1978, pp. 228–230.

———. "Prichinno-sledstvennye struktury poeticheskikh proizvedenii," *Issledovaniya po poetike i stilistike,* ed. V. V. Vinogradov, Leningrad: Nauka, 1971, pp. 212–247.

Sokolov, V. N. "Iz stati '*Maskarad* v Aleksandrinskom teatre,' " PBG, pp. 144–146. Orig. *Apollon,* nos. 2–3 (1917).

———. "Slovo ob Akhmatovoi," TsS, pp. 9–13.

Somova, Svetlana. "Anna Akhmatova v Tashkente," VOAA, pp. 369–374.

———. "Mne dali imya—Anna: Anna Akhmatova v Tashkente," *Moskva,* no. 3 (1984), pp. 183–193, and *Moskva,* no. 4 (1984), pp. 188–193.

———. "Ten na glinyanoi stene: Anna Akhmatova v Tashkente," Ch. 2, *Moskva,* no. 10 (1986), pp. 180–187.

Sophocles. *Oedipus the King,* trans. R. C. Jebb in *Seven Famous Greek Plays.* New York: Random House, 1950, pp. 117–182.

Sorokina, Yelena. "Vspominaya Akhmatovu," *Neva,* no. 1 (1988), pp. 206–208.

Spassky, Sergey. "Iz stati 'Pisma o poezii,' " *Requiem,* p. 169. Orig. *Zvezda,* no. 1 (1945).

Spender, Stephen. "Views," *The Listener* (September 12, 1968), pp. 52–53.

Sreznevskaya, Valeriya. "Dafnis i khloya," OAA, pp. 15–25.

———. "Dafnis i Khloya," VOAA, pp. 5–19. (The two excerpts from Sreznevskaya's memoirs differ in each book.)

———. "Iz vospominanii," DG, pp. 14–20, 37–38, 213–214. Orig. *Vestnik russkogo khristyanskogo dvizheniya.* Paris, no. 146 (1986).

———. "Iz vospominanii V. S. Sreznevskoi," Nikolay Gumilyov, *Neizdannoye i nesobrannoye,* pp. 157–168.

Stanislavsky, Constantine. *My Life in Art,* trans. J. J. Robbins. Cleveland and New York: World Publishing Company, 1948 (first published 1924).

Stankiewicz, Edward. "Centripetal and Centrifugal Structures in Poetry," *Semiotica,* nos. 3–4, XXXVIII (1982), pp. 217–242.

Stepanov, Evgeny. "Dom poeta," LO, no. 6 (1989), pp. 79–81.

———. "Vtoraya rodina," *Nashe naslediye,* no 9, III (1989), pp. 89–95.

Stepun, Fyodor. "Iz knigi *Byvsheye i nesbyvsheyesya,*" PBG, p. 95. Orig. *Byvsheye i nesbyvsheyesy,* I, New York, 1956, p. 297.

"Stikhi i pisma. Anna Akhmatova. N. Gumilyov," ed. E. G. Gershtein, *Novyi mir,* no. 9 (September 1986), pp. 196–227.

Strakhovsky, Leonid. "O Gumilyove (1886–1921)," NGVS, pp. 200–202.

———. *Three Poets of Modern Russia.* Cambridge, MA: Harvard University Press, 1949.

Stroganov, M. V. "*Poema bez geroya* i yeyo kommentatory," *Russkaya literatura,* no. 4 (1980), pp. 177–178.

Struve, Gleb. "Akhmatova i Boris Anrep," S-F, III, pp. 428–438.

———. "Akhmatova i Nikolay Nedobrovo," S-F, III, pp. 371–418.

———. "Blok and Gumilyov: A Double Anniversary," *Slavonic and East European Review,* XXV (1946), pp. 176–180.

———. "K istorii russkoi literatury 1910-kh godov. Pisma N. V. Nedobrovo k B. V. Anrepu," *Slavica Hierosolymitana,* nos. 5–6 (1981), pp. 425–466.

———. "N. S. Gumilyov: Zhizn i lichnost," in Nikolay Gumilyov, *Sobraniye sochinenii,* S-F, I, pp. vii–xliv.

———. *Russian Literature Under Lenin and Stalin.* Norman, OK: University of Oklahoma Press, 1971.

———, and Boris Filipoff. "Poemy bez geroja," S-F, II, pp. 603–605.

Struve, Nikita. "Kolebaniya vdokhnoveniya v poeticheskom tvorchestve Akhmatovoi," AS, pp. 155–164.

————. "O 'Polnochnykh stikhakh,' " AA, pp. 186–193.

————. "Vosem chasov s Annoi Akhmatovoi," S-F, II, 1968, pp. 325–349.

Subbotin, Aleksandr. "Mayakovsky i Akhmatova," *Ural*, no. 6, LXXXVI (1983), pp. 177–184.

Sukhanova, Maria. "Fuga Temporum," *Russian Literature*, XXX (1991), pp. 337–342.

Sumerkin, Aleksandr. "Neizvestnoye stikhotvoreniye Tsvetayevoi," AS, pp. 199–202.

Superfin, Gabriel, and Roman Timenchik. "A propos de deux lettres de A. A. Akhmatova à V. Brjusov," *Cahiers du Monde russe et soviétique*, nos. 1–2, XV (January–June 1974), pp. 183–200.

Surkov, A. "Iz otchyote ob obsuzhdenii knig o Mayakovskom," *Requiem*, p. 164. Orig. *Literaturnaya gazeta*, December 1, 1940.

————. "Iz stati 'Nezabyvayemoye,' " *Requiem*, p. 262. Orig. *Literaturnaya gazeta*, May 9, 1947.

————. "Vstupitelnaya statya," in Akhmatova, *Stikhotvoreniya i poemy*, 1979, pp. 5–18.

Suvorova, K. N. "Samyi neprochitannyi poet: Zametki Anny Akhmatovoi o Nikolaye Gumilyove," *Novyi mir*, no. 5 (May 1990), pp. 219–223.

"Svidetelstvo no. 4379" [Akhmatova's gymnasium final grade report], DG, p. 6.

Svoyu mezh vas yeshchyo ostaviv ten . . . , Akhmatovskiye chteniya, vyp. III. Ed. N. V. Korolyova and S. A. Kovalenko. Moscow: Naslediye, 1992.

Svyatopolk-Mirsky, Prince D. "Poety i Rossiya," PV, pp. 67–71. Orig. *Versty*, no. 1 (Paris, 1926).

Tager, Elena. "Iz vospominanii," *Requiem*, pp. 93–94. Orig. *Vozdushnye puti*, IV (New York, 1965).

Tainy remesla, Akhmatovskiye chteniya, vyp. II. Ed. N.V. Korolyova and S. A. Kovalenko. Moscow: Naslediye, 1992.

Tamarchenko, Anna. "Tak ne zrya my vmeste byvali" (Tema emigratsii v poezii Anny Akhmatovoi), TsS, pp. 71–88.

Taranovsky, Kiril. "Zametka k state M. B. Meilakha i V. N. Toporova 'Akhmatova i Dante,' " *International Journal of Slavic Linguistics and Poetics*, XVI (1973), pp. 177–178.

————. "Zhizn dayushchii golos: Zametka o Pasternake i Akhmatovoi," in *Vozmi na radost': To Honour Jeanne van der Eng-Liedmeier*, ed. V. J. Amsenga, et al. Amsterdam: Slavic Seminar, 1980, pp. 149–156.

Tarasenkov, A. "Iz stati 'Pafos sovetskoi zhizni,' " *Requiem*, pp. 261–262. Orig. *Literaturnaya gazeta*, August 2, 1947.

————. "Iz stati 'Zametki kritika," *Requiem*, p. 265. Orig. *Znamya*, no. 10 (1949), p. 173.

Tarkovsky, Arseny. "Predisloviye," in *Golosa poetov: stikhi zarubezhnykh poetov v perevode Anna Akhmatovoi*, pp. 5–11.

Tatarinova, N. "Anna Akhmatova v Tashkente," *Prostor*, no. 2 (1971), pp. 97–101. (Also in English in SL, no. 6 [1986], pp. 108–118.)

Tauber, Ekaterina. "Neukrotimaya sovest," *Grani*, no. 53 (1963), pp. 80–86.

Taubman, Jane Andelman. "Tsvetaeva and Akhmatova: Two Female Voices in a Poetic Quartet," RLT, no. 9 (Spring 1974), pp. 355–370.

Tavis, Anna. "A Journey from Petersburg to Stockholm: Preliminary Biography of Joseph Brodsky," *Slavic Review*, no. 3, XLIII (Fall 1988), pp. 499–501.

Temnenko, G. M. "Pushkinskiye traditsii v 'Poeme bez geroya,' A. Akhmatovoi," *Voprosy russkoi literatury*, no. 54, II (1989), pp. 12–19.

Terekhov, G. A. "Vozvrashchayas k delu N. S. Gumilyova," *Novyi mir*, no. 23 (December 1987), pp. 257–258.

Text. Symbol. Weltmodell, ed. Johanna Renata Döring-Smirnov, Peter Rehder, and Wolf Schmid. Munich: Verlag Otto Sagner, 1984.

Thomson, R. D. B. "The Anapestic Dolnik in the Poetry of Akhmatova and Gumilev," *Russian Literature* (Spring 1975 supplement), pp. 42–58.

Three Russian Women Poets: Anna Akhmatova, Marina Tsvetaeva, Bella Akhmadulina, trans. Mary Murdoch, intro. Edward J. Brown. Trumansburg, NY: Crossing Press, 1983.

Timenchik, R. D. "Akhmatova i Pushkin (Razbor stikhotvoreniya 'Smuglyi otrok brodil po alleyam')," *Pushkinskii sbornik.* Uchyonye zapiski Latvia State University, 106. Riga: Latvia State University, 1968, pp. 124–131.

———. "Akhmatova i Pushkin: Zametki k teme," *Pushkinskii sbornik,* II. Uchyonye zapiski Latvia State University, 215. Riga: Latvia State University, 1974, pp. 32–55.

———. "Akhmatova's *Macbeth,*" trans. Howard Goldman. *Slavic East European Journal,* no. 4, XXIV (1980), pp. 362–368.

———. "Anna Akhmatova: 1922–1966," PV, p. 2–17.

———. "Anna Akhmatova i Pushkinskii Dom," *Pushkinskii Dom: Stati, dokumenty, bibliografiya.* Leningrad: Nauka, 1982, pp. 102–118.

———. "Avtometaopisaniye u Akhmatovoi," *Russian Literature,* 10/11 (1975), pp. 213–226.

———. "Chuzhoye slovo u Akhmatovoi," *Russkaya rech,* no. 3 (May–June 1989), pp. 33–36.

———. "Innokenty Annensky i Nikolay Gumilyov," *Voprosy literatury,* no. 2 (1987), pp. 271–278.

———. "K analizu 'Poemy bez geroya,' " *Materialy XXII nauchnoi studencheskoi konferentsii.* Tartu: Tartu State University, 1967, pp. 121–123. (Excerpt cited in S-F, II, pp. 604–605.)

———. "K semioticheskо interpretatsii *Poemy bez geroya,*" *Trudy po znakovym sistemam,* vyp. 308. Tartu: Tartu State University, 1973, pp. 438–442.

———. "K voprosu ob istochnikakh dlya zhizneopisanii Gumilyova i Akhmatovoi," AS, pp. 251–256.

———. "Khram premudrosti boga: stikhotvoreniye Anny Akhmatovoi 'Shiroko raspakhnuty vorota . . . ,' " *Slavica Hierosolymitana,* 5–6 (1981), pp. 297–317.

———. " 'Nad sedoyu, vspenennoi Dvinoi . . . , N. Gumilyov v Latvii: 1916–1917," *Daugava,* 8 (110) (August 1986), pp. 115–121.

———. "Neizvestnoye stikhotvoreniye Anny Akhmatovoi," *Oktyabr,* no. 10 (1989), pp. 182–184.

———. "Neizvestnye ekspromty Nikolaya Gumilyova," *Daugava,* 6 (120) (June 1987), pp. 111–116.

———. "Neopublikovannye prozaicheskiye zametki Anny Akhmatovoi," *Izvestiya AN SSSR. Seriiya literatury i yazyka,* XLIII (1984), pp. 75–76.

———. "Neskolko primechanii k state T. Tsivyan," *Trudy po znakovym sistemam,* vyp. 284. Tartu, 1971, pp. 278–280.

———. "Nikolay Gumilyov i vostok," *Pamir,* no. 3 (1987), pp. 123–136.

———. "Ob odnom iz poslednikh sobesednikov Akhmatovoi: Yubileinye zametki," *Daugava* (June 6, 1989), pp. 100–102.

———. "Otryvok iz perevoda *Makbeta,*" LO, no. 5 (1989), pp. 18–21.

———. "Po povodu *Antologii peterburgskoi poezii epokhi akmeizma,*" *Russian Literature,* no. 4, V (October 1977), pp. 315–323.

———. "Posle vsego: Neakademicheskiye zametki," LO, no. 5 (1989), pp. 22–26.

———. "Poslesloviye," DG, pp. 263–278.

———. "Predisloviye," *Requiem,* pp. 3–25.

———. "Ranniye poeticheskiye opyty Anny Akhmatovoi," *Pamyatniki kultury. Novye otkrytiya. Ezhegodnik 1979.* Leningrad: Nauka, 1980, pp. 140–143.

———. "Rizhskii epizod v *Poeme bez geroya* Anny Akhmatovoi," *Daugava*, 2 (80) (February 1984), pp. 113–121.

———. "Tekst v tekste u akmeistov," *Tekst v tekste: trudy po znakovym sistemam*, vyp. 567, XIV (Tartu, 1977), pp. 65–75.

———. "Verses from *A Burnt Notebook*," *Soviet Literature*, no. 6 (1989), pp. 74–78.

———. "Zametki o *Poeme bez geroya*," PBG, pp. 3–25.

———. "Zametki ob akmeizme: I," *Russian Literature*, no. 7/8 (1974), pp. 23–47.

———. "Zametki ob akmeizme: II," *Russian Literature*, no. 3, V (1977), pp. 281–300.

———. "Zametki ob akmeizme: III," *Russian Literature*, no. 2, IX (1981), pp. 175–191.

———, and A. V. Lavrov. "Innokenty Annensky v neizdannykh vospominaniyakh," *Pamyatnik. Kultury. Novye otkrytiya. Ezhegodnik 1981*. Leningrad: Nauka, 1983, pp. 61–117.

———, and A. V. Lavrov. "Materialy A. A. Akhmatovoi v rukopisnom otdele Pushkinskogo Doma," *Ezhegodnik rukopisnogo otdela Pushkinskogo Doma za 1974*, ed. Alekseyev, et al., pp. 53–83.

———, V. N. Toporov and T. V. Tsivyan, "Akhmatova i Kuzmin," *Russian Literature*, no. 3, VI (July 1978), pp. 213–300.

Tishchenko, Boris. "Velikiye khudozhniki," *Sovetskaya kultura* (October 15, 1988), p. 5.

Titov, L. "K shestidesyatiletiyu knigi *Vecher*," in *Pamyati Anny Akhmatovoi*, pp. 213–218.

Tjalsma, H. W. "The Petersburg Poets," in Gibian and Tjalsma, eds., *Russian Modernism*, pp. 65–85.

Tlusty, Isabel. *Anna Akhmatova and the Composition of Her "Poema bez geroya" 1940–1962*. Ph.D. Dissertation, Oxford University, 1984.

Tolstoy, Aleksey. "N. Gumilyov," NGVS, pp. 38–44.

Tomashevskaya, Z. B. "Ya—kak peterburgskaya tumba," OAA, pp. 417–438.

Toporov, V. N. *Akhmatova i Blok*. Modern Russian Literature and Culture, 5. Berkeley: Berkeley Slavic Specialties, 1981.

———. "Dve glavy iz istorii russkoi poezii nachala veka: I. V. A. Komarovsky—II. V. K. Shileiko (k sootnosheniyu poetiki simvolizma i Akmeizma)," *Russian Literature*, VII (1979), pp. 249–326.

———. "K otzvukam zapadnoyevropeiskoi poezii u Akhmatovoi (T. S. Eliot)," *International Journal of Slavic Linguistics and Poetics*, XVI (1973), pp. 157–176.

———. "Ob istorizme Akhmatovoi (dve glavy iz knigi)," AA, pp. 194–237.

———. "Ob odnom pisme k Anne Akhmatovoi," AS, pp. 12–32.

———, and T. V. Tsivyan, "O nervalianskom podtekste v russkom akmeizme (Akhmatova i Mandelshtam)," *Russian Literature*, XV (1984), pp. 29–50.

Tregub, S. "Iz stati 'Mirovozzreniye poeta,' " *Requiem*, pp. 245–246. Orig. *Literaturnaya gazeta*, September 7, 1946.

———. "Iz stati 'Ob oshibkakh leningradskikh kritikov,' " *Requiem*, p. 243. Orig. *Leningradskaya pravda*, September 6, 1946.

———. "Iz stati 'Poeziya, vrednaya i chuzhdaya narodu,' " *Requiem*, p. 249. Orig. *Leningradskaya pravda*, September 14, 1946.

Trifonova, T. "Iz stati 'Cherty neodolimogo dvizheniya,' " *Requiem*, p. 183. Orig. *Zvezda*, no. 6 (1950), p. 171.

Tropkina, N. E. "O proiskhozhdenii dvukh obrazov narodnogo teatra v *Poeme bez geroya* A. Akhmatovoi," *Russaya literatura i folklornaya traditsiya*. Gosudarstvennyi pedagogicheskii institut im. A. S. Serafimovicha, 1983, pp. 112–118.

Trotsky, L. "Iz knigi *Literatura i revolyutsiya*," *Requiem*, p. 62. Orig. *Literatura i revolyutsiya*, Moscow, 1923.

———. *Literature and Revolution*, trans. Rose Strunsky. Ann Arbor: University of Michigan Press, 1971.

Trushchenko, E. "Rob-Griie ishchot tochki opory," *Novyi mir,* no. 7 (July 1962), pp. 218–221.

Tsarstvennoye slovo, Akhmatovskiye chteniya, vyp. 1. Ed. N. V. Korolyova and S. A. Kovalenko. Moscow: Naslediye, 1992.

"Tsentralnyi Literaturnyi Klub . . ." [poster, Simferopol, 1921], *Requiem,* pp. 36–37.

Tsivyan, T. V. "Akhmatova i muzyka," *Russian Literature,* 10/11 (1975), pp. 173–212.

———. "Antichnye geroini—zerkala Akhmatovoi," *Russian Literature,* 7/8 (1974), pp. 103–119.

———. "Kassandra, Didona, Fedra: antichnye geroini—zerkala Akhmatovoi," LO, no. 5 (1989), pp. 29–33.

———. "Materialy k poetike Anny Akhmatovoi," *Trudy po znakovym sistemam,* III. Tartu: Tartu State University, 1967, pp. 180–208.

———. "Nablyudeniya nad kategoriei opredelyonnosti-neopredelyonnosti vo poeticheskom tekste (Poetika A. Akhmatovoi)," *Kategoriya opredelyonnosti-neopredelyonnosti v slavyanskikh i balkanskikh yazykakh,* pp. 348–363.

———. *"Poema bez geroya:* yeshchyo raz o mnogovariantnosti," AS, pp. 123–130.

———. "Two Hypostases of *Poema bez geroya,*" SUE, I, pp. 113–122.

———. "Zametki k deshifrovke *Poemy bez geroya,*" *Trudy po znakovym sistemam,* V, vyp. 284. Tartu: Tartu State University, 1971, pp. 255–280.

Tsvetayeva, Marina. "Geroi truda," *Requiem,* pp. 32–33.

———. "Iz dnevnika [3 October 1940]," PBG, p. 367.

———. "Iz ocherka 'Nezdeshnii vecher,' " PBG, pp. 354–356.

———. "Pismo k Akhmatovoi [April 1921]," PBG, pp. 357–358.

———. "Pismo k Akhmatovoi [12 November 1926]," *Requiem,* pp. 83–84.

———. "Pismo k Anne Akhmatovoi [August 1921]," *Requiem,* pp. 34–36.

Tucker, Janet G. *Innokentij Annenskij and the Acmeist Doctrine.* Columbus, OH: Slavica Publishers, 1986.

Tynyanov, Yuri. "Iz stati 'Promezhutok,' " PV, pp. 65–67. Orig. *Russkii sovremennik,* no. 4 (1924).

Tyrkov, A. M. *Aleksandr Blok: Zhizn i tvorchestvo.* Moscow: Russkii yazyk, 1986.

Tyrkova-Williams, Ariadna. "Teni minuvshego," DG, pp. 28–38. Orig. *Vozrozhdeniya,* no. 41 (Paris, 1955).

Tyshler, A. G. "Ya pomnyu Annu Akhmatovu," VOAA, pp. 401–403.

Tyutchev, F. I. *Polnoye sobraniye stikhotvorenii.* Biblioteka poeta, Bolshaya seriya, 3rd ed. Ed. A. A. Nikolayev. Leningrad: Sovetskii pisatel, 1987.

Ulam, Adam. *Stalin: The Man and His Era.* Boston: Beacon Press, 1973.

Urban, Adolf. " 'I upala kamennoye slovo . . . ," *Literaturnaya gazeta,* April 22, 1989, p. 4.

———. "Obraz Anny Akhmatovoi," *Zvezda,* no. 6 (1989), pp. 8–18.

"Utro 'O Rossii,' " *Requiem,* pp. 29–30. Orig. *Nash vek,* January 24, 1918.

"Utro 'O Rossii,' ustroyennoe v Tenishevskom zale . . . ," *Requiem,* pp. 28–29. Orig. *Novyi vechernii chas.,* January 22, 1918.

Usov, D. "Iz pisma k E. Arkhippovu," *Requiem,* p. 93.

———. "Iz pisma k E. Gollerbakhu," *Requiem,* p. 92.

———. "Iz pisma k V. Rozhdestvenskomu," *Requiem,* p. 91.

"V Chrezvychainuyu komissiyu po borbe s kontrrevolyutsiyei i spekulyatsiyei," DG, p. 255. Orig. *Russkaya literatura,* no. 3 (1988).

"V glavnuyu voyennuyu prokuraturu," *Requiem,* pp. 285–286. Orig. E. G. Gershtein, "Memuary i fakty (ob osvobozhdenii Lva Gumilyova)," in Anna Akhmatova, *Stikhi. Perepiska. Vospominaniya. Ikonografiya.*

Valkenier, Nina. "Anna Akhmatova *Anno Domini*," PV, pp. 52–53. Orig. *Germes,* no. 1 (Moscow, 1922).

Valsomova-Bondi, N. "Dialog uchyonogo i poeta," *Literaturnaya gazeta,* October 25, 1989, p. 5.

Vaneyev, Anatoly. "Iz ocherka 'Dva goda v Abezi," *Requiem,* pp. 266–277.

Vasilyev, Igor. " 'Yeyo udivitelnoye litso . . .": Pismo Yu. Annenkova," LO, no. 5 (1989), pp. 85–87.

Vasilyeva, Larisa. "S. V. Shervinskomu—95 let," *Literaturnaya gazeta,* November 11, 1987, p. 7.

Vecheslova, Tatyana. "Yeyo tainstvennyi golos," OAA, pp. 282–289.

———. "Ob Anne Akhmatovoi," VOAA, pp. 460–464.

Verheul, Kees. "Public Themes in Poetry of Anna Akhmatova," in Akhmatova, *Tale Without a Hero,* pp. 9–47.

———. *The Theme of Time in the Poetry of Anna Axmatova.* The Hague: Mouton, 1971.

———. "Tishina u Akhmatovoi," TsS, pp. 14–20.

Verigina, Valentina. "Iz *Vospominanii o khudozhnike S. Yu. Sudeikina,*" PBG, pp. 219–223. Orig. D. Kogan, *S. Yu. Sudeikin.* Moscow, 1974.

Vidre, K. "Tam, v Tashkente . . . ," *Neva,* no. 6 (1989), pp. 198–201.

Vilenkin, Vitaly. "Memoirs with a Commentary," trans. John Crowfoot. SL, no. 6 (1989), pp. 80–93.

———. "On a *Poem Without a Hero,*" AA, pp. 249–266.

———. "Stimuly tochnosti v tvorchestve Anny Akhmatovoi," *Voprosy literatury,* no. 6 (1983), pp. 144–176.

———. " 'V sto pervom zerkale': Novye stranitsy: K 100-letiyu so dnya rozhdeniya Anny Akhmatovoi," *Oktyabr,* no. 2 (February 1989), pp. 192–197.

———. *V sto pervom zerkale.* Moscow: Sovetskii pisatel, 1987.

———. *Vospominaniya s kommentariyami.* Moscow: Iskusstvo, 1991.

Vinogradov, V. V. *Anna Akhmatova.* Munich: Wilhelm Fink Verlag, 1970. (Reprint of *O poezii Anny Akhmatovoi,* Leningrad, 1925, and "O simvolike A. A. Akhmatovoi," *Literaturnaya mysl,* I [1922].)

———. *O poezii Anny Akhmatovoi (Stilicheskiye nabroski).* Leningrad, 1925. Reprinted in Vinogradov, *Poetika russkoi literatury.* Moscow: Nauka, 1976, pp. 346–359.

Vishnyak, Mark. "Iz stati 'Na rodine,' " *Requiem,* p. 45. Orig. *Sovremennye zapiski,* no. 19 (1922).

Volkov, Solomon. *Brodsky: Vospominaya Akhmatovu.* Moscow: Nezavisimaya gazeta, 1992. (Also in SMV, pp. 60–101.)

———. *Die Memoirendes Dmitrij Schostakowitsch,* trans. Heddy Pross-Weerth. Hamburg: Albrecht Knaus, 1979. (Original title *Svidetelstvo.* English title *Testimony.*)

Volkovsky, Nikolay. "Delo N. S. Gumilyova," DG, pp. 257–260. Orig. *Segodnya,* Riga, February 3, 1923.

Voloshin, Maksimilian. "Vospominaniya o Cherubine de Gabryak," NGVS, pp. 145–147.

Voogd-Stojanova, T. "Tsezura i slovorazdely v poeme A. Akhmatovoi *Rekviem,*" in *Dutch Contributions to the Seventh International Congress of Slavists,* ed. Van Holk, pp. 317–333.

Vospominaniya ob Anne Akhmatovoi, ed. V. Ya. Vilenkin and V. A. Chernykh. Commentary A. V. Kurt and K. M. Polivanov. Moscow: Sovetskii pisatel, 1991.

Vozdvizhensky, V. G. "Sudba pokoleniya v poezii Anny Akhmatovoi," TsS, pp. 21–28.

Vozmi na radost': To Honour Jeanne van der Eng-Liedmeier, ed. V. J. Amsenga, et al. Amsterdam: Slavic Seminar, 1980.

Vygotsky, Lev. *Thought and Language,* trans. Eugenia Hanfmann and Gertrude Vakar. Cambridge, MA: MIT Press, 1962.

Vysotsky, Orest. "Vozvrashchaya veru v spravedlivost." Interview A. Pasechnik. *Sotsialisticheskaya industriya* (March 27, 1988).

Ware, Timothy. *The Orthodox Church.* New York: Penguin Books, 1963.

Weidle, Wladimir. "Iz stati 'Tri Rossii,' " PBG, p. 90. Orig. *Sovremennye zapiski,* no. 65 (Paris, 1937).

———. "Petersburgskaya poetika," in Gumilyov, *Sobraniye sochinenii,* S-F, IV, pp. v–xxxvi.

———. "The Poetry and Prose of Boris Pasternak," *Pasternak*-Davie, pp. 108–125.

Weissbort, Daniel. "Translating Anna Akhmatova: A Conversation with Stanley Kunitz," in Daniel Weissbort, ed., *Translating Poetry: The Double Labyrinth.* Iowa City: University of Iowa Press, 1989, pp. 107–124.

Wells, David. "Akhmatova and French Literature," *Australian Slavonic and East European Studies,* no. 1, III (1989), pp. 27–47.

———. "Akhmatova and the Nineteenth-Century Poetic Tradition: The Genres of Elegy and Ballad," *Slavonic and East European Review* (1993), pp. 38–45.

———. *Akhmatova and Pushkin: A Study of Literary Relationship.* Ph.D. Dissertation, Oxford University, 1988.

———. "In Expectation of a Thaw: Literary Tradition as Code in Akhmatova's *Poem Without a Hero,*" in *Glasnost in Context,* ed. M. Pavlyshyn. New York: Berg, 1990, pp. 143–156.

———. "Folk Ritual in Anna Akhmatova's *Poema bez geroya,*" *Scottish Slavonic Review,* no. 7 (1986), pp. 69–88.

———. "The Function of the Epigraph in Akhmatova's Poetry," AA, pp. 266–281.

———. "Three Functions of the Classical in Akhmatova's Poetry," SUE, II, pp. 183–199.

Werth, Alexander. "Akhmatova: The Tragic Queen Anna," *The Nation* (August 22, 1966), pp. 157–160.

Weststeijn, Willem G. "Futurism or Acmeism: Some Notes on the Succession to Russian Symbolism," in *Vozmi na radost': To Honour Jeanne van der Eng-Liedmeier,* pp. 99–110.

Whittaker, Robert T., Jr. "Nikolai Gumilev and Acmeist Criticism," RLT, no. 1 (Fall 1971), pp. 139–140.

Wilson, Elizabeth. *Shostakovich: A Life Remembered.* Princeton: Princeton University Press. 1994.

Woodward, James B. "Semantic Parallelism in the Verse of Akhmatova," *Slavic and East European Journal,* no. 4, XV (1971), pp. 455–465.

Woroszylski, Wiktor. *The Life of Mayakovsky,* trans. Boleslaw Taborski. New York: Orion Press, 1970.

Yakovlev, V. "O semantike nekotorykh proizvedenii Anny Akhmatovoi," *Russkaya literatura,* I (1992), pp. 170–174.

Yegolin, A. "Iz stati 'Za vysokuyu ideinost sovetskoi literatury,' " *Requiem,* p. 243. Orig. *Zvezda,* no. 10 (1946).

Yenisherlov, Vladimir. "Anna Akhmatova: K 90-letiyu so dnya rozhdeniya," *Ogonyok,* no. 25 (1979), pp. 26–27.

———. *Vremyon proslezhivala svyaz.* Moscow: Sovremennik, 1985.

Yermilov, V. "Iz vystupleniya na obshchemoskovskom sobranii pisatelei," *Requiem,* p. 249. Orig. *Literaturnaya gazeta,* September 21, 1946.

Yeroshok, E. "Razlucheniye nashe mnimo," *Komsomolskaya pravda,* June 21, 1989, p. 4.

Yesipov, V. M. " 'Dvukh golosov pereklichka . . . ,' " *Russkaya literatura,* III (1991), pp. 159–163.

Yeventov, I. S. "Ob Anne Akhmatovoi," *Voprosy literatury,* no. 3 (1987), pp. 176–194.
———. "Ot Fontanki do Sitsilii," OAA, pp. 360–379.
"Za bolshevistskuyu ideinost!," *Requiem,* p. 244. Orig. *Literaturnaya gazeta,* September 3, 1946.
Zaitsev, Boris. "Dni," *Requiem,* pp. 297–299. Orig. *Russkaya mysl* (Paris, January 7, 1964).
Zamyatin, E. I. "Iz pisma k L. N. Zamyatinoi," *Requiem,* pp. 85–86.
———. "Pismo k Z. Shakhovskoi," *Requiem,* p. 104.
Zelinsky, Bodo. "Dido und Äneas bei Anna Achmatowa und Iosif Brodskij," *Jubiläumsschrift zum 25-jährigen Bestehen des Instituts für Slawistik der Universität Giessen,* ed. Gerhard Giesemann/Herbert Jelittle. Beiträge zur Slavistik, VII. Verlag Peter Lang, 1987, pp. 265–277.
Zenkevich, Mikhail. *Elga: belletricheskiye memuary.* Moscow: "Kor-inf," 1991.
———. "U kamina s Annoi Akhmatovoi," PV, pp. 20–23. Orig. *Muzhitskii sfinks.* Copy of manuscript in collection of M. S. Lesman. (See also "U kamina s Annoi Akhmatovoi," VOAA, pp. 91–95).
Zernov, Nicolas. *The Russians and Their Church.* 3rd ed. Crestwood, NY: St. Vladimir's Seminary Press, 1978.
Zhirmunsky, V. M. "Anna Akhmatova i Aleksandr Blok," *Russkaya literatura,* no. 3 (1970), pp. 57–82.
———. "O tvorchestve Anny Akhmatovoi" (K vosmidesyatiletiyu so dnya rozhdeniya), *Novyi mir,* no. 6, XLV (June 1969), pp. 240–251.
———. "The Poetry of Alexander Blok," *Alexander Blok: An Anthology of Essays and Memoirs,* pp. 144–167.
———. "Poeziya Aleksandra Bloka," in Zhirmunsky, *Voprosy teorii literatury,* pp. 190–269.
———. "Preodolevshiye simvolizma," in Zhirmunsky, *Voprosy teorii literatury,* pp. 278–322.
———. "Symbolism's Successors," trans. Stanley Rabinowitz. In *The Noise of Change: Russian Literature and the Critics: 1891–1917.* Ann Arbor: Ardis, 1986, pp. 217–247.
———. *Tvorchestvo Anny Akhmatovoi.* Leningrad: Nauka, 1973.
———. "Two Tendencies of Contemporary Lyric Poetry," trans. John Glad, RLT, no. 4 (Fall 1972), pp. 175–182.
———. *Voprosy teorii literatury: stati 1916–1926.* Slavistic Printings and Reprintings. The Hague: Mouton, 1962.
Zhukova, Lydia. "Iz knigi *Epilogi,*" *Requiem,* pp. 155–156. From *Epilogi,* I, New York, 1983.
Zhuravlev, D. N. "Anna Akhmatova," VOAA, pp. 326–331.
Zorgenfrei, V. A. "Iz vospominanii," DG, p. 252.
Zykov, Leonid. "Nikolai Punin-Adresat i geroi lirik Anny Akhmatovoi," *Zvezda* I (1995), p. 77–114.

NOTES: AAA stands for Anna Andreyevna Akhmatova (pseud. of Anna Gorenko); cited works are by Akhmatova unless otherwise noted.